PHILIP'S

STREET ATLAS
Gloucestershire
South Gloucestershire
and Bristol

www.philips-maps.co.uk
First published in 2001 by
Philip's, a division of
Octopus Publishing Group Ltd
www.octopusbooks.co.uk
Carmelite House
50 Victoria Embankment
London EC4Y 0DZ
An Hachette UK Company
www.hachette.co.uk

Third edition with interim revision 2015
First impression 2015
GLOCA

ISBN 978-1-84907-366-0 (spiral)

© Philip's 2015

Ordnance Survey®

Contents

III **Key to map symbols**

IV **Key to map pages**

VI **Route planning**

X Major administrative and Postcode boundaries

1 **Street maps** at 3½ inches to 1 mile

140 **Street maps** at 1¾ inches to 1 mile

193 **Street maps** of centres of Bristol, Cheltenham and
Gloucester at 7 inches to 1 mile

197 **Index** of towns and villages, streets, hospitals,
industrial estates, railway stations, schools,
shopping centres, universities and places of interest

Key to map symbols

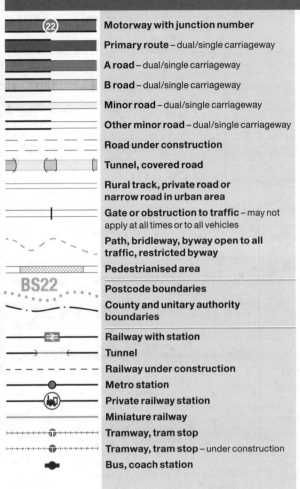

Motorway with junction number	
Primary route – dual/single carriageway	
A road – dual/single carriageway	
B road – dual/single carriageway	
Minor road – dual/single carriageway	
Other minor road – dual/single carriageway	
Road under construction	
Tunnel, covered road	
Rural track, private road or narrow road in urban area	
Gate or obstruction to traffic – may not apply at all times or to all vehicles	
Path, bridleway, byway open to all traffic, restricted byway	
Pedestrianised area	
Postcode boundaries	
County and unitary authority boundaries	
Railway with station	
Tunnel	
Railway under construction	
Metro station	
Private railway station	
Miniature railway	
Tramway, tram stop	
Tramway, tram stop – under construction	
Bus, coach station	

Ambulance station	
Coastguard station	
Fire station	
Police station	
Accident and Emergency entrance to hospital	
H	**Hospital**
+	**Place of worship**
i	**Information centre** – open all year
P	**Shopping centre, parking**
P&R / PO	**Park and Ride, Post Office**
	Camping site, caravan site
	Golf course, picnic site
Church / ROMAN FORT	**Non-Roman antiquity, Roman antiquity**
Univ	**Important buildings, schools, colleges, universities and hospitals**
	Woods, built-up area

River Medway **Water name**

	River, weir
	Stream
	Canal, lock, tunnel
	Water
	Tidal water

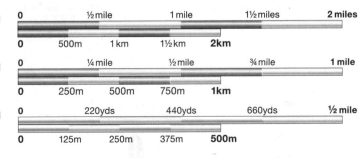

58 87 246 Adjoining page indicators and overlap bands – the colour of the arrow and band indicates the scale of the adjoining or overlapping page (see scales below)

The dark grey border on the inside edge of some pages indicates that the mapping does not continue onto the adjacent page

The small numbers around the edges of the maps identify the 1-kilometre National Grid lines

Acad	**Academy**	Meml	**Memorial**
Allot Gdns	**Allotments**	Mon	**Monument**
Cemy	**Cemetery**	Mus	**Museum**
C Ctr	**Civic centre**	Obsy	**Observatory**
CH	**Club house**	Pal	**Royal palace**
Coll	**College**	PH	**Public house**
Crem	**Crematorium**	Recn Gd	**Recreation ground**
Ent	**Enterprise**	Resr	**Reservoir**
Ex H	**Exhibition hall**	Ret Pk	**Retail park**
Ind Est	**Industrial Estate**	Sch	**School**
IRB Sta	**Inshore rescue boat station**	Sh Ctr	**Shopping centre**
Inst	**Institute**	TH	**Town hall / house**
Ct	**Law court**	Trad Est	**Trading estate**
L Ctr	**Leisure centre**	Univ	**University**
LC	**Level crossing**	W Twr	**Water tower**
Liby	**Library**	Wks	**Works**
Mkt	**Market**	YH	**Youth hostel**

Enlarged maps only

Railway or bus station building

Place of interest

Parkland

The map scale on the pages numbered in green is 1¾ inches to 1 mile
2.76 cm to 1 km • 1:36 206

0   ½ mile   1 mile   1½ miles   **2 miles**
0   500m   1 km   1½ km   **2km**

The map scale on the pages numbered in blue is 3½ inches to 1 mile
5.52 cm to 1 km • 1:18 103

0   ¼ mile   ½ mile   ¾ mile   **1 mile**
0   250m   500m   750m   **1km**

The map scale on the pages numbered in red is 7 inches to 1 mile
11.04 cm to 1 km • 1:9 051

0   220yds   440yds   660yds   **½ mile**
0   125m   250m   375m   **500m**

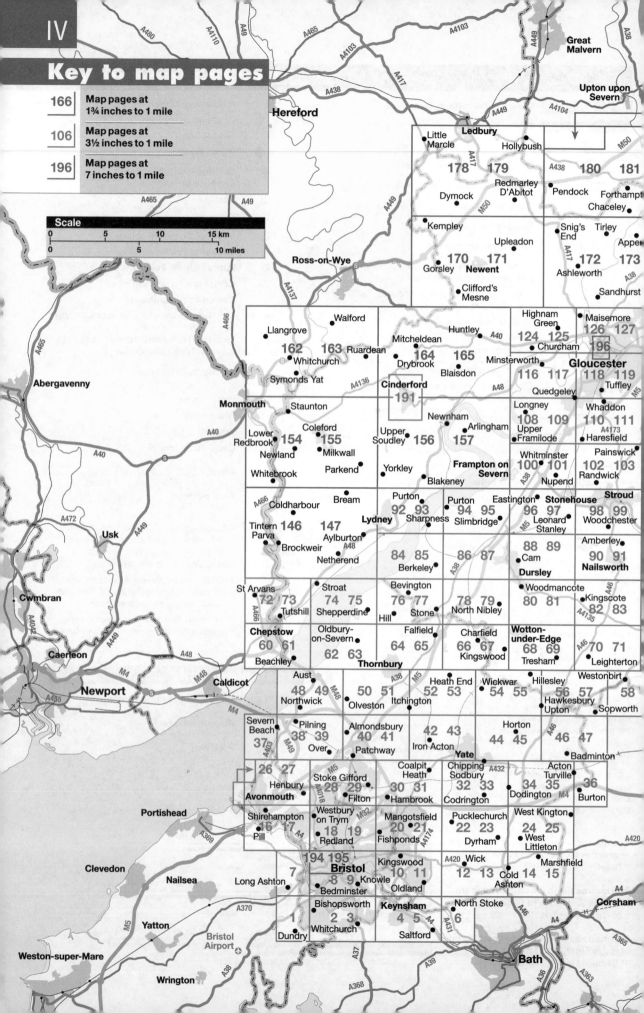

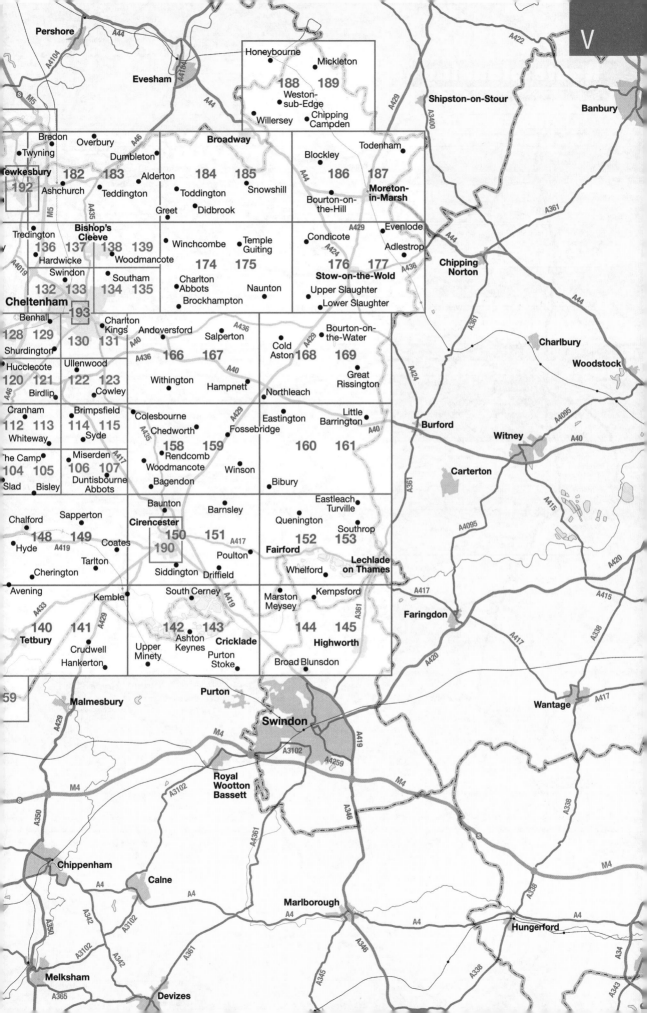

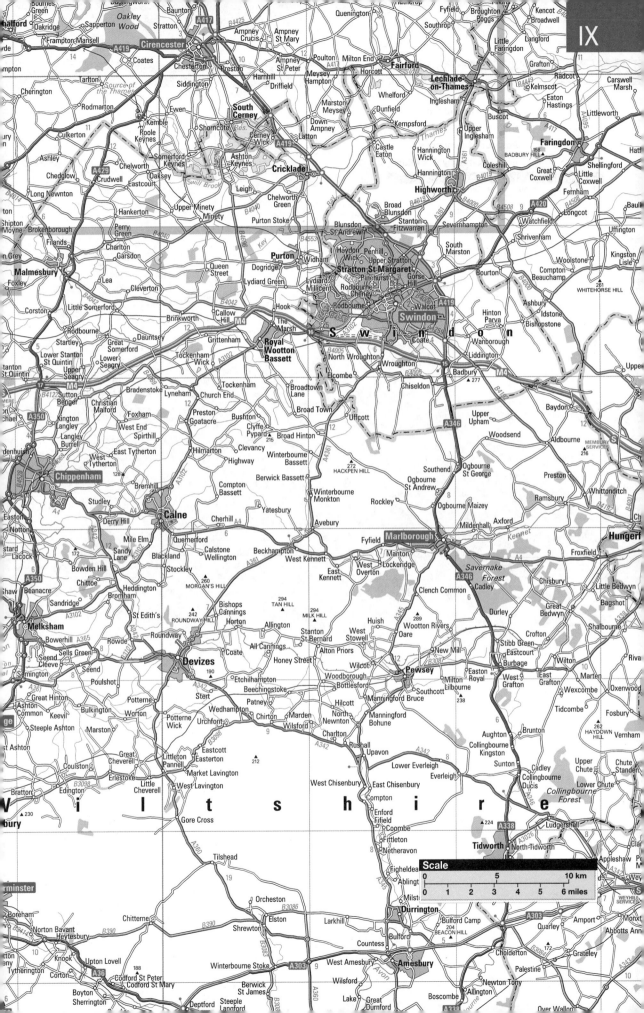

Major administrative and Postcode boundaries

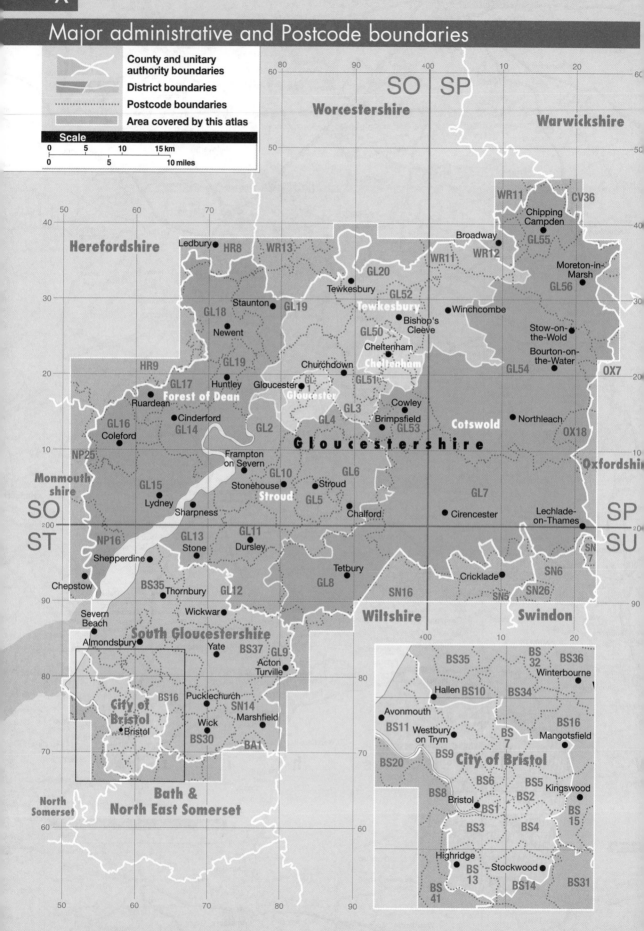

County and unitary authority boundaries
District boundaries
Postcode boundaries
Area covered by this atlas

Scale
0 5 10 15 km
0 5 10 miles

Worcestershire
Warwickshire
SO SP

Herefordshire
Ledbury HR8 WR13
WR11 CV36
Chipping Campden
GL55
Broadway
WR12
Moreton-in-Marsh
GL56

GL20
Staunton GL19
Tewkesbury
Tewkesbury GL52
Winchcombe
Bishop's Cleeve
Stow-on-the-Wold
GL18
Newent
HR9
GL50
Cheltenham
Cheltenham
GL54
Bourton-on-the-Water
OX7

GL19
GL17
Huntley Gloucester
GL51
Forest of Dean
Ruardean
GL1
GL3
Cowley
Gloucester
Brimpsfield
Cotswold
Northleach
GL16
Cinderford
GL4
GL53
Coleford
GL14
GL2
Gloucestershire
OX18

NP25
Frampton on Severn
GL10
GL6
Stroud
GL7
Oxfordshire
Monmouthshire
GL15
Stonehouse
Stroud
Cirencester
Lechlade-on-Thames
SO
Lydney
GL5
Chalford
SP
ST
Sharpness
GL11
SN7
SU
NP16
GL13
Dursley
Shepperdine
Stone
Tetbury
SN6
Chepstow
BS35
Thornbury
GL12
GL8
Cricklade
SN26
SN5
Severn Beach
Wickwar
SN16
Swindon
South Gloucestershire
Wiltshire
Almondsbury
Yate
BS37 GL9
Acton Turville
BS16
Pucklechurch
SN14
City of Bristol
Wick Marshfield
Bristol
BS30
BA1
North Somerset
Bath & North East Somerset

BS35
BS32 BS36
Winterbourne
Hallen BS10
BS34
Avonmouth
BS16
BS11 Westbury on Trym
BS7
Mangotsfield
BS20
BS9 City of Bristol
BS8
BS6
BS5
Kingswood
Bristol
BS1
BS2
BS15
BS3
BS4
Highridge
BS13
Stockwood
BS14 BS31
BS41

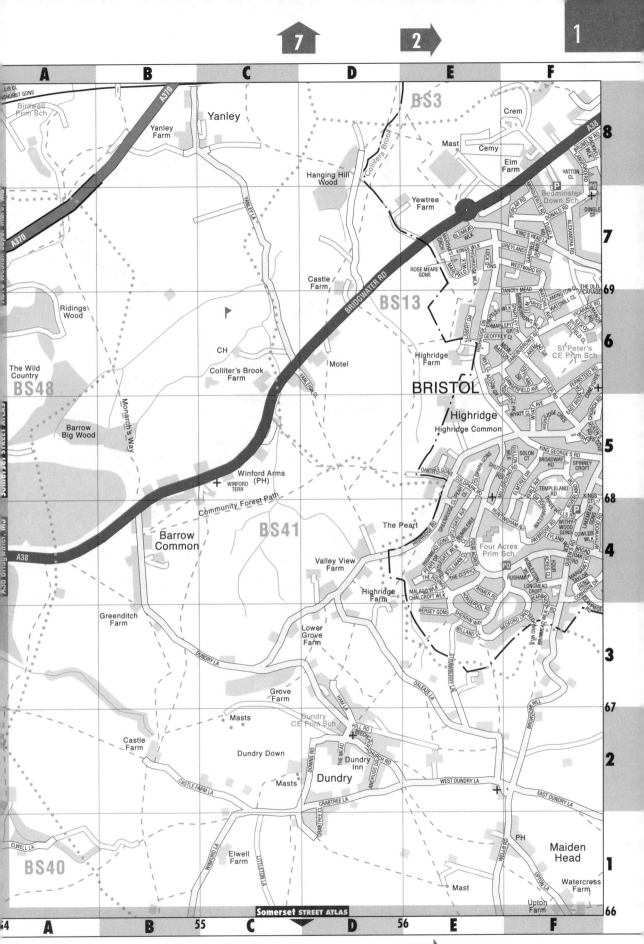

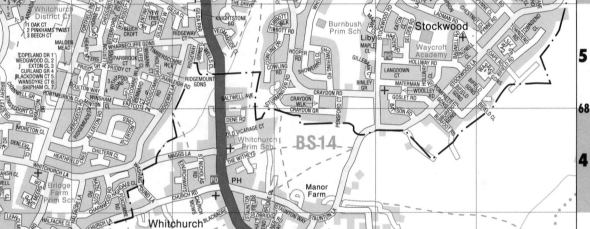

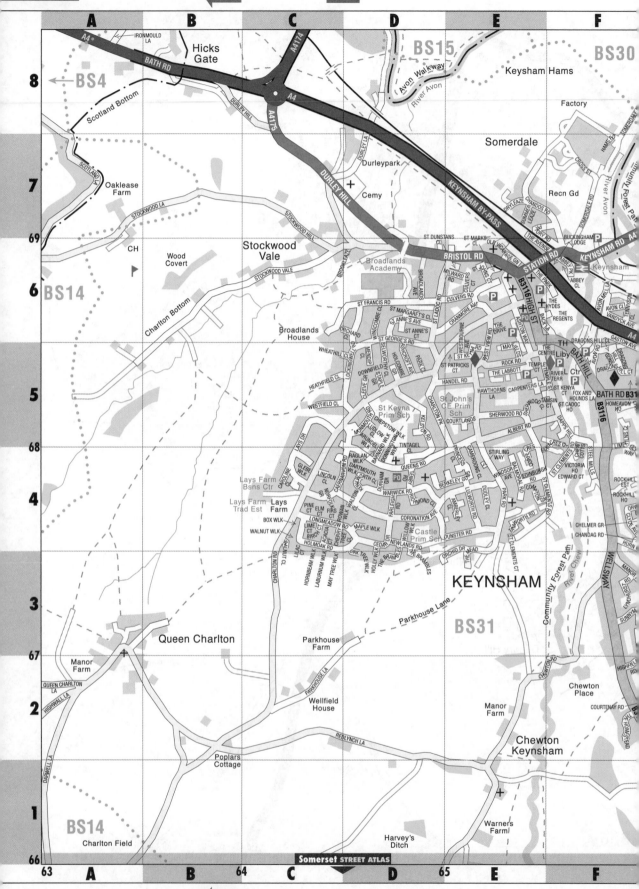

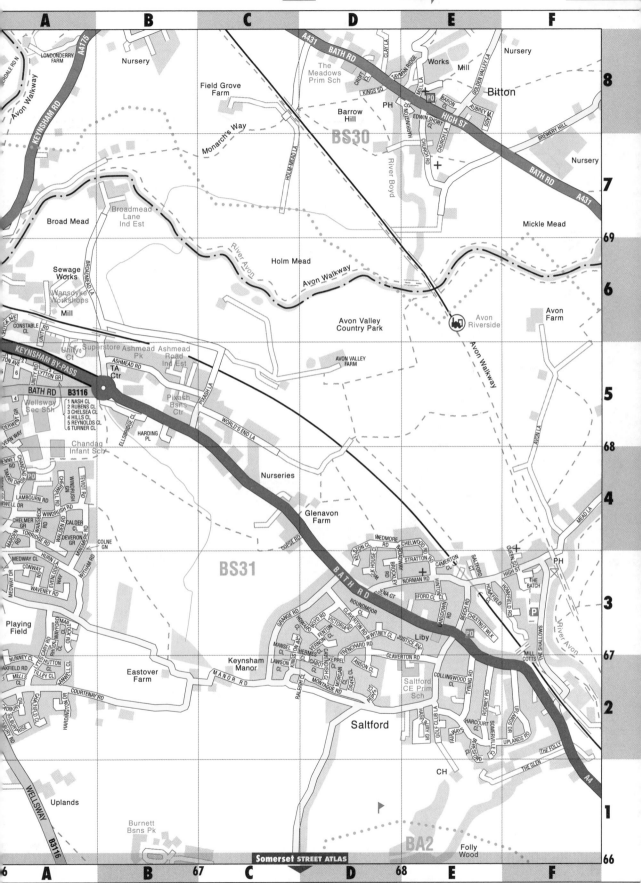

A · B · C · D · E · F

8
7
69
6
5
68
4
3
67
2
1
66

LONDONDERRY FARM
Nursery
Field Grove Farm
Barrow Hill
BS30
The Meadows Prim Sch
BATH RD A431
Works
Mill
Nursery
Bitton
BREWERY HILL
Nursery
BATH RD A431
River Boyd
Mickle Mead
Avon Farm
Monarch's Way
River Avon
Holm Mead
Avon Walkway
Avon Valley Country Park
Avon Riverside
Avon Walkway
Broad Mead
Broadmead Lane Ind Est
Sewage Works
Wansdyke Workshops
Mill
Superstore Ashmead Pk
Ashmead Road Ind Est
KEYNSHAM BY-PASS
BATH RD B3116
Wellsway Sec Sch
Pixash Bsns Ctr
AVON VALLEY FARM
WORLD'S END LA
Chandag Infant Sch
Nurseries
Glenavon Farm
BS31
BATH RD
Keynsham Manor
Playing Field
Eastover Farm
Saltford
Saltford CE Prim Sch
Liby
River Avon
THE BATCH
PH
MILL COTTS
THE SHALLOWS
CH
THE GLEN
THE FOLLY
A4
Uplands
WELLSWAY B3116
Burnett Bsns Pk
BA2
Folly Wood

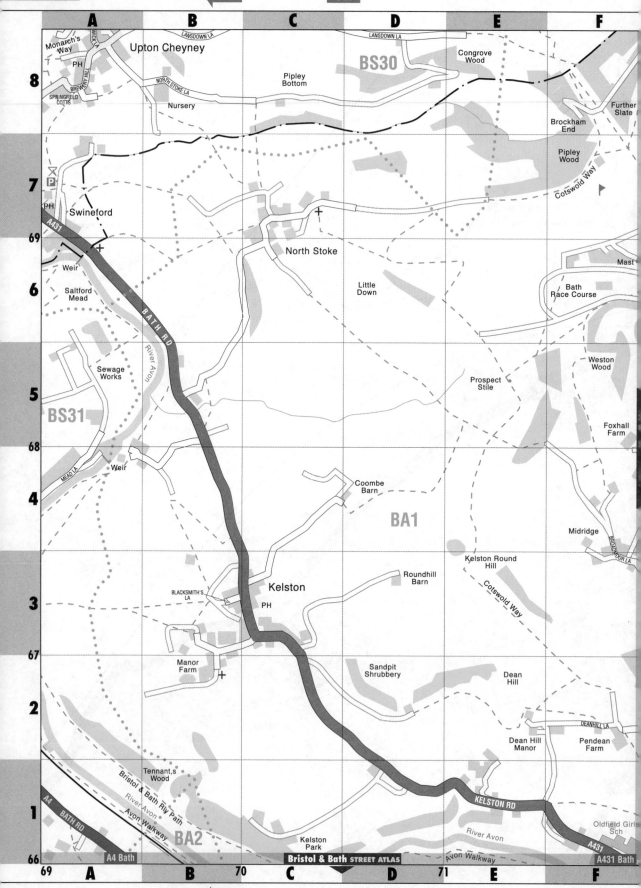

F5
1 BRISTOL GATE
2 FARADAY RD
3 DOWRY PL
4 LITTLE CAROLINE PL
5 GRENVILLE CHAPEL
6 HUMPHRY DAVY WAY

7 GRENVILLE PL
8 ASHMEAD WAY
9 CUMBERLAND RD
10 BRUNSWICK PL

F6
1 HABERFIELD HO
2 ALBERMARLE TERR
3 DAWES CT
4 CLEVE CT
5 BROWNE CT
6 ADAMS CT

7 CUMBERLAND PL
8 CARRICK HO
9 SOUTH GREEN ST
10 ALBERMARLE ROW
11 HOPECHAPEL HILL
12 NORTH GREEN ST
13 HINTON LA

F6
14 WINDSOR CT
15 VICTORIA TERR
16 THE POLYGON
17 GLENDALE
18 WELLINGTON TERR
19 OXFORD PL

F7
1 CLIFTON CL
2 HARLEY MEWS
3 HARLEY CT
4 HARLEY PL
5 GLENDOWER HO
6 CLIFTON DOWN RD

7 GLOUCESTER ROW
8 BEAUFORT BLDGS
9 BEAUFORT MEWS
10 GUARDIAN CT
11 WATERLOO ST
12 GLOUCESTER ST
13 CARTER'S BLDGS

17   8   7

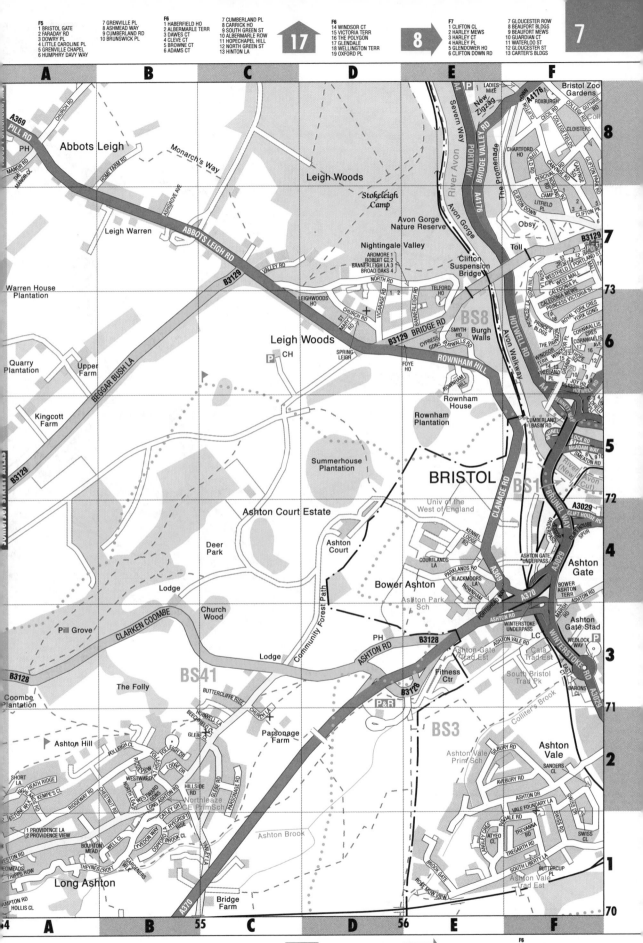

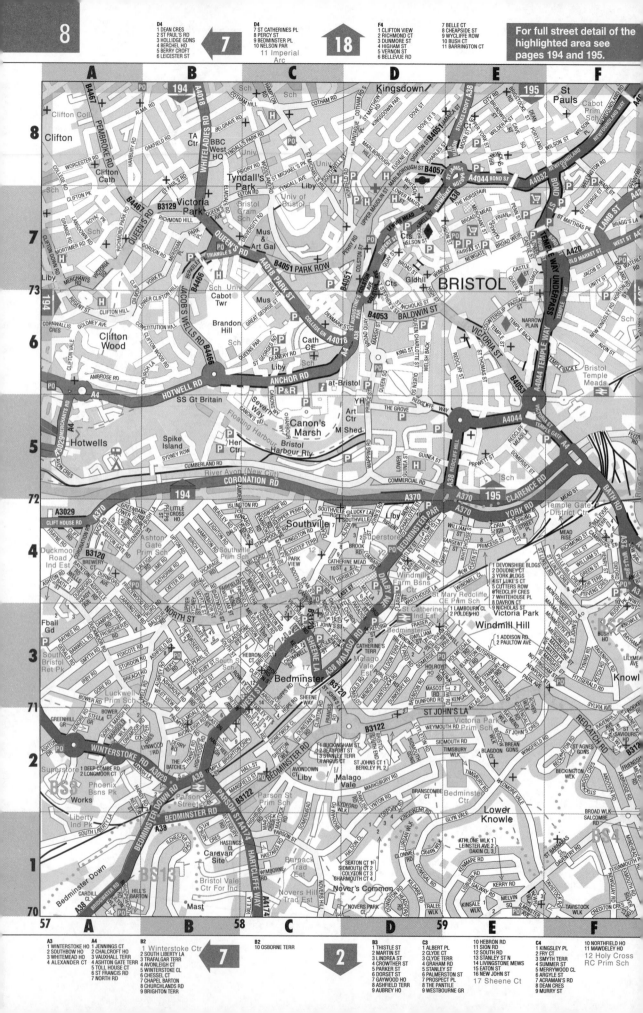

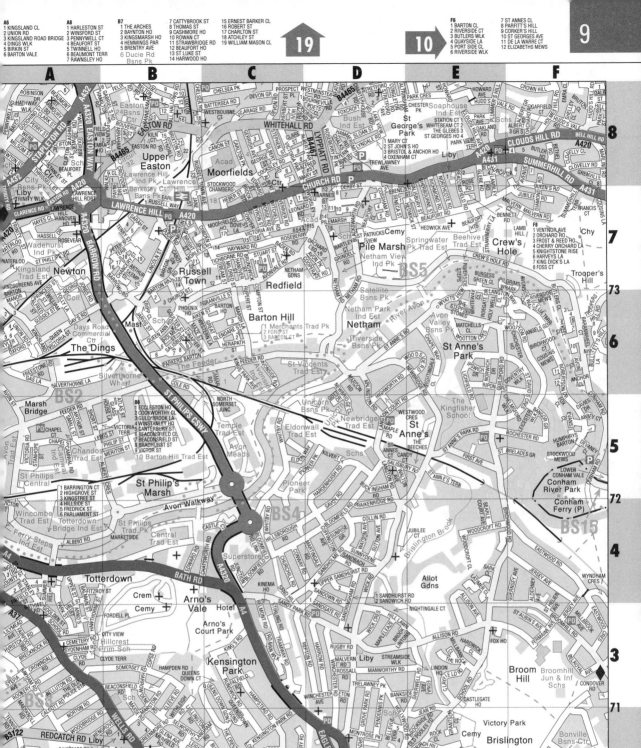

A6
1 Kingsland Cl
2 Union St
3 Kingsland Road Bridge
4 Dings Wlk
5 Birkin St
6 Barton Vale

A8
1 Harleston St
2 Winsford St
3 Pennywell Ct
4 Beaufort St
5 Twinnell Ho
6 Beaumont Terr
7 Rawnsley Ho

B7
1 The Arches
2 Baynton Ho
3 Kingsmarsh Ho
4 Hemmings Par
5 Brentry Ave
6 Ducie Rd Bsns Pk

7 Cattybrook St
8 Thomas St
9 Cashmore Ho
10 Rowan Cl
11 Strawbridge Rd
12 Beaufort Ho
13 St Luke St
14 Harwood Ho

15 Ernest Barker Cl
16 Robert St
17 Charlton St
18 Atchley St
19 William Mason Cl

F6
1 Barton Cl
2 Riverside Ct
3 Butlers Wlk
4 Quayside La
5 Port Side Cl
6 Riverside Wlk

7 St Annes Cl
8 Parfitt's Hill
9 Corker's Hill
10 St Georges Ave
11 De La Warre Ct
12 Elizabeths Mews

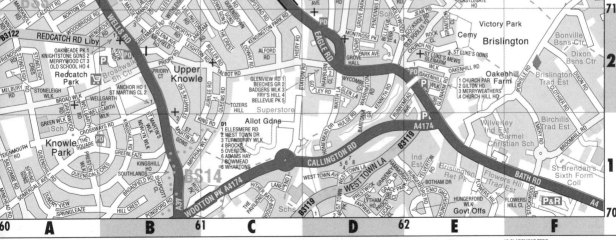

A8
1 Croydon Ho
2 Lansdowne Ct
3 Shaw Cl
4 Vining Wlk
5 Hilton Ct
6 Lansdown Rd
7 Thomson Rd
8 Westbourne Rd
9 Eastbourne Rd

10 Elmgrove Ave
11 All Hallows Ct
12 Adelaide Pl
13 Compactory La
14 Lawnwood Ind Units
15 Lawnwood Rd
16 Brighton Pk
17 Kilburn St
18 Owen St

19 Kilburn St
20 Windsor Gr
21 Clayton St
22 Brixton Road Mews
23 Cattybrook St
24 St Gabriel's Bsns Pk

C7
1 Milton Pk
2 Weight Rd
3 Draper Ct
4 Chester St
5 Barker Ct
6 Adryan Ct
7 Oxford St
8 Cambridge St
9 York St

10 Lancaster St
11 Corbett St
12 Ashmead Ho
13 Langham Ho
14 Garvey Ho
15 Osprey Rd
16 Howett Rd
17 Matthew's Rd
18 Russell Town Ind Pk

C8
1 Johnsons Rd
2 Ida Rd
3 Samuel St
4 Whitehall Trad Est
5 Lillian St
6 Albion St
7 Arthur St
8 William St
9 Lynton Pl

D7
1 Seneca Pl
2 Handel Ave
3 Parkfield Ave
4 Weston Ave
5 Speedwell Ave
6 Blacksworth Ho
7 Padmore Ct
8 Shaftesbury Terr
9 Lewin St

10 Claremont Terr
11 George & Dragon La
12 St George's Hts
13 Gladstone St
14 Terrell Gdns
15 Gibbs Ct
16 Frampton Ct
17 Edwards Ct
18 Dillon Ct
19 Orchard Ct

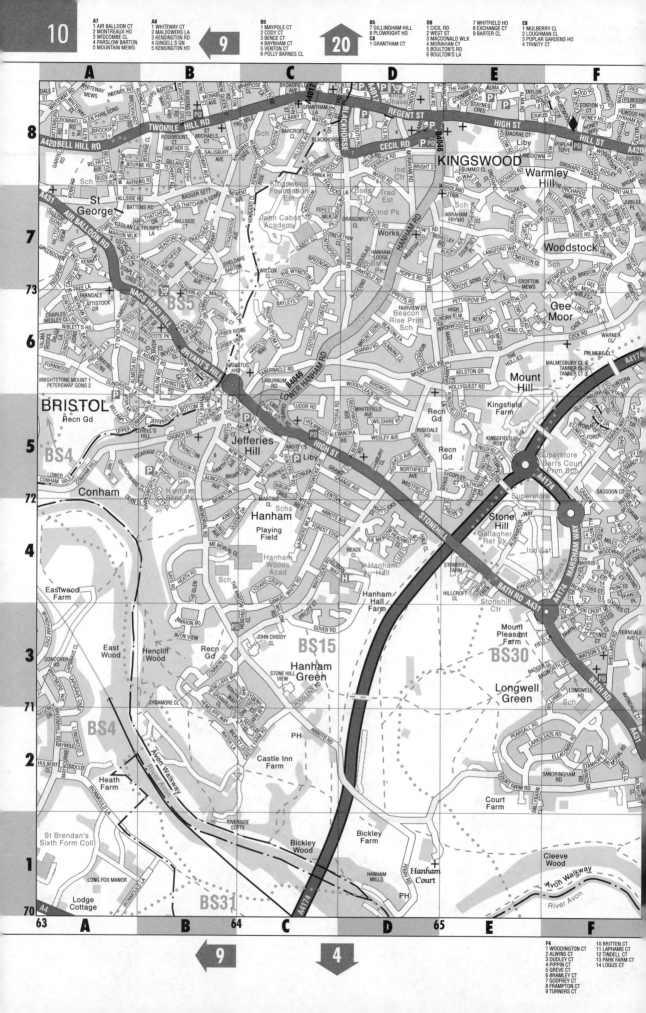

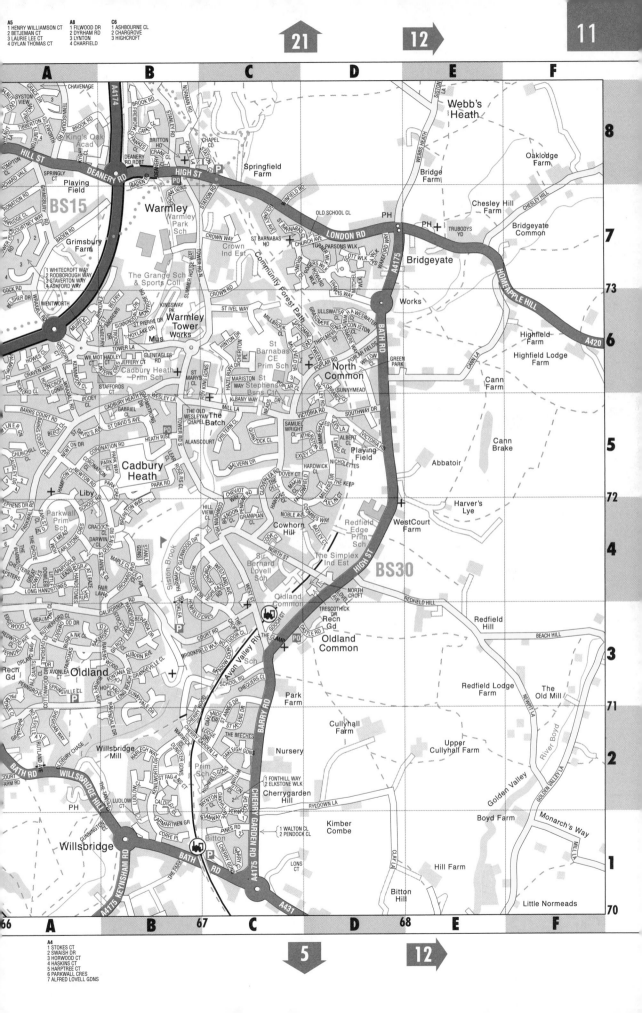

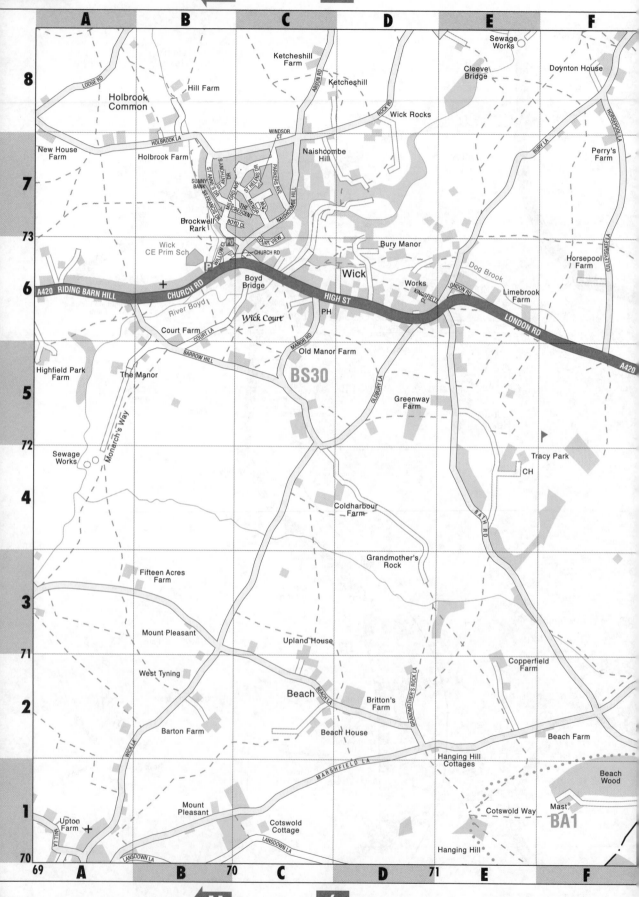

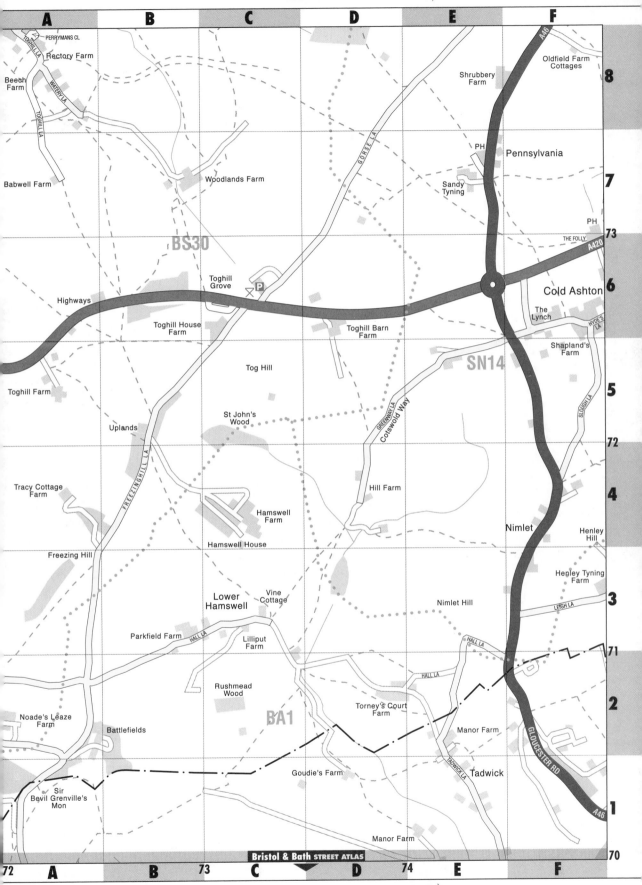

A B C D E F

Rectory Farm

PERRYMANS CL

Beech Farm

Babwell Farm

Highways

Toghill Farm

Tracy Cottage Farm

Freezing Hill

Noade's Leaze Farm

Sir Bevil Grenville's Mon

Woodlands Farm

BS30

Toghill Grove

Toghill House Farm

Tog Hill

St John's Wood

Uplands

Hamswell Farm

Hamswell House

Lower Hamswell

Vine Cottage

Parkfield Farm

Lilliput Farm

Rushmead Wood

Battlefields

BA1

Goudie's Farm

Toghill Barn Farm

Hill Farm

Cotswold Way

GREENWAY LA

Nimlet Hill

Torney's Court Farm

Manor Farm

Shrubbery Farm

GORSE LA

PH

Sandy Tyning

Pennsylvania

PH

THE FOLLY

A420

Cold Ashton

The Lynch

HYDE'S LA

Shapland's Farm

SN14

SLOUGH LA

Nimlet

Henley Hill

Henley Tyning Farm

LEIGH LA

HALL LA

HALL LA

HALL LA

Manor Farm

Tadwick

TADWICK LA

GLOUCESTER RD

A46

Oldfield Farm Cottages

8

7

73

6

5

72

4

3

71

2

1

70

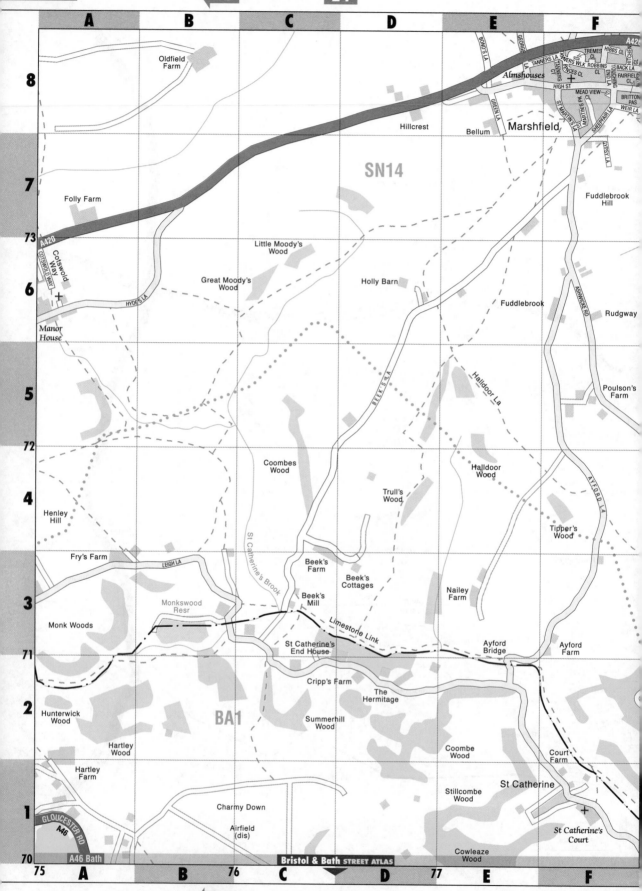

A B C D E F

8

Oldfield
Farm

Almshouses

BOND'S LA
GEORGE

TANNERS LA
TANNERS WLK
HIBBS CL
HITCHEN CL
ROBBINS CL
BACK LA
FAIRFIELD
CL
A42

TREMES
CL

HIGH ST
GREEN LA

MEAD VIEW
CL
ST MARTIN'S
BRITTON
PAS
WEIR LA

Hillcrest

Bellum

Marshfield

ST MARTIN'S LA

SHEPFAIR LA

GREEN LA

GIPSY LA

7

SN14

Fuddlebrook
Hill

Folly Farm

73

A420

Cotswold
Way

Little Moody's
Wood

COTSWOLD WAY

6

Great Moody's
Wood

Holly Barn

Fuddlebrook

Rudgway

ASHWICKE RD

HYDE'S LA

Manor
House

BEEK'S LA

Halldoor La

Poulson's
Farm

5

72

Coombes
Wood

Halldoor
Wood

AYFORD LA

4

Henley
Hill

Trull's
Wood

Tipper's
Wood

St Catherine's Brook

Fry's Farm

LEIGH LA

Beek's
Farm

Beek's
Cottages

Nailey
Farm

3

Monkswood
Resr

Beek's
Mill

Limestone Link

Ayford
Bridge

Ayford
Farm

Monk Woods

St Catherine's
End House

71

Cripp's Farm

The
Hermitage

2

Hunterwick
Wood

BA1

Summerhill
Wood

Coombe
Wood

Court
Farm

Hartley
Wood

St Catherine

Hartley
Farm

Stillcombe
Wood

1

GLOUCESTER RD

Charmy Down

A46

Airfield
(dis)

St Catherine's
Court

Cowleaze
Wood

70

A46 Bath

75 A B 76 C D 77 E F

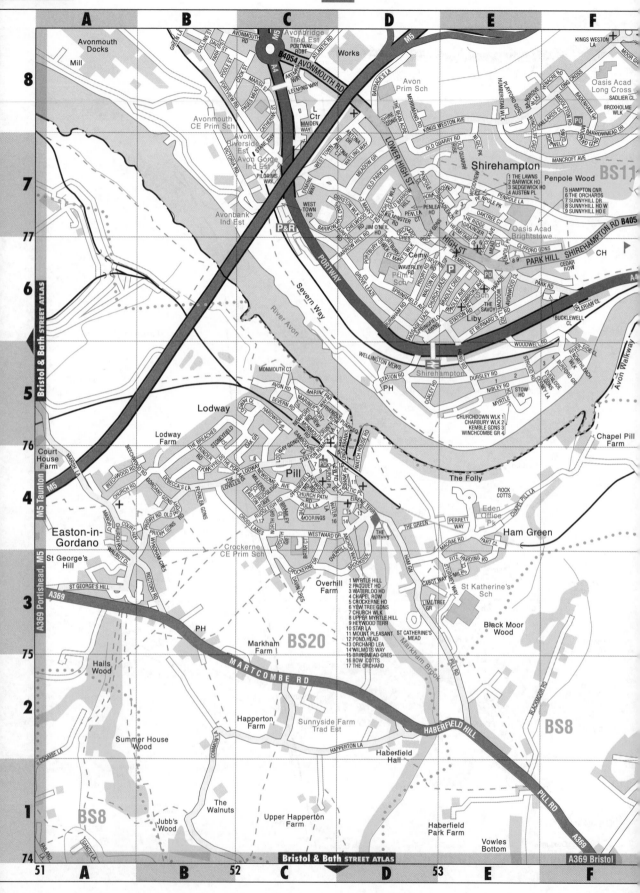

This is a street map page showing the Bristol area (Sea Mills, Coombe Dingle, Stoke Bishop, Sneyd Park, Westbury on Trym, Leigh Woods).

A B C D E F

8
7
77
6
5
76
4
3
75
2
1
74

BROADLANDS DR
DEANS MEAD
BANFIELD CL
Sch
ROCKINGHAM GDNS
HOWMEAD AVE
TUTTON AVE
KNELLER CL
NAPIER MILES RD
DRAYTON RD
BENVILLE AVE
CHARDSTOCK AVE
BEECHFIELD GR
Potter's Point
CH
Camphill Community
Coombe Farm
WESTOVER GDNS 1
WESTOVER RD 2
CEDAR CT 4
MARLE CT 3
RAVEN CT 5
ASHDOWN CT 6
STRATFORD CT 7
HYLAND GR
FALCON CL
HEBBURN RD
FENBURY RD
B4055
1 2

ALDERDOWN CL
Evergreens Wood
SOUTHWOOD DR E
Coombe Dingle
GROVE RD
THE GRANGE
CEDAR CT
PITCHCOMBE GDNS
FAIRVIEW RD
MERLIN CL
WOODHILL RD
HILLSDON
A4018
8

Kingsweston House
BS11
BRISTOL
INN COTTS
Sch
KINGS WESTON RD
Kings Weston Hill
Mast
B4457
B4057
Community Forest Path
FERNDOWN CL
ARDERN CL
SOUTHWOOD DR
ALDERCOMBE RD
CRANBERRY WLK
MULBERRY WLK
WYEDALE AVE
RAIG CL
SOUTHSIDE CL
BOWEN RD
HARFORD
THE GRANGE
CNG
TRYM BANK
CHURCH
DINGLE
BEVERLEY GDNS
HUTTON CL
SANDY LEANE
HAMMOND GDNS
GREENACRES
Cemy
Canford Park
CANFORD LA
A4162
CANFORD RD
Crem
Westbury on Trym
Liby
CANFORD HO
GRAYLING RD
FALCONDALE RD
A4162
CANFORD LA
7

Shirehampton Park
Shirehampton RD
SHIREHAMPTON RD
ELBERTON RD
LUX FURLONGS
HIGH GR
Liby
WESTBURY LA
MOORGROVE HO
DOWNFIELD CL
COMPTON DR
HALL END DR
Sch
WESTON CL
DINGLE VIEW
SUNNY HILL
ASHCROFT RD
THE DINGLE
DINGLE RD
DINGLEWOOD CL
BRIERCLIFFE RD
WEST ROCKE AVE
RAY LEIGH RD
COOMBE ROCKE
Coombe Dingle Sports Complex
CHARLECOMBE RD
CONISTON AVE
LYNDHURST RD
NEWCOMBE RD
ABBEY RD
RISDALE RD
BK STONE LA
COOMBE RD
DOWNS COTE DR
BRIARWOOD
A4018
77

SYLVAN WAY
WEST PAR
BLAISE WLK
THE CRESCENT
EAST PAR
SILKLANDS GR
HAYTOR PK
BARN RD
POPLAR AVE
WOODLAND RD
WEST DENE
COOMBE LA
COOMBE GR
RED ROCKS
STOKE GR
COTE LA
PO
GREAT BROCKERIDGE
BRAINSFIELD
6

Sea Mills
A4162
BLUEBELL CL
WOODLEAZE
THE PENTAGON
EAZY
ST EDYTH'S RD
FAILAND WLK
MEDWAY
DINGLE RD
TRYM LEYE DR
HILHOUSE
TRYMWOOD
NEWLYN AVE
ELLBRIDGE CL
CEDAR GR
CEDAR AVE
LYNDALE AVE
KINGSMILL
Prim Sch
DRUID HILL
SUNNY SIDE
WITHY CL W
GROVE CT
LITTLE WITHY CL
MEAD CL
REEDLEY RD
OAKHURST
Elmlea Jun & Inf Schs
WESTFIELD HO
BS9
5

Prim Sch
BROOKLEAZE WLK
STOKE LEIGH
TRYM SIDE DR
FAILAND CRES
TRYM CROSS
ABLETON WLK
CLAPTON WLK
SEA MILLS LA
BOWERLEAZE
TRIMNELLS
WEST DENE
EBENEZER LA
SOUTH DENE
EBENEZER LA
CROSS ELMS LA
YEOMANS CL
PARRYS GR
DRUID STOKE AVE
HOLLYBUSH
HIGH KINGSDOWN
CN HIGH KNOLL
DRUID HILL
STOKE COTTS
TUNSTALL CL
NEWSTOKE GDNS
CRANLEIGH GDNS
HOWECROFT GDNS
BIRBECK RD
LITTLE STOKE
ORMEROD RD
SHAPLANDS
PARRY'S LA
CN STONE LA
ELM LEA
COTE PADDOCK
B4054
76

HORSESHOE DR
AVON WAY
NEWBRIDGE HO
ABON HO
ROMAN WAY
BEANSCOMBE RD
AVON VALE
STOKE HILL
AVON WAY
DRUID WOODS
PYALTY CL
GLEN DR
Stoke Bishop
PO
OLD SNEED AVE
OLD SNEED RD
OLD SNEED COTTS
MARINERS DR
EASTMEAD LA
EASTMEAD CT
STOKE PARK RD
1 LODGE CT
2 HOWECROFT CT
SAVILLE GATE CL
THE GRANGE
Trinity Coll
5

HADRIAN CL
HARBOUR WALL
Sea Mills
Avon Walkway
CAVENDISH GDNS
CEDAR CT 1
WESTONIAN CT 2
GLENAVON CT 3
Old Sneed Park
GLENAVON PK
1 2 3
NEWCOMBE DR
PINE RIDGE CL
MARINERS DR
WOODLANDS
MARINERS' PATH
CHURCH AVE
SHARLAND CL
Sneyd Park
STOKE HILL
BISHOPS CL
SEVERNLEIGH GDNS
SAVILLE RD
SPRINGFORT
4

PORTWAY
River Avon
Severn Way
SYKBRINA
Leigh Court Bsns Ctr
Paradise Bottom
Oak Wood
CHURCH RD
BISHOPS KNOLL CT
BRAMLEY
ORCHARD CL
BRAMBLE CL
CHANCEL CL
SANCTUARY GDNS
Goodeve PK
GOODEVE RD
KNOLL HILL
WOODSIDE
HAZELWOOD CT
HAZELWOOD RD
JULIAN CL
MARKLANDS
PITCH AND PAY PK
PITCH AND PALLA
SEVERNLEIGH HO
STOKE PARK RD S
CHATTENDEN HO
The Heath
JULIAN RD
ROCKLEAZE RD
JULIAN CT
ROCKLEAZE CT
STOKE RD
DOWNLEAZE
SAVILLE RD
3

BS8
WOODLAND CT
BISHOPS KNOLL
THE OAK
RIDGEWOOD
KNOLL CT 1
TOWERLEAZE 2
LEIGH CT 3
SNEYD PARK HO 4
AVONDALE CT 5
DUNMURRY 6.
SCHOOL
GOODEVE RD
CHANTLEY
AVON GR
SEAWALLS RD
AVON CL
CYPRESS GR
WELL HOUSE
THE AVENUE
VYVELL RD
ROCKLEAZE RD
Community Forest Path
Durdham Down
75

Leigh Woods
SEAWALLS
CIRCULAR RD
2

Vicarage
CHURCH RD
Leigh Woods
Rifle Range
Leigh Woods Forest Walks
Avon Gorge
A4
LADIES MILE
Clifton Down
Zoo Gdns
A4176 CLIFTON DOWN
NORTHCOTE
BS8
Sch
1

P
P
P
74

A7
1 WESTMINSTER CL
2 CARLTON HO
3 CARLTON CT
4 IVY LODGE
5 BELLEVUE COTTS
6 WESTBURY MEWS

F1
1 ASHLEY CT
2 CARY ST

B6
1 CRANFORD CT
2 BLANDFORD CL
3 ST PETER'S WLK

F1
1 CARR HO
2 WINKWORTH PL
6 COREY CL
5 LANGSDOWN HO
7 DAVEY TERR
8 NEWFOUNDLAND RD

F1
9 FRANKLYN LA
10 DERMOT ST
11 CAIRNS' CRES
12 LOWER ASHLEY RD
13 GORDON RD
14 MARY CARPENTER PL
15 St Barnabas CE VC Prim Sch

F2
1 SOMMERVILLE RD S
2 ASHLEY COURT RD
3 BALMORAL MANS
4 FALKLAND RD
5 CUMBERLAND GR
6 Ashley Trad Est

7 ASHLEY GROVE RD
8 Minto Road Ind Ctr
9 THE MINT
10 Parkway Trad Est
11 LYNMOUTH RD
12 St Barnabas CE VC Prim Sch

F4
1 CARLTON CT
2 COULSON HO
3 ATHENA CT
4 LILSTOCK AVE

A2
1 ST VINCENT'S HILL
2 YORK ST
3 HIGHLAND CRES
4 HIGHLAND SQ
5 BELGRAVE RD
6 RICHMOND DALE
7 RICHMOND CT
8 QUARRY STEPS
9 SUTHERLAND PL
10 WORRALL MEWS
11 WORRALL PL
12 HAYDON CT
13 HIGHLAND PL
14 MORNINGTON RD
15 ANGLESEA PL
16 NORMANTON RD

B1
1 KING'S PARADE AVE
2 GROSVENOR CT

3 COMPTON LODGE
4 COLLINGWOOD RD
5 PLIMSOLL RD
6 OAKLAND RD
7 TYNDALE CT
8 IMPERIAL RD
9 WHATLEY CT
10 CLIFTON METRO
11 Clifton Down Sh Ctr

13 HOPKINS CT
14 BIRKRAFT CT
15 CLOTHAM GDNS
16 PITVILLE PL
17 BURLINGTON CT
18 HAMPTON LA

B2
1 FERNLEIGH CT
2 LOWER REDLAND MEWS
3 EAST SHRUBBERY
4 SHRUBBERY COTTS
5 WEST SHRUBBERY
6 SOUTH TERR
7 FITZROY TERR
8 REDLAND TERR
9 LLANARTH VILLAS
10 ARLEY COTTS
11 HAMPTON RD

C2
1 ERMLEET RD
2 FERNBANK CT
3 CLYDE MEWS
4 HILLSIDE HO
5 VICTORIA ST
7 VICTORIA GDNS
8 FREMANTLE LA
9 THORPE LODGE

D1
1 ELMGROVE PK
2 CHELTENHAM CRES
10 ST MATTHEW'S AVE
11 PRIOR'S HILL
12 THOMAS ST N

D2
1 PROSPECT PL
2 BROOKFIELD LA
3 BROOKFIELD RD
4 GILLHAM HO
5 ELTON MANS

E1
1 MONTPELIER CENTRAL
2 THE MONT
3 MILLBROOK CT
4 ARMIDALE AVE
5 ARMIDALE COTTS
6 PICTON MEWS
7 WOODMANCOTE RD
8 NORRISVILLE RD
9 BARNABAS ST
10 DALRYMPLE RD
11 WELLINGTON CT
12 BRIGHTON ST
13 HERBURN RD
14 CATHERINE CT
15 SYDENHAM CT
16 NINE TREE HILL
17 DOVE ST
18 ARMADA HO
19 ARMADA PL

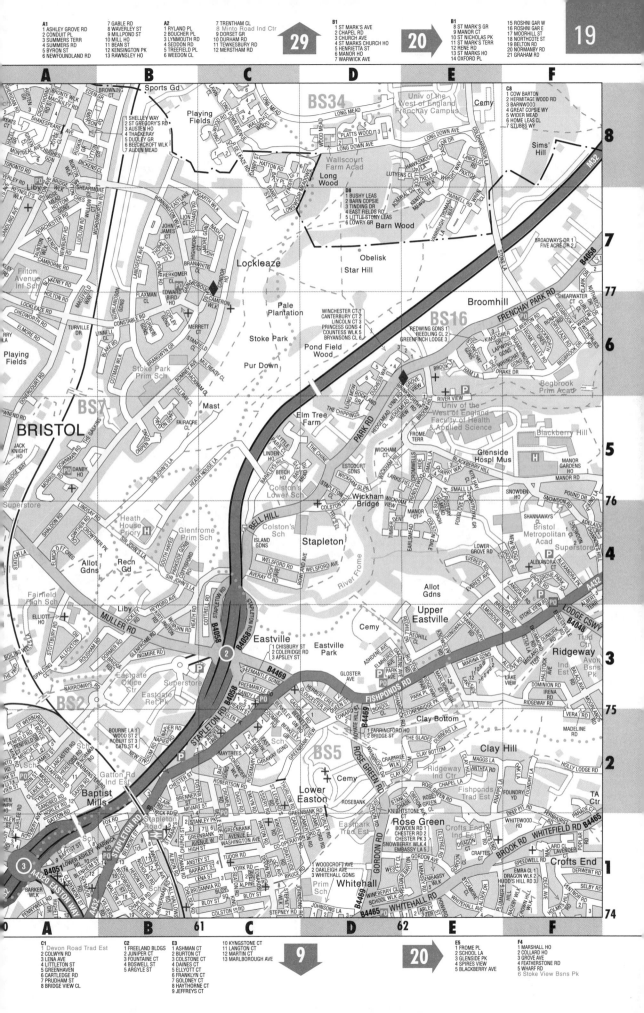

D5
1 BRITANNIA CT
2 OVERNHURST CT
3 GARTON HO
4 PLEASANT HO
5 PENDENNIS HO
6 SHRUBBERY CT

7 BERKELEY HO
8 NELSON HO
9 JOHN WESLEY CT
10 ORCHARD COTTS
11 VICARAGE COTTS

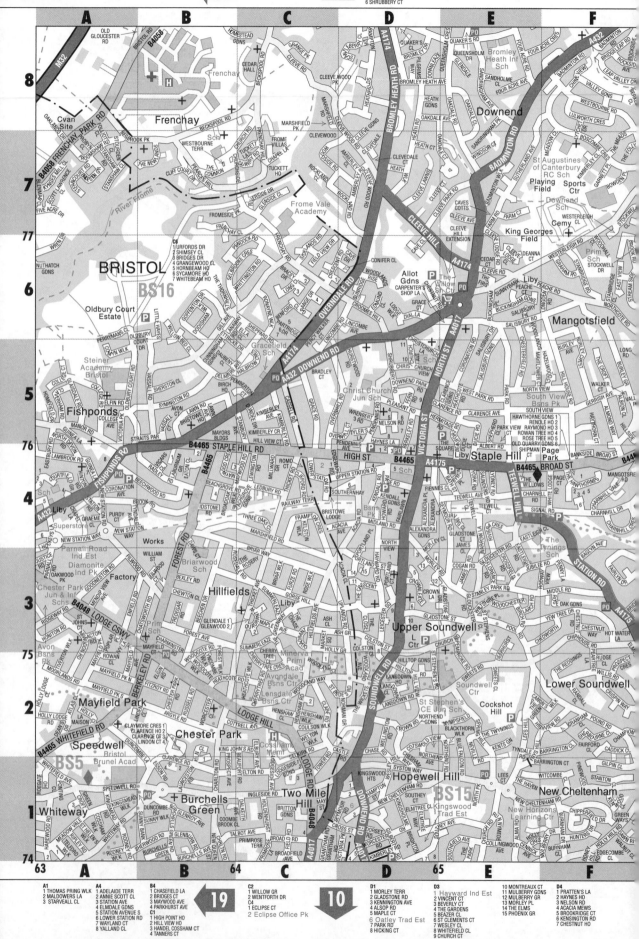

A1
1 THOMAS PRING WLK
2 MALDOWERS LA
3 STARVEALL CL

A4
1 ADELAIDE TERR
2 ANNIE SCOTT CL
3 STATION AVE
4 ELMDALE GDNS
5 STATION AVENUE S
6 LOWER STATION RD
7 WAYLAND CT
8 YALLAND CL

B4
1 CHASEFIELD LA
2 BRIDGES CT
3 MAYWOOD AVE
4 PARKHURST AVE

C1
1 HIGH POINT HO
2 HILL VIEW HO
3 HANDEL COSSHAM CT
4 TANNERS CT

C2
1 WILLOW GR
2 WENTFORTH DR
C4
1 ECLIPSE CT
2 Eclipse Office Pk

D1
1 MORLEY TERR
2 GLADSTONE CT
3 KENNINGTON AVE
4 ALSOP RD
5 MAPLE CT
6 Oatley Trad Est
7 PARK RD
8 HICKING CT

D3
1 Hayward Ind Est
2 VINCENT CT
3 WESVEY CT
4 THE GARDENS
5 BEAZER CL
6 ST CLEMENTS CT
7 WESLEY CL
8 WHITEFIELD CL
9 CHURCH CT

10 MONTREAUX CT
11 MULBERRY GDNS
12 MULBERRY GR
13 MORLEY PL
14 THE ELMS
15 PHOENIX GR

D4
1 PRATTEN'S LA
2 HAYNES HO
3 NELSON RD
4 ACACIA MEWS
5 BROOKRIDGE CT
6 KENSINGTON RD
7 CHESTNUT HO

A   B   C   D   E   F

8
7
77
6
5
76
4
3
75
2
1
74

M4

Lyde
Green

Chy

Lydegreen
Farm

Green Tree
Farm

Grove
Farm

Whitehouse
Farm

Hallen
Farm

Newlands

LYDE GREEN
RDBT

New
England

Blackhorse

Vinney
Green

Emersons
Green Prim
Sch

St LUKES CL

Liby

The Village
Superstore
PO

THE ROSARY
RDBT

THE
ROSARY

Works
(dis)

THE VALE

City of Bristol
Coll,
Downend Ctr

Emerson's
Green

Shortwood
Farm

Shortwood
Lodge

BS16

Barley Close
Com Prim
Sch

The Laurels

Vinney Green
Secure Unit

GREEN SIDE
RODWAY

Teaching Unit

Hillhouse

COSSHAM ST

Pomphrey

The
Vale

Rock House
Farm

DRAMWAY
RDBT

B4465

CATTYBROOK RD N

MANGOTSFIELD RD

POMPHREY HILL   MAIN RD

PH

Shortwood

SHORTWOOD HILL

B4465

Charn
Hill

Rodway
Hill

Orchard
Farm

Mangotsfield
Sch

RODWAY HILL

Lodge
Farm

Long
Plantation

Community Forest Path

Gingell's
Farm

Siston
Court

Siston

Station Road
Workshops
Station Road
Bsns Ctr

Kings' Forest
Prim Sch
The
Siston
Ctr

STATION RD

BRIDGE
FARM WK

Syston
Farm

CH

Hanging
Wood

St Anne's
Bridge

SISTON LA

STATION ROAD LINK

A4175

SISTON HILL
RDBT

SISTON COMM
PH

WHISTLE
RD

Withy
Bed

Mill
Farm

Siston Brook

Tut's
Wood

BS15

NEW CHELTENHAM
RD
FISHER RD

Siston
Hill

SISTON HILL

GOOSE GN

Cherry Orchard
Farm

Myrtle
Farm

Goose
Green

BS30

Webb's Heath
Farm

THE RIDE

SISTON
COMMON

Brook
Farm

Meadow
Farm

WEBBS HEATH

A4174

CHAVENAGE

HOBBS LA

NORMAN RD

Mounds Court
Farm

Warmley Brook

6

67

68

74

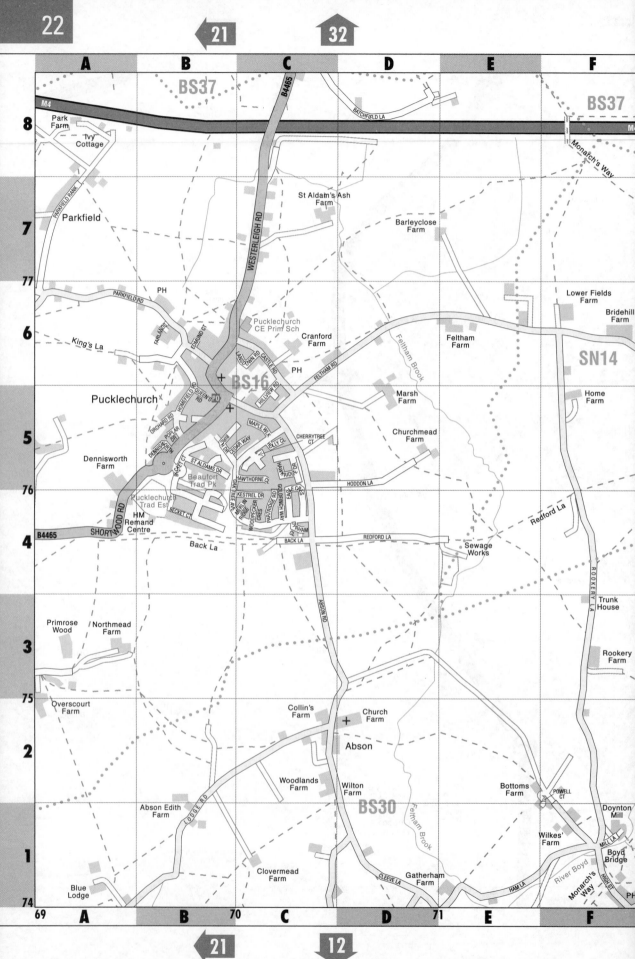

A B C D E F

BS37

BS37

M4

M4

Monarch's Way

Park
Farm

8

Ivy
Cottage

St Aldam's Ash
Farm

Batchfield La

Barleyclose
Farm

PARKFIELD PARK

Parkfield

7

WESTERLEIGH RD

B4465

Feltham
Farm

Lower Fields
Farm

Bridehill
Farm

77

PH

Parkfield RD

PH

Pucklechurch
CE Prim Sch

Cranford
Farm

Feltham Brook

SN14

6

King's La

FARLANDS

EDMUND CT

LANSDOWN RD
CASTLE RD

PH

FELTHAM RD

Marsh
Farm

Home
Farm

Pucklechurch

BS16

HOMEFIELD
QUEEN'S RD
PO

HILLVIEW RD

Churchmead
Farm

5

Dennisworth
Farm

ORCHARD RD
DENNISWORTH
POPLAR

MAPLE WLK

KELLY CL

CHERRYTREE
CT

76

BECKET CT
CEDAR WAY
ST ALDAMS DR
HAWTHORNE CL
RIDGEWAY

KESTREL DR
PARTRIDGE RD

EAGLE CL

HODDON LA

Redford La

Pucklechurch
Trad Est

Beaufort
Trad Pk

OAK TREE AVE
WOODPECKER
CRES

Trunk
House

HM
Remand
Centre

SHORTWOOD RD

BECKET CT

BACK LA

REDFORD LA

ROOKERY LA

B4465

Back La

REDFORD LA

Sewage
Works

4

ABSON RD

Primrose
Wood

Northmead
Farm

Rookery
Farm

3

75

Overscourt
Farm

Collin's
Farm

Church
Farm

LODGE RD

Abson

2

Woodlands
Farm

Wilton
Farm

Bottoms
Farm

POWELL
CT

Doynton
Mill

Abson Edith
Farm

BS30

Feltham Brook

Wilkes'
Farm

River Boyd

MILL LA

HIGH ST

Boyd
Bridge

1

Clovermead
Farm

CLEEVE LA

Gatherham
Farm

HAM LA

Monarch's Way

Blue
Lodge

74

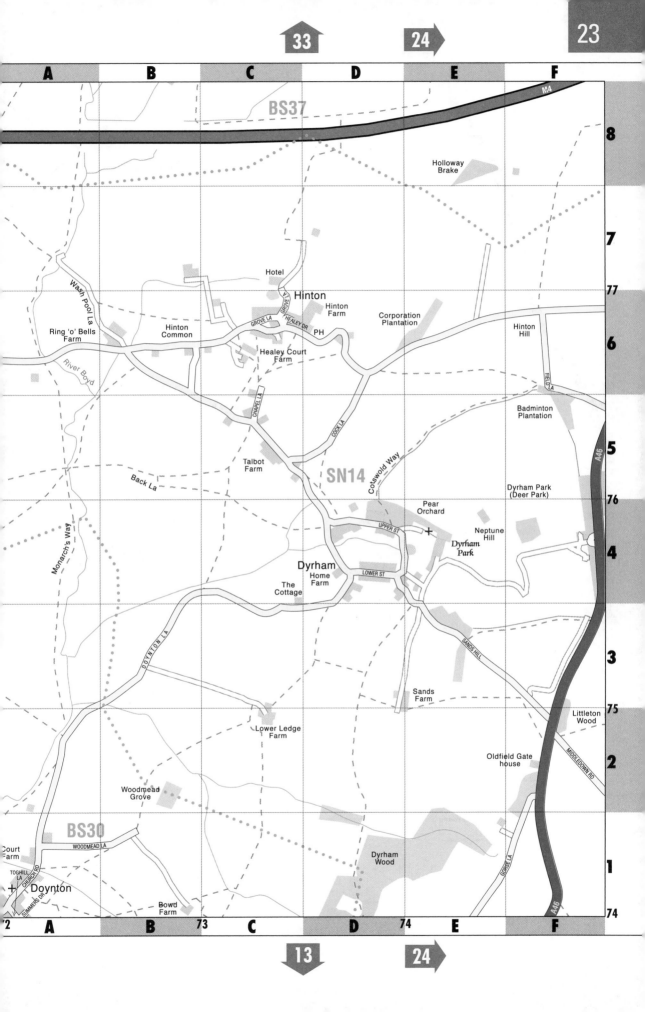

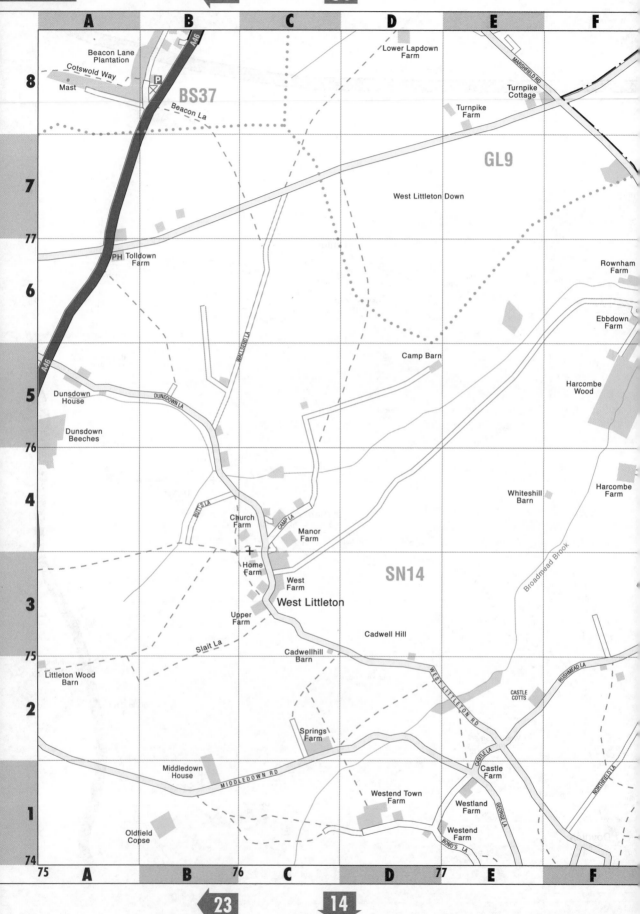

A B C D E F

8

BS37

Beacon Lane
Plantation
Cotswold Way
Mast
Beacon La

Lower Lapdown
Farm

MARSHFIELD RD

Turnpike
Cottage

Turnpike
Farm

GL9

7

West Littleton Down

77

PH Tolldown
Farm

Rownham
Farm

6

Ebbdown
Farm

Camp Barn

Harcombe
Wood

5

Dunsdown
House

DUNSDOWN LA

WALLSEND LA

A46

Dunsdown
Beeches

76

Whiteshill
Barn

Harcombe
Farm

4

BUTT'S LA

Church
Farm

CAMP LA

Manor
Farm

Home
Farm

SN14

Broadmead Brook

West
Farm

3

West Littleton

Upper
Farm

Cadwell Hill

Slait La

Cadwellhill
Barn

WEST LITTLETON RD

RUSHMEAD LA

75

Littleton Wood
Barn

CASTLE
COTTS

2

Springs
Farm

CASTLE LA

Castle
Farm

NORTHFIELD LA

Middledown
House

MIDDLEDOWN RD

Westend Town
Farm

Westland
Farm

GEORGE LA

1

Oldfield
Copse

Westend
Farm

BOND'S LA

74

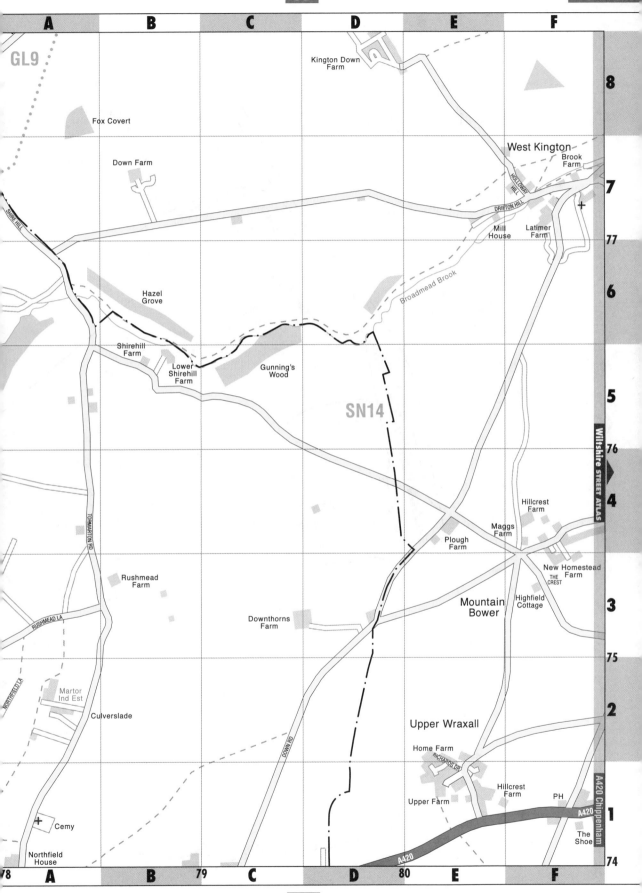

A **B** **C** **D** **E** **F**

GL9

Kington Down Farm

Fox Covert

Down Farm

SHIRE HILL

West Kington

Brook Farm

HOLLOWAY HILL

DRIFTON HILL

77

Mill House

Latimer Farm

Broadmead Brook

Hazel Grove

Shirehill Farm

Lower Shirehill Farm

Gunning's Wood

SN14

76

Wiltshire STREET ATLAS

Hillcrest Farm

Maggs Farm

TORMARTON RD

Plough Farm

New Homestead Farm

THE CREST

Rushmead Farm

Highfield Cottage

RUSHMEAD LA

Downthorns Farm

Mountain Bower

75

Martor Ind Est

NORTHFIELD LA

Culverslade

DOWN RD

Upper Wraxall

Home Farm

RICHARDS DR

Hillcrest Farm

PH

A420 Chippenham

Cemy

Upper Farm

A420

A420

The Shoe

Northfield House

A **B** **C** **D** **E** **F**

A | B | C | D | E | F

Jetty
(dis)

79

Piers

BS11   Docks   8

River Avon
Swash Channel   7

BS20   81

505   Holes
Mouth   6

A   B

Fuel Storage
Depot

River Severn

Bristol & Bath STREET ATLAS

BANK RD

RIVER RD

Hallen Marsh
Junction

SMOKE LA

A403

SEVERN RD

Works

BRISLION LA

SEVERN RD

Chittening
Ind Est

CHITTENING RD

GREENSA COTT RD

WORTHY RD

BANK RD

LC's

WASHINGPOOL LA

BS10

West
House
Farm

CABOT PK

Severn Way

Works

POPLAR WAY W

MOOREND FARM AVE

IO Ctr

POPLAR
RDBT

BS11

POPLAR WAY E

MOORHOUSE LA

BS10

LAWRENCE WES LN RD

MEREBANK ROAD

5

80

4

3

79

2

1

78

Fuel
Storage
Depot

Severnside
Trad Est

LC

IRONCHURCH RD

SEVERN RD

DEAN RD

BURCOTT RD

HUMBER WAY

STORES RD

CCC OMMUNAL RD

ACID RD

WORKSHOP RD

SPAR RD

ZINC RD

Works

FIRST RD

LC's RD

I.S.E RD

BOUNDARY RD

KINGS WESTON LA

Katherine
Farm

Sewage
Works

Mere Bank Rhine

M49

St Andrews
Road

St Georges
Ind Est

Royal Edward Dock

Royal Edward Dock

Avonmouth
Docks

P

P

International
Trad Est

St Andrews
Trad Est

Haslemere
Ind Est

JUBILEE WAY

THIRD WAY

ST ANDREWS
GATE RDBT

KING ROAD
AVE

P

A403

FIRE STATION LA

AVONMOUTH WAY W

Motorway
Distribution
Ctr

Avonmouth

AVONMOUTH WAY

FIRST WAY

SECOND WAY

WILLMENT WAY

LESCREN WAY

THE
POLYGON

BALLAST LA

FIFTH WAY

18a

M49

A4 CROWLEY WAY

BRISTOW BROADWAY

M5

NEW WAY

Nova
Distribution
Ctr

Island
Trad Pk

FOURTH WAY

AVONMOUTH WAY

M5

1 Campbell Farm
2 Campbell Ct

CAMPBELL

KING ST

NAPIER SQ

CLAXTON

QUEEN ST

RICHMOND RD

LENNOX RD

JUTLAND RD

ST ANDREWS RD

MEADOW ST

MCLAREN

EVELYN LA

NOVA WAY

ST BRENDAN'S WAY

ACTING CL

Liby

Nova
Distribution
Ctr

P

GLOUCESTER RD

AVONMOUTH RD

GREEN

COLLINS ST

PORTVIEW
RD

Avonmouth

PO

A4

Avonbridge
Trad Est

ATLANTIC RD

M5   18

M5

FIM CL

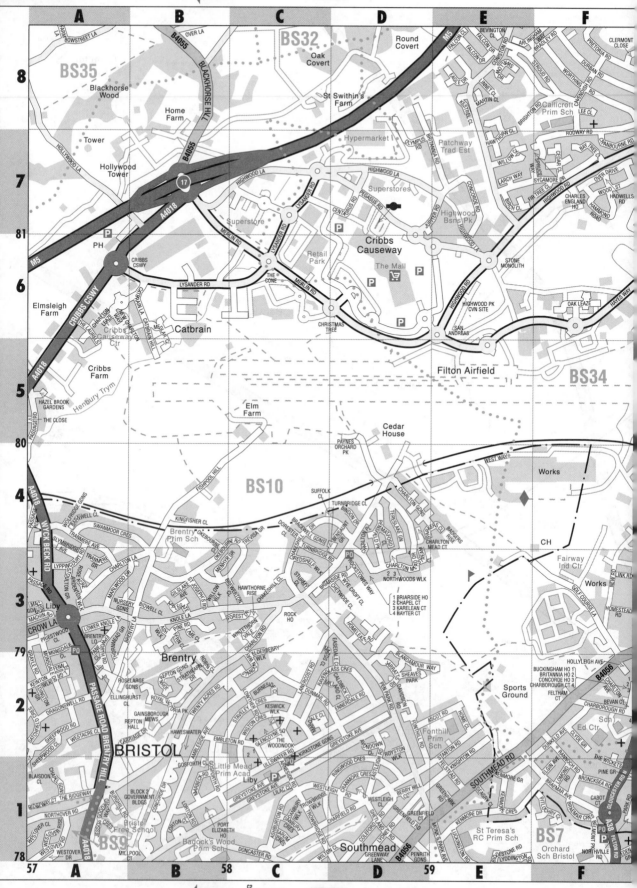

C2
1 GLENCOYNE CT
2 ST STEPHENS CL

D7
1 MINSTER CT
2 FOUNTAIN CT
3 MONKS HO
4 FRIARS HO
5 ABBEY HO
6 PRINKNASH CT

D8
1 AVONLEA
2 OAK LODGE
3 STANSHAWES DR
4 BROOKTHORPE CT
5 HOLLYBROOK MEWS
6 LYDBROOK CL

A B C D E F

8
7
81
6
5
80
4
3
79
2
1
78

Says Court Farm

BS36

Say's Wood

Westerleigh Common

YATE

Beech Hill

Elm Farm

Rodford

Immanuel Christian School

BS37

Pool Farm

Wapley Bushes

Wapley Common

Cliff Farm

Chescombe Farm

Dodmoor Farm

Grove Farm

Besom La

Wapley Bank

Jorrocks Ind Est

Westerleigh

Brook Farm

Wychwell Farm

Church Farm

Brice's Farm

Mill House Farm

Beanwood Farm

Bean Wood

Bush's Farm

Wapley

Wayleaze

B4465

Kidney Hill Sunnybank

Westerleigh Rd

Westerleigh Hill Farm

Mast

Westerleigh Hill

B4465

Beanwood Pk (CVN Site)

Burbarrow La

B4465

Abattoir

Dewshill Wood

Cliff Farm

Crem

Gorse Covert

Leigh La

Leigh Farm

69 A B 70 C D 71 E F

Abbotswood Prim Sch

Wellesley Prim Sch

Shire Way

Brockworth

Edgeworth

Badgeworth

Kingscote

Raysfield Infants Sch

Kingsgate Park

Woodchester

Macemore

Cherington

Littledean

Maisemore

Harescombe

Harescombe

Blaisdon

Glenfall

Hatherley

Brean

Heron Way

Robin Way

Kestrel Cl

Goldcrest Rd

Scott Way

Merlin Way

Hudson Cl

Finch Cl

Shackleton Ave

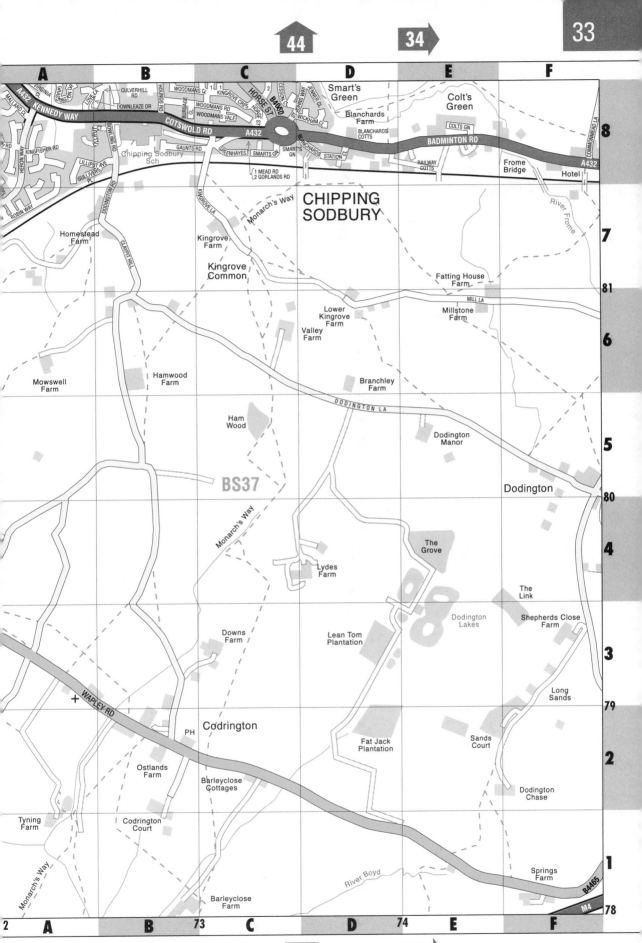

A **B** **C** **D** **E** **F**

A432
KENNEDY WAY
MALLARD CL
VIRGINIA GRDS
GRASMERE RD
LOVS LA
HOUNDS RD
CULVERHILL RD
DOWNLEAZE DR
WOODMANS CL
1 KINGROVE CRES
WOODMANS RD
WOODMANS VALE
HORSE ST
B4060
CESSON CL
NW SINGL KI
JENNER CL
WICKHAM CL
Smart's Green
Blanchards Farm
Colt's Green
COMMONMEAD LA

8

COTSWOLD RD
A432
BURGAGE CL
GAUNTS RD
GREENHAYES
SMARTS GN
SMART'S GN
BLANCHARDS
COTTS
BLANCHARDS STATION CL
COLTS GN
BADMINTON RD
A432

Kingfisher RD
HERON WAY
ROBIN WAY
LILLIPUT AVE
GULLIVERS PL
Chipping Sodbury Sch
1 MEAD RD
2 GORLANDS RD
RAILWAY COTTS
Frome Bridge
Hotel

River Frome

Homestead Farm
CLAPPIT HILL
DODINGTON RD
BOWLING RD
Monarch's Way
KINGROVE LA
Kingrove Farm
CHIPPING SODBURY

7

Kingrove Common
Fatting House Farm

81

Lower Kingrove Farm
MILL LA
Millstone Farm

Valley Farm

6

Mowswell Farm
Hamwood Farm
Branchley Farm
DODINGTON LA

5

Ham Wood
Dodington Manor
Dodington

80

BS37
Monarch's Way
The Grove

4

Lydes Farm
The Link
Dodington Lakes
Shepherds Close Farm

Downs Farm
Lean Tom Plantation
Long Sands

3

WAPLEY RD
79

Codrington
PH
Fat Jack Plantation
Sands Court

2

Ostlands Farm
Barleyclose Cottages
Dodington Chase

Tyning Farm
Codrington Court

1

Springs Farm
B4465

Monarch's Way
Barleyclose Farm
River Boyd
M4
78

A **B** **C** **D** **E** **F**

2 73 74

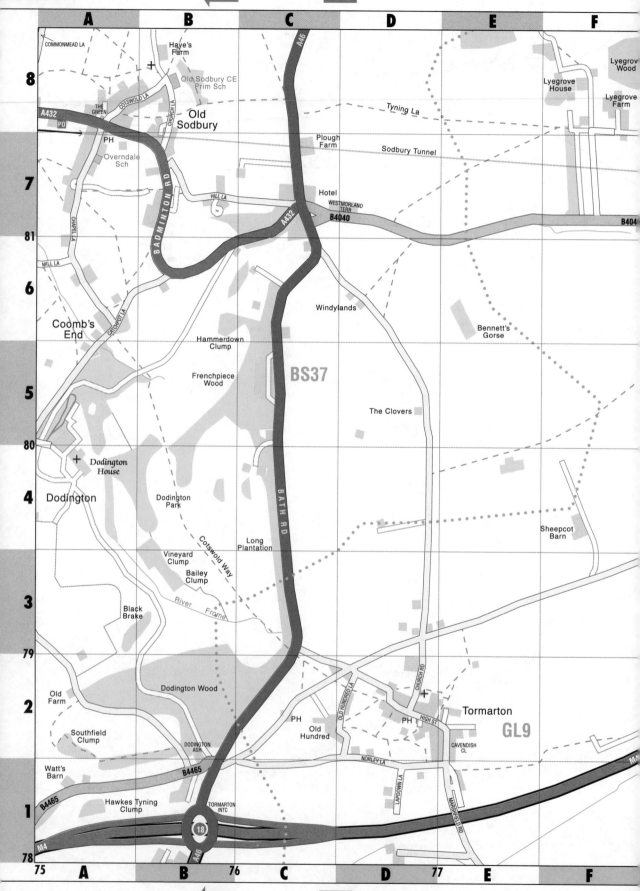

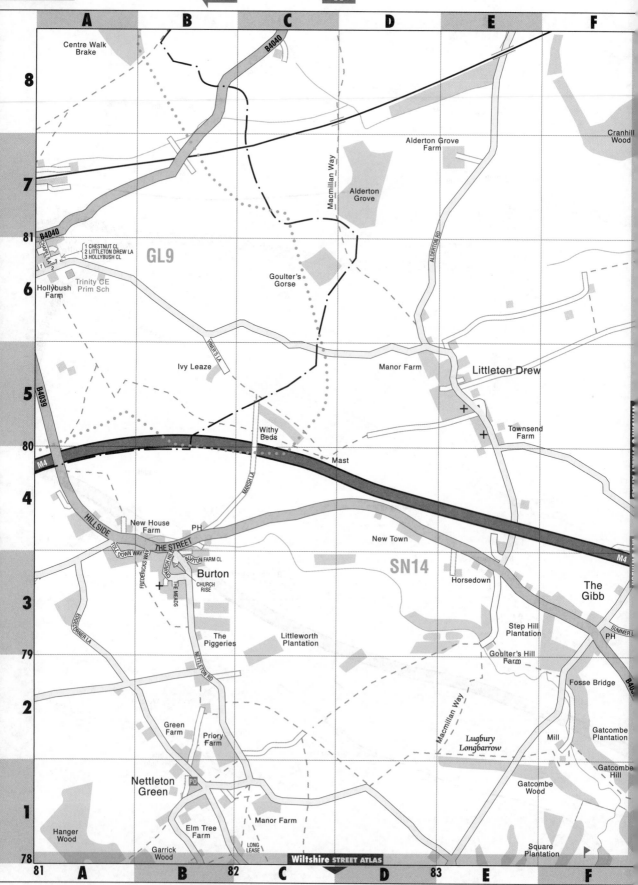

A B C D E F

8

7

81

6

5

80

4

3

79

2

1

78

Centre Walk Brake

B4040

Macmillan Way

Alderton Grove Farm

Alderton Grove

Cranhill Wood

B4040

GL9

1 CHESTNUT CL
2 LITTLETON DREW LA
3 HOLLYBUSH CL

CHAPEL LA

Hollybush Farm

Trinity CE Prim Sch

Goulter's Gorse

ALDERTON RD

B4039

VINER'S LA

Ivy Leaze

Manor Farm

Littleton Drew

Townsend Farm

M4

Withy Beds

MARSH LA

Mast

HILLSIDE

New House Farm

PH

THE STREET

New Town

SN14

M4

The Gibb

TOLL DOWN WAY

FREDERICKS WAY

CHURCH HILL

Burton

BURTON FARM CL

THE MEADS

CHURCH RISE

Horsedown

SUMMER L

PH

EDGECORNER LA

The Piggeries

Littleworth Plantation

Step Hill Plantation

Goulter's Hill Farm

Fosse Bridge

B4039

NETTLETON RD

Green Farm

Priory Farm

Macmillan Way

Lugbury Longbarrow

Mill

Gatcombe Plantation

Gatcombe Hill

Nettleton Green

PO

Gatcombe Wood

Hanger Wood

Elm Tree Farm

Manor Farm

LONG LEASE

Square Plantation

Garrick Wood

81 A 82 B C 83 D E F

A   B   C   D   E   F

Herefordshire Monmouthshire STREET ATLAS

M4 Newport
M4
Second Severn Crossing
M4

8

The Binn Wall

7

BEACH RD
B4064
BEACH AVE
85

RUSTIC PK
PO
STATION RD

Severn
Beach

6

RIVERSIDE PK

5

A403
84

4

River Severn

Severn Way

CENTRAL AVE

3

SEVERN RD
BS10

New Pill
Gout
Works
83

Chittening Warth

Red Rhine

2

Power
Station

BS11

1

Stup Pill

A403

Crook's Marsh

82

Severn Way

M4

22

B4064
REDWICK RD

B4064

Southworthy Farm

A403

PH

B4055

M4

REDHAM LA

Works

8

SHAFT RD

GREEN LA

Redwick

NORTHWICK RD

Laurel Farm

SALTHOUSE FARM PK

KINGS ARMS Inn

The Pill

Pilning

BEACH RD

B4064 BEACH AVE

LITTLE GREEN LA

REDWICK RD

REDWICK CROSSROADS

WICK RD

WHITEHOUSE LA

CHESTNUT AVE
VICARS CL
THE GR

REDWICK RDNS

PO

B4064

St Peter's Farm

East Redham Farm

7

OSBORNE RD

GORSE CORNER RD
GORSE COVER RD

CHURCH LA

CHURCH RD

B4055

B4064
W

B4055
JACKSON CL

PH

CROSS HANDS RD

NORTHOVER CT

BANK RD

Gumhurn Farm

Torrs Farm

85

RUSTIC PK

SALMON

STATION RD

CHURCH RD

WINBRIDGE CRES
CRANMOOR GN

St Peter's Anglican / Methodist VC Prim Sch

PILNING ST

Severn Beach Prim Sch

ABLETON CT
SOLWAY

ACRES
DENNY ISLE DR
PROSPECT RD

Whitehouse Farm

Redwick Common Rhine

The Plough (PH)

6

ALBERT RD
A VICTORIA CRES

Severn Beach

ABLETON LA

LANSON ROBERTS ROAD

Ellinghurst Rhine

Pilning

Stati Farm

ABBOTT RD

SEVERNWOOD GDNS

Depot

5

A403

Ellinghurst Farm

SHAYMOOR LA

STATION RD

Grove Farm

Western Approach Distribution Pk

BS35

84

Gilslake

4

ABLETON LA

GOWER WAY

HOLLOWAY RD

Marsh Common

MARSH COMMON RD

Swanmoor Rhine

COLLINS DR
PALMER AVE

Noor Rhine

Swanmoor Bridge

3

P

CENTRAL AVE

P

Dyer's Common

Middle Compton Rhine

Avlon Works

GREEN LA

GOLDCREST WAY

83

ROAD TWO

Mast

Upper Compton Rhine

SPANIORUM VIEW

B40

2

Severnside Works

BS10

FARM LA

THE LANE

Lyde Brook

Brook Farm

LC

How Street Rhine

VIMPENNYS LA

1

ABLETON LA

BS11

BERWICK LA

82

Crook's Marsh

A B C D E F

8
7
85
6
5
84
4
83
3
2
1
82

REDHAM LA

Waining Farm

Pear Tree Farm

Poplar Farm

Home Farm

Willow Farm

AWKLEY LA

Awkley Hill

M4

Kenora Farm

PILNING ST

Awkley

HARDY LA

MOOR LA

Ostbridge Manor Farm

Pilning New Rhine

Bunsham Rhine

The Niatts

Niatt Rhine

Orchard Farm

Laurel Farm

Sandy Rhine

Pilning Farm

Tockington Mill Rhine

Gussy's Withy Bed

The NAS Anderson Sch

ROOKERY LA

Hayes Farm

Mill Rhine Plantation

MARSHWALL LA

Pilning Farm

Middle Rhine

Square Covert

Rookery Farm

Old Withy Bed

Rednend Farm

Round Hill

Lower Knowle Farm

TOWNSEND LA

Bellhouse

Bell lane

BS35

Newman's Hill

84

TOWNSEND

KING CL

CHURCH VIEW

Pilning Junction

SHAYMOOR LA

BS32

MONMOUTH HILL

Almondsbury

Brynleaze Farm

Catbrain Wood

KNOLE LN

Cattybrook Farm

Brick Works

Washingpool Farm

Bailey's Mead Rhine

Over Brook

BADGER'S LA

Nursery

M5

Village Farm

PROSPECT CL

Lower Over Farm

Over Farm

Pegwell Brake

Mast

Aztec West

Easter Compton

Community Forest Path

ASH LA

OVER LA

BRISTOL

CABLE CT

Over

PARK AVE

Coniston Prim Sch

1 CHARLTON CT
2 NORTON HO
3 TIRLEY HO
4 KEMBLE HO
5 ASHLEY HO
6 KENTON HO

The Fox (PH)

PO

HOME FARM WY

Over Court Farm House

Basin Covert

BS34

Church Farm

COOKS LN

CHURCH RD

Over Court

PO

RICHMOND CT

B4055

BLACKHORSE HILL

FARM LA

CONISTON RD

ARLINGHAM WHY

BRADLEY RD

D1
1 SHEPHERDS WK
2 THE PASTURE
3 THE HEDGEROWS
4 LITTLE GREEN

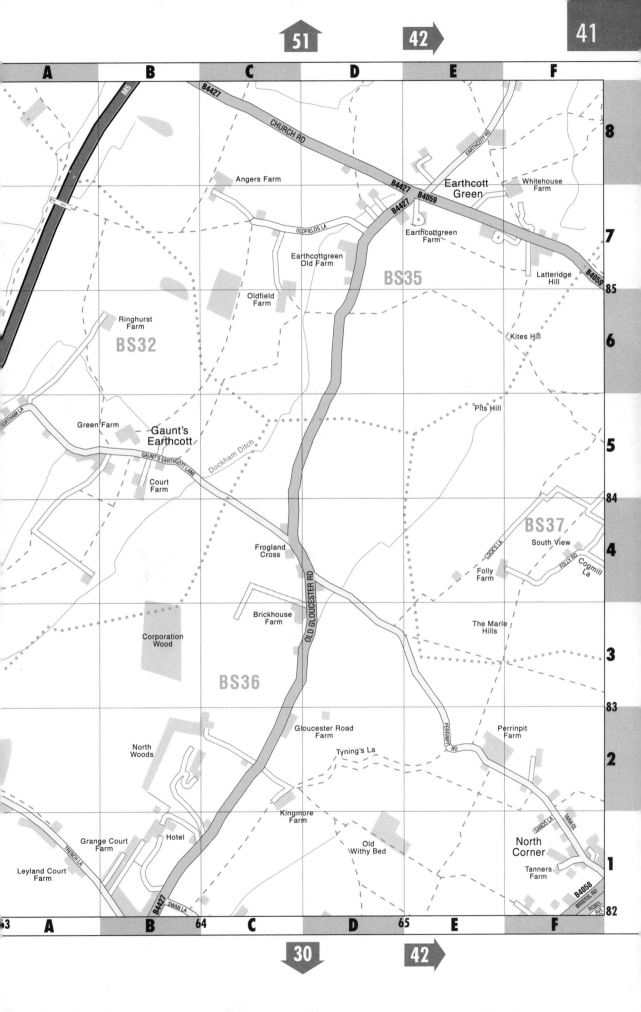

A **B** **C** **D** **E** **F**

8

BS35

Lower Lark's Farm

Dowells Farm

Patch Elm Farm

7

PATCH ELM LA

B4059

85

Mudgedown Farm

B4059

LATTERIDGE LA

LARK'S LA

Northend Farm

6

Ladden Bows Bridge

CHAINGATE LA

Chaingate House

WOTTON RD

Latteridge

LC

Two Pools Farm

Backfield Farm Bsns Pk

5

Acton Court

Ladden Brook

Sheephouse Farm

FOLLY RD

Acton Lodge

BS37

84

Hill House

B4059

4

THE GREEN

B4058

B4058

LATTERIDGE RD

PH

Iron Acton

PARK ST

PH

Isle of Rhee

B4059

Laddenside Farm

PH

HIGH ST

PH

WOTTON RD

YATE RD

Elm Farm

Cogmill La

STATION RD

HOLLY HILL

Iron Acton CE Prim Sch

B4059

3

River Frome

LC

CHILLWOOD

ALGARS DR

Robins Wood

Lavenham Farm

NIBLEY LA

BRISTOL RD

HOOVER'S LA

Brake Farm

Algars Manor

83

Cog Mill Farm

2

FRAMPTON END RD

Tubb's Bottom

HOOVER'S LA

BS36

Chestnut Farm

1

PH

Frampton Cotterell

B4058

MILL LA

BADMINTON RD

Cemy

Mayshill

MAYS HILL

WESTERN AVE

LOWER CL

CHURCH RD

SCHOOL RD

A4432

82

66 **A** **B** **67** **C** **D** **68** **E** **F**

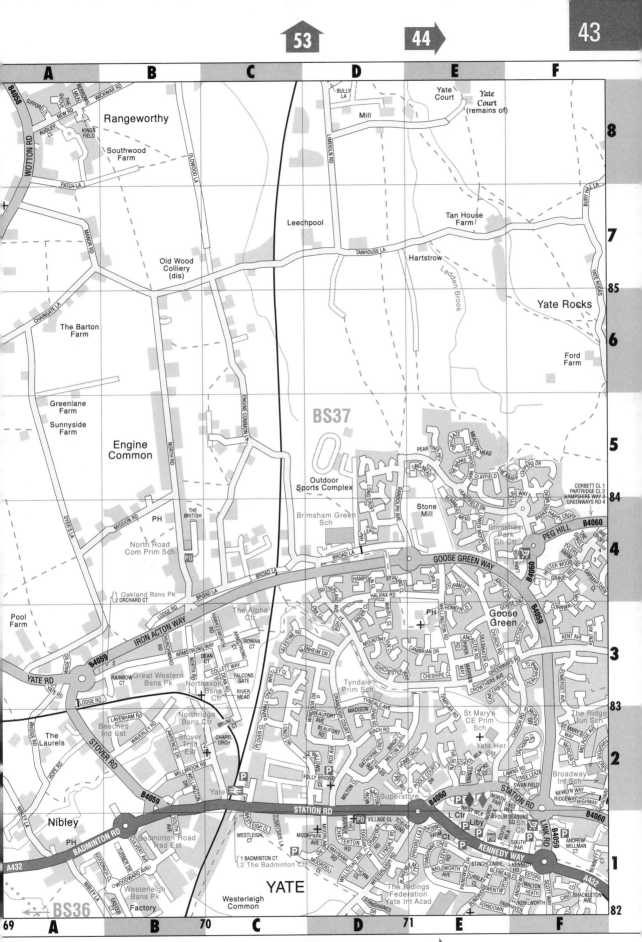

A B C D E F

8

Oxwick Farm

Lady's Wood

Horwood Riding Farm

B4060

BURY HILL LA

The Chase

Springfield Farm

VINNEY LA

7

Bury Hill

Lattimore Farm

Little Wood

Brinsham Wood

85

Brinsham Farm

Brinsham Bridge

Hares Farm

MAPLERIDGE LA

Ashlea Farm

6

BRINSHAM LA

WICKWAR RD

Horton Bushes

5

Home Farm

Quarry

Quarry

Quarry

GRAVEL HILL RD

BS37

Sodbury Common

Totteroak

Rockwood

Totteroak Farm

84

ROCKWOOD HO

B4060

PEG HILL

SOUTHFIELD WAY

Star Vale Farm

Little Sodbury End

Winchcombe Farm

4

LOVE LA

LIME CROFT

BARNHILL CL

HORTON RD

Greystone Ct

CARMARTHEN CL

WILTSHIRE RD

GREEN WAYS RD

Stub Riding

Mead Riding

CH
The Windmill

Great House Farm

3

YATE

DORSET WAY

Lodge

Monarch's Way

83

W.J.MHRST GDNS

WALNUT RD

JUBILEE GDNS

MELROSE AVE

2

BROADWAY

FIRGROVE CR

STACY

MELROSE CL

DOWDING CL

CAROLINE

COUZENS CL

HORTON RD

BROOKFIELD CL

MANOR WAY

ST JOHNS WAY

PORTWAY LA

Hardwoodgate Farm

RIDGEWAY

ROSS CL

Park's Farm

HIGHWAY

Works

Bowling Hill Bsns Pk

Cemy

BARNHILL RD

BROOK

STONE HOUSE MEWS

Chipping Edge Est

BEAUFORT MEWS

HATTERS

River Frome

RIDINGS

1

STATION RD

B4060

Mill

BOWLING HILL

EDWARD RD

THE PARADE

ROUNCEVAL ST

HORSESHOE LA

B4060

HIGH ST

BROAD ST

BATTEN CT

ROGERS CL

MELBOURNE

GLOUCESTER RD

GRACE CL

FROME RD

BRANDASH RD

WHITEFIELDS

WALSHE AVE

KWI SHOP

CHIPPING SODBURY

BENNET

CHERRY RD

STREAMSIDE RD

RIVER

VIRGINIA AVE

CHESTNUT DR

CULVERHILL RD

MEADOW

HIGHFIELD RD

EAMAN

ARNOLD CT

COTSWOLD

HOUNDS CL

B4060 HORSE ST

MEAD RD

CESSON CL

HARTLEY CL

82

Prim Sch

WISTARIA AVE

GRASSINGTON DR

ABBEYFIELD HO

HOUNDS CL

A432

72 A B 73 C D 74 E F

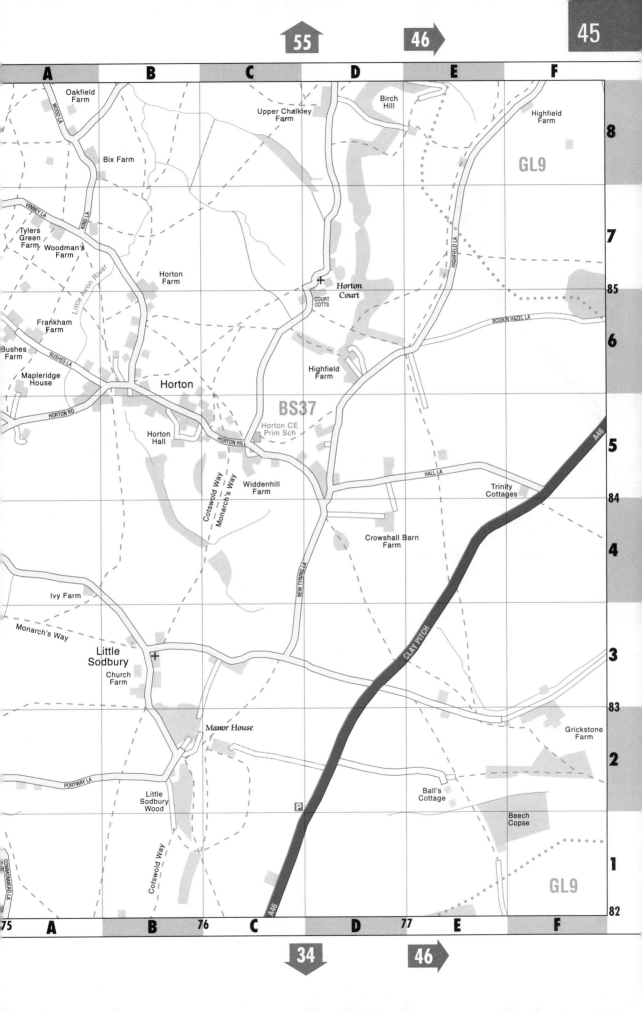

A B C D E F

8

Petty France
Farm

THE STABLE
YD

Hotel

Petty France

Swangrove
House

Bodkin
Wood

7

85 Bodkin Hazel
Wood

BODKIN HAZEL LA

Worcester Avenue

6

Shepherd's
Lodge

Worcester Clump

A46

Seven Mile Plantation

Withy
Bed

Little
Badminton
Farm

Little
Badminton

5 American
Barn

CHURCH LA

GL9

WELL LA

84

BS37

4

Peaked Down
Clump

Badminton Park

Mount
Pond

Deer Park

The
Mount

Landing Strip

Park
Pond

3

83

Slait
Lodge

Badminton
House

2 Castle
Barn

The Tyning

KENNEL DR

SHOP LA

Bath
Lodge

Bath Verge

ROACH'S LA

PO

HIGH ST

Badminton

LIME AVE

THE LIMES

SCHOOL LA

HAYES LA

Vicarage
Plantation

1

LIME AVE

KENNEL DR

STATION RD

Badminton
Farm

82

OLD DOWN RD

Cape
Farm

78 A 79 B C 80 D E F

A B C D E F

Duchess's Clump

GL9

Badminton Down

Luckley Brake

Hundred Acres Farm

SN16

SHALLOWBROOKS LA

Sandy Farm

Ivy Leaze Cottage

Luckley Farm

Lord's Copse

Wick Farm

SN14

Cherry Orchard

CHERRY ORCHARD LA

NORTH END

North End Farm

North End House

SHERSTON RD

B4040

Luckington Court

BROOK END

Lyppiatt Barn

Luckington Com Sch

PH

THE PYGHTELL

Luckington Court Gardens

Wiltshire STREET ATLAS

The Green

THE MERCHANTS

The Farm

CHURCH RD

Hermit's Cell

THE BELL FIELD

THE STREET

CHAPEL ROW

HOLLIS GDNS

AVON RISE

THE MEADOWS

Luckington

Allengrove Farm

ALLENGROVE LA

POLAR GDNS

BEAUFORT VIEW

Allen Grove

Oak Plantation

Hebden Leaze Farm

BRISTOL RD

Macmillan Way

GL9

Giant's Cave

Alderton

Splash Pond

Townfield Farm

Fatting Barn

Hebden Leaze

Hebden Farm

B4040

A B C D E F

Herefordshire Monmouthshire STREET ATLAS

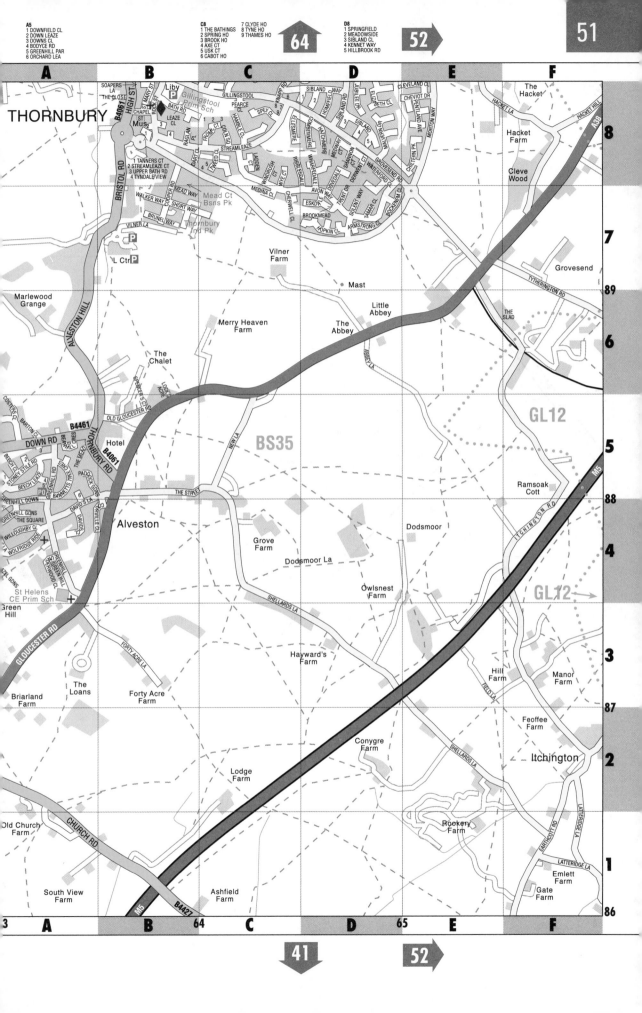

A38
Garden Ctr
Lodge Farm
Acorn Farm
Corbets
GREEN LA

Cromhall La
Hope Farm
M5
Mast
Cuttsheath
Priest Wood
Jones's Wood
Trapwell Bridge
RECTORY LA

BS35
Barmer's Land Farm
Baden Hill
CUTSHEATH RD

89
Quarry
WOODLANDS SOUTH RD

Tytherington Rd
WOODLANDS
STOW HILL RD
Quarry
NEW RD
THE JAYS
STOWELL HILL RD
BADEN HILL RD
Tytherington Hill
Stidcot
Stidcot Farm
Ashworthy Farm

M5
The Castle
THE ORCHARD
PH
PO
WEST ST
DUCK ST
Tytherington
Lower Hill Farm
STIDCOT LA
Pendicks Farm
Stidcot Plat
STIDCOTE LA

Brook Farm
West Street Farm
THE NURSERIES
Newhouse Farm
Summer Bridge

88
SOUTHLANDS
Mill Farm
GL12

ITCHINGTON RD

BAGSTONE RD
B4058

3
Moorleaze
Ladden Brook

87

Lower Farm
BS35
BS37

Hotel
Rangeworthy

1
Cemy
CHURCH LA
WOTTON RD
Rangeworthy CE Prim Sch

LATTERIDGE LA
Stockhill Cottage

86

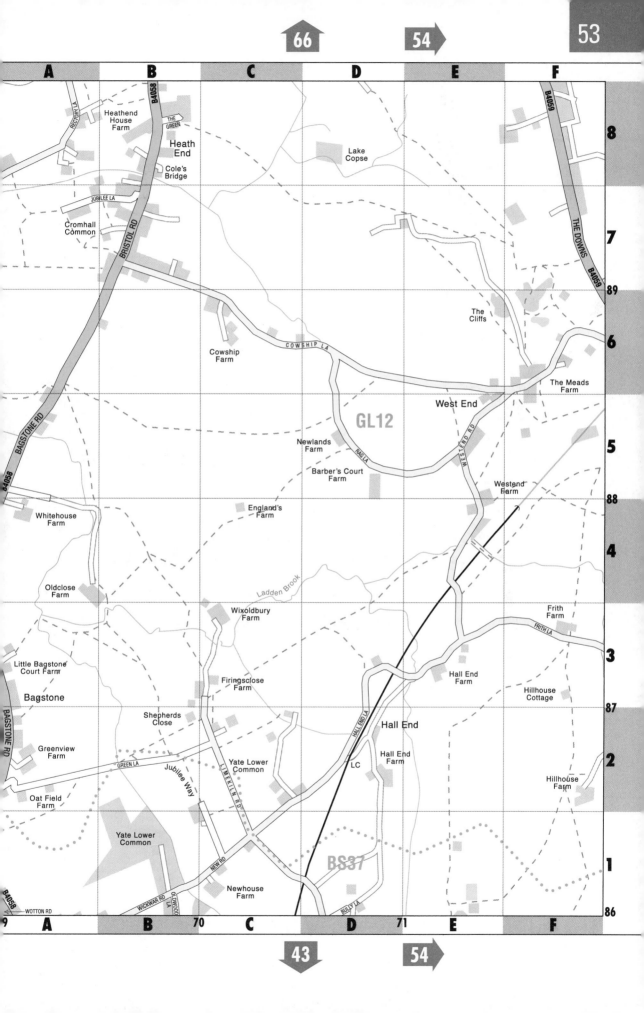

A   B   C   D   E   F

8

Southwood
Farm

Bunsall
Bridge

B4060

Archfield
Nursery

Cherryrock
Farm

Cherryrock
Brake

Mounteney's
Farm

Haroldsfield
Farm

7

Station
House

STATION RD

Trad
Est

Chasehouse
Farm

Kites
Farm

Mounteney's
Farm

89

CHURCH LA

CHASE LA

MOUNTENEY'S LA

B4059

THE DOWNS

B4060

Saltmoors Ditch

Chaselane
Farm

Chase Hill

Inglestone
Farm

6

WESTEND
RD

PH

TURNPIKE

NORTH ST

AVON CRES

AVON CRES

COTSWOLD VIEW

HONEYBOURNE WAY

South Moon
Ridings

GL12

Arnolds Field
Trad Est

TH

HIGH ST

ARKELLS LA

BACK LA

INGLESTONE RD

Alexander Hosea
Prim Sch

Sturt
Farm

The Walk

Little Stanley
Wood

Lower Woods
Lodge

5

THE
BUTHAY

BUTHAY LA

PO

SOUTHEND
HO

AMBERLEY WAY

BURLEIGH WAY

CANTERS LEAZE

Wickwar

Sturt
Bridge

88

South
Farm

Little Avon River

GL9

POPLAR LA

Horwood
Farm

Wetmoor
Nature Reserve

4

Poplar
Farm

HORWOOD LA

SODBURY RD

Bishop's Hill
Wood

Upper
Wetmoor

Lower Wetmoor
Wood

Littley
Wood

3

FRITH LA

Hill View
Farm

Bishop's Hill Brook

Sturgeon
Wood

87

PINCOTS LA

Pincots
Farm

Burnt
Wood

2

Bedford's
Wood

Bays Wood

BS37

Shortwood
Farm

Stonybridge
Wood

Haskin's
Farm

WOOD LA

1

WICKWAR RD

Little Shortwood
Farm

Birdsbush
Farm

B4060

86

72   A   73   B   C   73   D   74   E   F

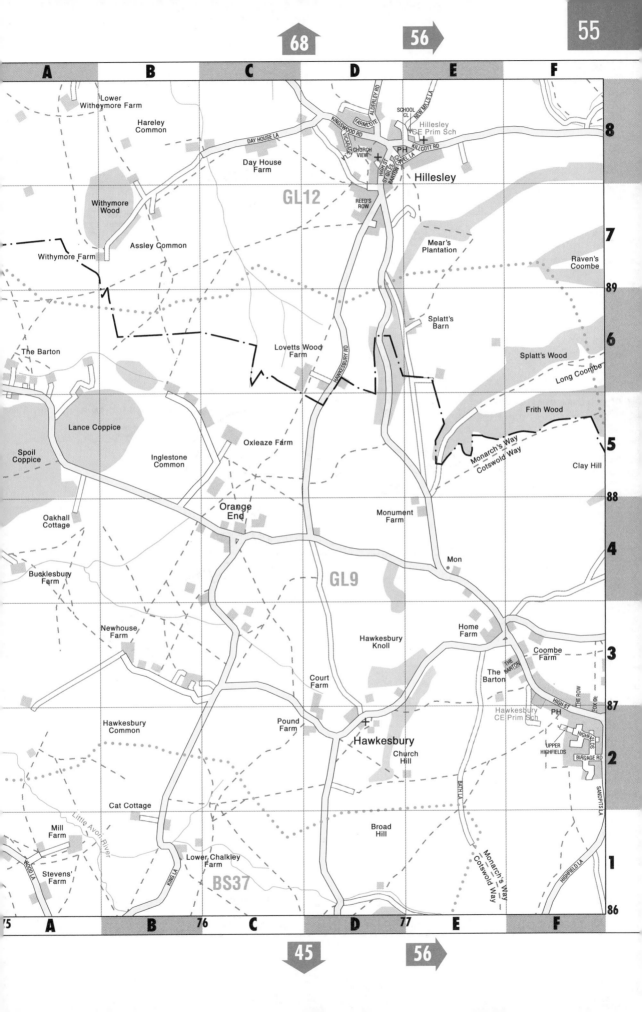

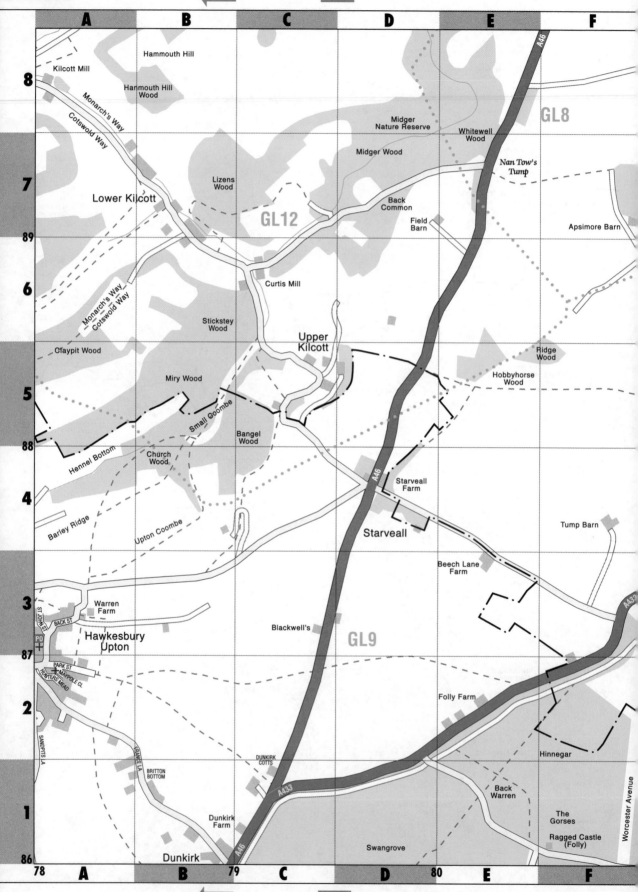

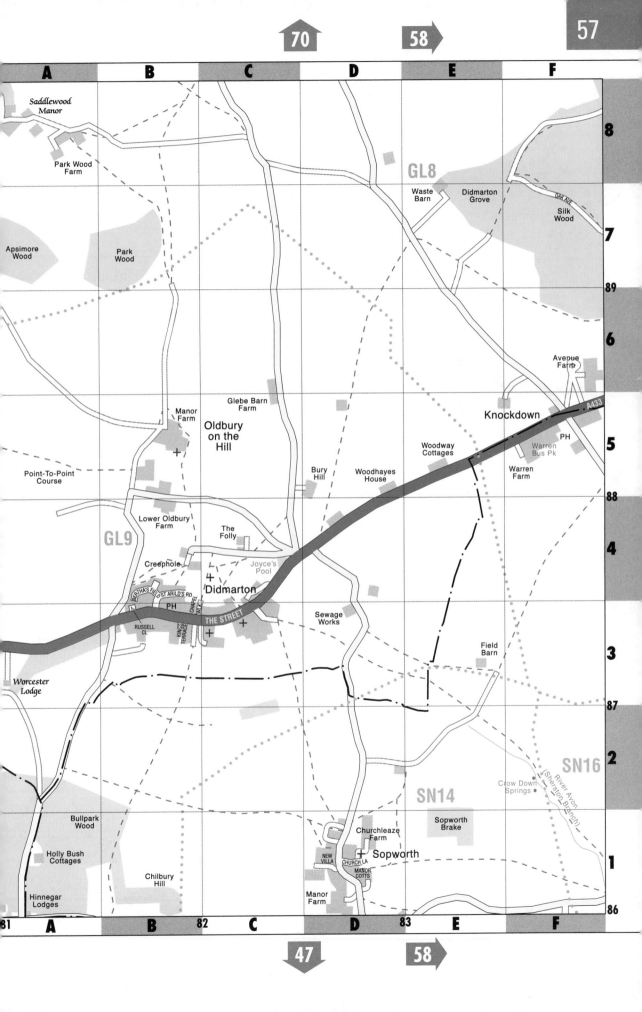

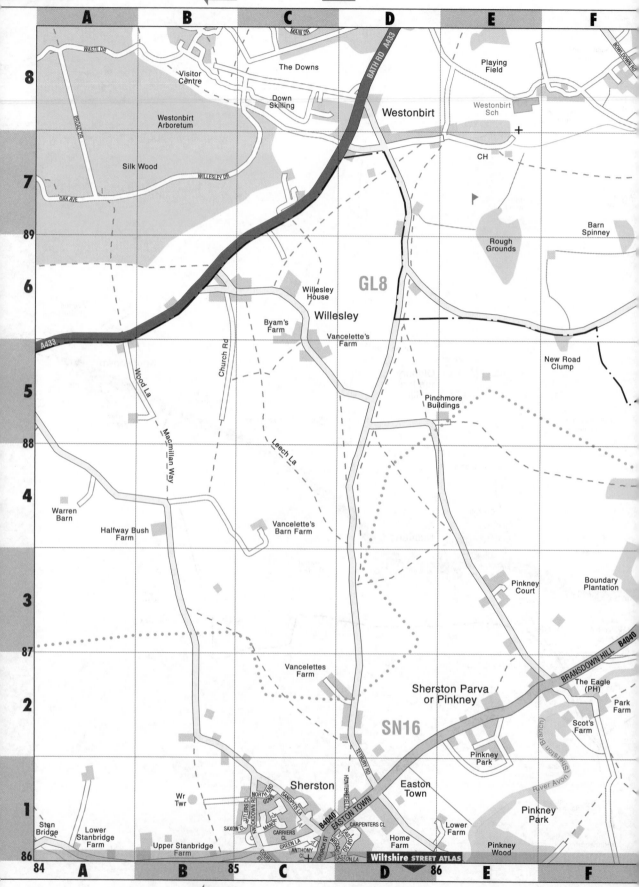

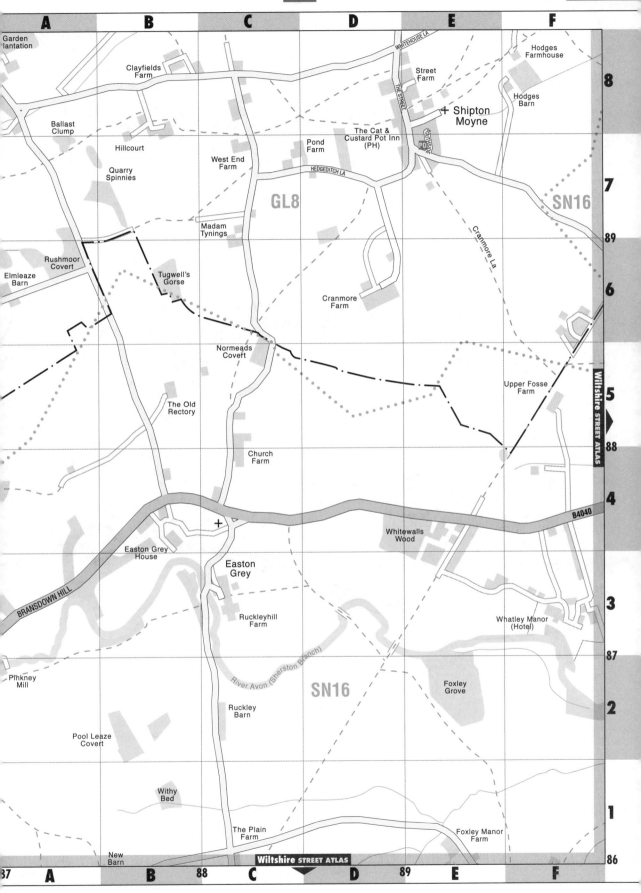

A B C D E F

8
7
89
6
5
88
4
3
87
2
1
86

Garden Plantation

Clayfields Farm

WHITEHOUSE LA

Hodges Farmhouse

Street Farm

THE STREET

✝ Shipton Moyne

Hodges Barn

Ballast Clump

Hillcourt

West End Farm

Pond Farm

The Cat & Custard Pot Inn (PH)

SOUTHSIDE

PO

Quarry Spinnies

GL8

HEDGEDITCH LA

SN16

Madam Tynings

Cranmore La

Rushmoor Covert

Tugwell's Gorse

Cranmore Farm

Elmleaze Barn

Normeads Covert

Upper Fosse Farm

The Old Rectory

Wiltshire STREET ATLAS

Church Farm

✝

Easton Grey House

Easton Grey

Whitewalls Wood

B4040

BRANSDOWN HILL

Ruckleyhill Farm

Whatley Manor (Hotel)

Pinkney Mill

River Avon (Sherston Branch)

SN16

Foxley Grove

Ruckley Barn

Pool Leaze Covert

Withy Bed

The Plain Farm

Foxley Manor Farm

New Barn

37 A B 88 C D 89 E F

E8
1 ALBION SQ
2 LIBRARY PL
3 OLD BELL CHAMBERS
4 HOCKER HILL ST
5 BEAUFORT SQ
6 BANK SQ

7 MIDDLE ST
8 ST MARY ST
9 ST MARY STREET ARC
10 OXFORD ST
11 RESTWAY WALL
12 GARDEN CITY WAY

13 School Hill Ind Est
14 EXEMOUTH PL

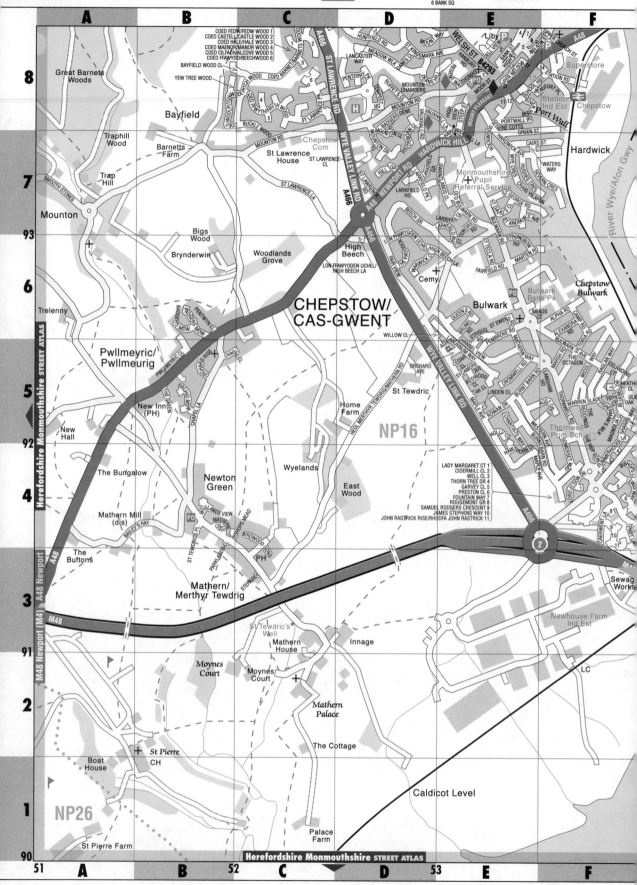

CHEPSTOW/
CAS-GWENT

NP16

NP26

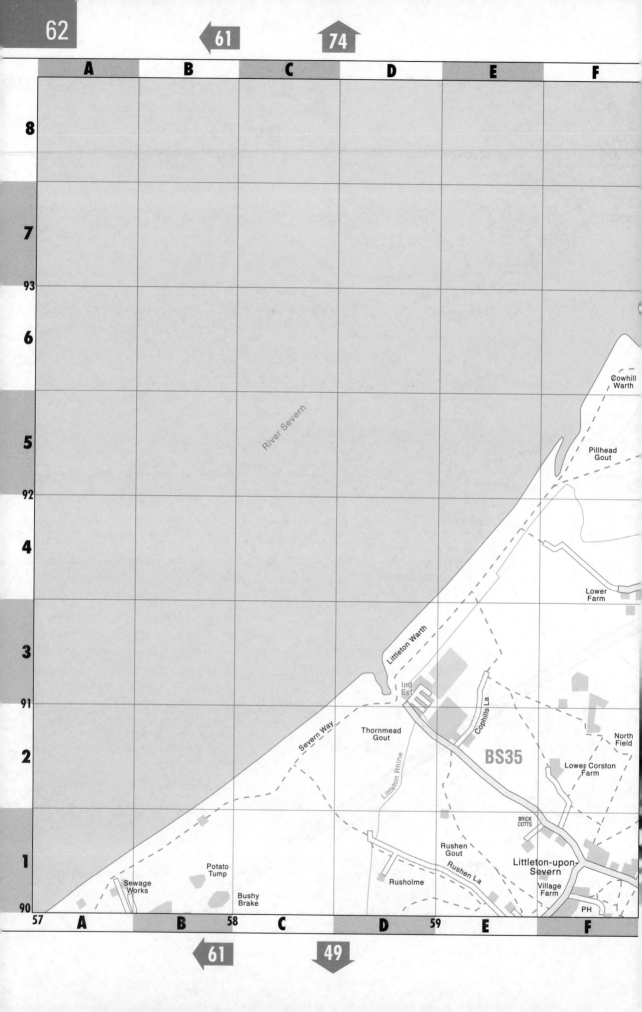

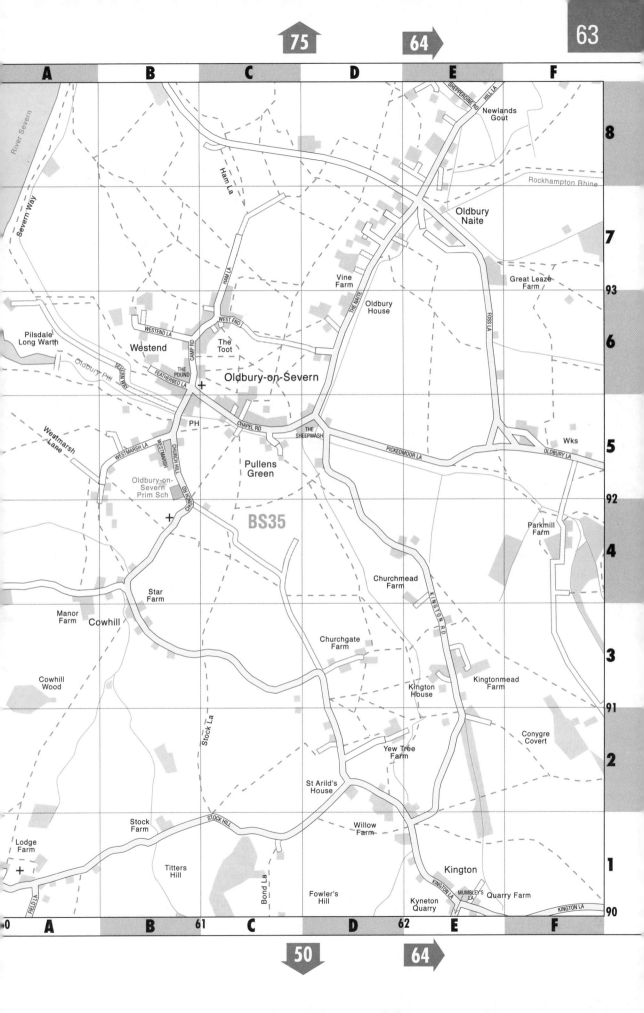

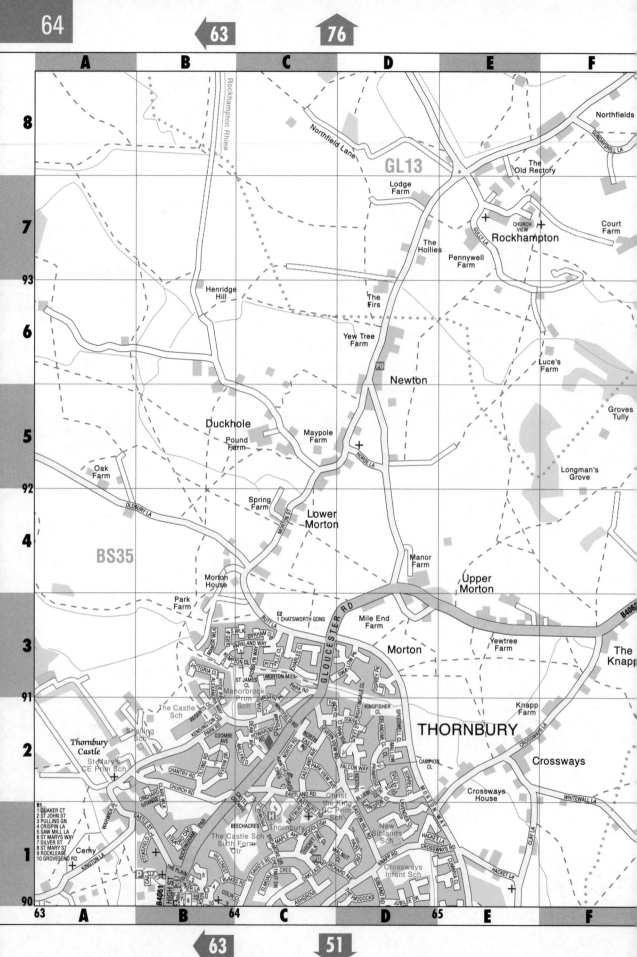

A   B   C   D   E   F

8

Northfields

Northfield Lane

GL13

Lodge
Farm

The
Old Rectory

7

CHURCH
VIEW
Rockhampton

Court
Farm

The Hollies

Pennywell
Farm

93

Henridge
Hill

The Firs

Luce's
Farm

6

Yew Tree
Farm

Newton

Groves
Tully

5

Duckhole

Maypole
Farm

Longman's
Grove

Pound
Farm

Oak
Farm

HORSE LA

92

OLDBURY LA

Spring
Farm

Lower
Morton

4

BS35

Manor
Farm

Upper
Morton

Morton
House

Park
Farm

BUTT LA

C2
1 CHATSWORTH GDNS

Mile End
Farm

GLOUCESTER RD

The
Knapp

3

Morton

Yewtree
Farm

B4061

MANOR WALK

S WLK

DYRHAM CL

PARKLAND WAY

PITT LE CL

CHARLES CL

SWALLOW PK

KINGFISHER
CL

Knapp
Farm

THORNBURY

91

VICTORIA CL

HYDE AVE

ALEXANDRA WAY

KEMPTON CL

ST JAMES
CL

MORTON MILL

PARK RD

OSPREY PK

SPEEDWELL CL

CROSSWAYS LA

Manorbrook
Prim
Sch

FINCH CL

KESTREL CL

MOORLAND CL

The Castle
Sch

REGENTS CL

KENSINGTON CL

WHITTIELD RD

SEVERN AVE

KINGFISHER CL

DELANCEY CL

MALLOW

Shelving
Sch

COOMBE
AVE

MILLS RD

NORTH

HAWTHORN

PARK VIEW AVE

FALCON WAY

PRIMROSE CL

SORREL CL

CAMPION
CL

Crossways

2

Thornbury
Castle

CHANTRY RD

SEVERN DR

HOWARDOCKS

EASTLAND RD

KESTREL

BLUEBELL CL

LAVENDER CL

MORTON WAY

Crossways
House

St Mary's
CE Prim Sch

CHURCH RD

ORCHARD
GRANGE

CASTLE
COOMBE

EASTLAND RD

Christ
the King
RC Prim
Sch

New
Siblands
Sch

Crossways
Rd

WHITEWALL LA

CLAY LA

WARWICK PL

KINGTON LA

CLARE WLK

STOKEFIELD CL

BUCKINGHAM PL

BEECHACRES

MAPLE AVE

WOODLEIGH

THICKET AVE

HAZEL CRES

HACKET LA

CROSSWAYS RD

1

B1
1 QUAKER CT
2 ST JOHN ST
3 PULLINS GN
4 CRISPIN LA
5 SAW MILL LA
6 ST MARYS WAY
7 SILVER ST
8 ST MARY ST
9 ROCKLEASE
10 GROVESEND RD

Cerny

The Castle Sch
Sixth Form
Ctr

H
Thornbury

SYCAMORE AVE

CHESTNUT CL

WALNUT CL

ELM CL

OAKLEAZE RD

KNAPP RD

SIBLAND RD

HACKET LA

CUMBRIA CL

Crossways
Infant Sch

HIGH ST

THE PLAIN

HILLCREST

BLAKES RD

ST DAVID'S RD

ELMDALE CRES

ASHGROVE

The
Pyddocks

JUBILEE DR

90

B4061

CASTLE
CT

PARK LA

COLIN CL

63   A   B   64   C   D   65   E   F

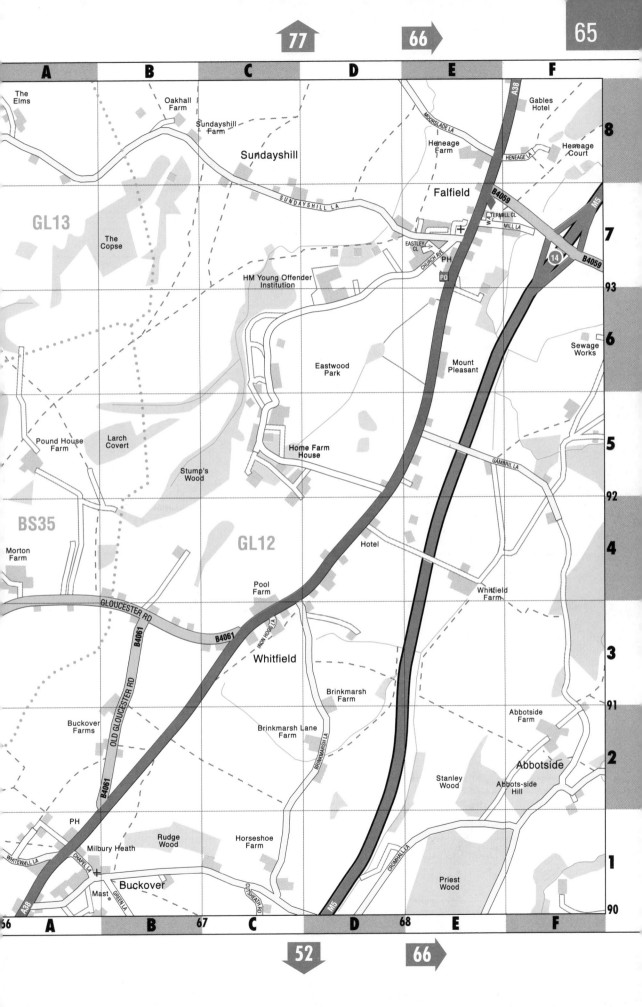

A | B | C | D | E | F

8

The Elms

Oakhall Farm

Sundayshill Farm

Sundayshill

Moorslade La

A38

Gables Hotel

Heneage Farm

Heneage La

Heneage Court

GL13

The Copse

Sundayshill La

Falfield

B4059

M5

7

93

HM Young Offender Institution

W.C.

Termill Cl

Mill La

Eastley Cl

Church Ave

PH

PO

14

B4059

6

Sewage Works

Eastwood Park

Mount Pleasant

BS35

Pound House Farm

Larch Covert

Stump's Wood

Home Farm House

Gambril La

5

92

Morton Farm

GL12

Hotel

4

Pool Farm

Whitfield Farm

Gloucester Rd

B4061

Iron Hogg La

B4061

Whitfield

Brinkmarsh Farm

3

91

Old Gloucester Rd

Buckover Farms

Brinkmarsh Lane Farm

Brinkmarsh La

Abbotside Farm

Abbotside

2

B4061

Stanley Wood

Abbots-side Hill

PH

Rudge Wood

Horseshoe Farm

Cromhall La

Priest Wood

1

Whitewall La

Chapel La

Milbury Heath

Outsheath Rd

M5

90

A38

Mast

Green La

Buckover

A | B | C | D | E | F

A B C D E F

8

M5

Daniel's Wood

Huntingford

Huntingfo Farm

Old Court Farm

Avening Green

7

Brook Farm

Howcroft Cottages

Tortworth

Old Court

Little Tortworth Copse

Hotel

Chestnut

93

Tortworth Prim Sch

Old Lodge Farm

Kennel Plantation

Tortworth Copse

Underwood Farm

B4059

6

Gall Pond

Arboretum

Lodge

Tortworth Court

Tortworth Green

Elmtree Farm

Poolfield Farm

Charfield Prim Sch

5

HM Prison

Charfield Hill

WOTTON RD B405

92

The Lake

Tortworth Park

Leyhill

Tafarn-bach

B4059

The Old Rectory

4

Harris's Wood

PARK RD

WOODLAND RD

MEADOW RD

Woodend Farm

GL12

Hammerley Down

B4059

Poundhouse Farm

CHURCHEND LA

Bloody Acre

3

Parkend

Royal Oak (PH)

KNAPP LA

Brand Wood

Manor Farm

Churchend

DEVIL'S LA

91

Wick's Hill

Bibstone

Church Farm

2

Sodam Mill

FARLEIGH LA

THE BURLTONS

PO

Townwell

Mulberry Tree Steiner School

DUDIE CL

LONGCROSS

Talbotsend Farm

CHURCH LA

St Andrew's CE Prim Sch

Talbot's End

1

Court Farm

Cromhall

BRISTOL RD

RECTORY LA

B4058

B4059

90

69 A 70 B C 70 D 71 E F

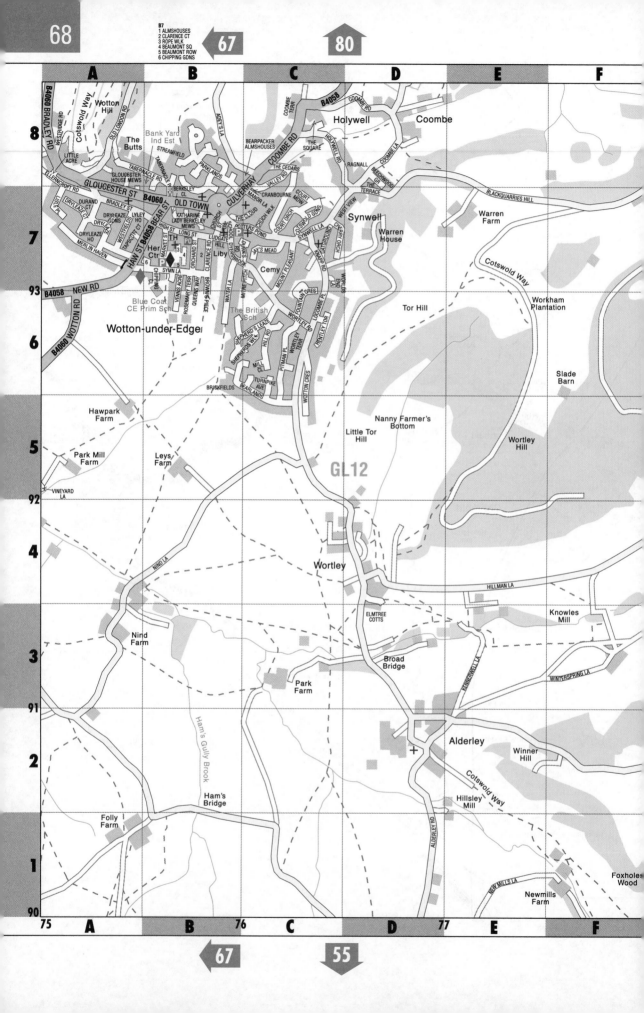

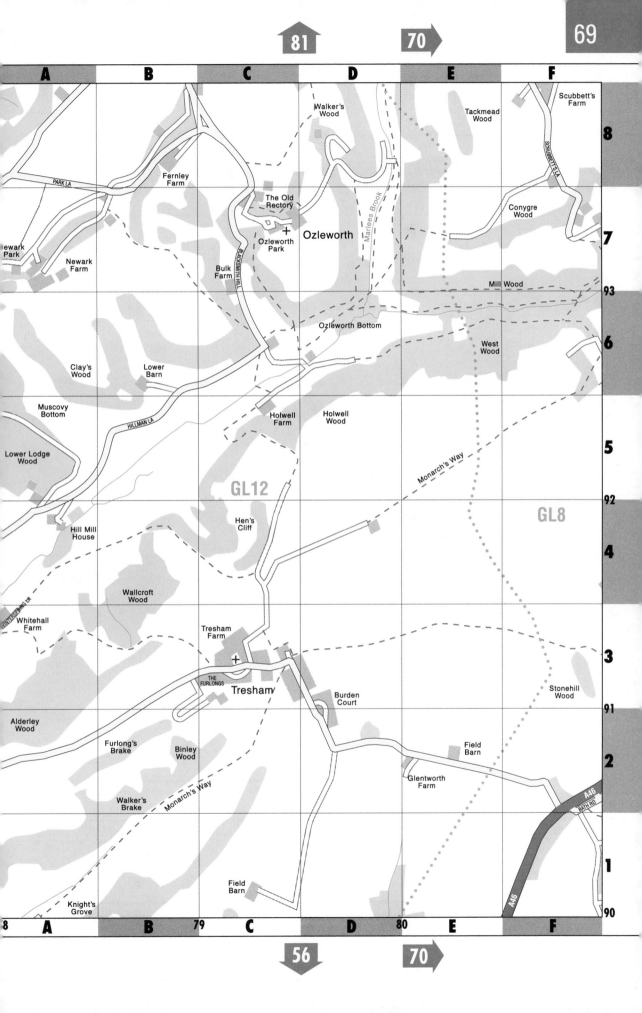

A | B | C | D | E | F

8

Brockhill Covert

Home Covert

Lasborough Park

Brock Hill

Ash Covert

Lasborough Cottages

Lodge Farm

A46

Tum Cove

Long Covert

7

Goss Covert

BOWLDOWN RD

Nursery Wood

93

6

Kitesnest

Boxwell Court +

Boxwell

The Box Wood

Bowldown Farm

Boxwell Farm

GL8

5

Haymead Covert

Monarch's Way

BOXWELL RD

HAYMEAD LA

Slait Barn

92

Cross Roads Lodge

4

WHITEWATER RD

Whitwewater Farm

Sheephouse Covert

3

Leighterton Prim Sch

Leighterton

Drews Farm

TETBURY LA

Cemy

Bennetts Farm

91

BACK LA

PARK LA

THE STREET

THE MEADS

CASTLE FARM CL

Poole Farm

Church Farm

Hillsid Farm

Hamgreen Covert

2

A46

BATH RD

Ashtree Farm

Didmarton Piece

Monarch's Way

1

Castle Farm

Waste Bottom

90

Payne's Barn

81 | A | B | 82 | C | D | 83 | E | F

A B C D E F

8
7
93
6
5
92
4
3
91
2
1
90

Beverston

A4135
A4135

Chavenage La

Park
Farm

Babdown
Ind Est

Park
Bottom

Nesley
Farm

Oldown

BOWLDOWN
COTTS

GL8

Hare
Covert

Hookshouse

HOOKSHOUSE LA

Macmillan Way

CHARLTON DOWN
COTTS

Charlton
Down

Bowldown
Wood

Charltondown
Covert

Monarch's Way

Reservoir
Farm

BOWLDOWN RD

Down
Farm

Field Barn
Farm

A433

Hollybush
Clump

Ellick's
Wood

Three Corner
Covert

Monarch's Way
Macmillan Way

Hare and Hounds
Hotel

BATH RD

Bennett's
Spinney

Down
Plantation

Home
Farm

CIRCULAR DRIVE   MAIN DRIVE

Down
Covert

Westonbirt Arboretum

A433

Garden
Plantation

Hawkesbury
Spinney

4   A   B   85   C   D   86   E   F

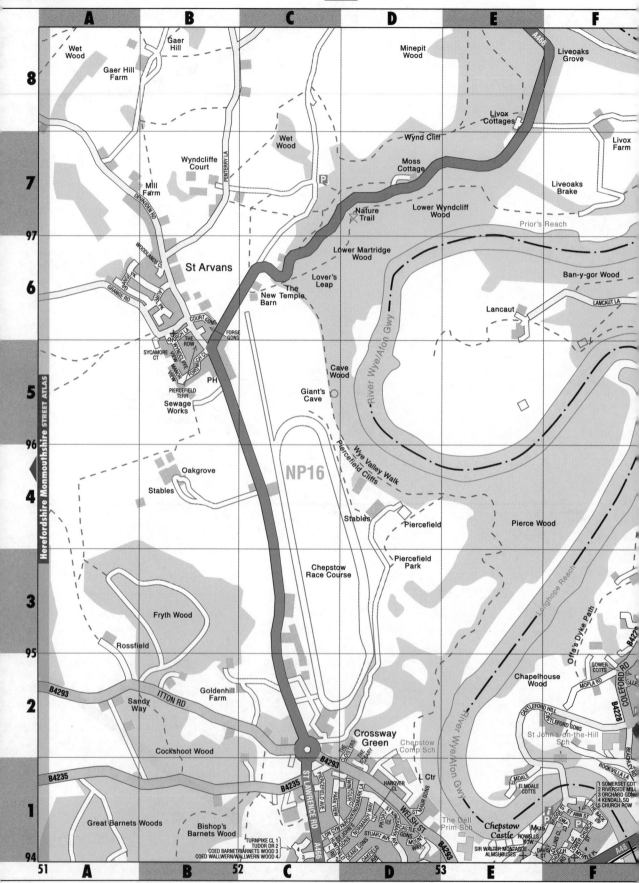

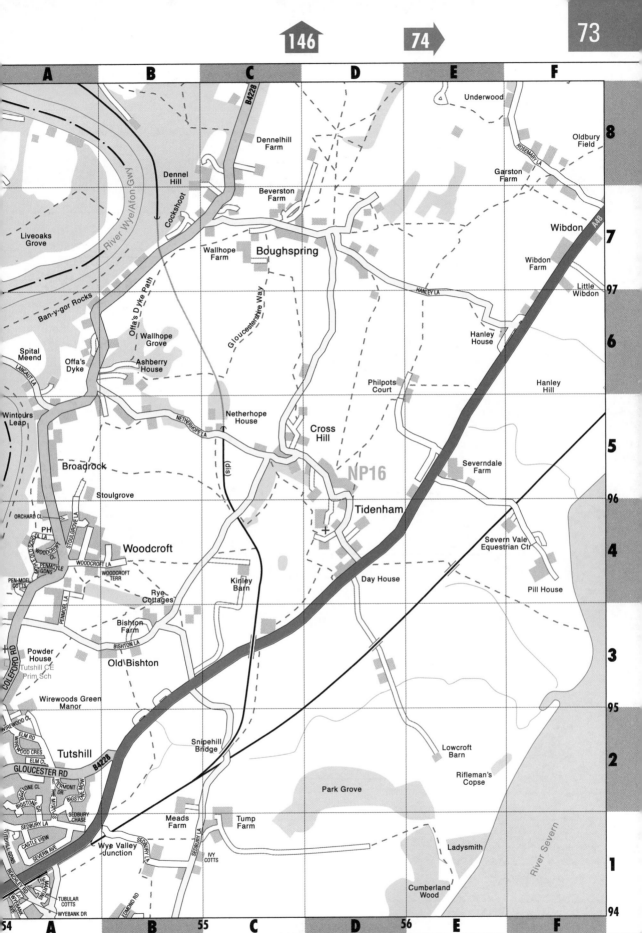

73
147

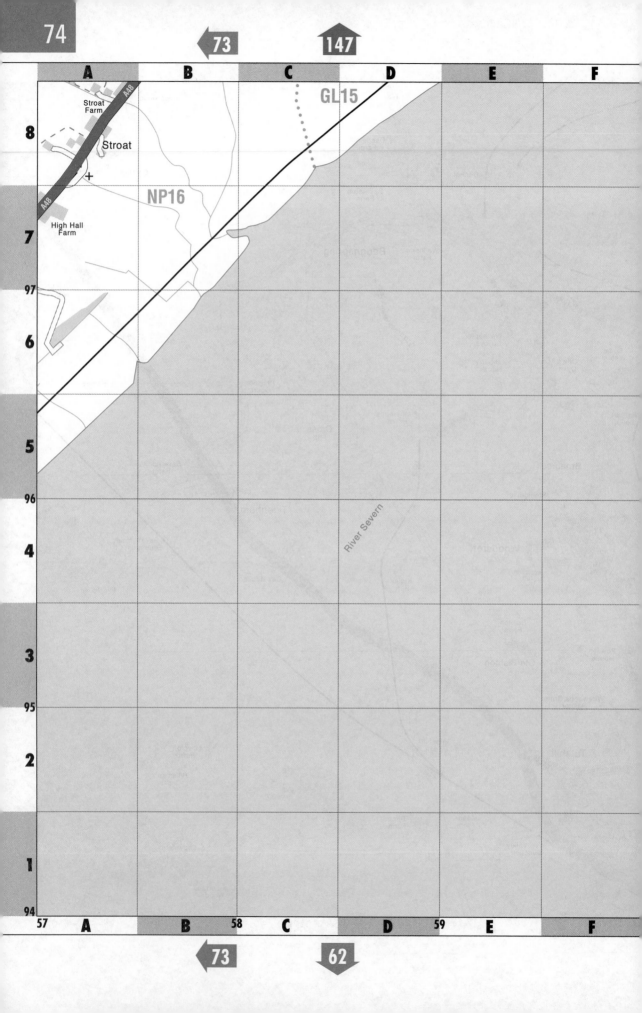

A   B   C   D   E   F

8

GL15

Stroat
Farm

Stroat

NP16

High Hall
Farm

7

97

6

5

96

River Severn

4

3

95

2

1

94

57   A   B   58   C   D   59   E   F

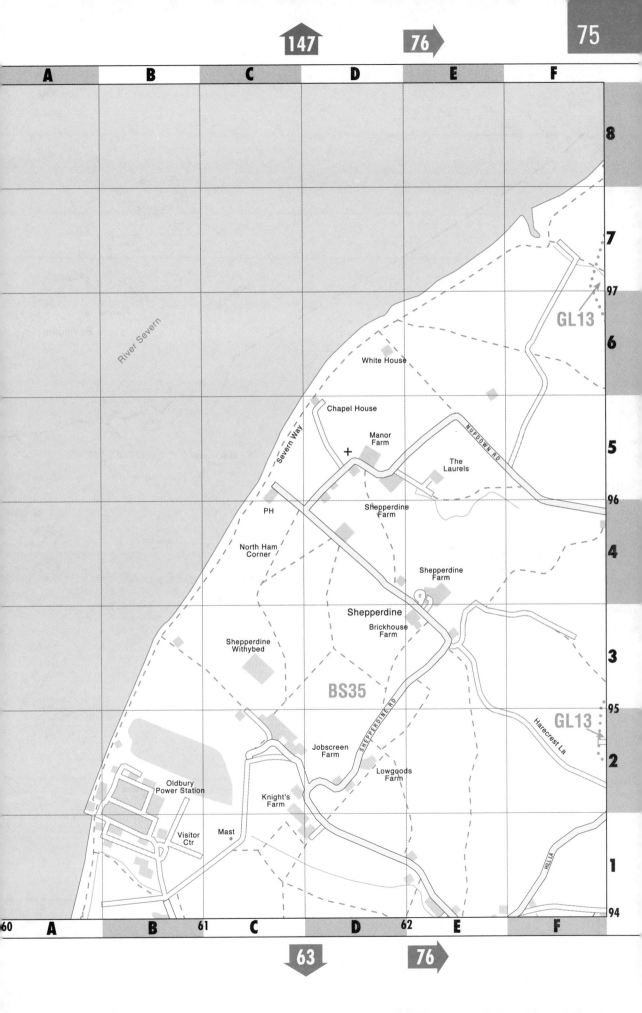

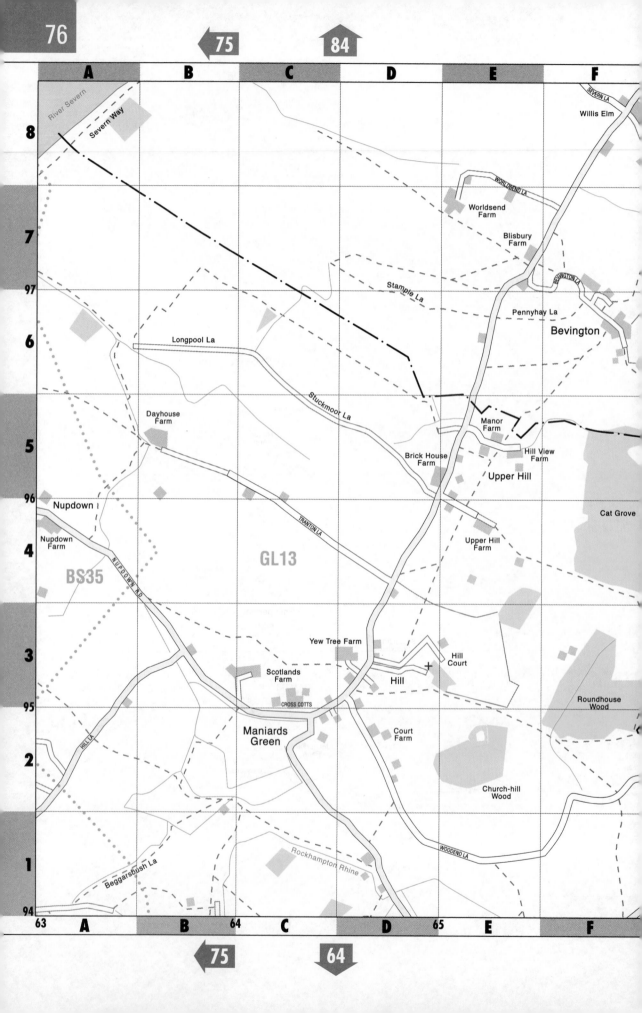

A B C D E F

8

Bluegates
Farm

Tanhouse
Farm

Doverte Brook

Park
Farm

7

Park
House

Lobthorn
Covert

97

Comeley
Farm

Whitcliff Park
(Deer Park)

Pedington
Elm

6

Pedington
Elm Farm

Matford
Bridge

Pedington
Manor Farm

Little Avon River

Pedington
Farm

The
Quarries

5

Hystfield

96

Hystfield
Farm

Appleridge
Farm

GL13

MATFORD LA

A38

DAMERY LA

4

APPLERIDGE LA

Westend
House

Stone with
Woodford
Prim CE Sch

Dog-gate Lane

PH

Newpark
Farm

Lowerstone
Farm

COURT MDW
COURT MDW
COURT MDW
COURT MEAD

Stone

3

DAMERY LA

GLOUCESTER
RD

95

Manor
Farm

Stone
Bridge

2

WOODEND LA

Lowerstone
Wood

Green
Farm

Lower
Stone

MOORSLADE LA

A38

1

Glen
Farm

The
Mount

Chestnut
Farm

GL12

Moorslade

94

66 A B 67 C D 68 E F

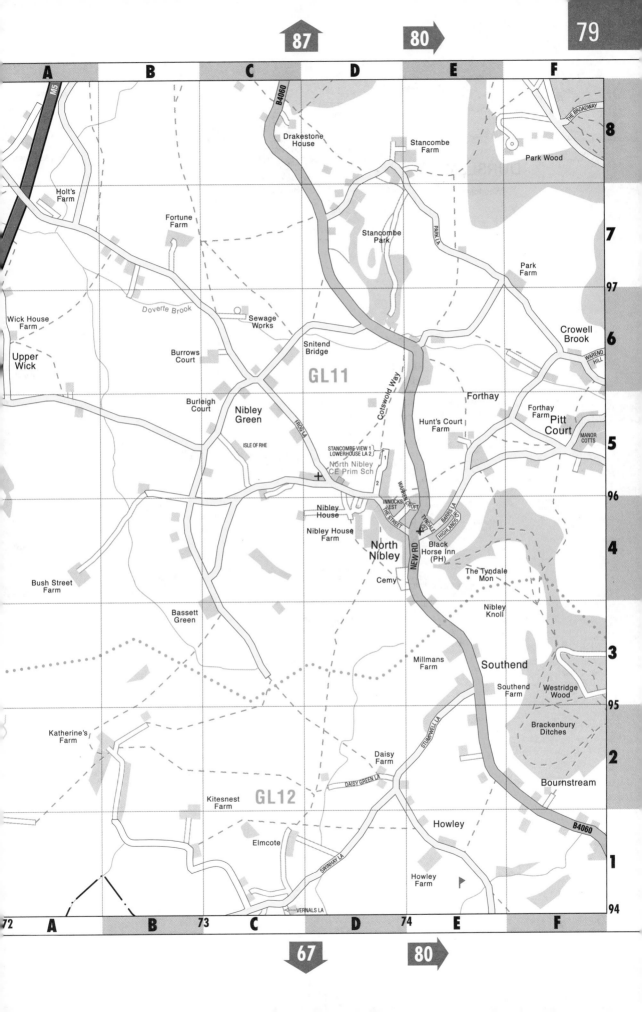

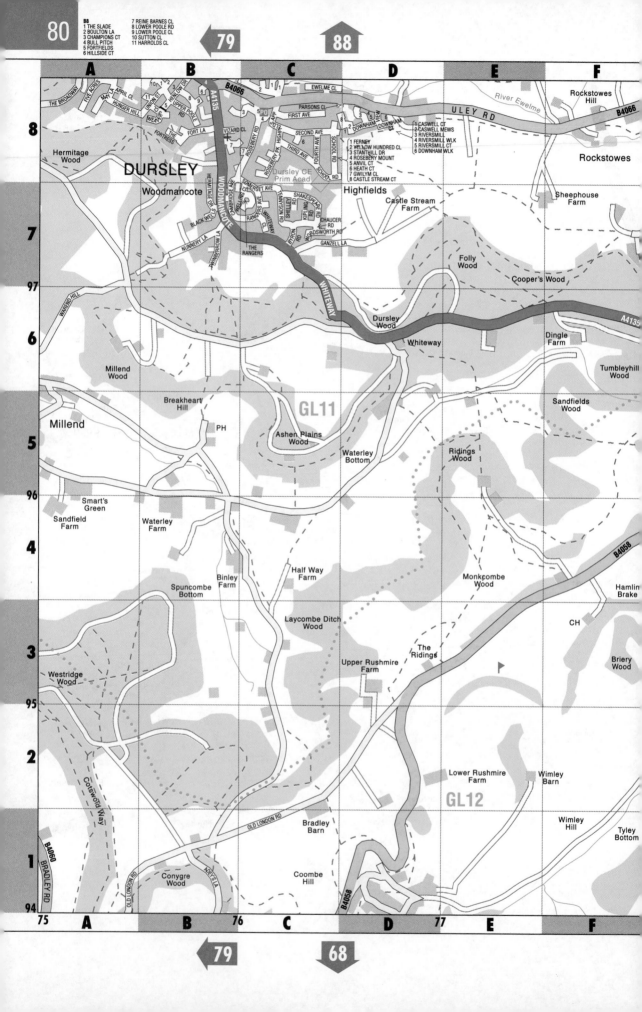

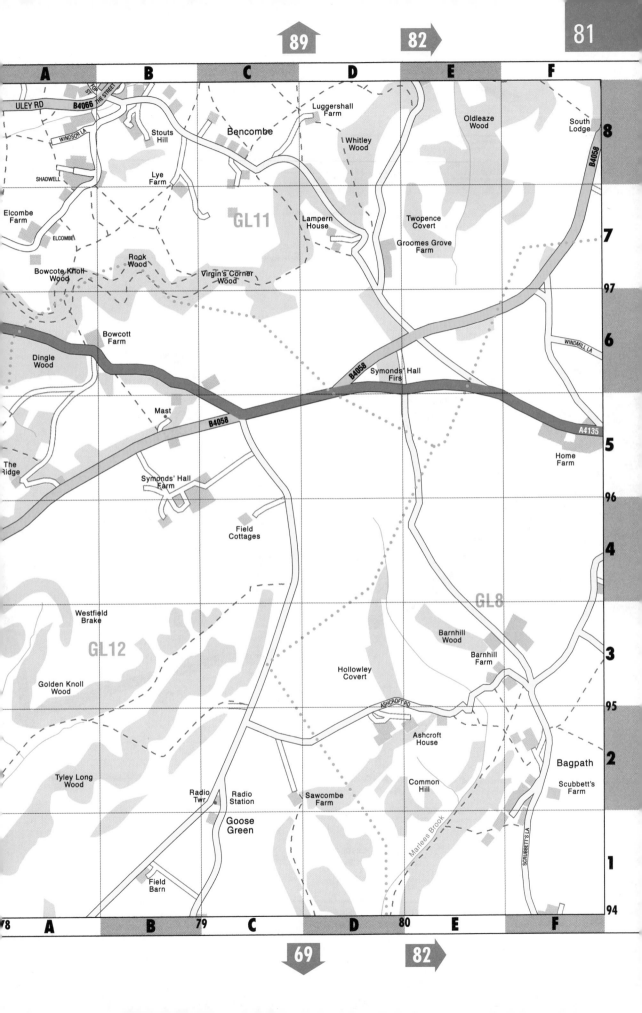

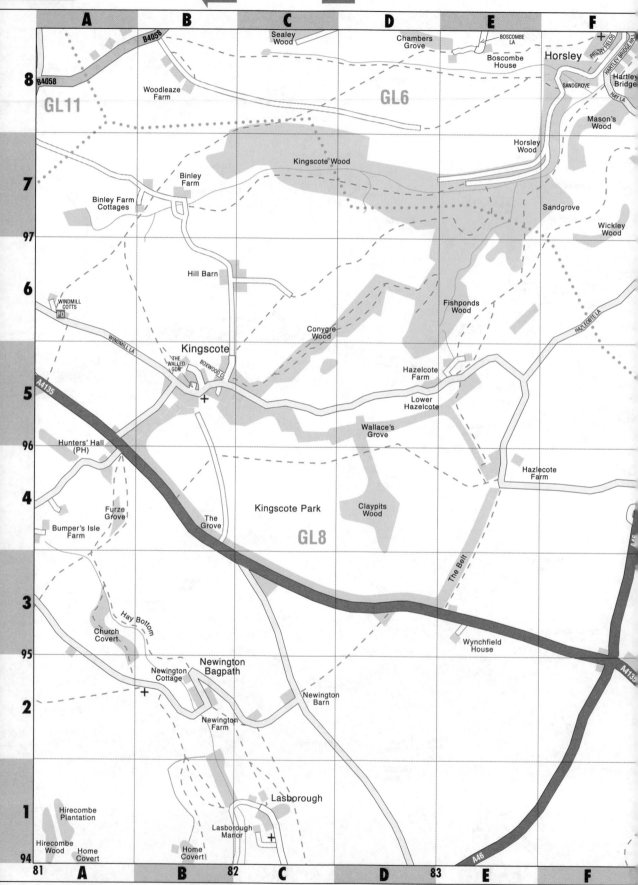

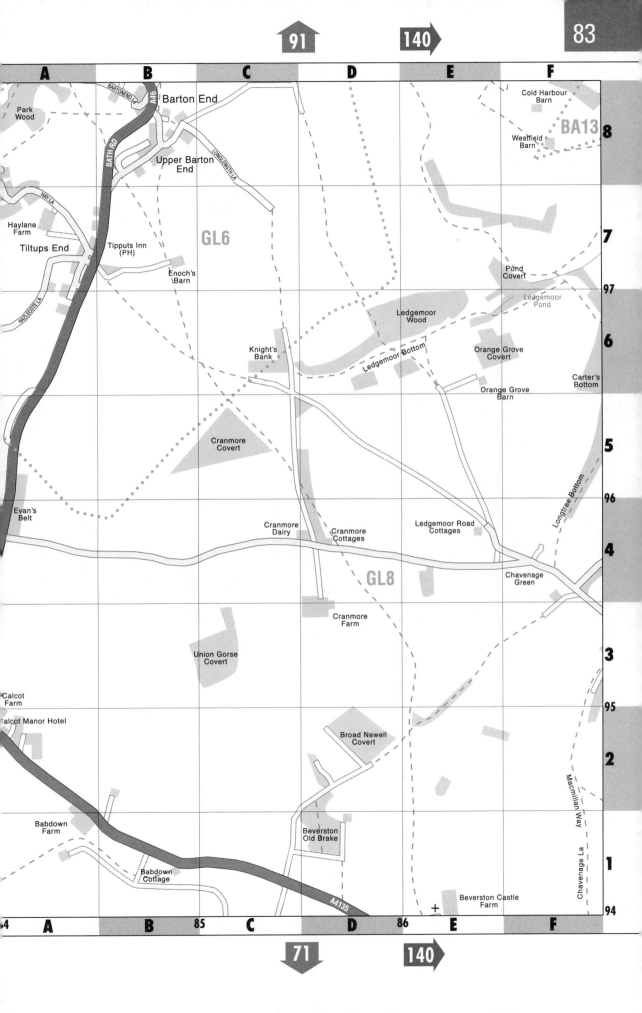

Park
Wood

Barton End

Cold Harbour
Barn

BA13

Westfield
Barn

Haylane
Farm

Upper Barton
End

GL6

Tiltups End

Tipputs Inn
(PH)

Enoch's
Barn

Pond
Covert

Ledgemoor
Pond

Ledgemoor
Wood

Knight's
Bank

Ledgemoor Bottom

Orange Grove
Covert

Carter's
Bottom

Orange Grove
Barn

Cranmore
Covert

Evan's
Belt

Longtree Bottom

Ledgemoor Road
Cottages

Cranmore
Dairy

Cranmore
Cottages

Chavenage
Green

GL8

Cranmore
Farm

Union Gorse
Covert

Calcot
Farm

Calcot Manor Hotel

Broad Newell
Covert

Macmillan Way

Babdown
Farm

Beverston
Old Brake

Babdown
Cottage

A4135

Chavenage La

Beverston Castle
Farm

A   B   C   D   E   F

STATION RD

MEAD LA

Ward
Ind Est

STATION RD

Lydney
COOKSON
TERR

LC

RAILWAY
TERR

THE MARINA

GL15

HARBOUR RD

Lydney Harbour

Lydney Marsh

New Grounds

Marina
Bsns Park

Lydney
Ind Est

CH

Naas
House

HARBOUR RD

River Severn

GL13

Severn Way

Severn House
Farm

SEVERN LA

8

7

01

6

5

00

4

3

99

2

1

98

63   A   B   64   C   D   65   E   F

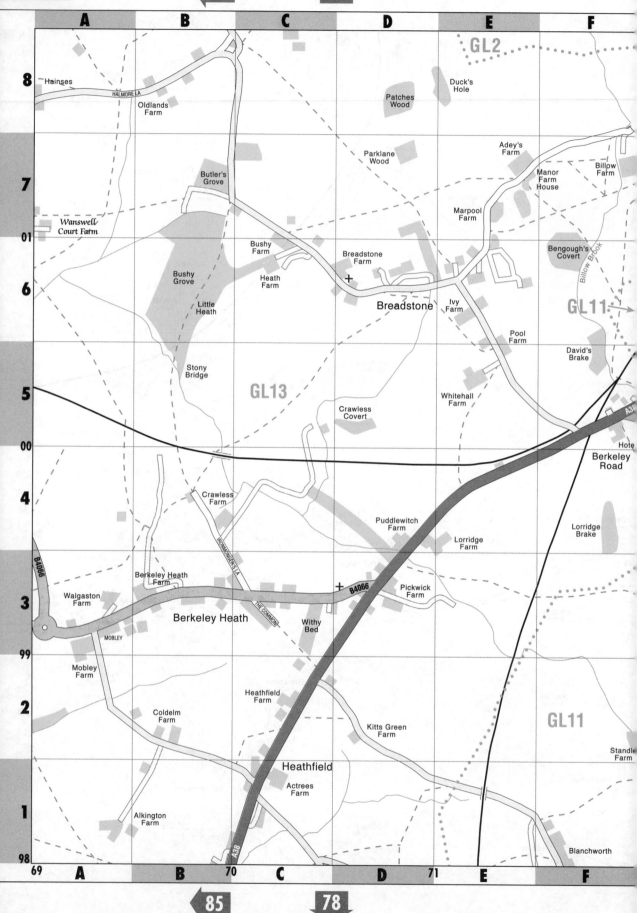

A B C D E F

8 Hainses
HALMORE LA
Oldlands Farm
GL2
Patches Wood
Duck's Hole

7 Butler's Grove
Parklane Wood
Adey's Farm
Manor Farm House
Billow Farm

01 Wanswell Court Farm
Bushy Farm
Marpool Farm
Bengough's Covert
Billow Brook

6 Bushy Grove
Heath Farm
Breadstone Farm
Breadstone
Ivy Farm
GL11
Little Heath
Pool Farm
David's Brake

5 Stony Bridge
GL13
Crawless Covert
Whitehall Farm

00 Berkeley Road
Hote

4 Crawless Farm
Puddlewitch Farm
Lorridge Farm
Lorridge Brake
A38

3 B4066
Berkeley Heath Farm
BROADMONGERS LA
Walgaston Farm
THE COMMON
Berkeley Heath
Withy Bed
B4066
Pickwick Farm

MOBLEY

99 Mobley Farm

2 Coldelm Farm
Heathfield Farm
Kitts Green Farm
GL11
Standle Farm

1 Alkington Farm
Heathfield
Actrees Farm
Blanchworth

98
69 A 70 B C 71 D E F

A B C D E F

8
7
01
6
5
00
4
3
99
2
1
98

GL2
GL13
GL13
GL11

Tumpy Green Farm
Green Farm
Tumpy Green
Horns Hill
Mast
Quercus
Leathern Bottle
Hengaston Farm
Nubbis Ashe
A4066
New Clingre Farm
Clingre House
Tait's Hill
Clingre LA
OLDHILL LANE
CLINGRE DOWN
Taits Hill Ind Est
TAIT'S HILL
Mast
Clingre Farm
The Quarry
TAIT'S HILL RD
ORCHARD LEAZE
COOMBE GDNS
THE BUILDINGS
Street Farm
Church Farm
ECHO LA
THE AVENUE
STANDLE LA
Stinchcombe
Whitehouse Farm
Southend Farm
B4060
B4060
M5

Gossington Bridge
A38
M5
Draycott
BOX ROAD AVE
TOCKNELL CT
BOX RD
Draycott Bsns Pk
DRAYCOTT
Mills
DRAYCOTT CRES
THE VENNINGS
Mill
EVERSIDE LA
Everside La
Woodend Green Farm
WOODEND LA
EVERSIDE CL
JUBILEE CL
JUBILEE AVE
BEYON CL
MANOR CL
BEYON DR
STEPS CL
COURTHOUSE GDNS
HIGH ST
Lower Knapp Farm
Lower Cam
MORRIS ORCH
KNAPP LA
SPARK HILL
NOEL LEE WAY
PO
Fieldlane Farm
FIELD LA
Mast
TYTHE CT
BOWLERS LEA
RYELANDS
MANOR AVE
WHITEHAY DR
POSSE DR
BARTIN
WITH VW
Summerhayes
HIGH FURLONG
THE HAWTHORNS
CHAPEL ST
ORCHARD
Woodfield
ADDYMORE
GLEBELANDS
CAM PITCH
MEAD
Cam Woodfield Junior School
MAY EVANS CL
SUNRISE
ELSTUB LA
SCHOOL CL
THE CLOSE
DELKIN RD
THE DELKIN
SPOUTHOUSE LA
TROTMAN
HICKS
FREDERICK AVE
WILEY
MILL WAY
THE QUARRY
UNION
TURNER RD
PADLEY RD
LITTLE QUILLET CT
ANGLE
THE CRESCENT
VALLEY VIEW
Norman Hill
CHAPEL CT
TYNDALE RD
STONELEA
ROCK RD
QUARRY GDNS
WORKMANS CL
PHILLIMORE
SEVERN RD
THE SPINNEY
SPRINGFIELD
TILSDOWN
MEADOW VALE
ELM GR
NORMAN CRES
NORDOWN RD
B4060
TILSDOWN
WOODEND RD
PO
MARMENT RD
WOODFIELD RD
SPRINGFIELD
NEW RD
EXELL CL
ORCHARD CL
PARKLAND RD
YEWTREE CL
PH
B4060
BROADMERE
Tilsdown
DURSLEY RD
LAMBSDOWNE
BROADMERE RD
ORCHARD VIEW
Ct
B4066
KINGSHILL RD
A4135
Sandpits
F4
1 WINTERBOTTOM RD
2 NORDOWN CL
3 MARLSTONE RD
Sheep Path Wood
Cemy
Kingshill
LAWRENCE GR
ST DAVID'S CRES
BEECHWOOD RISE
Cotswold Way
Stinchcombe Hill
Westfield Wood
Yercombe Lodge
P
Hollow Combe
CH

A B C D E F

8

Halmore Mill

River Cam

The Elms

Coaley CE Prim Sch

Church Farm

WATKINS TERR

Coaley

PH

CIDER ORCHARD

Silver Street House

Draycott Farm

7

Meadbridge's Grove

Pinnells End Farm

BETWORTHY
THE CLOSE
THE STREET

Betworthy Farm

HAW ST

Trenley House

FIELD LA

FRENLEY RD

01

Field Farm

HAMSHILL

6

Upthorpe

Pear Orchard Farm

Upper Upthorpe Farm

UPTHORPE LA

GREEN ST

Far Green

Upthorpe Farm

Green Street

Ashmead Covert

Ashmead Farm

5

ROWLEY MEWS
THE BRASS CT
ROWLEY
GLEBELANDS
CHAPEL ST
SPOUTHOUSE LA
THE CORRAL
STATION RD

UPTHORPE

CAM GR

GL11

Ashmead House

Myles House

Ashmead Green

00

THE CROFT
MILL BANK
ELM LODGE

Cam

Cam Hopton CE Prim Sch

Dulkin Brook

4

Cam Everlands Prim Sch
LEASIDE CL
WOODVIEW RD
MARLSTONE RD
HOLTWELL RD
RYDER CL
BIRCH RD
WILLOW CL
EVERLANDS
HOPTON RD
RIVERSIDE

Everlands

Upper Cam

Church Farm

3

Norman Hill
BRAMBLE DR
MAPLE GR
ROWAN GR
ACACIA DR
OAK DR
HILL SQ
ST GEORGE'S RD
ST GEORGE'S CL
CHURCH RD
ALEXANDRA
RICARDO
SPRINGHILL (OLD COURT)

St George's

+

Downhouse Farm

P

Cotswold Way

Nature Reserve

Cam Long Down

99

A4135
KINGSHILL RD
KINGSWAY
BLACKNEST
NELMS
LISTER RD
ASHWORTH
BUDDING WAY

PRIORY CT
KINGSDOWN
KINGSHILL LA
REDNOCK Sch

SPRINGHILL

Farfield

The Grove

Uleyfield

Hydegate

2

LAWRENCE
EKWINS
OLIVE GR
WOOD AND AVE
WOODLAND DR
REDNOCK DR
WESTFIELD

Kingshill

Peak Academy

CAM HOUSE COTTS

DRAKE LA

Coldharbour Farm

1

THE BROADWAY 1
FIVE ACRES 2
DURSLEY CT
BARNT OAK
GARDEN SUBURB
CAR DR
HARDINGS DR
HILL RD
TORCHACRE RISE
HARDINGS

Sports Ctr
THE KNAPP
WINDSOR RD
CASTLE ST
PARSONAGE ST

Liby

P

P

P

DURSLEY

VICTORIA CL
LONG ST
CHESTAL
MARKET PL
PHELPS MILL CL
WATERS RD
SILVER ST
A4135
PRIORY DL
TOWNSEND CL
BROWNINGS LA
PROSPECT PL
MAIN LA

Home Farm

Chestal

1 BOULTON LA
2 BULL PITCH
3 BROADWELL TERR
4 YELLOW HUNDRED CL
5 FERNEY

Downham Hill

Newbrook Farm

98

Ferney Hill

Wresden Farm

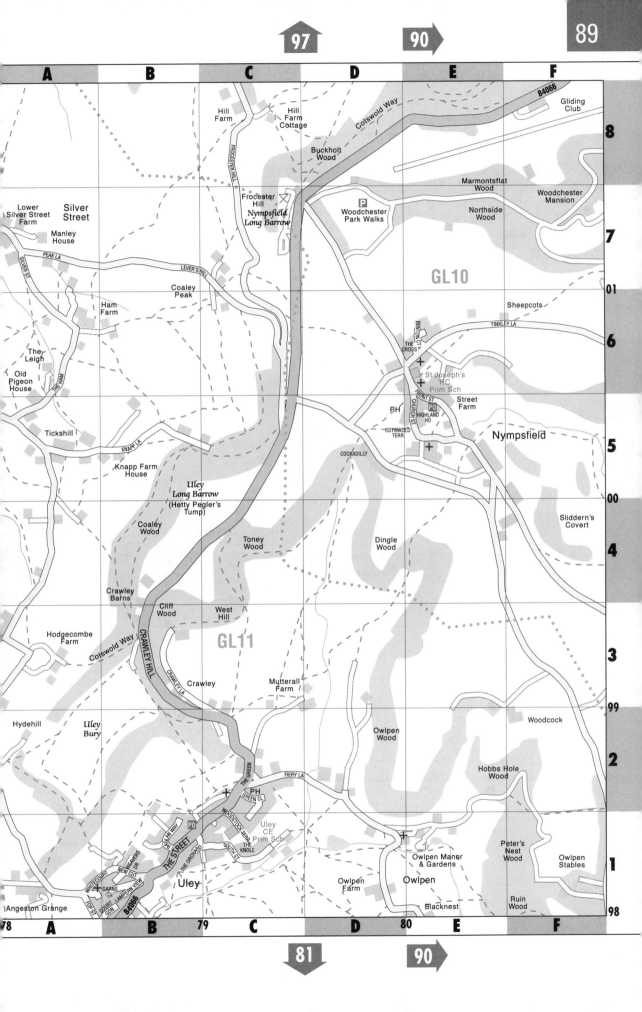

A B C D E F

Gliding Club

B4066

Hill Farm

Hill Farm Cottage

Cotswold Way

Buckholt Wood

Marmontsflat Wood

Woodchester Mansion

Frocester Hill

Nympsfield Long Barrow

Woodchester Park Walks

Northside Wood

Lower Silver Street Farm

Silver Street

GL10

Manley House

Sheepcots

PEAK LA

SILVER ST

FROCESTER HILL

LEVER'S HILL

Coaley Peak

Tinkley La

BENTON CL

THE CROSS

St Joseph's RC Prim Sch

Ham Farm

The Leigh

Old Pigeon House

THE HAM

FRONT ST

CHURCH ST

PO

HIGHLAND HO

Street Farm

PH

Nympsfield

Tickshill

KNAPP LA

Knapp Farm House

COTSWOLD TERR

Uley Long Barrow (Hetty Pegler's Tump)

COCKADILLY

Sliddern's Covert

Coaley Wood

Toney Wood

Dingle Wood

Crawley Barns

Cliff Wood

West Hill

GL11

Hodgecombe Farm

Cotswold Way

CRAWLEY HILL

CRAWLEY LA

Crawley

Mutterall Farm

Woodcock

Hydehill

Uley Bury

Owlpen Wood

Hobbs Hole Wood

THE GREEN

FIERY LA

PH

GREEN CL

Peter's Nest Wood

Owlpen Stables

WOODSTOCK TERR

Uley CE Prim Sch

THE KNOLL

SOUTH ST

THE ORCHARD

ASHLAN WAY

THE STREET

PO

Owlpen Manor & Gardens

Owlpen

WEAVERS DR

NEW CUT

WHITECOURT

GARNS CL

COURT GDN

LAMPERN VIEW

TOP ST

B4066

Uley

Owlpen Farm

Ruin Wood

Angeston Grange

Blacknest

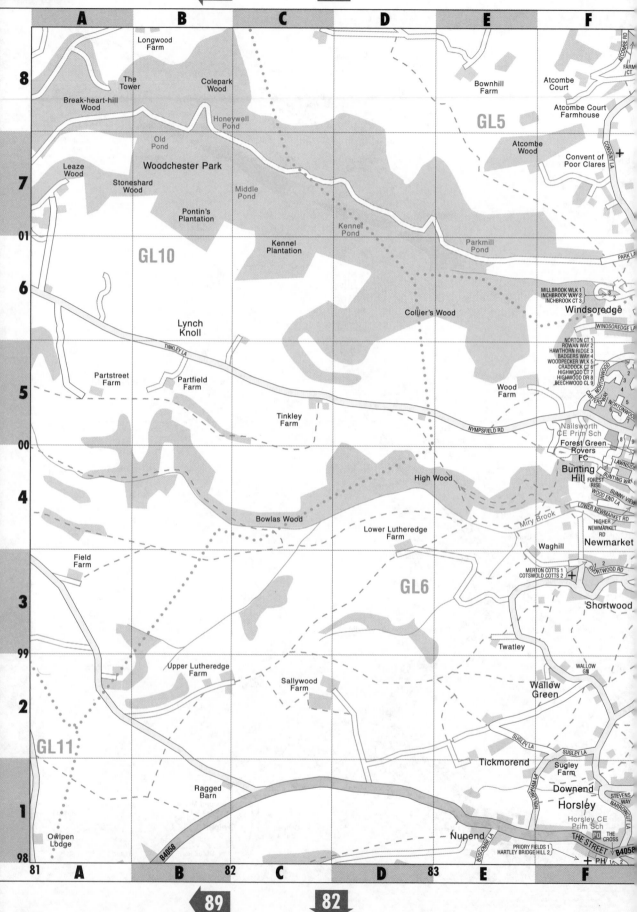

89
98

A　B　C　D　E　F

8

Longwood
Farm

Colepark
Wood

The
Tower

Bownhill
Farm

Atcombe
Court

Atcombe Court
Farmhouse

ATCOMBE RD

FARM
/CT

Break-heart-hill
Wood

Honeywell
Pond

GL5

Atcombe
Wood

Old
Pond

Convent of
Poor Clares

Leaze
Wood

Woodchester Park

7

CONVENT LA

Stoneshard
Wood

Middle
Pond

01

Pontin's
Plantation

Kennel
Pond

Parkmill
Pond

PARK LA

GL10

Kennel
Plantation

6

Millbrook WLK 1
Inchbrook Way 2
Inchbrook CT 3

3
2

Collier's Wood

Windsoredge

WINDSOREDGE L

Lynch
Knoll

NORTON CT 1
ROWAN WAY 2
HAWTHORN RIDGE 3
BADGERS WAY 4
WOODPECKER WLK 5
CRADDOCK CT 6
HIGHWOOD CT 7
HIGHWOOD DR 8
BEECHWOOD CL 9

TINKLEY LA

5

Partstreet
Farm

Partfield
Farm

Wood
Farm

NORTONWOOD

CARTERS WAY

NORTONWOOD L

Tinkley
Farm

NYMPSFIELD RD

Nailsworth
CE Prim Sch

Forest Green
Rovers
FC

00

High Wood

LAWNSIDE

Bunting
Hill

BUNTING WAY

4

FOREST
RISE

WOOD END LA

SUNNY VIEW

Bowlas Wood

Miry Brook

LOWER NEWMARKET RD

HIGHER
NEWMARKET
RD

Field
Farm

Lower Lutheredge
Farm

Waghill

Newmarket

MERTON COTTS 1
COTSWOLD COTTS 2

2

SHORTWOOD RD

GL6

Shortwood

3

Twatley

99

Upper Lutheredge
Farm

Sallywood
Farm

WALLOW
GN

Wallow
Green

2

GL11

SUGLEY LA

SUGLEY LA

Tickmorend

Sugley
Farm

Ragged
Barn

TICKMOREND LA

Downend
Horsley

STEVENS
WAY

NARROW CUT LA

1

Horsley CE
Prim Sch

PO

THE
CROSS

Owlpen
Lodge

B4058

Nupend

BISCOMBE LA

THE STREET

B4058

98

PRIORY FIELDS 1
HARTLEY BRIDGE HILL 2

PH

81　A　82　B　C　83　D　E　F

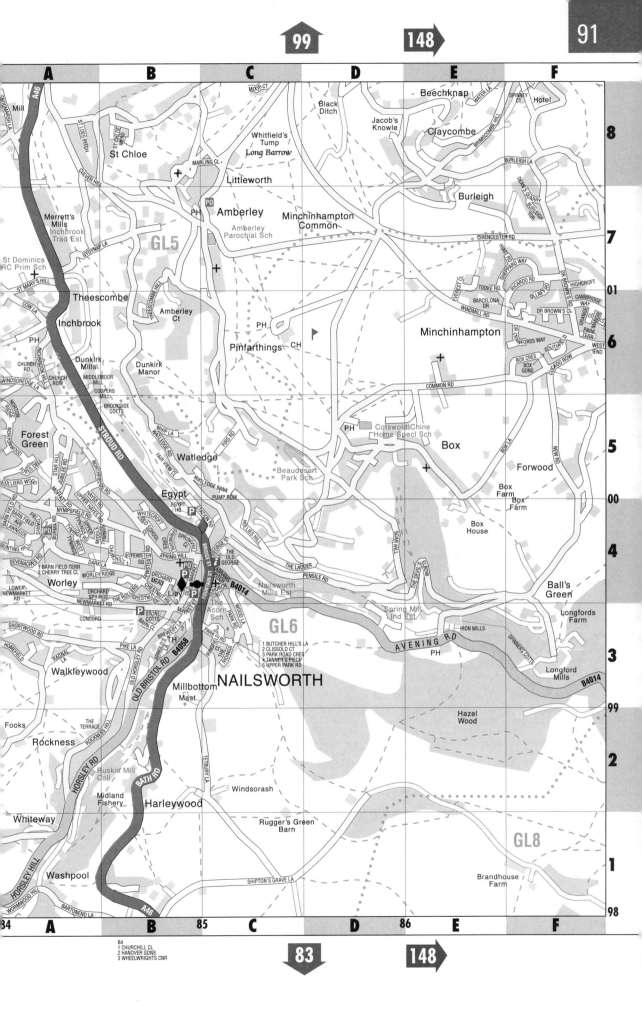

A   B   C   D   E   F

8

7

05

6

5

04

4

3

03

2

1

02

63   A   B   64   C   D   65   E   F

Shaphouse Farm

Oldcroft
1 BRIERLEY WAY
2 CHURCH WLK

Needs Top

Little Purlieu

Hulks Farm

Soilwell Farm

Purlieu End Farm

Soilwell Manor

The Purlieu

Ten Acre Wood

Allaston Meend

Plummer's Brook

Tingley Wood

Little Allaston

Billings Barn

Allaston

Nursehill Wood

Nursehill

Driffield Farm

Mast

GL15

New Mills

Millrough Wood

Allaston Court

Primrose Hill CE Prim Acad

Warren

Highfield La

Wellhouse Grove

Primrose Hill

Willow Hts

Minerva Wlk

Juno Dr

Cross Hands

Middle Forge

Lime Way

Almond Wlk

Centurion Rd

1 NODENS WAY
2 NERO CL
3 CAESARS CL

Rodley Manor

Highfield

Hurst Farm

Warren Grove

The Springs

Spring Meadow Rd

Newerne

Lydney

Water Mead

1 TUTHILL RISE
2 THE FOLDERS
3 HAWTHORN CT
4 HIGHFIELD RISE

Severnbanks Prim Sch

Crump Farm

Lydney CE Com Sch

Newerne St

Manor Ct

Kears Wood

Liby

Lydney Town

Hampton Mews

Klondike Ave

Rodley Sq

Shepherdine

Bream Rd

Forest Rd

Apple Blossom Cl

1 WYNTOUR'S PAR
2 DARTERS CL
3 HERBERT HOWELLS CL
4 STEEPLE VIEW
5 VICARAGE CL
6 BREHAL CL

Pylers Way

Rushyleaze

Harrison Way

Purton Pl

High St

Superstore

Bathurst Park

Tutnalls

Summerleaze

1 THE BUNGALOWS
2 MOUNT PLEASANT CL

Plummer's Farm

Cliff Farm

The Dean Acad

St Mary's Halt

Lakeside Gdns

Lakeside Ave

Naas Crossing (LC)

Feathers

A48

Bledisloe Wy

Naas Court

Lydney Junc

Naas

A3
1 RAGLAN GDNS
2 GOODE CT
3 CAVENDISH BLDGS
4 FOREST PAR
5 REGENTS WLK

← 147   84

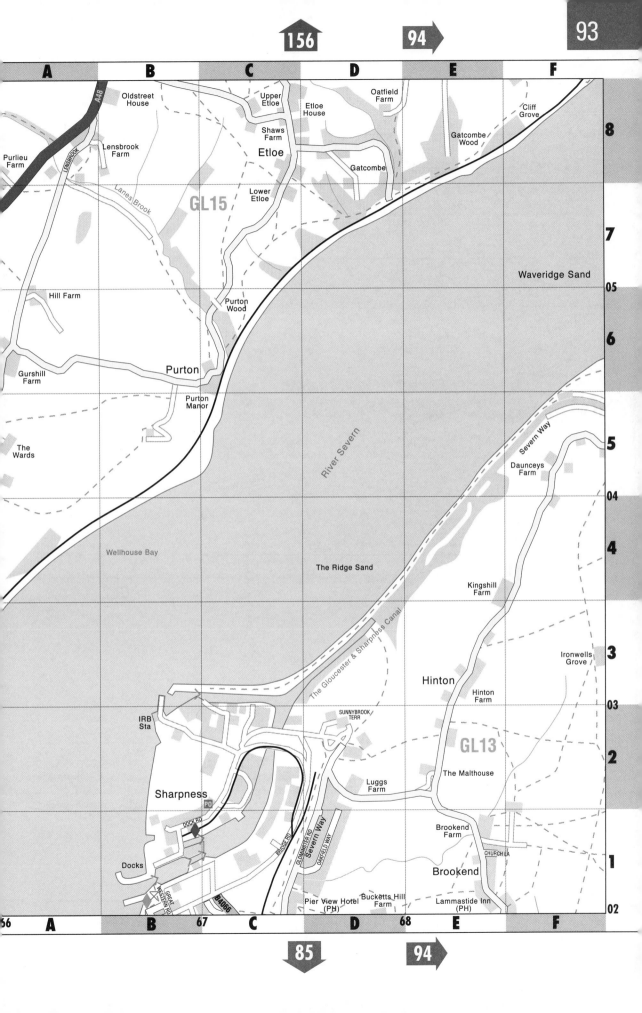

8

Purlieu Farm

Oldstreet House

Lensbrook Farm

A48

LENSBROOK

Lanes Brook

GL15

Upper Etloe

Shaws Farm

Etloe House

Etloe

Lower Etloe

Oatfield Farm

Gatcombe Wood

Cliff Grove

Gatcombe

7

05

Hill Farm

Purton Wood

Waveridge Sand

6

Gurshill Farm

Purton

Purton Manor

Severn Way

5

The Wards

River Severn

Dauceys Farm

04

Wellhouse Bay

The Ridge Sand

4

Kingshill Farm

Ironwells Grove

3

The Gloucester & Sharpness Canal

Hinton

Hinton Farm

03

IRB Sta

SUNNYBROOK TERR

GL13

2

Sharpness

PO

DOCK RD

BRIDGE RD

Luggs Farm

The Malthouse

OLDMINSTER RD

Severn Way

OAKFIELD WAY

Brookend Farm

CHURCH LA

1

Docks

GREAT WESTERN RD

B4066

Pier View Hotel (PH)

Bucketts Hill Farm

Brookend

Lammastide Inn (PH)

02

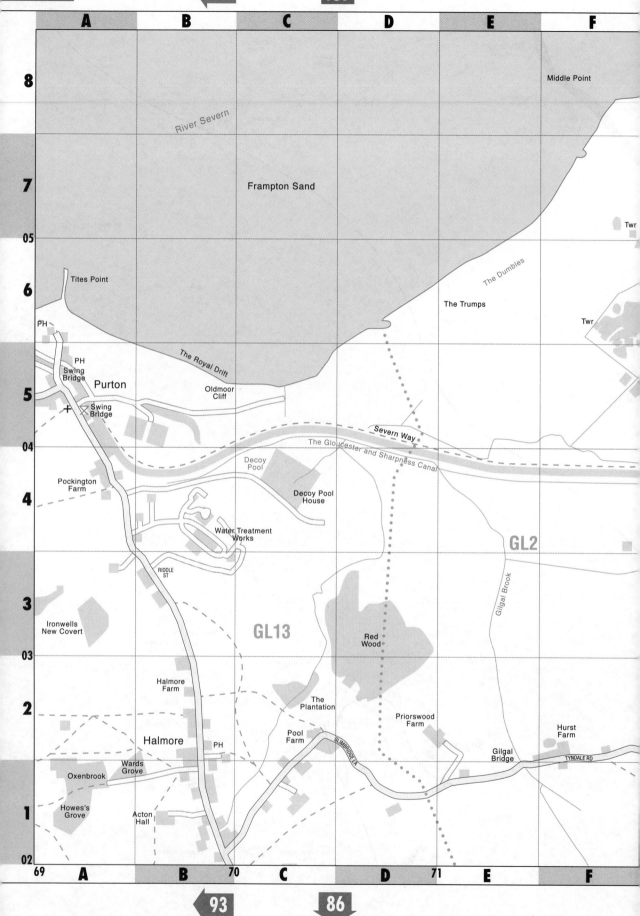

A   B   C   D   E   F

8

Middle Point

River Severn

Frampton Sand

7

05   Twr

Tites Point   The Dumbles

6   The Trumps   Twr

PH   The Royal Drift

PH
Swing
Bridge   Purton   Oldmoor
5   Cliff

✚   Swing
            Bridge   Severn Way

04   The Gloucester and Sharpness Canal

Pockington   Decoy
Farm   Pool

4   Decoy Pool
                                     House   GL2

                        Water Treatment
                        Works   Gilgal Brook

                    RIDDLE
                    ST   Red
3   Wood

Ironwells   GL13
New Covert

03

                        Halmore
                        Farm

2   The Plantation   Priorswood
                                                              Farm   Hurst
                                                                                 Farm
            Halmore   PH   Pool
                                       Farm   Gilgal
                                                                       Bridge   TYNDALE RD
            Wards   SLIMBRIDGE LA
            Grove
Oxenbrook

1   Howes's
     Grove   Acton
                    Hall

02
69   A   B   70   C   D   71   E   F

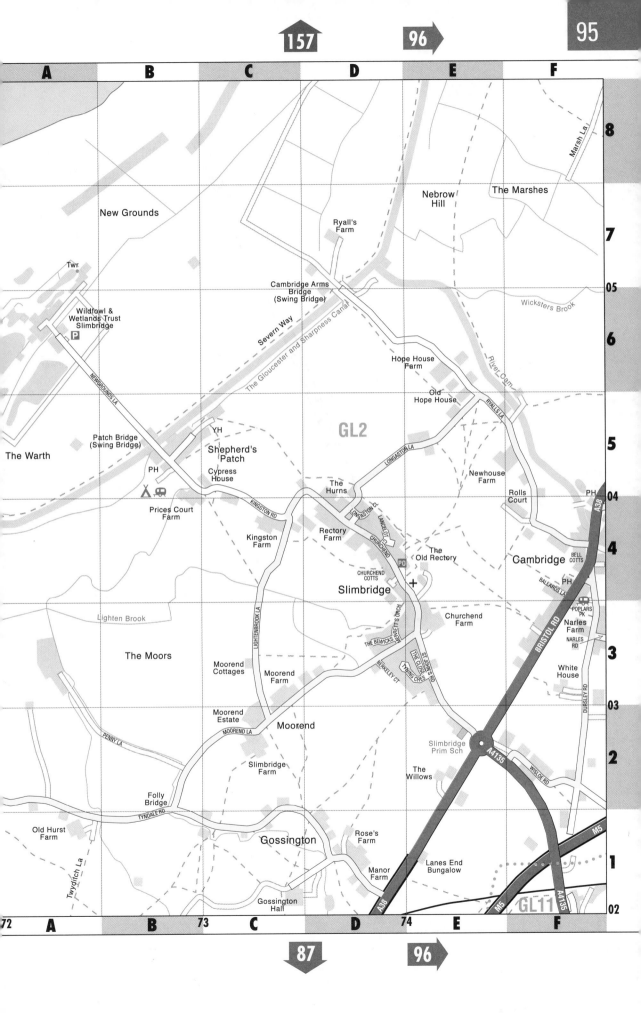

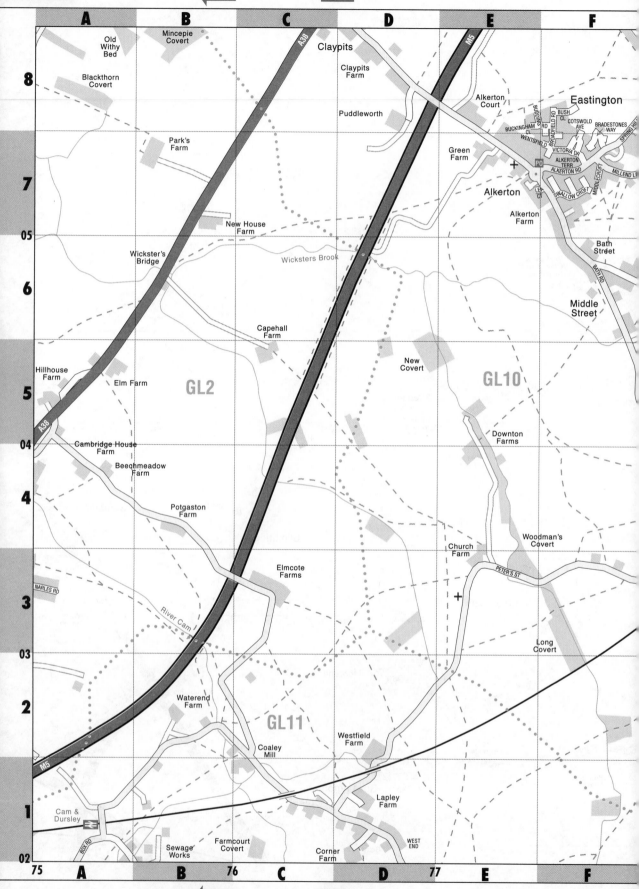

A B C D E F

8

7

05

6

5

04

4

03

3

02

2

1

75 A B 76 C D 77 E F

Old Withy Bed
Mincepie Covert
Blackthorn Covert
Claypits
Claypits Farm
Puddleworth
Alkerton Court
Eastington
Park's Farm
Green Farm
BUDDING RD
BROADFIELD RD
BUSH
BUCKINGHAM CL
COTSWOLD AVE
BRADESTONES WAY
WENTSFIELD
VICTORIA DR
SPRING HILL
ALKERTON TERR
ALKERTON RD
Alkerton
LEAZE CL?
SWALLOW CROFT
MIDDLECROFT
MILLEND LA
New House Farm
Alkerton Farm
Wickster's Bridge
Wicksters Brook
Bath Street
BATH RD
Middle Street
Capehall Farm
New Covert
GL2
GL10
Hillhouse Farm
Elm Farm
Downton Farms
A38
Cambridge House Farm
Beechmeadow Farm
Woodman's Covert
Potgaston Farm
Church Farm
PETER'S ST
NARLES RD
Elmcote Farms
River Cam
Long Covert
Waterend Farm
GL11
Westfield Farm
Coaley Mill
M5
Lapley Farm
Cam & Dursley
WEST END
BOX RD
Sewage Works
Farmcourt Covert
Corner Farm
PO
A38
M5

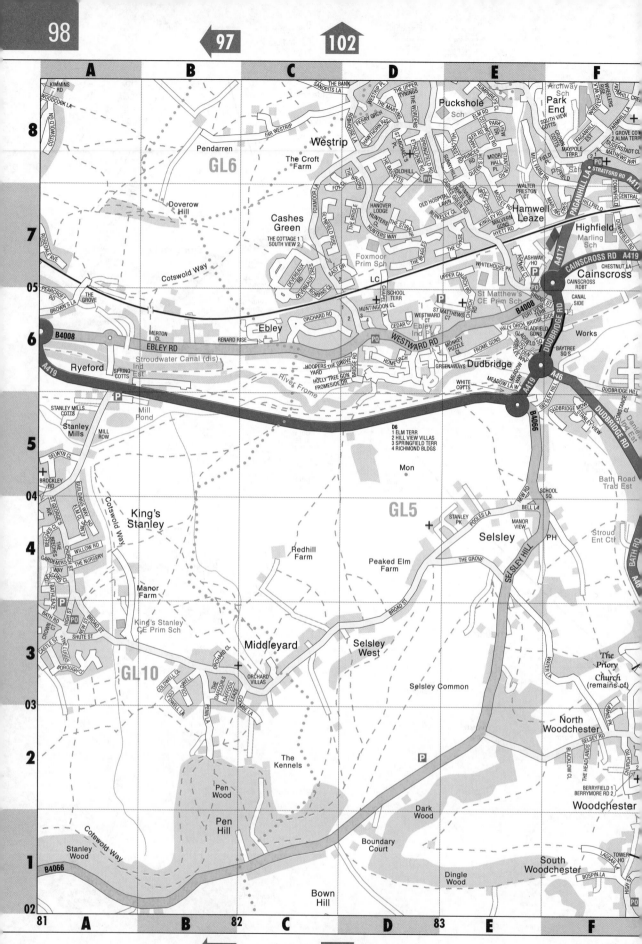

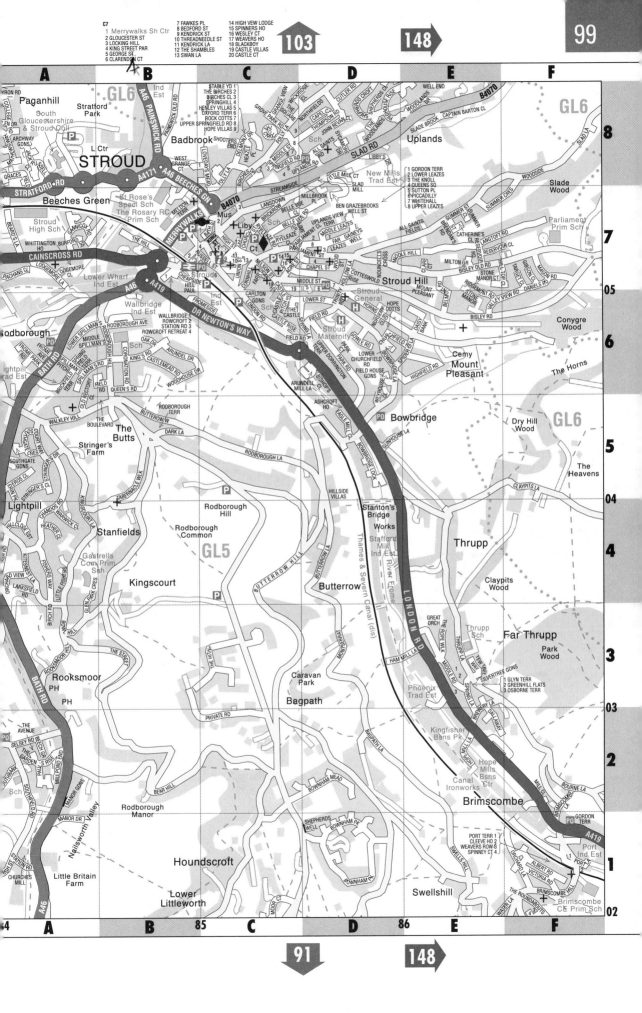

157
108

A B C D E F

8

The Gloucester and Sharpness Canal

Spring Rhyne

Moreton Valence Rhyne

Barracks Farm

CHURCH LA

Packthorne Farm

7

SANDFIELD CRES

CHURCH LA

Junction Bridge

Whitminster House

Sandfield Bridge (Swing Bridge)

09

Wheatenhurst

Grain Store

Walk Bridge

Oatfield

Whitminster Bridge

6

Sanfurlong

Jaxons farm

Berrows

Lakefield CE Prim Sch

LAKE LA

DATFIELD RD

THE SQUARE

LIMMORE GDNS

ANN WICKS RD

WHITMINSTER LA

Highfield House

HYDE LA

GL2

5

Frampton on Severn

SCHOOL FIELD CL

HOLBURY CRES

KIDNAM WLK

VAISEY

PAYNES MDW

THE CLOSE

RICKYARD WAY

Whitminster CE Prim Sch

SCHOOL LA

UPCOTS GDN

Stonepitts Bridge

Whitminster

BRIDGE RD

B4071

River Frome

Stroudwater Canal (dis)

HENRY WITHERS PL

PO

Hotel

MANOR CT

GROVE LA

PH

Parklands

08

Frampton Court

Occupation Bridge

Grove End Farm

4

Netherhills Covert

3

Townfield Farm

PERRY WAY

Netherhills Farm

Mill

A419

The Grove

GL10

Fromebridge

Frome Bridge

07

Park Corner Cottage

Nastfield Farm

Hillsborough

B4071

Fromebridge Cottages

Depot

M5

2

13

A419

Parkfield Covert

CLAYPITS HILL

The Hawthornes

GL10

M5

1

A38

Claypits

Eastington Trad Est

06

Mincepie Covert

75 A B 76 C D 77 E F

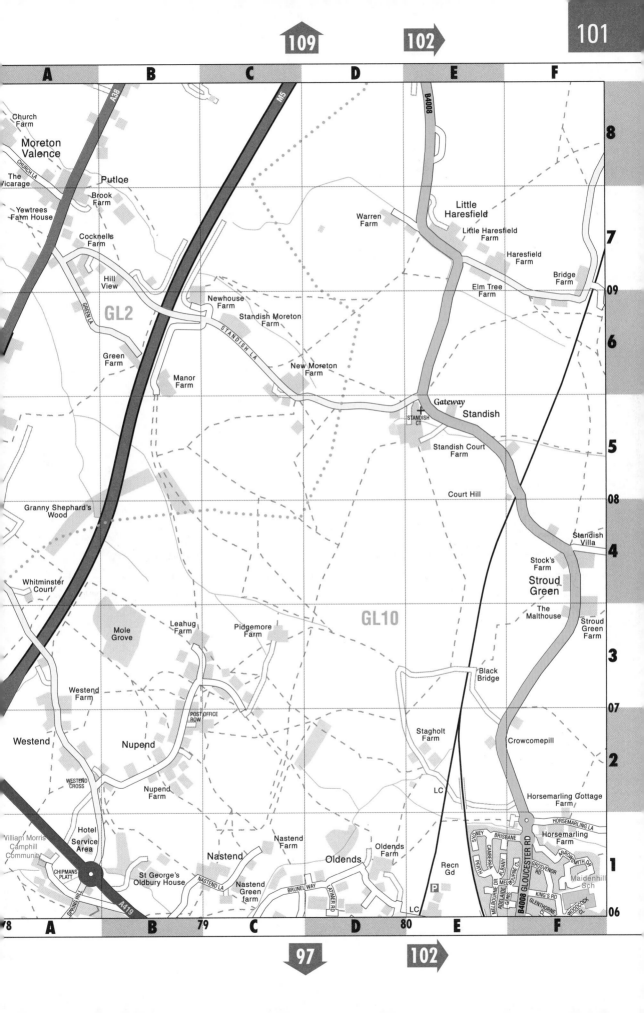

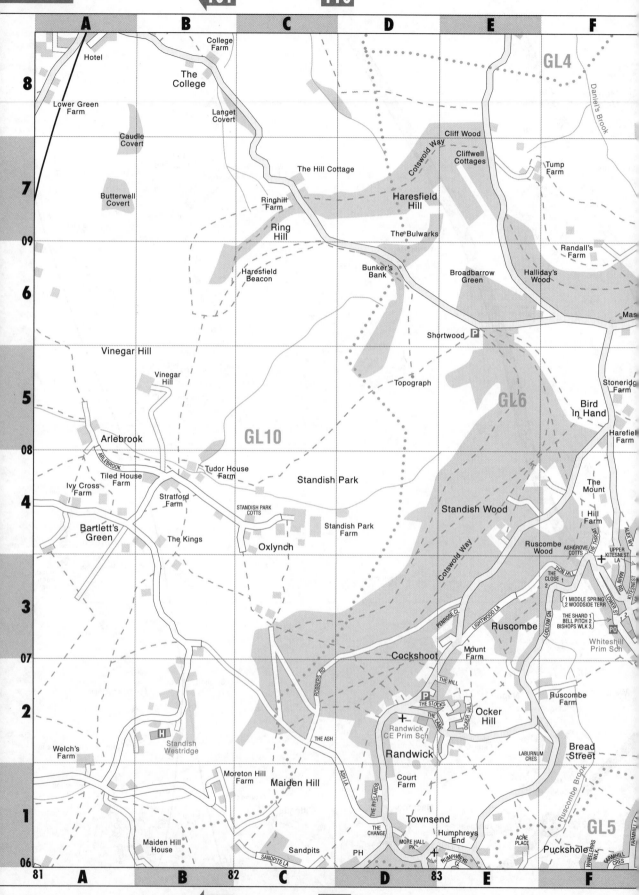

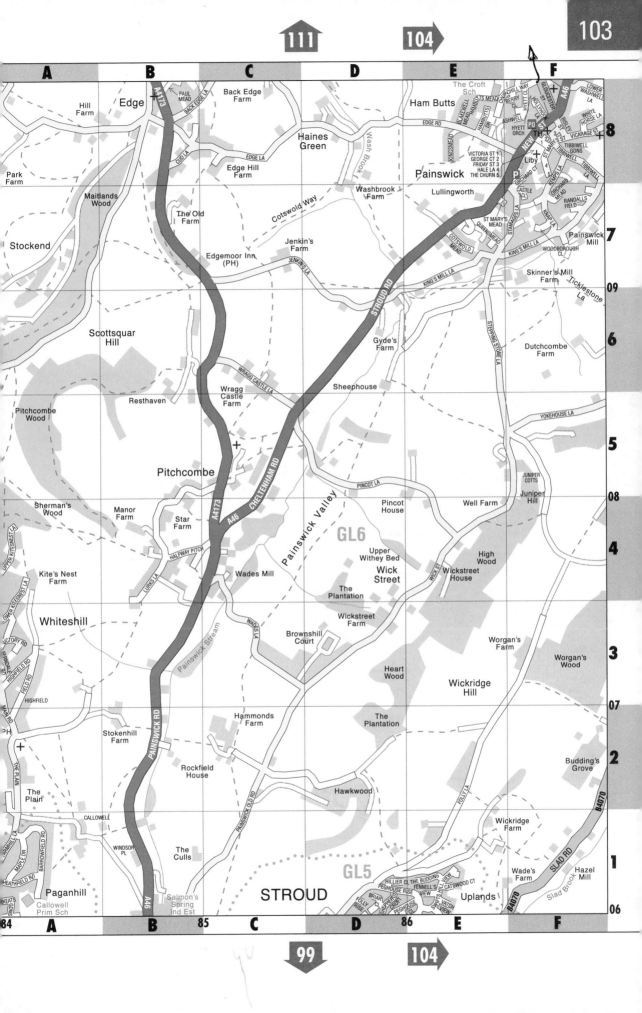

103
112

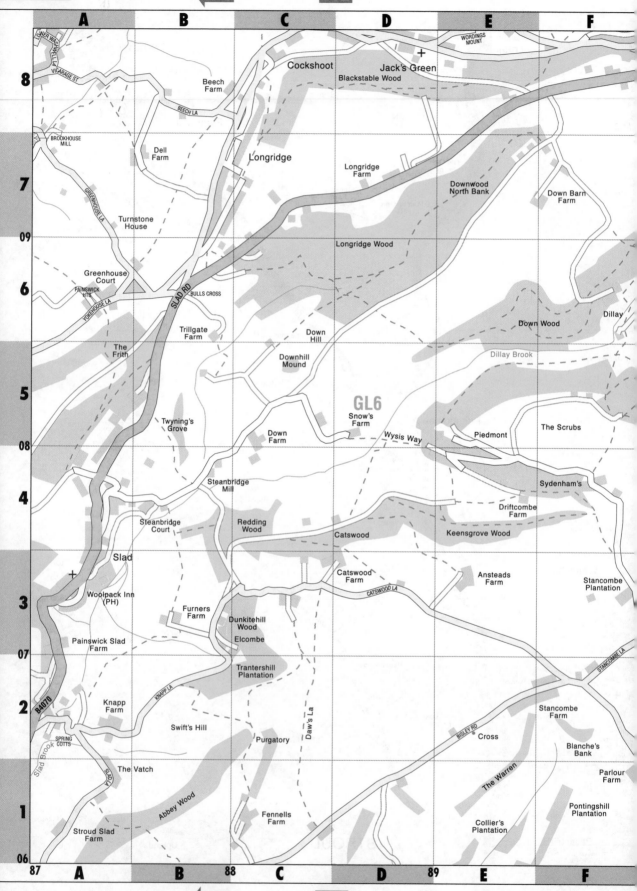

A   B   C   D   E   F

8

LOWER WASHWELL LA
VICARAGE ST
BROOKHOUSE MILL
Beech Farm
Cockshoot
Jack's Green
Wordings Mount
Blackstable Wood

7

Dell Farm
BEECH LA
Longridge
Longridge Farm
Downwood North Bank
Down Barn Farm

09

GREENHOUSE LA
Turnstone House

6

Greenhouse Court
PAINSWICK HTS
YOKEHOUSE LA
SLAD RD
BULLS CROSS
Trillgate Farm
Down Hill
Longridge Wood
Down Wood
Dillay

The Frith
Downhill Mound
Dillay Brook

5

Twyning's Grove
GL6
Snow's Farm
Wysis Way
Piedmont
The Scrubs

08

Down Farm
Sydenham's

4

Steanbridge Mill
Driftcombe Farm

Steanbridge Court
Redding Wood
Catswood
Keensgrove Wood

Slad
Catswood Farm
Ansteads Farm
Stancombe Plantation

3

Woolpack Inn (PH)
Furners Farm
Catswood Farm
CATSWOOD LA

Painswick Slad Farm
Dunkitehill Wood
Elcombe

07

Trantershill Plantation
STANCOMBE LA

KNAPP LA
DAW'S LA

2

B4070
Knapp Farm
Stancombe Farm

SPRING COTTS
Swift's Hill
Purgatory
BISLEY RD
Cross
Blanche's Bank

SLAD LA
The Vatch
The Warren
Parlour Farm

1

Slad Brook
Abbey Wood
Fennells Farm
Pontingshill Plantation

Stroud Slad Farm
Collier's Plantation

06

87   A   B   88   C   D   89   E   F

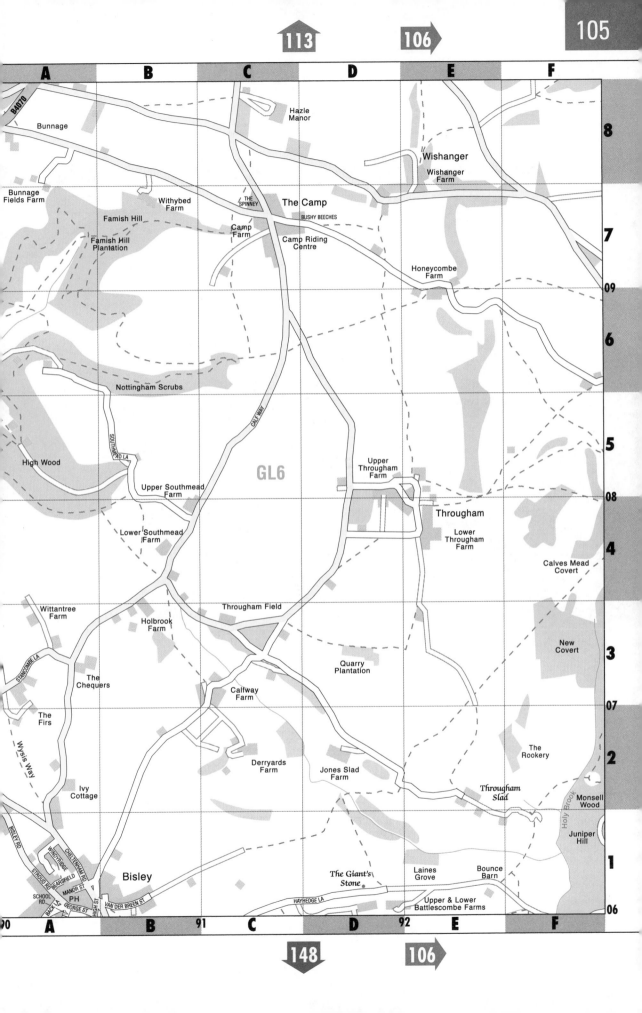

A   B   C   D   E   F

8

Bunnage

Hazle
Manor

Wishanger

Wishanger
Farm

7

Bunnage
Fields Farm

Withybed
Farm

THE
SPINNEY

The Camp

BUSHY BEECHES

Famish Hill

Camp
Farm

Camp Riding
Centre

09

Famish Hill
Plantation

Honeycombe
Farm

6

Nottingham Scrubs

CALF WAY

5

High Wood

SOUTHMEAD LA

Upper
Througham
Farm

GL6

08

Upper Southmead
Farm

Throughham

Lower Southmead
Farm

Lower
Througham
Farm

Calves Mead
Covert

4

Wittantree
Farm

Holbrook
Farm

Throughham Field

New
Covert

3

STANCOMBE LA

The
Chequers

Quarry
Plantation

07

The
Firs

Calfway
Farm

The
Rookery

2

Wysis Way

Derryards
Farm

Jones Slad
Farm

Throughham
Slad

Monsell
Wood

Ivy
Cottage

Juniper
Hill

BISLEY RD

WINDYRIDGE

Bisley

The Giant's
Stone

Laines
Grove

Bounce
Barn

1

SCHOOL
RD.

BEARSFIELD

MANOR ST
BACK ST
HIGH ST
GEORGE ST

STROUD RD

CHELTENHAM RD

PH

VAN DER BREEN ST

HAYHEDGE LA

Upper & Lower
Battlescombe Farms

Holy Brook

06

90   A   B   91   C   D   92   E   F

A B C D E F

8

Park Farm

Woodside Cottage

Henley Farm

Noel's Copse

Winstone Hill

Pound Cottage

Furze Wood

Townsend Farm

7

Lodge

Gaskill's Farm

09

Miserden

Misarden Park Woodland Trail

Misarden Park Lake

Ashgrove Farm

PO

Miserden CE Prim Sch

PH

Misarden Park Gardens

Misarden Park

6

Francombe

Pillow Mound

Bull Banks Lake

Lypiatt Farm

Lypiatt

Lamphill Wood

River Frome

GL6

Bull Banks

GL7

5

Sudgrove House Farm

Sandy Flats Plantation

Sudgrove

BIRDS BUSH LA

08

Warneford House

Sudgrove Farm

Parson's Hill

4

Sudgrove House

Ashcombe Bottom

Thick Wood

Jackbarrow Cottages

Fox Wood

Valley Farm

Jackbarrow Farm

3

Waverley Farm

Quarry Plantation

07

Stonewall Belt

Duntisbourne Common

2

Edgehill Plantation

Edgeworth Mill

Eight Acre Plantation

Monsell Wood

Juniper Hill

Redshed Belt

ASHLETTS RD

Brook Grove

Duntisbourne House

1

Red Shed

FARM RD

Edgeworth

SCHOOL LA

North Farm

Knightswood Common

06

93 A B 94 C D 95 E F

115
158
149
158

A B C D E F

Cot Abbey

Selscomb
Wood

Cotswold
Park

GL53

Winstone

North
Bank

South
Bank

8

Manor
Farm

Cotswold
Farm

7

PH

The
Grove

Playing
Field

09

Field's
Copse

6

Rectory
Farm

EALY
HILL

Field's
Farm

GL7

BURCOMBE LA

Long Furlong
Barn

5

Yew Tree
Farm

Dix's
Barn

08

Rendcombury

Abbots
Farm

Duntisbourne
Abbots

Sly's Wall
Plantation

4

Fords

Ford

Duntisbourne
Leer

Nutbeam
Farm

3

07

New Barn
Farm

CRABTREE LA

Beech
Copse

Manor
Farm

WELSM WAY

2

Hoar Stone

Middle
Duntisbourne

Longhill

Duntisbourne
Grove

Macmillan Way

LONGHILL RD

Rough
Plantation

Macmillan Way

Duntisbourne
Rouse

1

06

A B C D E F

96 97 98

PIKE RD
CROSS FIELD
SCHOOL HILL
BACK LA
CROFT LA
XBARROW RD
NOTCH RD
A417

157
116

	A	B	C	D	E	F

8

Downend

Bow Lane
Farm

Poolpits
Wood

7

Castle End
Farm

Patterills
Farm

Monks
Hill

Clarke's
Farm

13

Bollow
Pool

Hillfield
Farm

Madam's End
Farm

Ellis's
Farm

6

Churchend

POST OFFICE
COTTS

Vicarage

Longney

GL2

Severn Way

Longney
C.E. Prim Sch

Manor
Farm

5

Logney
Sands

High
Green

Bellamy's
Farm

12

Brush
Crib

River Severn

Lynch
Farm

GL14

4

Longney
Crib

3

Upper
Dumball

Oakey
Farm

Epney

11

PH

Parkend Bridge
(Swing Bridge)

2

CASTLE LA

Upper
Framilode

Lea Court
Farm

The Gloucester and Sharpness Canal

CANAL ROW

Baldwins

Moreton Valence Rhyne

River Frome

1

PH

Moor
Farm

MOOR ST

10

75	A	B	76	C	D	77	E	F

157
100

A B C D E F

Hockley Hill

Hardwick Farm Covert

Grove End Wood

Grove End Villas

Grove End Farm

Hardwicke Farm

Sellars Bridge (Swing Bridge)

GOSS WOOD CNR 1
SEVERNVALE DR 2
CHACERLEY CL 3

Fisher's Bridge

School La

PARKLANDS

BRUIDS OAK

Inf Sch

DARLEYDALE WAY
DOVEDALE CL
WHARFDALE CL
ROSEDALE
AIRDALE CL
ARKENDALE CL
BEKDALE CL
STOCKDALE CL
TEVONBUS
SUNNYFIELD RD

PH
BRIDGE KEEPERS WAY

PIPEWOOD RD
MULBERRY CL
MAPLE CL
CHERRY CL
BECH CL
OVERBROOK RD

ASHLEWORTH GDNS

CHILTERN RD
BRECON
PENHILL RD
QUANTOCK CL
MENDIP RD
HENLEY
WATERLEY

CORNFIELD RD

FIELDCOURT FARMHOUSE

COURTFIELD RD

FIELD COURT DR

SQUIRREL CL

CHESTNUT CL
WATERCRESS
MDN

HARVEST WAY
LOWER MDW

CHURCH DR
GILES COX
KNOLLYS END
HOLLY END
GUISE WAY

DAWES
DARBY CL
LANHAM GDNS
MANSFIELD MEWS

NAAS LA RDBT

BRISTOL RD

NAAS LA

A38

PH
EDISON WAY
TELFORD WAY
WATERWELLS DR
DAVY CL

13

ELMGROVE RD W
COLLETT CL
SELLARS RD
HEMBURY CL
DANOR CL

WESTLAND RD

WESTDRONE DR
ASHGROVE CL

THE PLANTATION
ORCHARD CL
POPLAR
OAK TREE CL
PEAR TREE CL
ELMGROVE WEST

ST NICHOLAS CL

SPRINGFIELD
LLOYD BAKER CT

CORNFIELD DR
ELMGROVE RD E

BARLEY CL
PLOUGHMANS WAY
CLOVER PK

WARD CL
FIELD CL

CHAPEL GDNS

GREEN PK

PO

Hardwicke Prim Sch

GREEN LA

Old Hall

CHURCH LA

STANK LA

Hardwicke

STICKY LA

GL2

Ellis Farm

Four Mile Elm

The Perry Ctr

Quedgeley Dist Ctr

School Farm

Stockpits Wood

The Gloucester and Sharpness Canal

Laynes Farm

Southfield Farm

Church Farm

POUND LA

Quedgeley West Bsns Pk

A38

B4008

PH
CROSS KEYS RDBT

BATH RD

A38

Colethrop Farm

Hardwicke Court

Summerhouse Farm

Road Farm

Mast

M5

Quedgeley East Bsns Pk

Parkend Covert

Broadfield Farm

Hiltmead

Mast

B4008

GL10

Royston

The Mount

Parkend Lodge

Parkend

Parkend Farm

Javelin Park

Lodge

A38

M5

B4008

Putloe Farm

Putloe Court

Gables Farm

78 A 79 B C 80 D E F

8 7 6 5 4 3 2 1

12 13 11 10

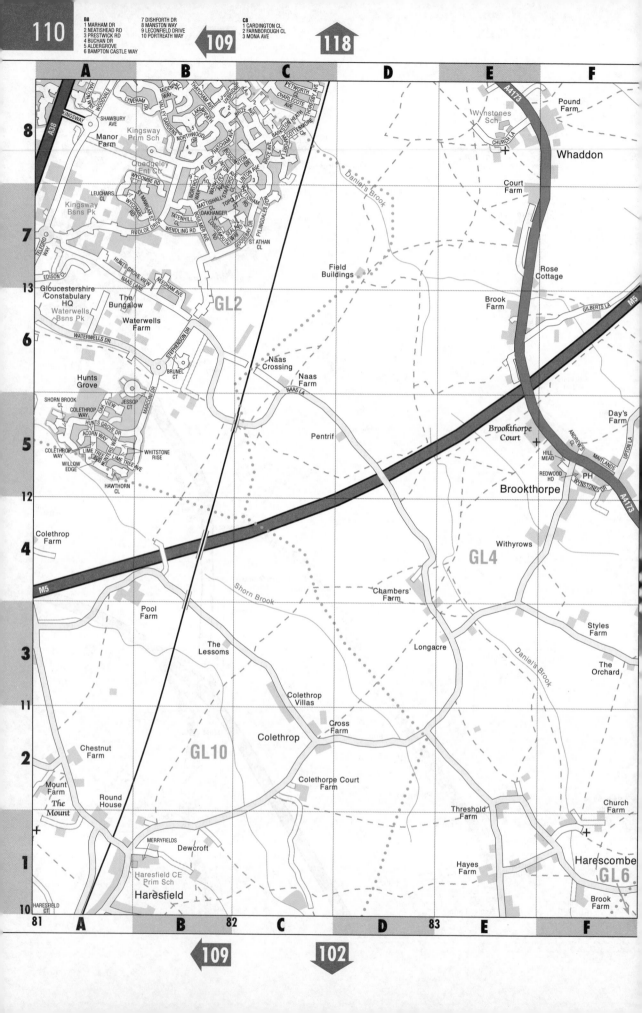

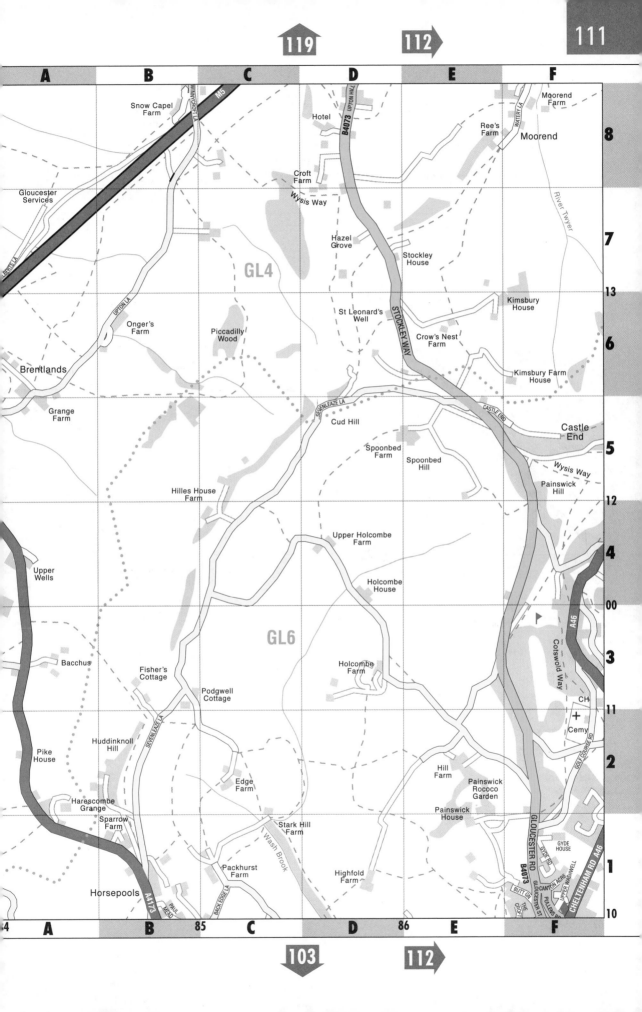

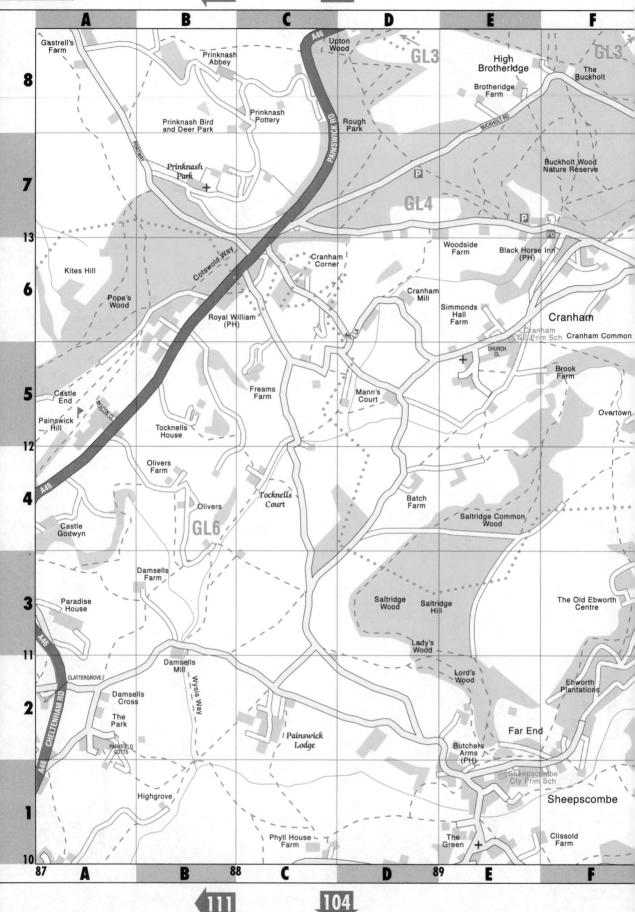

A   B   C   D   E   F

8

Gastrell's Farm

Prinknash Abbey

Upton Wood

GL3

High Brotheridge

Brotheridge Farm

The Buckholt

GL3

Prinknash Bird and Deer Park

Prinknash Pottery

Rough Park

BUCKHOLT RD

Buckholt Wood Nature Reserve

PORTWAY

A46

PAINSWICK RD

7

Prinknash Park

P

GL4

13

Cotswold Way

Cranham Corner

Woodside Farm

P

Black Horse Inn (PH)

PO

6

Kites Hill

Pope's Wood

Royal William (PH)

Cranham Mill

MILL LA

Simmonds Hall Farm

Cranham

Cranham CE Prim Sch

Cranham Common

CHURCH CL

Brook Farm

5

Castle End

Painswick Hill

BEACON CL

Tocknells House

Freams Farm

Mann's Court

Overtown

12

Olivers Farm

A46

4

Castle Godwyn

Olivers

Tocknells Court

GL6

Batch Farm

Saltridge Common Wood

3

Paradise House

Damsells Farm

Saltridge Wood

Saltridge Hill

The Old Ebworth Centre

11

CLATTERGROVE

Damsells Mill

Wysis Way

Lady's Wood

Lord's Wood

Ebworth Plantations

2

Damsells Cross

The Park

Painswick Lodge

Far End

CHELTENHAM RD

PARKFIELD COTTS

Butchers Arms (PH)

Sheepscombe Cty Prim Sch

1

Highgrove

Phyll House Farm

The Green

Sheepscombe

Clissold Farm

10

87   A   88   B   C   88   D   89   E   F

A B C D E F

8
7
13
6
5
12
4
3
11
2
1
10

Hawcote Hill
Hawcote Copse
Sidelands
Yew Tree Farm
NEWCOMBE
Brimpsfield
Long Acre
GL4
Groveridge Hill
Stonyhill Farm
Round Hill Wood
Morcombe
Quarry Farm House
New Seal Wood
Fishcombe Bank
Warren Hill
GL6
Caudle Green
Eddington Wood

A417
Nettleton
PH
Birtlands Grove
Watercombe Farm
The Rookery
Brimpsfield Park
Poston Wood
Ostrich Wood
Longmead Wood
River Frome
Winstone Wood

Harding's Barn
Harcombe Bottom
Cowley Wood
Highgate House
Highgate Farm
Park Wood
Round Wood
Pit Wood
Gloucester Beeches
The Clump
GL53
Harcombe Faem
Manor Farm
Syde
Harcombe Wood
GL7
Saltershill Barn
A417

93 A B 94 C D 95 E F

A B C D E F

A435 Lower Cockleford

Cockleford Farm

Ward's Wood

Bubb's Hill Wood

Trout Farm

Churn Bank

River Churn

A435

8

Bubb's Hill

Butlers Hill Farm

Butler's Farm

The Bungalow

7

HIGH CROSS

High Cross

13

Enfield Farm

HILL VIEW

Ward's Hey

Sparrowthorn

Slutswell

6

Ivy Cottage Farm

Elkstone

GL53

Manor Farm

Hillclose Grove

Paynters Cottage

Hall's Grove

5

12

Lion's Grove

Sadlers Farm

Hall's Grove

Elkstone Farm

Combend Manor

Power's Wood

4

Hailer's Wood

The Clumps

Westedge Wood

3

Ermin House Farm

Combend Farm

Pine Tree Cottage

Watercombe Farm

11

Beechpike

PH

The Ash

Bromsley Wood

Shewel Wood

2

Damson Grove

Adder Bank

PIKE RD

Fosse Farm

GL7

GL7

1

Winstone Radio Station

A417

10

165
124

| A | B | C | D | E | F |

8

Oakle Street

The Hill

Hook's Farm

PH

Clayhill Wood

7

Oakle House

Clay Hill

Minsterworth

Minsterworth CE Prim Sch

LYNCROFT

A48

The Elms

BURY LA

CHURCH LA

17

Green Farm

Brook Farm

Gloucestershire Way

Duni Farm

River Severn

Elmore Back

6

Denny Hill

Elmore Back Farm

Lake Street Farm

Bagley Farm

LEY RD

Severn Way

GL2

5

Lower Ley Farm

16

LAKE ST

4

The Flat

PO

Farleys End Farm

PH

Church Farm

Hartland's Hill

Farley's End

Pleasure Farm

3

ROOKERY VILLAS

Bridgemacote Farm

15

A48

BROADWAY LA

Kenton Green

Broadway Farm

2

The Noards

GL14

Church Covert

Hill Farm

1

Wicksgreen

Waterend

Yew Tree Farm

Shatford Grove

Velthouse Farm

14

| 75 | A | B | 76 | C | D | 77 | E | F |

Long Brook

165
108

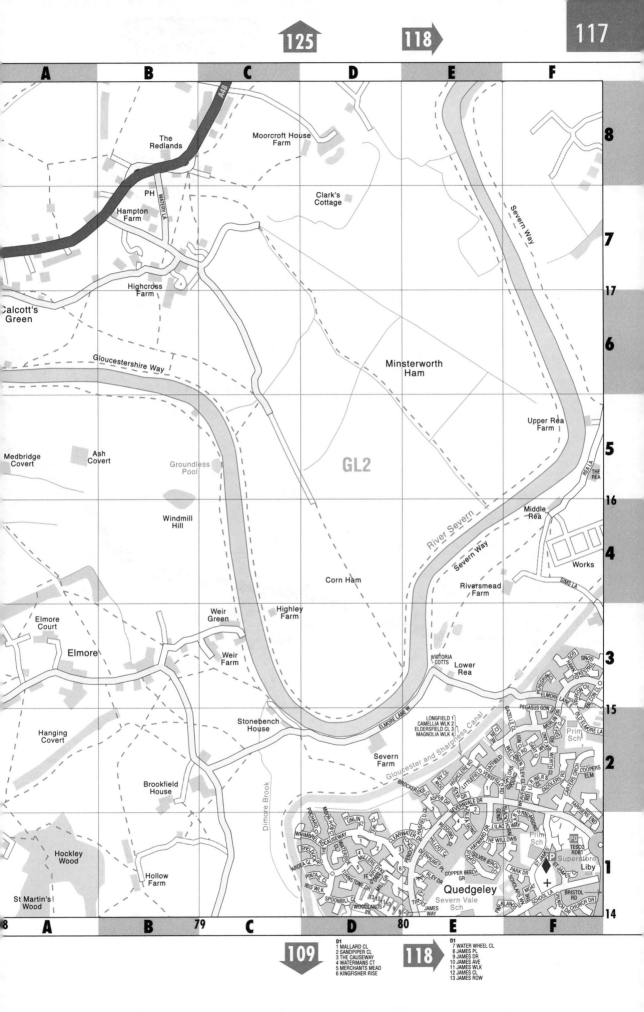

D1
1 MALLARD CL
2 SANDPIPER CL
3 THE CAUSEWAY
4 WATERMANS CT
5 MERCHANTS MEAD
6 KINGFISHER RISE

D1
7 WATER WHEEL CL
8 JAMES PL
9 JAMES DR
10 JAMES AVE
11 JAMES WLK
12 JAMES CL
13 JAMES ROW

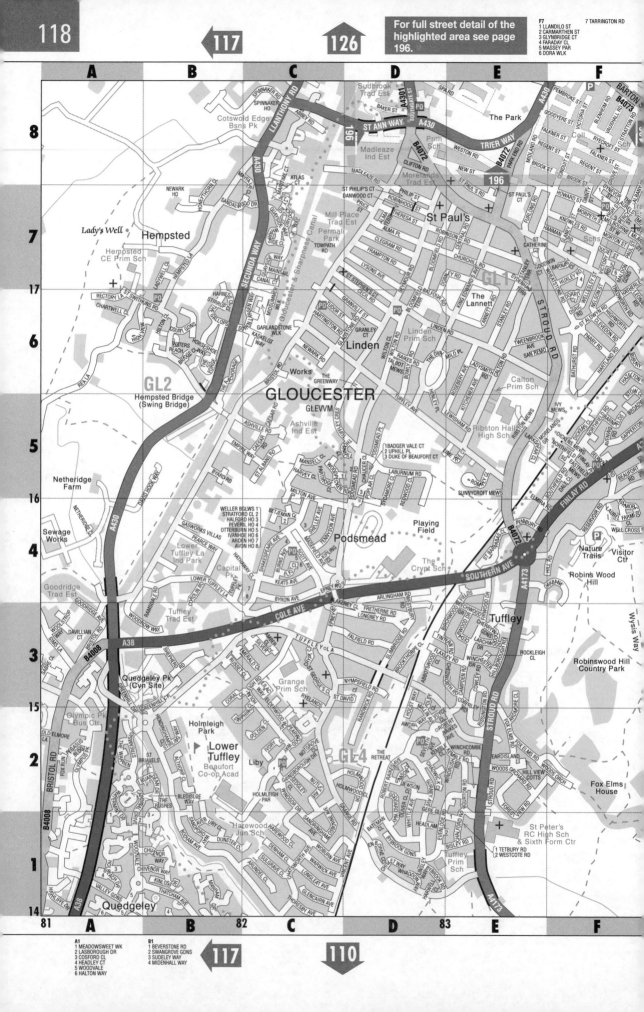

A8
1 SALISBURY HO
2 RED LION CT
3 ST JAMES MEWS
4 BURFORD MEWS
5 St James Trad Est

6 Francis Woodcock Trad Est

C7
1 DRUIDS LA
2 PEGGOTTY BGLWS

127

120

E6
1 CENTURION CL
2 SPARTAN CL
3 BENSON CL
4 PILGRIM CL
5 WIGMORE CL

F5
1 HOWGATE CL
2 MARJORAM CL
3 CAMOMILE CL
4 VIBURNUM VIEW
5 BILBERRY CL

119

C4
1 DRAYTON CL
2 PAINSWICK LODGE
3 SEVERN LODGE
4 PARK VIEW
5 GEORGE WHITEFIELD CL
6 ABBEY VIEW
7 PRINKNASH CL
8 PRINKNASH RD
9 ACORN CT

10 WINSLEY CT
11 ROBINSWOOD PL
12 UNDERHILL CT
13 MATSON LODGE
14 CHERRY TREE CT
15 FAIRFIELD CT
16 CULVERIN CL

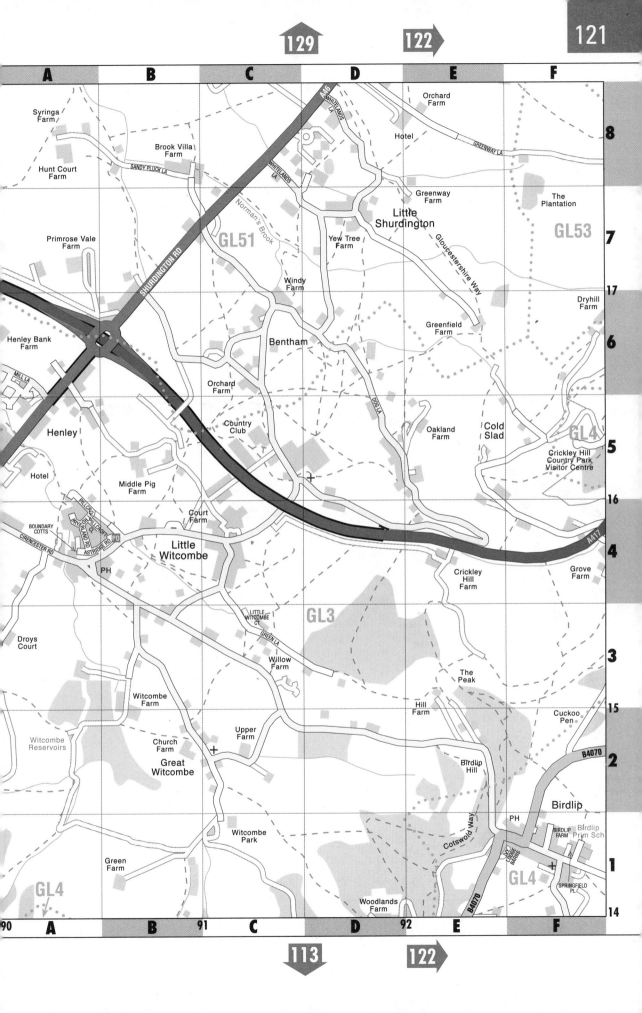

A **B** **C** **D** **E** **F**

8

Crippets

GL51

Shurdington
Hill

Hartley
Farm

Blackhedge
Farm

HARTLEY LA

P

LECKHAMPTON HILL

7

Mast

GREENWAY LA

SALTERLEY
GRANGE

Cotswold Way

Barrow Piece
Plantation

Hartley
Bottom

Ullenwood Court
Bsns. Pk

17

Ullenwood
Court

MANOR
BARN

GL53

6

Shortwood
Farm

The
National Star
Coll

CH

Poolpiece
Langet

GL3

Shortwood Flat

A436

Short
Wood

P

The
Scrubbs

Ullen
Wood

Dowman
Farm

5

Crickley Hill
Country Park

A436

Clerk's
Patch

Town
End

16

A417

Air Balloon
(PH)

South
Hill

4

A417

Cuckoopen
Barn Farm

Barrow
Wake

GL3

P

Mast

Rushwood
Kennels

Coldwell
Bottom

3

Birdlip
Radio Station

Masts

Gloucestershire Way

GL4

Mast

Shab
Hill

Shab
Hill
Farm

Cally Hill
Plantation

15

2

Green
Hatch
Farm

Hill
Barn

1

Parson's
Pitch

Stockwell

The
Rise

Harcombe
Bottom

14

A417

93 **A** **B** 94 **C** **D** 95 **E** **F**

A   B   C   D   E   F

8

GL54

Pegglesworth
Home Farm

A435

CIRENCESTER RD

Windmill
Farm

Wistley
Grove

Chatcombe
Wood

Little
Grove

7

Hartley
Wood

Sandford
Sch

A436

PH

Home
Farm

Seven
Springs

Cotswold Way

Slack's
Barn

Bogdon
Bank

17

Needlehole

6

Gloucestershire Way

Coberley

HAMBLINS
COTTS

Coberley
CE Prim Sch

PO

New
Farm

GL53

Hilcot
Wood

5

16

Close
Farm

Coberley
Court

The
Rookery

Upper
Coberley

Mercombe
Wood

4

Pinswell

3

Pinswell
Plantation

15

Park
Farm

Cowley

Cowley
Manor

The
Forest

2

Hill
Covert

Cowley
View

Cockleford

PH

River Churn

A435

Tomtit's
Bottom

Westbury
Farm

Chescombe
Bottom

1

14

96   A   B   C   97   C   D   98   E   F

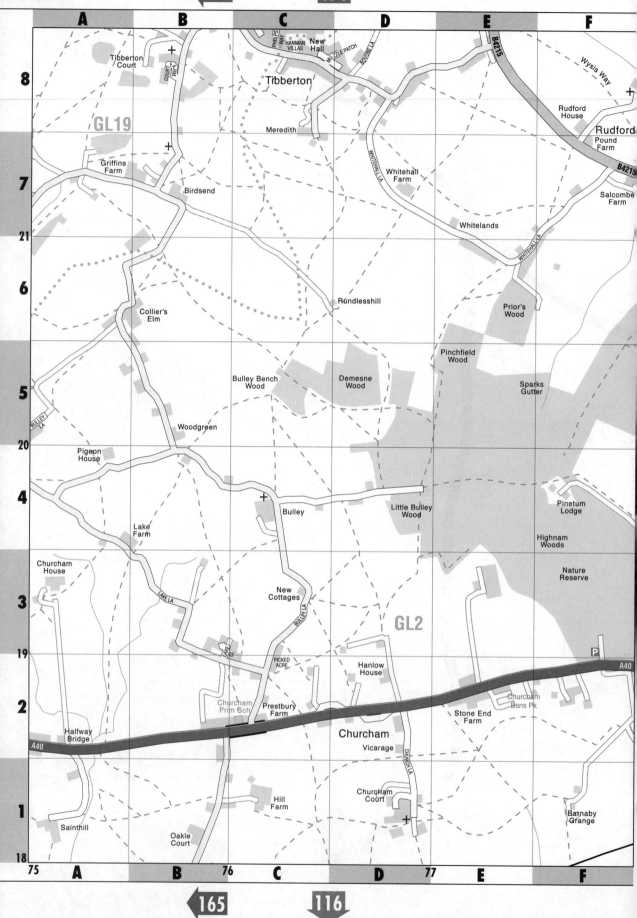

A B C D E F

GL19

Hooper's Covert

River Leadon

The Roughett

Wysis Way

Lassington Court

+ruin

Lassington

The Reddings

Astman's Farm

Rodwayhill Covert

PINCOATE 1
TUNACRE 2
POPPY FIELD 3
WOODLEIGH FIELD 4
MICKLE MEAD 5
BLACKSMITHS GROUND 6
STONEY FIELD 7
PETERS FIELD 8
CLAYBURN CL 9
WETHERLEIGH DR 10

Persh Farm

Rodway Hill

Lassington Hill

Lassington Wood
(Nature Reserve)

Highnam

LIMEKILN GR
MARY GR
THE RANGE
CHESTNUT COTTS
Prim Acad

POOLE GROUND

PIPERS RISE

MAIDENHALL

HIGHNAM GN

LAS SINGTON GR

PO

THE PADDOCKS

CH

Highnam
Bsns Ctr

TWO MILE LA

GL2

BRIMSOME MDW
POPES MC

WILLIAMS ORCH

LITTLE LANCARRIDGE
FARTHING
PARK BRAKE
BEECH CL
LIDO VC
TURNERS CL

Over Farm

Pope's Pool Cottages

Home Farm

B4215

Linton Farm

A40

Highnam Court

The Lake

A48

Beachamp Lodge

PINETUM DR

19

Corseless Brake

Beachamp House

Piper's Grove

Gloucestershire Way

Highnam Bridge

Upper Moorcroft Farm

River Severn

Severn Way

Hygrove House

HYGROVE LA

A48

Murcott Farm

A B C D E F

8

The Steadings Bsns Ctr

White House

Abbott's Lodge

BASE LA

Maisemore Court

Maisemore

THE RIDGE

CHURCH RD

Upper Parting

Works

Gloucestershire Way

Abloads Court

7

ORCHARD WAY

PERSH WAY

PERSH LA

CHURCH RISE

PH

STANLEIGH TERR

THE RIDINGS

SEVERN CL

BRIDGE FARM

Maisemore Bridge Cross

21

Rectory Farm

6

Persh Farm

West Channel

Maisemore Ham

Alney Island

PH

Queen's Dyke

Longford

CHESTERTON CT 1
LONGFORD MEWS 2
FINCHMOOR MEWS 3
TAURUS CL 4

AUSTIN DR

LEWIS AVE

SHERWOOD

A40

A38

MEADOW CL

HAYES CL

VICTORIA RD

TEASEL CL

ADONIS CT

TITHCROFT CT

TEWKESBURY RD

5

East Channel

Severn Way

SANDHURST LA

WILLOW CVN SITE

Winfield Hospl

H

Playing Field

STAMP'S MDW

PLOCK CT

FAIRMILE GDNS

HIGHBANK PK

20

Herefordshire & Gloucestershire Canal

GL2

Alney Island

Walham

Frogcastle Fram

ORCHARD CL

WESTFIELD TERR

THE LIMES

RIVERMEAD CL

GAMBIER

PARRY GDNS

CHESMANN CT

4

WYSIS WAY

WOOD MEWS

CANAL WAY

HORSE WY

HORSEL RD

Over

The STOCKYARDS

WALHAM LA

LAWRENCE WAY N

WALHAM LA

SUFFOLK DR

GREVILLE CL

A417

A38

ESTCOURT RD

A430

A38

River Twyer

LONGHORN AVE

GL1

St Oswalds Ret Pk

ST OSWALD'S RD

SANDHURST RD

BIJOU CT

HINTON RD

MALVERN RD

HEATHVILLE RD

Girls High Sch

Kingsholm

Over Bridge

A417

Town Ham

DEXTER WY

GAVEL WAY

LAWRENCE WAY

KINGSHOLM RD

DEANS ROW

MERCIA RD

196

DEAN'S WLK

ST MARK ST

EDWY PAR

SWAN RD

SEBERT ST

RFC Ground

Kingsholm CE Prim Sch

OXFORD ST

HONYATT RD

SHERBORNE ST

HENRY ST

A40

PH

P&R

Pool Meadow

FAIR VIEW CVN PK

POOL MEADOW CVN PK

WESTEND TERR

WESTEND PAR

ALNEY TERR

St Mark's Sch

SWEETBRIAR ST

UNION ST

HENRY ST

3

River Severn

Port Ham

Richard's Wood

A417

Mean Ham

L Ctr

ST CATHERINE ST

Works

DEAN'S WAY

ALVIN ST

CLARENCE ROW

London RD

B4063

196

19

GL1

WESTGATE

A417

PRIORY RD

GOUDA WAY

The King's Sch

WORCESTER ST

BLACK DOG WAY

H

Gloucester Royal

2

Lower Parting

Oxlease

196

WESTGATE

A430 ROYAL OAK RD

QUAY ST

CLARE ST

ST MARY'S SQ

PITT ST

Cath

P

PO

P

HARE LA

P

P

NORTHGATE ST

ALDGATE ST

THE OXEBODE

NEW INN LA

STATION RD

RUSSELL ST

Gloucester

GREAT WESTERN RD

CLARENCE ST

METZ WAY

A4302

GLOUCESTER

GLEVVM

Mus

Shire Hall

BARRACK SQ Ct

Prison

Mus

Mus

WESTGATE ST

LONGSMITH ST

SOUTHGATE ST

BRUNSWICK RD

RUSSELL ST

BRUTON WAY

Widden Prim Sch

1

Severn Way

Sud Meadow

Castle Meads

THE QUAY

COMMERCIAL RD

SEVERN RD

The Docks

Mus

Mus

P

Mus

KIMBROSE WAY

PARLIAMENT ST

ST MICHAEL'S

HAMPDEN WAY

BRUNSWICK SQ

BELGRAVE RD

WELLINGTON ST

ARTHUR ST

L Ctr

CHARLES ST

WIDDEN ST

NAPIER ST

B4073

PO

Severnside Trad Est

Llanthony Ind Est

SUDMEADOW RD

HEMMINGSDALE RD

LLANTHONY RD

SEVERN RD

125 Bsns Pk

Coll

ALBION ST

OLD TRAM RD

NORFOLK ST

CROMWELL ST

BARTON ST

A430

A4073

18

Sports Gd

Llanthony Secunda Priory (rems of)

High Orchard

A4301

SOUTHGATE ST

A430

81 A 82 B C 82 D 83 E F

For full street detail of the highlighted area see page 196.

A B C D E F

8 7 21 6 5 20 4 3 19 2 1 18

Hotel
TEWKESBURY RD
A38
Twigworth CE Prim Sch
Broadboard Bridge
Longford Bridge
Horsbere Brook
DAWN DR
Longford La

Hatherley Brook
Gloucestershire Way
Drymeadow Farm
Drymeadow Lodge
DRY MEADOW LA
Innsworth Tech Pk
Sewage Works

Sewage Works
Innsworth House Farm
Innsworth
GL3
RAF Innsworth

CHAFFINCH CL 1
BULLFINCH WAY 2
INNSWORTH LA
ROBINS END
FINCH RD
FALCO
WREN TERR
ROOKES
Innsworth Jun Sch
NIGHTINGALE CROFT
PEN
PELICAN

Innsworth La
GRAY RD
HANNAH PL
WARD AVE
SWALLOW CRES
SHEARWATER
THOMPSON WAY
JACKSON CL
BARTON CL
RYDER ROW
TANDEY WLK
Larkfield Inf Sch

GIBSON RD
CHESHIRE RD
NOTTINGHAM DR
MIDDLETON LAWN
NICOLSON CL

Sports Gd
SHAMROCK CL 1
LOVAGE CL 2
MISTLETOE MEWS 3
ELDERBERRY MEWS 4
BLAKELEY CT 5
HEATHDEAN RD 6
HAWTHORN CL 7

ARAGON WAY 1
PARR CL 2
PRINCES MEWS 3
ZINNIA CL
SALVIA CL
PARKSIDE DR

GLENDOWER CL 1
FROBISHER MEWS 2
MINSTREL WAY 3
HIGHGROVE WAY
TUDOR CL
SHEPHERDS WAY
MARY ROSE
SELCOCK
DRAKE CL
BOLEYN

GREVILLE CL
KATHERINE CL
TALLIS
RALEIGH
ROBERTS
CAMPBELL
CLARKIA CL
CORNFIELD
LANCET RD
GROVE RD
B4063
CHELTENHAM ROAD E
LIME
A40

WENTWORTH CL 1
THE TULWORTHS 2
WOODCOTE 3
FOXCOTE 4
HORNBEAM MEWS 5

EVERGREEN WLK 1
CYPRESS GDNS 2
SHEEVAUN CL 3
LACCA CL 4

1 MELODY WAY
2 SAYLITTLE MEWS
3 MUTSILVER MEWS
4 PATSEAMUR MEWS

Playing Field
GL2
The Milestone Sch

LACY CL
DURAND
MAINARD SQ
THISTLEBANK
WHITEBEAM
FLEMING RD
FIRETHORN CL
ASHFIELD
MILFORD CL
ABENHALL
MONTFORT RD
CRISPIN CL
MANDEVILLE
LITTLE WLK
PARK ASH
GRISEDALE CL
GIFFORD CL
MALT
SAXON
LITTLE NORMANS
GILBERT CL
DANE CL
SIMON RD
MANLEY GDNS
KENTON DR
HAYDALE GDNS
LANGDALE GDNS
PADDOCK GDNS
COTSWOLD
BROOKLANDS PK
ENNERDALE AVE
HURST CL
WESTMEAD RD
MILLER RD
PALLINSKA MEWS
CLOMONEY WAY
WALT
BLACKWATER CL

Longlevens
Longlevens Inf Sch
CALSPICK WAY
SANGSTAR
COLLEGE FIELDS
DOVERDALE
PERRY CL
BRADSHAW GDNS
FOXLEIGH CRES
MARS CL
CANNING RD
B4063
A40

Allot Gdns
ESTCOURT CL
COOKS ORCH
Univ of Gloucestershire (Oxstalls Campus)
ESTCOURT RD
BEECHCROFT RD
OXSTALLS DR
REDLAND
RODNEY CL
FLOWER WAY
THE HEDGEROW
GARDEN WAY
GLEVUM CL
OXSTALLS WAY
SOUTH CL
CHANNELS WAY
PD

LONGLAND GDNS
LONGLAND CT

LAVINIA
LAURA
Liby
ALDER CL
BRADLEY CL
GRASMERE RD
RYDAL RD
KESWICK CL
KENDAL RD
WELLSPRINGS RD
THE TRIANGLE
WINDERMERE RD
Longlevens Jun Sch
COWNSTONE
CHURCH RD
LEVEN CL
THE ELMS
OLD CHELTENHAM RD
P PO
CONISTON RD

KIMBERLEY
MANOR RD
WISFORD CL
NINE ELMS RD
LITTLE ELMBRIDGE
LIDDINGTON RD
ORCHARD RD
THE PARADE
LAMBOURN CL
LOSBOURNE
LAVINGTON RD

Wells' Bridge

Elmbridge Playing Fields
CHELTENHAM RD
ELMLEAZE
OAKLEAZE
PILLOWELL
WILLOWLEAZE
Sir Thomas Rich's Sch
GL4
Factory
Imperial Gate Bsns Pk

GL1
HEALEY CL
St Margarets
THE COURTYARD
ROYAL CL
Coll
Wotton Lawn
HILLFIELD COURT RD
HILLFIELD
TUDOR CT
ALEXANDRA CT
DENMARK RD
MICHAELMAS
HAMPTON CT
HOLLAND CT
GRAHAM GDNS
CHELTENHAM RD
KENILWORTH AVE
B4063

LANSDOWN RD
WALLBANK HO
DENMARK HO

ARGYLL RD
GRAFTON RD
GROSVENOR RD
RIVERSLEY RD
LONSDALE RD
WAVERLEY
SISSON RD
COLEBRIDGE
MEREVALE RD
BRAEBURN CL
PICKWICK CL
MEADOWLEAZE
HAVEN CT
SANDYLEAZE

Elmbridge Inf & Jun Schs
Bsns Ctr

BIRDLIP HO
FLAXLEY HO
MAYHILL WAY
Gloucestershire Royal
H
St Peter's RC Prim Sch
WOTTON ELMS CT
BARNWOOD RD
WOLSELEY RD
W & S ELEY RD
WINDFALL WAY
GREEN PIPPIN CL
THE GRANGE
CORONATION GR
Wotton
WOTTON BROOK

GREAT WESTERN RD
THE CRESCENT
CARESCOMBE
PEART CL
COLDRAY CL
MYERS RD
ETHERIDGE PL
NORMAN BALL WAY
CASEY
COLTMAN CL
BROOKSIDE GR
ARMSCROFT CRES
ARMSCROFT WAY
ARMSCROFT GDNS
BROOKFIELD MEWS
BLINKHORNS BRIDGE LA
ARMSCROFT CT
NORTHBROOK RD
CAMSEL CL
SOUTHBROOK RD
WELLS RD

METZ WAY
A4302
A38
EASTERN AVE
CORINIUM AVE
A417
A38
TA Ctr
The Limes
Barnwood CE Prim Sch
Barnwood
Superstore
Barnwood Fields Bsns Pk
GL3
Hotel
A417

HAMMOND WAY
BAIRNWATER
BARNETT WAY
HAZEL CT
SAW MILLS END
GROVE CRES
FAIRWATER
BARNWOOD AVE
MELVERLAND RD
KEVIN CL
COLIN RD
PEGASUS CT
GROVELANDS
CREDON RD
GREENWAYS
KINGSTON RD
INSLEY GDNS
KNIGHTON AVE
CHOSEN WAY
GATTON RD
MAYFIELD DR
DUNCROFT
BARRINGTON DR
BARNSIDE
CREST WAY
GIPPIN AVE

A1
1 MAGDALA RD
2 BECKSIDE CT
3 GREAT WESTERN CT
4 LOBB CT
5 COUNTY CRES
6 MILLBROOK CL
7 ALINGTON CL

B2
1 ALDERNEY FLATS
2 KENCOURT CL
3 WESTMINSTER CT
4 WOTTON ELMS CT
5 BRADFORD RD

127
173

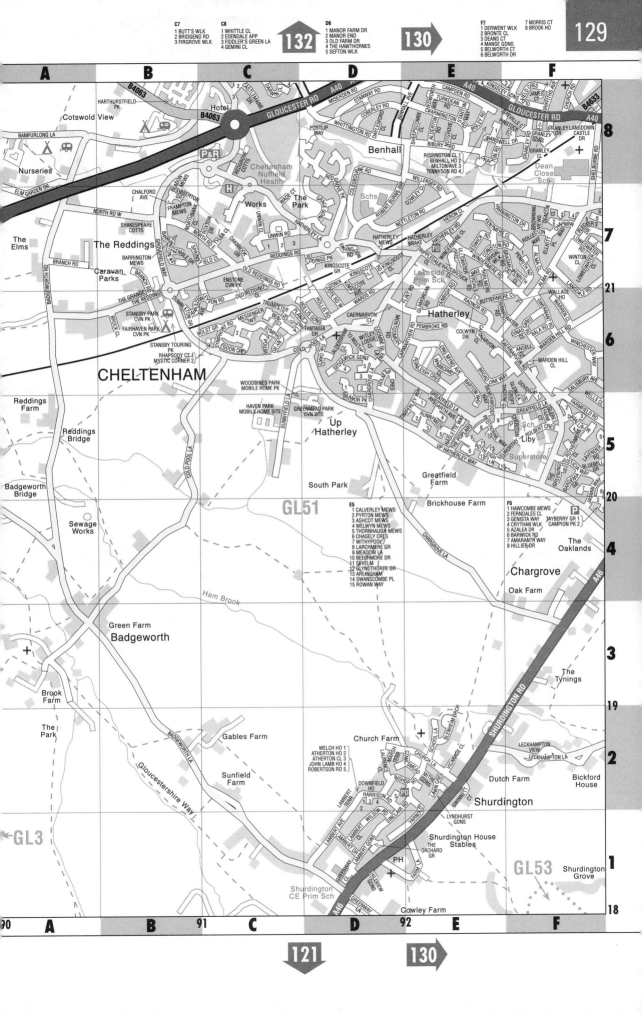

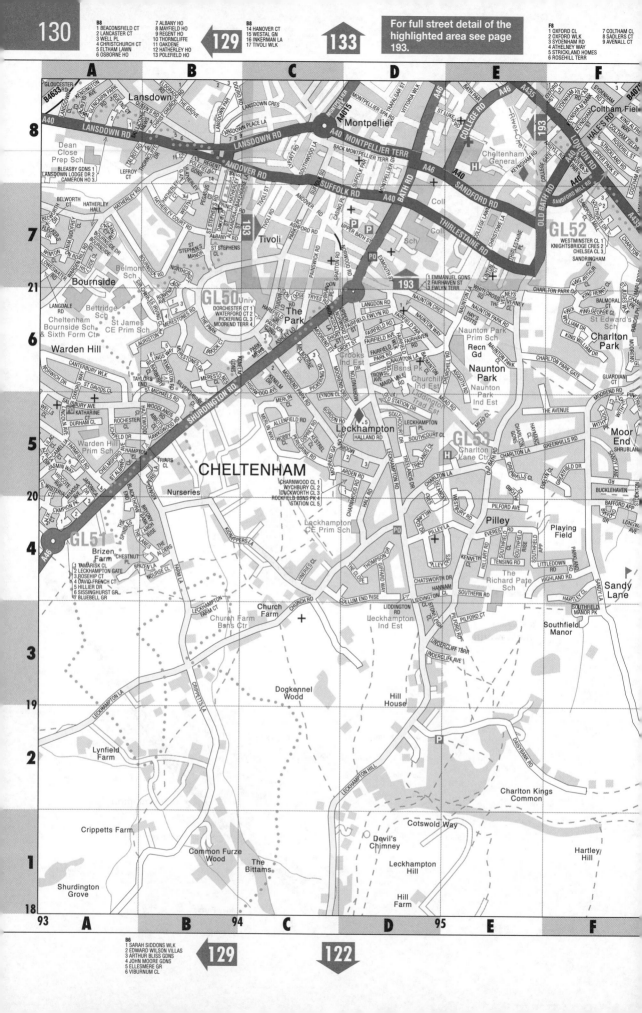

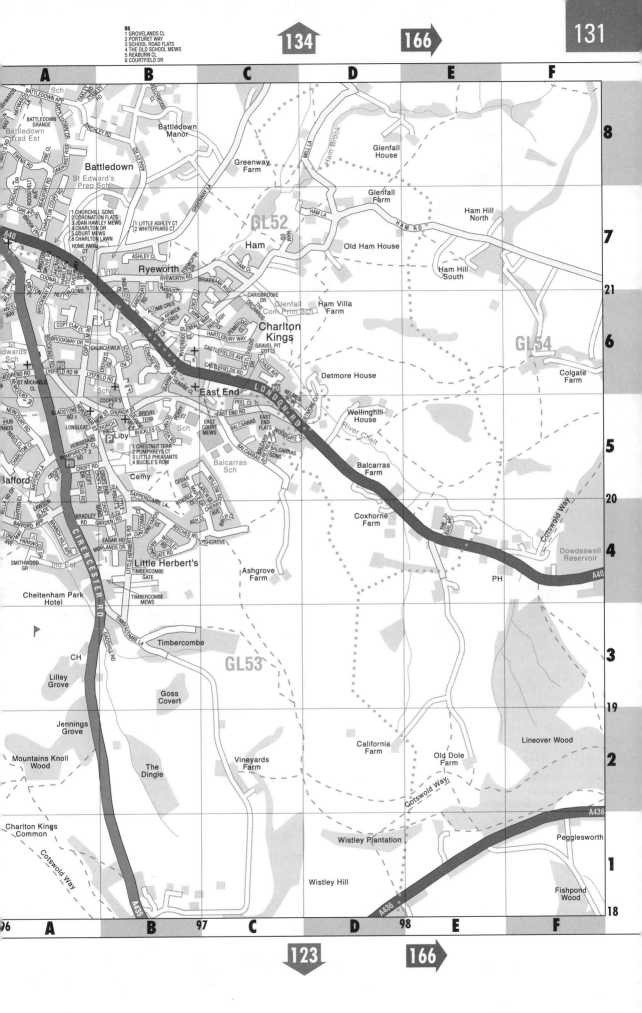

D2		E2		
1 MAGNOLIA CT	10 SHAFTESBURY PL	6 FRANKLYN CT	15 ANAPA MEWS	F3
2 MULBERRY CT	11 GLEVUM CT	7 EVINGTON CT	16 YALTA CL	1 AUCKLAND HO
3 SYCAMORE CT	12 DE FERRIERES WLK	8 EVINGTON RD	17 SOCHI MEWS	2 NEW ZEALAND HO
4 REDWOOD CT	13 DORINGTON WLK	9 AMBERLEY RD	E3	3 LYGON WLK
5 PEACOCK CL	E2	10 AMBERLEY CT	1 LECHMERE RD	4 BROOKLYN CT
6 SWALLOWTAIL CL	1 PAKISTAN HO	11 COATES HO	2 EDWARD WILSON HO	F4
7 EMPEROR CL	2 INDIA HO	12 ARUNDEL HO	3 KENILWORTH HO	1 RHODESIA HO
8 HEAPEY CL	3 TYLER CT	13 CHEPSTOW HO	4 BERKELEY HO	2 SOUTH AFRICA HO
9 ROYAL CT	4 TASMANIA HO	14 EASTNOR HO	5 SUDELEY HO	3 GREVIL RD
	5 GRESHAM CT			4 DURBAN HO

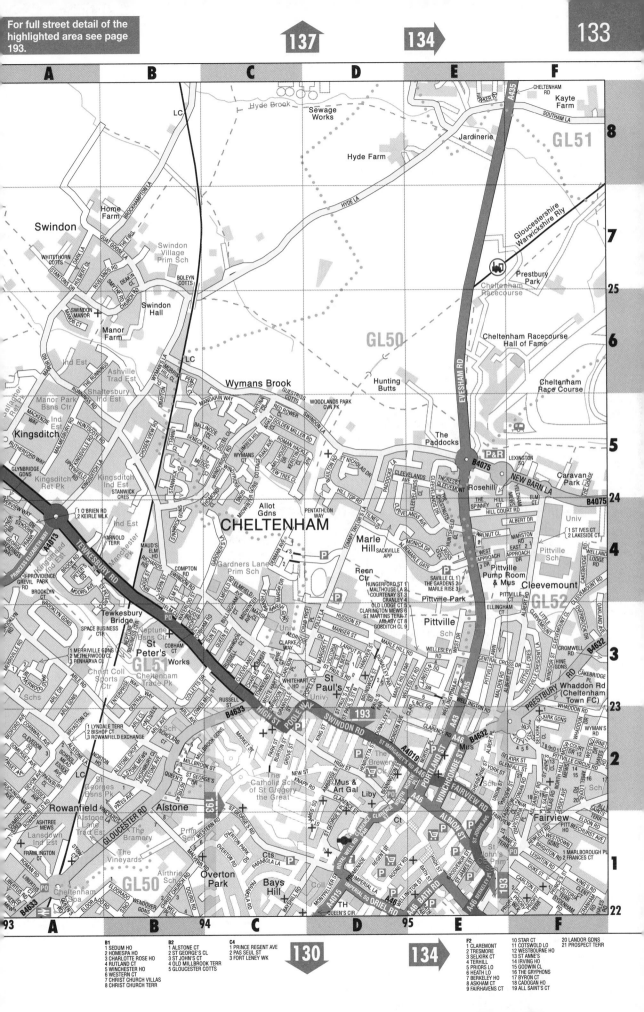

133
138

A B C D E F

8

Southam

Thrift Wood

Cleve Cloud

Cleve Common

Gloucestershire & Warwickshire Rly

SOUTHAM LA

RATCLIFF

THE CLOSE

SCHOOL LA

OLD RD

SUNSET LA

SUNSET LA

Nutterswood

Ellenborough Park (Hotel)

B4632

NEW RD

THE BANK / LEWIS

GRAVEL WLK

BENTLEY LA

7

Hyde Brook

GL50

25

Queen's Wood

Cotswold Way

Southam Bridge

6

Cheltenham Race Course

White's Barn

PARK LA

SPRING LA

SHAW GREEN LA

Shaw Green

Knoll Holl House

UPPER MILL LA

BOWBRIDGE LA

Bow Bridge

LAKE ST

GRAVEL PIT LA

QUEENWOOD GR

Lower Hill Farm

5

APPLE ORCH

WATERSHOOT CL

LINDEN CT

Prestbury Manor House

GL52

Whitehill

APPLE CL

ACACIA CL

LIME CL

BROADWAY

LINDEN AVE

BRYMORE CL

THE BURGAGE

MILL ST

Prestbury

1 MORNINGSIDE CTYD
2 MORNINGSIDE CL
3 ANN GOODRICH CL
4 THE OLD MANSION

24

B4075

CUMMING CT 1
BRYMORE AVE 2

NEW BARN LA

The Priory

Liby

IDSAL DR

THE STABLES

MILL LA

1 BULA WAY
2 MILL REEF DR
3 TREMBLANT CL
4 MIDNIGHT CT

RUSHY LA

NEW BARN CL

TATCHLEY LA

B4075

DEEP ST

HIGH ST

PO

BAY TREE CT

PRESTBURY

FLORIDA GREEN

COURT RD

BEECH CL

DESERT ORCHID RD

RUSHY MEWS

AUREL DR

GLEBE RD

BLACKSMITHS LA

LYNWORTH TERR

SOUTH VIEW WAY

NOVERTON AVE

NOVERTON LA

4

CLEEVEMOUNT

WELLAND LODGE

STEIM

Prestbury St Mary's CE Jun Sch

STUDLAND DR

PURBECK WAY

HONEYSUCKLE DR

FAWLEY DR

IVY BANK CL

MUSCROFT RD

FINCHCROFT LA

PICCADILLY WAY

Noverton

Noverton Farm

PRESTBURY RD

PRESCOTT

KINDER

CORONATION RD

FIR TREE CL

CHEVIOT

PENNINE RD

BUSH CT

CHILTERN RD

WHITE'S

HORN CL

BRAMBLE RISE

BLACK BERRY FIELD

THREE SISTERS

GALLOPS LA

ROBERTS RD

CLEEVE CLOUD LA

BUTTERCROSS LA

WESTWOOD LA

DILLY WAY

Lynworth

Sch

MENDIP RD

LYNWORTH PL

COTSWOLD RD

BRENDON WLK

BETTRIDGE CT

Sch

B4632

MENDIP CL

CROMWELL RD

CAM RD

CHELT RD

BOUNCER'S LA

WILLOWHERB CL

NEWLAND CT

3

WYMAN'S RD

STEVENS RD

BOWEN

PRIORS RD

BURMA AVE

PRIORS CT

Cemy

Crem

Piccadilly Farm

23

HAYES CT

THAMES RD

TAMAR RD

Whaddon

Sch

DART RD

SLOANE RD

LADYSMITH RD

MANCA

ROBINS

WHADDON RD

PO

CLYDE CRES

WYE RD

BOURNE

SEVERN RD

KIMBERLEY WLK

CHELTENHAM

2

HAYES RD

HOMESPRING

CLEVE VIEW RD

MERSEY RD

CHURCH AVE

AVON RD

HUMBER RD

IMJIN RD

Oakley

GOODRICH RD

ALVINGTON DR

The Hewletts

JAMES DONOVAN CT

BELL VW CL

HILLVIEW

KEMPLEY RD

CLEARWELL GDNS

YORKLEY RD

BROCKWEIR

GL54

HEWLETT RD

OAK CT

OAK MANOR DR

HYDE

ESSEX DR

WYE DR

PILLOWELL CL

Oakley Farm

1 ALEXANDRIA WLK
2 REDMARLEY RD
3 JOYFORD PASSAGE
4 DYMOCK WLK
5 BICKNOR DR
6 RUARDEAN WLK

Lower Hewletts Farm

ELDON RD

HALE'S CL

GROVE DR

Battledown Children's Ctr

Battledown Mead

Hewletts Resr

AGGS HILL

1

ELDON RD

HALE'S RD

THE GROVE

Battledown Hill

STANLEY RD

ASHLEY RD

HARP HILL

CAMP RD

GREENWAY

MILL LA

Northfield Farm

Cotswold Way

B4075

BATTLEDOWN

BATTLEDOWN WN CL

Holy Apostles CE Prim Sch

22

96

A

B

97

C

D

98

E

F

139
174

A   **B**   **C**   **D**   **E**   **F**

Cotswold Way

8

Cleeve Common

Breakheart
Plantation

Hill Barn
Farm

7

25

GL52

Radio
Masts

6

Cotswold Way

Wontley
Farm

Upper Hill
Farm

5

Westwood
House

GL54

West
Wood

West Down

24

4

Cotswold Way

Wardens
Wood

Drypool
Farm

3

23

Quietways

Whitehall
Farm

Puckham
Woods

2

Puckham Woods
House

Puckham
Scrubs

Woodlands
Farm

Cotswold Way

1

Puckham
Farm

22

9   **A**   **B**   **00**   **C**   **D**   **01**   **E**   **F**

166
174

173
182

| | A | B | C | D | E | F |

8

Warders Farm

Gothic Farm

Tredington Court

ST JOHN'S CT

BOZARD LA

Tredington

LLANTHONY COTTS

GL20

M5

7

Tredington House

29

Tredington Com Prim Sch

River Swilgate

6

Phillant Farm

WHITE CT

ARMSTRONG RD

Old Forge Cotts

MILLER CT

DEAN LA

BANADY LA

Wks

CLEEVE VIEW

5

Rudgeway Farm

CURSEY LA

Manor Farm

Stoke Orchard

STOKE RD

Waterloo House

SWAN LA

ARCHERS LA

MILL LA

28

Harrow Farm

GL52

4

Mill Farm

Waterloo Farm

MILL LA

Hardwicke

3

Manor Farm

Red House Farm

Green Farm

WESTFIELD COTTS

Mast

River Swilgate

27

Wks

GL51

2

Colman's Farm

Hardwicke Brake

LOWGLOW LA

Barn Farm

Villa Farm

1

Piff's Elm

Elmstone Hardwicke

Church Lane Farm

26

| 90 | A | | B | 91 | C | D | 92 | E | | F |

M5

173
132

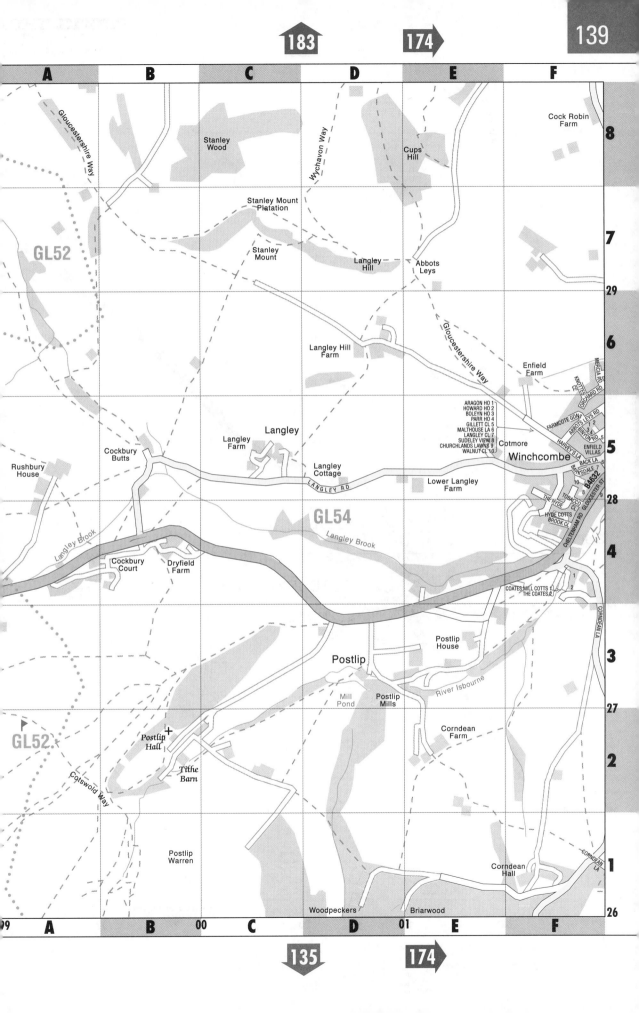

A   B   C   D   E   F

Cock Robin
Farm

Gloucestershire Way

Stanley
Wood

Wychavon Way

Cups
Hill

8

GL52

Stanley Mount
Platation

7

Stanley
Mount

Langley
Hill

Abbots
Leys

29

Gloucestershire Way

6

Langley Hill
Farm

Enfield
Farm

MERCIA RD

KNOTTRESCL
ORCHARD RD

ARAGON HO 1
HOWARD HO 2
BOLEYN HO 3
PARR HO 4
GILLETT CL 5
MALTHOUSE LA 6
LANGLEY CL 7
SUDELEY VIEW 8
CHURCHLANDS LAWNS 9
WALNUT CL 10

FARMCOTE GDN
ABBOTS LEYS RD
BINYON RD

Langley

Langley
Farm

Cockbury
Butts

HARVEY'S LA
ENFIELD
VILLAS

Cotmore

Winchcombe   5

Rushbury
House

Langley
Cottage

BACK LA
BARKSDALE

B4632

LANGLEY RD

Lower Langley
Farm

28

THE HYDE
CL
TOBACCO
CL
GLOUCESTER ST

GL54

Langley Brook

HYDE COTTS
CHELTENHAM RD
BROOK CL

4

Langley Brook

Cockbury
Court

Dryfield
Farm

COATES MILL COTTS 1
THE COATES 2

CORNDEAN LA

Postlip
House

3

Postlip

River Isbourne

27

Corndean
Farm

GL52

Mill
Pond

Postlip
Mills

Postlip
Hall

Cotswold Way

Tithe
Barn

2

Postlip
Warren

Corndean
Hall

1

CORNDEAN LA

Woodpeckers   Briarwood

26

09   A   B   00   C   D   01   E   F

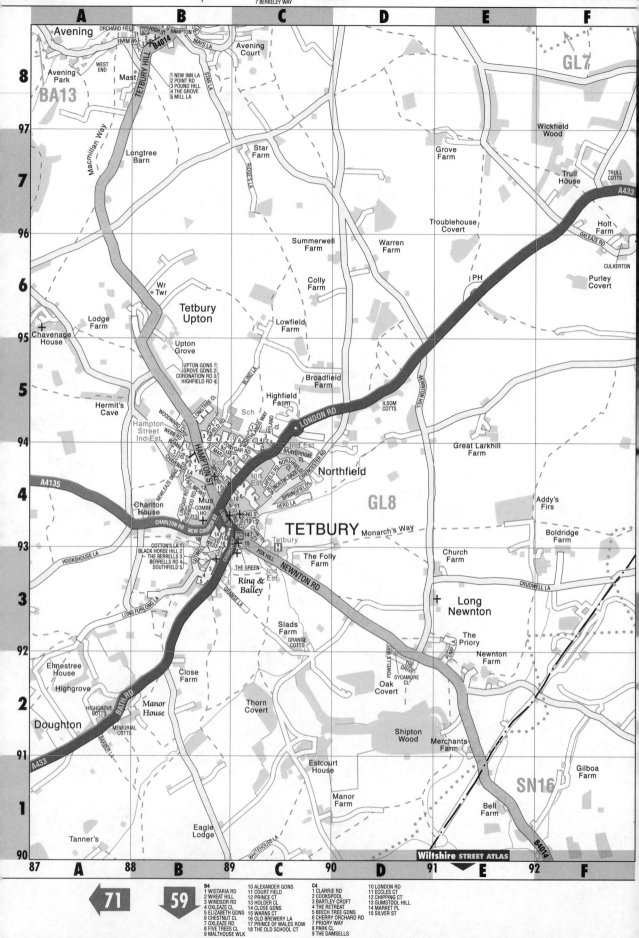

C5
1 CHEVIOT CL
2 SUFFOLK CL
3 SHEPHERDS MEAD
4 JACOBS CL
5 COTSWOLD CL
6 TALBOY'S WLK
7 BERKELEY WAY

B4
1 WISTARIA RD
2 WHEAT HILL
3 WINDSOR RD
4 OXLEAZE CL
5 ELIZABETH GDNS
6 CHESTNUT CL
7 OXLEAZE RD
8 FIVE TREES CL
9 MALTHOUSE WLK

10 ALEXANDER GDNS
11 COURT FIELD
12 PRINCE CT
13 HOLDER CL
14 CLOSE GDNS
15 WARNS CT
16 OLD BREWERY LA
17 PRINCE OF WALES ROW
18 THE OLD SCHOOL CT

C4
1 CLARRIE RD
2 COOKSPOOL
3 BARTLEY CROFT
4 THE RETREAT
5 BEECH TREE GDNS
6 CHERRY ORCHARD RD
7 PRIORY WAY
8 PARK CL
9 THE DAMSELLS

10 LONDON RD
11 ECCLES CT
12 CHIPPING CT
13 GUMSTOOL HILL
14 MARKET PL
15 SILVER ST

E

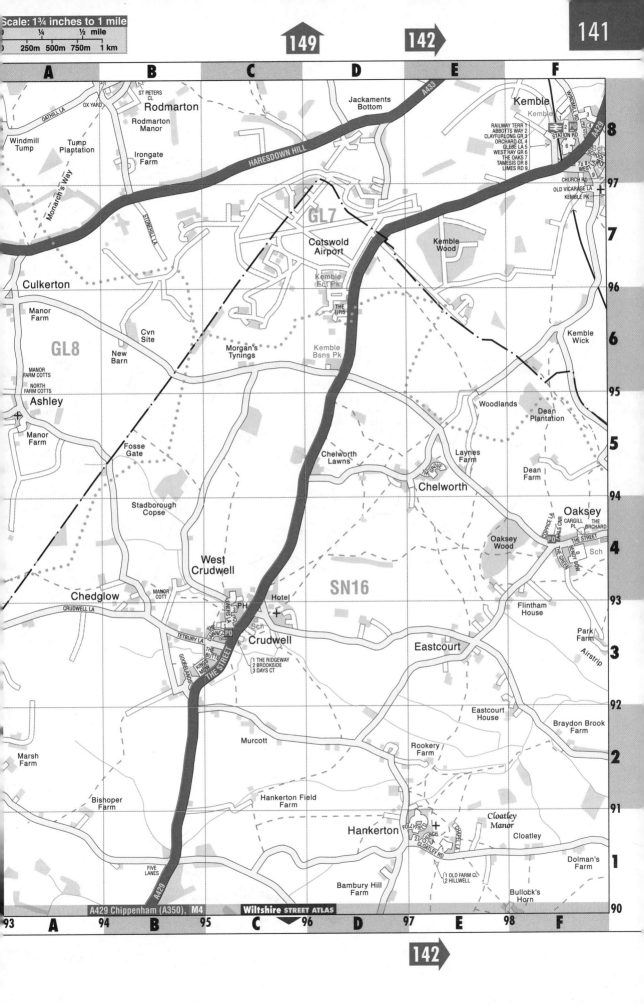

Scale: 1¾ inches to 1 mile

¼   ½ mile
250m 500m 750m 1 km

149   142

A   B   C   D   E   F

ST PETERS CL
Rodmarton
OX YARD
OATHILL LA

Windmill Tump

Tump Plantation

Rodmarton Manor

Irongate Farm

STONEHILL LA

Monarch's Way

HARESDOWN HILL

A433

Jackaments Bottom

Kemble
Kemble
RAILWAY TERR 1
ABBOTTS WAY 2
CLAYFURLONG GR 3
ORCHARD CL 4
GLEBE LA 5
WEST HAY GR 6
THE OAKS 7
TAMESIS DR 8
LIMES RD 9
WINDMILL RD
PO
STATION RD
A429
SCHOOL
YARD WEST
CHURCH RD
OLD VICARAGE LA
KEMBLE PK

GL7

Cotswold Airport

Kemble Ent Pk

Kemble Wood

THE FIRS

Culkerton

Manor Farm

Cvn Site

New Barn

Morgan's Tynings

Kemble Bsns Pk

Woodlands

Dean Plantation

Kemble Wick

GL8

MANOR FARM COTTS
NORTH FARM COTTS

Ashley

Manor Farm

Fosse Gate

Chelworth Lawns

Laynes Farm

Dean Farm

THE GROVE
EARLS LA

Chelworth

Oaksey

COPPICE LA
CARGILL PL
PO
THE ORCHARD
THE STREET
THE GREEN
BENDY BOW
SCH

Stadborough Copse

Oaksey Wood

West Crudwell

Chedglow

MANOR COTT

CRUDWELL LA

TANNERS LA
THE
PH
Sch
Hotel

SN16

Flintham House

Park Farm

Airstrip

TETBURY LA
THE
DAMNERS
PO
KINGS MDW
THE BUTTS
GOOSELANDS
THE STREET

Crudwell

1 THE RIDGEWAY
2 BROOKSIDE
3 DAYS CT

Eastcourt

Eastcourt House

Braydon Brook Farm

Murcott

Rookery Farm

Marsh Farm

Bishoper Farm

Hankerton Field Farm

Hankerton

FOLLY FIELD
CHURCH LA
CLOATLEY RD
CHAPEL LA

Cloatley Manor

Cloatley

Dolman's Farm

FIVE LANES

A429

Bambury Hill Farm

1 OLD FARM CL
2 HILLWELL

Bullock's Horn

93   A   94   B   95   C   96   D   97   E   98   F

142

8
97
7
96
6
95
5
94
4
93
3
92
2
91
1
90

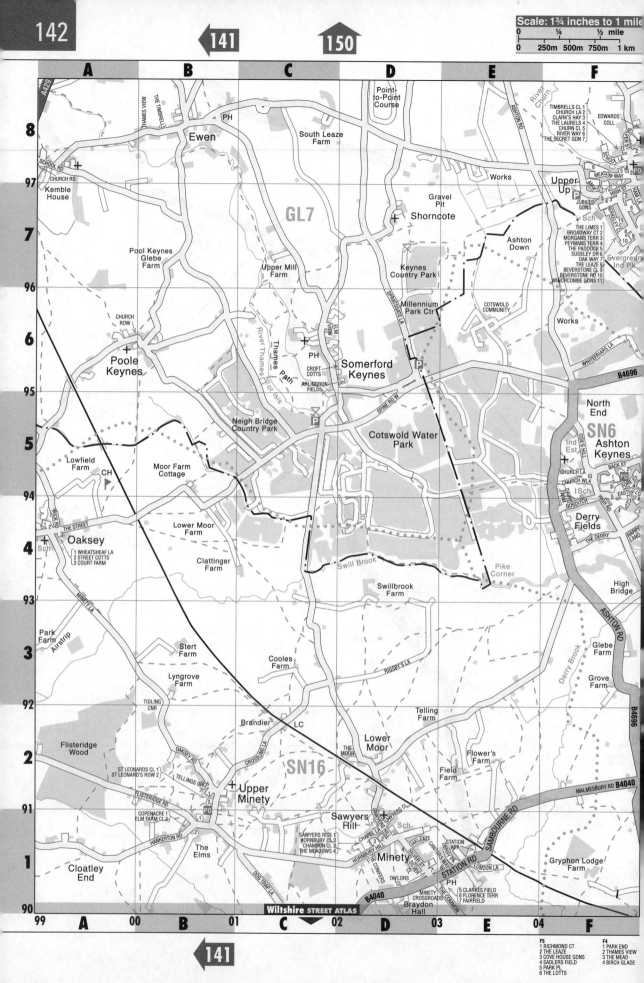

Scale: 1¾ inches to 1 mile
0   ¼   ½   mile
0 250m 500m 750m 1 km

A   B   C   D   E   F

8

Point-to-Point
Course

Ewen

South Leaze
Farm

THE TIMBRELLS

THAMES VIEW

PH

River Churn

TIMBRELLS CL 1
CHURCH LA 2
CLARK'S HAY 3
THE LAURELS 4
CHURCH CL 5
RIVER WAY 6
THE SECRET GDN 7

EDWARDS'
COLL

97

SCHOOL RD

CHURCH RD

Kemble
House

Works

GL7

Shorncote

Gravel
Pit

Upper
Up

P

JUBILEE
GDNS

Sch

SCHOOL LA

MEADOW WAY

HIGH ST

HALL LA

BERKELEY CL

B320

7

Pool Keynes
Glebe
Farm

Upper Mill
Farm

Keynes
Country Park

Ashton
Down

THE LIMES 1
BROADWAY CT 2
MORGANS TERR 3
PEYMANS TERR 4
THE PADDOCK 5
SUDELEY DR 6
OAK WAY 7
THE LEAZE 8
BEVERSTONE CL 9
BEVERSTONE RD 10
WINCHCOMBE GDNS 11

Evergreen
Ind Pk

96

CHURCH
ROW

Millennium
Park Ctr

COTSWOLD
COMMUNITY

Works

WHITEFRIARS LA

B4696

6

Poole
Keynes

River Thames

Thames
Path

PH

CROFT
COTTS

ARLINGDON
FIELDS

ELM VIEW

Somerford
Keynes

SPRATSGATE LA

P

SPINE RD W

North
End

SN6

Ashton
Keynes

COX'S HILL

Ind
Est

CHURCH LA
CHURCH WLK

BACK ST

FORE ST

EASTCOMBE

95

Neigh Bridge
Country Park

P

Cotswold Water
Park

Derry
Fields

DAIRY
FARM

GOSDITCH

HIGH RD

THE DERRY

HAPPY
LAND

5

Lowfield
Farm

CH

Moor Farm
Cottage

Pike
Corner

High
Bridge

94

WICK RD

THE STREET

Oaksey

Sch

1 WHEATSHEAF LA
2 STREET COTTS
3 COURT FARM

Lower Moor
Farm

Swill Brook

4

MINETY LA

Clattinger
Farm

Swillbrook
Farm

ASHTON RD

Glebe
Farm

Grove
Farm

B4696

93

Park
Farm
Airstrip

Stert
Farm

Cooles
Farm

RIGSBY'S LA

Telling
Farm

Derry Brook

3

Lyngrove
Farm

TIDLING
CNR

Brandier

LC

Lower
Moor

Flower's
Farm

2

Flisteridge
Wood

OAKSEY RD

CROSSING LA

SN16

THE
MOOR

Field
Farm

MALMESBURY RD   B4040

B4040

SAMBOURNE RD

ST LEONARDS CL 1
ST LEONARD'S ROW 2

TELLINGS ORCH

Upper Minety

PO

COPENACRE 1
ELM FARM CL 2

FLISTERIDGE RD

Sawyers
Hill

SAWYERS CL

Sch

STATION
APR

DERRY PK

1

Cloatley
End

HAWKERTON RD

The
Elms

DOG TRAP LA

CHAPEL LA

HORNBURY HILL

THE CONIFERS

SILVER ST

SAWYERS RISE 1
HORNBURY CL 2
CHAMBON CL 3
THE MEADOWS 4

Minety

TAYLORS
CL

OAKLEAZE

SILVER ST

STATION RD

LONDON LA

Gryphon Lodge
Farm

PH

90

Wiltshire STREET ATLAS

B4040

MINETY
CROSSROADS

Braydon
Hall

THE COMMON

5 CLARKES FIELD
6 FLORENCE TERR
7 FAIRFIELD

99   A   00   B   01   C   02   D   03   E   04   F

F5
1 RICHMOND CT
2 THE LEAZE
3 COVE HOUSE GDNS
4 SADLERS FIELD
5 PARK PL
6 THE LOTTS

F4
1 PARK END
2 THAMES VIEW
3 THE MEAD
4 BIRCH GLADE

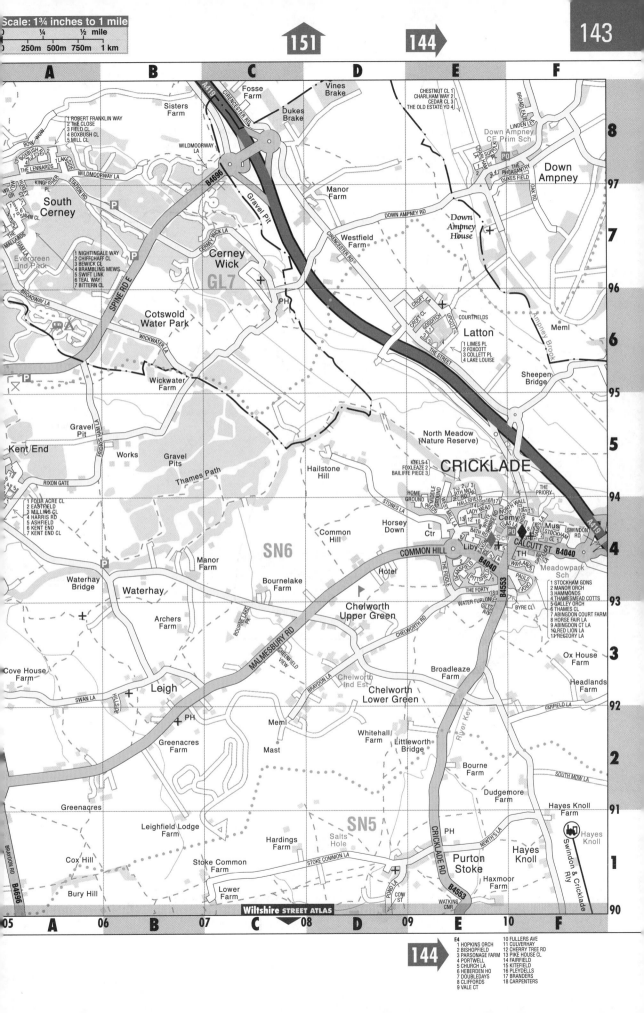

¼   ½   mile
250m 500m 750m 1 km

A   B   C   D   E   F

8

Fosse Farm
Vines Brake
CHESTNUT CL 1
CHARLHAM WAY 2
CEDAR CL 3
THE OLD ESTATE YD 4
Down Ampney CE Prim Sch

97

Sisters Farm
Dukes Brake
Down Ampney
Down Ampney House

1 ROBERT FRANKLIN WAY
2 THE CLOSE
3 FIELD CL
4 BOXBUSH CL
5 MILL CL

WILDMOORWAY LA
Manor Farm
DOWN AMPNEY RD

South Cerney
WILDMOORWAY LA
7

Westfield Farm
CIRENCESTER RD
96

Cerney Wick
GL7
Latton
1 LIMES PL
2 FOXCOTT
3 COLLETT PL
4 LAKE LOUISE
GOSDITCH
THE STREET

6

Cotswold Water Park
PH
Sheepen Bridge
WICKWATER LA
95

1 NIGHTINGALE WAY
2 CHIFFCHAFF CL
3 BEWICK CL
4 BRAMBLING MEWS
5 SWIFT LINK
6 TEAL WAY
7 BITTERN CL

Wickwater Farm
North Meadow (Nature Reserve)

Kent End
Gravel Pit
Works
CRICKLADE
KEELS 1
FOXLEAZE 2
BAILIFFE PIECE 3

Gravel Pits
Hailstone Hill
STONES LA
THE PRIORY
94

Thames Path
1 FOUR ACRE CL
2 EASTFIELD
3 MILLING CL
4 HARRIS RD
5 ASHFIELD
6 KENT END
7 KENT END CL
RIXON GATE
Common Hill
Horsey Down
L Ctr
CALCUTT ST
B4040

SN6
Manor Farm
Bournelake Farm
Hotel
1 STOCKHAM GDNS
2 MANOR ORCH
3 HAMMONDS
4 THAMESMEAD COTTS
5 GALLEY ORCH
6 THAMES CL
7 ABINGDON COURT FARM
8 HORSE FAIR LA
9 ABINGDON CT LA
10 RED LION LA
11 REGTORY LA
Meadowpark Sch
93

Waterhay Bridge
Waterhay
Chelworth Upper Green
THE FIDDLE
Water Furlongs
GILES AVE
BYRE CL
Archers Farm
CHELWORTH RD
Ox House Farm
92

Cove House Farm
MALMESBURY RD
Broadleaze Farm
Headlands Farm
Leigh
BRAYDON LA
Chelworth Ind Est
Chelworth Lower Green
River Key
FARFIELD LA

SWAN LA
HILLSIDE
PH
GREENFIELD VIEW
Whitehall Farm
Littleworth Bridge
2

Greenacres Farm
Meml
Mast
Bourne Farm
SOUTH MDW LA

Greenacres
Leighfield Lodge Farm
Salts Hole
Dudgemore Farm
Hayes Knoll Farm
91

Cox Hill
Hardings Farm
SN5
PH
Purton Stoke
Hayes Knoll
Swindon & Cricklade Rly
Hayes Knoll

Bury Hill
Stoke Common Farm
STOKE COMMON LA
POND LA
COW ST
CRICKLADE RD
Haxmoor Farm
WATKINS CNR
B4553
90

B4696
Lower Farm
B4696

E4
1 HOPKINS ORCH
2 BISHOPFIELD
3 PARSONAGE FARM
4 PORTWELL
5 CHURCH LA
6 HEBERDEN HO
7 DOUBLEDAYS
8 CLIFFORDS
9 VALE CT
10 FULLERS AVE
11 CULVERHAY
12 CHERRY TREE RD
13 PIKE HOUSE CL
14 FAIRFIELD
15 KITEFIELD
16 PLEYDELLS
17 BRANDERS
18 CARPENTERS

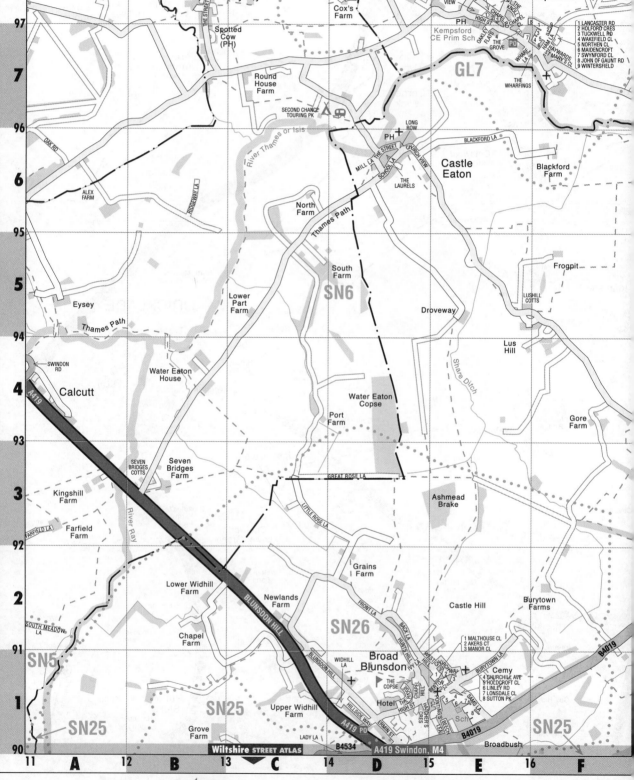

A   B   C   D   E   F

Castle Hill Farm

Fairford Airfield

GREENLEAZE

Marston Meysey

Dunfield

MIDDLE FARM CT
CROSS TREE CRES
BROADWAY
CROSS TREE FLATS

Kempsford

WASHPOOL LA

THE STREET

Spotted Cow (PH)

Cox's Farm

MEADOW VIEW

TOP RD

Kempsford CE Prim Sch

PH

THE GROVE

PO

1 LANCASTER RD
2 HOLFORD CRES
3 TUCKWELL RD
4 WAKEFIELD CL
5 NORTHEN CL
6 MAIDENCROFT
7 SWYNFORD CL
8 JOHN OF GAUNT RD
9 WINTERSFIELD

Round House Farm

GL7

THE WHARFINGS

SECOND CHANCE TOURING PK

River Thames or Isis

LONG ROW

PH

BLACKFORD LA

Blackford Farm

OAK RD

MILL LA

THE STREET

SCHOOL LA

CHURCH VIEW

Castle Eaton

THE LAURELS

ALEX FARM

RIDGEWAY LA

North Farm

Thames Path

Frogpit

Eysey

Lower Part Farm

South Farm

SN6

Droveway

LUSHILL COTTS

Thames Path

Lus Hill

Share Ditch

SWINDON RD

Calcutt

Water Eaton House

Water Eaton Copse

Gore Farm

A419

Port Farm

SEVEN BRIDGES COTTS

Seven Bridges Farm

GREAT ROSE LA

Ashmead Brake

Kingshill Farm

River Ray

LITTLE ROSE LA

FARFIELD LA

Farfield Farm

Grains Farm

Castle Hill

Burytown Farms

B4019

Lower Widhill Farm

Newlands Farm

FRONT LA

BACK LA

HUNTS HILL

1 MALTHOUSE CL
2 AKERS CT
3 MANOR CL

SOUTH MEADOW LA

SN5

Chapel Farm

BLUNSDON HILL

WIDHILL LA

Broad Blunsdon

THE COPSE

Hotel

Cemy

4 CHURCHILL AVE
5 HOLDCROFT CL
6 LINLEY RD
7 LONSDALE CL
8 SUTTON PK

SN26

SN25

Upper Widhill Farm

HILLSIDE WAY

ERMIN ST

A419 PO

Sch

SN25

SN25

Grove Farm

LADY LA

B4534

Wiltshire STREET ATLAS

A419 Swindon, M4

Broadbush

11   A   12   B   13   C   14   D   15   E   16   F

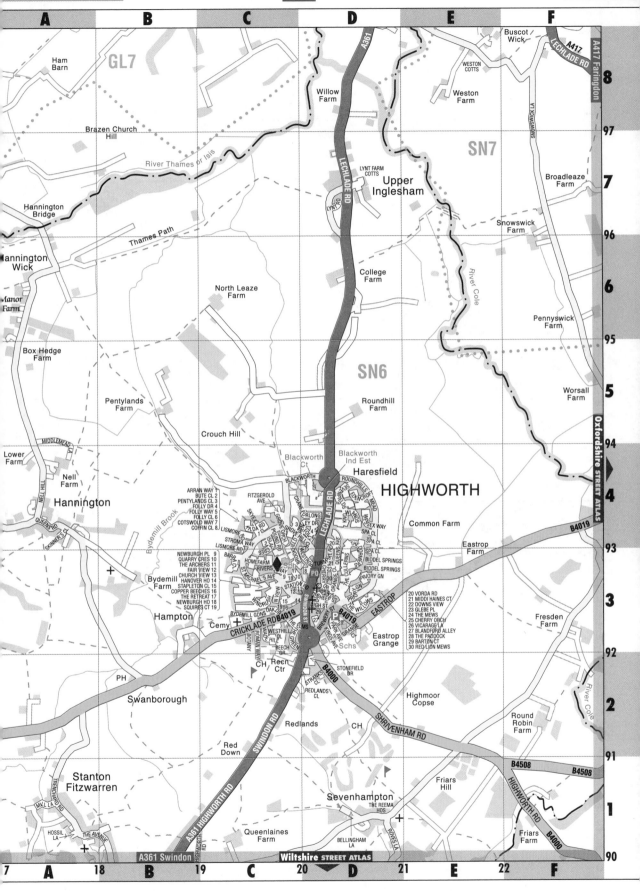

A   B   C   D   E   F

GL7

Ham Barn

8

Brazen Church Hill

97

River Thames or Isis

Willow Farm

SN7

Upper Inglesham

Lynt Farm Cotts

Buscot Wick

A417

LECHLADE RD

A417 Faringdon

7

Broadleaze Farm

Hannington Bridge

Thames Path

LECHLADE RD

LYNT RD

Weston Cotts

Weston Farm

Snowswick Farm

SNOWSWICK LA

96

Hannington Wick

North Leaze Farm

College Farm

River Cole

Pennyswick Farm

6

Manor Farm

Box Hedge Farm

Pentylands Farm

Crouch Hill

Roundhill Farm

SN6

Worsall Farm

5

Oxfordshire STREET ATLAS

Lower Farm

MIDDLEMEAD

Nell Farm

NELL HILL

Hannington

Bydemill Brook

QUEENS RD

SKINNER'S CL

Blackworth Ct

Blackworth Ind Est

Haresfield

HIGHWORTH

Common Farm

B4019

94

4

ARRAN WAY 1
BUTE CL 2
PENTYLANDS CL 3
FOLLY DR 4
FOLLY WAY 5
FOLLY CL 6
COTSWOLD WAY 7
COFFIN CL 8

FITZGEROLD AVE

BLACKWORTH

LECHLADE RD

ROUNDHILL'S MEAD

WSEX WAY

SPA CL

SPA CL

Eastrop Farm

93

NEWBURGH PL 9
QUARRY CRES 10
THE ARCHERS 11
FAIR VIEW 12
CHURCH VIEW 13
HANOVER HO 14
STAPLETON CL 15
COPPER BEECHES 16
THE RETREAT 17
NEWBURGH HO 18
SQUIRES CT 19

LISMORE LA

STROMA WAY

LISMORE RD

BARRA CL

HOMEFARM RIVERS

ST MICHAEL'S AVE

STATION

BIDDEL SPRINGS

BIDDEL SPRINGS

PRIORY GN

THE CULLERNS

Bydemill Farm

Hampton

KINGROFT

Cemy

BYDEMILL GDNS

OAK

BREWERY ST

HIGH ST

20 VORDA RD
21 MIDDL HAINES CT
22 DOWNS VIEW
23 GLEBE PL
24 THE MEWS
25 CHERRY ORCH
26 VICARAGE LA
27 BLANDFORD ALLEY
28 THE PADDOCK
29 BARTON CT
30 RED LION MEWS

EASTROP

Fresden Farm

3

CRICKLADE RD

B4019

WESTHILL

ROMAN WAY

BOTANY

SWINDON'S ROUNDS CL

PARK AVE

KING'S AVE

B4019

PARK AVE

Eastrop Grange

92

CH

Recn Ctr

Stonefield Dr

Highmoor Copse

Round Robin Farm

2

PH

Swanborough

SWINDON RD

Redlands

B4000

REDLANDS CL

CH

SHRIVENHAM RD

B4508

B4508

91

Red Down

HIGHWORTH RD

Stanton Fitzwarren

TRENCHARD RD

MILL LA RD

HOSSIL LA

THE AVENUE

Queenlaines Farm

Sevenhampton

THE REEMA HOS

BELLINGHAM LA

ROVES LA

Friars Hill

Friars Farm

B4000

1

154

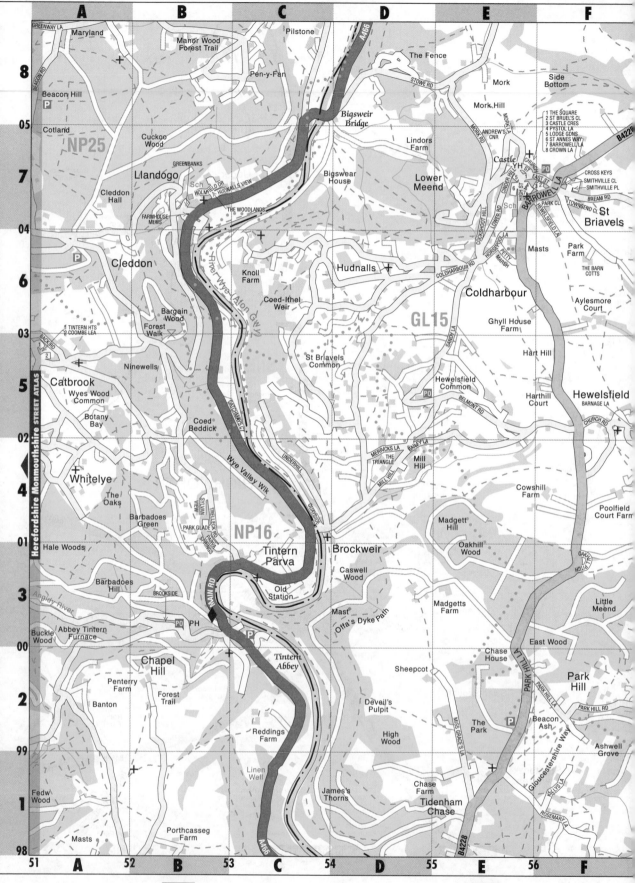

Scale: 1¾ inches to 1 mil

0   ¼   ½ mile
0   250m 500m 750m 1 km

A   B   C   D   E   F

8

05

NP25

7

04

6

03

5

02

Herefordshire Monmouthshire STREET ATLAS

4

01

3

00

2

99

1

98

51   A   52   B   53   C   54   D   55   E   56   F

72

73

Maryland
Manor Wood Forest Trail
Pilstone
Pen-y-Fan
The Fence
Mork
Side Bottom
Beacon Hill
Cotland
Cuckoo Wood
Bigsweir Bridge
Lindors Farm
Mork Hill
ANDREW'S CNR

1 THE SQUARE
2 ST BRUEL'S CL
3 CASTLE CRES
4 PYSTOL LA
5 LODGE GDNS
6 ST ANNES WAY
7 BARROWELL LA
8 CROWN LA

Cleddon Hall
Greenbanks
Llandogo
Bigswear House
Lower Meend
Castle
BARROWELLA
CROSS KEYS
SMITHVILLE CL
SMITHVILLE PL
St Briavels
HUDNALLS VIEW
THE WOODLANDS
FARMHOUSE MEWS
Cleddon
Knoll Farm
Hudnalls
Coldharbour
Masts
Park Farm
THE BARN COTTS
Bargain Wood
Forest Walk
Coed-Ithel Weir
GL15
Ghyll House Farm
Aylesmore Court
1 TINTERN HTS
2 COOMBE LEA
Catbrook
Wyes Wood Common
Ninewells
St Briavels Common
Hewelsfield Common
Hart Hill
Hewelsfield
BARNAGE LA
Harthill Court
Botany Bay
Coed Beddick
BELMONT RD
CHURCH RD
Whitelye
UNDERHILL
MERRYCKS LA
THE TRIANGLE
BAILEY LA
Mill Hill
Cowshill Farm
The Oaks
PARK GLADE
MILL HILL
Madgett Hill
Oakhill Wood
Poolfield Court Farm
Barbadoes Green
NP16
Tintern Parva
Brockweir
Hale Woods
Caswell Wood
Madgetts Farm
Little Meend
Barbadoes Hill
BROOKSIDE
Old Station
Mast
Offa's Dyke Path
East Wood
Buckle Wood
Abbey Tintern Furnace
Chase House
Park Hill
Chapel Hill
Tintern Abbey
Sheepcot
The Park
Beacon Ash
Penterry Farm
Forest Trail
Devil's Pulpit
Banton
Reddings Farm
High Wood
Ashwell Grove
Fedw Wood
Linen Well
James's Thorns
Chase Farm
Tidenham Chase
Masts
Porthcasseg Farm

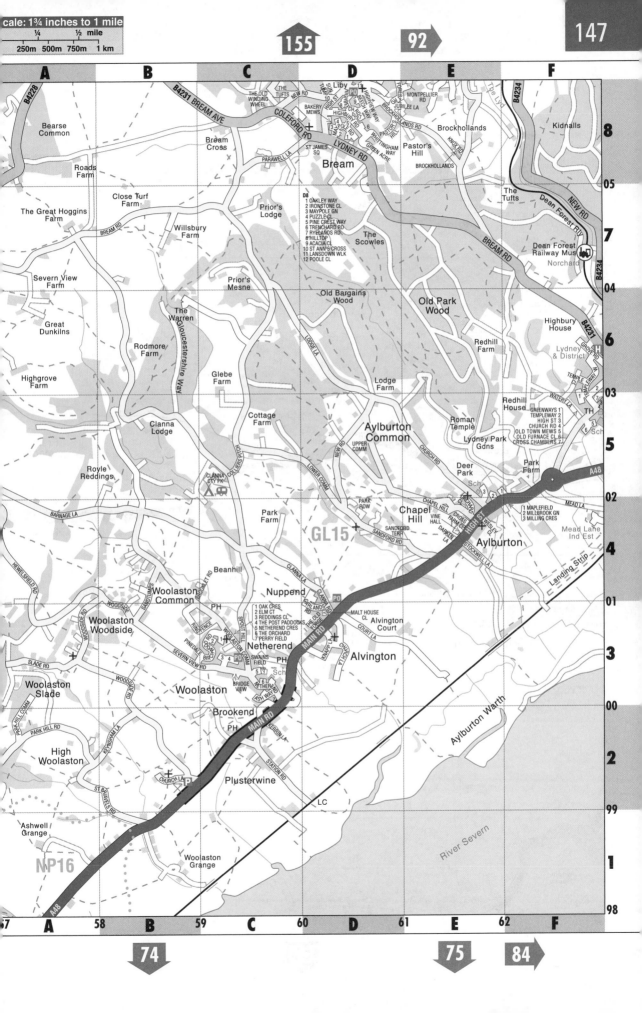

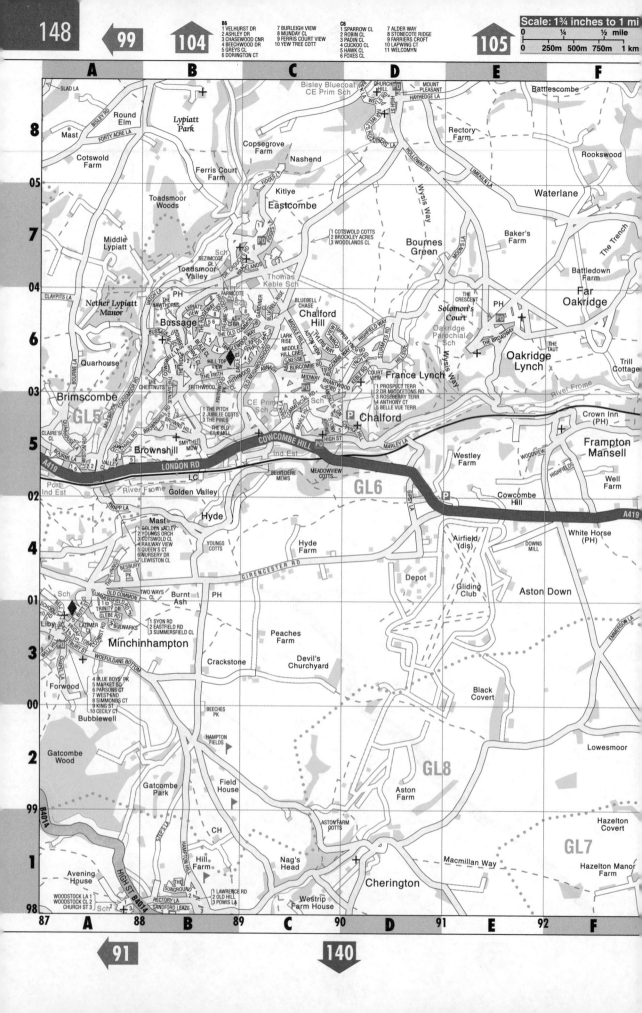

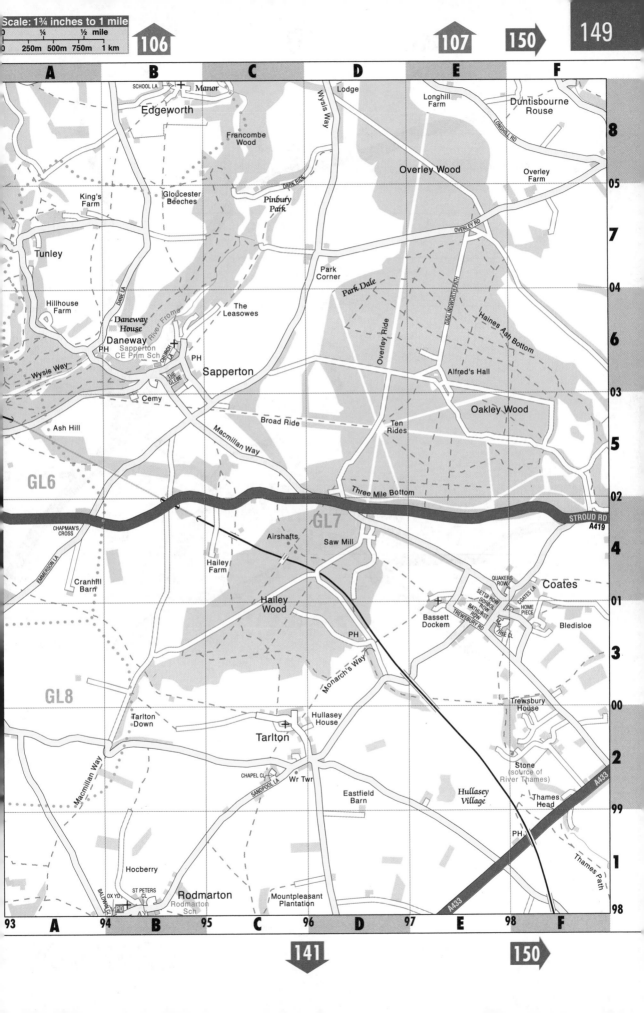

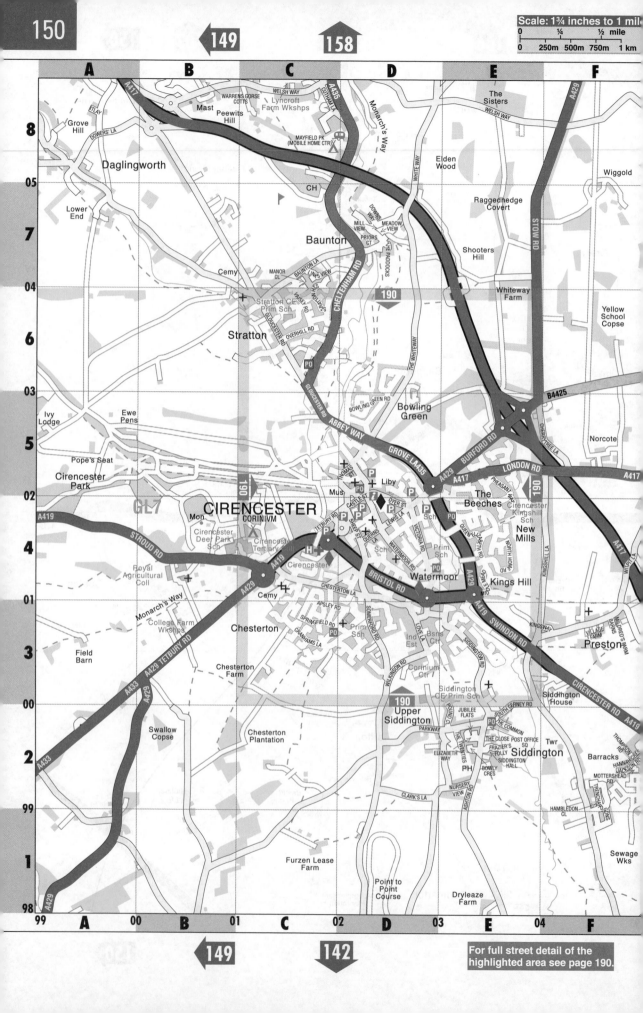

Scale: 1¾ inches to 1 mile
0   ¼   ½   mile
0 250m 500m 750m 1 km

A   B   C   D   E   F

8
05
7
04
6
03
5
02
4
01
3
00
2
99
1
98

99   A   00   B   01   C   02   D   03   E   04   F

Grove Hill
Daglingworth
Lower End
ITLAY
DOWERS' LA
A417
WARRENS GORSE COTTS
Mast
Peewits Hill
WELSH WAY
Lyncroft Farm Wkshps
CUTHAM LA
A435
Monarch's Way
The Sisters
WELSH WAY
A429
STOW RD
MAYFIELD PK (MOBILE HOME CTR)
CH
Baunton
Elden Wood
Raggedhedge Covert
Wiggold
DOWNS WAY
MILL VIEW
MEADOW VIEW
PRIORS CT
CHE PADDOCKS
BAUNTON LA
LINS VIEW
MANOR CL
Cemy
Stratton CE Prim Sch
Shooters Hill
Whiteway Farm
190
Yellow School Copse
CHELTENHAM RD
VASEY RD
OVERHILL RD
Stratton
THE WHITEWAY
WHITE WAY
GLOUCESTER RD
PO
GLOUCESTER RD
BOWLING GREEN RD
Bowling Green
B4425
Norcote
ABBEY WAY
GROVE LA A435
BURFORD RD
CHERRY TREE LA
A429
A417
LONDON RD
A417
Ivy Lodge
Ewe Pens
Pope's Seat
Cirencester Park
GL7
190
THOMAS ST
P
Liby
Mus
CASTLE ST
i
DYER ST
Sch
PHEASANT WAY
Cirencester Kingshill Sch
A429
CIRENCESTER
CORINIVM
Mon.
Cirencester Deer Park Sch
TETBURY RD
SHEEP ST
P
P
P
QUERNS
LEWIS RD
VICTORIA RD
NORTH HOME RD
QUEEN
KINGSHILL LA
The Beeches
New Mills
A419
A419
STROUD RD
A419
Cirencester Tertiary
Cirencester
Royal Agricultural Coll
Cemy
CHESTERTON LA
BRISTOL RD
H
WATERMOOR RD
Prim Sch
Watermoor
PO
Kings Hill
A429
A417
Monarch's Way
College Farm Wkshps
Chesterton
A429 TETBURY RD
APSLEY RD
SPRINGFIELD RD
CRANHAMS LA
Prim Sch
SOMERFORD RD
PO
Ind Est
LOVE LA
Bsns Ctr
SWINDON RD
KINGSWAY
VILLAGE FARM
MILDRED'S LA
Preston
Field Barn
A433
A429
Chesterton Farm
WILKINSON RD
Corinium Ctr
SIDDINGTON RD
THOMPSON RD
HANNAH CRES
JACKSON RD
A419 CIRENCESTER RD
Swallow Copse
Chesterton Plantation
190
Upper Siddington
SOUTH CERNEY RD
Siddington CE Prim Sch
Siddington House
Twr
Barracks
PARKWAY
JUBILEE FLATS
THE COMMON
PO
THE CLOSE POST OFFICE SQ
FRAZIER'S FOLLY
SIDDINGTON HALL
Siddington
MOTTERSHEAD RD
FRENCHAY GDNS
A433
ELIZABETH WAY
THE THWAITES
PH
BOWLY CRES
NURSERY VIEW
CLARK'S LA
ASHTON RD
HAMBLEDON CL
Furzen Lease Farm
Point to Point Course
Dryleaze Farm
Sewage Wks
A429

For full street detail of the highlighted area see page 190.

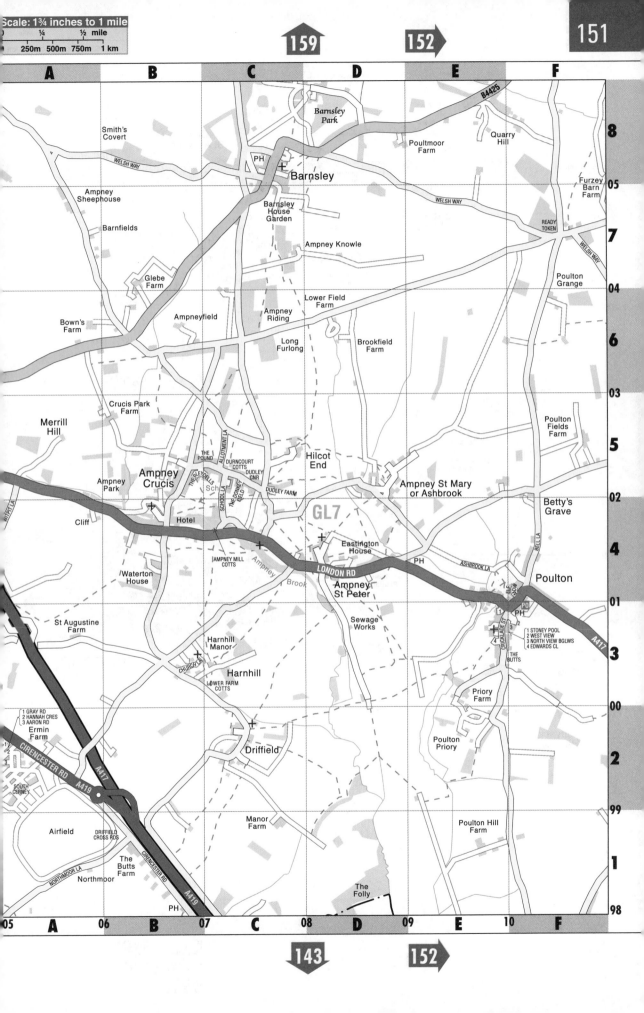

Scale: 1¾ inches to 1 mil
¼   ½ mile
0   250m 500m 750m 1 km

A   B   C   D   E   F

8

Williamstrip Park

Furzey Barn Farm

05

Coln St Aldwyns

Hatherop

Coneygar Farm

Hatherop Castle Sch

Hatherop CE Prim Sch

THE PIECE

7

Coneygar Wood

CONEYGAR RD

PAINTERS FIELD

Cemy

FOWLER'S HILL

Netherton

Quenington

Donkeywell Farm

LIME TREE COTTS

GREENVIEW

MAWLEY RD

CHURCH RD

PH

PO

Hartwell Farm

04

Leafield Farm

6

Lea Wood

03

Sunhill

River Coln

Farhill Farm

WELSH WAY

5

Honeycomb Leaze Farm

GL7

02

Broad Water

Farmor's Sch

4

Manor Farm

Toms Plantation

WEST END GDNS

CORONATION ST

Fairford CE Prim Sch

MOUNT PLEASANT

ST MARYS RD

CRABTREE PK

1 VICTORY VILLAS
2 HOMEGROUND LA
3 ALDSWORTH CL

Queens

HATHEROP RD

DYNEVOR TERR 1
LONGLANDS 2
THE GARRETTS 3
SUNHILL CL 4
SAXON WAY 5
MILTON PL 6
FAYRE GDNS 7

MILL LA

PARK ST

Liby

LOWER CROFT

LONDON RD

East End

A417

01

Milton End

BRIDGE ST

MILTON ST

BACK LA

KEBLE LAWNS

BEALMOOR PL

1 GROVES PL
2 WHITE HART CT
3 THE PLIES
4 EASTBOURNE TERR
5 MOOR LANE CT
6 GABLE COTTS

Horcott

Coln House Sch

Horcott Ind Est

LITTLE HORCOTT LA

COURTBROOK

FAIRFORD

Wr Twr

3

Verge Farm

CIRENCESTER RD

TAME WY 1
LAMBE CL 2
JACOBS PIECE 3
BUCKLER CL4
PIPS FIELD WY 5

FLORIDA BVD

KANSAS DR

WESTFIELD GN

GREENACRES PK

HAMPTON GR

ELIZABETH GDNS

MEYSEY CL

DAWES CL

GEORGIA RD

VIRGINIA AVE

00

Meysey Hampton CE Prim Sch

ST MARYS FIELD

BEECH LEA

STRAWBERRY LA

MARSTON HILL

Gravel Pit

Horcott Hill

IDAHO ST

MAINE ST

PO

PH

CHURCH CROFT

SCHOOL LA

HIGH ST

2

Meysey Hampton

Furzey Hill

TOTTERDOWN LA

OHIO AVE

ALASKA AVE

LANE END

99

Ash Copse

NEBRASKA CIRCLE

WESTPOOL LA

1

SN6

Fairford Airfield

98

11   A   12   B   13   C   14   D   15   E   16   F

E4
1 BARKER PL
2 BEAUCHAMP CL
3 WARWICK CL
4 JOHN TAME CL
5 GOODMANS TERR
6 PRINCE CHARLES RD
7 JEFFERIES CL
8 MANOR CL
9 CHURCHILL PL
10 THE QUARRY
11 MARKET PL
12 CROFT LA
13 THE ORCHARD
14 THE CROFT
15 MANOR CT

A8
1 MONKSWELL RD
2 MONKSWELL CL
3 JONES HO
4 BURGAGE
5 Hadnock Rd Ind Est

A7
1 NEWLAND WAY
2 CHURCH FARM
3 ORCHARD CT
4 RHODFA WYESHAM/WYESHAM AV
5 CLAYPATCH RD
6 Y PADDGAU/ THE PADDOCKS

7 CHESTNUT TERR
8 CILGANT DEFIW/OAK CRES
9 LIMETREE AVE
10 CHESTNUT CT
11 HEATH ST
12 READE ST
13 BLAKE ST

A7
14 THE DOWNHAMS
15 HILLCREST CL
16 GREENLANDS CL
17 WYEBRIDGE ST
18 ST JAMES' ST
19 WHITECROSS ST

20 ST JAMES' SQ
21 GRANVILLE ST
22 YR HEN HEOL/THE OLD RD
23 RIVERSIDE PK

24 Mayhill Ind Est
25 Wyeside Com Ctr

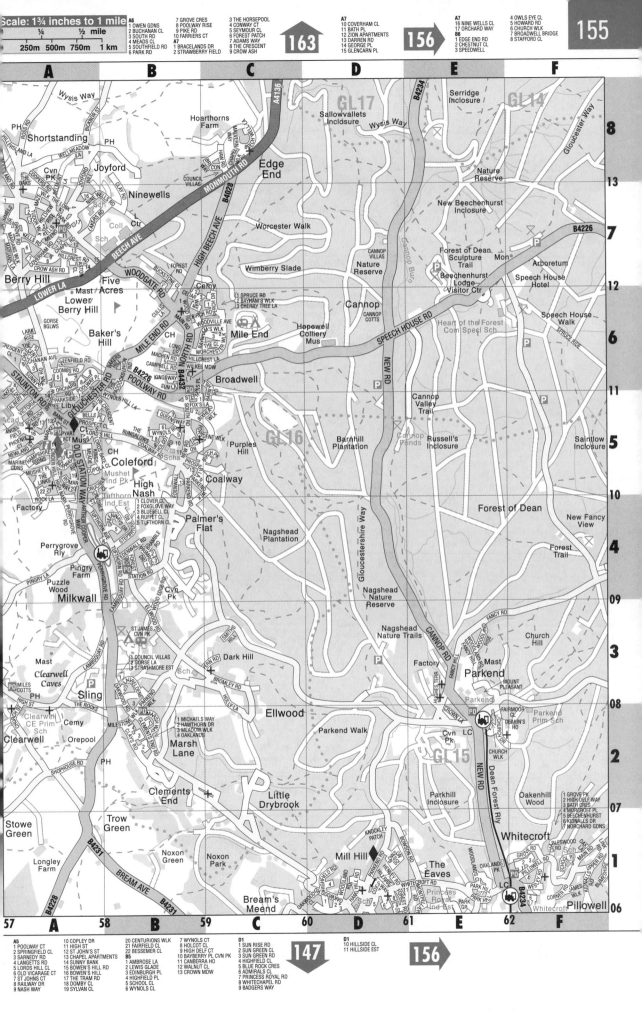

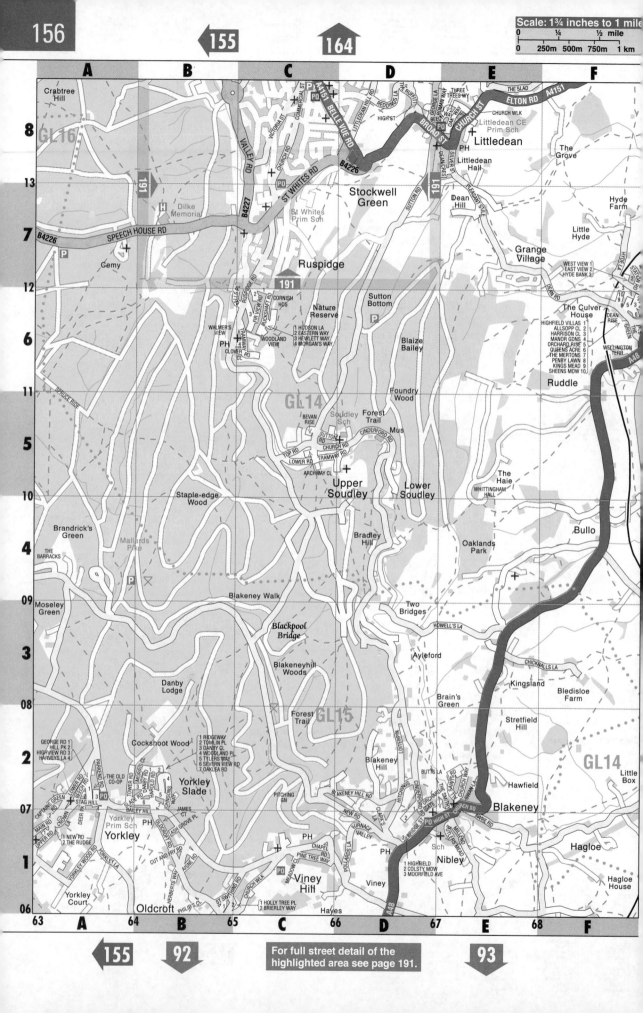

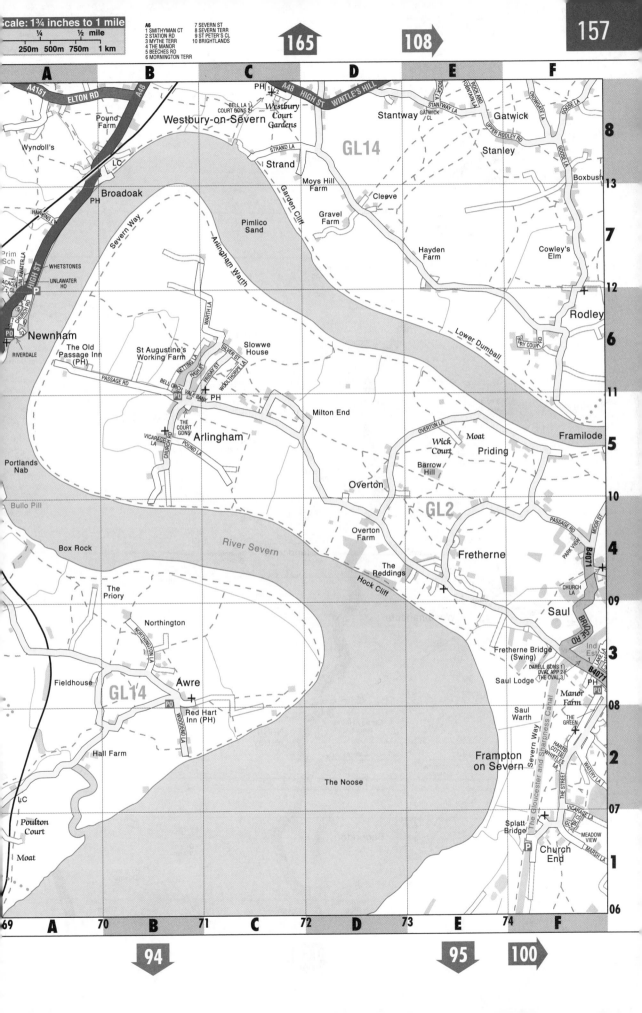

| A | B | C | D | E | F |

8

M435
Southbury
Farm
Colesbourne
Park
Little
Colesbourne
The
Gulf Scrubs
Withington
Woods
Chedworth
Woods

13
PO
PH
DINGLE
BGLWS
Colesbourne
GL53
Boy's
Grove
Woodlands
Pinswell

7
Pen
Hill
Monkham
Wood
River Churn
Iffcomb
Wood

12
Penhill
Plantation
Marsden
Manor
Shawswell
Newport
Farm
GL54
Chedworth
Beacon

6
Clifferdine
Wood
Chedworth
Laines
THE LAINES
EST
Macmillan Way
Setts
Farm House

11
Rapsgate
Park
Eycot
Wood
Green Meadow
Farm
Chittlegrove

5
Aycote
Farm
Rendcomb
Park
Rendcomb
Coll
Ashwell
Lodge

10
GLEBE
VIEW.
PO

4
Macmillan Way
Old Park
Rendcomb
GL7
Rendcomb
Buildings
Airfield

09
ROBINSON LA
Burcombe
BURCOMBE LA
HAYES LA
HOBBS LA 1
WOODLAND VIEW 2
MOOR WOOD
COTTS
Woodmancote
Monarch's Way
Nordown
Calmsden

3
Halfpenny
Hill
BURCOMBE LA
Moor
Wood
North
Cerney
CE Prim
Sch
CHURN HILL
CHAPEL LA
DARK LA
North Cerney Downs

08
Voxhills
Farm
THE ORCHARD
HILLVIEW
PH
BANKSIDE
Calmsden
Gorse

2
Dartley
Farm
Merchants'
Downs
Cerney House
Gardens
Cerney
House
North
Cerney

07
A417
WELSH WAY
CHURNSIDE
River Churn
STOW RD

1
Upper
End
Bagendon
CUTHAM LA
Downs
Farm
Ampney
Downs

06
Bagendon
Downs
Perrott's
Brook
A435
WELSH WAY
Baunton
Downs
The Dillies
Farm
A429

| 99 | A | 00 | B | 01 | C | 02 | D | 03 | E | 04 | F |

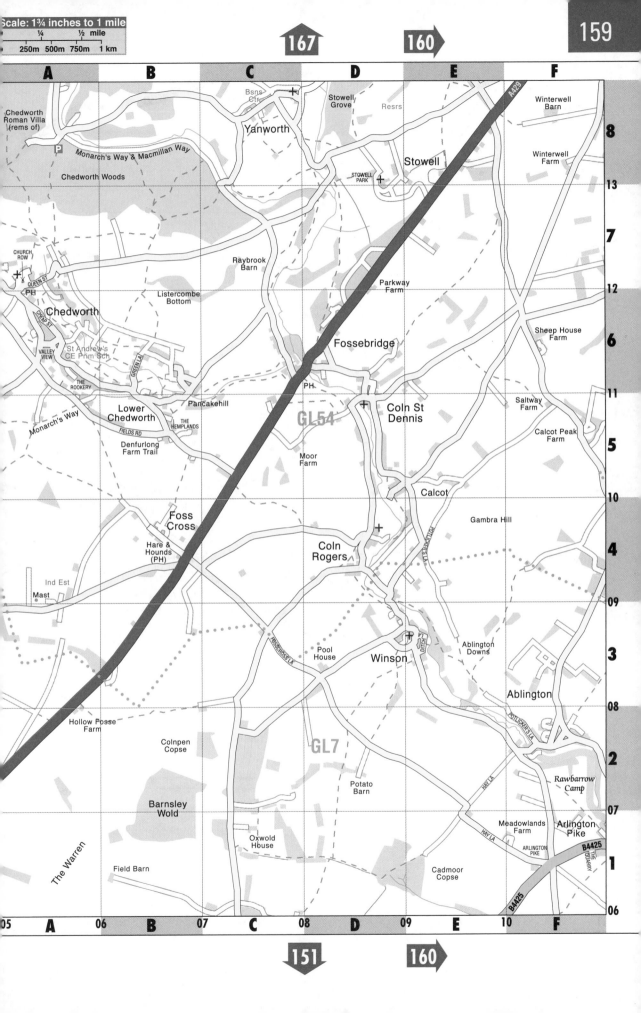

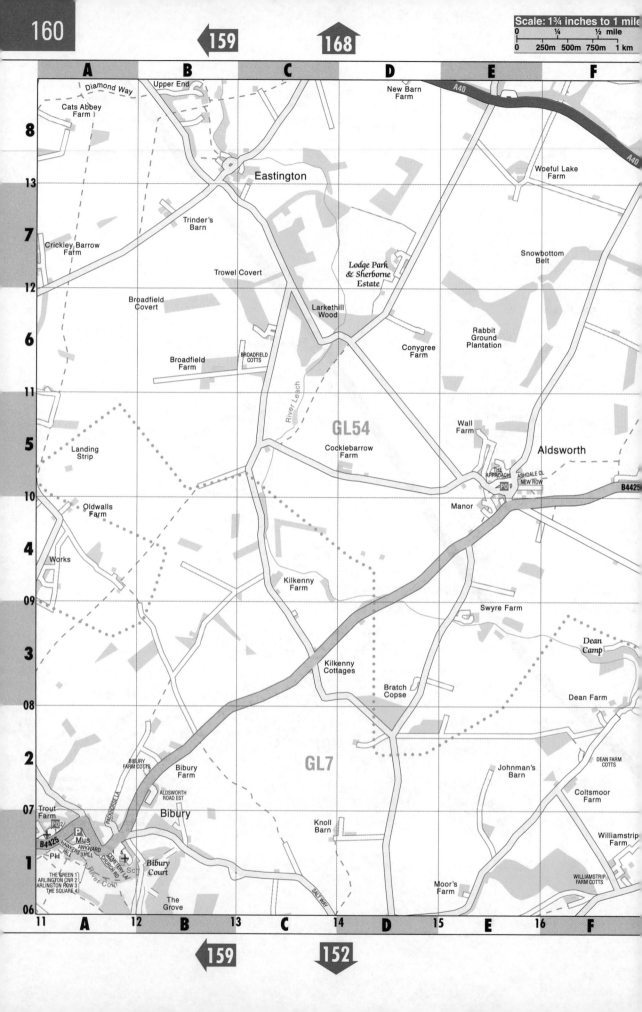

A   B   C   D   E   F

Diamond Way
Upper End
New Barn Farm
A40

Cats Abbey Farm

8

13   Eastington

Woeful Lake Farm

Trinder's Barn

7

Crickley Barrow Farm

Snowbottom Belt

Trowel Covert

12   Broadfield Covert

Lodge Park & Sherborne Estate

Larkethill Wood

6

Broadfield Farm
BROADFIELD COTTS

Conygree Farm

Rabbit Ground Plantation

11   River Leach

GL54

Wall Farm

5   Landing Strip

Cocklebarrow Farm

Aldsworth

THE APPROACH
ASHDALE CL
NEW ROW
PO

10   Oldwalls Farm

Manor

B4425

4   Works

Kilkenny Farm

Swyre Farm

09

Dean Camp

3

Kilkenny Cottages

Dean Farm

Bratch Copse

08

2   GL7

Johnman's Barn

DEAN FARM COTTS

BIBURY FARM COTTS
Bibury Farm

ALDSWORTH ROAD EST

Coltsmoor Farm

07   Trout Farm
PO
Bibury

Knoll Barn

Williamstrip Farm

P
Mus
AWKWARD
B4425
HAWKERS HILL 3
PH

1   THE GREEN 1
ARLINGTON CNR 2
ARLINGTON ROW 3
THE SQUARE 4

Bibury Court

Moor's Farm

WILLIAMSTRIP FARM COTTS

River Coln

Sch
PACKHORSE LA
COLN FERRY LA
CHURCH RD

The Grove

SALT WAY

06

11   A   12   B   13   C   14   D   15   E   16   F

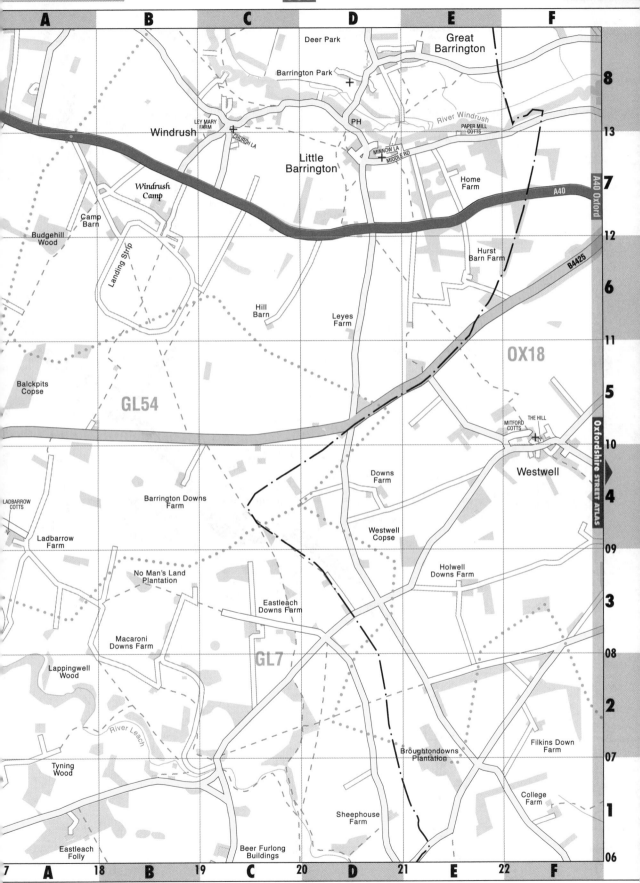

169

cale: 1¾ inches to 1 mile

¼ ½ mile

250m 500m 750m 1 km

A B C D E F

Deer Park

Great
Barrington

Barrington Park

Windrush

LEY MARY
FARM

CHURCH LA

PH

River Windrush

PAPER MILL
COTTS

Little
Barrington

MINNOW LA

MIDDLE RD

Home
Farm

A40

A40 Oxford

Windrush
Camp

Camp
Barn

Budgehill
Wood

Hurst
Barn Farm

B4425

Landing Strip

Hill
Barn

Leyes
Farm

OX18

Balckpits
Copse

GL54

THE HILL

MITFORD
COTTS

Westwell

Oxfordshire STREET ATLAS

Downs
Farm

LADBARROW
COTTS

Barrington Downs
Farm

Westwell
Copse

Ladbarrow
Farm

Holwell
Downs Farm

No Man's Land
Plantation

Eastleach
Downs Farm

Macaroni
Downs Farm

GL7

Lappingwell
Wood

Broughtondowns
Plantation

Filkins Down
Farm

River Leach

Tyning
Wood

College
Farm

Sheephouse
Farm

Eastleach
Folly

Beer Furlong
Buildings

7 A 18 B 19 C 20 D 21 E 22 F

8
13
7
12
6
11
5
10
4
09
3
08
2
07
1
06

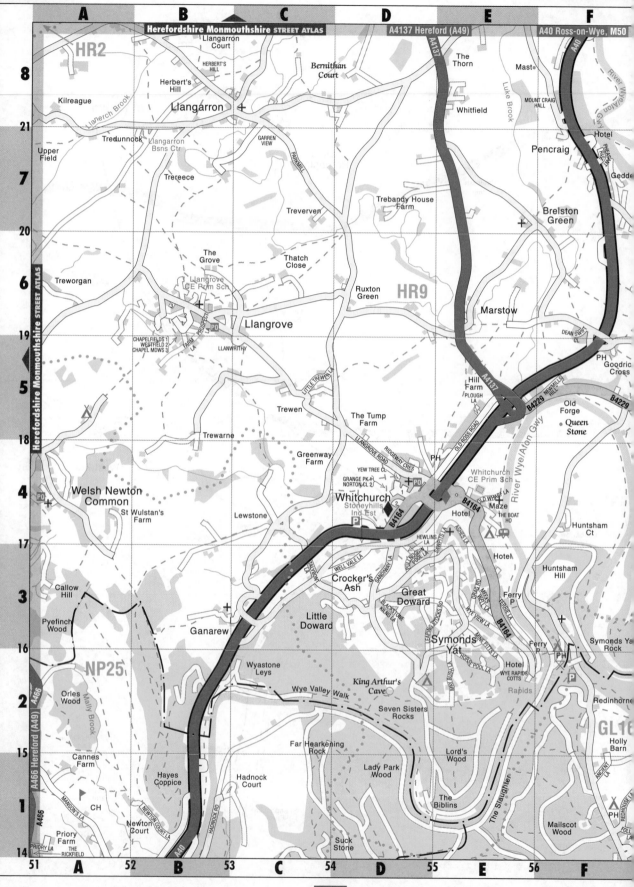

0   ¼   ½ mile
0   250m 500m 750m 1 km

Herefordshire Monmouthshire STREET ATLAS

A4137 Hereford (A49)

A40 Ross-on-Wye, M50

HR2

Kilreague
Upper Field
Treworgan

Llangarron Court
Herbert's Hill
Herbert's Hill
Llangarron
Tredunnock
Llangarron Bsns Ctr
Trereece
Treverven
The Grove
Llangrove CE Prim Sch
Thatch Close
Llangrove
CHAPELFIELDS 1
WESTFIELD 2
CHAPEL MDWS 3
Llanwrithy
Trewen

Bernithan Court
GARREN VIEW
PARKMILL

Trebandy House Farm
Ruxton Green

HR9

The Thorn
Whitfield
Mast
MOUNT CRAIG HALL
Pencraig
Hotel
Gedde
Brelston Green
Marstow
DEAN SWFE CL
PH
Goodrich Cross
Old Forge
Queen Stone

The Tump Farm
Greenway Farm
YEW TREE CL
GRANGE PK 1
NORTON CL 2
Welsh Newton Common
St Wulstan's Farm
Lewstone
Trewarne
LITTLE TREWEN LA
LLANGROVE ROAD
RIDGEWAY CRES
Hill Farm
PLOUGH LA
A4137
OLD ROSS ROAD
B4229
B4229
PH
Whitchurch CE Prim Sch

Whitchurch
Stoneyhills Ind Est
B4164
HEWLINS LA
ASHES LA
SANDPITS LA
Hotel
OLD WHARF LA
B4164
Maze
THE BOAT HO
Huntsham Ct

WELL VALE LA
SANDWAY LA
Crocker's Ash
BULL MEADOW
PINON POOL LA
DRAG RD
BLACKSTONE KILNS LA
Great Doward
Hotel
MEEND LA
WYE VIEW LA
Huntsham Hill
Ferry P
FERRIE LA
B4164

Callow Hill
Pyefinch Wood
Ganarew
Little Doward
LEAPING STOCKS RD
HORSE POOL LA
Symonds Yat
Hotel
WYE RAPIDS COTTS
Rapids
Ferry P
PH
Symonds Ya Rock
P

NP25
Orles Wood
Mally Brook
Cannes Farm
Hayes Coppice
Newton Court
Wyastone Leys
Wye Valley Walk
Hadnock Court
HADNOCK RD
King Arthur's Cave
Seven Sisters Rocks
Far Hearkening Rock
Lady Park Wood
Lord's Wood
The Biblins
THE SLAUGHTER
Mailscot Wood
Redinhorne
GL16
Holly Barn

MANSON'S LA
CH
Priory Farm
THE RICKFIELD
PRIORY LA
A466
NEWTON COURT LA
A40
Suck Stone
ANCIENT
PH

A466 Hereford (A49)

154

Herefordshire Monmouthshire STREET ATLAS

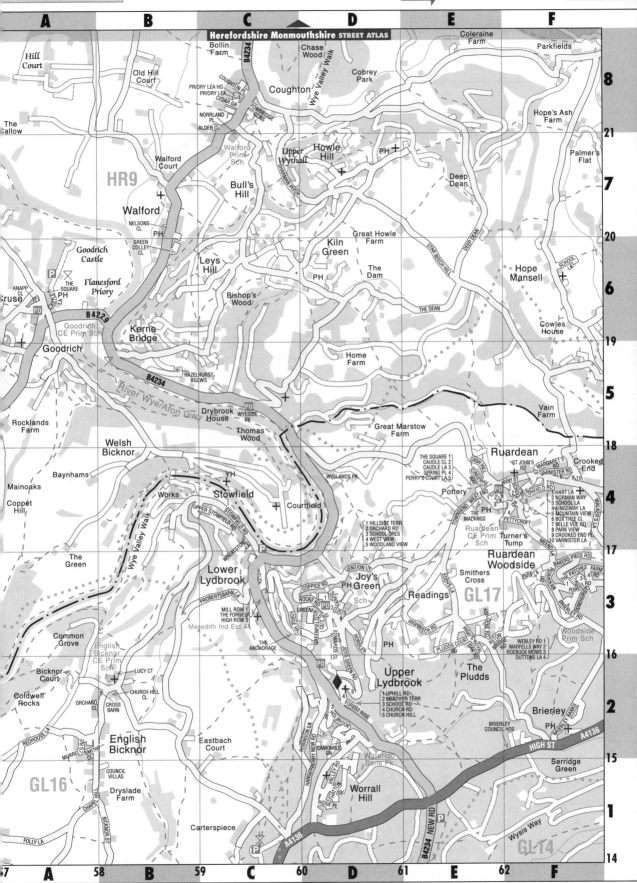

Scale: 1¾ inches to 1 mile

¼   ½   mile

250m 500m 750m 1 km

Scale: 1¾ inches to 1 mile

0 ¼ ½ mile
0 250m 500m 750m 1 km

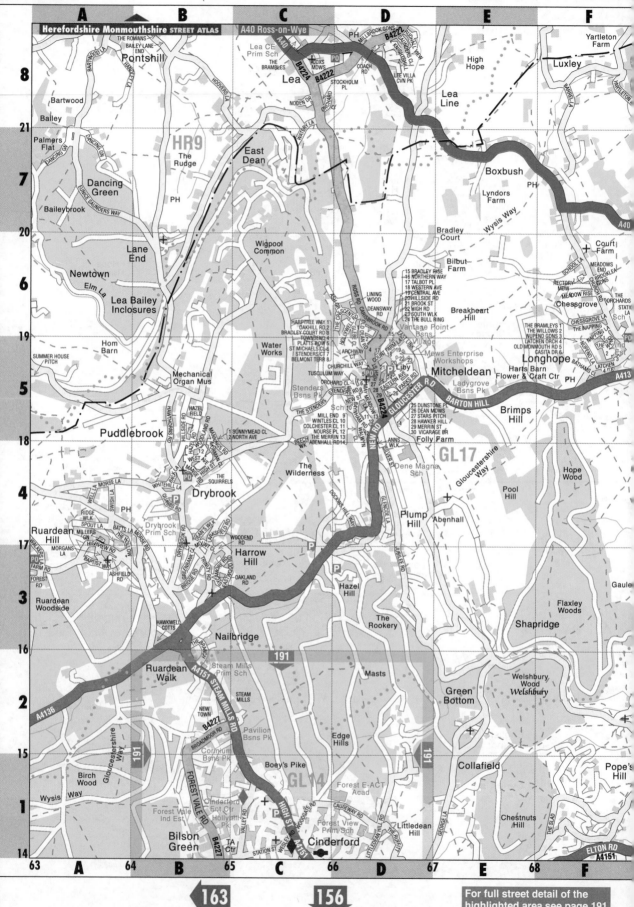

Herefordshire Monmouthshire STREET ATLAS
A40 Ross-on-Wye

For full street detail of the highlighted area see page 191.

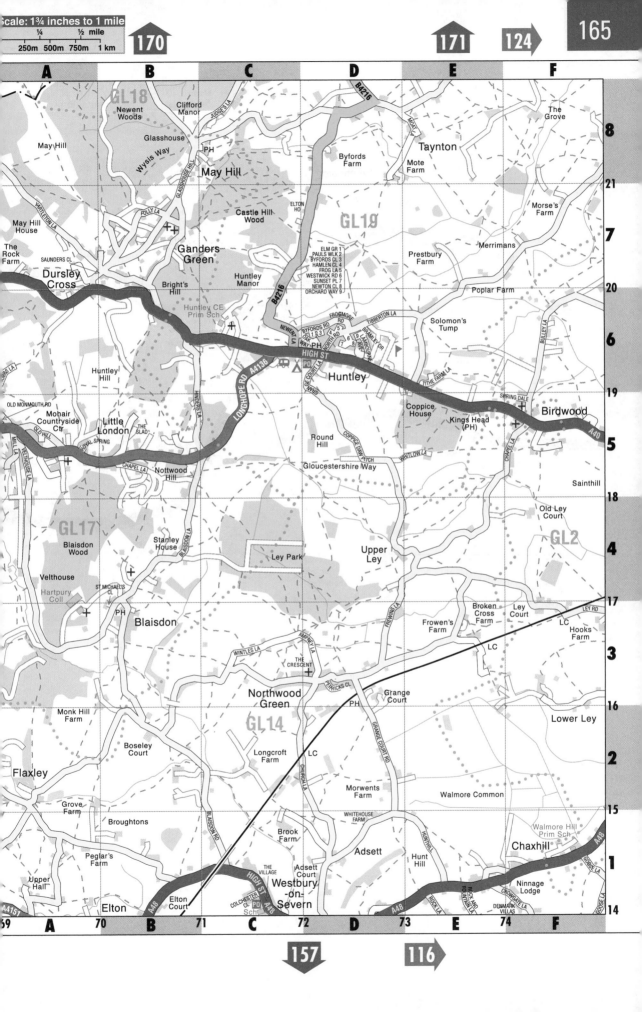

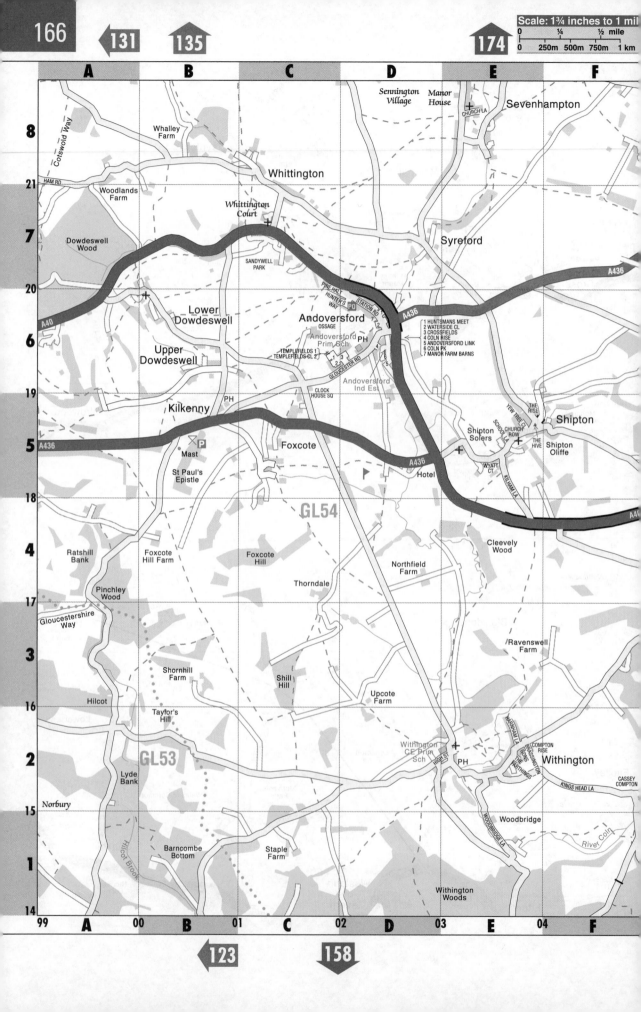

Scale: 1¾ inches to 1 mil
0   ¼   ½   mile
0   250m 500m 750m 1 km

A   B   C   D   E   F

Sennington Village
Manor House
CHURCH LA
Sevenhampton

8

Whalley Farm

Cotswold Way

21

HAM RD
Woodlands Farm

Whittington

7
Whittington Court

Syreford

Dowdeswell Wood

SANDYWELL PARK

A436

20

A40

Lower Dowdeswell

PINE HALT
HUNTER'S WAY
STATION RD
PO

A436

1 HUNTSMANS MEET
2 WATERSIDE CL
3 CROSSFIELDS
4 COLN RISE
5 ANDOVERSFORD LINK
6 COLN PK
7 MANOR FARM BARNS

6
Upper Dowdeswell

OSSAGE
Andoversford Prim Sch
Andoversford
PH

TEMPLEFIELDS 1
TEMPLEFIELDS CL 2
GLOUCESTER RD

Andoversford Ind Est

19
Kilkenny

PH

CLOCK HOUSE SQ

YEW TREE CL
THE RISE
Shipton

5
A436
Mast

Foxcote

Shipton Solers
SCHOOL LA
CHURCH ROW
THE HIVE
Shipton Oliffe

Hotel

WYATT CT
KILHAM LA

A40

St Paul's Epistle

18

GL54

4
Ratshill Bank

Foxcote Hill Farm

Foxcote Hill

Northfield Farm

Cleevely Wood

Pinchley Wood

Thorndale

17

Gloucestershire Way

3

Ravenswell Farm

Hilcot

Shornhill Farm

Shill Hill

16

Tailor's Hill

Upcote Farm

2

GL53

Withington CE Prim Sch
HIGH ST
PH

MARKHAM LA
BRASSINGTON
THE HAYTHINGS
COMPTON RISE
Withington

Lyde Bank

KINGS HEAD LA
CASSEY COMPTON

15

Norbury

WOODBRIDGE LA
Woodbridge

River Coln

Hilcot Brook

1

Barncombe Bottom

Staple Farm

Withington Woods

14

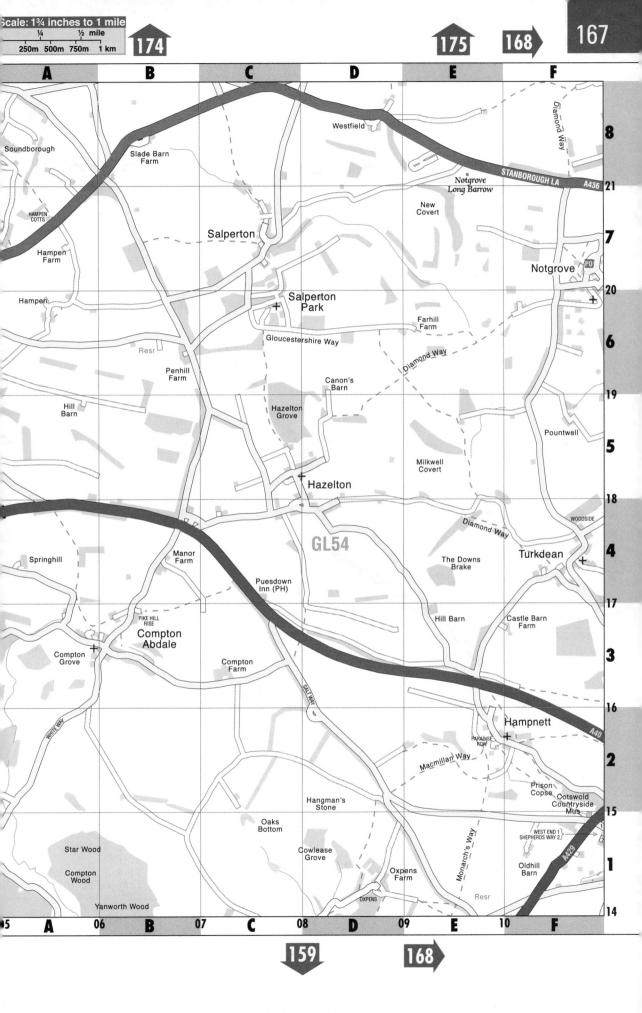

A   B   C   D   E   F

8

Soundborough

Slade Barn
Farm

Westfield

Diamond Way

STANBOROUGH LA   A436   21

HAMPEN
COTTS

Salperton

Notgrove
Long Barrow

New Covert

Notgrove   PO   7

20

Hampen
Farm

Salperton
Park

Farhill
Farm

6

Hampen

Gloucestershire Way

Diamond Way

Resr

Penhill
Farm

Canon's
Barn

19

Hill
Barn

Hazelton
Grove

Pountwell

5

Hazelton

Milkwell
Covert

18

Diamond Way

WOODSIDE

GL54

Turkdean   4

Springhill

Manor
Farm

The Downs
Brake

Puesdown
Inn (PH)

17

PIKE HILL
RISE

Hill Barn

Castle Barn
Farm

Compton
Abdale

Compton
Grove

Compton
Farm

3

WHITE WAY

Hampnett   16

SALT WAY

PARADISE
ROW

Macmillan Way

2

Prison
Copse

Cotswold
Countryside
Mus

Hangman's
Stone

15

Oaks
Bottom

WEST END 1
SHEPHERDS WAY 2

A429

Star Wood

Cowlease
Grove

Monarch's Way

Oldhill
Barn

1

Compton
Wood

Oxpens
Farm

Resr

Yanworth Wood

OXPENS

14

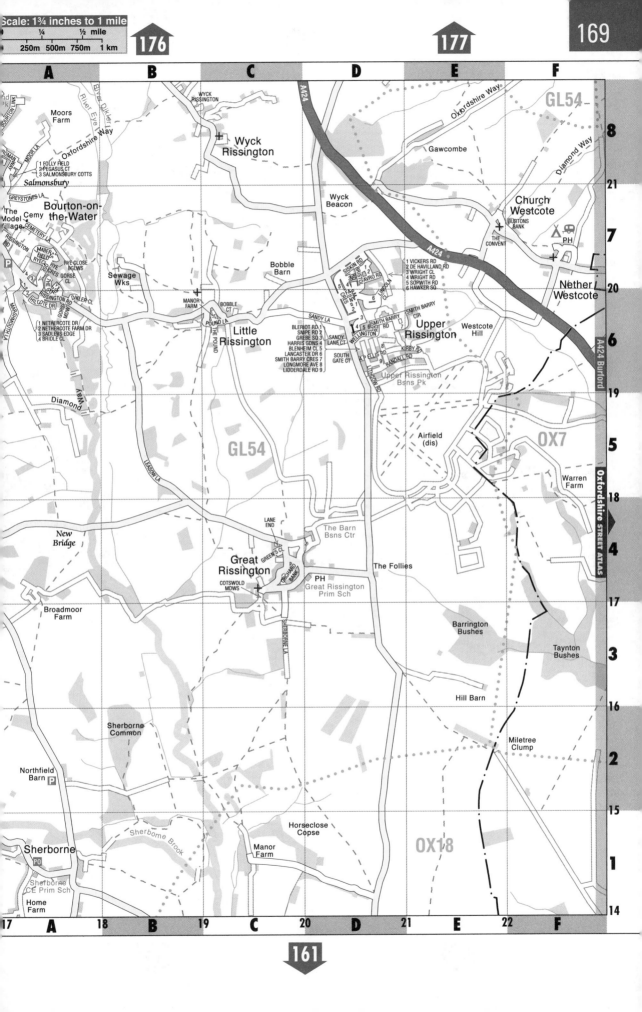

Scale: 1¾ inches to 1 mile
¼   ½ mile
250m 500m 750m 1 km
176
177
169

A B C D E F

8
21
7
20
6
19
5
18
4
17
3
16
2
15
1
14

Moors Farm
River Eye Dikler
WYCK RISSINGTON
GL54
Oxfordshire Way
Diamond Way
Oxfordshire Way
ROMAN...
1 FOLLY FIELD
2 PEGASUS CT
3 SALMONSBURY COTTS
Salmonsbury
Wyck Rissington
Gawcombe
Church Westcote
BURTONS BANK
PH
GREYSTONES LA
The Model Village
Cemy
Bourton-on-the-Water
Wyck Beacon
A424
THE CONVENT
AMBER FIELD
RYE CLOSE BGLWS
RYE CRES
GORSE CL
Sewage Wks
Bobble Barn
1 VICKERS RD
2 DE HAVILLAND RD
3 WRIGHT CL
4 WRIGHT RD
5 SOPWITH RD
6 HAWKER SQ
Nether Westcote
SISKIN RD
TAVRO RD
LINCOLN LA
P
RISSINGTON RD
HILLCOTE CL
DIKLER CL
MANOR FARM
BOBBLE CT
THE POUND
POUND LA
Little Rissington
SANDY LA
SMITH BARRY RD
SMITH BARRY CIR
Upper Rissington
Westcote Hill
1 NETHERCOTE DR
2 NETHERCOTE FARM DR
3 SADLERS EDGE
4 BRIDLE CL
MARGOT...
BLERIOT RD 1
SNIPE RD 2
GREBE SQ 3
HARRIS GDNS 4
BLENHEIM CL 5
LANCASTER DR 6
SMITH BARRY CRES 7
LONGMORE AVE 8
LIDDERDALE RD 9
WELLINGTON...
SANDY LANE CT
SOUTH GATE CT
ELLIS RD
LIGHTON RD
KIRBY...
RANDALL RD
Upper Rissington Bsns Pk
A424 Burford
Diamond Way
GL54
Airfield (dis)
OX7
Warren Farm
Oxfordshire STREET ATLAS
New Bridge
LANE END
The Barn Bsns Ctr
GREEN'S CL
ORCHARD BANK
Great Rissington
The Follies
Barrington Bushes
Taynton Bushes
Broadmoor Farm
COTSWOLD MDWS
PH
Great Rissington Prim Sch
LEASOW LA
SHERBORNE LA
Hill Barn
Sherborne Common
Miletree Clump
Northfield Barn
P
OX18
Sherborne Brook
Horseclose Copse
Sherborne
PO
Manor Farm
Sherborne CE Prim Sch
Home Farm

178

Scale: 1¾ inches to 1 mile

0   ¼   ½   mile
0 250m 500m 750m 1 km

Herefordshire Monmouthshire STREET ATLAS

M50 Ross-on-Wye

Row labels (left): 8, 29, 7, 28, 6, 27, 5, 26, 4, 25, 3, 24, 2, 23, 1, 22

Column labels (top): A, B, C, D, E, F

Fishpool
Kempley
The New Grange
Boyce Court
Little Woodland Farm
Welsh House La
Castletump
Aylesmore
Wantridge
Kempley Green
Timber Hill Farm
Three Choirs Vineyard
Daubies Farm
Queens Wood Forest Trails
Dymock Wood
Hillend Green
Botloe's Green
The Parks
Birches La
Oxenhall Wood
Four Oaks
Woodview
Queen's Wood
Shaw Common
Holder's Farm
Tedgewood
Hay Wood
Peter's Farm
Hilter Farm
Three Ashes
CH
Coldharbour La
Linton Wood
White House
Oxenhall
FURNACE LA 1
OLD STATION RD 2
GREENWAYS 3
GLEBE WAY 4
GLEBE CT 5
Picklenash
SWAGWATER LA
Haywood Pitch
North Pitch
Hawthorne Hill
Whitehouse La
GL18
Crooke's Farm
Sch
ROSS RD
B4221
Jay's Gn
CH
IVY HOUSE EST 1
COCKATOOS LA 2
PH
Ivy House La
Burrus La
Sterrys Cnr
Brookmoor La
Lower House
GARDNERS WAY 6
JOHNSTONE RD 7
CRADDOCK RD 8
WINFIELD 9
TYTHINGS MEWS 10
WEST VIEW 11
BRADFORDS CT 12
KNIGHTS CRES 13
BRADFORDS CL 14
TYTHINGS CRES 15
BLACKMANS GL 16
B4221
Mast
Gorsley Common
CHAPEL BGLWS
MANSE LA
ROWENS LA
Sugar Tump
PO
FORTY'S PITCH
DYERS WLK
COURT LA
Gorsley
Kews La
Blue La
PH
VAUXHALL ORCH
Cemy
Sch
Sports Ctr
GORSLEY GDNS 3
SPRINGDALE 4
DALEBROOK 5
SUNDEW
LINTON RD
PROSPECT ROW
OLD LA (SIMMONDS LA)
Sterrys Rd
Ford Farm
Kilcot
Conigree Court
THE TYTHINGS
KNIGHTS WAY
HR9
Linton
The Lanes
LAMBS CROSS
SARGENTS LA
Stoney Rd
Place Hill
Ford La
B4222
Wood La
Commonfields
CULVER ST
Woodend La
Great Woodend Farm
Darnell's La
Little Gorsley
PIGS CROSS
Hill View La
Briery Hill
Linton Hill
THE LINE
Darnell's Farm
Beavan's Hill
SHOTTS LA
Gypsy La
Darks Rd
Mill La
Kilcot Wood
Ravenshill
Acorn Wood
Boulsden
Cut Throat La
Withymoor Farm
Cowley Bank
Aston Bank
Nailers La
Reslaw Wood
International Centre of Birds of Prey
Stallion Hill
Anthony Cross
The Green
Woodgate
Aston Crews
PH
Aston Ingham
Oaks La
Chapel Pitch
Southall Terr
Clifford's Mesne
Warren La
New House Farm
Barrel La
GL17
PH
Hay Farm
Aston Mills
Crews Hill
Barrel Farm
Newents Wood
Black House Farm
GL19
Judge's La
B4222
B4216

164
165

Column labels (bottom): A, B, C, D, E, F

Bottom scale numbers: 66, 67, 68, 69, 70, 71

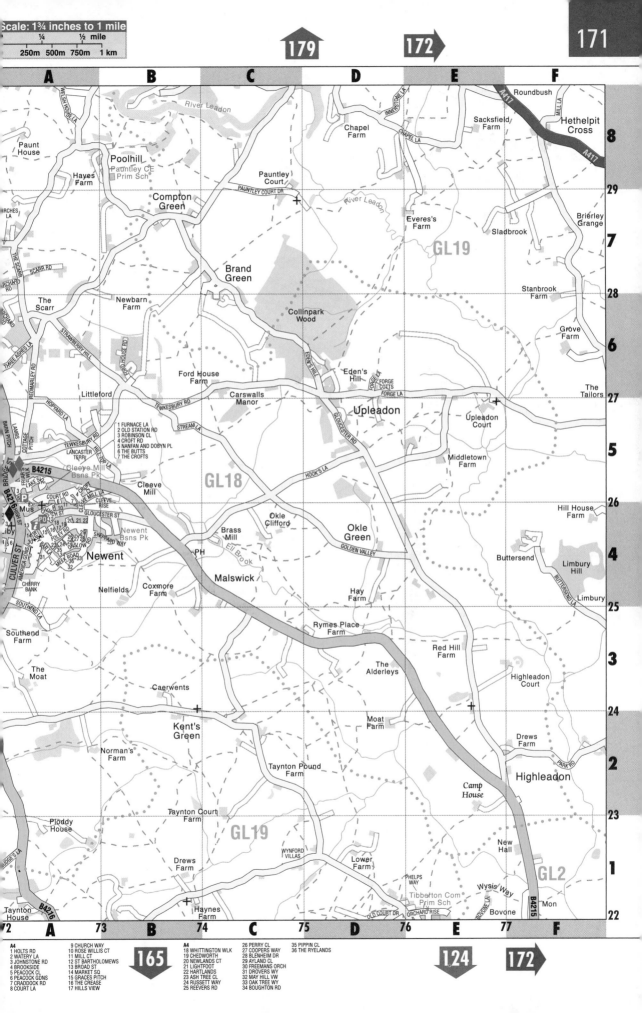

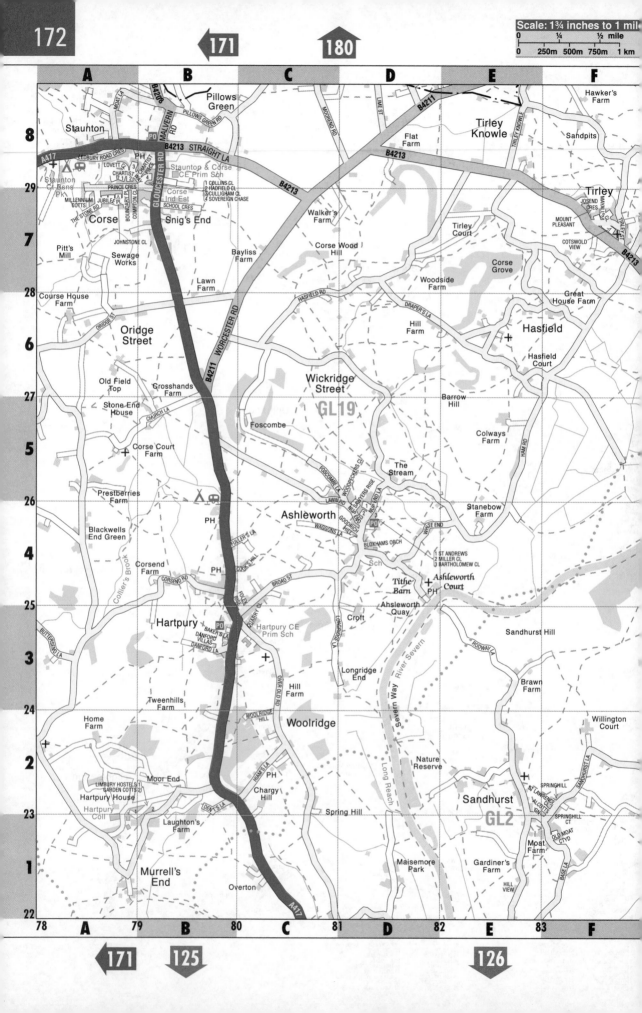

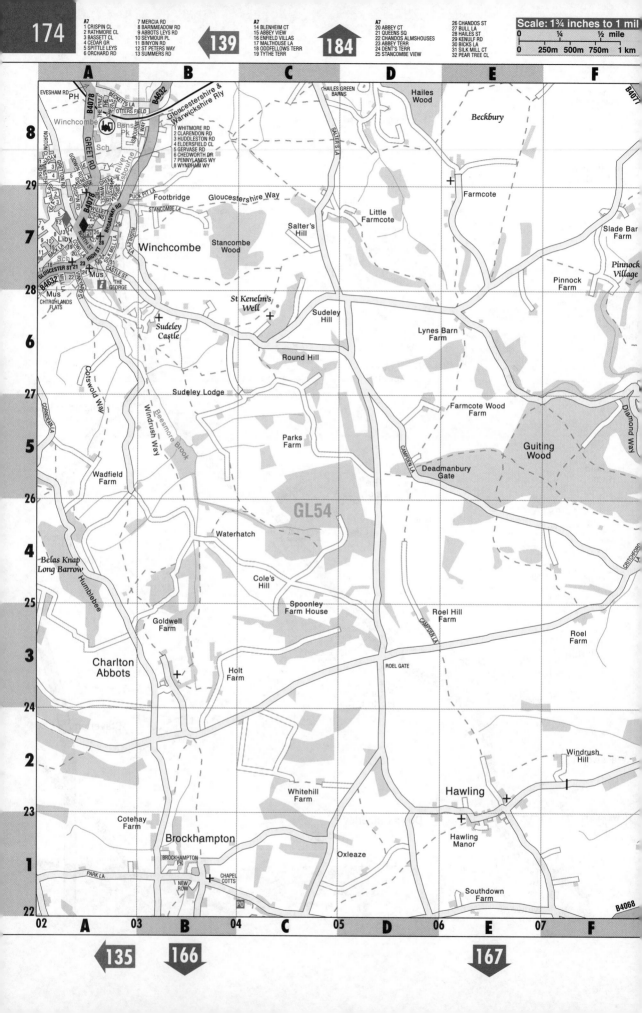

174

Scale: 1¾ inches to 1 mil
0   ¼   ½   mile
0   250m 500m 750m 1 km

139
184
135
166
167

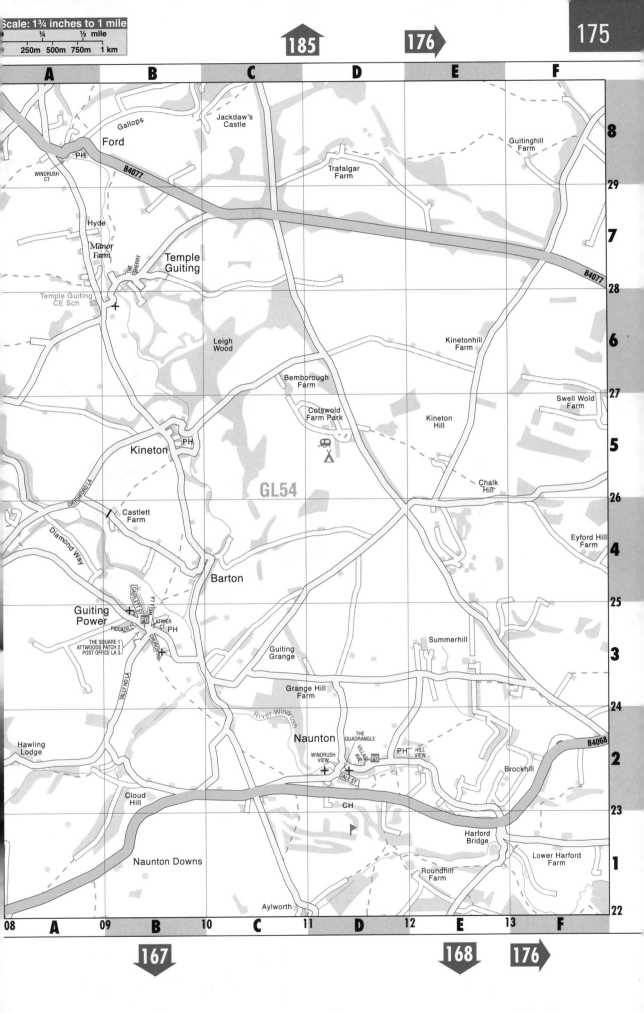

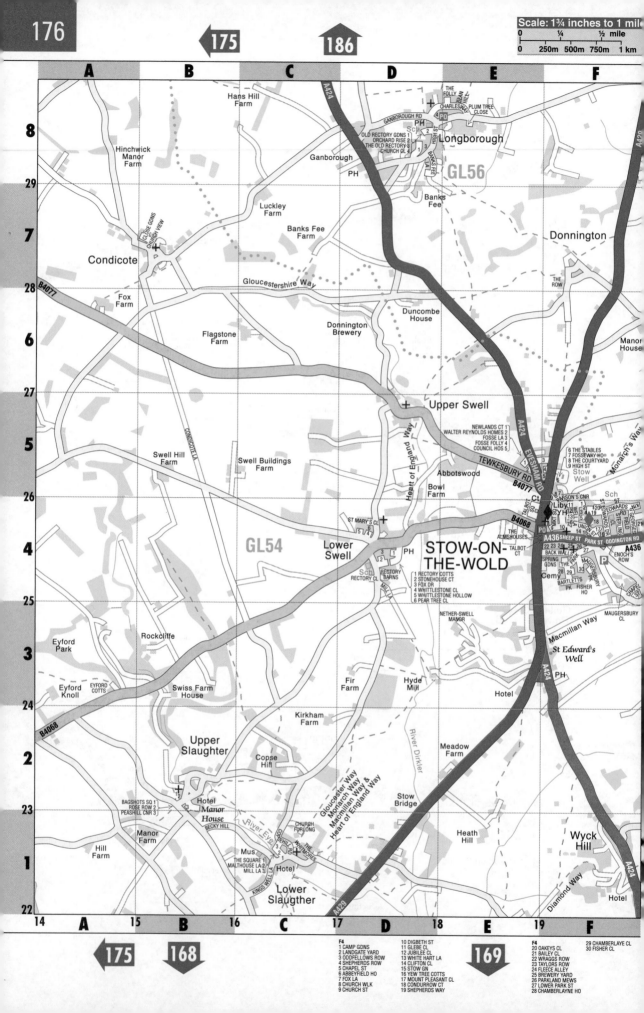

F4
1 CAMP GDNS
2 LANDGATE YARD
3 ODDFELLOWS ROW
4 SHEPHERDS ROW
5 CHAPEL ST
6 ABBEYFIELD HO
7 FOX LA
8 CHURCH WLK
9 CHURCH ST

10 DIGBETH ST
11 GLEBE CL
12 JUBILEE CL
13 WHITE HART LA
14 CLIFTON CL
15 STOW GN
16 YEW TREE COTTS
17 MOUNT PLEASANT CL
18 CONDURROW CT
19 SHEPHERDS WAY

F4
20 OAKEYS CL
21 BAILEY CL
22 WRAGGS ROW
23 TAYLORS ROW
24 FLEECE ALLEY
25 BREWERY YARD
26 PARKLAND MEWS
27 LOWER PARK ST
28 CHAMBERLAYNE HO

29 CHAMBERLAYE CL
30 FISHER CL

187

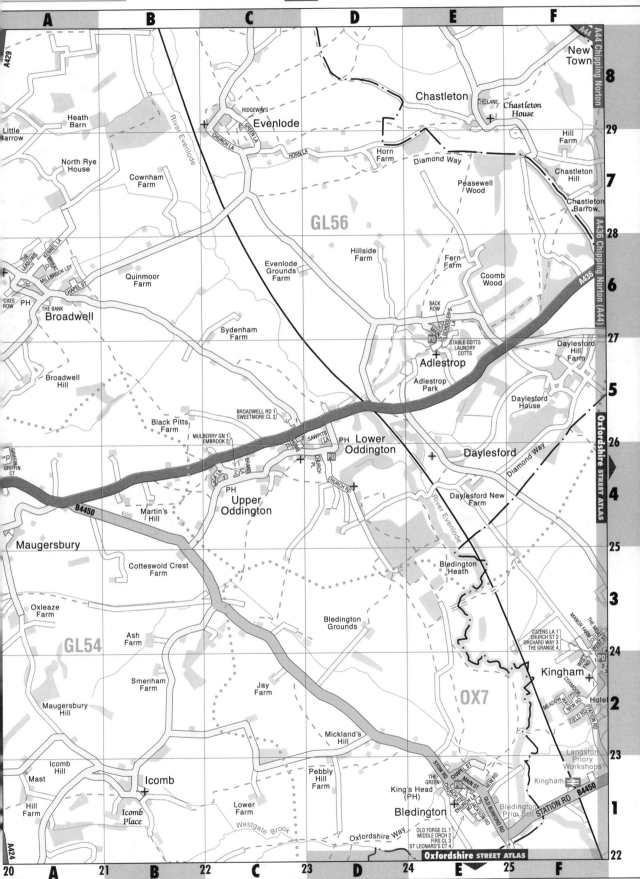

Scale: 1¾ inches to 1 mile
¼ ½ mile
250m 500m 750m 1 km

New Town

Chastleton

Chastleton House

THE LANE

Hill Farm

Chastleton Hill

Chastleton Barrow

Little Barrow

Heath Barn

North Rye House

Cownham Farm

RIDGEWAYS

Evenlode

CHURCH LA

GREEN LA

HORN LA

Horn Farm

Diamond Way

Peasewell Wood

GL56

Hillside Farm

Fern Farm

Coomb Wood

Daylesford Hill Farm

THE LEASOWS
KENNEL LA
MILLBROOK LBY
CHAPEL ST
FOXES ROW
PH
THE BANK

Broadwell

Quinmoor Farm

Sydenham Farm

Evenlode Grounds Farm

BACK ROW

SCHOOLS LA

MAIN ST

PO

STABLE COTTS
LAUNDRY COTTS

Adlestrop

Daylesford Hill Farm

Broadwell Hill

Black Pitts Farm

BROADWELL RD 1
SWEETMORE CL 2

MULBERRY GN 1
EMBROOK 2

SAWPITS LA

PH Lower Oddington

PO

Adlestrop Park

Daylesford House

Daylesford

GRIFFIN CL 1
GRIFFIN CT

B4450

BACK LA

BRANS LA

CHURCH PL

CHURCH RD

PH

Upper Oddington

Daylesford New Farm

River Evenlode

Diamond Way

Maugersbury

Cotteswold Crest Farm

Bledington Heath

Oxleaze Farm

GL54

Ash Farm

Bledington Grounds

MANOR FARM CL

WEST END

COZENS LA 1
CHURCH ST 2
ORCHARD WAY 3
THE GRANGE 4

PO

Kingham

Smenham Farm

Jay Farm

OX7

COXMOOR

MEADOW WAY

NEW RD

FIELD CL

STATION RD

Hotel

Maugersbury Hill

Mickland's Hill

Langston Priory Workshops

Kingham

Mast

Icomb Hill

Icomb

Pebbly Hill Farm

King's Head (PH)

THE GREEN

STOW RD

CHAPEL ST

MAIN ST

NEW RD

PO

B4450

Hill Farm

Icomb Place

Lower Farm

Oxfordshire Way

Bledington

CHURCH ST
CHURCH LA
JACKSON RD
OLD BURFORD RD

Bledington Prim Sch

STATION RD

Westgate Brook

OLD FORGE CL 1
MIDDLE ORCH 2
FIRS CL 3
ST LEONARD'S CT 4

A429

A44

A44 Chipping Norton

A436 Chipping Norton (A44)

A436

Oxfordshire STREET ATLAS

A424

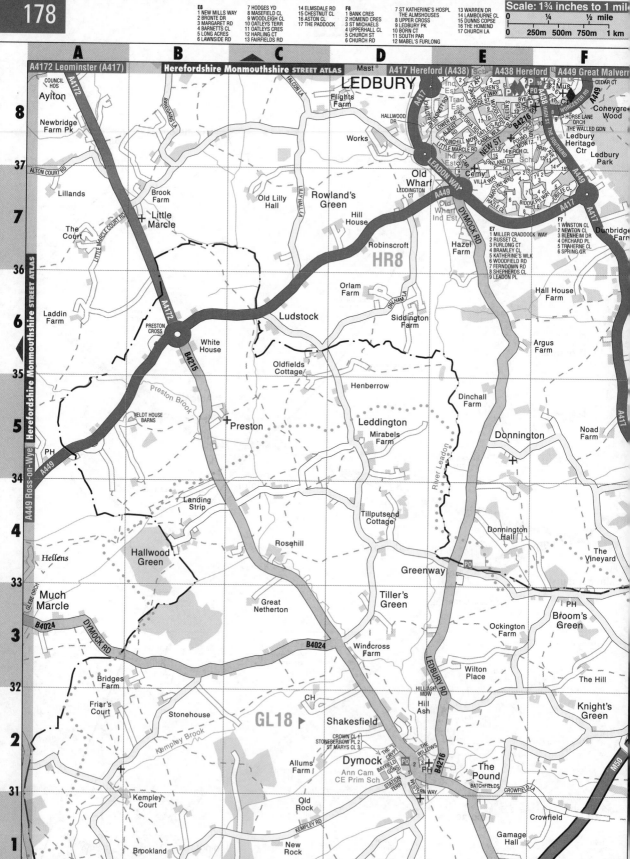

E8
1 NEW MILLS WAY
2 BRONTE DR
3 MARGARET RD
4 BARNETTS CL
5 LONG ACRES
6 LAWNSIDE RD

7 HODGES YD
8 MASEFIELD CL
9 WOODLEIGH CL
10 OATLEYS TERR
11 OATLEYS CRES
12 HARLING CT
13 FAIRFIELDS RD

14 ELMSDALE RD
15 CHESTNUT CL
16 ASTON CL
17 THE PADDOCK

F8
1 BANK CRES
2 HOMEND CRES
3 ST MICHAELS
4 UPPERHALL CL
5 CHURCH ST
6 CHURCH RD

7 ST KATHERINE'S HOSPL
THE ALMSHOUSES
8 UPPER CROSS
9 LEDBURY PK
10 BORN CT
11 SOUTH PAR
12 MABEL'S FURLONG

13 WARREN DR
14 LAMBOURNE CL
15 DUNNS COPSE
16 THE HOMEND
17 CHURCH LA

Scale: 1¾ inches to 1 mile

E7
1 MILLER CRADDOCK WAY
2 RUSSET CL
3 FURLONG CT
4 BRAMLEY CL
5 KATHERINE'S WLK
6 WOODFIELD RD
7 FERNDOWN RD
8 SHEPHERDS CL
9 LEADON PL

F7
1 WINSTON CL
2 NEWTON CL
3 BLENHEIM DR
4 ORCHARD PL
5 TRAHERNE CL
6 SPRING GR

scale: 1¾ inches to 1 mile
¼ ½ mile
250m 500m 750m 1 km

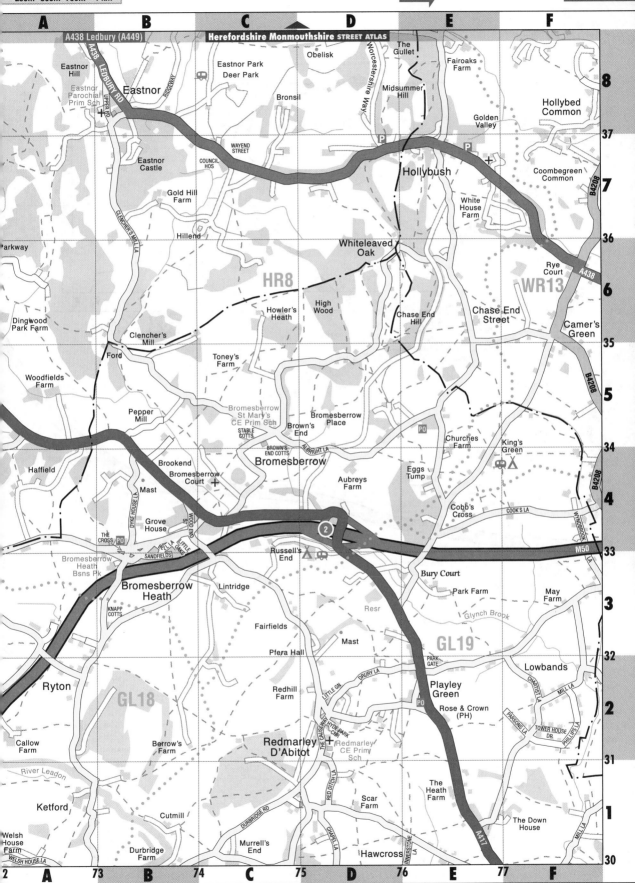

Herefordshire Monmouthshire STREET ATLAS

A438 Ledbury (A449)

Eastnor Hill
Eastnor Parochial Prim Sch
Eastnor
LEDBURY RD
UPPER RD
Eastnor Castle
RIDGEWAY
Eastnor Park Deer Park
Obelisk
Bronsil
WAYEND STREET
COUNCIL HOS
The Gullet
Fairoaks Farm
Midsummer Hill
Golden Valley
Hollybush
Hollybed Common
Coombegreen Common
White House Farm
B4208
A438
Gold Hill Farm
CLENCHER'S MILL LA
Hillend
Parkway
Whiteleaved Oak
HR8
Rye Court
WR13
Dingwood Park Farm
Clencher's Mill
Ford
Howler's Heath
High Wood
Chase End Hill
Chase End Street
Camer's Green
B4208
Woodfields Farm
Toney's Farm
Pepper Mill
Bromesberrow St Mary's CE Prim Sch
STABLE COTTS
Brown's End
Bromesberrow Place
PO
Churches Farm
King's Green
Haffield
Brookend
Bromesberrow Court
BROWN'S END COTTS
ALBRIGHT LA
Bromesberrow
Aubreys Farm
Eggs Tump
Mast
DYKE HOUSE LA
Grove House
WOOD END ST
LITTLE OAKS
Cobb's Cross
COOK'S LA
WINDBROOK
B4208
THE CROSS
PO
BELL LA
SANDFIELDS
Russell's End
2
Bury Court
M50
LA
Bromesberrow Heath Bsns Pk
Bromesberrow Heath
Lintridge
Resr
Park Farm
May Farm
KNAPP COTTS
Glynch Brook
GL18
Fairfields
Mast
GL19
PARK GATE
Lowbands
CHARTISTS LA
MILL LA
Ryton
Pfera Hall
DRURY LA
Playley Green
PARSONS LA
TOWER HOUSE DR
PHILLIPS LA
Callow Farm
Redhill Farm
LITTLE GN
PO
Rose & Crown (PH)
THE CHUSEWAY
HYDE PARK CNR
Berrow's Farm
Redmarley D'Abitot
Redmarley CE Prim Sch
The Heath Farm
The Down House
Ketford
RED DITCH LA
River Leadon
Cutmill
DURBRIDGE RD
Scar Farm
A417
MILL LA
Welsh House Farm
WELSH HOUSE LA
Durbridge Farm
Murrell's End
CHAPEL LA
INNERSTONE LA
Hawcross

8
37
7
36
6
35
5
34
4
33
3
32
2
31
1
30

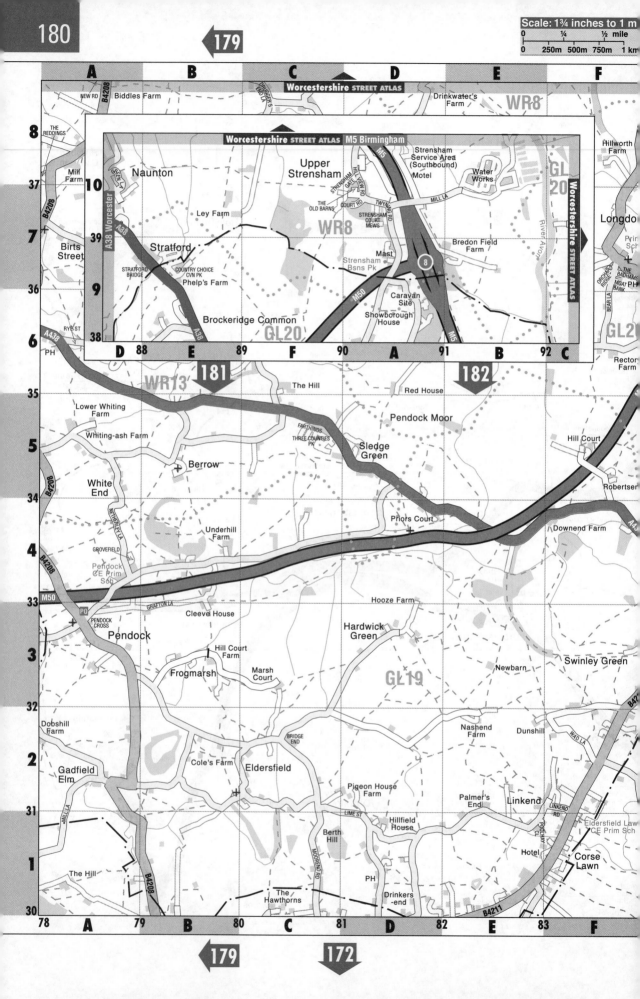

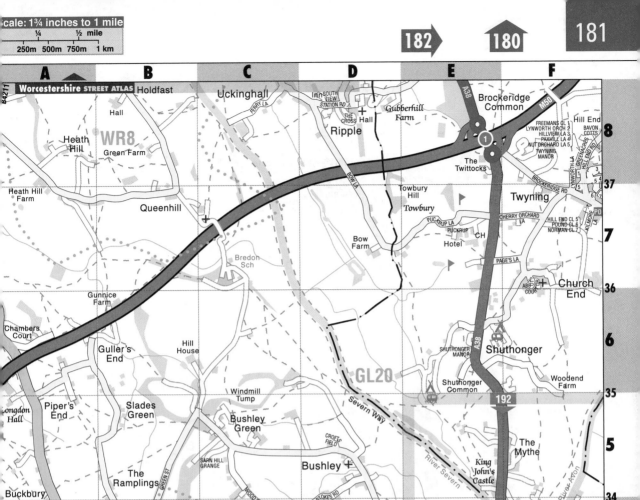
A   B   C   D   E   F

Worcestershire STREET ATLAS Holdfast

Uckinghall

Inn SOUTH
VIEW
STATION RD

Brockeridge
Common

M50

Hall

Heath
Hill

WR8

Green Farm

FERRY LA

THE
CROSS Hall

Gubberhill
Farm

Ripple

Hill End

FREEMANS CL 1
LYNWORTH ORCH 2
HILLVIEW LA 3
PAXHILL LA 4
NUT ORCHARD LA 5
TWYNING
MANOR

BAVON
COTTS

8

Heath Hill
Farm

Queenhill

BOW LA

The
Twittocks

BROCKERIDGE
RD

Twyning

CYNWORTH LA

KILMORE

37

Towbury
Hill

Towbury

CHERRY ORCHARD

Hotel

Bredon
Sch

Bow
Farm

PUCKRUP LA

PUCKRUP

CH

HILL END CL 5
POUND CL 6
NORMAN CL 7

Church
End

36

Gunnice
Farm

Hill
House

PAGE'S LA

ABF
COURT

Chambers
Court

Guller's
End

SHUTHONGER
MANOR

Shuthonger

Woodend
Farm

6

Longdon
Hall

Piper's
End

Slades
Green

Windmill
Tump

Severn Way

Shuthonger
Common

192

35

Bushley
Green

The
Mythe

Buckbury

The
Ramplings

GREEN ST

SARN HILL
GRANGE

CROFT
FIELD

Bushley

King
John's
Castle

River Severn

River Avon

5

PH

Sarn Hill
Wood

WOOD ST

STOKES RD

A438

Marinas

BREDON RD

B4080

34

Long
Green

B4211

Massey
Farm

Bushley
Park

Works

MYTHE RD

Mitton

BRAMLEY CL
CARRANT RD

4

Upper
Lode

192

HIGH ST

Liby

STATION RD

Cold
Elm

BISHOPS WALK

ARBOUR
ELMS

CHURCH LA

Alcock's
Farm

PO

Mills

TH

CHANCE ST

Seh

P

33

TEWKESBURY

BARTON ST

BARTON RD

A438

DUNSMORE GN

BISHOP'S WALK

Forthampton

Mus CHURCH ST

Mus

H

3

GL19

Home Farm

Severn Ham

Abbey

Cemy

Priors
Park

A38

Forthampton
Court

PH

Lower Lode La

LINCOLN GREEN LA

GLOUCESTER RD

ABBOT'S RD

QUEENS RD

P

Margaret's
Camp

VAN WAY

32

Lawn Farm

Severn Way

Lower
Lode

CH

Tewkesbury
Park

192

31

Hillend
Farm

Chaceley

ROCK ST

WREATH LA

Rayer's
Hill

Southwick
Park

GLOUCESTER RD

Stonehouse
Farm

1

Rye Court
Farm

Park Farm

Southwick
Farm

A38

30

A   B   C   D   E   F

84   85   86   87   88   89

173 ▼   182 ▼

For full street detail of the
highlighted area see page
192.

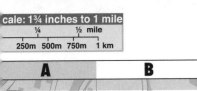

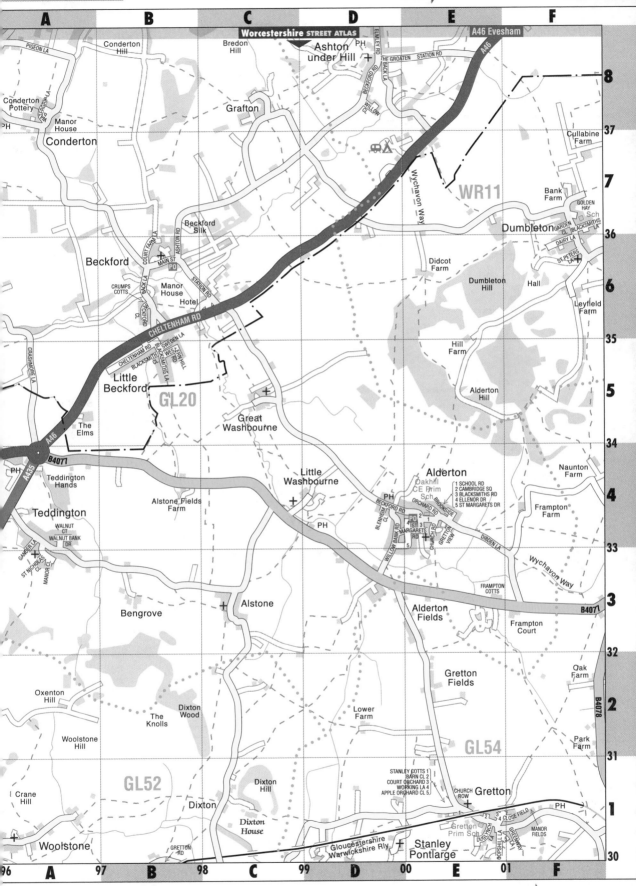

A   B   C   D   E   F

8

37

7

36

6

35

5

34

4

33

3

32

2

31

1

30

Worcestershire STREET ATLAS

CHURCH RD

Aston
Somerville

Buckland
Fields

Peasebrook
Farm

Mast

Little
Buckland

CHELTENHAM RD

B4632

THE
LANE

Wormington

Leasow
House

WR12

Buckland

1 DOUGHMEADOW COTTS
2 MEADOW COTTS

WR11

Mill
Farm

River Isbourne

Cotton's
Farm

Stanton
Fields

Laverton

Raymeadow
Farm

Wormington
Grange

WEDGEWOOD
COTTS

CHURCH LA

Stanton

Manorway
THE VINEYARD

HIGH ST

Cross

PH

SHEPPEY
CNR

Berry
Wormington

STANWAY RD

CHESTNUT
CNR

CULLS
MDW

Lydes
Farm

Cotswold Way

Shenberrow
Hill

Toddington
Manor

Stanway
Grounds

Lidcombe
Hill

Gateway

Orchard
Ind Est

THE
SQUARE

OLDE LA

CHURCH LA

NURSERY LA

BROADWAY RD

Papermill
Farm

Lidcombe
Wood

B4077

CHURCH MDWS

Toddington

NEW TOWN

Tithe
Barn

Stanway
House

B4078

Toddington
Prim Sch

CONSELL
GN

PH

Toddington

PO

Stanway

Didbrook
Fields

GL54

Warren
Farm

Groveleys

Didbrook

Wood
Stanway

Gloucestershire Warwickshire Rly

Isbourne
Valley Sch

OLD FORGE
COTTS

Millhampost
Farm

Lower
Coscombe

B4078

GROVE
VIEW

NEAR FARM

Mill
Farm

Ireley
Farm

Hailes

SALTERS LA

Hailes
Abbey
(rems of)

Hailes
Wood

Stump
Cross

EVESHAM RD

SMITHY LA

MARKET LA

MILL LA

Greet

B4632

Mus

Upper
Coscombe

B4077

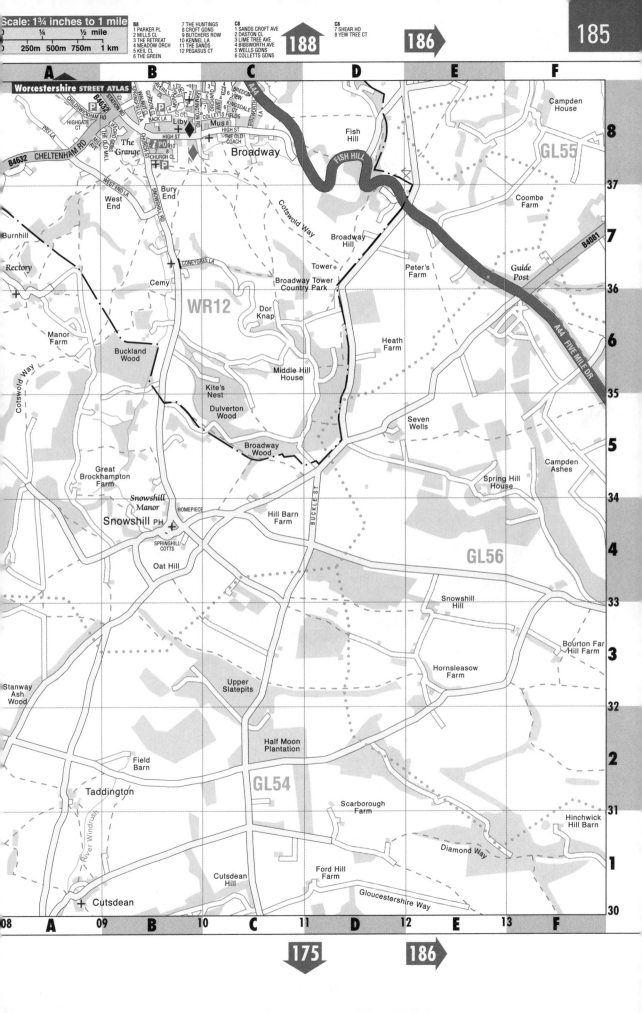

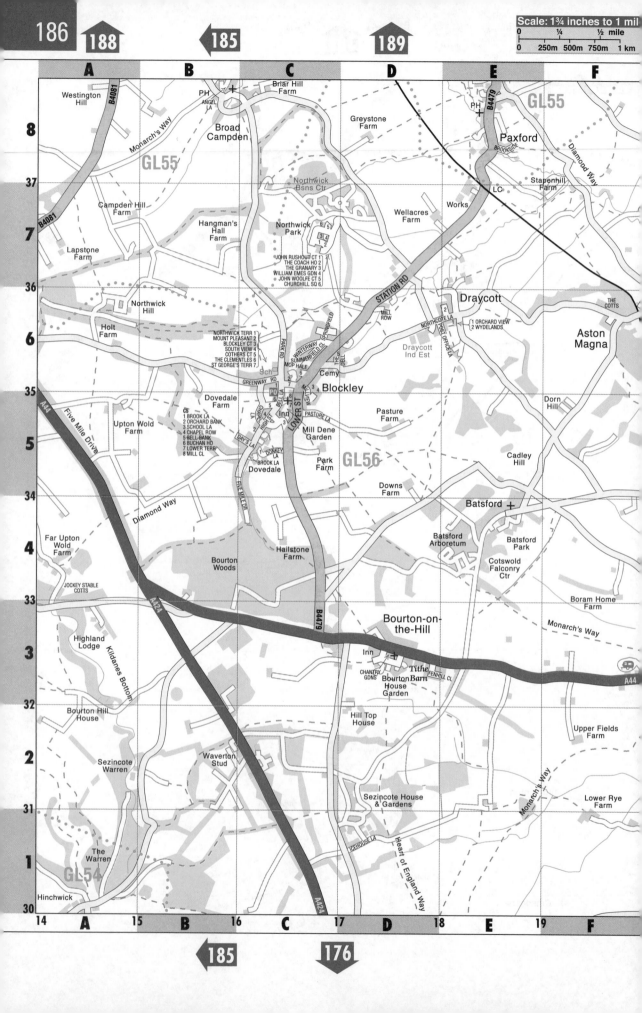

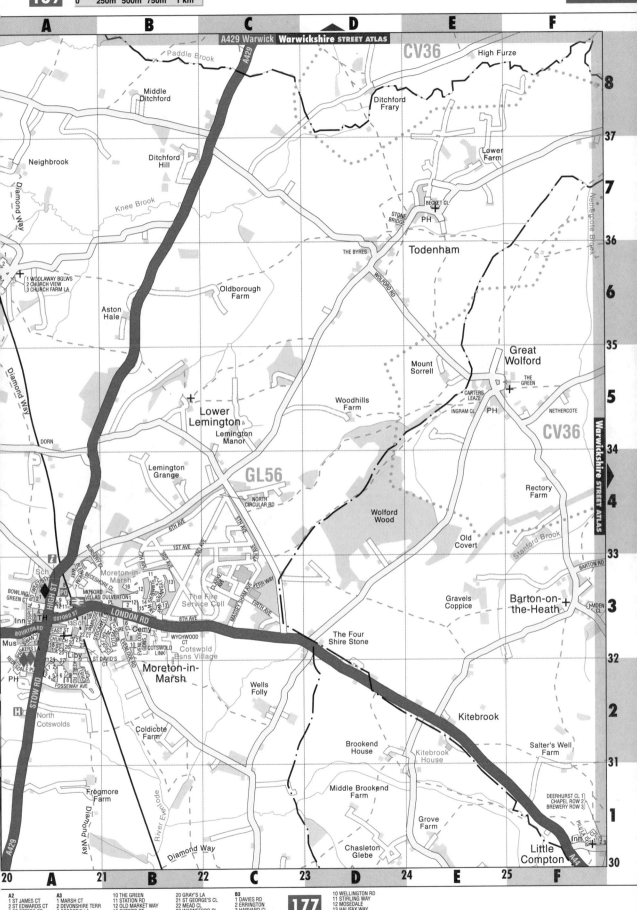

Scale: 1¾ inches to 1 mile

0 ¼ ½ mile

0 250m 500m 750m 1 km

189

187

A429 Warwick **Warwickshire** STREET ATLAS

CV36

High Furze

Middle
Ditchford

Ditchford
Frary

Neighbrook

Ditchford
Hill

Lower
Farm

Knee Brook

BECKET CL

STONE
BRIDGE

PH

1 WOOLAWAY BGLWS
2 CHURCH VIEW
3 CHURCH FARM LA

THE BYRES

Todenham

Oldborough
Farm

WOLFORD RD

Aston
Hale

Mount
Sorrell

Great
Wolford

THE GREEN

Lower
Lemington

Woodhills
Farm

CARTERS
LEAZE

INGRAM CL

PH

NETHERCOTE

Lemington
Manor

CV36

Lemington
Grange

GL56

NORTH
CIRCULAR RD

Wolford
Wood

Rectory
Farm

Diamond Way

DORN

6TH AVE

1ST AVE

Old
Covert

Stanford Brook

BARTON RD

Moreton-in-
Marsh

The Fire
Service Coll

KERR WAY

Gravels
Coppice

Barton-on-
the-Heath

CAMDEN CL

BOWLING
GREEN CT

HIGH ST

Inn

PO

LONDON RD

8TH AVE

The Four
Shire Stone

OXFORD ST

EAST ST

Cemy

Mus

WYCHWOOD
CT

Cotswold
Link

Cotswold
Bsns Village

Libry

ST DAVID'S
CT

Moreton-in-
Marsh

Wells
Folly

Kitebrook

PH

H

North
Cotswolds

Coldicote
Farm

Salter's Well
Farm

STOW RD

Brookend
House

Kitebrook
House

Frogmore
Farm

Diamond Way

Middle Brookend
Farm

Grove
Farm

DEERHURST CL 1
CHAPEL ROW 2
BREWERY ROW 3

A429

River Evenlode

Diamond Way

Chaselton
Glebe

Little
Compton

A44

Warwickshire STREET ATLAS

CV36

177

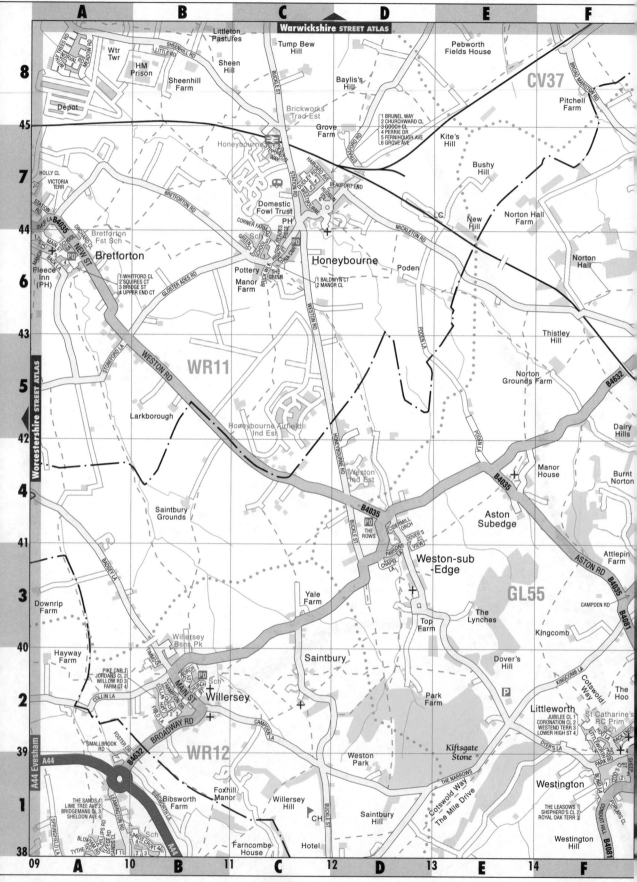

Warwickshire STREET ATLAS

Worcestershire STREET ATLAS

CV37

GL55

WR11

WR12

A44 Evesham

Littleton Pastures

Tump Bew Hill

Pebworth Fields House

Baylis's Hill

Pitchell Farm

Wtr Twr

Sheen Hill

HM Prison

Sheenhill Farm

Grove Farm

Kite's Hill

Bushy Hill

Depot

Brickworks Trad Est

New Hill

Norton Hall Farm

1 BRUNEL WAY
2 CHURCHWARD CL
3 GOOCH CL
4 PERRIE DR
5 FERNIHOUGH AVE
6 GROVE AVE

Honeybourne Station Way

LC

Norton Hall

HOLLY CL

VICTORIA TERR

BRETFORTON RD

Domestic Fowl Trust

BEAUFORT END

MICKLETON RD

Poden

Bretforton Fst Sch

CORNER FARM

Bretforton

NEW ST

Honeybourne

1 WHITFORD CL
2 SQUIRES CT
3 BRIDGE ST
4 UPPER END CT

GLOSTER ADES RD

Pottery

Manor Farm

THE GREEN

1 BALDWYN CT
2 MANOR CL

Fleece Inn (PH)

Thistley Hill

WESTON RD

Norton Grounds Farm

B4632

Larkborough

Honeybourne Airfield Ind Est

Dairy Hills

STONEFORD LA

HONEYBOURNE RD

Manor House

Burnt Norton

Saintbury Grounds

Weston Ind Est

B4035

Aston Subedge

Attlepin Farm

Downrip Farm

THE ROWS

CIDERMILL ORCH

DOVER'S VIEW

ASTON RD

B4081

BADSEY LA

Yale Farm

CHAPEL LA

Weston-sub-Edge

CAMPDEN RD

Kingcomb

Hayway Farm

Willersey Bsns Pk

Saintbury

Top Farm

The Lynches

Dover's Hill

KINGCOMB LA

Cotswold Way

The Hoo

PIKE CNR 1
JORDANS CL 2
WILLOW RD 3
FARM CT 4

MAIN ST

Willersey

Park Farm

St Catharine's RC Prim Sch

Littleworth

COLLIN LA

FOSTER DR

BROADWAY RD

CAMPDEN LA

Weston Park

Kiftsgate Stone

1 JUBILEE CL 1
CORONATION CL 2
WESTEND TERR 3
LOWER HIGH ST 4

THE LEASOWS 1
SHEPHERD'S CL 2
ROYAL OAK TERR 3

SMALLBROOK RD

B4632

Bibsworth Farm

Foxhill Manor

Willersey Hill

THE NARROWS

Cotswold Way

The Mile Drive

Westington

THE SANDS 1
LIME TREE AVE 2
BRIDGEMANS CL 3
SHELDON AVE 4

A44

CH

Saintbury Hill

Westington Hill

Farncombe House

Hotel

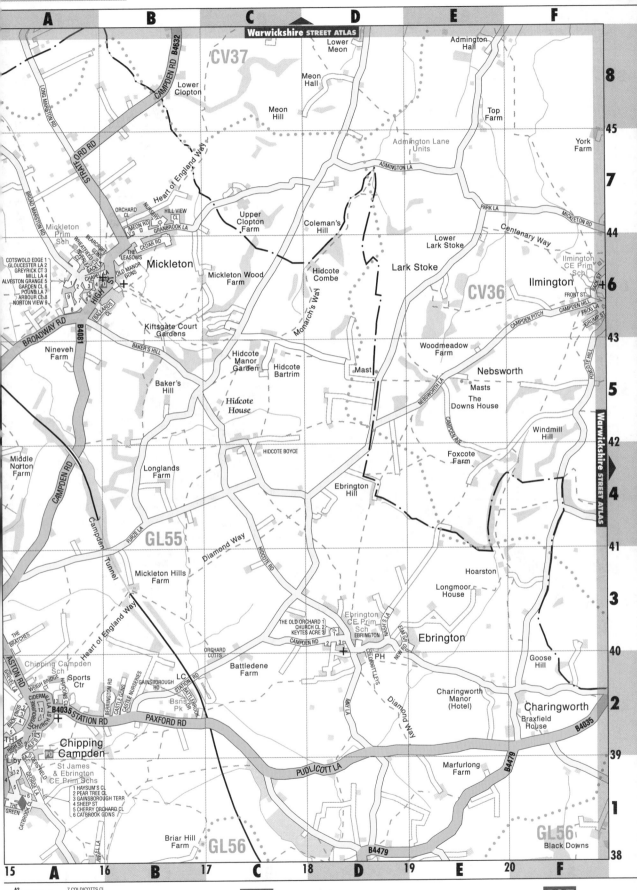

CV37

Lower Meon
Admington Hall
Lower Clopton
Meon Hall
Top Farm
York Farm
Meon Hill
Admington Lane Units
ADMINGTON LA
PARK LA
MICKLETON RD

Heart of England Way
STRATFORD RD
CAMPDEN RD B4632

ORCHARD CL
HILL VIEW
Upper Clopton Farm
Coleman's Hill
Lower Lark Stoke
Centenary Way
Ilmington CE Prim Sch
MEON RD
NURSERY LA
GRANBROOK LA
CL
Lark Stoke
Ilmington

Mickleton Prim Sch
THE LEASOWS
THE CEDAR RD
Mickleton Wood Farm
Hidcote Combe
CV36
FRONT ST

COTSWOLD EDGE 1
GLOUCESTER LA 2
GREYRICK CT 3
MILL LA 4
ALVESTON GRANGE 5
GARDEN CL 6
POUND LA 7
ARBOUR CL 8
NORTON VIEW 9

Mickleton
Woodmeadow Farm
Nebsworth
CAMPDEN PITCH
CAMPDEN HILL
FROG LA
BRUMP ST

Kiftsgate Court Gardens
Hidcote Manor Garden
Hidcote Bartrim
Mast
Masts
The Downs House
NEBSWORTH LA
FOXCOTE HILL

BROADWAY RD B4081
BAKER'S HILL
Nineveh Farm

Baker's Hill
Hidcote Boyce
Windmill Hill

Hidcote House
Foxcote Farm
CAMPDEN AVE

Middle Norton Farm
Longlands Farm
Ebrington Hill

CAMPDEN RD

GL55
Diamond Way
HIDCOTE RD
Hoarston
Longmoor House

Mickleton Hills Farm
FURZE LA
Campden Tunnel

THE BRATCHES
Heart of England Way
THE OLD ORCHARD 1
CHURCH CL 2
KEYTES ACRE 3
Ebrington CE Prim Sch
EBRINGTON
Ebrington
ELM GR
NASH'S LA
Goose Hill

Chipping Campden Sch
Sports Ctr
WEIGH BRIDGE
ORCHARD COTTS
Battledene Farm
CAMPDEN RD
PH
COLDICOTTLEY'S
Charingworth Manor (Hotel)
Charingworth

ASTON RD
GRETELLA
CIDERMILL
BERRINGTON RD
CASTLE EDNS
CASTLE NURSERIES
Gainsborough Ho
LC
STATION RD
ST BATTLEBROOK
Bsns Pk
MAY LA
Diamond Way
Braxfield House
B4035

B4035
STATION RD
PAXFORD RD
Chipping Campden
Marfurlong Farm
B4479

TH
HIGH ST
CALF'S LA
PO
Liby
St James & Ebrington CE Prim Schs
1 HAYSUM'S CL
2 PEAR TREE CL
3 GAINSBOROUGH TERR
4 SHEEP ST
5 CHERRY ORCHARD CL
6 CATBROOK GDNS
PUDLICOTT LA

THE GREEN
CATBROOK LA
Briar Hill Farm
GL56
GL56
Black Downs
B4479

186
187

A2
1 BARRELS PITCH
2 WOLDS END CL
3 GRIGGS CL
4 ROLLING STONES
5 SEYMOUR GATE
6 THE SQUARE
7 COLDICOTTS CL
8 NOEL CT
9 THE OLD GRAMMAR SCHOOL MEWS
10 GLEBE FOLD
11 ALMSHOUSES
12 VICARAGE COTTS
13 CHURCH COTTS

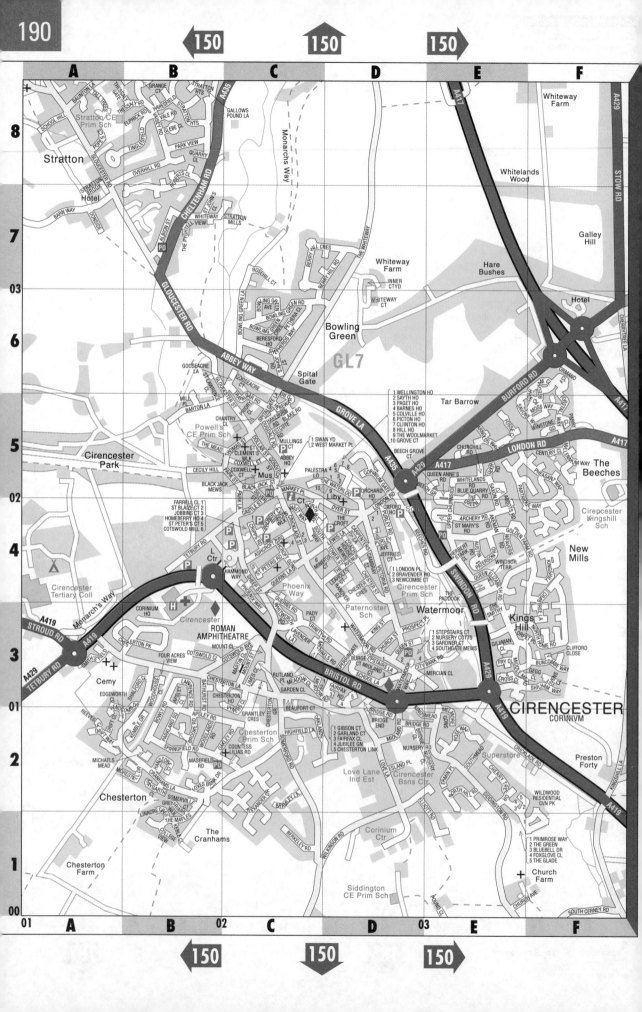

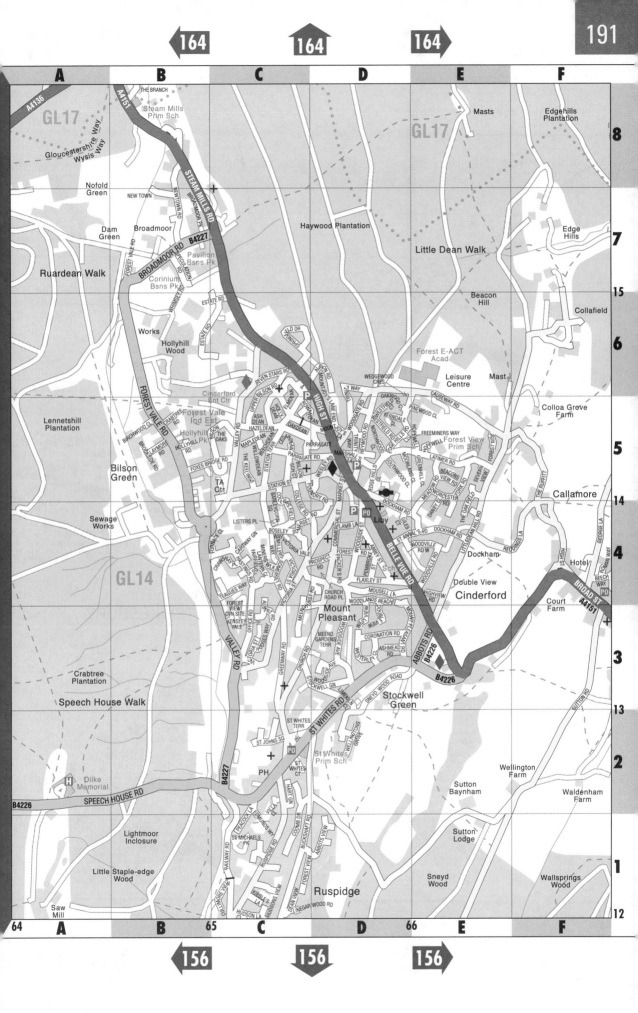

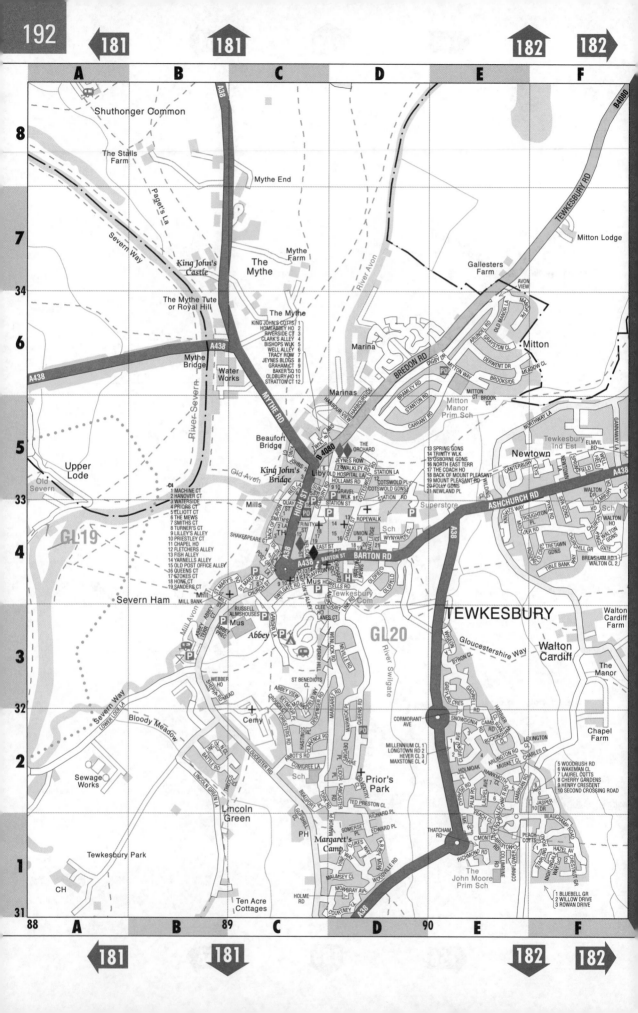

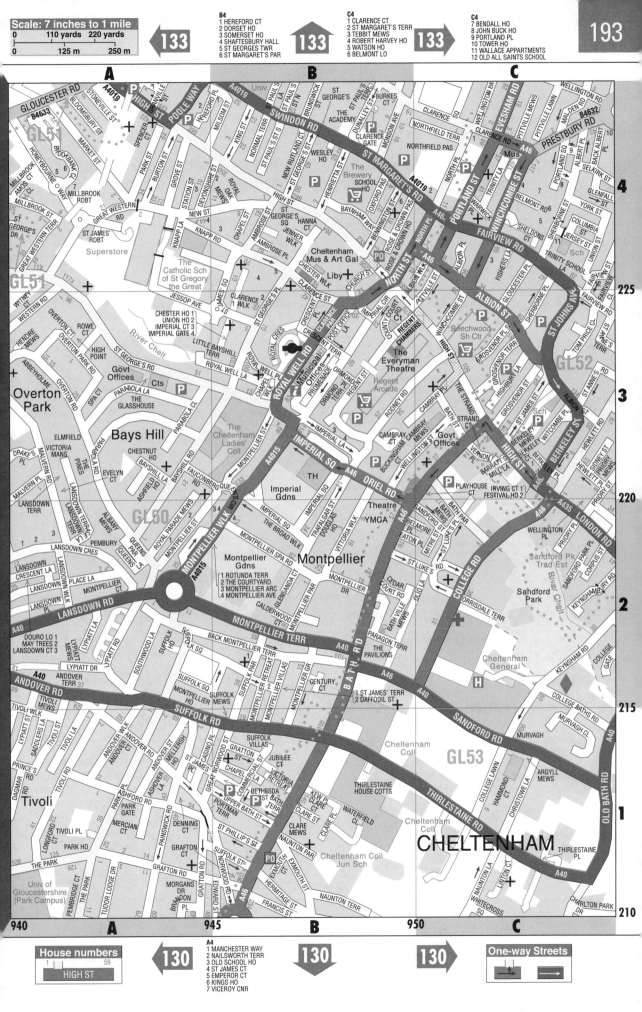

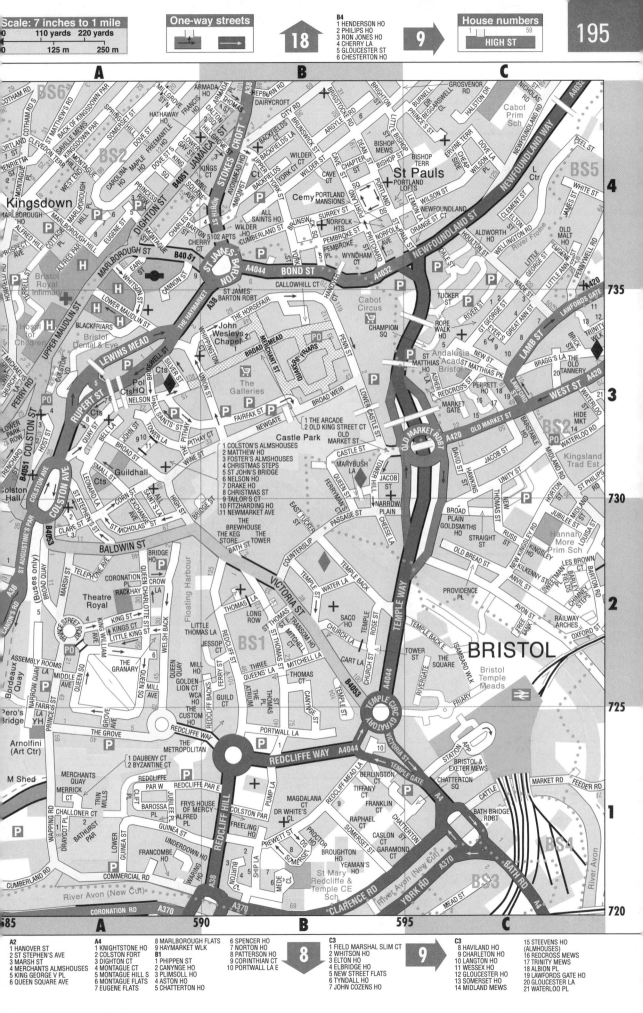

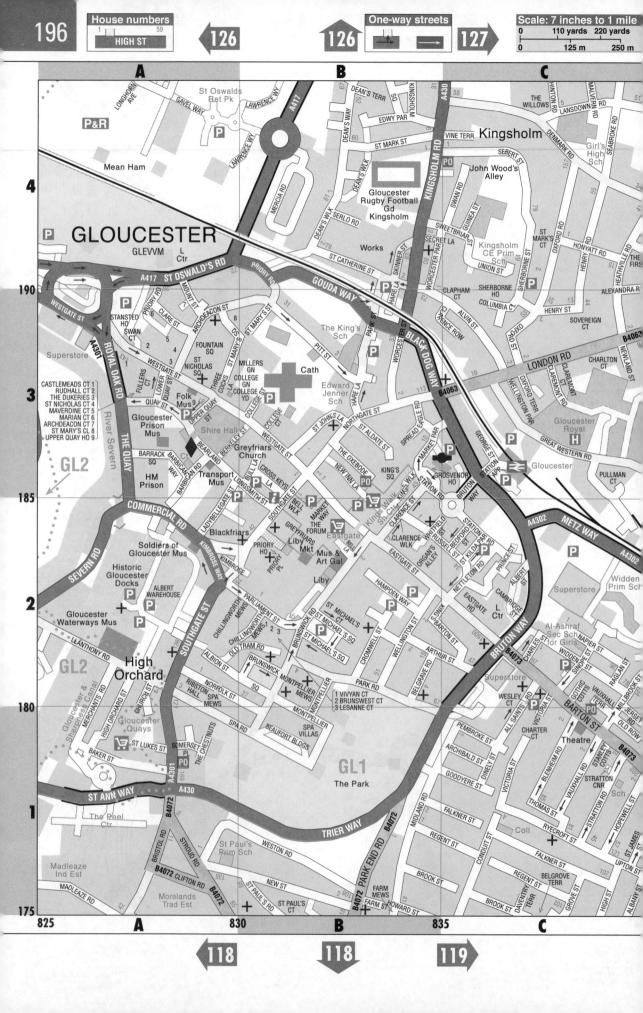

Index

Place name May be abbreviated on the map

Location number Present when a number indicates the place's position in a crowded area of mapping

Locality, town or village Shown when more than one place has the same name

Postcode district District for the indexed place

Page and grid square Page number and grid reference for the standard mapping

Church Rd **6** Beckenham BR2.........**53** C6

Cities, towns and villages are listed in CAPITAL LETTERS

Public and commercial buildings are highlighted in magenta **Places of interest** are highlighted in blue with a star★

Abbreviations used in the index

Acad	**Academy**	Comm	**Common**	Gd	**Ground**	L	**Leisure**	Prom	**Promenade**
App	**Approach**	Cott	**Cottage**	Gdn	**Garden**	La	**Lane**	Rd	**Road**
Arc	**Arcade**	Cres	**Crescent**	Gn	**Green**	Liby	**Library**	Recn	**Recreation**
Ave	**Avenue**	Cswy	**Causeway**	Gr	**Grove**	Mdw	**Meadow**	Ret	**Retail**
Bglw	**Bungalow**	Ct	**Court**	H	**Hall**	Meml	**Memorial**	Sh	**Shopping**
Bldg	**Building**	Ctr	**Centre**	Ho	**House**	Mkt	**Market**	Sq	**Square**
Bsns, Bus	**Business**	Ctry	**Country**	Hospl	**Hospital**	Mus	**Museum**	St	**Street**
Bvd	**Boulevard**	Cty	**County**	HQ	**Headquarters**	Orch	**Orchard**	Sta	**Station**
Cath	**Cathedral**	Dr	**Drive**	Hts	**Heights**	Pal	**Palace**	Terr	**Terrace**
Cir	**Circus**	Dro	**Drove**	Ind	**Industrial**	Par	**Parade**	TH	**Town Hall**
Cl	**Close**	Ed	**Education**	Inst	**Institute**	Pas	**Passage**	Univ	**University**
Cnr	**Corner**	Emb	**Embankment**	Int	**International**	Pk	**Park**	Wk, Wlk	**Walk**
Coll	**College**	Est	**Estate**	Intc	**Interchange**	Pl	**Place**	Wr	**Water**
Com	**Community**	Ex	**Exhibition**	Junc	**Junction**	Prec	**Precinct**	Yd	**Yard**

Index of towns, villages, streets, hospitals, industrial estates, railway stations, schools, shopping centres, universities and places of interest

1st Ave GL56............ **187** B4
2nd Ave GL56............ **187** B4
3rd Ave GL56............ **187** B3
5th Ave GL56........... **187** C4
6th Ave GL56............ **187** B4
7th Ave GL56........... **187** B3
8th Ave GL56........... **187** B3
125 Bsns Pk GL2....... **126** C1
5102 Apartments BS1... **195** B4

A

Aaron Rd GL7............ **150** F2
Abbenesse GL6......... **148** C6
Abbey Cl BS31 ....4 F6
Abbey Ct
 Bristol BS4................9 F5
 Tewkesbury GL20....... **192** B3
 20 Winchcombe GL54 ... **174** A7
Abbeydale BS36 .... **30** E6
Abbeydale Ct GL4..... **119** C4
Abbeyfield Ho
 Chipping Sodbury BS37... **44** C1
 6 Stow-on-t-W GL54 .... **176** F4
Abbey Ho
 Cirencester GL7........ **190** C5
 5 Yate BS37............ **32** D7
Abbeyholme BS36...... **193** A3
Abbey La BS35.......... **51** D6
Abbey Mdw GL20....... **192** D1
Abbeymead Ave GL4 .. **119** C6
Abbeymead Prim Sch
 GL4................... **119** F5
Abbey Mews GL12...... **67** F4
Abbey Pk BS31..............4 F6
Abbey Prec GL20....... **192** B3
Abbey Rd
 Bristol BS9............. **17** F7
 Gloucester GL2........ **118** C8
Abbey's Mills Ind Est
 GL12................... **67** F5
Abbey St
 Cinderford GL14 .... **191** D4
 Kingswood GL12....... **67** F5
Abbey Terr
 Tewkesbury GL20 ...... **192** B3
 23 Winchcombe GL54 ... **174** A7

Abbey Tintern Furnace★
 NP16................... **146** A3
Abbey View
 6 Gloucester GL4...... **119** C4
 15 Winchcombe GL54 ... **174** A7
Abbey Vw GL20......... **192** C3
Abbey Way GL7........ **190** C6
Abbeywood Dr BS9 ... **17** C5
Abbeywood Pk BS34... **29** C2
Abbey Wood Ret Pk BS34 **29** C2
Abbots Ave BS15....... **10** C4
Abbots Cl
 Bristol BS14.............3 A3
 Cheltenham GL51....... **130** B5
Abbots Court Dr GL20 .. **181** F7
Abbotsford Rd BS6...... **18** B1
Abbots Leigh Rd BS8... **7** C7
Abbots Leys Rd GL54 .. **139** F5
Abbots Mews GL52..... **137** E2
Abbots Rd
 Bristol BS15........... **10** C2
 Cinderford GL14 ...... **191** E3
 Cirencester GL7........ **190** E4
 Gloucester GL4........ **119** E6
Abbot's Rd GL20....... **192** C2
Abbots View GL14...... **191** D1
Abbots Way
 Bristol BS9............. **18** E6
 Stonehouse GL10......... **97** E6
Abbots Wlk GL7........ **153** E2
Abbotswood
 Bristol BS15........... **10** D7
 Yate BS37.............. **29** C2
Abbotswood Cl GL4.... **118** D3
Abbotswood Prim Sch
 BS37.................. **32** D6
Abbotswood Rd GL3 .. **120** F4
Abbott Rd BS35........ **38** A5
Abbotts Way GL7...... **141** F8
Abenhall Rd GL17...... **164** D5
Aberdeen Rd BS6...... **194** B4
Abingdon Court La SN6 . **143** F4
Abingdon Rd BS3........ **8** E3
Ableton Ct BS35....... **38** A6
Ableton La
 Compton Greenfield BS10.. **38** A1
 Severn Beach BS35....... **38** A5
Ableton Wlk BS9....... **17** C5

Abnash GL6 .... **148** C6
Abon Ho BS9 .... **17** C4
Abraham Cl BS5 ....9 B8
Abraham Fry Ho BS15... **10** E7
Abson Rd
 Pucklechurch BS16...... **22** C3
 Wick BS30............. **12** C8
Acacia Ave BS16....... **20** D4
Acacia Cl
 9 Bream GL15........ **147** D8
 Bristol BS16........... **20** D3
 Cheltenham GL52....... **134** A5
 Newnham GL14 .... **157** A7
Acacia Ct
 Cheltenham GL51....... **132** C2
 Keynsham BS31............4 C4
Acacia Dr GL11......... **88** A3
Acacia Mews **4** BS16 .. **20** D4
Acacia Pk GL52........ **137** D4
Acacia Rd BS16........ **20** D4
Academy The GL50..... **193** B4
Acer Cres BS32 .... **40** E5
Acer Gr GL2 .... **117** E2
Acer Village BS14...... **3** C7
Acid Rd BS11.......... **26** C4
Acomb Cres GL52...... **131** B6
Acorn Ct **9** GL4 ...... **119** C4
Acorn Gr BS13 ....1 E6
Acorn Sch The GL6.... **91** C4
Acorn Wy GL2 .... **110** A5
Acraman's Rd **7** BS3 ... **8** C4
Acresbush Cl BS13....... **2** A5
Acre St GL5........... **99** C7
Acton Rd BS16.......... **20** A3
Acton Turville Rd GL9 .. **35** B4
Adams Ct **6** BS8........ **7** F6
Adams Hay **6** BS4 ..... **9** D1
Adams Land BS36....... **31** C7
Adams Way **7** GL16... **155** A7
Adderly Gate BS16..... **21** B7
Addiscombe Rd BS14.... **3** B5
Addison Rd BS3..........8 E3
Addis Rd GL51 .... **133** B3
Addymore Cl GL11...... **87** F5
Adelaide Gdns GL10.... **101** F1
Adelaide Pl
 Bristol, Fishponds BS16 ... **19** F4

Adelaide Pl *continued*
 12 Bristol, Upper Easton BS5 **9** B8
Adelaide St GL1........ **119** A7
Adelaide Terr **1** BS16... **20** A4
Adelante Cl BS34 ...... **30** A4
Adey's La GL12 .... **68** B8
Admington La CV36 .... **189** D7
Admington Lane Units
 CV36.................. **189** E7
Admiral Cl
 Bristol BS16........... **19** E7
 Cheltenham GL51....... **132** D2
Admirals Cl **6** GL15.... **155** D1
Adryan Ct **6** BS5 ...... **9** C7
Aesops Orch GL52 ..... **138** C3
Agate St BS3 ....8 B3
Aggs Cl GL52 .... **138** A8
Aggs Hill GL54 .... **134** D1
Aggs La GL52 .... **138** A8
Aiken St BS5 ....9 B6
Aintree Dr BS16........ **30** F1
Air Balloon Ct **1** BS5 .... **10** A7
Air Balloon Hill Prim Sch
 BS5.................. **10** A7
Air Balloon Rd BS5..... **10** A7
Airport Rd BS14.......... **3** A8
Airthrie Sch GL50...... **133** B1
Aisne Rd GL15 .... **156** B1
Akeman Rd GL7........ **190** E4
Akeman Way BS11 ..... **16** C8
Akermans Orch GL18.... **170** F4
Akers Ct SN26 .... **144** E1
Alanscourt BS30 .... **11** B5
Alard Rd BS4............2 F7
Al-Ashraf Prim Sch GL1 **196** C1
Al-Ashraf Sec Sch for Girls
 GL1................... **196** C2
Alaska Ave GL7 .... **152** E1
Albany GL10 .... **101** E1
Albany Gate BS34 ..... **29** E5
Albany Ho **7** GL50 .... **130** B8
Albany Mews GL50..... **193** A2
Albany Rd
 Bristol BS6............. **18** F1
 Cheltenham GL50....... **130** B7
Albany St
 Bristol BS15........... **10** C8
 Gloucester GL1 .... **118** F7

1st–Alb

Albany Way BS30 ...... **11** C5
Albemarle Gate GL50... **133** E4
Albemarle Rd GL3..... **128** D5
Albemarle Row **10** BS8...**7** F6
Albemarle Terr **2** BS8 ...**7** F6
Albert Cl BS30......... **11** D5
Albert Cres BS2..........9 B5
Albert Ct GL52 .... **133** F3
Albert Dr GL52........ **133** F4
Albert Gr BS5.............9 F8
Albert Gr S BS5...........9 F8
Albert Pk BS16........ **19** F6
Albert Par BS5.......... **9** D8
Albert Park Pl BS6 ..... **18** F1
Albert Pk BS6.......... **18** F1
Albert Pl
 1 Bristol, Bedminster BS3.. **8** C3
 Bristol, Eastfield BS9...... **18** A7
 Cheltenham GL52....... **193** C4
Albert Rd
 Brimscombe GL5 ...... **99** F1
 Bristol, Hanham BS15 ..... **10** D5
 Bristol, St Philip's Marsh BS2 **9** A4
 Bristol, Staple Hill BS16 ... **20** E4
 Cheltenham GL52....... **133** F3
 Cinderford GL14 ...... **191** C3
 Coleford GL16......... **155** A5
 Keynsham BS31.......... **4** E5
 Ledbury HR8 .... **178** E8
 Severn Beach BS35...... **38** A6
Albert St
 Bristol BS5.............. **9** C8
 Cheltenham GL50....... **133** D3
 Gloucester GL1 .... **196** C2
 Lydney GL15........... **92** B3
Albert Terr BS16....... **19** F4
Albion Cl BS16......... **20** F5
Albion Ct GL10......... **97** F7
Albion Pl
 18 Bristol BS2.......... **195** C3
 Cheltenham GL52....... **193** C4
Albion Rd
 Bristol BS5............ **19** B1
 Cinderford GL14 ...... **191** D6

Albion Sq **1** NP16 . . . . 60 E8
Albion St
  6 Bristol BS5 . . . . 9 C8
  Cheltenham GL52 . . . . 193 C3
  Gloucester GL1 . . . . 196 A6
  Stratton GL7 . . . . 190 B7
Albion Terr
  Bristol BS34 . . . . 40 B1
  Stonehouse GL10 . . . . 97 E6
Albion Wlk GL50 . . . . 193 C4
Albright La HR8 . . . . 179 D4
Alcotts Gn GL2 . . . . 172 F4
Alcove Rd BS16 . . . . 19 F3
Alcove Wood/Coed Cilfach
  NP16 . . . . 60 C8
Alden Ho BS36 . . . . 30 D4
Alder Cl
  Gloucester GL2 . . . . 127 C4
  Walford HR9 . . . . 163 C8
Alder Ct
  Bristol BS14 . . . . 3 B5
  Cheltenham BS11 . . . . 132 C2
Alderdale GL15 . . . . 92 B4
Alderdown Cl BS11 . . . . 17 A8
Alder Dr BS5 . . . . 19 E1
Aldergate St GL10 . . . . 97 F7
Aldergate Terr **6** GL10 . . . 97 F7
Aldergrove **5** GL12 . . . . . 110 B8
Alderley Rd GL12 . . . . 68 D1
Alderman Knight Sch
  GL20 . . . . 182 B4
Alderman Twr BS6 . . . . 18 C3
Aldermoor Way BS30 . . . . 10 E4
Alderney Ave BS4 . . . . 9 F4
Alderney Flats **1** GL2 . . . 127 B2
Alders Gn GL2 . . . . 127 B5
Aldershaw Cl GL51 . . . . 129 D6
Alders The
  Bristol BS16 . . . . 30 B1
  Cheltenham GL53 . . . . 130 B4
Alderton Cl GL4 . . . . 119 E4
Alderton Rd
  Bristol BS7 . . . . 18 E8
  Burton SN14 . . . . 36 D6
  Cheltenham GL51 . . . . 129 E8
Alder Way **7** GL6 . . . . . . 148 C6
Aldridge Cl GL50 . . . . 133 C3
Aldsworth Cl GL7 . . . . 152 F4
Aldsworth Road Est GL7 . 160 D8
Aldwick Ave BS13 . . . . 2 C3
Aldworth Ho BS2 . . . . 195 C4
Alexander Ct **4** BS3 . . . . . 8 A3
Alexander Dr GL7 . . . . 190 C2
Alexander Gdns **10** GL8 . 140 B4
Alexander Hosea Prim Sch
  GL12 . . . . 54 B5
Alexandra Apartments
  BS6 . . . . 18 C3
Alexandra Cl
  Bristol BS16 . . . . 20 D4
  Dursley GL11 . . . . 88 B3
Alexandra Ct BS16 . . . . 19 F4
Alexandra Gdns BS16 . . . . . . 20 D4
Alexandra Pk
  Bristol, Cotham BS6 . . . . 18 C2
  Bristol, Ridgeway BS16 . . . . . 19 F4
Alexandra Pl BS16 . . . . 20 D4
Alexandra Rd
  Bristol, Clifton BS8 . . . . 194 B4
  Bristol, Eastfield BS10 . . . . . 18 C8
  Bristol, Hanham BS15 . . . . . . 10 D5
  Bristol, Highridge BS13 . . . . . .1 F7
  Chepstow/Cas-Gwent NP16 60 F6
  Coalpit Heath BS36 . . . . 31 D7
  Gloucester GL1 . . . . 127 A3
Alexandra St GL50 . . . . 130 B7
Alexandra Way
  Northway GL20 . . . . 182 B4
  Thornbury BS35 . . . . 64 B3
Alexandria Wlk GL52 . . . . . . 134 B2
Alex Farm SN6 . . . . 144 B4
Alex Wy
  Randwick GL6 . . . . 102 F4
  Whiteshill GL7 . . . . 102 F4
Alford Rd BS4 . . . . 9 C2
Alfred Hill BS2 . . . . 195 A4
Alfred Lovell Gdns **7**
  BS30 . . . . 11 A4
Alfred Par BS2 . . . . 195 A4
Alfred Pl
  Bristol BS1 . . . . 195 A1
  Bristol, Tyndall's Park BS2 194 C4
Alfred Rd
  Bristol, Westbury Park
    BS6 . . . . 18 A4
  Bristol, Windmill Hill BS3 . . . . 8 D3
Alfred St
  Bristol, Moorfields BS5 . . . . . 9 D8
  Bristol, Newton BS2 . . . . 9 A6
  Gloucester GL1 . . . . 119 A8
Algars Dr BS37 . . . . 42 E3
Algiers St BS3 . . . . 8 D3
Alice Cres NP16 . . . . 61 A4
Alington Cl **7** GL1 . . . . . 127 A1
Alkerton Cl GL10 . . . . 96 F7
Alkerton Terr GL10 . . . . 96 F7
All Alone GL54 . . . . 168 A1
Allanmead Rd BS14 . . . . .3 B8
Allaston Rd GL15 . . . . 92 B6
Allendale Cl GL2 . . . . 127 C4
Allen Dr GL5 . . . . 99 A8
Allenfield Rd GL53 . . . . 130 C5

Allengrove La SN14 . . . . 47 C3
Allen's Almhouses The **12**
  GL54 . . . . 168 A1
Allerton Cres BS14 . . . . .3 B4
Allerton Gdns BS14 . . . . .3 B4
Allerton Rd BS14 . . . . .3 B4
Allfoxton Rd BS7 . . . . 19 A3
All Hallows Ct **11** BS5 . . . . 9 B8
All Hallows Rd BS5 . . . . .9 B8
Allington Dr BS30 . . . . 10 F4
Allington Rd BS3 . . . . 194 C1
Allison Ave BS4 . . . . 9 F4
Allison Rd BS4 . . . . 9 E3
Allotment La GL7 . . . . 151 C5
All Saints' Acad GL51 . . . . . 132 F4
All Saints Cl BS30 . . . . 11 A3
All Saint's Ct **19** GL52 . . 133 F2
All Saints Fields GL5 . . . . 99 E7
All Saints Ho BS2 . . . . 195 B4
All Saint's La BS1 . . . . 195 A3
All Saints Mans BS8 . . . . 194 A4
All Saints Rd
  Blakeney GL15 . . . . 156 E2
  Stroud GL5 . . . . 99 D8
All Saints' Rd
  Bristol BS8 . . . . 194 A4
  Cheltenham GL52 . . . . 133 F2
  Gloucester GL1 . . . . 196 C1
All Saints' St BS1 . . . . 195 A3
All Saints' Terr GL52 . . . . . . 133 F1
All Saints' Villas Rd GL52 133 F2
Allsopp Cl GL14 . . . . 156 F6
Alma Cl
  Bristol BS15 . . . . 10 E8
  Cheltenham GL51 . . . . 129 F7
Alma Dr NP16 . . . . 61 A4
Alma Pl GL1 . . . . 118 D7
Alma Rd
  Bristol, Clifton BS8 . . . . 194 B4
  Bristol, Kingswood BS15 . . . . 20 E1
  Cheltenham GL51 . . . . 129 F7
Alma Road Ave BS8 . . . . 194 B4
Alma St BS8 . . . . 18 B1
Alma Terr
  Gloucester GL1 . . . . 118 D7
  Stroud GL5 . . . . 98 F8
Alma Vale Rd BS8 . . . . 194 A4
Almeda Rd BS5 . . . . 10 A6
Almhouses GL7 . . . . 190 C4
Almond Cl GL4 . . . . 119 D3
Almond Cl GL51 . . . . 132 C2
Almondsbury Bsns Ctr
  BS32 . . . . 40 D3
Almondsbury CE Prim Sch
  BS32 . . . . 40 E4
Almondsbury Intc BS32 . . . 40 E4
Almond Way BS16 . . . . 20 F5
Almond Wlk GL15 . . . . 92 B4
Almorah Rd BS3 . . . . .8 E3
Alms Cl GL3 . . . . 128 B5
Almshouses
  11 Chipping Campden
    GL55 . . . . 189 A2
  Marshfield SN14 . . . . 14 E8
  1 Wotton-u-E GL12 . . . . 68 B7
Almshouses Rd GL16 . . . . . . 154 E4
Almshouses The GL54 . . . . . 176 F4
Alney Terr GL1 . . . . 126 C3
Alpha Cl GL20 . . . . 182 B4
Alpha Ctr The BS37 . . . . 43 C3
Alpha Rd
  Bristol BS3 . . . . 8 D4
  Chepstow/Cas-Gwent NP16 60 F6
Alpine Cl GL4 . . . . 119 B6
Alpine Rd BS5 . . . . 19 C1
Alsop Rd **8** BS15 . . . . 20 D1
Alstone Ave GL51 . . . . 133 B2
Alstone Croft GL51 . . . . 133 B2
Alstone Ct **1** GL51 . . . . . 133 B2
Alstone La GL51 . . . . 133 A2
Alstone Lane Trad Est
  GL51 . . . . 133 A1
Alstone Mews GL51 . . . . 133 B2
Althorp Cl GL4 . . . . 118 B2
Alton Court Rd HR8 . . . . 178 A7
Alton Rd BS7 . . . . 18 F5
Altringham Rd BS5 . . . . 9 D8
Alverstoke BS14 . . . . .2 F7
Alverton Dr GL52 . . . . 137 C2
Alveston Grange GL51 . . . . 189 A6
Alveston Hill BS35 . . . . 51 A6
Alveston Rd BS32 . . . . 50 D3
Alveston Wlk BS9 . . . . 17 B7
Alvington Dr GL52 . . . . 134 C2
Alvin St GL1 . . . . 196 C3
Alwins Ct **2** BS30 . . . . 10 F4
Amaranth Way **4** GL51 . 129 F5
Amazing Hedge Puzzle The★
  HR9 . . . . 162 E4
Amber Cl GL4 . . . . 118 C3
Amberley Cl
  Bristol BS16 . . . . 20 D7
  Keynsham BS31 . . . . 4 E4
Amberley Ct **10** GL20 . . . . 182 B4
Amberley House Sch BS8 18 A1
Amberley Parochial Sch
  GL5 . . . . 91 C7
Amberley Rd
  Bristol, Kingswood BS16 . . . . 20 D7
  Bristol, Patchway BS34 . . . . . 29 B8
  9 Cheltenham GL51 . . . . 132 E2
  Gloucester GL4 . . . . 119 B5
Amberley Way GL12 . . . . 54 B4
Amble Cl BS15 . . . . 10 F7
Ambleside Ave BS10 . . . . 28 B2

Ambra Ct BS8 . . . . 194 A2
Ambra Terr BS8 . . . . 194 A2
Ambra Vale BS8 . . . . 194 A2
Ambra Vale E BS8 . . . . 194 A2
Ambra Vale S BS8 . . . . 194 A2
Ambra Vale W BS8 . . . . 194 A2
Ambrose La **1** GL16 . . . . 155 B5
Ambrose Pl GL50 . . . . 193 B4
Ambrose Rd BS8 . . . . 194 A2
Ambrose St GL50 . . . . 193 B4
Amercombe Wlk BS14 . . . . . . 3 D7
America Gdns GL18 . . . . 171 A4
Amos Cl GL50 . . . . 193 A4
Ampney Crucis CE Prim Sch
  GL7 . . . . 151 C5
Ampney La GL14 . . . . 165 D3
Ampney Mill Cotts GL7 . . 151 C4
Amport La GL4 . . . . 110 C8
Anapa Mews **15** GL51 . . . 132 E2
Anbrook Cres GL4 . . . . 119 E7
Anchorage The
  Gloucester GL4 . . . . 118 B6
  Lower Lydbrook GL17 . . . . 163 C3
Anchor Cl BS5 . . . . 9 F6
Anchor Ho BS4 . . . . .9 B2
Anchor La BS1 . . . . 194 C2
Anchor Rd
  Bristol, Canon's Marsh
    BS1 . . . . 194 C2
  Bristol, Kingswood BS15 . . . 21 A2
Anchor Sq BS1 . . . . 194 C2
Anchor Way BS20 . . . . 16 D4
Ancient Rd GL16 . . . . 162 F1
Andalusia Acad Bristol
  BS2 . . . . 195 C3
Andereach Cl BS14 . . . . .3 B8
Anderson Cl GL52 . . . . 138 B3
Anderson Dr **3** GL10 . . . . 97 F7
Andorra Way GL3 . . . . 128 B6
Andover Cl GL50 . . . . 193 A1
Andover Rd
  Bristol BS4 . . . . .8 F2
  Cheltenham GL50 . . . . 193 A1
Andoversford Ind Est
  GL54 . . . . 166 A2
Andoversford Link GL54 166 D6
Andoversford Prim Sch
  GL54 . . . . 166 D6
Andover St GL50 . . . . 193 A1
Andover Terr GL50 . . . . 193 A2
Andover Wlk GL50 . . . . 193 A1
Andrew Millman Ct BS37 . 43 F1
Andrew's Cl GL4 . . . . 110 F5
Andrew's Cnr GL15 . . . . 146 E7
Andruss Dr BS41 . . . . 1 D2
Angel Field GL16 . . . . 155 A5
Angelica Way GL4 . . . . 119 F5
Angel La GL55 . . . . 186 B8
Angels Gd BS4 . . . . 9 F6
Angers Rd BS4 . . . . 9 A4
Anglesea Pl **16** BS8 . . . . . 18 A2
Anlaby Ct GL52 . . . . 133 F2
Ann Cam CE Prim Sch
  GL18 . . . . 178 D2
Ann Edwards CE Prim Sch
  GL7 . . . . 142 F7
Anne Edwards Mews
  GL4 . . . . 119 D4
Anne Hathaway Dr GL3 . . . 128 E5
Ann Goodrich Cl GL52 . . . 134 C4
Annie Scott Cl **2** BS16 . . 20 A4
Anns Wlk GL17 . . . . 164 D4
Ann Wicks Rd GL2 . . . . 100 A5
Ansdell Dr GL3 . . . . 120 E6
Ansell Cl GL51 . . . . 129 F6
Anson Bsns Pk GL51 . . . . . 173 E1
Anson Cl BS31 . . . . 5 D2
Ansteys Cl BS15 . . . . 10 B5
Anstey's Ct BS15 . . . . 10 C5
Anstey's Rd BS15 . . . . 10 C5
Anstey St BS5 . . . . 19 B1
Antelope Paddock **11**
  GL54 . . . . 168 A1
Anthea Rd BS5 . . . . 19 E2
Anthony Cl SN16 . . . . 58 C1
Anthony Ct GL6 . . . . 148 C5
Antona Cl BS11 . . . . 16 D7
Antona Dr BS11 . . . . 16 D7
Antrim Rd BS9 . . . . 18 B6
Anvil Cl GL11 . . . . 80 C8
Anvil St BS2 . . . . 195 C2
A P Ellis Rd GL54 . . . . 169 D6
Apna Ghar Ct GL1 . . . . 119 A8
Apperley Cl BS37 . . . . 32 E8
Apperley Dr GL2 . . . . 117 C1
Apperley Pk GL19 . . . . 173 C7
Apple Blossom Cl GL15 . . 92 B3
Appleby Wlk BS4 . . . . 2 D7
Apple Cl GL52 . . . . 134 A5
Apple Orch GL52 . . . . 134 A5
Apple Orchard Cl GL54 . 183 E1
Apple Orch The GL20 . . . . . 182 C5
Appleridge La GL13 . . . . 77 C4
Appleton Ave GL51 . . . . 129 B6
Appleton Way GL3 . . . . 120 A6
Apple Tree Cl
  4 Churchdown GL3 . . . 128 C4
  Gloucester GL4 . . . . 119 E4
  Woodmancote GL52 . . . . . . 138 C2
Appleyard Cl GL51 . . . . 132 E5
Applin Gn BS16 . . . . 21 C6
Apprentice Cl NP16 . . . . 61 B4
Approach The GL54 . . . . 160 E5
April Cl GL11 . . . . 80 A8

Apseleys Mead BS32 . . . . . 40 C2
Apsley Cl GL7 . . . . 190 B3
Apsley Garden Apartments
  BS6 . . . . 18 E2
Apsley Mews BS8 . . . . 18 A2
Apsley Rd
  Bristol BS8 . . . . 18 A1
  Cirencester GL7 . . . . 190 B2
Apsley St BS5 . . . . 19 C3
Aragon Ho GL54 . . . . 139 F5
Aragon Way GL3 . . . . 127 C4
Arbour Cl GL25 . . . . 189 A6
Arbour Elms GL19 . . . . 181 C5
Arbutus Dr BS9 . . . . 17 C8
Arcade Mews BS8 . . . . 194 A3
Arcade The BS1 . . . . 195 B3
Archdeacon Ct GL1 . . . . 196 A3
Archdeacon St GL1 . . . . 196 A3
Archer Ct BS30 . . . . 10 F3
Archers La GL52 . . . . 136 D5
Archers The SN6 . . . . 145 C3
Archer Wlk BS14 . . . . 3 E6
Archery Rd GL7 . . . . 190 E4
Arches The **1** BS5 . . . . 9 B7
Archfield Ct BS6 . . . . 18 C1
Archfield Rd BS6 . . . . 18 C1
Archibald St GL1 . . . . 196 C1
Archway Cl GL14 . . . . 156 C5
Archway Ct GL17 . . . . 164 D5
Archway Gdns GL5 . . . . 99 A8
Archway Sch GL5 . . . . 98 F8
Ardagh Ct BS7 . . . . 18 F7
Ardea Ct GL2 . . . . 117 D1
Arden Cl BS32 . . . . 29 E6
Arden Ho GL2 . . . . 118 C4
Arden Rd GL53 . . . . 130 C5
Ardenton Wlk BS10 . . . . 28 A3
Ardern Cl BS9 . . . . 17 B8
Ardmore BS8 . . . . 7 D7
Ardmore Ct GL4 . . . . 118 E2
Argus Ct BS3 . . . . 8 C2
Argus Rd BS3 . . . . 8 C3
Argyle Ave BS5 . . . . 19 C2
Argyle Pl BS8 . . . . 194 A2
Argyle Rd
  Bristol, Chester Park
    BS16 . . . . 20 B2
  Bristol, St Pauls BS2 . . . . . 195 B4
Argyle St
  5 Bristol, Eastville BS5 . . 19 C2
  6 Bristol, Southville BS3 . . 8 C4
Argyll Mews GL53 . . . . 193 C1
Argyll Pl GL2 . . . . 127 B2
Argyll Rd
  Cheltenham GL53 . . . . 130 F8
  Gloucester GL2 . . . . 127 B2
Ariel Lodge Rd GL52 . . . . . 133 F2
Arkells Ct GL12 . . . . 54 A6
Arkendale Dr GL2 . . . . 109 D8
Arkle Cl GL50 . . . . 133 C5
Arle Ave GL51 . . . . 133 B2
Arle Cl GL51 . . . . 133 A3
Arle Cotts GL51 . . . . 132 F4
Arle Gdns GL51 . . . . 133 A3
Arlebrook GL10 . . . . 102 A5
Arley Cotts **4** BS6 . . . . . . 18 D1
Arley Hill BS6 . . . . 18 D1
Arley Pk BS6 . . . . 18 D1
Arley Terr BS5 . . . . 19 E1
Arlingdon Fields GL7 . . . . 142 D6
Arlingham **13** GL51 . . . . . 129 E5
Arlingham Rd GL4 . . . . 118 D4
Arlingham Way BS34 . . . . . . 39 F1
Arlington Cnr GL7 . . . . 160 A1
Arlington Ct NP16 . . . . 61 B8
Arlington Mews BS8 . . . . . . 194 B4
Arlington Mill Mus★
  GL7 . . . . 160 A1
Arlington Pike GL7 . . . . 159 F1
Arlington Rd
  Bristol BS4 . . . . 9 D5
  Gloucester GL3 . . . . 120 B4
  Tewkesbury GL20 . . . . 192 E2
Arlington Row★ GL7 . . . . 160 A1
Arlington Villas BS8 . . . . . . 194 B3
Armada Cl GL3 . . . . 127 F7
Armada Ho BS2 . . . . 195 A4
Armada Pl BS1 . . . . 195 A4
Armada Rd BS14 . . . . 3 A6
Armidale Ave **4** BS6 . . . . 18 E1
Armidale Cotts **5** BS6 . . 18 E1
Armoury Sq BS5 . . . . 9 A8
Armscroft Cres GL2 . . . . . . 127 B2
Armscroft Ct GL2 . . . . 127 C1
Armscroft Gdns GL2 . . . . . 127 B1
Armscroft Pl GL2 . . . . 127 B1
Armscroft Rd GL2 . . . . 127 C1
Armscroft Way GL2 . . . . 127 B1
Armstrong Cl BS35 . . . . 51 D7
Armstrong Ct BS37 . . . . 43 C3
Armstrong Dr BS30 . . . . 11 B5
Armstrong Rd GL52 . . . . . . 136 D5
Armstrong Way BS37 . . . . . 43 B3
Arnall Dr BS10 . . . . 27 F1
Arncliffe BS10 . . . . 18 C8
Arneside Rd BS10 . . . . 28 C1
Arnold Ct BS37 . . . . 44 B1
Arnold Rd BS16 . . . . 21 B3
Arnolds Field Trad Est
  GL12 . . . . 54 A5
Arnold's La GL6 . . . . 91 B3
Arnolds Way GL7 . . . . 190 E5
Arnolfini (Art Ctr)★ BS1 195 A1

Arno's St BS4 . . . . 9 A3
Arran Way SN6 . . . . 145 C4
Arreton Ave GL4 . . . . 119 C6
Arrowfield Cl BS14 . . . . 3 A2
Arrowhead Cl GL4 . . . . 119 B4
Arrowsmith Dr GL10 . . . . . 101 F1
Arthur Bliss Gdns **3**
  GL50 . . . . 130 B6
Arthur Cooper Way
  GL16 . . . . 155 A4
Arthur Milton St BS7 . . . . . 18 F4
Arthurs Cl BS16 . . . . 21 C6
Arthur Skemp Cl BS5 . . . . . .9 B7
Arthur St
  7 Bristol, Moorfields BS5 . . 9 C8
  Bristol, St Philip's Marsh BS2 9 A5
  Gloucester GL1 . . . . 196 B2
Arthurswood Rd BS13 . . . . . 2 A4
Arundel Cl
  Bristol BS13 . . . . 2 B5
  Gloucester BS13 . . . . 118 C1
Arundel Ct BS7 . . . . 18 D3
Arundel Dr GL5 . . . . 99 B6
Arundel Ho **12** GL51 . . . 132 E2
Arundell Mill La GL5 . . . . . . 99 D6
Arundel Rd
  Bristol BS7 . . . . 18 D3
  Tewkesbury GL20 . . . . 192 E6
Arundel Wlk BS31 . . . . 4 D5
Ascot Cl BS16 . . . . 30 F1
Ascot Ct GL1 . . . . 119 A8
Ascot Rd BS10 . . . . 28 E2
Ashbed Cl GL4 . . . . 119 E6
Ashbourne Cl **1** BS30 . . . 11 C6
Ashbrittle Rd GL3 . . . . 120 B4
Ashbrook La GL7 . . . . 151 E4
Ashburton Rd BS10 . . . . 28 C1
Ashchurch for Tewkesbury
  Sta GL20 . . . . 182 C4
Ashchurch Ind Est GL20 . 182 C4
Ashchurch Prim Sch
  GL20 . . . . 182 C4
Ashchurch Rd GL20 . . . . . . 192 E4
Ash Cl
  Bristol, Hillfields BS16 . . . . . 20 C3
  Bristol, Little Stoke BS34 . . . 29 D7
  Charlton Kings GL53 . . . . . 131 C4
  Chepstow/Cas-Gwent NP16 60 E5
  Dursley GL11 . . . . 88 A4
  Lydney GL15 . . . . 92 B4
  Yate BS37 . . . . 43 B3
Ashcombe Cres BS30 . . . . 11 D6
Ashcot Mews **3** GL51 . . 129 E5
Ashcott BS14 . . . . .2 F7
Ashcroft Cl GL4 . . . . 119 D2
Ashcroft Ave BS31 . . . . 4 D5
Ashcroft Gdns GL7 . . . . 190 C4
Ashcroft Ho GL5 . . . . 99 D5
Ashcroft Rd
  Bristol BS9 . . . . 17 C7
  Cirencester GL7 . . . . 190 C4
  Wotton-u-E GL8, GL12 . . . . 81 D3
Ash Ct BS14 . . . . 3 A6
Ashdale Cl GL54 . . . . 160 E5
Ashdean GL14 . . . . 191 C5
Ashdene Ave BS5 . . . . 19 D3
Ash Dene Rd GL17 . . . . 163 E3
Ashdown Ct BS9 . . . . 17 F8
Asher La BS2 . . . . 195 C3
Ashes La HR9 . . . . 162 E4
Ashfield SN6 . . . . 143 A5
Ashfield Cl GL52 . . . . 138 A3
Ashfield Ho GL50 . . . . 193 A3
Ashfield Pl BS6 . . . . 18 F1
Ashfield Rd
  Bristol BS3 . . . . 8 B3
  Ruardean Hill GL17 . . . . . . 164 A3
Ashfield Terr **8** BS3 . . . . . .8 B3
Ashford Rd
  Bristol BS34 . . . . 29 A7
  Cheltenham GL50 . . . . 193 A4
Ashford Way BS15 . . . . 11 A2
Ash Gr
  Bristol BS16 . . . . 20 D3
  Bussage GL6 . . . . 148 B6
  Mitcheldean GL17 . . . . 164 D6
  Upton St Leonards GL4 . . . 119 E3
Ashgrove
  Charlton Kings GL53 . . . . . 131 C4
  Thornbury BS35 . . . . 64 C1
Ashgrove Ave
  Abbots Leigh BS8 . . . . 7 B7
  Bristol BS7 . . . . 18 F4
  Gloucester BS13 . . . . 119 C6
Ashgrove Cl
  Bristol BS7 . . . . 18 F4
  Hardwicke GL2 . . . . 109 E7
Ashgrove Cotts GL6 . . . . . . 102 F4
Ash Grove Pl GL15 . . . . 156 B3
Ashgrove Rd
  Bristol, Ashley Down BS7 . . 18 F4
  Bristol, Bedminster BS3 . . . . 8 B3
Ashgrove Way GL4 . . . . 119 C6
Ash La
  Down Hatherley GL2 . . . . . 173 B1
  Over BS32 . . . . 39 D2
  Randwick GL6 . . . . 102 C3
Ashland Rd BS13 . . . . 2 A4
Ashlands Cl GL51 . . . . 132 E3
Ashlands Rd GL51 . . . . 132 E3
Ashlea Mdws GL52 . . . . 137 D4
Ashleigh La GL52 . . . . 138 D1
Ashletts Rd GL6 . . . . 106 C1
Ashleworth CE Prim Sch
  GL19 . . . . 172 D4
Ashleworth Gdns GL2 . . . 109 E8

Ashleworth Tithe Barn★
GL19 . . . .**172** D4
Ashley BS15 . . . . **10** F8
Ashley Cl
  Bristol BS7 . . . . **18** F4
  Charlton Kings GL52 . . **131** B7
Ashley Court Rd 2 BS7 . . **18** F2
Ashley Ct BS2 . . . . **18** F1
Ashley Down Rd BS7 . . . . **18** F4
Ashley Down Schs BS7 . . **18** F5
Ashley Dr 2 GL6 . . . . . . **148** B6
Ashley Grove Rd
  7 Bristol BS2 . . . . **18** F2
  1 Bristol BS2 . . . . **19** A1
Ashley Hill BS6, BS7 . . . . **18** F2
Ashley Ho BS34 . . . . **39** F1
Ashley Lo GL53 . . . . **130** C6
Ashley Par BS2 . . . . **18** F2
Ashley Pk BS6 . . . . **18** F3
Ashley Rd
  Bristol BS6 . . . . **18** E1
  Cheltenham GL52 . . . . **131** B8
Ashley St BS2 . . . . **19** A1
Ashley Trad Est **6** BS2 . . **18** F2
Ashman Cl BS5 . . . . **9** A8
Ashman Ct 1 BS16 . . . . . **19** E3
Ashmead BS34 . . . . **127** B5
Ashmead Ct GL3 . . . . **128** A7
Ashmead Dr GL52 . . . . . . **138** A8
Ashmead Ho 12 BS5 . . . . . . **9** C7
Ashmead Pk BS31 . . . . **5** B5
Ashmead Rd
  Cinderford GL14 . . . . . **191** D3
  Keynsham BS31 . . . . **5** B5
Ashmead Road Ind Est
  BS31 . . . . **5** B5
Ashmead Way 8 BS1 . . . . **7** F5
Ashmore Rd GL4 . . . . **118** F4
Ashover La GL50 . . . . **193** A1
Ash Path The GL4 . . . . . . **119** E3
Ash Rd
  Bristol BS7 . . . . **18** E5
  Northway GL20 . . . . . . **182** C4
  Stroud GL5 . . . . **99** A4
Ash Ridge Rd BS32 . . . . . **40** B3
Ash The GL6 . . . . **102** C2
Ashton BS16 . . . . **30** C1
Ashton Ave BS1 . . . . **194** A1
Ashton Cl GL4 . . . . **119** E3
Ashton Court Estate★
  BS41 . . . . **7** C4
Ashton Dr BS3 . . . . **7** C4
Ashton Gate Prim Sch BS3 . **8** A4
Ashton Gate Rd BS3 . . . . . . **8** A4
Ashton Gate Stad(Bristol City
  FC) BS3 . . . . **7** F3
Ashton Gate Terr 4 BS3 . . **8** A4
Ashton Gate Trad Est BS3 . . **7** E3
Ashton Gate Underpass
  BS3 . . . . **7** F3
Ashton Keynes CE Prim Sch
  SN6 . . . . **142** F5
Ashton Park Sch BS3 . . . . . **7** E4
Ashton Rd
  Ashton Keynes SN6 . . . **142** F3
  Beckford GL20 . . . . **183** B6
  Bristol, Ashton Gate BS3 . . **7** F4
  Bristol, Bower Ashton BS3,
    BS41 . . . . **7** D3
  Siddington GL7 . . . . . . **150** E1
Ashton Vale Prim Sch BS3 . . **7** F2
Ashton Vale Rd BS3 . . . . . . **7** E2
Ashton Vale Trad Est BS3 . . **7** F1
Ashton Way BS31 . . . . **4** E6
Ash Tree Cl 28 GL18 . . . . **171** A4
Ashtree Mews GL51 . . . . **133** A1
Ashville Bsns Pk GL2 . . . . **173** B8
Ashville Ind Est GL2 . . . . **118** C5
Ashville Rd
  Bristol BS3 . . . . **8** A4
  Gloucester GL2 . . . . . . **118** C5
Ashville Trad Est GL51 . . . **133** B6
Ashway 17 GL54 . . . . **168** A1
Ash Way GL15 . . . . **147** C3
Ashway Ct GL5 . . . . **98** E7
Ashway Ho GL5 . . . . **98** E7
Ashwell GL6 . . . . **103** F8
Ashwell Cl BS14 . . . . **3** E6
Ashwicke BS14 . . . . **3** A6
Ashwicke Rd SN14 . . . . . . **15** B3
Ashwood Way GL3 . . . . . . **119** F6
Ashworth Cl GL11 . . . . **88** B3
Askham Ct 8 GL52 . . . . **133** F2
Askwith Rd GL4 . . . . **119** B6
Aspen Cl SN14 . . . . **15** F6
Aspen Dr GL2 . . . . **117** E2
Asquith Rd GL53 . . . . **130** E6
Assembly Rooms La BS1 . . **195** A2
Aston Bank HR9 . . . . **170** C2
Aston Bridge Rd GL17 . . . **163** E3
Aston Cl
  Berry Hill GL54 . . . . . . **155** A4
  16 Ledbury HR8 . . . . . **178** E8
Aston Farm Cotts GL8 . . **148** C1
Aston Gr
  Cheltenham GL51 . . . . **132** D2
  Cold Aston GL54 . . . . . **168** B6
Aston Ho 4 BS1 . . . . **195** B4
Aston Rd GL55 . . . . **188** F3
Aston View GL6 . . . . **148** C6
Astor Cl GL3 . . . . **120** D6
Astridge Rd GL3 . . . . **121** A4
Astry Cl BS11 . . . . **27** A1
at-Bristol★ BS1 . . . . **194** C2
Atchley St 18 BS5 . . . . **9** B7

Atcombe Rd GL5 . . . . **90** F8
Athelney Way 4 GL52 . . . **130** F8
Athena Ct 3 BS7 . . . . **18** F4
Atherston BS30 . . . . **11** D5
Atherstone Cl GL51 . . . . . **132** C3
Atherton Cl GL51 . . . . . . **129** D2
Atherton Ho GL51 . . . . . . **129** D2
Athlone Wlk BS4 . . . . **8** L1
Atkins Cl BS14 . . . . **3** E6
Atlantic Rd BS11 . . . . **16** C8
Atlas Cl BS5 . . . . **20** A2
Atlas Ct GL2 . . . . **118** C7
Atlas Rd BS3 . . . . **8** E3
Atlas St BS2 . . . . **9** B5
Atrium The BS1 . . . . **195** B2
Attwood Cl GL51 . . . . **132** F5
Attwoods Patch GL54 . . . **175** B3
Atwell Dr BS32 . . . . **40** B1
Atwood Dr BS11 . . . . **27** B2
Atyeo Cl BS3 . . . . **7** E1
Aubrey Ho 9 BS3 . . . . **8** B3
Aubrey Meads BS30 . . . . . . **5** E8
Aubrey Rd BS3 . . . . **8** B3
Auburn Ave BS30 . . . . **11** B3
Auburn Rd BS6 . . . . **18** B1
Auckland Ho 1 GL51 . . . **132** F3
Auden Mead BS7 . . . . **19** A8
Audley Cl BS37 . . . . **43** A8
Audrey Wlk BS9 . . . . **18** D7
Augustine Way GL4 . . . . . **119** F6
Augustus Ho BS15 . . . . . . **10** B6
Augustus Way GL15 . . . . . **92** B4
Aust Cres NP16 . . . . **60** F5
Austen Gr BS7 . . . . **19** A8
Austen Ho BS7 . . . . **19** A8
Austin Cl BS11 . . . . **16** E7
Austin Dr GL2 . . . . **126** F6
Australia Ho GL51 . . . . . . **132** E1
Aust La BS9 . . . . **18** A8
Aust Rd
  Northwick BS35 . . . . . . **48** D3
  Olveston BS35 . . . . **49** F5
Autumn Rise GL4 . . . . . . **119** D4
Avalon La BS5 . . . . **10** C1
Avalon Rd BS5 . . . . **10** B6
Avebury Cl GL4 . . . . **118** B1
Avebury Rd BS3 . . . . **7** F2
Avenall Ct 9 GL52 . . . . . **130** F8
Avenall Par GL51 . . . . **132** F5
Avening Prim Sch GL8 . . **148** A1
Avening Rd
  Bristol BS15 . . . . **10** A8
  Gloucester GL4 . . . . . . **118** F5
  Nailsworth GL6 . . . . **91** E3
Avenue Terr GL10 . . . . **97** D7
Avenue The
  Bourton-on-t-W GL54 . . **168** F8
  Brimscombe GL6 . . . . . **148** B5
  Bristol, Ashley Down BS7 . **18** E3
  Bristol BS34 . . . . **40** B2
  Bristol, Clifton BS8 . . . . **18** A1
  Bristol, Crew's Hole BS5 . . **9** F8
  Bristol, Frenchay BS16 . . **29** C6
  Bristol, Little Stoke BS34 . **29** C6
  Bristol, Sneyd Park BS9 . **17** E3
  Cheltenham GL53 . . . . **130** F5
  Churchdown GL3 . . . . . **128** D5
  Cirencester GL7 . . . . . . **190** D4
  Dursley GL11 . . . . **87** D3
  Gloucester GL2 . . . . . . **127** C4
  Keynsham BS31 . . . . **4** E6
  Stanton Fitzwarren SN6 . **145** A1
  Woodchester GL5 . . . . . **99** A2
  Yate BS37 . . . . **43** D1
Averay Rd BS16 . . . . **19** C4
Averill Cl WR12 . . . . **185** B8
Avonbank Ind Est BS11 . . **16** B7
Avonbridge Trad Est
  BS11 . . . . **16** C6
Avon Bsns Pk BS16 . . . . . . **20** A3
Avon Cl
  Bristol BS5 . . . . **9** F6
  Keynsham BS31 . . . . **4** F6
Avon Cres
  Bristol BS1 . . . . **194** A1
  Brockworth GL3 . . . . . . **120** F5
  Wickwar GL12 . . . . **54** B6
Avon Ct
  Bristol, Clifton BS8 . . . . **18** A1
  Bristol, Fishponds BS16 . . **20** B5
Avondale Ct
  Bristol, Oldland BS30 . . . . **8** C2
  Bristol, Sneyd Park BS9 . **17** D3
Avondown Cl BS10 . . . . . . **28** D2
Avondown Ct BS3 . . . . **8** C2
Avondowns Ct BS8 . . . . . **194** A4
Avon Gorge Ind Est BS11 . **16** C7
Avon Gorge Nature
  Reserve★ BS8 . . . . **7** E7
Avon Gr BS9 . . . . **17** D2
Avon Ho GL2 . . . . **118** C4
Avon La BS31 . . . . **5** F5
Avonlea
  Bristol BS15 . . . . **10** C5
  1 Yate BS37 . . . . **32** D8
Avonlea Ct BS30 . . . . **11** A3
Avonleigh Ct 4 BS3 . . . . . . **8** B2
Avonleigh Rd BS3 . . . . **8** B2
Avonmead Ho BS1 . . . . . . **195** B4
Avon Meads BS2 . . . . **9** C5
Avon Mill La BS31 . . . . **4** F6

Avonmouth CE Prim Sch
  BS11 . . . . **16** C8
Avonmouth Rd
  Avonmouth BS11 . . . . . **16** C8
  Bristol BS11 . . . . **26** B1
Avonmouth Sta BS11 . . . . **26** B1
Avonmouth Way
  Avonmouth BS11 . . . . . **26** D1
  Bristol BS10 . . . . **27** E3
Avonmouth Way W BS11 . **26** B1
Avon Pk BS5 . . . . **9** D7
Avon Prim Sch BS11 . . . . . **16** D8
Avon Rd
  Bristol BS13 . . . . **2** A6
  Charfield GL12 . . . . **67** A4
  Cheltenham GL52 . . . . **134** A2
  Keynsham BS31 . . . . **4** F5
  Pill BS20 . . . . **16** C5
Avon Rise SN14 . . . . **47** E4
Avon Riverside Est BS11 . . **16** C7
Avon Riverside Sta★ BS31 . **5** E6
Avonside Ind Est BS2 . . . . . . **9** C6
Avonside Rd BS2 . . . . **9** C6
Avonside Way BS4 . . . . **9** F6
Avonsmere Residential Pk
  BS34 . . . . **29** C3
Avon St BS2 . . . . **195** B3
Avon Trad Est BS2 . . . . **9** A5
Avonvale Rd BS5 . . . . **9** C7
Avon Valley Bsns Pk BS4 . . **9** E6
Avon Valley Ctry Pk★ BS31 . **5** D6
Avon Valley Rly★ BS30 . . . **11** C3
Avon View
  Bristol BS15 . . . . **10** B3
  Tewkesbury GL20 . . . . **192** E6
Avon Way
  Bristol, Sneyd Park BS9 . **17** C4
  Bristol, Southmead BS10 . **18** D7
  Thornbury BS35 . . . . **51** D7
Avonwood Cl BS11 . . . . . . **16** E6
Avro Rd GL51 . . . . **169** D7
Awdelett Cl BS11 . . . . **27** B1
Awdry Way GL4 . . . . **118** D2
Awebridge Way GL4 . . . . **119** C4
Awkward Hill GL7 . . . . . . **160** A1
Awre Rd GL15 . . . . **156** E1
Axbridge Rd BS4 . . . . **8** F2
Axe Ct 8 BS35 . . . . **51** C8
Axis BS14 . . . . **2** D5
Aycote Cl GL4 . . . . **119** B5
Ayford La SN14, BA1 . . . . . **14** F4
Ayland Cl 29 GL18 . . . . . . **171** A4
Ayland Gdns GL1 . . . . **119** A8
Aylburton CE Prim Sch
  GL15 . . . . **147** E5
Aylesbury Cres BS3 . . . . **8** B1
Aylesbury Rd BS3 . . . . **8** B1
Aylmer Cres BS14 . . . . **3** B6
Aylminton Wlk BS11 . . . . . **27** B2
Aylton Cl GL51 . . . . **129** D6
Aysgarth Ave GL51 . . . . . **129** E5
Azalea Dr GL51 . . . . **130** A5
Azalea Gdns GL2 . . . . **117** E1
Aztec Ctr The BS32 . . . . . . **40** A2
Aztec West BS32 . . . . **40** A2

B

Babdown Ind Est GL8 . . . . **71** B8
Back Albert Pl GL52 . . . . **193** C4
Back Edge La GL6 . . . . . . **103** B8
Back Ends GL55 . . . . **189** A2
Backfield Farm Bsns Pk
  BS37 . . . . **42** F5
Backfields BS2 . . . . **195** B4
Backfields Ct BS2 . . . . . . **195** B4
Backfields La BS2 . . . . . . **195** B4
Back La
  Ashton under Hill WR11 . **183** D8
  Beckford GL20 . . . . **183** B6
  Bisley GL6 . . . . **148** D8
  Bredon GL20 . . . . **182** C8
  Bretforton WR11 . . . . . **188** A6
  Broad Blunsdon SN26 . . **144** D2
  Broadway WR12 . . . . . . **185** B8
  Drybrook GL17 . . . . **164** B4
  Fairford GL7 . . . . **152** E3
  Keynsham BS31 . . . . **4** E6
  Leighterton GL8 . . . . **70** C3
  Marshfield SN14 . . . . **14** F8
  Mickleton GL55 . . . . . . **189** A6
  Pill BS20 . . . . **16** C5
  Pucklechurch BS16 . . . . . **22** C4
  Upper Oddington GL56 . **177** C4
  Wickwar GL12 . . . . **54** A5
  Winchcombe GL54 . . . . **174** A7
  Winstone GL7 . . . . **107** A8
Back Montpellier Terr
  GL50 . . . . **193** B2
Back Of Avon GL20 . . . . . **192** C4
Back Of Kingsdown Par
  BS6 . . . . **195** A4
Back Of Mount Pleasant
  GL20 . . . . **192** D4
Back Rd
  Bristol BS3 . . . . **8** A4
  Llandogo NP16 . . . . **146** A5
Back Row GL56 . . . . **177** E6
Back St
  Ashton Keynes SN6 . . . **142** F5
  Hawkesbury Upton GL9 . . **56** A3
  Ilmington CV36 . . . . . . **189** F6
Back Stoke La BS9 . . . . . . **17** F6

Back The NP16 . . . . **72** F1
Back Walls GL54 . . . . **176** F4
Backwell Wlk BS13 . . . . **1** F8
Badenham Gr BS11 . . . . . . **16** F8
Baden Hill Rd GL12 . . . . . . **52** C6
Baden Rd
  Bristol, Kingswood BS15 . **11** A7
  Bristol, Redfield BS5 . . . . . **9** C7
Bader Ave GL3 . . . . **128** C5
Bader Ct BS37 . . . . **43** D3
Badger Cl
  Bristol BS30 . . . . **10** F3
  Gloucester GL4 . . . . . . **119** D3
Badgers Cl BS32 . . . . **40** D3
Badgers Dene
  NP16 . . . . **60** D8
  Narth The NP25 . . . . . . **154** D1
Badger Sett BS5 . . . . **10** B7
Badgers Field GL55 . . . . . **189** A2
Badgers Holt BS14 . . . . **3** C6
Badger's La GL52 . . . . **39** C3
Badgers Mdw NP16 . . . . . . **60** B6
Badgers Rise BS10 . . . . . . **28** E4
Badgers Way
  9 Bream GL15 . . . . . . **155** D1
  Nailsworth GL6 . . . . **90** F5
Badgers Wlk BS4 . . . . **9** D2
Badger Vale Ct GL2 . . . . . **118** C5
Badgeworth BS37 . . . . **32** D6
Badgeworth La GL51 . . . . **129** B2
Badgeworth Rd GL51 . . . . **129** A7
Badhams The GL20 . . . . . **180** F7
Badminton BS16 . . . . **30** C1
Badminton Cl GL53 . . . . . **130** D6
Badminton Ct BS37 . . . . . . **43** C2
Badminton Ctr The BS37 . . **43** C2
Badminton Rd
  Bristol, Downend BS16 . . . **20** E7
  Bristol, Montpelier BS2 . . **18** F1
  Chipping Sodbury BS37 . . **34** B7
  Frampton Cotterell BS36,
    BS37 . . . . **31** C6
  Gloucester GL4 . . . . . . **119** B5
Badminton Road Trad Est
  BS37 . . . . **43** B1
Badminton Sch BS9 . . . . . **18** A5
Badminton Wlk BS16 . . . . **20** E7
Badock's Wood Prim Sch
  BS10 . . . . **28** B1
Badsey La WR12 . . . . **188** A3
Bafford App GL53 . . . . . . **131** A4
Bafford Gr GL53 . . . . **130** F4
Bafford La GL53 . . . . **131** A5
Baglyn Ave BS15 . . . . **20** F3
Bagnell Cl BS14 . . . . **3** E5
Bagnell Rd BS14 . . . . **3** E5
Bagpath La GL5 . . . . **99** D2
Bagshots Sq GL54 . . . . . . **176** B2
Bagstone Rd BS37, GL12 . . **53** A2
Bagworth Dr BS30 . . . . **10** F3
Bailey Cl 21 GL54 . . . . . . **176** F4
Bailey Hill GL15 . . . . **156** B1
Bailey La NP16, GL15 . . . . **146** D4
Bailey's Court Prim Sch
  BS32 . . . . **29** F6
Baileys Court Rd BS32 . . . **29** F6
Bailey's Hay NP16 . . . . **60** B4
Baileys Mead Rd BS16 . . . **19** C5
Bailiffe Piece SN6 . . . . . . **143** E5
Baily Pl BS7 . . . . **19** C8
Baines St GL54 . . . . **168** F7
Bakehouse La GL50 . . . . . **130** B7
Bakersfield BS30 . . . . **11** B3
Bakers Ground BS34 . . . . . **30** A5
Bakers Hill GL16 . . . . **155** B6
Baker's Hill GL55 . . . . . . **189** B5
Baker's La GL19 . . . . **172** B3
Bakers Piece GL17 . . . . **2** B6
Bakers Piece Rd GL17 . . . **163** F3
Baker Sq GL20 . . . . **192** D5
Baker St
  Cheltenham GL51 . . . . **133** C3
  Gloucester GL2 . . . . . . **196** A1
Bakery Mews GL15 . . . . . **147** D8
Balaclava Ind Est BS16 . . **19** F3
Bala Rd GL51 . . . . **129** F6
Balcarras Gdns GL53 . . . . **131** C5
Balcarras Rd GL53 . . . . . . **131** C5
Balcarras Retreat GL53 . . **131** C5
Balcarras Sch GL53 . . . . . **131** C5
Baldwin Cl GL7 . . . . **149** B1
Baldwin St BS1 . . . . **195** A2
Baldwyn Ct WR11 . . . . . . **188** C6
Balfour Rd
  Bristol BS3 . . . . **8** B3
  Gloucester GL1 . . . . **118** D6
Ballards Cl GL53 . . . . **189** A6
Ballards La GL2 . . . . **95** F4
Ballast La BS11 . . . . **26** E2
Ballinode Cl GL50 . . . . . . **133** B5
Ballinska Mews GL2 . . . . . **127** D5
Balmain St 4 BS4 . . . . **9** A4
Balmoral Cl BS34 . . . . **29** D4
Balmoral Rd
  Bristol BS16 . . . . **21** A5
  Cheltenham GL51 . . . . **130** F6
  Keynsham BS31 . . . . **4** E5
Balmoral Mans 3 BS7 . . . **18** F2

Baltic Pl BS20 . . . . **16** D4
Baltimore Ct GL3 . . . . . . **120** C4
Bamel Wy GL3 . . . . **120** D4
Bamfield BS14 . . . . **3** A6
Bamfurlong Ind Pk GL51 . **173** E1
Bamfurlong La
  Bamfurlong GL51 . . . . . **128** D8
  Bamfurlong GL51 . . . . . **129** A8
  Cheltenham GL51 . . . . **173** F1
Bampton Castle Wy 6
  GL2 . . . . **110** B8
Bampton Cl
  Bristol, Emerson's Green
    BS16 . . . . **21** C6
  Bristol, Headley Park BS13 . **2** B7
Bampton Croft BS16 . . . . **21** C6
Bampton Dr BS16 . . . . **30** D1
Banady La GL52 . . . . **136** E5
Banbury Rd GL4 . . . . **119** A4
Banfield Cl BS11 . . . . **17** A8
Bangor Gr BS4 . . . . **9** F5
Bangrove Wlk BS11 . . . . . **16** E8
Bangup La GL54 . . . . **168** B6
Banister Gr BS4 . . . . **2** D7
Bank Cres 1 HR8 . . . . . . **178** F8
Bank Pl BS20 . . . . **16** D4
Bank Rd
  Avonmouth BS11 . . . . . **26** D7
  Bristol BS15 . . . . **10** D8
  Pilning BS35 . . . . **38** E6
Banks Fee La GL56 . . . . . **176** D8
Bankside
  Bristol BS16 . . . . **20** F4
  North Cerney GL7 . . . . **158** D3
Bankside Ind Est HR8 . . . **178** E8
Bankside Rd BS4 . . . . **9** D3
Bank Sq 6 NP16 . . . . **60** E8
Bank St
  Chepstow/Cas-Gwent
    NP16 . . . . **60** E8
  Coleford GL16 . . . . **155** A5
Bank The
  Broadwell GL56 . . . . . . **177** A6
  Cheltenham GL52 . . . . **134** C4
  Stroud GL6 . . . . **98** D8
Bank Yard Ind Est GL12 . . **68** B8
Bannerleigh La BS8 . . . . **7** E6
Bannerleigh Rd BS8 . . . . . . **7** E6
Bannerman Rd BS5 . . . . . . **9** B8
Bannerman Road Com Acad
  BS5 . . . . **19** B1
Banner Rd BS6 . . . . **18** E1
Bannetts Tree Cres BS35 . **51** A5
Bantock Cl BS4 . . . . **2** D6
Bantry Rd BS4 . . . . **2** E8
Banwell Cl
  Bristol BS13 . . . . **2** A8
  Keynsham BS31 . . . . **5** A2
Banwell Rd BS3 . . . . **8** A3
Banyard Cl GL51 . . . . **132** D2
Baptist Cl GL4 . . . . **119** F6
Baptist St BS5 . . . . **19** A1
Baptist Way GL17 . . . . . . **164** A3
Baranwheel Ct BS5 . . . . **9** F6
Barber La GL8 . . . . **140** A2
Barberry Cl GL50 . . . . **130** B6
Barbican Rd GL1 . . . . **196** A3
Barbican Way GL1 . . . . . . **196** A3
Barbour Gdns BS13 . . . . **2** D3
Barbour Rd BS13 . . . . **2** D3
Barbridge Rd GL51 . . . . . **132** E3
Barcelona Dr GL6 . . . . **91** F6
Barcroft Cl BS15 . . . . **10** C8
Baregains La HR8 . . . . . . **178** B8
Barker Ct 5 BS5 . . . . **9** C7
Barker Pl 1 GL7 . . . . **152** E4
Barker's Leys GL52 . . . . . **138** B4
Barker Wlk BS5 . . . . **19** A1
Barkers Mead BS37 . . . . . . **43** F4
Barkston Heath GL4 . . . . . **110** C8
Barlands Ho BS10 . . . . **27** F3
Barlands The GL52 . . . . . **131** E4
Barley Cl
  Bristol BS16 . . . . **21** A6
  Cheltenham GL51 . . . . **132** D5
  Frampton Cotterell BS36 . **31** C8
  Hardwicke GL2 . . . . . . **129** E6
Barley Close Com Prim Sch
  BS16 . . . . **21** A6
Barleycorn Sq GL14 . . . . . **191** C4
Barley Croft BS9 . . . . **17** F5
Barleycroft GL4 . . . . **119** D2
Barley Fields BS2 . . . . **195** C2
Barlow Cl GL10 . . . . **97** E7
Barlow Rd GL51 . . . . **132** F4
Barnabas St 9 BS2 . . . . . . **18** E1
Barnaby Cl GL1 . . . . **118** F7
Barnaby Rd GL52 . . . . . . **138** A5
Barnack Trad Est BS3 . . . . . **8** C1
Barnacre Dr GL3 . . . . **127** F1
Barnage La GL15 . . . . **147** A4
Barnard Par 5 GL10 . . . . . **97** F7
Barnard Wlk BS31 . . . . **4** E5
Barn Bsns Ctr The GL54 . **169** D4
Barn Cl
  Bristol BS16 . . . . **21** B6
  Gloucester GL4 . . . . . . **119** E4
  Gretton GL54 . . . . **183** E1
  Nailsworth GL6 . . . . **91** B3
Barn Copsie 2 BS16 . . . . . **19** D8
Barn Cotts The GL15 . . . . **146** F6

Barn End SN14 . . . . 15 A8
Barnes Ho GL7 . . . . 190 D5
Barnes St BS5 . . . . 9 D8
Barnes Wallis Way GL3 . . 128 C5
Barnets Wood/Coed Barnet
NP16 . . . . 60 C8
Barnett Ave HR8 . . . . 178 E8
Barnett Cl GL51 . . . . 132 E5
Barnetts Cl 4 HR8 . . . . 178 E8
Barnett Way
Gloucester GL4 . . . . 127 D1
5 Northleach GL54 . . . . . . 168 A1
Barn Field 5 GL52 . . . . 134 A1
Barn Field Ave GL6 . . . . 91 A4
Barn Field Rd GL6 . . . . 91 A4
Barnfields GL4 . . . . 118 F5
Barn Field Terr GL6 . . . . 91 A4
Barn Ground GL2 . . . . 125 D5
Barnhay GL3 . . . . 128 C4
Barnhill Cl BS37 . . . . 44 A4
Barnhill Rd BS37 . . . . 44 B1
Barn Hill Rd GL16 . . . . 155 C6
Barn La GL17 . . . . 163 F3
Barnmeadow Rd 8
GL54 . . . . 174 A7
Barn Owl Way BS34 . . . . 29 F5
Barnsley House Garden★
GL7 . . . . 151 C7
Barnsley Wy GL54 . . . . 168 F8
Barnstaple Ct BS4 . . . . 2 E8
Barnstaple Rd BS4 . . . . 2 E8
Barnstaple Wlk BS4 . . . . 2 E8
Barn Way GL7 . . . . 190 A7
Barnwell Cl BS10 . . . . 28 A4
Barnwood 3 BS7 . . . . 78 C8
Barnwood Ave GL4 . . . . 119 D8
Barnwood CE Prim Sch
GL4 . . . . 127 D1
Barnwood Fields Bsns Ctr
GL4 . . . . 127 E1
Barnwood Park Arts Coll
GL4 . . . . 119 D8
Barnwood Rd
Gloucester GL2 . . . . 127 C2
Yate BS37 . . . . 32 C7
Baron Cl BS30 . . . . 5 E8
Barons Cl BS3 . . . . 7 F3
Barossa Pl BS1 . . . . 195 A1
Barrack's La BS11 . . . . 16 D8
Barrack Sq GL1 . . . . 196 A3
Barracks The GL15 . . . . 156 A4
Barra Cl SN6 . . . . 145 C3
Barratt's Mill La GL53 . . . . 193 C3
Barratt St BS5 . . . . 9 C1
Barrel La GL17 . . . . 164 F8
Barrels Pitch 1 GL55 . . . . . 189 A2
Barrington Cl BS15 . . . . 20 F2
Barrington Ct
11 Bristol, Knowle BS2 . . . . . 8 F4
Bristol, New Cheltenham
BS15 . . . . 20 E1
Barrington Dr GL3 . . . . 119 F8
Barrington Mews GL51 . . . 129 B7
Barrow GL51 . . . . 173 E3
Barrow Cl GL2 . . . . 109 F8
Barrowell La GL15 . . . . 146 F7
Barrow Elm Barns GL7 . . . 152 F7
Barrowfield Rd GL5 . . . . . . 103 A1
Barrow Hill
Churchdown GL3 . . . . 128 D3
Wick BS30 . . . . 12 B5
Barrow Hill Cres BS11 . . . . . 16 C7
Barrow Hill Rd BS11 . . . . . . 16 D6
Barrowmead Dr BS11 . . . . . 16 F7
Barrow Rd BS2 . . . . 9 A7
Barrs Court Ave BS30 . . . . . 11 A5
Barrs Court Prim Sch
BS30 . . . . 10 F5
Barrs Court Rd BS30 . . . . . . 10 F5
Barrs La GL11 . . . . 79 E4
Barry Cl BS30 . . . . 11 C1
Barry Rd BS30 . . . . 11 C2
Barstable Ho BS2 . . . . 195 C3
Barter Cl 9 BS15 . . . . 10 D8
Bartholomew Cl GL19 . . . . 172 D4
Bartholomew Sq BS7 . . . . . . 18 F7
Bartletts Pk GL54 . . . . 176 F4
Bartlett's Rd BS3 . . . . 8 C2
Bartley Ct BS5 . . . . 9 D7
Bartley St BS3 . . . . 8 D4
Barton Cl
Alveston BS35 . . . . 51 A5
1 Bristol BS4 . . . . 9 F6
Charlton Kings GL53 . . . . . 131 A4
Innsworth GL3 . . . . 127 E6
Winterbourne BS36 . . . . 30 E5
Barton Ct
Bristol BS5 . . . . 9 C6
Highworth SN6 . . . . 145 C3
Bartonend La GL6 . . . . 91 A1
Barton Gn BS5 . . . . 9 B7
Barton Hill GL17 . . . . 164 E5
Barton Hill Prim Sch BS5 . . . 9 B6
Barton Hill Rd BS5 . . . . 9 B7
Barton Hill Trad Est 10 BS5 . 9 B6
Barton Ho BS5 . . . . 9 C6
Bartonia Br BS4 . . . . 9 D1
Barton La GL7 . . . . 190 B5
Barton Manor BS2 . . . . 9 A6
Barton Mews GL20 . . . . 192 D4

Barton Rd
Barton-on-t-H GL56 . . . . . . 187 F3
Bristol BS2 . . . . 195 C2
Tewkesbury GL20 . . . . 192 D4
Barton St
Bristol BS1 . . . . 195 A4
Gloucester GL1 . . . . 119 A8
Tewkesbury GL20 . . . . 192 C4
Barton The
Bristol BS15 . . . . 10 C4
Hawkesbury Upton GL9 . . . 55 F3
Barton Vale 6 BS2 . . . . 9 A6
Barton Way BS1 . . . . 129 E6
Bartwood La HR9 . . . . 164 A8
Barwick Ho BS11 . . . . 16 E7
Barwick Rd 6 GL51 . . . . . . 129 F5
Barwood Cl BS15 . . . . 10 F8
Base La GL2 . . . . 172 F1
Basil Cl GL4 . . . . 119 D4
Bassett Cl 3 GL54 . . . . 174 A7
Bassett Rd GL54 . . . . 168 A1
Bassetts The GL5 . . . . 98 D8
Batches The BS3 . . . . 8 B2
Batchfield La BS16, BS37 . . 22 D8
Batchfields GL18 . . . . 178 E2
Batch The BS31 . . . . 5 F3
Bateman Cl GL4 . . . . 118 D1
Bates Cl BS5 . . . . 9 A8
Bathams Cl GL17 . . . . 164 F5
Bath Bldgs BS6 . . . . 18 E1
Bath Bridge Rdbt BS1 . . . . 195 C1
Bath Cres GL15 . . . . 155 F1
Bath Hill BS31 . . . . 4 F5
Bathings The 1 BS35 . . . . . 51 C8
Bath La GL9 . . . . 55 E2
Bath Mews GL53 . . . . 193 C2
Bath Par GL53 . . . . 193 C2
Bath Pl
11 Berry Hill GL16 . . . . 155 A7
Lydney GL15 . . . . 92 B3
Bath Race Course★ BA1 . . . . 6 F6
Bath Rd
Bitton BS30, BA1 . . . . 5 F7
Bristol, Brislington BS4 . . . . 9 F9
Bristol BS3 . . . . 195 C1
Bristol, Longwell Green
BS30 . . . . 10 F3
Bristol, North Common
BS30 . . . . 11 D6
Bristol, Totterdown BS4 . . . . 9 B4
Bristol, Upper Knowle BS4 . . 9 D2
Bristol, Willsbridge BS30 . . 11 C1
Cheltenham GL50, GL53 . . 193 B2
Chipping Sodbury BS37, GL9 34 C4
Colerne SN14 . . . . 15 E2
Cricklade SN6 . . . . 143 E4
Eastington GL10 . . . . 96 F6
Hardwicke GL2 . . . . 109 E4
Leighterton GL8 . . . . 70 B2
Leonard Stanley GL10 . . . . 97 E4
Nailsworth GL6 . . . . 91 B2
Saltford BS31 . . . . 5 D3
Stonehouse GL10 . . . . 97 F7
Tetbury GL8 . . . . 140 B2
Thornbury BS35 . . . . 51 B8
Wick BS30 . . . . 12 E4
Woodchester GL5 . . . . 99 A3
Bath Road Trad Est GL5 . . . 98 F5
Bath St
Bristol, Ashton Gate BS3 . . . 8 A4
Bristol BS1 . . . . 195 B2
Bristol, Staple Hill BS16 . . . 20 E4
Cheltenham GL50 . . . . 193 C3
Stroud GL5 . . . . 99 C7
Bath Terr GL53 . . . . 193 B1
Bathurst Par BS1 . . . . 195 A1
Bathurst Park Rd GL15 . . . . 92 A3
Bathurst Rd
Cirencester GL7 . . . . 190 B3
Gloucester GL1 . . . . 118 F6
Bathurst Row GL7 . . . . 149 E3
Bath Ville Mews GL53 . . . . 193 B2
Bathwell Rd BS4 . . . . 9 A3
Batley Ct BS30 . . . . 11 D4
Batsford Arboretum★
GL56 . . . . 186 E4
Batsford Cl GL54 . . . . 168 F8
Batt Cl BS32 . . . . 40 E5
Battenburg Rd BS5 . . . . 10 A8
Batten Ct BS37 . . . . 44 C1
Batten's La BS5 . . . . 10 A6
Battens Rd BS5 . . . . 10 B7
Battersby Way BS10 . . . . 27 E2
Battersea Rd BS5 . . . . 9 C8
Battlebrook Dr GL55 . . . . . 189 B2
Battledown App GL52 . . . . 131 A8
Battledown Childrens Ctr
GL52 . . . . 134 C4
Battledown Cl GL52 . . . . . . 134 A1
Battledown Dr GL52 . . . . . . 131 A8
Battledown Grange
GL52 . . . . 131 A8
Battledown Mead GL52 . . . 134 A1
Battledown Priors GL52 . . 134 A1
Battledown Trad Est
GL52 . . . . 131 A8
Battle Rd GL20 . . . . 192 B2
Batts La GL17 . . . . 164 A4
Battson Rd BS14 . . . . 3 E4
Baugh Gdns BS16 . . . . 30 E1
Baugh Rd BS16 . . . . 30 E1
Baunton La GL7 . . . . 150 C7
Bavon Cotts GL20 . . . . 181 F8
Baxter Cl BS15 . . . . 10 F8
Baxters Barns GL7 . . . . 153 D6

Bayberry Pl Cvn Pk 10
GL16 . . . . 155 B5
Bayfield Gdns GL18 . . . . . . 178 D2
Bayfield Wood Cl NP16 . . . . 60 B8
Bay Gdns BS5 . . . . 19 C2
Bayham Rd BS4 . . . . 9 A3
Bayham's Wlk GL16 . . . . . . 155 C6
Baylands GL13 . . . . 85 D8
Bayleys Dr BS15 . . . . 10 C6
Bayliss Ho GL51 . . . . 132 E4
Bayliss Rd GL20 . . . . 182 E8
Baynham Ct 4 BS15 . . . . . . 10 B5
Baynham Rd GL17 . . . . 164 D5
Baynham's Wlk GL16 . . . . . 155 B6
Baynton Ho 2 BS5 . . . . 9 B7
Baynton Mdw BS16 . . . . 21 C6
Baynton Rd BS3 . . . . 8 A4
Bays Hill GL13 . . . . 85 D8
Bayshill La GL50 . . . . 193 A3
Bayshill Rd GL50 . . . . 193 A3
Bayswater Ave BS6 . . . . 18 B3
Bayswater Rd BS7 . . . . 18 F7
Bay Tree Cl BS34 . . . . 28 F7
Bay Tree Ct GL52 . . . . 134 C4
Bay Tree Rd GL4 . . . . 119 F5
Baytree Sq S GL5 . . . . 98 B4
Bazeley Rd GL4 . . . . 119 B2
Beach Ave BS35 . . . . 38 A7
Beachgrove Gdns BS16 . . . . 20 C4
Beachgrove Rd BS16 . . . . . . 20 B4
Beach Hill BS30 . . . . 11 F3
Beach La BS30 . . . . 12 C2
Beachley Rd
Beachley NP16 . . . . 61 B4
Tutshill NP16 . . . . 73 A1
Beachley Wlk BS11 . . . . 16 D7
Beach Rd BS35 . . . . 37 F7
Beacon Cl GL6 . . . . 112 A5
Beacon La BS16 . . . . 30 C6
Beaconlea BS15 . . . . 10 D6
Beacon Rd
Gloucester GL4 . . . . 119 B2
Llandogo NP25 . . . . 146 A8
Beacon Rise Prim Sch
BS15 . . . . 10 D6
Beaconsfield Ct 1 GL50 . . 130 B8
Beaconsfield Rd
Bristol, Clifton BS8 . . . . 18 A1
Bristol, Crew's Hole BS5 . . . 9 E7
Bristol, Kensington BS4 . . . 9 B3
Beaconsfield St 7 BS5 . . . . . 9 B6
Beacons View Rd GL14 . . . 191 E5
Beagles The GL5 . . . . 98 D7
Beale Cl
Bristol BS14 . . . . 3 E6
Bussage GL6 . . . . 148 B6
Beale Rd GL61 . . . . 132 D3
Beam St BS5 . . . . 9 C7
Bean Acre The BS11 . . . . 16 D8
Bean Hill GL56 . . . . 176 B8
Beanhill Cres BS35 . . . . 51 A5
Bean St 11 BS5 . . . . 19 A1
Beanwood Pk (Cvn Site)
BS37 . . . . 32 E3
Bearbridge Rd BS13 . . . . 1 F4
Bearcroft Gdns GL55 . . . . . 189 B6
Beard's La GL5 . . . . 99 A4
Bear Hill GL15 . . . . 92 B2
Bear La BS20 . . . . 180 F6
Bearland GL1 . . . . 196 A3
Bearlands GL12 . . . . 68 C6
Bearpacker Almshouses
GL12 . . . . 68 C8
Bearsfield GL6 . . . . 105 A1
Bear St GL12 . . . . 68 B7
Bear Yard Mews BS8 . . . . . . 194 A2
Beauchamp Cl 2 GL7 . . . . 152 E4
Beauchamp Mdw GL15 . . . . 92 C4
Beauchamp Rd
Bristol BS7 . . . . 18 D4
Tewkesbury GL20 . . . . 192 F1
Beaudesert Park Sch GL6 91 C5
Beaufort BS16 . . . . 30 C1
Beaufort Ave BS37 . . . . 43 D2
Beaufort Bldgs
8 Bristol BS8 . . . . 7 F7
Gloucester GL1 . . . . 196 B1
Beaufort Cl BS5 . . . . 9 D7
Beaufort Co-operative Acad
GL4 . . . . 118 B2
Beaufort Cres BS34 . . . . 29 E4
Beaufort Ct
Bristol BS16 . . . . 21 A8
Cirencester GL7 . . . . 190 C3
Beaufort Dr GL15 . . . . 92 B2
Beaufort End WR11 . . . . . . 188 C7
Beaufort Ho 12 BS5 . . . . 9 B7
Beaufort Hts BS5 . . . . 9 E7
Beaufort Mews
9 Bristol BS8 . . . . 7 F7
Chipping Sodbury BS37 . . . 44 B1
Beaufort Pl
Bristol, Frenchay BS16 . . . . 30 B2
Bristol, Upper Easton BS5 . . 9 A8
Chepstow/Cas-Gwent NP16 60 E8
Tewkesbury GL20 . . . . 192 C2
Beaufort Rd
Bristol, Clifton BS8 . . . . 18 A1
Bristol, Horfield BS7 . . . . . . 18 F6
Bristol, Kingswood BS15 . . 20 C1
Bristol, Pile Marsh BS5 . . . . 9 F7
Bristol, Staple Hill BS16 . . . 20 E5
Bristol, Vinney Green BS16 . 21 A8
Cheltenham GL52 . . . . 131 A7

Beaufort Rd continued
Frampton Cotterell BS36 . . . 31 A8
Gloucester GL4 . . . . 119 A5
14 Moreton-in-M GL56 . . . 187 B3
Yate BS37 . . . . 43 D2
Beaufort Sq 5 NP16 . . . . . . 60 E8
Beaufort St
Bristol, Bedminster BS3 . . . . 8 C2
4 Bristol, Upper Easton BS5 9 A8
Beaufort Trad Pk BS16 . . . . 22 B5
Beaufort Vw SN14 . . . . 47 E4
Beaufort Way BS10 . . . . 18 B4
Beauley Rd BS3 . . . . 8 B4
Beaumont Cl BS30 . . . . 11 A3
Beaumont Dr GL51 . . . . 132 D4
Beaumont Pl GL15 . . . . 92 A2
Beaumont Rd
Cheltenham GL51 . . . . 132 D3
Gloucester GL2 . . . . 127 C5
Beaumont Row 5 GL12 . . . . 68 B7
Beaumont Sq 4 GL12 . . . . . 68 B7
Beaumont St BS5 . . . . 9 A8
Beaumont Terr 6 BS5 . . . . . . 9 A8
Beaumoor Pl GL7 . . . . 152 E3
Beaver Cl BS36 . . . . 30 F7
Beazer Cl 5 BS16 . . . . 20 D3
Beceshore Cl GL56 . . . . 187 A3
Beck Cl BS16 . . . . 21 C7
Becket Cl GL56 . . . . 187 E7
Becket Ct BS16 . . . . 22 B5
Becketts La GL54 . . . . 174 A8
Beckford Cl GL20 . . . . 183 B6
Beckford Gdns BS14 . . . . 3 A3
Beckford Rd
Alderton GL20 . . . . 183 D4
Ashton under Hill WR11 . . 183 D8
Gloucester GL4 . . . . 119 E4
Beckford Silk★ GL20 . . . . . 183 B6
Beck Ho BS34 . . . . 29 A8
Beckingham Rd BS3 . . . . 8 F2
Beckington Wlk BS3 . . . . . . 8 F2
Beckside Ct 2 GL1 . . . . 127 A1
Beckspool Rd BS16 . . . . 30 C1
Becky Hill GL54 . . . . 176 B1
Beddome Way GL54 . . . . . . 168 F8
Bedford Ave GL51 . . . . 133 A2
Bedford Cres BS7 . . . . 18 F5
Bedford St
Gloucester GL1 . . . . 196 C2
8 Stroud GL5 . . . . 99 C7
Bedminster Down Rd BS3,
BS13 . . . . 8 B1
Bedminster Down Sch
BS13 . . . . 1 F7
Bedminster Par BS3 . . . . 8 D4
Bedminster Pl 9 BS3 . . . . . . 8 D4
Bedminster Rd BS3 . . . . 8 C2
Bedminster Sta BS3 . . . . 8 D3
Beechacres BS35 . . . . 64 C1
Beecham Cl GL7 . . . . 190 F5
Beech Ave GL16 . . . . 155 B7
Beech Cl
Alveston BS35 . . . . 51 A5
Bristol BS30 . . . . 11 A5
Cheltenham GL52 . . . . 134 C4
Hardwicke GL2 . . . . 109 E7
Highnam GL2 . . . . 125 D4
Beechcroft BS41 . . . . 1 D2
Beechcroft Rd BS7 . . . . 18 D3
Beechcroft Wlk BS7 . . . . 19 A8
Beech Ct BS14 . . . . 3 A5
Beechdean GL14 . . . . 191 C5
Beechen Dr BS16 . . . . 20 B3
Beechenhurst GL15 . . . . 155 F1
Beechenhurst Lodge Visitor
Ctr★ GL16 . . . . 155 E7
Beeches Cl GL10 . . . . 98 A4
Beeches Gn GL5 . . . . 99 B8
Beeches Gr BS4 . . . . 9 D2
Beeches Ind Est BS37 . . . . . 43 B2
Beeches Pk GL6 . . . . 148 B2
Beeches Rd
Charlton Kings GL53 . . . . . 131 B4
Cirencester GL7 . . . . 190 E5
5 Newnham GL14 . . . . 157 A6
Beeches The
Bristol, Bradley Stoke
BS32 . . . . 29 D8
Bristol, Frenchay BS16 . . . . 30 B1
Bristol, Oldland Common
BS30 . . . . 11 C2
King's Stanley GL10 . . . . . . 98 A4
Beechfield Cl BS41 . . . . 7 C2
Beechfield Gr BS9 . . . . 17 C8
Beech Gr
Chepstow/Cas-Gwent
NP16 . . . . 60 D7
Cirencester GL7 . . . . 190 E5
Highworth SN6 . . . . 145 C3
Woodchester GL5 . . . . 99 A2
Beech Green Prim Sch
GL2 . . . . 117 F1
Beech Grove Ct GL7 . . . . . . 190 E5
Beech Ho BS16 . . . . 19 C5
Beech La GL6 . . . . 104 B8
Beech Lea
Broad Blunsdon SN26 . . . . 144 E1
Meysey Hampton GL7 . . . . 152 B3
Beech Leaze BS35 . . . . 51 A5
Beechmore Dr 10 GL51 . . . 129 E5
Beechmount Ct BS14 . . . . . . 3 B8
Beechmount Gr BS14 . . . . . . 3 B8
Beech Rd
Bristol BS7 . . . . 18 E5

Beech Rd continued
Saltford BS31 . . . . 5 E3
Yorkley GL15 . . . . 156 A2
Beech Tree Gdns 5 GL8 140 C4
Beechurst Ave GL52 . . . . . . 133 F1
Beechurst Way GL52 . . . . . 137 D4
Beech Way
Bream GL15 . . . . 147 C5
Littledean GL14 . . . . 156 E8
Beech Well La GL16 . . . . . . 155 C8
Beech Wlk GL17 . . . . 164 C5
Beechwood Ave BS15 . . . . . 10 D5
Beechwood Cl
Bristol BS14 . . . . 3 C8
Cheltenham GL52 . . . . 131 B8
Nailsworth GL6 . . . . 90 F5
Beechwood/Coed Ffawydd
NP16 . . . . 60 C8
Beechwood Dr 4 GL6 . . . . 148 B6
Beechwood Gr
Gloucester GL4 . . . . 118 C3
Wotton-u-E GL12 . . . . 68 C8
Beechwood Rd
Bristol BS16 . . . . 20 B4
Easton-in-G BS20 . . . . 16 A4
Beechwood Rise BS11 . . . . . 87 F2
Beechwood Sh Ctr GL50 193 C3
Beehive Trad Est BS5 . . . . . . 9 E7
Beek's La SN14, BA1 . . . . . . 14 D5
Beesmoor Rd BS36 . . . . 31 B6
Begbrook Dr BS16 . . . . 19 F6
Begbrook La BS16 . . . . 19 F6
Begbrook Pk BS16 . . . . 20 A7
Begbrook Prim Acad
BS16 . . . . 19 F6
Beggar Bush La BS8 . . . . 7 B1
Beggarswell Cl BS2 . . . . 195 C4
Bekdale Cl GL2 . . . . 129 D8
Belas Knap Long Barrow★
GL54 . . . . 174 A4
Belfast Wlk BS4 . . . . 2 E8
Belfry BS30 . . . . 11 B6
Belfry Ave BS5 . . . . 10 A8
Belfry Cl GL4 . . . . 119 E4
Belfry The NP16 . . . . 61 C8
Belgrave Hill 5 BS8 . . . . . . 18 A2
Belgrave Ho 4 BS8 . . . . . . 194 A3
Belgrave Pl BS8 . . . . 194 A3
Belgrave Rd
Bristol BS8 . . . . 194 A4
Gloucester GL1 . . . . 196 C1
Belgrove Terr GL1 . . . . 196 C1
Bellamy Ave BS13 . . . . 2 C4
Bellamy Cl BS15 . . . . 10 A5
Belland Dr
Bristol BS14 . . . . 2 F4
Charlton Kings GL53 . . . . . 131 A4
Bella Vista GL52 . . . . 138 B3
Bell Bank 5 GL56 . . . . 186 C5
Bell Barn Rd BS9 . . . . 17 C6
Bell Cl BS10 . . . . 18 E7
Bell Cotts GL2 . . . . 95 F4
Belle Ct 7 BS2 . . . . 8 F4
Bellevue BS8 . . . . 194 B2
Belle Vue Cl GL5 . . . . 99 C7
Bellevue Cotts
5 Bristol BS9 . . . . 18 A7
Bristol, Clifton Wood BS8 . 194 B2
Bellevue Cres BS8 . . . . 194 B2
Bellevue Ct BS8 . . . . 194 B2
Bellevue Pk BS4 . . . . 9 D2
Bellevue Rd
Bristol, Kingswood BS15 . . 10 F7
Bristol, St George BS5 . . . . 10 A8
6 Bristol, Windmill Hill BS2 . 8 F4
Belle Vue Rd
Bristol BS5 . . . . 19 C1
Cinderford GL14 . . . . 191 C6
Ruardean GL17 . . . . 163 F4
Stroud GL5 . . . . 99 C7
Bellevue Terr
Bristol, Brislington BS4 . . . . 9 D2
Bristol, Clifton Wood BS8 . 194 B2
Bristol, Windmill Hill BS2 . . 8 F4
Belle Vue Terr GL6 . . . . 148 C5
Bellfields La BS16 . . . . 30 C1
Bell Field The SN14 . . . . 47 E4
Bellflower Rd GL20 . . . . 192 E2
Bell Hill BS16 . . . . 19 C4
Bell Hill Rd BS5 . . . . 9 F8
Bellhouse Wlk BS11 . . . . 27 B1
Bellingham La SN6 . . . . 145 C3
Bell La
Blockley GL56 . . . . 186 C5
Bristol BS1 . . . . 195 A3
Bromesberrow Heath
GL18 . . . . 179 B4
Gloucester GL1 . . . . 196 B2
Lechlade on T GL7 . . . . . . 153 C2
Minchinhampton GL6 . . . . 148 A3
Poulton GL7 . . . . 151 F4
Stroud GL5 . . . . 98 E4
Westbury-on-S GL14 . . . . . 157 C3
Bell Orch GL2 . . . . 157 B6
Bell Pitch GL6 . . . . 102 F3
Bell Rd BS36 . . . . 31 C6
Bells Pl
Cinderford GL14 . . . . 156 C6
Coleford GL16 . . . . 155 A5
Bell Sq SN14 . . . . 15 A8
Belluton Rd BS4 . . . . 9 A3
Bell Vw Cl GL52 . . . . 134 A2
Bell Wlk GL1 . . . . 196 B2
Belmont Ave GL3 . . . . 120 B7
Belmont Dr BS34 . . . . 29 E5

Belmont La GL16......155 A8
Belmont Lo **6** GL52......193 C4
Belmont Pk BS7.........28 F1
Belmont Rd
　Bristol, Arno's Vale BS4....9 C3
　Bristol, Montpelier BS6....18 E2
　Cheltenham GL52......193 C4
　Hewelsfield GL15....146 E5
　Stroud GL5............99 E6
Belmont St GL51......130 A7
Belmont St BS5..........19 B1
Belmont Terr GL17....164 D5
Belmore Pl GL53......193 B2
Beloe Rd BS7..........18 E5
Belroyal Ave BS4........9 F3
Belsher Dr BS15.......11 A6
Belstone Wk BS4......2 C8
Belton Rd BS5...........9 B8
Belvedere Mews GL6..148 C5
Belvedere Rd BS6......18 B3
Belvoir Rd BS6.........18 E2
Belworth Ct **5** GL51...129 F7
Belworth Dr GL51....130 A7
Bence Ct **3** BS15.....10 B5
Bences Cl SN14.......14 F8
Bendall Ho **7** GL52...193 C4
Bendy Bow SN16.....141 F4
Benford Cl BS16.......20 C6
Ben Grazebrooks Well St
　GL5................99 D7
Benhall Ave GL51....129 E8
Benhall Gdns GL51....132 E1
Benhall Ho GL51.....129 F8
Benhall Inf Sch GL51..129 D7
Beni Cl GL51..........129 C6
Bennett Rd BS5..........9 F7
Bennett's Ct BS37.....44 A1
Bennett Way BS1, BS8...7 F5
Bennington St GL50...193 B4
Bensaunt Gr BS10.....28 D4
Benson Cl **3** GL4....119 E6
Bentley Cl
　Bristol BS14............2 F3
　Quedgeley GL2......117 F2
Bentley La GL52......134 D7
Benton Ct GL10........89 E6
Benville Ave BS9.......17 C8
Berchel Ho **4** BS3....8 D4
Berenda Dr BS30.......11 B3
Beresford Cl BS31.......5 E2
Beresford Ho GL7....190 C6
Berkeley Ave
　Bristol, Bishopston BS7....18 D3
　Bristol, Brandon Hill BS8..194 C3
Berkeley Castle & Butterfly
　House ★ GL13........85 F2
Berkeley Cl
　Bristol BS16...........21 A8
　Charfield GL12.......67 A5
　Gloucester GL3.....120 C6
　South Cerney GL7...142 F7
　Stroud GL5............98 D7
　Wotton-u-E GL12....68 B7
Berkeley Cres
　Bristol BS8..........194 B3
　Lydney GL15..........92 B5
Berkeley Ct
　Bristol, Bishopston BS7....18 D3
　Cheltenham GL52....193 C3
　Slimbridge GL2.......95 D3
Berkeley Bsns Pk BS5...9 B7
Berkeley Gdns BS31.....4 E4
Berkeley Gn BS16.......30 B1
Berkeley Gn Rd BS5....19 D2
Berkeley Gr BS5........19 C2
Berkeley Ho
　Bristol, Brandon Hill BS1..194 C3
　7 Bristol, Staple Hill BS16..20 D5
　7 Cheltenham GL52....133 F7
　4 Cheltenham, Hester's Way
　GL51................132 E3
Berkeley Mews GL52...193 C3
Berkeley Pl
　Bristol BS8..........194 B3
　Cheltenham GL52....193 C3
Berkeley Prim Sch GL13..85 E3
Berkeley Rd
　Bristol, Bishopston BS7....18 D3
　Bristol, Kingswood BS15...10 D7
　Bristol, Mayfield Park BS16..20 D2
　Bristol, Staple Hill BS16...20 D5
　Bristol, Westbury Park BS6..18 B4
　Cirencester GL7.....190 C1
Berkeleys Mead BS34...30 A6
Berkeley Sq BS8......194 C3
Berkeley St
　Bristol BS5...........19 C3
　Cheltenham GL52....193 C3
　Gloucester GL1.....196 A3
Berkeley Sta GL13.....85 F5
Berkeley Vale Pk GL13..85 D4
Berkeley Way
　Bristol BS16...........21 B7
　7 Tetbury GL8.......140 C5
Berkhampstead Sch
　GL52................134 A2
Berkley Pl BS3...........8 D2
Berkshire Rd BS7......18 D3
Berlington Ct BS1....195 B1
Berners Cl BS4..........2 D7
Berrells Rd GL8......140 B3
Berrells The GL8.....140 B3
Berrow Rd GL55.....189 B2
Berrows Mead BS37....43 A8
Berrow Wlk BS3........8 E2
Berry Cl GL6.........103 F8

Berrycroft GL13........85 E4
Berry Croft **5** BS3.....8 D4
Berryfield GL5.........98 F2
Berryfield Glade GL3..128 A6
Berry Hill Cl BS10.....28 D1
Berry Hill Cres GL7...190 C7
Berry Hill Prim Sch
　GL16................155 A7
Berry Hill Rd GL7....190 D7
Berry La BS7...........18 F6
Berry Lawn GL4.......119 D3
Berrymore Rd GL5.....98 F2
Bertha's Field GL9....57 B4
Berton Cl SN26.......144 E1
Berwick Cl BS10.......27 E8
Berwick Ct BS10.......27 B5
Berwick Dr BS10.......27 E5
Berwick La BS10.......27 D7
Berwick Rd
　Bishop's Cleeve GL52....137 F5
　Bristol BS5............19 B2
Beryl Gr BS14...........3 C8
Beryl Rd BS3...........8 B3
Besbury Pk GL6......148 A4
Besford Rd GL52.....138 E3
Besom La BS37.........32 D5
Bessemer Cl **22** GL16..155 A5
Beta Cl GL20.........182 B4
Bethel Rd BS5...........9 F8
Bethesda St GL50....193 B1
Betjeman Cl GL2.....118 C4
Betjeman Rd **2** BS30...11 A5
Bettenson Rise **10** GL54..168 A1
Bettertons Cl GL7....152 D3
Bettridge Ct GL52....134 B3
Betts Gn BS16.........21 C7
Betworthy Est GL11...88 E8
Bevan Cl BS34.........28 F7
Bevan Gdns GL20....182 C5
Bevan Rise GL14.....156 C5
Bevans Hill GL13......85 D4
Beverley Ave BS16....30 F1
Beverley Cl BS5.......10 B6
Beverley Croft GL51..132 C2
Beverley Gdns
　Bristol BS9............17 D7
　Woodmancote GL52..138 C3
Beverley Rd BS7......18 F8
Beverly Ct **3** BS16....20 D3
Beverstone BS15.......10 C8
Beverstone Ct GL7...142 F7
Beverstone Rd
　1 Gloucester GL2...118 B1
　South Cerney GL7...142 F7
Beverston Gdns BS11..27 B2
Bevington Cl BS34....39 E1
Bevington La GL13....76 F7
Bevington Wlk BS34..39 E1
Bewick Cl GL47......143 A7
Bewicks The GL2......95 D3
Bewley Way GL3.....128 A6
Bexley Rd BS16........20 B3
Beyon Cl GL11........87 F6
Beyon Dr GL11........87 F6
Bibstone BS15.........11 A8
Bibsworth Ave **4** WR12..185 C8
Bibsworth La
　Broadway WR12.....185 C8
　Broadway WR12.....188 B1
Bibury Ave BS34.......29 B8
Bibury CE Prim Sch GL7..160 A1
Bibury Cl BS9.........18 D7
Bibury Cnr GL54.....168 F8
Bibury Cres
　Bristol, Hanham BS15...10 C3
　Bristol, Henleaze BS9...18 D7
Bibury Farm Cotts GL7..160 B2
Bibury Rd
　Cheltenham GL51...129 E8
　Gloucester GL4.....119 A6
Bibury Trout Farm ★
　GL7................160 A1
Bickerton Cl BS10.....27 F3
Bickford Cl BS30......11 A6
Bickley Cl BS15.......10 C2
Bicknor Dr GL52.....134 B2
Bicknor St GL16......155 A6
Bicks La **30** GL54....174 A7
Biddel Springs SN6..145 D3
Biddestone Rd BS7....28 E1
Biddulph Way WR8...178 E7
Bideford Cres BS4......2 F1
Bidwell Cl BS10.......28 B3
Bifield Cl BS14..........3 F5
Bifield Gdns BS14......3 E5
Bifield Rd BS14.........3 F5
Bigstone Cl BS14.......3 F5
Bigstone Gr BS14.......3 F5
Bigstone Mdw NP16...73 A2
Bigwood La BS1......194 C2
Bijou Ct GL1..........126 F4
Bilberry Cl
　Bristol BS9............17 C8
　5 Gloucester GL4..119 F5
Bilbie GL1 **5** BS10....18 E7
Billand Cl BS13.........1 E3
Billbrook Rd GL3.....120 A7
Billingham Cl GL4....119 B6
Billings Way GL50...130 B6
Bilsham La BS35.......48 D2
Bilson GL14...........191 C5
Bilson School GL14..191 C5
Bindon Dr BS10.......28 D4
Binley Gr BS14..........3 D5
Binmead Gdns BS13....2 B4

Binyon Rd GL54.....139 F5
Birbeck Rd BS9.......17 E5
Birchall Ave GL4.....119 C3
Birchall Rd BS6........18 C4
Birch Ave GL4.......119 C6
Birch Cl
　Bishop's Cleeve GL52....138 B4
　Bristol BS34...........28 E7
　Charlton Kings GL53...131 C4
　Ledbury HR8.........178 E8
Birch Croft BS14........3 A3
Birch Ct
　Keynsham BS31........4 C4
　Yate BS37.............43 D2
Birchdale Rd BS14......3 A8
Birch Dr
　Alveston BS35........50 F4
　Pucklechurch BS16....22 B5
Birches Cl GL5.........99 C8
Birches Dr GL5.........99 C8
Birches La GL18.....170 F7
Birches The NP25....154 B5
Birches The GL5........99 C8
Birchfield Rd GL52...138 A4
Birch Glade **4** SN6..142 F4
Birch Ho BS16.........20 B5
Birchills Trad Est BS4..9 F1
Birchley Rd GL52....131 B8
Birchmore Rd GL1...119 A8
Birch Pk GL16........155 C5
Birch Rd
　Bristol, Kingswood BS15...20 E3
　Bristol, Southville BS3....8 B4
　Dursley GL11.........88 A4
　Mile End GL16......155 C6
　Woodchester GL5....99 A3
　Yate BS37.............43 D2
Birchwood Cl GL14..191 B5
Birchwood Ct BS4......9 F6
Birchwood Fields GL4..118 E3
Birchwood Rd
　Bristol BS4............9 F4
　Woolaston GL15....147 C3
Birdale Cl BS10.......27 E3
Birdland ★ GL54.....168 F7
Birdlip Fm GL4......121 F1
Birdlip Ho GL11......127 A2
Birdlip Prim Sch GL4..121 F1
Bird Rd GL3.........120 B6
Birds Bush La GL6...106 B5
Birdwell Prim Sch BS41...1 A8
Birdwood BS15.......10 D6
Birdwood Cl GL4....119 D6
Birdwood Gdns NP16...60 C4
Birgage Rd GL9.......55 F2
Birkdale
　Bristol BS30..........11 B6
　Yate BS37.............32 E8
Birkin St **5** BS2.......9 A6
Bishop Cl GL51......133 A2
Bishop Manor Rd BS10..18 D7
Bishop Mews BS2....195 B4
Bishop Rd
　Bristol, Bishopston BS7....18 D4
　Bristol, Emerson's Green
　BS16................21 C6
　Shurdington GL51..129 E2
Bishop Road Prim Sch
　BS7.................18 D4
Bishop's Castle Way
　GL1.................119 A8
Bishops Cl
　Bishop's Cleeve GL52....138 A3
　Bristol BS9............17 C3
　Chepstow/Cas-Gwent NP16..60 F4
Bishop's Cl GL5........99 D6
Bishop's Cleeve Prim Sch
　GL52................137 F3
Bishops Cove BS13......1 F5
Bishops Ct BS9.......17 C3
Bishops Dr GL52.....137 F3
Bishopsfield **2** SN6..143 E4
Bishops Gate GL15....92 A2
Bishops Knoll BS9.....17 C3
Bishops Mdw GL52...137 E4
Bishops Mead NP16...60 B4
Bishops Rd GL4.....119 E6
Bishop St BS2.......195 B4
Bishopston Cl GL51..132 C1
Bishopstone Rd GL1..119 A8
Bishops Wlk
　Cirencester GL7.....190 C4
　Forthampton GL19...181 B3
　Tewkesbury GL20...192 C5
　Whiteshill GL6......102 F3
Bishop's Wlk GL19...181 C3
Bishop's Wood BS32...40 C6
Bishopsworth Rd BS13...2 A7
Bishop Terr BS2.....195 C4
Bishopthorpe Rd BS10..18 E7
Bishton La NP16.......73 B3
Bishport Ave BS13......2 C3
Bishport Cl BS13.......2 B4
Bishport Gn BS13......2 C3
Bishton La NP16.......73 B3
Blake Rd
　Bristol BS7............19 B6
　Cirencester GL7.....190 C5
Blakes Rd BS35........64 B1
Blake St **13** NP25...154 A7
Blakewell Mead GL6..103 E8
Blanchards BS37.......33 D8
Blanchards Cotts BS37..33 D8
Blandamour Wy BS10..28 D2
Blandford Alley SN6..145 D3
Blandford Cl BS9......18 B6
Blandford Rd **2** BS9...18 B6
Blands Row BS35......48 B1
Bleasby Gdns GL50...130 A4

Bittern Ave GL4.....119 D6
Bittern Cl GL7.......143 A7
Bitterwell Cl BS36.....31 D3
Bittlemead BS13.........2 E1
Bitton Sta ★ BS30....11 B1
Bixhead Wlk GL16...155 C5
Blaby Cl GL4........119 F5
Blackacre GL4.......119 C3
Blackberry Ave **5** BS16..19 E5
Blackberry Cl GL4...119 E4
Blackberry Dr BS36....31 C6
Black Berry Field GL52..134 C3
Blackberry Gr GL52..137 E4
Blackberry Hill BS16..19 E5
Blackberry Hill Hospl
　BS16................19 F5
Blackbird Ave GL3...127 D6
Blackbird Ct GL10.....97 F8
Blackboy **18** BS15....99 C7
Blackboys GL11........88 A3
Blackburn Rd GL52...137 E1
Black Dog Way GL1...196 B3
Blackdown Ct BS14.....3 B5
Blackford La GL7....144 E6
Blackfriars BS1......195 A3
Blackfriars Church ★
　GL1.................196 A2
Blackhorse Ct BS15...10 C8
Blackhorse Hill BS35,
　BS10................28 B8
Black Horse Hill GL8..140 B3
Blackhorse La BS15...21 A6
Blackhorse Pl BS15...21 A6
Blackhorse Prim Sch
　BS16................21 A8
Blackhorse Rd
　Bristol, Kingswood BS15...10 D8
　Bristol, Mangotsfield BS16..21 A7
Black Jack Mews GL7..190 C5
Black Jack St GL7....190 C5
Blacklow Cl GL5.......98 F2
Blackmans Cl GL18..170 F4
Blackmoor Rd BS8....16 E2
Blackmoors La BS3.....7 E4
Blackquarries Hill GL12..68 E7
Blacksmith Cl GL20..183 B5
Blacksmith Hill GL12..69 C7
Blacksmith La
　Churchdown GL3....128 D4
　The Leigh GL19.....173 D5
Blacksmiths Ground
　GL2.................125 D3
Blacksmiths La
　Beckford GL20......183 B5
　Cheltenham GL52...134 C4
　Dumbleton WR11...183 F7
　Highnam GL2........125 F7
Blacksmith's La BA1...6 B3
Blacksmiths Rd GL20..183 B4
Black Stone Kilns La
　HR9.................162 D3
Blackswarth Ho **6** BS5...9 D7
Blackswarth Rd BS5....9 D7
Blackthorn Cl BS13.....2 D5
Blackthorn Dr BS32...29 D7
Blackthorn End GL53..130 A4
Blackthorn Gdns GL2..117 F1
Blackthorn Rd BS13....2 D5
Blackthorn Wlk BS15..20 E2
Blackwater Way GL2..127 E5
Black Wells GL11......80 B7
Blackworth SN6.....145 D4
Blackworth Ct SN6...145 D4
Blackworth Ind Est SN6..145 D4
Bladon Mews GL51..129 B7
Blagdon Cl BS3.........8 E2
Blagrove Cl BS13.......2 C3
Blagrove Gdns BS13....2 C3
Blaisdon BS37.........32 E7
Blaisdon Cl
　Bristol BS10..........28 A1
　Gloucester GL4.....119 E4
Blaisdon La GL17.....165 B4
Blaisdon Rd GL14....165 C1
Blaisdon Way **5** BS10..27 E2
Blaise Castle Mus ★ BS10..27 E2
Blaisedell Wy BS10....27 D3
Blaise Hamlet BS11...27 D2
Blaise Prim Sch BS10..27 E2
Blaise Wlk BS9........17 C6
Blake Croft GL51....132 E4
Blake Hill Way GL4..119 D7
Blakeley Ct GL3.....127 F6
Blakeney Cl GL4.....118 D3
Blakeney Hill Rd GL15..156 C2
Blakeney Mills BS37...43 E1
Blakeney Prim Sch GL15..156 D1
Blakeney Rd
　Bristol BS34..........39 E1
　Bristol, Horfield BS7...19 A7

Bledington Prim Sch
　OX7.................177 E1
Bledisloe Wy
　Gloucester GL4.....118 B2
　Lydney GL15..........92 C1
Blenheim Cl
　Alderton GL20......183 D4
　Upper Rissington GL54..169 D6
Blenheim Ct
　Bristol BS32..........40 D3
　14 Winchcombe GL54..174 A7
Blenheim Dr
　Bredon GL20.........182 C7
　Bristol BS34..........29 B4
　3 Ledbury HR8....178 F7
　28 Newent GL18..171 A4
　Yate BS37.............43 D3
Blenheim Ho GL3....120 A7
Blenheim Orch GL51..129 E2
Blenheim Rd
　Bristol BS6...........18 B3
　Gloucester GL1.....196 C1
Blenheim Sq GL51...132 E3
Blenheim St BS5.......19 A1
Blenheim Way GL56..187 A3
Blenheim Ct BS16.....20 A7
Bleriot Rd GL54.....169 D6
Blethwin Cl BS10......27 F1
Blimeshire GL15.....155 F1
Blind La
　Chipping Campden GL55..188 F1
　Tetbury GL8.........140 C5
Blinkhorns Bridge La
　GL2.................127 B1
Block 2 Government Bldgs
　BS10................28 B1
Blockley CE Prim Sch
　GL56................186 C6
Blockley Ct GL56....186 C6
Bloomfield Rd
　Bristol BS4............9 D4
　Gloucester GL1.....118 D7
Bloomfield Road Link GL4..9 C4
Bloomfield Terr GL1..118 D6
Bloomsbury St GL51..193 A4
Bloxham Rd WR12...188 A1
Bloxhams Orch GL19..172 D4
Bloy Sq BS55.........19 C1
Bloy St BS55.........19 C1
Bluebell Chase GL6..148 C6
Bluebell Cl
　Bristol BS9...........17 B6
　Gloucester GL4.....119 D5
　Milkwall GL16......155 B4
　Thornbury BS35......64 D2
Bluebell Ct GL52.....137 F5
Bluebell Dr
　Chepstow/Cas-Gwent
　NP16................60 F5
　Cirencester GL7.....190 E2
Bluebell Gr
　Cheltenham GL51...130 A5
　Tewkesbury GL20...192 F1
Bluebell Rise GL6...148 C6
Bluebells The BS32...29 F7
Blue Boys' Pk GL6...148 A4
Blue Coat CE Prim Sch
　GL12.................68 B6
Blue Falcon Rd BS15..20 E1
Blue La GL18.........170 D4
Blue Quarry Rd GL7..190 D5
Blue Rock Cres **5** GL15..155 D1
Blunsdon Hill SN26..144 C2
Blunts Hay GL7......153 C8
Boakes Dr GL10.......97 E6
Boat Ho The HR9....162 E4
Boating Lake La GL15..92 C1
Bobble Ct GL54......169 C6
Bockenem Cl BS35....51 D7
Boddington Dr GL2..110 B8
Bodenham Field GL4..119 E6
Bodey Cl BS30........11 A5
Bodiam Ave GL4.....118 B1
Bodmin Wlk BS4.......2 F8
Bodnam Rd GL51....132 E4
Bodyce Rd **3** BS35...51 A5
Boiling Wells La BS2...19 A3
Boleyn Cl **3** GL4....127 F7
Boleyn Cotts GL51...133 B7
Boleyn Ho GL54.....139 F5
Bolton Rd BS7........18 E3
Bondend Rd GL4.....119 F2
Bond's La GL11........24 E1
Bonds Mill Est GL10..97 C3
Bond St BS1.........195 B3
Bonnington Wlk BS7..19 B7
Bonville Bsns Ctr BS4...9 F2
Bonville Rd BS4........9 F2
Book End GL17......164 F5
Bootenhay Rd GL52..138 A4
Booth Rd BS3..........8 C4
Boot La BS3............8 D4
Borage Cl GL4......119 F5
Bordesley Rd BS14.....3 A3
Borkley St BS34.......29 A7
Borleyton Wlk BS13....1 F4
Born Ct **10** HR8....178 F8
Borough Cl GL10......98 A3
Borver Gr BS13.........2 B4
Boscombe Cres BS16..20 F7
Boscombe La GL6.....90 E1
Boseley Way GL14...191 C4
Bospin La GL5..........98 F1

Boston Rd BS7 . . . . 18 F8
Boswell St **4** BS5 . . . . . . 19 C2
Botany SN6 . . . . 145 C3
Botham Dr BS4 . . . . .9 E1
Boucher Pl **2** BS2 . . . . . . 19 A2
Boughton Rd **34** GL18 . . . 171 A4
Boughton Wy GL4 . . . . . . 119 C7
Boulevard The
  Bristol BS14 . . . . 2 E5
  Stroud GL5 . . . . 99 B5
Boulmer Ave GL2 . . . . . . 110 B7
Boulters Rd BS13 . . . . 2 C4
Boulton La
  2 Dursley GL11 . . . . . . 80 B8
  Dursley GL11 . . . . 88 B1
Boulton Rd GL50 . . . . . . 133 D5
Boulton's La **6** BS15 . . . 10 D8
Boulton's Rd **5** BS15 . . . 10 D8
Bouncer's La GL52 . . . . . 134 B3
Boundary Cotts GL3 . . . . 121 A4
Boundary Pl GL19 . . . . . . 172 A7
Boundary Rd
  Avonmouth BS11 . . . . . . 26 D3
  Coalpit Heath BS36 . . . . 31 D7
Bourchier Gdns BS13 . . . . .2 B3
Bourne Cl
  Bristol BS15 . . . . 10 B8
  Winterbourne BS36 . . . . 30 E7
Bourne La
  Brimscombe GL5, GL6 . . 148 A6
  Bristol BS5 . . . . 19 B2
Bourne Lake Pk SN6 . . . 143 C3
Bourne Rd BS15 . . . . 10 A8
Bourne The GL7 . . . . 153 D8
Bourneville Rd BS5 . . . . . . 9 B8
Bournside Cl GL51 . . . . . 130 A7
Bournside Dr GL51 . . . . . 130 A7
Bournside Rd GL51 . . . . . 130 B7
Boursland Cl BS32 . . . . . . 40 C2
Bourton Ave BS34 . . . . . . 29 C8
Bourton Cl BS34 . . . . 29 C8
Bourton House Garden★
  GL56 . . . . 186 D3
Bourton Ind Pk GL54 . . . 169 A8
Bourton Link GL54 . . . . . 169 A8
Bourton Mead BS41 . . . . . 7 A1
Bourton-on-the-Water Prim
  Sch GL54 . . . . 168 F8
Bourton Rd
  Gloucester GL4 . . . . . . 118 E2
  Moreton-in-M GL56 . . . 187 A3
Bourton Wlk BS13 . . . . . . 2 A8
Bouverie St BS5 . . . . 9 B8
Boverton Ave GL3 . . . . . . 120 E6
Boverton Dr GL3 . . . . 120 D6
Boverton Rd BS34 . . . . . . 29 B4
Bovone La GL2 . . . . 124 D8
Bowbridge La
  Cheltenham GL52 . . . . . 134 B5
  Stroud GL5 . . . . 99 D6
Bowbridge Lock GL5 . . . . 99 D5
Bow Cotts BS20 . . . . 16 C4
Bowden Cl BS9 . . . . 17 C8
Bowden Pl BS16 . . . . 20 F7
Bowden Rd BS5 . . . . 19 E1
Bowen Cl GL52 . . . . 134 A3
Bowen's Hill **16** GL16 . . 155 A5
Bowen's Hill Rd **15** GL16 . 155 A5
Bower Ashton Terr BS3 . . . .7 F4
Bower Ct BS3 . . . . 8 A2
Bowerleaze BS9 . . . . 17 C5
Bower Rd BS3 . . . . 8 A3
Bower Wlk BS3 . . . . .8 E3
Bowes Lyon Cl **4** GL56 . . 187 A2
Bow La
  5 Bourton-on-t-W GL54 . 168 F7
  Ripple GL20 . . . . 181 D8
Bowland Ct BS32 . . . . 40 D1
Bowldown Cotts GL8 . . . . 71 A5
Bowldown Rd GL8 . . . . . . 71 C3
Bowler Rd GL20 . . . . 182 C5
Bowlers Lea GL11 . . . . . . 87 F5
Bowl Hill GL5 . . . . 99 A3
Bowling Green Ave GL7 . . 190 C6
Bowling Green Cres GL7 . 190 C6
Bowling Green Ct GL56 . . 187 A3
Bowling Green La GL7 . . . 190 C6
Bowling Green Rd GL7 . . . 190 C6
Bowling Hill BS37 . . . . . . 44 A1
Bowling Hill Bsns Pk
  BS37 . . . . 44 A1
Bowling Rd BS37 . . . . 33 B8
Bowly Cres GL7 . . . . 150 E2
Bowly Rd
  Cirencester GL7 . . . . . . 190 B2
  Gloucester GL1 . . . . . . 118 D6
Bowmead **7** BS4 . . . . . . 9 D1
Bownham Mead GL5 . . . . . 99 D2
Bownham Pk GL5 . . . . 99 D1
Bowood BS16 . . . . 30 C1
Bowood Dr GL3 . . . . 120 C4
Bowring Cl BS13 . . . . 2 C3
Bowsland BS32 . . . . 40 E2
Bowsland Green Prim Sch
  BS32 . . . . 40 E2
Bowsland Way BS32 . . . . . 40 D2
Bowson Rd GL15 . . . . . . 155 D1
Bowson Sq GL15 . . . . . . 155 D1
Bowstreet La BS35 . . . . . . 28 A8
Bow Wow GL7 . . . . 143 A8
Boxbush Cl GL7 . . . . 143 A8
Boxbush Rd
  Coleford GL16 . . . . . . 155 A5

Boxbush Rd continued
  South Cerney GL7 . . . . . 143 A8
Box Cres GL6 . . . . 91 F6
Box Gdns GL6 . . . . 91 F6
Boxhedge Farm La BS36 . . 31 E3
Box La GL6 . . . . 91 F5
Box Rd GL11 . . . . 88 A8
Box Road Ave GL11 . . . . . 88 A8
Box Tree Cl GL17 . . . . . . 163 F4
Boxwell Rd GL8 . . . . 70 B4
Box Wlk BS31 . . . . 4 C4
Boxwood Cl GL8 . . . . 82 B5
Boyce Cl GL4 . . . . 119 E3
Boyce Dr BS2 . . . . 19 A2
Boyce's Ave BS8 . . . . 194 A3
Boyd Cl BS30 . . . . 12 B7
Boyd Rd BS31 . . . . 5 D3
Bozard La GL20 . . . . 136 B8
Brabazon Rd BS34 . . . . . . 29 B2
Bracelands GL6 . . . . 148 C7
Bracelands Dr **1** GL6 . . . 155 A7
Bracewell Gdns BS10 . . . . 28 C4
Bracey Dr BS16 . . . . 20 C6
Brackenbury Dr BS34 . . . . 29 F5
Bracken Cl GL15 . . . . 92 C3
Brackendene BS32 . . . . . . 40 C1
Bracken Dr GL15 . . . . 92 B3
Bracton Dr BS4 . . . . 3 A5
Bradestones Wy GL10 . . . 96 F8
Bradford Rd **5** GL2 . . . 127 B2
Bradfords Cl GL18 . . . . . 170 F4
Bradfords Ct GL18 . . . . . 170 F4
Bradfords La GL18 . . . . . 170 F4
Bradhurst St **8** BS5 . . . . .9 B6
Bradley Ave
  Bristol BS11 . . . . 16 E6
  Winterbourne BS36 . . . . 30 E5
Bradley Cl GL2 . . . . 127 C4
Bradley Court Rd GL17 . . 164 D6
Bradley Cres BS11 . . . . . . 16 E6
Bradley Ct BS16 . . . . 20 C5
Bradley Pavilions BS32 . . . 40 C2
Bradley Rd
  Bristol BS34 . . . . 39 F1
  Charlton Kings GL53 . . . 131 A4
  Wotton-u-E GL12 . . . . . 68 A8
Bradley Rise GL17 . . . . . 164 C6
Bradley St GL12 . . . . 68 A7
Bradley Stoke Com Sch
  BS32 . . . . 40 E1
Bradley Stoke Way BS32 . . 29 F2
Bradshaw Cl GL2 . . . . . . 127 C5
Bradstone Rd BS36 . . . . . 30 D5
Bradwell Gr BS10 . . . . . . 18 C8
Braeburn Cl
  Cheltenham GL51 . . . . . 132 E2
  Gloucester GL2 . . . . . . 127 C2
Braemar Ave BS7 . . . . . . 28 F1
Braemar Cres BS7 . . . . . . 28 F1
Braemor Ct BS9 . . . . 18 A8
Brae Wlk GL4 . . . . 119 D4
Bragg's La BS2 . . . . 195 C3
Braikenridge Rd BS4 . . . . . 9 D4
Brainsfield BS9 . . . . 17 F6
Brake Cl
  Bristol, Bradley Stoke
   BS32 . . . . 29 E7
  Bristol, Warmley Hill BS15 . 10 F7
Brake The
  Coalpit Heath BS36 . . . . 31 C5
  Yate BS37 . . . . 43 E5
Brakewell Gdns BS14 . . . . 3 A4
Bramble Chase GL52 . . . 137 F4
Bramble Dr
  Bristol BS9 . . . . 17 D3
  Dursley GL11 . . . . 88 A3
Bramble La
  Bristol BS9 . . . . 17 C3
  Stonehouse GL10 . . . . . 97 F8
Bramble Lawn GL4 . . . . . 119 D3
Bramble Rd GL16 . . . . . . 155 B4
Bramble Rise GL52 . . . . . 134 C3
Brambles The
  Berkeley GL13 . . . . 85 E4
  Bristol BS13 . . . . 2 C4
  Keynsham BS31 . . . . . . 4 D3
  Lea HR9 . . . . 164 C8
Brambling Mews GL4 . . . 143 A7
Brambling Wlk BS16 . . . . 19 F6
Bramery The GL51 . . . . . 133 B2
Bramley Cl
  Kingswood GL12 . . . . . . 67 F4
  4 Ledbury HR8 . . . . . 178 E7
  Olveston BS35 . . . . 50 A3
  Pill BS20 . . . . 16 C4
Bramley Ct **6** BS30 . . . . 10 F4
Bramley Dr GL19 . . . . . . 165 D6
Bramley La GL7 . . . . 190 C2
Bramley Mews GL4 . . . . . 120 A6
Bramley Rd
  Cheltenham GL51 . . . . . 132 F3
  Tewkesbury GL20 . . . . . 192 D6
Bramleys The GL17 . . . . . 164 F5
Branche Gr BS13 . . . . 2 D3
Branch Hill Rise GL53 . . . 131 A4
Branch Rd
  Bamfurlong GL51 . . . . . 129 A7
  Cheltenham GL51 . . . . . 129 B7
Branch The GL17 . . . . . . 164 B3
Brandash Rd BS37 . . . . . . 44 C1
Branders **17** SN6 . . . . . 143 E4
Brandon Cl GL3 . . . . 128 A8
Brandon Ho BS8 . . . . . . 194 B1
Brandon Pl GL50 . . . . . . 193 A1
Brandon St BS1 . . . . 194 C2

Brandon Steep BS1 . . . . . 194 C2
Brangwyn Gr BS7 . . . . . . 19 B6
Branksome Cres BS34 . . . . 29 B3
Branksome Dr
  Bristol BS34 . . . . 29 B3
  Winterbourne BS36 . . . . 30 E6
Branksome Rd BS6 . . . . . . 18 B3
Brannigan Ct GL20 . . . . . 182 C5
Branscombe Ct BS3 . . . . . . 8 D2
Branscombe Rd BS9 . . . . . 17 C4
Bransdown Hill SN16 . . . . 59 A3
Brans La GL56 . . . . 177 C4
Brantwood Rd BS16 . . . . 148 C6
Branwhite Cl BS7 . . . . 19 B7
Brasenose Rd GL20 . . . . . 182 C7
Brassington Gdns GL54 . . 166 E2
Bratches The GL55 . . . . . 189 A3
Bratton Rd BS4 . . . . 2 D7
Braunton Rd BS3 . . . . 8 C3
Bravender Ho GL7 . . . . . . 190 D4
Bray Ave HR8 . . . . 178 F8
Braybrooke Cl GL8 . . . . . 140 C4
Braydon Ave BS32 . . . . . . 29 D7
Braydon La SN6 . . . . 143 D3
Braydon Rd SN6 . . . . 143 A1
Brayne Ct BS30 . . . . 10 F3
Breaches Cl GL52 . . . . . . 138 C4
Breaches Gate BS32 . . . . . 29 F6
Breaches The BS20 . . . . . . 16 B5
Bream Ave GL15 . . . . 155 B1
Bream CE Prim Sch
  GL15 . . . . 155 D1
Bream Rd
  Bream GL15 . . . . 147 E7
  St Briavels GL15 . . . . . 147 B7
Brean Down Ave BS9 . . . . 18 B5
Brean Gdns BS3 . . . . 8 E2
Brecknock Rd BS4 . . . . 9 A3
Brecon Cl
  Bristol BS9 . . . . 18 B6
  Quedgeley GL2 . . . . . . 109 E8
Brecon Rd BS9 . . . . 18 B6
Brecon Way GL16 . . . . . . 155 C8
Bredon BS37 . . . . 32 D7
Bredon Cl BS15 . . . . 10 F7
Bredon Hancock's Endowed
  Fst Sch The GL20 . . . . 182 C8
Bredon Lodge GL20 . . . . 182 C7
Bredon Nook Rd BS10 . . . 18 C7
Bredon Rd GL20 . . . . 192 D6
Bredon Sch GL20 . . . . . . 181 C7
Bredon Tythe Barn★
  GL20 . . . . 182 B7
Bredon View WR12 . . . . . 185 C8
Bregawn Cl GL52 . . . . . . 137 E2
Brehal Cl GL15 . . . . 92 A2
Breinton Way GL2 . . . . . . 127 D5
Brendon Cl BS30 . . . . 11 C4
Brendon Rd BS3 . . . . 8 D3
Brendon Wlk GL52 . . . . . 134 B3
Brenner St BS5 . . . . 19 B2
Brensham Ct GL3 . . . . . . 120 A7
Brent Rd BS7 . . . . 18 F5
Brentry Ave **5** BS5 . . . . .9 B7
Brentry La BS10 . . . . 28 B3
Brentry Lo BS10 . . . . 28 A3
Brentry Prim Sch BS10 . . . 28 B4
Brentry Rd BS16 . . . . 19 F3
Brereton Way BS30 . . . . . 11 B4
Bretforton Fst Sch
  WR11 . . . . 188 A6
Bretforton Rd WR11 . . . . 188 B7
Brevel Terr GL53 . . . . . . 131 B5
Brewerton Cl BS10 . . . . . 28 C3
Brewery Cotts NP25 . . . . 154 C5
Brewery Ct
  Bristol BS3 . . . . 8 A4
  Cirencester GL7 . . . . . . 190 C4
Brewery Hill BS30 . . . . . . .5 F7
Brewery La
  Nailsworth GL6 . . . . . . 91 B3
  Thrupp GL5 . . . . 99 E2
Brewery Row GL56 . . . . . 187 F1
Brewery St SN6 . . . . 145 D3
Brewery The GL50 . . . . . 193 B4
Brewery Yard **25** GL54 . . 176 F4
Brewhouse The BS1 . . . . 195 B2
Briarbank Rise GL52 . . . . 131 C7
Briar Cl BS15 . . . . 103 D1
Briar Ct BS20 . . . . 16 C4
Briarfield Ave BS15 . . . . . 10 C5
Briar Lawn GL4 . . . . 119 D3
Briarleaze BS35 . . . . 50 F2
Briars Cl GL3 . . . . 128 A6
Briarside Ho BS10 . . . . . . 28 D3
Briarside Rd BS10 . . . . . . 28 D3
Briar Way BS16 . . . . 20 C3
Briar Wlk
  Bristol BS16 . . . . 20 C3
  Cheltenham GL52 . . . . . 134 C3
Briarwood BS9 . . . . 17 F6
Briarwood Sch BS16 . . . . 20 B3
Briary Rd GL15 . . . . 153 E3
Briavels Gr BS6 . . . . 18 F2
Brick Cotts BS35 . . . . 62 E1
Brickfield Terr GL5 . . . . . 99 A6
Brickfields GL12 . . . . 68 B6
Bricknell Ave GL20 . . . . . 182 C7
Brickrow GL5 . . . . 99 C7
Brick St BS2 . . . . 195 C3
Brick Wlk WR11 . . . . 188 C6
Brickworks Trad Est
  WR11 . . . . 188 C8
Bridewell St BS1 . . . . . . 195 A3
Bridge Access Rd BS35 . . . 49 A7

Bridge Cl
  Cirencester GL7 . . . . . . 190 D2
  Gloucester GL2 . . . . . . 118 B6
  Lechlade on T GL7 . . . . 153 F2
  Whitchurch BS14 . . . . . . 3 C4
Bridge End
  Cirencester GL7 . . . . . . 190 D3
  Staunton GL19 . . . . . . 180 C2
Bridge Farm GL2 . . . . . . 126 B7
Bridge Farm Cl BS14 . . . . . 3 A3
Bridge Farm Prim Sch
  BS14 . . . . 3 A4
Bridge Farm Wlk BS16 . . . 21 B3
Bridge Ho
  Alveston BS35 . . . . 50 F5
  Bristol BS1 . . . . 195 A2
Bridge Keepers Wy GL2 . . 109 D7
Bridgeleap Rd BS16 . . . . . 20 F8
Bridge Learning Campus
  BS13 . . . . .2 E4
Bridgemans Cl WR12 . . . . 188 B1
Bridgend Ct GL10 . . . . . . 97 E6
Bridgend Rd **2** GL51 . . . 129 C7
Bridge Rd
  Bristol, Eastville BS5 . . . . 19 B3
  Bristol, Lower Soundwell
   BS15 . . . . 21 A3
  Bristol, Shortwood BS16 . . 21 C4
  Cirencester GL7 . . . . . . 190 D2
  Frampton on Severn GL2 . 157 F3
  Harrow Hill GL17 . . . . . 164 B3
  Leigh Woods BS8 . . . . . . 7 E6
  Sharpness GL13 . . . . . . 93 C1
  Stroud GL5 . . . . 98 D6
  Yate BS37 . . . . 43 A2
Bridges Ct **2** BS16 . . . . 20 B4
Bridges Dr **3** BS16 . . . . 20 C6
Bridgeside GL54 . . . . 168 F8
Bridge-Side GL5 . . . . 98 F6
Bridge St
  Blakeney GL15 . . . . 156 D1
  Bretforton WR11 . . . . . 188 A6
  Bristol BS1 . . . . 195 A2
  Bristol, Eastville BS5 . . . . 19 D2
  Cheltenham GL52 . . . . . 133 B4
  Chepstow/Cas-Gwent NP16 . 72 F1
  Fairford GL7 . . . . 152 E4
  Ledbury HR8 . . . . 178 E8
  Nailsworth GL6 . . . . . . 91 C4
  Newent GL18 . . . . 171 A5
  Stroud GL5 . . . . 98 E6
Bridget Dr NP16 . . . . 61 A7
Bridge Valley Rd BS8 . . . . .7 E8
Bridge Vw GL15 . . . . 147 C3
Bridge Vw Cl **8** BS5 . . . 19 C1
Bridge Way BS36 . . . . 31 B8
Bridge Wlk BS7 . . . . 19 A8
Bridgman Gr BS34 . . . . . . 29 B3
Bridgwater Rd BS41, BS13,
  BS48 . . . . .1 D6
Bridle Cl GL54 . . . . 169 A7
Bridle The GL5 . . . . 98 D7
Bridle Way BS35 . . . . 50 F4
Briercliffe Rd BS9 . . . . . . 17 D7
Brierley Banks GL17 . . . . 163 F2
Brierley Cl GL4 . . . . 119 E5
Brierley Council Hos
  GL17 . . . . 163 F2
Brierley Rd GL17 . . . . . . 163 F3
Brierley Way GL15 . . . . . 156 B1
Brierly Furlong BS34 . . . . 29 D3
Briery Leaze Rd BS14 . . . . 3 A4
Brightlands **10** GL14 . . . 157 A6
Brighton Cres BS3 . . . . . . .8 B2
Brighton Mews BS8 . . . . . 194 B4
Brighton Pk **16** BS5 . . . . .9 B8
Brighton Pl BS15 . . . . 20 D1
Brighton Rd
  Bristol, Kingswood BS15 . . 10 D8
  Bristol, Russell Town BS5 . . 9 B7
Brigstocke Rd BS2 . . . . . 195 B4
Brimbles The BS7 . . . . . . 29 B2
Brimley GL10 . . . . 97 F4
Brimscombe CE Prim Sch
  GL5 . . . . 99 F1
Brimscombe Hill GL5 . . . . 91 E8
Brimscombe La GL5 . . . . . 99 F2
Brimsham Green Sch
  BS37 . . . . 43 D4
Brimsham Park Sh Ctr
  BS37 . . . . 43 F4
Brimsome Mdw GL2 . . . . 125 D5
Brindle Cl GL4 . . . . 119 C4
Brinkmarsh La GL12 . . . . . 65 D2
Brinkworthy Rd BS16 . . . . 19 E6
Brinmead Wlk BS13 . . . . . .1 F3
Brins Cl BS34 . . . . 29 F4
Brinsham La BS37 . . . . . . 44 A6
Brinsmead Cres BS20 . . . . 16 D4
Brionne Way GL2 . . . . . . 127 B5
Brisbane GL10 . . . . 101 F1
Briscoes Ave BS13 . . . . . . .3 F8
Brislington Enterprise Coll
  BS4 . . . . .3 F8
Brislington Hill BS4 . . . . . . .9 E1
Brislington Ret Pk BS4 . . . . .9 E1
Brislington Trad Est BS4 . . .9 E1
Bristol & Anchor Ho BS5 . . 9 D8
Bristol Bsns Pk BS16 . . . . 29 E1

Bristol Cathedral★ BS1 . . 194 C2
Bristol Dental Hospl
  BS1 . . . . 195 A3
Bristol & Exeter Mews
  BS1 . . . . 195 C1
Bristol Eye Hospl BS1 . . . 195 A3
Bristol Free Sch BS10 . . . . 28 B1
Bristol Gate **1** BS8 . . . . .7 F5
Bristol Gateway Sch BS11 . 27 B1
Bristol Gateway Sch The
  BS2 . . . . 19 A2
Bristol Gram Sch BS8 . . . 194 C3
Bristol Harbour Rly★
  BS1 . . . . 194 B1
Bristol Hill BS4 . . . . 9 D2
Bristol Metropolitan Acad
  BS16 . . . . 19 F4
Bristol Old Vic Theatre Sch
  BS8 . . . . 18 A1
Bristol Parkway N BS34 . . . 30 A5
Bristol Parkway Sta BS34 . 29 E4
Bristol Rd
  Bristol BS16 . . . . 30 C4
  Cambridge GL2 . . . . . . 95 F3
  Cirencester GL7 . . . . . . 190 D2
  Cromhall GL12 . . . . 53 B7
  Frampton Cotterell BS36 . . 42 B3
  Gloucester GL1, GL2 . . . 118 C6
  Keynsham BS31 . . . . . . 4 E6
  Luckington SN14 . . . . . 47 E3
  Stonehouse GL10 . . . . . 97 E7
  Thornbury BS35 . . . . . . 51 B8
  Upper Rissington GL54 . . 169 D7
  Whitchurch BS14 . . . . . . 3 D3
  Winterbourne BS16 . . . . 30 C4
Bristol Royal Hospital for
  Children BS1 . . . . 195 A4
Bristol Royal Infmy BS2 . . 195 A4
Bristol South End BS3 . . . . 8 D2
Bristol Steiner Sch BS6 . . 18 B2
Bristol Tech & Engineering
  Acad BS34 . . . . 29 D3
Bristol Vale Ctr For Ind
  BS3 . . . . .8 E1
Bristol Zoo Gdns★ BS8 . . 17 F1
Bristow Broadway BS11 . . 26 C1
Bristowe Ho BS16 . . . . . . 20 B5
Bristowe Lodge BS16 . . . . 20 C4
Bristow Rd GL20 . . . . 192 E1
Britannia Cl **4** BS16 . . . . 30 F1
Britannia Cres BS34 . . . . . 29 B5
Britannia Ct **1** BS16 . . . 20 D5
Britannia Ho BS34 . . . . . . 28 F2
Britannia Rd
  Bristol, Kingswood BS15 . . 10 C8
  Bristol, Lower Easton BS5 . 19 C1
  Bristol, Patchway BS34 . . 28 E7
Britannia Way GL52 . . . . 138 E3
British Rd BS3 . . . . 8 C3
British Sch The BS37 . . . . 43 B4
Briton Cl NP16 . . . . 61 A4
Brittania Bldgs BS8 . . . . 194 B1
Britten Ct **10** BS30 . . . . . 10 F4
Britten Pl GL51 . . . . 132 E2
Britton Bottom GL9 . . . . . 56 B1
Britton Gdns BS15 . . . . . . 20 C1
Britton Ho BS15 . . . . 11 B8
Brittons Pas SN14 . . . . . . 14 F8
Brixham Rd BS3 . . . . 8 C1
Brixton Rd BS5 . . . . 9 B8
Brixton Road Mews **22** BS5 . .9 B8
Brize Ave GL2 . . . . 110 C8
Brizen La GL53 . . . . 130 B4
Broadacre Cl GL20 . . . . . 182 C7
Broadbury Rd BS4 . . . . . . .2 E8
Broad Croft BS32 . . . . . . 40 C2
Broadclose Rd GL2 . . . . . 173 B2
Broad Dr GL8 . . . . 57 A8
Broadfield Ave BS15 . . . . 20 C1
Broadfield Cotts GL54 . . . 160 C6
Broadfield Rd
  Bristol BS4 . . . . .9 B1
  Eastington GL10 . . . . . . 96 F6
Broad La
  Coalpit Heath BS36 . . . . 31 B5
  Westerleigh BS37 . . . . . 32 A4
  Yate BS37 . . . . 43 C4
Broadlands Acad BS31 . . . . 4 D6
Broadlands Ave BS31 . . . . . 4 D6
Broadlands Ct GL54 . . . . 168 F7
Broadlands Dr BS11 . . . . . 27 A1
Broadleas BS13 . . . . 2 C7
Broadleaze
  Bristol BS11 . . . . 16 E7
  Down Ampney GL7 . . . . 143 F8
Broadleys Ave BS9 . . . . . . 18 C7
Broad Leys Rd GL4 . . . . . 119 D7
Broad Marston Rd GL55 . . 189 A7
Broad Mdw GL10 . . . . 97 C4
Broadmead BS1 . . . . 195 B3
Broadmead La BS31 . . . . . . 5 A3
Broadmead Lane Ind Est
  BS31 . . . . .5 B3
Broadmere GL11 . . . . 87 E4
Broadmere Ct GL11 . . . . . 87 E3
Broadmoor La BA1 . . . . . . .6 F4
Broadmoor Pk GL14 . . . . 191 B7
Broadmoor Rd GL14 . . . . 191 B7
Broadoak Hill BS41 . . . . . .1 F2
Broad Oak Rd BS13 . . . . . .1 F4
Broad Oaks BS8 . . . . .7 E6
Broad Oak Way BS15 . . . 129 F6
Broadoak Wlk BS16 . . . . . 20 B4
Broad Plain BS2 . . . . 195 C2
Broad Quay BS1 . . . . 195 A3

Broad Rd BS15 . . . 20 C1
Broad St
Bristol BS1 . . . 195 A3
Bristol, Staple Hill BS16 . . . 20 F4
Chipping Sodbury BS37 . . . 44 B1
Hartpury GL19 . . . 172 C4
King's Stanley GL10 . . . 98 A3
Littledean GL14 . . . 191 F4
13 Newent GL18 . . . 171 A4
Stroud GL5 . . . 98 D3
Broadstone Cl GL4 . . . 119 E8
Broadstone Wlk BS13 . . . 2 D5
Broadwalk Sh Ctr BS4 . . . 9 B2
Broadway
Gloucester GL4 . . . 118 F5
Saltford BS31 . . . 5 D3
Yate BS37 . . . 43 F2
Broadway Ave BS9 . . . 18 D6
Broadway Bears & Dolls Mus★ WR12 . . . 185 C8
Broadway Cl
Cheltenham GL52 . . . 134 A5
Kempsford GL7 . . . 144 E8
Broadway Ct GL7 . . . 142 F7
Broadway Fst Sch WR12 . 188 B1
Broadway Inf Sch BS37 . . . 43 F2
Broadway La
Minsterworth GL2 . . . 116 A2
South Cerney GL7 . . . 143 A6
Broadway Rd
Bristol, Bishopston BS7 . . . 18 D3
Bristol, Bishopsworth BS13 . . 1 F5
Mickleton GL55 . . . 189 A6
Toddington GL54 . . . 184 C3
Willersey WR12 . . . 188 B2
Winchcombe GL54 . . . 174 A7
Broadway, St Mary's RC Prim Sch WR12 . . . 185 B8
Broadways Dr BS16 . . . 19 F7
Broadway The
Chalford GL6 . . . 148 E6
Dursley GL11 . . . 80 A8
North Nibley GL11 . . . 79 F8
Broadway Tower Ctry Pk★ WR12 . . . 185 D4
Broad Weir BS1 . . . 195 B3
Broadwell Bridge 7 GL16 . . . 155 B6
Broadwell Cl GL4 . . . 119 E5
Broadwell Rd GL56 . . . 177 C5
Broadwell Terr GL11 . . . 88 B1
Broad Wlk BS4 . . . 9 A2
Broad Wlk The GL50 . . . 193 B2
Brock Cl GL51 . . . 129 B6
Brockeridge Cl GL2 . . . 117 E2
Brockeridge Rd GL20 . . . 181 F7
Brockhampton La GL51 . . 133 B7
Brockhampton Pk GL54 . 174 B1
Brockhollands GL15 . . . 147 E8
Brockhollands Rd GL15 . . 147 D8
Brockhurst Gdns BS15 . . . 10 A8
Brockhurst Rd BS15 . . . 10 A8
Brockley Acres GL6 . . . 148 C7
Brockley Cl BS34 . . . 29 C7
Brockley Rd
Leonard Stanley GL10 . . . 97 F4
Saltford BS31 . . . 5 D3
Brockley Wlk BS13 . . . 2 A8
Brockmoor La HR9 . . . 170 C4
Brockridge La BS36 . . . 31 C7
Brocks 4 BS4 . . . 9 D1
Brocks Rd BS13 . . . 2 C3
Brockweir Rd GL52 . . . 134 C2
Brockworth BS37 . . . 32 C6
Brockworth Cotts GL3 . . . 120 F4
Brockworth Cres BS16 . . . 19 F6
Brockworth Prim Acad GL3 . . . 120 E5
Brockworth Rd GL3 . . . 128 E2
Brome Rd GL4 . . . 119 F5
Bromesberrow Heath Bsns Pk HR8 . . . 179 B3
Bromesberrow St Mary's CE Prim Sch HR8 . . . 179 C5
Bromfield Wlk BS16 . . . 21 B7
Bromley Dr BS16 . . . 20 D8
Bromley Heath Ave BS16 . 20 D8
Bromley Heath Inf Sch BS16 . . . 20 E8
Bromley Heath Rd BS16 . . 20 D8
Bromley Rd
Bristol BS7 . . . 18 F5
Ellwood GL16 . . . 155 C3
Brompton Cl BS15 . . . 11 A8
Broncksea Rd BS7 . . . 28 F1
Bronte Cl 2 GL51 . . . 129 F7
Bronte Dr 2 HR8 . . . 178 E8
Bronte Wlk BS7 . . . 19 A8
Bronze Cl GL3 . . . 120 E5
Brookbank Cl GL50 . . . 193 A4
Brook Cl
Long Ashton BS41 . . . 7 B1
15 Northleach GL54 . . . 168 A1
Winchcombe GL54 . . . 139 F4
Brookcote Dr BS34 . . . 29 D6
Brook Ct
Cheltenham GL50 . . . 130 B6
Tewkesbury GL20 . . . 192 E5
Brookdale Rd BS13 . . . 2 B6
Brook End SN14 . . . 47 F5
Brooke Rd GL7 . . . 190 B2
Brookfield SN6 . . . 145 C3
Brookfield Ave BS7 . . . 18 D3
Brookfield Cl BS37 . . . 44 C2
Brookfield La
2 Bristol BS6 . . . 18 D2
Brookfield La *continued*
Churchdown GL3 . . . 128 E5
Brookfield Mews GL4 . . . 127 C1
Brookfield Rd
8 Bristol, Montpelier BS6 . . . 18 D2
Bristol, Patchway BS34 . . . 29 B8
Churchdown GL3 . . . 128 D5
Gloucester GL3 . . . 119 F7
Brookfield Wlk BS30 . . . 11 C3
Brook Gate BS3 . . . 7 E1
Brook Hill BS6 . . . 18 F1
Brook Ho
Bristol BS34 . . . 29 C8
8 Cheltenham GL51 . . . 129 F7
3 Thornbury BS35 . . . 51 C8
Brookhouse Mill GL6 . . . 104 A7
Brook La
1 Blockley GL56 . . . 186 C5
Blockley GL56 . . . 186 C5
Bristol, Montpelier BS6 . . . 18 F1
Bristol, Stapleton BS16 . . . 19 E6
Down Hatherley GL2 . . . 173 B1
Brookland Rd BS6 . . . 18 D5
Brooklands Pk GL2 . . . 127 D5
Brooklea BS30 . . . 11 B3
Brooklea Gdns GL17 . . . 164 F6
Brookleaze
Bristol BS9 . . . 17 C5
Keynsham BS31 . . . 4 D6
Brooklet Rd GL15 . . . 147 B4
Brook Lintons BS4 . . . 9 D3
Brooklyn Cl 4 GL51 . . . 132 F3
Brooklyn Ct GL51 . . . 133 A4
Brooklyn Gdns GL51 . . . 133 A3
Brooklyn Rd
Bristol BS13 . . . 2 B8
Cheltenham GL51 . . . 132 F2
Brookmead BS35 . . . 51 D7
Brook Office Pk BS16 . . . 31 B2
Brook Rd
Bristol, Hillfields BS16 . . . 20 B4
Bristol, Mangotsfield BS16 . 20 F6
Bristol, Montpelier BS6 . . . 18 F1
Bristol, Southville BS3 . . . 8 D4
Bristol, Speedwell BS5 . . . 19 F1
Bristol, Warmley BS15 . . . 11 B8
Cheltenham GL51 . . . 133 A4
Brookridge Ct 5 BS16 . . . 20 D4
Brookridge Ho BS10 . . . 27 F3
Brooksdale La GL53 . . . 130 C6
Brookside
Alderton GL20 . . . 183 E4
Crudwell SN16 . . . 141 C3
4 Newent GL18 . . . 171 A4
Paxford GL55 . . . 186 E8
Pill BS20 . . . 16 D3
Tewkesbury GL20 . . . 192 E6
Tintern Parva NP16 . . . 146 B3
Brookside Cotts GL5 . . . 91 B5
Brookside Dr BS36 . . . 31 B8
Brookside Rd
Bristol BS4 . . . 9 E2
Cinderford GL14 . . . 191 B5
Brookside Villas GL2 . . . 127 B2
Brook St
Bristol BS5 . . . 9 C7
Chipping Sodbury BS37 . . . 33 A8
Gloucester GL1 . . . 196 B1
Mitcheldean GL17 . . . 164 D5
Brookthorpe BS37 . . . 32 D8
Brookthorpe Ave BS11 . . . 27 A1
Brookthorpe Cl GL4 . . . 118 D3
Brookthorpe Ct 4 BS37 . . 32 D8
Brook Vale GL52 . . . 131 A7
Brookview Wlk BS13 . . . 2 B7
Brook Way BS32 . . . 29 D8
Brookway Dr GL53 . . . 131 A6
Brookway Rd GL53 . . . 131 A6
Broom Bglws GL4 . . . 119 A5
Broom Hill
Bristol BS16 . . . 19 E5
Coleford GL16 . . . 154 F7
Broom Hill Forest Trail★ GL16 . . . 154 F7
Broomhill Inf Sch BS4 . . . 9 F3
Broomhill Jun Sch BS4 . . . 9 F3
Broomhill Rd BS4 . . . 10 A2
Broom Ho GL4 . . . 119 A5
Brooms The BS16 . . . 31 A1
Brosnan Dr GL51 . . . 132 C1
Brotherswood Ct BS32 . . . 40 D4
Broughton Ho BS1 . . . 195 B1
Brown Cl GL51 . . . 132 E3
Browne Ct 5 BS8 . . . 7 F6
Browning Ct BS7 . . . 19 B8
Browning Mews GL51 . . . 129 F7
Brownings La GL11 . . . 88 B1
Brown's End Cotts HR8 . . 179 C5
Browns Hill GL6 . . . 148 B5
Brownshill Rd GL6 . . . 148 B5
Brown's La GL10 . . . 98 A6
Brown's Piece GL12 . . . 68 B7
Broxholme Wlk BS11 . . . 16 F8
Bruce Ave BS5 . . . 19 C1
Bruce Rd BS5 . . . 19 C1
Brummels Dr GL16 . . . 155 A7
Brunel Cl BS30 . . . 11 C7
Brunel Ct
Quedgeley GL2 . . . 110 B6
Yate BS37 . . . 43 C2
Brunel Lock Rd BS1 . . . 7 F5
Brunel Rd
Bristol BS13 . . . 2 A8
Chepstow/Cas-Gwent NP16 60 E6
Brunel Way
Bristol BS1, BS3 . . . 7 F4
Honeybourne WR11 . . . 188 C7
Stonehouse GL10 . . . 101 C1
Thornbury BS35 . . . 51 B7
Brunswest Ct GL1 . . . 196 B2
Brunswick Pl 10 BS1 . . . 7 F5
Brunswick Rd GL1 . . . 196 B2
Brunswick Sq
Bristol BS2 . . . 195 B4
Gloucester GL1 . . . 196 B2
Brunswick St
Bristol, Redfield BS5 . . . 9 C7
Bristol, St Pauls BS2 . . . 195 B4
Cheltenham GL50 . . . 133 D3
Brush The GL5 . . . 98 D8
Bruton Cl BS5 . . . 9 F8
Bruton La GL12 . . . 67 F5
Bruton Pl BS8 . . . 194 B3
Bruton Way GL1 . . . 196 C3
Bryansons Cl BS16 . . . 19 D6
Bryants Cl BS16 . . . 30 C1
Bryant's Hill BS5 . . . 10 B6
Bryaston Cl GL51 . . . 133 A2
Bryerland Rd GL3 . . . 121 A4
Brymore Ave GL52 . . . 134 A5
Brymore Cl GL52 . . . 134 A5
Brynland Ave BS7 . . . 18 E4
Bryony Bank GL53 . . . 130 B4
Bryworth La GL7 . . . 153 C3
Buchanan Ave GL16 . . . 155 A6
Buchanan Cl 2 GL16 . . . 155 A6
Buchan Dr 4 GL2 . . . 110 B8
Buchan Ho 6 GL56 . . . 186 C5
Buckholt Rd GL4 . . . 112 E8
Buckholt Way GL3 . . . 120 E5
Buckholt Wood Nature Reserve★ GL4 . . . 112 F7
Buckingham Ave GL51 . . 132 F2
Buckingham Cl
Eastington GL10 . . . 96 E8
Tewkesbury GL20 . . . 192 E2
Buckingham Ct
Bristol BS32 . . . 40 D3
Cheltenham GL50 . . . 193 B3
Buckingham Dr
Bristol BS34 . . . 29 D5
2 Churchdown GL3 . . . 128 A7
Buckingham Gdns BS16 . . 20 E6
Buckingham Ho BS34 . . . 28 F2
Buckingham Lodge BS31 . . . 4 F5
Buckingham Par BS35 . . . 64 B1
Buckingham Pl
Bristol, Mangotsfield BS16 . . . 20 E6
Bristol, Victoria Park BS8 . 194 A3
Buckingham Rd BS4 . . . 9 D5
Buckingham St BS3 . . . 8 C2
Buckingham Vale BS8 . . . 194 A4
Buckland Cl GL52 . . . 137 F3
Bucklehaven GL53 . . . 130 F5
Buckler Cl GL7 . . . 152 D3
Buckles Cl GL53 . . . 131 B5
Buckle's Row GL53 . . . 131 B5
Buckle St
Broadway WR12, GL54, GL56 . . . 185 D5
Honeybourne WR11 . . . 188 C8
Weston-s-E GL55 . . . 188 D4
Bucklewell Cl BS11 . . . 16 F6
Buckle Wood NP16 . . . 60 C8
Buckleys Rd BS34 . . . 29 A7
Buckshaft Rd GL14 . . . 191 C1
Buckstone Cl GL16 . . . 155 B7
Budding Rd GL10 . . . 96 E8
Budding The GL5 . . . 103 E1
Budding Wy GL11 . . . 88 B2
Buddleia Cl GL4 . . . 119 F4
Buddleia Ct 7 GL3 . . . 128 A7
Bude Ave BS5 . . . 10 A8
Bude Rd BS34 . . . 29 B4
Buildings The GL11 . . . 87 D3
Bula Wy GL52 . . . 134 D4
Bulford Cl GL3 . . . 120 C6
Bullens Cl BS32 . . . 40 D2
Buller Rd BS4 . . . 9 C2
Bulley La
Birdwood GL2 . . . 165 F6
Churcham GL2 . . . 124 C3
Bullfinch Rd GL4 . . . 119 C6
Bullfinch Way GL3 . . . 127 D7
Bullingham Ct GL51 . . . 133 C3
Bull La
Bristol BS5 . . . 9 F6
Gloucester GL1 . . . 196 B3
Pill BS20 . . . 16 C4
27 Winchcombe GL54 . . . 174 A7
Bull Pitch
4 Dursley GL11 . . . 80 B8
Dursley GL11 . . . 88 B1
Bull Ring The GL17 . . . 164 D5
Bulls Cross GL6 . . . 104 B6
Bully La BS37 . . . 53 D1
Bulwark Ave NP16 . . . 60 F5
Bulwark Bsns Pk NP16 . . . 60 E6
Bulwark Rd NP16 . . . 60 E7
Bulwarks The GL6 . . . 148 A3
Bumblebee Cl BS13 . . . 1 E4
Buncombe Wy GL7 . . . 190 F3
Bungalows The
Coleford GL16 . . . 155 B5
Lydney GL15 . . . 92 C2
Bunting Hill GL6 . . . 91 A4
Bunting Way GL6 . . . 90 F4
Burbank Cl BS30 . . . 11 A3
Burchells Ave BS15 . . . 20 B1
Burchells Green Cl BS15 . 20 B1
Burchells Green Rd BS15 . 20 B1
Burcombe GL7 . . . 158 B4
Burcombe Cl BS36 . . . 31 D6
Burcombe La GL7 . . . 158 A3
Burcombe Rd GL6 . . . 148 C6
Burcombe Way GL6 . . . 148 C6
Burcott Rd BS11 . . . 26 D5
Burden Cl BS32 . . . 29 F6
Burdett Cl GL10 . . . 97 F7
Burdett Ho 10 GL10 . . . 97 F7
Burdett Rd GL10 . . . 97 F7
Burfoote Gdns BS14 . . . 3 E4
Burfoot Rd BS14 . . . 3 E4
Burford Ave BS34 . . . 29 C8
Burford Dr GL5 . . . 99 A7
Burford Gr BS11 . . . 16 F5
Burford Mews GL1 . . . 119 A8
Burford St GL7 . . . 153 E2
Burgage 4 NP25 . . . 154 A8
Burgage Cl BS37 . . . 33 B8
Burgage The GL52 . . . 134 B5
Burge Ct GL7 . . . 190 D3
Burgess Green Cl BS4 . . . 9 E7
Burghill Rd BS10 . . . 28 A1
Burghley Ct BS36 . . . 30 E5
Burghley Rd BS6 . . . 18 E2
Burgis Rd BS14 . . . 3 D6
Burkes Ct GL50 . . . 193 B4
Burleigh Croft GL3 . . . 119 F8
Burleigh La GL5 . . . 91 F8
Burleigh Tor GL5 . . . 91 F7
Burleigh View 7 GL6 . . . 148 B6
Burleigh Way GL12 . . . 54 B5
Burley Ave BS16 . . . 20 F5
Burley Crest BS16 . . . 20 F5
Burley Gr BS16 . . . 20 F5
Burlington Ct 9 BS6 . . . 18 B2
Burlington Rd BS6 . . . 18 B2
Burltons The GL12 . . . 66 B2
Burma Ave GL52 . . . 134 B2
Burma Rd GL6 . . . 91 A4
Burnbush Cl BS14 . . . 3 E6
Burnbush Prim Sch BS14 . . 3 D5
Burnell Dr BS2 . . . 195 C4
Burneside Cl BS10 . . . 28 C2
Burnet Cl GL4 . . . 119 A4
Burnett Bsns Pk BS31 . . . 5 B1
Burney Way BS30 . . . 11 A3
Burnham Cl BS15 . . . 20 F1
Burnham Dr BS15 . . . 20 F1
Burnham Rd BS11 . . . 16 D6
Burns Ave GL2 . . . 118 C4
Burnt Barn Rd NP16 . . . 60 F4
Burnt Oak GL11 . . . 88 A2
Burrington Wlk BS13 . . . 2 A8
Burrough Way BS36 . . . 30 E6
Burrups La HR9 . . . 170 B5
Burton Cl BS1 . . . 195 B1
Burton Ct
2 Bristol, Upper Eastville BS16 . . . 19 E3
Bristol, Victoria Park BS8 . 194 B3
Burton Farm Cl SN14 . . . 36 B3
Burton Rd GL9 . . . 35 F6
Burtons Bank OX7 . . . 169 F7
Burton St GL50 . . . 193 A4
Burwalls Rd BS8 . . . 7 E6
Bury Bar La GL18 . . . 171 A4
Burycourt Cl BS11 . . . 27 A1
Bury Court Rd GL14 . . . 157 F6
Bury Hill BS36 . . . 30 F3
Bury Hill La BS37 . . . 44 A8
Bury Hill View BS16 . . . 30 E1
Bury La
Doynton BS30 . . . 12 F7
Minsterworth GL2 . . . 116 E7
Burytown La SN26 . . . 144 E1
Bury Vw BS36 . . . 30 E4
Buscombe Gdns GL3 . . . 120 B7
Bush Ave BS34 . . . 29 D5
Bush Cl GL10 . . . 96 F8
Bushcombe Cl GL52 . . . 138 C3
Bushcombe La GL52 . . . 138 D4
Bush Ct
Alveston BS32 . . . 50 F5
10 Bristol BS4 . . . 8 F4
Cheltenham GL52 . . . 134 B3
Bushes La BS37 . . . 45 A6
Bush Hay GL3 . . . 128 B5
Bush Ind Est BS5 . . . 9 D8
Bushy Beeches GL6 . . . 105 D7
Bushy Ho BS2 . . . 8 F3
Bushy Leas 1 BS16 . . . 19 D8
Bushy Pk BS2 . . . 8 F3
Bushy Rd BS34 . . . 29 A7
Bushy Way GL51 . . . 132 D5
Business Park The BS13 . . . 2 E3
Bussage CE Prim Sch GL6 . . . 148 B6
Bussage Hill GL6 . . . 148 B6
Butcher Hill's La GL6 . . . 91 B3
Butcher Row Folk Mus★ HR8 . . . 178 F8
Butchers Row 9 WR12 . . 185 B8
Butcombe Wlk BS14 . . . 3 B5
Bute Cl SN6 . . . 145 C4
Buthay La GL12 . . . 54 A5
Buthay The GL12 . . . 54 A5
Butler Ho BS5 . . . 9 F8
Butlers Cl
Bristol BS5 . . . 9 F7
Sherston SN16 . . . 58 C1
Butler's Field GL7 . . . 153 E3
Butlers Mead GL15 . . . 156 E1
Butlers Wlk 3 BS5 . . . 9 F6
Buttercliffe Rise BS41 . . . 7 C3
Buttercross La GL52 . . . 134 D3
Buttercup Lawn GL4 . . . 119 D2
Buttercup Pl BS3 . . . 7 F1
Butterfield Cl
Bristol BS10 . . . 18 E7
Frampton Cotterell BS36 . . . 31 B6
Butterfield Ct GL52 . . . 137 F5
Butterfield Rd BS10 . . . 18 E7
Buttermere Cl GL51 . . . 129 F6
Buttermilk La GL3 . . . 128 C6
Butterow W GL5 . . . 99 B5
Butterrow Hill GL5 . . . 99 C4
Butterrow La GL5 . . . 99 D4
Buttersend La GL19 . . . 171 F4
Butterworth Ct BS4 . . . 2 D7
Butt Gn GL6 . . . 111 F1
Buttington GL4 . . . 119 F5
Buttington Hill NP16 . . . 61 B7
Buttington Rd NP16 . . . 61 A7
Buttington Terr NP16 . . . 61 B6
Butt La BS35 . . . 64 C3
Button Cl BS14 . . . 3 A6
Button Mills Est GL10 . . . 97 E6
Butts Farm The★ GL7 . . . 151 B1
Butts La GL15 . . . 156 E2
Butt's La
Dyrham SN14 . . . 24 B4
Woodmancote GL52 . . . 138 C4
Butt St GL6 . . . 148 A3
Butts The
Crudwell SN16 . . . 141 C3
Gloucester GL4 . . . 119 A4
Newent GL18 . . . 171 A5
Poulton GL7 . . . 151 F3
Butt's Wlk 1 GL51 . . . 129 C7
Buxton Wlk BS7 . . . 19 A8
Byard Rd GL2 . . . 118 B5
Bybrook Gdns GL4 . . . 118 D1
Bybrook Rd GL4 . . . 118 D1
Bydemill Gdns SN6 . . . 145 C3
Bye Mead BS16 . . . 21 B8
Bye St HR8 . . . 178 E8
Byfield Cl GL52 . . . 138 C2
Byfords Cl GL19 . . . 165 D6
Byfords Rd GL19 . . . 165 D6
Byre Cl SN6 . . . 143 F4
Byres The GL56 . . . 187 D6
Byron Ave GL2 . . . 118 C4
Byron Cl GL20 . . . 192 E3
Byron Ct 17 GL52 . . . 133 F2
Byron Pl
Bristol, Brandon Hill BS8 . . 194 B3
Bristol, Staple Hill BS16 . . 20 E4
Byron Rd
Cheltenham GL51 . . . 132 F1
Dursley GL11 . . . 80 C7
Stroud GL5 . . . 99 A8
Byron St
Bristol, Moorfields BS5 . . . 9 C7
5 Bristol, St Pauls BS2 . . . 19 A1
Bythesea Ave BS10 . . . 18 E7
Byzantine Ct BS1 . . . 195 A1

C

Cabot Circus BS1 . . . 195 B3
Cabot Cl
Bristol BS15 . . . 10 C7
Saltford BS31 . . . 5 D2
Yate BS37 . . . 43 F1
Cabot Ct BS7 . . . 28 F1
Cabot Gn BS5 . . . 9 B7
Cabot Ho 6 BS35 . . . 51 C8
Cabot Pk BS11 . . . 26 E5
Cabot Prim Sch BS2 . . . 195 C4
Cabot Twr★ BS1 . . . 194 B2
Cabot Way
Bristol BS8 . . . 7 F5
Pill BS20 . . . 16 D3
Cadbury Cl GL3 . . . 120 B6
Cadbury Heath Prim Sch BS30 . . . 11 B6
Cadbury Heath Rd BS30 . . 11 B5
Cadbury Rd BS31 . . . 5 A2
Caddick Cl BS15 . . . 20 F2
Cade Cl
Bristol, Kingswood BS15 . . . 10 F6
Bristol, Stoke Gifford BS34 . 29 E5
Cadmium Rd BS11 . . . 26 C4
Cadogan Ho 18 GL52 . . . 133 F2
Cadogan Rd BS14 . . . 3 A8
Caen Rd BS3 . . . 8 D3
Caernarvon Cl GL51 . . . 129 E6
Caernarvon Ct GL51 . . . 129 D6
Caernarvon Rd
Cheltenham GL51 . . . 129 F6
Keynsham BS31 . . . 4 C4
Caerwent La NP16 . . . 60 F4
Caesar Rd GL2 . . . 118 C5
Caesars Cl GL15 . . . 92 C4
Caine Rd BS7 . . . 18 F7
Caine Sq GL51 . . . 132 C1
Cains Cl BS15 . . . 10 E6
Cainscross Rd GL5 . . . 98 F7
Cainscross Rdbt GL5 . . . 98 F7
Caird St NP16 . . . 60 E7
Cairn Gdns BS36 . . . 30 E4
Cairns' Cres 12 BS2 . . . 18 F1
Cairns Ct BS6 . . . 18 C4
Cairns Rd BS6 . . . 18 C4
Caitlin Ct BS14 . . . 3 D6

Cakebridge Pl GL52 . . . . 133 F3
Cakebridge Rd GL52 . . . 133 F4
Cala Trad Est BS3 . . . . . . .7 F3
Calcott Rd BS4 . . . . 9 A3
Calcutt St SN6 . . . . . . 143 F4
Caldbeck Cl BS10 . . . . 28 D2
Calder Cl BS31. . . . . 5 A4
Calderdale GL4 . . . . . . 119 F5
Calderwood Ct GL50 . . 193 B2
Caldicot Cl
  Bristol, Lawrence Weston
  BS11. . . . . 27 C2
  Bristol, Willsbridge BS30. . 11 B2
Caledonia Mews BS8. . . . .7 F6
Caledonian Rd
  Bristol BS1. . . . . 194 B1
  Gloucester GL4 . . . . . 119 C2
Caledonia Pl BS8 . . . . . . .7 F7
Calf's La GL55 . . . . 189 A2
Calf Way GL6 . . . . 105 C5
California Rd BS30 . . . . . 11 B3
Callicroft Prim Sch BS34 . 28 F8
Callicroft Rd BS34 . . . . . 29 A7
Callington Rd BS4 . . . . . . 9 D1
Callowell GL6. . . . . 103 A1
Callowell Prim Sch GL5 . 103 A1
Callowhill Ct BS1. . . . . 195 B3
Calspick Way GL2. . . . . 127 D5
Calton Prim Sch GL1. . . 118 E5
Calton Rd GL1 . . . . 118 E6
Calverley Mews 1 GL51. 129 E5
Camberley Cl GL3. . . . . 120 A8
Camberley Dr BS36 . . . . 30 F8
Camberley Rd BS4 . . . . . 2 D8
Camberwell Rd GL51. . . 132 D2
Camborne BS7 . . . . 19 A7
Cambourne Pl GL15. . . . 92 B2
Cambray Ct
  Cheltenham GL50. . . . 193 B3
  Cirencester GL7. . . . . 190 D4
Cambray Mews GL50 . . 193 C3
Cambray Pl GL50. . . . . 193 C3
Cambrian Dr BS37 . . . . . 43 E3
Cambrian Rd GL20 . . . . 192 E2
Cambridge Ave
  Cheltenham GL51. . . . 132 F1
  Dursley GL11. . . . . 80 B7
Cambridge Cres BS9. . . . 18 A7
Cambridge Pk BS6 . . . . . 18 B3
Cambridge Rd BS7. . . . . 18 E4
Cambridge Sq GL20 . . . 183 E4
Cambridge St
  8 Bristol, Redfield BS5 . . 9 C7
  Bristol, Windmill Hill BS3. . .8 F4
  Gloucester GL1 . . . . . 196 C2
Cambridge Way GL6 . . . 91 F6
Camden Cl GL56. . . . . . 187 F3
Camden Rd BS3 . . . . . . 194 B1
Camden Terr BS8 . . . . . 194 A2
Camden La
  Hawling GL54 . . . . . . 174 D5
  Willersey WR12. . . . . 188 C2
Camden Pitch CV36. . . . 189 F6
Camden Rd
  Cheltenham GL51. . . . 129 E8
  Chipping Campden GL55 . 189 A4
  Ebrington GL55 . . . . . 189 C3
  Gloucester GL4 . . . . . 118 E3
  Mickleton GL55 . . . . . 189 B8
Camp Gdns 1 GL54 . . . 176 F4
Campian Wlk BS4 . . . . . . 2 D6
Campion Cl
  Gloucester GL4 . . . . . 119 B4
  Thornbury BS35. . . . . . 64 D2
Campion Dr BS32 . . . . . 40 D2
Campion Pk GL51. . . . . 130 A4
Cam Pitch GL11. . . . . . . 87 F5
Camp La SN14 . . . . 24 C4
Camp Rd
  Bristol BS8. . . . . .7 F7
  Cheltenham GL52. . . . 134 C1
  Chepstow/Cas-Gwent NP16 60 F6
  Oldbury-on-S BS35 . . . . 63 B6
Camp View BS36. . . . . . 30 E4
Cam Rd GL52 . . . . 134 B3
Cams Ground GL2. . . . . 125 D6
Camwal Ind Est BS2. . . . .9 A5

Camwal Rd BS2. . . . . . .9 A5
Cam Woodfield Jun Sch
  GL11. . . . . 87 E5
Canada Way BS1. . . . . 194 B1
Canal Ct GL2 . . . . 118 C7
Canal Ironworks GL5. . . 99 E2
Canal Row GL2 . . . . . . 108 A1
Canal Side GL5 . . . . . . 98 F6
Canal Way GL2 . . . . . . 126 B4
Canal Wlk HR8. . . . . . . 178 E8
Canberra GL10. . . . . . . 101 E1
Canberra Gr BS34. . . . . 29 B4
Canberra Ho
  Cheltenham GL51. . . . 132 E1
  11 Coleford GL16 . . . . 155 B5
Candy Ct BS4. . . . . 9 D5
Canford La BS9. . . . . . . 17 E8
Canford Rd BS9. . . . . . . 17 F8
Cannans Cl BS36. . . . . . 30 E7
Canning Rd GL2. . . . . . 127 E5
Cann La BS30. . . . . 11 E6
Cannon Conner GL4. . . 120 A4
Cannon St
  Bristol, Kingsdown BS1. . 195 A4
  Bristol, Southville BS3. . . 8 C4
Cannop Cotts GL16. . . . 155 D6
Cannop Rd GL15. . . . . . 155 E3
Cannop Valley Trail★
  GL16. . . . . 155 E5
Cannop Villas GL16. . . . 155 D7
Canonbury St GL13. . . . . 85 F3
Canon Pk GL13 . . . . 85 F4
Canons Dr GL7. . . . . . . 153 F2
Canons Rd BS1 . . . . . . 194 C2
Canon St BS5 . . . . .9 C8
Canons Way BS1. . . . . 194 C1
Canon's Wlk BS15. . . . . 20 F2
Canowie Rd BS6 . . . . . . 18 B3
Cantell Gr BS14. . . . . . . .3 F5
Canterbury Cl BS37 . . . . 43 E3
Canterbury Ct BS16 . . . . 19 E6
Canterbury Leys GL20 . . 192 E5
Canterbury St 5 BS5 . . . .9 B6
Canterbury Wlk GL51. . . 130 A6
Canters Leaze GL12 . . . . 54 B4
Cantock's Cl BS8. . . . . . 194 C3
Canton Acre GL6. . . . . . 111 F1
Cantors Ct GL52 . . . . . 137 F2
Cantors Dr GL52 . . . . . 137 E2
Cantors Way SN16 . . . . 142 E1
Canvey Cl BS10 . . . . . . 18 E7
Canynge Ho 2 BS1. . . . 195 B1
Canynge Rd BS8 . . . . . . .7 F8
Canynge Sq BS8 . . . . . . .7 F8
Canynge St BS1. . . . . . 195 B2
Capel Cl BS15. . . . . 11 B8
Capel Ct GL5 . . . . 99 D8
Capel Rd
  Bristol BS11. . . . . 27 B1
  Gloucester GL4 . . . . . 119 C2
Capgrave Cl BS4. . . . . . 10 A3
Capgrave Cres BS4. . . . . 10 A3
Capital Edge BS8 . . . . . 194 B2
Capricorn Pl BS1 . . . . . 194 B2
Captain Barton Cl GL5. . . 99 E8
Captains Green Rd GL15. 156 A2
Caraway Gdns BS5. . . . . 19 C2
Cardigan Mews BS9. . . . 18 B5
Cardigan Rd BS9. . . . . . 18 B6
Cardill Cl BS13. . . . . . . .2 A8
Cardinal Dr GL2. . . . . . 118 A2
Cardington Cl 1 GL4. . . 110 C8
Cares Ct GL52. . . . . . . 138 A4
Carfax Ct BS6. . . . . 18 A3
Cargill Pl SN16 . . . . . . 141 F4
Carisbrooke Dr GL52 . . 131 C6
Carisbrooke Lodge BS6 . 18 A3
Carisbrooke Rd
  Bristol BS4. . . . . 2 D7
  Gloucester GL3 . . . . . 120 A7
Carisbrook Rd GL17. . . . 164 D6
Carlow Rd BS4. . . . . . . .2 E8
Carlton Ct
  1 Bristol, Ashley Down
  BS7. . . . . 18 F4
  3 Bristol, Eastfield BS9 . . 18 A7
Carlton Gdns GL5. . . . . 99 C6
Carlton Ho 2 BS9 . . . . . 18 A7
Carlton Pk BS5 . . . . . . .9 C8
Carlton Pl GL50, GL51 . . 133 C3
Carlton St GL52. . . . . . 133 F1
Carlyle Gr GL51 . . . . . . 132 D4
Carlyle Rd BS5. . . . . . . 19 C1
Carmarthen Ct BS37. . . . 43 F4
Carmarthen Gr BS30 . . . 11 B1
Carmarthen Rd
  Bristol BS9. . . . . 18 A5
  Cheltenham GL51. . . . 129 E6
Carmarthen St 2 BS11. . 11 B8
Carmel Christian Sch BS4 . .9 F1
Carnarvon Rd BS6 . . . . . 18 D2
Carne Pl GL4 . . . . 127 C1
Carolina Ho BS2. . . . . . 195 A4
Caroline Cl
  Chipping Sodbury BS37 . . 44 B2
  Keynsham BS31. . . . . . . 4 C4
Carpenter Cotts GL16 . . 154 F3
Carpenters 18 SN6 . . . . 143 E4
Carpenters Cl SN16 . . . . 58 D1
Carpenters La
  Cirencester GL7. . . . . 190 D4
  Keynsham BS31. . . . . . . 4 E5
Carpenter's Shop La BS16 20 E6

Carrant Brook Jun Sch
  GL20. . . . . 182 C5
Carrant Rd GL20 . . . . . 192 D5
Carr Ho 3 BS2 . . . . 18 F1
Carriage Dr BS10 . . . . . 28 B2
Carrick Ho 8 BS8. . . . . . .7 F6
Carriers Cl SN16 . . . . . . 58 C1
Carrington Rd BS3. . . . . .8 A3
Carrol Gr GL51. . . . . . . 132 D4
Carroll Ct BS16 . . . . . . 29 E1
Carsons Rd BS16. . . . . . 21 B2
Carter Cl GL3. . . . . 120 B4
Carter Rd GL51 . . . . . . 132 F4
Carter's Bldgs 13 BS8 . . .7 F7
Carters Leaze CV36 . . . . 187 E5
Carters Orch GL2 . . . . . 117 F2
Carters Way GL2 . . . . . . 90 F5
Carter Wlk BS32. . . . . . 29 D8
Cart La BS1. . . . . 195 B2
Cartledge Rd 6 BS5 . . . . 19 C1
Cartway Gn GL14. . . . . 191 C4
Carwardine Field GL4. . . 119 E6
Cary Ct 2 BS2. . . . . 18 F1
Casey Cl GL11. . . . . . . 127 B1
Cashes Green Prim Sch
  GL5. . . . . 98 D8
Cashes Green Rd GL5 . . 98 E7
Cash Hill GL17 . . . . 163 E4
Cashmore Ho 9 BS5. . . . .9 B7
Casino Pl GL50. . . . . . . 193 A4
Casita Dr GL17. . . . . . . 164 F5
Caslon Ct BS1. . . . . . . 195 B1
Cassell Rd BS16. . . . . . . 20 C5
Cassey Bottom La BS5 . . 10 A7
Cassey Compton GL54. . 166 F2
Cassin Dr GL51 . . . . . . 132 E2
Casson Dr BS16. . . . . . . 19 E8
Castanum Ct GL51 . . . . 130 B7
Castle Cl
  Bristol BS10. . . . . 27 E2
  Painswick GL6. . . . . . 103 F7
Castle Coombe BS35 . . . . 64 C1
Castle Cotts
  Gloucester GL3 . . . . . 119 F8
  Marshfield SN14 . . . . . 24 E2
Castle Cres GL15. . . . . . 146 F7
Castle Ct
  Bristol, Arno's Vale BS4 . . 9 C4
  Bristol BS34. . . . . 30 A4
  20 Stroud GL5 . . . . . . 99 C7
  Thornbury BS35. . . . . . 64 B1
Castle End GL16 . . . . . . 111 E5
Castle Farm Cl GL8. . . . . 70 C3
Castle Farm La BS41 . . . . 1 B2
Castle Farm Rd BS15. . . . 10 C2
Castlefields Ave GL52 . . 131 C6
Castlefields Dr GL52 . . . 131 C6
Castlefields Rd GL52. . . 131 C6
Castleford Gdns NP16 . . 72 F2
Castleford Hill NP16 . . . 72 E2
Castlegate Ho BS4 . . . . .9 E3
Castle Gdns
  Chepstow/Cas-Gwent
  NP16. . . . . 72 D1
  Chipping Campden GL55 . 189 B2
Castle Hill Dr GL3. . . . . 120 F4
Castle Hill Prim Sch GL3 120 E4
Castle La
  Goodrich HR9 . . . . . . 163 A6
  Marshfield SN14 . . . . . 24 E2
  Moreton Valence GL2 . . 108 E2
Castlemaine Dr GL51. . . 129 C8
Castle Mead GL15. . . . . 146 F5
Castlemead Rd GL5 . . . . 99 B6
Castlemeads Ct GL1. . . . 196 A3
Castle Nurseries GL55. . 189 B2
Castle Pitch GL5 . . . . . . 99 C6
Castle Prim Sch BS31 . . . 4 D4
Castle Rd
  Bristol, Kingswood BS15. . 20 D2
  Bristol, Oldland Common
  BS30. . . . . 11 D3
  Pucklechurch BS16 . . . 22 C6
Castle Rise GL5 . . . . . . 99 C6
Castle Sch Sixth Form Ctr
  The BS35. . . . . 64 B1
Castle Sch The BS35 . . . 64 B2
Castle St
  Bristol BS1. . . . . 195 B3
  Cirencester GL7. . . . . 190 C4
  Dursley GL11. . . . . . . 88 B1
  King's Stanley GL10. . . 98 A3
  Stroud GL5. . . . . 99 C6
  Thornbury BS35. . . . . . 64 B1
  Winchcombe GL54 . . . 174 A7
Castle Stream Ct GL11 . . 80 C8
Castle The GL5 . . . . 99 C6
Castleton Rd GL4 . . . . . 119 D8
Castle View NP16 . . . . . 73 A1
Castle Villas 19 GL5 . . . . 99 C7
Castle Wood/Coed Castell
  NP16. . . . . 60 C8
Caswell Ct GL11 . . . . . . 80 D8
Caswell Mews GL11. . . . 80 D8
Catbrain Hill BS10 . . . . . 28 B6
Catbrain La BS10 . . . . . . 28 B6
Catbrook Cl GL55 . . . . . 189 A1
Catbrook Gdns GL55 . . . 189 A1
Catchmays Ct NP16,
  NP25. . . . . 146 C5
Catchpot La BS37 . . . . . 34 A6
Cater Rd BS13 . . . . .2 B6
Cathedral Church of St Peter
  & the Holy Family★
  GL1. . . . . 196 B3

Cathedral Prim Sch BS1 194 C2
Catherine Ct 14 BS6. . . . 18 E1
Catherine Hill BS35 . . . . 49 F2
Catherine Mead St BS3. . .8 D4
Catherine's Cl GL5. . . . . 99 E7
Catherine St BS11. . . . . 16 C8
Catholic Sch of St Gregory
  the Great The GL50 . . 193 A4
Catkin Cl GL2. . . . . 109 E7
Catley Gr BS41. . . . . . . .7 B2
Cato St BS5. . . . . 19 B2
Catswood Cl GL5. . . . . . 103 E1
Catswood La GL6 . . . . . 104 D3
Cattistock Dr BS5 . . . . . 10 A6
Cattle Market Rd BS1 . . 195 C1
Cattybrook Rd N BS16. . . 21 D5
Cattybrook St
  7 Bristol BS5. . . . . . . .9 B7
  23 Bristol BS5. . . . . . . .9 B8
Caudle Cl GL17 . . . . . . 163 E4
Caudle La GL17. . . . . . . 163 E4
Causeway Rd GL14. . . . 191 E5
Causeway The
  Coalpit Heath BS36 . . . . 31 D7
  3 Quedgeley GL2. . . . . 117 D1
  Redmarley D'Abitot GL19 . 179 D2
Causley Dr BS30 . . . . . . 11 A5
Cavan Wlk BS4 . . . . 8 D1
Cave Cl BS16 . . . . 20 D6
Cave Ct BS2 . . . . 195 B4
Cave Dr BS16 . . . . 20 D6
Cave Gr BS16. . . . . 21 B7
Cavendish Ave GL3. . . . 128 D5
Cavendish Bldgs 3 GL15 . 92 A3
Cavendish Cl
  Saltford BS31. . . . . . . .5 D2
  Tormarton GL9. . . . . . . 34 E2
Cavendish Gdns BS9 . . . 17 C4
Cavendish Rd
  Bristol, Henleaze BS9 . . . 18 A5
  Bristol, Patchway BS34. . 28 F8
Caves Cotts BS16 . . . . . 20 E7
Cave St BS2 . . . . 195 B4
Cecil Ave BS5. . . . . 19 F1
Cecil Rd
  Bristol, Clifton BS8. . . . .7 F8
  Bristol, Kingswood BS15. . 10 D8
  Gloucester GL1 . . . . . 118 D6
Cecily Ct GL6 . . . . 148 A3
Cecily Hill GL7 . . . . 190 B5
Cedar Cl
  Bristol, Oldland BS30. . . 11 B4
  Bristol, Patchway BS34. . 28 F7
  Charlton Kings GL53. . . 131 B5
  Chepstow/Cas-Gwent NP16 60 E5
  Down Ampney GL7. . . . 143 E8
  Stroud GL5. . . . . 98 D6
Cedar Court Rd GL53. . . 193 B2
Cedar Ct
  Bristol, Coombe Dingle
  BS9. . . . . 17 D7
  Bristol, Mangotsfield BS16 . 20 E6
  Bristol, Sneyd Park BS9. . . 17 C4
  Bristol, Westbury on Trym
  BS9. . . . . 17 F8
  Ledbury HR8 . . . . 178 F8
Cedardean GL14 . . . . . 191 C5
Cedar Dr
  Dursley GL11. . . . . . . 88 A1
  Keynsham BS31. . . . . . . 4 D4
Cedar Gdns GL10 . . . . . 97 F8
Cedar Gr
  Bristol BS9. . . . . 17 D5
  Walford HR9 . . . . 163 C8
  4 Winchcombe GL54 . . 174 A7
Cedar Hall BS16 . . . . . . 20 C8
Cedar Pk BS9. . . . . 17 D5
Cedar Rd
  Brockworth GL3. . . . . 120 D7
  Mickleton GL55 . . . . . 189 B6
  Northway GL20 . . . . . 182 C4
Cedar Row BS11 . . . . . . 16 F6
Cedars The
  Gloucester GL3 . . . . . 120 A8
  Wotton-u-E GL12 . . . . 68 C8
Cedar Way
  Mile End GL16 . . . . . . 155 B6
  Pucklechurch BS16 . . . 22 C6
  Winterbourne BS36. . . . 30 D5
Cedarwood Dr GL4. . . . 118 E3
Celandine Bank GL52. . . 138 B4
Celandine Cl BS35 . . . . . 64 D2
Celandine Ct NP16 . . . . 60 F5
Celestine Rd BS37 . . . . . 43 C3
Celia Terr BS4 . . . . .9 F6
Cemetery La
  Bibury GL7 . . . . 160 A1
  Bourton-on-t-W GL54 . . 169 A7
Cemetery Rd
  Bristol BS4. . . . . 9 A3
  Gloucester GL4 . . . . . 119 A6
Cennick Ave BS15. . . . . 20 E1
Centaurus Rd BS34. . . . 28 D7
Central Ave
  Bristol BS15. . . . . 10 C5
  Mitcheldean GL17 . . . . 164 D5
  Severn Beach BS10. . . . 38 A3
Central Cross Dr GL50,
  GL52. . . . . 133 E3
Central Pk BS14 . . . . . . .3 B7
Central Rd
  Gloucester GL1 . . . . . 118 E7
  Stroud GL5. . . . . 98 F7
Central Trad Est BS4 . . . .9 B4
Central Way
  Bristol BS10. . . . . 18 E8

Central Way continued
  Cheltenham GL51. . . . 133 B3
Centre for Science & Art★
  GL5. . . . . 99 C7
Centre The BS31. . . . . . .4 F5
Centurion Cl 1 GL4. . . . 119 E6
Centurion Rd GL15. . . . . 92 B4
Centurions Wlk 20 GL16 . 155 A5
Century Cl GL7 . . . . . . 190 F5
Century Ct
  Brockworth GL3. . . . . 120 E5
  Cheltenham GL50. . . . 193 B2
Ceres Cl BS30. . . . . 10 F2
Cerimon Gate BS34 . . . . 29 E5
Cerney House Gardens★
  GL7. . . . . 158 C2
Cerney La BS11. . . . . . . 16 E5
Cerney Wick La GL7. . . . 143 E5
Cesson Cl BS37 . . . . 33 C8
Ceylon Ho GL51. . . . . . 132 F4
Chaceley Cl
  Gloucester GL4 . . . . . 119 E5
  Quedgeley GL2. . . . . . 109 E8
Chadbournes GL3. . . . . 128 B6
Chadleigh Gr BS4. . . . . . 2 D7
Chad Rd GL51. . . . . . . 132 F1
Chadwick Cl GL4. . . . . . 118 D2
Chaffinch Cl GL3. . . . . . 127 D5
Chaffinch Ct 5 GL10. . . . 97 F8
Chaingate La BS37. . . . . 43 A6
Chakeshill Cl BS10 . . . . 28 C3
Chakeshill Dr BS10. . . . . 28 C4
Chalcombe Cl BS34 . . . . 29 C8
Chalcroft Ho 2 BS3. . . . . 8 A4
Chalcroft Wlk BS13. . . . .1 C1
Chalet The BS10 . . . . . . 27 F3
Chalfield Cl BS31. . . . . . 5 A2
Chalford Ave GL51 . . . . 129 B7
Chalford Cl BS37. . . . . . 32 D8
Chalford Hill Prim Sch
  GL6. . . . . 148 C5
Chalford Ind Est GL6. . . 148 C5
Chalford Rd GL4 . . . . . . 118 E1
Chalks Rd BS5. . . . . 9 D8
Challender Ave BS10 . . . 27 F2
Challoner Ct BS1 . . . . . 195 A1
Chamberlayne Cl 29
  GL54. . . . . 176 F4
Chamberlayne Ho 28
  GL54. . . . . 176 F4
Chambon Cl SN16. . . . . 142 D1
Champion Rd BS15. . . . . 21 A2
Champions Ct 3 GL11 . . 80 B7
Champion Sq BS2. . . . . 195 C3
Champneys Ave BS10 . . . 27 F3
Champs Sur Marne BS32. 29 E8
Chamwells Ave GL2 . . . 127 B4
Chamwells Wlk GL2. . . . 127 B4
Chancel Cl
  Bristol BS9. . . . . 17 D3
  Gloucester GL4 . . . . . 127 C1
Chancel Pk GL53. . . . . . 130 F4
Chancel Way
  Charlton Kings GL53 . . 131 A6
  Lechlade on T GL7 . . . 153 C2
Chancery St GL5 . . . . . .9 B7
Chance St GL20. . . . . . 192 D4
Chandag Infant Sch BS31. .5 A4
Chandag Rd BS31. . . . . .5 A4
Chandler Rd GL52. . . . . 137 F2
Chandos 5 BS5 . . . . . . 18 C2
Chandos Almshouses 22
  GL54. . . . . 174 A7
Chandos Dr GL3 . . . . . . 120 E5
Chandos Rd
  Bristol BS6. . . . . 18 C1
  Keynsham BS31. . . . . . . 4 E7
  Stroud GL5. . . . . 99 A4
Chandos St 26 GL54. . . 174 A7
Chandos Trad Est BS2. . . .9 A5
Change The GL6. . . . . . 102 D1
Channell's Hill BS9 . . . . 18 A8
Channel View NP16 . . . . 60 E5
Channon's Hill BS16 . . . 19 F4
Chantry Cl
  Cirencester GL7. . . . . 190 C5
  Lydney GL15. . . . . . . 92 A1
Chantry Ct
  Bristol BS1. . . . . 194 C2
  Tetbury GL8. . . . . 140 C4
Chantry Gate GL52 . . . . 137 E2
Chantry Gdns GL56. . . . 186 D3
Chantry Gr BS11. . . . . . 27 C2
Chantry La BS16 . . . . . . 30 F1
Chantry Rd
  Bristol BS8. . . . . 18 B1
  Thornbury BS35. . . . . . 64 B2
Chapel Apartments 13
  GL16. . . . . 155 B5
Chapel Barton 7 BS3. . . .8 B2
Chapel Bglws HR9 . . . . 170 B4
Chapel Cl
  Bristol BS15. . . . . 11 B8
  Chepstow/Cas-Gwent NP16 60 E5
  Kempsford GL7 . . . . . 144 E8
  Monmouth/Trefynwy
  NP25. . . . . 154 A7
  Tarlton GL7 . . . . 149 C2
Chapel Cotts GL54 . . . . 174 B1
Chapel Ct
  Bristol, Brentry BS10. . . . 28 D3
  Bristol, St Philip's Marsh BS2 9 A5
  Dursley GL11. . . . . . . 87 D4
Chapelfields HR9 . . . . . 162 B6
Chapel Gdns
  Bristol BS10. . . . . 28 A1

Chapel Gdns *continued*
Hardwicke GL2 .... 109 F7
Chapel Green La BS6.... 18 B2
Chapel Hay Cl GL3 .... 128 C4
Chapel Hay La GL3 .... 128 D4
Chapel Hill
  Aylburton GL15 .... 147 E4
  Broad Blunsdon SN26 .. 144 D1
  English Bicknor GL16.. 163 A1
  Newport GL13 .... 78 B7
Chapel Ho [11] GL20 ... 192 C4
Chapel La
  Acton Turville GL9 .... 36 A6
  Birdwood GL2 .... 165 F5
  Blockley GL56 .... 186 C5
  Bristol, Clay Hill BS5 ... 19 E2
  Bristol, Fishponds BS16 .. 20 A4
  Bristol, Frenchay BS16 .. 20 C7
  Bristol, Lawrence Weston
    BS11................. 27 C2
  Bristol, Warmley BS15 .. 11 B8
  Cheltenham GL50...... 193 B1
  Chepstow/Cas-Gwent NP16 60 B5
  Chipping Sodbury BS37... 34 A7
  Cold Aston GL54 ...... 168 B6
  Gorsley HR9. .... 170 B4
  Hankerton SN16 ...... 141 E1
  Hillesley GL12 .... 55 E8
  Hinton SN14. .... 23 C5
  Kinsham GL20......... 182 D6
  Longhope GL17 .... 165 B5
  Mickleton GL55....... 189 A6
  Minchinhampton GL6.. 148 A3
  Minety SN16.......... 142 D1
  North Cerney GL7 ..... 158 D3
  Staunton GL19........ 171 E8
  Stroud GL5. .... 98 D6
  Thornbury BS35....... 65 A1
  Westmancote GL20.... 182 D8
  Weston-s-E GL53...... 188 D3
  Woodmancote GL52.... 138 C3
Chapel Mdws HR9 ..... 162 B6
Chapel Orch BS37...... 43 C2
Chapel Pill La BS20 .... 16 E4
Chapel Pitch GL18 ..... 170 D2
Chapel Rd
  Berry Hill GL16 .... 155 A4
  Bristol, Bishopsworth BS13... 2 A6
  [2] Bristol, Lower Easton
    BS5................. 19 B1
  Kempsford GL7 .... 144 E8
  Oldbury-on-S BS35 ... 63 C5
  Viney Hill GL15 .... 156 C1
Chapel Row
  [4] Blockley GL56..... 186 C5
  Little Compton GL56 .. 187 F1
  Luckington SN14 ...... 47 E4
  Pill BS20 .... 16 C4
  [4] Stonehouse GL10 .. 97 F7
Chapel St
  Bledington OX7 .... 177 E1
  Bristol BS2. .... 9 A5
  Broadwell GL56....... 177 A6
  Cheltenham GL50..... 193 B4
  Dursley GL11......... 88 A5
  [5] Stow-on-t-W GL54.. 176 F4
  Stroud GL5. .... 99 D7
  Thornbury BS35....... 51 B8
Chapel Way BS4 .... 9 E6
Chapel Wlk
  Cheltenham GL50...... 193 B3
  Didmarton GL9....... 57 B3
  Edge End GL16........ 155 C8
Chapel Wy BS10 .... 18 D8
Chaplin Rd BS5........ 19 B1
Chapman's Cross GL6.. 149 A4
Chapman Way GL51.... 129 F7
Chapter St BS2 .... 195 B4
Chapter Wlk BS36..... 18 B3
Charbon Gate BS34.... 29 F5
Charborough Ct
  Bristol BS34.......... 28 F2
  Bristol BS34.......... 29 A2
Charborough Rd BS34... 28 F2
Charborough Road Prim Sch
  BS34................. 28 F2
Charbury Wlk BS11 .... 16 E5
Chard Ct BS14.......... 3 B6
Chardstock Ave BS9.... 17 D8
Chardwar Gdns [7] GL54.. 168 F7
Charfield GL11 .... 11 A8
Charfield Prim Sch GL12.. 66 F5
Charfield Rd
  Bristol BS10.......... 28 D1
  Kingswood GL12...... 67 E5
Chargrove
  [2] Bristol BS30........ 11 C6
  Yate BS37 .... 32 D7
Chargrove La GL51..... 129 E4
Charis Ave BS10 ...... 18 C7
Charlecombe Ct BS9.. 17 F6
Charlecombe Rd BS9... 17 F6
Charlecote Ave GL4.... 110 C8
Charlecote Cnr GL52... 137 C4
Charles Ave BS34 ..... 29 E4
Charles Cl
  Tewkesbury GL20 .... 192 E2
  Thornbury BS35....... 64 C3
Charles Ct BS8........ 194 A2
Charles England Ho BS34. 28 F7
Charles Pl BS8........ 194 A2
Charles Rd BS34 ...... 29 B3
Charles St
  Bristol BS1........... 195 A4
  Cheltenham GL51..... 133 C3

Charles St *continued*
  Gloucester GL1.......196 C2
Charlesway GL56.......176 E8
Charles Wesley Cl BS5.. 10 A6
Charleswood Rd GL15.. 155 F1
Charleton Ho [9] BS2.. 195 C3
Charlham La GL7 ...... 143 E8
Charlham Way GL7.... 143 E8
Charlock Cl GL4 .... 119 A4
Charlotte Rose Ho [3]
  GL50................. 133 B1
Charlotte St S BS1 .... 194 C2
Charlotte St BS1 ...... 194 C3
Charlton Ave BS34 .... 28 F2
Charlton Blvd BS34 .... 29 A7
Charlton Cl GL53....... 131 A5
Charlton Court Rd GL52.. 131 A7
Charlton Ct
  Bristol BS34.......... 39 F1
  Gloucester GL1....... 196 C3
Charlton Down Cotts GL8. 71 E4
Charlton Dr GL53 ...... 130 F7
Charlton Gdns
  Bristol BS10.......... 28 C4
  Cheltenham GL53..... 130 E5
Charlton Kings Inf Sch
  GL52................. 131 B6
Charlton Kings Jun Sch
  GL53................. 131 B5
Charlton La
  Bristol BS10.......... 28 A3
  Cheltenham GL53..... 130 D5
Charlton Lane Ctr Hospl
  GL53................. 130 E5
Charlton Lawn GL53.... 131 A7
Charlton Leaze GL53... 130 D4
Charlton Mead Ct BS10.. 28 D4
Charlton Mead Dr BS10.. 28 D4
Charlton Park Dr GL53.. 130 F7
Charlton Park Gate GL53 130 F6
Charlton Pk BS31 ...... 4 D5
Charlton Pl BS10....... 28 D4
Charlton Rd
  Bristol, Brentry BS10..... 28 C3
  Bristol, Kingswood BS15.. 20 B1
  Keynsham BS31, BS14.... 4 C3
  Tetbury GL8.......... 140 B4
Charlton St [17] BS5.....9 B7
Charlton Terr [7] GL56.. 187 B3
Charlton Way GL2..... 127 C5
Charminster Rd BS16... 20 B3
Charmouth Ct BS3 .... 8 D1
Charnell Rd BS16 ...... 20 F4
Charnhill Brow BS16... 21 A4
Charnhill Cres BS16.... 20 F4
Charnhill Dr BS16...... 20 F4
Charnhill Ridge BS16... 21 A4
Charnhill Vale BS16.... 20 F4
Charnwood BS16 ...... 21 A4
Charnwood Cl GL53.... 130 D5
Charnwood Ct GL15.... 92 B5
Charnwood Rd
  Bristol BS14.......... 3 B4
  Cheltenham GL53..... 130 D5
Charter Ct GL1. .... 196 C1
Charter Ho BS1....... 194 B2
Charterhouse Rd BS5... 9 D8
Charter Wlk BS14 ..... 3 A6
Chartfield Ho BS8...... 7 F8
Chartham Rd BS16.... 20 B3
Chartist La GL19 ...... 179 F2
Chartist Piece GL19 .. 172 B8
Chartist Way GL19 .... 172 A8
Chartley BS9.......... 17 D2
Chartwell Cl GL2...... 118 A6
Chase Ave GL52....... 131 C6
Chasefield La [1] BS16.. 20 B4
Chase La
  Gloucester GL4....... 119 B7
  Wickwar GL12........ 54 C6
Chasely Cres [6] GL51.. 129 E5
Chase Rd BS15........ 20 D2
Chase The
  Bristol BS16.......... 20 C3
  Cheltenham GL52..... 133 F5
  Churchdown GL3...... 128 D4
  Gloucester GL4....... 119 D5
  Stroud GL5........... 98 E7
Chasewood Cnr [3] GL6. 148 B6
Chatcombe GL52....... 32 E7
Chatcombe Cl GL53.... 131 B4
Chatcombe Ho GL4 .... 119 B5
Chatcombe Rd GL4.... 119 B5
Chatsworth Ave GL4... 118 C1
Chatsworth Dr GL53... 130 C4
Chatsworth Gdns [1] BS35 64 C2
Chatsworth Pk BS35 ... 64 C3
Chatsworth Rd
  Bristol, Arno's Vale BS4... 9 C4
  Bristol, Hillfields BS16... 20 B3
Chattenden Ho BS9 .... 17 E3
Chatterton Gn BS14.... 2 F3
Chatterton Ho [5] BS1.. 195 B1
Chatterton Rd BS37.... 43 D1
Chatterton Sq BS1 .... 195 C1
Chatterton St BS1..... 195 C1
Chaucer Cl GL1. ...... 118 D5
Chaucer Rd BS7....... 80 C7
Chaundey Gr BS13..... 2 B5
Chavenage BS15....... 21 A1
Chavenage House★ GL8 140 A6
Chavenage La GL8..... 140 B4
Cheapside
  Bristol BS2........... 195 C4
  Stroud GL5........... 99 B7
Cheapside St [8] BS3... 8 F4

Cheap St GL54 .... 159 A6
Cheddar Gr BS13....... 2 A8
Cheddar Grove Prim Sch
  BS13................. 2 A8
Chedworth
  Bristol BS15.......... 20 F3
  Yate BS37 .... 32 B7
Chedworth Dr GL54 ... 174 A8
Chedworth Rd
  Bristol BS7........... 19 A6
  Gloucester GL4....... 118 E3
Chedworth Roman Villas
  (rems of)★ GL54...... 159 A8
Chedworth Way GL51... 129 E8
Cheese La BS2......... 195 B2
Chelbury Mews [1] GL52 134 A3
Chelford Gr BS34 ..... 29 B8
Chelmer Gr BS31....... 4 F4
Chelmsford Ave GL51... 130 A5
Chelmsford Wlk BS4 .. 9 F5
Chelsea Cl
  Cheltenham GL53..... 130 F7
  Keynsham BS31....... 5 A5
Chelsea Pk BS5....... 9 C8
Chelsea Rd BS5........ 19 B1
Chelston Rd BS4....... 2 D7
Cheltenham Bournside Sch &
  Sixth Form Ctr GL51... 130 A6
Cheltenham Coll GL53.. 193 B1
Cheltenham Coll Jun Sch
  GL53................. 193 B1
Cheltenham Cres [2] BS6.. 18 D1
Cheltenham General Hospl
  GL53................. 193 C2
Cheltenham La BS6.... 18 D2
Cheltenham Ladies' Coll The
  GL50................. 193 B3
Cheltenham Mus & Art Gal★
  GL50................. 193 B4
Cheltenham Nuffield Health
  Hospl GL51........... 129 C7
Cheltenham Race Course★
  GL50, GL52........... 134 A6
Cheltenham Racecourse Hall
  of Fame★ GL50....... 133 F6
Cheltenham Racecourse
  Sta★ GL50........... 133 E7
Cheltenham Rd
  Beckford GL20........ 183 B6
  Bishop's Cleeve GL52... 137 F3
  Bisley GL6............ 105 A1
  Bredon GL20.......... 182 D7
  Bristol BS6........... 18 E1
  Broadway WR12....... 185 A8
  Gloucester GL2....... 127 D3
  Painswick GL6........ 112 A2
  Pitchcombe GL6....... 103 C4
  Stratton GL7.......... 150 D7
  Winchcombe GL54..... 139 F4
Cheltenham Rd E GL3... 128 A7
Cheltenham Spa Sta
  GL51................. 133 A1
Cheltenham Trade Pk
  GL51................. 133 B3
Chelt Rd GL52......... 134 B3
Chelvy Cl BS13........ 2 D3
Chelwood Rd
  Bristol BS11.......... 16 D7
  Saltford BS31......... 5 E4
Chelworth Ind Est SN6.. 143 D3
Chelworth Rd SN6 .... 143 E3
Chepstow Bulwark★
  NP16................. 60 F6
Chepstow Castle★ NP16.. 72 E1
Chepstow Com Hospl
  NP16................. 60 D8
Chepstow Comp Sch
  NP16................. 72 D2
Chepstow Rd BS4..... 2 D8
Chepstow Mus★ NP16.. 72 F1
Chepstow Pk BS30 .... 30 F1
Chepstow Race Course★
  NP16................. 72 C3
Chepstow Rd BS4..... 2 D8
Chepstow Sta NP16.... 60 F8
Chepstow Wlk BS31.... 4 D5
Chequers Cl BS30..... 11 C3
Chequers Ct BS34..... 30 A6
Chequers Rd GL4 ..... 119 B7
Cherington
  Bristol BS15.......... 10 B5
  Yate BS37 .... 32 D6
Cherington Rd BS10.... 18 D7
Cheriton Cl GL51...... 129 F5
Cheriton Pl
  Bristol, Eastfield BS9.... 18 B7
  Bristol, Warmley BS30... 11 C6
Cherrington Dr GL4.... 119 E5
Cherry Ave GL53....... 131 C4
Cherry Bank GL18...... 171 A4
Cherry Blossom Cl GL52 137 F5
Cherry Cl GL2......... 109 E7
Cherry Ct BS1........ 195 A4
Cherry Garden La BS30.. 11 B2
Cherry Garden Prim Sch
  BS30................. 11 C2
Cherry Garden Rd BS30.. 11 C1
Cherry Gdns
  Bristol BS30.......... 11 C1
  Gloucester GL3....... 120 A8
  Tewkesbury GL20..... 192 F2
Cherry Gr BS16........ 21 A6
Cherry La [4] BS1...... 195 B4
Cherry Orch
  Bredon GL20.......... 182 C7

Cherry Orch *continued*
  Highworth SN6 .... 145 D3
  Wotton-u-E GL12...... 68 C7
Cherry Orchard Cl GL55.. 189 A1
Cherry Orchard La
  [4] Bristol BS5....... 9 F8
  Luckington SN14..... 47 C5
  Twyning GL20........ 181 F7
Cherry Orchard Rd [6]
  GL8................. 140 C4
Cherry Orch The GL51.. 173 F2
Cherry Rd BS37....... 44 A1
Cherry Tree Cl
  Bristol BS16.......... 20 C2
  Churchdown GL3...... 128 A7
  Keynsham BS31....... 4 C4
  Nailsworth GL6....... 91 A4
Cherrytree Cres BS16... 20 C2
Cherrytree Ct BS16 .... 22 C5
Cherry Tree Ct [14] GL4.. 119 C4
Cherrytree La GL7 .... 150 F5
Cherry Tree La GL16 ... 155 C6
Cherrytree Rd BS16.... 20 C2
Cherry Tree Rd [7] SN6.. 143 E4
Cherry Wlk GL15....... 92 A4
Cherry Wood BS30..... 11 B2
Cherrywood Gdns GL4.. 118 C3
Cherston Ct GL4 ...... 119 E8
Chertsey Rd BS6...... 18 B1
Chervil Cl GL4 .... 119 B4
Cherwell Cl BS35...... 51 C7
Cherwell Rd BS31..... 5 A4
Chesford Dr GL3...... 128 C6
Chesham Way BS15.... 20 D1
Cheshire Cl BS37 ..... 43 E3
Cheshire Rd GL3...... 127 E6
Chesils The GL54...... 174 A8
Chesley Hill BS30..... 11 F7
Chesmann Ct GL1..... 126 F4
Chessel Cl BS32...... 40 C2
Chessel Ct [6] BS3..... 8 B3
Chessel Dr BS34 ..... 29 A7
Chessell Ave BS35 .... 38 C7
Chessel St BS3....... 8 B3
Chessgrove La GL17... 164 F6
Chessington Ave BS14... 3 B5
Chestal GL11 .... 88 B1
Chester Cl GL19....... 173 C7
Chester Cres GL7 ..... 190 D4
Chester Ct [4] BS5..... 9 C7
Chester Ho GL50...... 193 B1
Chestermaster Cl BS32.. 40 A5
Chester Park Jun & Inf Schs
  BS16................. 20 A3
Chester Park Rd BS16... 20 B2
Chester Pk BS5........ 19 E1
Chester Rd
  Bristol BS5........... 19 E1
  Gloucester GL4....... 119 C8
Chesters BS30........ 11 A4
Chester St
  Bristol BS5........... 19 B2
  Cirencester GL7...... 190 D4
Chesterton Cl GL2 .... 126 F6
Chesterton Gr GL7 .... 190 D3
Chesterton Ho
  [6] Bristol BS2....... 195 B4
  Cirencester GL7...... 190 C3
Chesterton La GL7 .... 190 D3
Chesterton Link GL7... 190 D3
Chesterton Pk GL7 .... 190 B4
Chesterton Prim Sch
  GL7................. 190 C2
Chester Wlk GL50..... 193 B1
Chestnut Ave GL10.... 97 F8
Chestnut Cl
  Acton Turville GL9 .... 36 A6
  Bristol BS14.......... 3 F5
  Down Ampney GL7.... 143 E8
  Hardwicke GL2....... 109 E7
  [15] Ledbury HR8..... 178 E6
  [2] Mile End GL16.... 155 B6
  Nailsworth GL6....... 91 B4
  [6] Tetbury GL8...... 140 B4
Chestnut Cnr WR12.... 184 E5
Chestnut Cotts GL21.. 125 D5
Chestnut Ct
  Bristol, Bishopsworth BS13.. 2 A7
  Bristol, Hillhouse BS16 .. 21 A5
  [10] Monmouth/Trefynwy
    NP25............... 154 A7
Chestnut Dr
  Chipping Sodbury BS37.... 44 A1
  Thornbury BS35....... 64 C1
Chestnut Gr GL20..... 192 F1
Chestnut Hill GL6..... 91 B4
Chestnut Ho
  Bristol, Hartcliffe BS13.... 2 D3
  [7] Bristol, Staple Hill BS16. 20 D6
  Cheltenham GL50..... 193 A3
Chestnut La GL51..... 98 F7
Chestnut Park Est GL12.. 67 F4
Chestnut Pk GL12..... 67 E4
Chestnut Pl GL53..... 130 E4
Chestnut Rd
  Bristol, Lower Soundwell
    BS15............... 20 F3

Chestnut Rd *continued*
  Bristol, Mangotsfield BS16.. 20 D6
  Gloucester GL3....... 120 B4
  Gloucester GL4....... 119 C5
  Long Ashton BS41..... 7 B2
Chestnuts The
  Bussage GL6.......... 148 B6
  Cheltenham GL52..... 133 E5
  Gloucester GL1....... 196 A1
Chestnut Terr
  Charlton Kings GL53... 131 A5
  [7] Monmouth/Trefynwy
    NP25............... 154 A7
Chestnut Way BS15.... 20 F3
Chestnut Wlk
  Bristol BS13.......... 2 A6
  Saltford BS31......... 5 E3
Chetwode Cl BS10 .... 28 D3
Chetwood Ho BS5..... 9 C6
Chevening Cl BS34.... 29 D4
Cheviot Cl
  Quedgeley GL2........ 109 E8
  [1] Tetbury GL8...... 140 C5
Cheviot Dr BS35...... 51 E8
Cheviot Rd GL52...... 134 B4
Cheviot Way BS30..... 11 C5
Chew Cotts BS31...... 4 F5
Chewton Cl BS16..... 20 B3
Chewton Rd BS31..... 4 F2
Cheyne Rd BS9 ...... 17 D6
Cheyney Cl GL4....... 119 B6
Chichester Ho BS4.... 9 F6
Chichester Way BS37... 43 D3
Chicknalls La GL15.... 156 F3
Chiffchaff Cl GL7 ..... 143 A7
Childer Rd HR8....... 178 D8
Childswickham Rd
  WR12................ 185 A8
Chillingworth Mews GL1 196 B2
Chillwood Cl BS37..... 42 E3
Chiltern Ave GL52..... 137 E4
Chiltern Cl
  Bristol, Warmley BS30..... 11 C5
  Bristol, Whitchurch BS14... 3 B4
Chiltern Pk BS35...... 51 E8
Chiltern Rd
  Cheltenham GL52..... 134 B3
  Quedgeley GL2........ 109 E8
Chilton Rd BS4 ...... 3 A8
Chilwood Cl BS37..... 42 E3
Chimney Steps BS2... 195 C2
China Cnr WR11...... 188 C6
Chine The BS16....... 19 D5
Chine View BS16...... 20 F8
Chiphouse Rd BS15... 20 F3
Chipmans Platt GL10... 101 A1
Chippenham Rd SN14... 15 A8
Chipperfield Dr BS15... 20 F1
Chipping Campden Bsns Pk
  GL55................. 189 B2
Chipping Campden Sch
  GL55................. 189 A2
Chipping Cl [12] GL12 ..... 68 B7
Chipping Edge Est BS37.. 44 C1
Chipping Gdns [6] GL12.. 68 B7
Chipping Sodbury Sch
  BS37................. 33 B8
Chipping St GL8....... 140 C4
Chippings The BS16.... 19 D5
Chipping The GL12..... 67 F4
Chisbury St BS5 ...... 19 C3
Chislet Way GL4....... 118 D1
Chittening Ind Est BS11.. 26 E8
Chittening Rd BS11.... 26 E7
Chivenor Wy GL2...... 118 B1
Chock La BS9......... 18 A7
Choirs Cl GL4......... 119 E6
Choke Wlk BS4 .... 3 E8
Chosen Dr GL3........ 128 B5
Chosen Hill Sch GL3... 128 E5
Chosen View Rd GL51.. 133 B5
Chosen Way GL3...... 119 F8
Christchurch Ave BS16.. 20 D5
Christ Church CE Inf Sch
  BS16................. 20 D5
Christ Church CE Prim Sch
  Bristol, Victoria Park
    BS8................. 194 A3
  Chalford GL6......... 148 C5
  Cheltenham BS16..... 20 D6
Christchurch Ct [4] GL50. 130 B8
Christ Church Hanham CE
  Prim Sch BS15........ 10 B4
Christ Church Jun Sch
  BS16................. 20 D5
Christchurch La BS16... 20 D5
Christchurch Rd BS8.... 194 A3
Christ Church Rd GL50.. 130 B8
Christ Church Terr [8]
  GL50................. 133 B1
Christ Church Villas [7]
  GL50................. 133 B1
Christ Coll Sports Ctr
  GL51................. 133 A3
Christina Terr BS8..... 194 A1
Christmas St BS1..... 195 A3
Christmas Steps BS1... 195 A3
Christmas Tree BS34... 29 E8
Christopher Brain St BS14.. 2 E5
Christowe La GL53..... 193 C1
Christ the King RC Prim Sch
  BS35................. 64 D1

Christy Cl BS36 . . . . 31 B6
Chubb Cl BS30 . . . . 10 F5
Chuch Wlk GL12 . . . . 68 C7
Churcham Bsns Pk GL2 .124 E2
Churcham Prim Sch GL2 124 C2
Church Ave
 Bristol, Sneyd Park BS9 . . 17 E4
 3 Bristol, Upper Easton
  BS5 . . . . 19 B1
 Bristol, Warmley BS30 . . . 11 D7
 Falfield GL12 . . . . 65 E7
 Siddington GL7 . . . . 190 E1
Church Cl
 Bristol BS10 . . . . 27 E2
 Broadway WR12 . . . . . . 185 B8
 Cranham GL4 . . . . 112 E5
 Ebrington GL55 . . . . . . 189 D3
 Frampton Cotterell BS36 . 31 B8
 Longborough GL56 . . . . 176 D8
Church Cotts 13 GL55 . 189 A2
Church Ct 9 BS16 . . . . . 20 D3
Churchdown La GL3 . . . . 120 C8
Churchdown Parton Manor
 Jun Sch GL3 . . . . 128 B6
Churchdown Sch GL3 . . . 128 B5
Churchdown Village Inf Sch
 GL3 . . . . 128 C5
Churchdown Village Jun Sch
 GL3 . . . . 128 C4
Churchdown Wlk BS11 . . 16 E5
Church Dr
 Bristol BS5 . . . . 9 E8
 Parkend GL15 . . . . 155 E2
 Quedgeley GL2 . . . . 117 F1
Churchend GL2 . . . . 95 D4
Churchend Cotts GL2 . . . . 95 D4
Churchend La GL12 . . . . . 66 F3
Churches Mill GL5 . . . . . . 99 A1
Church Farm 2 NP25 . . . 154 A7
Church Farm Bsns Ctr
 GL53 . . . . 130 C3
Churchfarm Cl BS37 . . . . 43 F3
Church Farm La GL56 . . 187 A6
Church Farm Rd BS16 . . . 21 C6
Churchfield Rd
 Stroud GL5 . . . . 99 D6
 Upton St Leonards GL4 . . 119 E3
Churchfields GL52 . . . . . 138 A4
Church Furlong GL54 . . . 176 C1
Church Gdns GL15 . . . . . 92 A2
Church Hill
 Bisley GL6 . . . . 148 D8
 Bristol BS4 . . . . 9 E2
 Burton SN14 . . . . 36 B3
 Oldbury-on-S BS35 . . . . . 63 B5
 Olveston BS35 . . . . 49 F3
 Upper Lydbrook GL17 . . . 163 D2
Church Hill Cl GL16 . . . . 163 B2
Church Hill Ho BS4 . . . . . .9 E2
Churchhill Rd GL5 . . . . . 148 A5
Church Ho BS7 . . . . 18 F8
Churchill Ave SN26 . . . . 144 E1
Churchill Cl
 Bristol BS30 . . . . 11 A5
 1 Nailsworth GL6 . . . . . 91 B4
Churchill Dr
 Bristol BS9 . . . . 17 D7
 Cheltenham GL52 . . . . . 131 A7
Churchill Gdns GL52 . . . 131 A7
Churchill Gr GL20 . . . . . 192 F4
Churchill Mdw HR8 . . . . 178 E8
Churchill Pl 9 GL7 . . . . . 152 E4
Churchill Rd
 Bristol BS4 . . . . 9 C4
 Cheltenham GL53 . . . . . 130 E6
 Cirencester GL7 . . . . . . 190 E5
 Gloucester GL1 . . . . 118 E7
 Nailsworth GL6 . . . . 91 B4
Churchill Sq GL56 . . . . . 186 C7
Churchill Way
 Mitcheldean GL17 . . . . . 164 D5
 Painswick GL6 . . . . 103 F8
Church La
 Ashton Keynes SN6 . . . . . 142 F5
 Badminton GL9 . . . . 46 E5
 Berkeley GL13 . . . . 85 E3
 Bitton BS30 . . . . 5 E7
 Bledington OX7 . . . . . . 177 E1
 Bristol, Bromley Heath BS16 30 F1
 Bristol BS1 . . . . 195 B2
 Bristol, Clifton Wood BS8 .194 B2
 Bristol, Henbury BS10 . . . 27 E2
 Bristol, Southville BS3 . . . . 8 D3
 Chipping Sodbury BS37 . . . 34 B8
 Churcham GL2 . . . . 124 D1
 Coalpit Heath BS36 . . . . . 31 C6
 Corse GL19 . . . . 172 B5
 5 Cricklade SN6 . . . . . . 143 E4
 Cromhall GL12 . . . . 66 A1
 Evenlode GL56 . . . . 177 C7
 Forthampton GL19 . . . . . 181 C3
 Gloucester GL4 . . . . 119 D8
 Hambrook BS16 . . . . 30 E2
 Hankerton SN16 . . . . . . 141 E1
 Hardwicke GL2 . . . . 109 D6
 Harnhill GL7 . . . . 151 B3
 17 Ledbury HR8 . . . . . . 178 F8
 Long Ashton BS41 . . . . . . 7 C2
 Marshfield SN14 . . . . . . 15 A8
 Minsterworth GL2 . . . . . 116 F7
 Moreton Valence GL2 . . . 101 A8
 Northwood Green GL14 . . 165 C1

Church La *continued*
 Rangeworthy BS37 . . . . . 52 F1
 Sapperton GL7 . . . . 149 B6
 Saul GL2 . . . . 100 A7
 Sevenhampton GL54 . . . 166 E8
 Sharpness GL13 . . . . 93 E1
 Shurdington GL51 . . . . . 129 E2
 Sopworth SN14 . . . . 57 D1
 South Cerney GL7 . . . . . 142 F8
 Stanton WR12 . . . . 184 E5
 St Arvans NP16 . . . . 72 B6
 Stonehouse GL10 . . . . . . 97 E7
 The Leigh GL19 . . . . . . 173 C4
 Toddington GL54 . . . . . 184 B3
 Whaddon GL4 . . . . 110 E8
 Whitchurch BS14 . . . . . . 3 B3
 Wickwar GL12 . . . . 54 A6
 Windrush OX18 . . . . . . 161 C7
 Winterbourne BS36 . . . . 30 C6
 Woolaston, Alvington
  GL15 . . . . 147 D3
 Woolaston, Plusterwine
  GL15 . . . . 147 B2
Churchlands Flats GL54 .174 A6
Churchlands Lawns
 GL54 . . . . 139 F5
Churchlands Rd 8 BS3 . . .8 B2
Church Leaze BS11 . . . . . 16 D6
Church Mdws
 Toddington GL54 . . . . . 184 B3
 Whitchurch BS14 . . . . . . 3 C4
Church Par BS4 . . . . .9 E2
Church Path Rd BS20 . . . 16 C4
Church Piece GL53 . . . . . 131 B5
Church Pl
 Lower Oddington GL56 . . 177 D4
 Pill BS20 . . . . 16 C4
Church Rd
 Abbots Leigh BS8 . . . . 7 A8
 Alderton GL20 . . . . 183 E4
 Almondsbury BS32 . . . . . 40 A5
 Alveston BS35 . . . . 51 A1
 Arlingham GL2 . . . . 157 B5
 Aylburton GL15 . . . . . . 147 E5
 Bibury GL7 . . . . 160 A1
 Bishop's Cleeve GL52 . . . 137 F4
 Bitton BS30 . . . . 5 E7
 Bristol, Bedminster BS3 . . . 8 C3
 Bristol, Bishopsworth BS13 . . 2 A6
 Bristol, Filton BS34 . . . . . 29 A3
 Bristol, Frenchay BS16 . . . 20 C7
 Bristol, Hanham BS15 . . . 10 B5
 Bristol, Horfield BS7 . . . . 18 E5
 Bristol, Kingswood BS15 . . 10 E8
 Bristol, Moorfields BS5 . . . 9 D8
 Bristol, Sneyd Park BS9 . . 17 D3
 Bristol, Stoke Gifford BS34 . 29 E4
 Bristol, Upper Soundwell
  BS16 . . . . 20 E3
 Bristol, Westbury on Trym
  BS9 . . . . 18 A7
 Cheltenham, Leckhampton
  GL53 . . . . 130 C3
 Cheltenham, St Mark's
  GL51 . . . . 129 F8
 Chepstow/Cas-Gwent NP16 72 F1
 Churchdown GL3 . . . . . . 128 C4
 Cinderford GL14 . . . . . . 191 C3
 Doynton BS30 . . . . 23 A1
 Dundry BS41 . . . . 1 D2
 Dursley GL11 . . . . 88 B3
 Easter Compton BS35 . . . 39 A1
 Easton-in-G BS20 . . . . . . 16 A4
 Frampton Cotterell BS36 . . 31 C8
 Gloucester GL2 . . . . 127 C4
 Guiting Power GL54 . . . . 175 B3
 Hewelsfield GL15 . . . . . 146 F5
 Kemble GL7 . . . . 141 F8
 6 Ledbury HR8 . . . . 178 F8
 Leigh Woods BS8 . . . . 7 D6
 Leonard Stanley GL10 . . . 97 E3
 Longhope GL17 . . . . . . 164 F6
 Lower Oddington GL56 . . 177 D4
 Luckington SN14 . . . . . . 47 F4
 Lydney GL15 . . . . 92 A2
 Maisemore GL2 . . . . . . 126 A7
 Nailsworth GL6 . . . . 91 A6
 Newnham GL14 . . . . . . 157 A6
 Oldbury-on-S BS35 . . . . . 63 B5
 Pilning BS35 . . . . 38 B7
 Quenington GL7 . . . . . . 152 D7
 Severn Beach BS35 . . . . . 38 A6
 Stanton WR12 . . . . 184 C8
 Stroud GL5 . . . . 98 C6
 Swindon GL51 . . . . 133 B6
 Thornbury BS35 . . . . 64 B2
 Tormarton GL9 . . . . 34 D2
 Upper Lydbrook GL17 . . . 163 D2
 Upper Soudley GL14 . . . 156 C5
 Whitchurch BS14 . . . . . . 3 C4
 Wick BS30 . . . . 12 B6
 Winterbourne BS36 . . . . 30 E4
 Woodchester GL5 . . . . . . 98 F2
 Yate BS37 . . . . 43 E3
 Yate BS37 . . . . 43 F2
Church Rise
 Burton SN14 . . . . 36 B3
 Maisemore GL2 . . . . . . 126 A7
Church Road Pl GL14 . . . 191 D4
Church Row
 Chedworth GL54 . . . . . . 159 A7
 Gretton GL54 . . . . 183 E1
 Nailsworth GL6 . . . . 91 A6
 Overbury GL20 . . . . 182 F8
 Poole Keynes GL7 . . . . . 142 A6
 Shipton GL54 . . . . 166 E5

Churchside BS16 . . . . . . 20 B7
Church Sq GL15 . . . . . . 156 E2
Church St
 Avening GL8 . . . . 148 A1
 Bledington OX7 . . . . 177 E1
 Bredon GL20 . . . . 182 C7
 Bristol BS1 . . . . 195 B2
 Bristol, Lower Easton BS5 . 19 B1
 Bristol, Russell Town BS5 . . 9 B6
 Broadway WR12 . . . . . . 185 B8
 Charlton Kings GL53 . . . 131 B5
 Cheltenham GL50 . . . . . 193 A4
 Chipping Campden GL55 . 189 A2
 Cirencester GL7 . . . . . . 190 D3
 Clearwell GL16 . . . . 155 A2
 Gloucester GL2 . . . . 196 A2
 Kingham OX7 . . . . 177 F2
 King's Stanley GL10 . . . . 98 A4
 5 Littledean GL14 . . . . 156 E8
 Meysey Hampton GL7 . . . 152 A2
 Moreton-in-M GL56 . . . . 187 A3
 Nailsworth GL6 . . . . 91 C4
 Newent GL18 . . . . 171 A4
 Nympsfield GL10 . . . . . . 89 E5
 Sherston SN16 . . . . 58 C1
 St Briavels GL15 . . . . . . 146 E7
 9 Stow-on-t-W GL54 . . 176 C4
 Stroud GL5 . . . . 99 C7
 Tetbury GL8 . . . . 140 B3
 Tewkesbury GL20 . . . . . 192 C4
 Willersey WR12 . . . . . . 188 B2
 Wotton-u-E GL12 . . . . . . 68 B7
Church View
 Almondsbury BS32 . . . . . 39 F4
 Aston Magna GL56 . . . . 187 A6
 Bristol, Filton BS34 . . . . . 29 A3
 Bristol, Staple Hill BS16 . . 20 D7
 Castle Eaton SN6 . . . . . . 144 D6
 Churchdown GL3 . . . . . . 128 D4
 Condicote GL54 . . . . . . 176 B7
 Gorsley HR9 . . . . 170 A4
 Highworth SN6 . . . . 145 C3
 Hillesley GL12 . . . . 55 D8
 Leonard Stanley GL10 . . . 97 E3
 Newport GL13 . . . . 78 C8
 Thornbury GL13 . . . . 64 E7
Churchview Dr GL4 . . . . . 119 D8
Churchward Cl
 Bristol BS15 . . . . 10 B5
 Honeybourne WR11 . . . . 188 C7
Churchward Rd BS37 . . . . 43 B3
Churchway SN26 . . . . . . 144 E1
Church Way
 Blakeney GL15 . . . . 156 E2
 Gloucester GL4 . . . . 119 C7
 9 Newent GL18 . . . . . . 171 A4
Churchways BS14 . . . . . . 3 C4
Churchways Ave BS7 . . . . 18 E6
Churchways Cres BS7 . . . 18 E6
Church Wlk
 Ashton Keynes SN6 . . . . . 142 F5
 Charlton Kings GL53 . . . 131 B6
 6 Coleford GL16 . . . . . 155 B6
 Littledean GL14 . . . . . . 156 E8
 23 Northleach GL54 . . . 168 A1
 Parkend GL15 . . . . 155 E2
 Pill BS20 . . . . 16 C4
 8 Stow-on-t-W GL54 . . 176 C4
 Viney Hill GL15 . . . . . . 156 C1
Churn Ave GL52 . . . . 134 A2
Churn Cl GL7 . . . . 142 F8
Churn Hill GL7 . . . . 158 D3
Churnside GL7 . . . . 158 D2
Churn The GL6 . . . . 103 F8
Churston Cl BS14 . . . . 3 A3
Cicely Way GL4 . . . . 119 C7
Cicester Terr 16 GL56 . . 187 A3
Cicil Rd 1 BS15 . . . . 10 D8
Cidermill Cl NP16 . . . . . . 60 F4
Cidermill La GL55 . . . . . 189 A2
Cidermill Orch GL55 . . . 188 D4
Cider Orchard GL11 . . . . 88 E8
Cilgant Defiw/Oak Cres 8
 NP25 . . . . 154 A7
Cinderford BS10 . . . . . . 18 D8
Cinderford Ent Ctr GL14 191 C5
Cinderford Rd GL15 . . . . 156 D2
Cinder Hill
 Coleford GL16 . . . . 155 A5
 St Briavels GL15 . . . . . . 146 E7
Cinderhill Way GL17 . . . 163 E4
Cinder La GL7 . . . . 152 F4
Circle The GL5 . . . . 99 C8
Circuit 32 BS5 . . . . .9 B8
Circular Rd BS9 . . . . 17 E2
Cirencester Bsns Ctr
 GL7 . . . . 190 D2
Cirencester Deer Park Sch
 GL7 . . . . 150 B4
Cirencester Hospl GL7 . .190 B4
Cirencester Kingshill Sch
 GL7 . . . . 190 F5
Cirencester Prim Sch
 GL7 . . . . 190 D3
Cirencester Rd
 Charlton Kings GL53 . . . 131 A4
 Fairford GL7 . . . . 152 C3
 Latton SN6 . . . . 143 D7
 Little Witcombe GL3 . . . 121 A4
 Minchinhampton, Burleigh GL5,
  GL6 . . . . 91 E7
 Minchinhampton, Hyde
  GL6 . . . . 148 C4
 South Cerney GL7 . . . . . 151 A2
 Tetbury GL8 . . . . 140 C4

Cirencester Tertiary Coll
 GL7 . . . . 190 A4
City Academy Bristol The
 BS5 . . . . 9 C8
City Bank Rd GL7 . . . . . . 190 D3
City Bsns Pk BS5 . . . . .9 A8
City Mus & Art Gal★
 BS8 . . . . 194 C3
City of Bristol Coll BS1 . .194 C2
City of Bristol Coll, Ashley
 Down Ctr BS7 . . . . 18 F4
City of Bristol Coll,
 Bedminster Ctr BS3 . . . . . .8 E2
City of Bristol Coll, Downend
 Ctr BS16 . . . . 21 A8
City of Bristol Coll (Folly La
 Ctr) BS2 . . . . 9 A6
City of Bristol Coll,
 Soundwell Ctr BS16 . . . . 20 E2
City Rd BS2 . . . . 195 B4
City View BS4 . . . . .9 A3
Claire's Cl GL5 . . . . 148 A5
Clamp The BS30 . . . . 11 C3
Clanage Rd BS3 . . . . .7 E4
Clanna Cty Pk GL15 . . . . 147 C5
Clanna La GL15 . . . . 147 C4
Clanna Rd GL15 . . . . 147 D4
Clapham St GL1 . . . . . . 196 C3
Clapton Row 8 GL54 . . . 168 F7
Clapton Wlk BS9 . . . . . . 17 C5
Clare Ave BS7 . . . . 18 C3
Clare Ct
 Cheltenham GL53 . . . . . 193 B1
 Stroud GL5 . . . . 99 E7
Clare Mews GL52 . . . . . 193 B1
Claremont GL52 . . . . . . 133 F2
Claremont Ave BS7 . . . . . 18 D3
Claremont Ct
 Bristol BS9 . . . . 18 C5
 Gloucester GL1 . . . . 196 C3
Claremont Rd
 Bristol BS7 . . . . 18 D3
 Gloucester GL1 . . . . 196 C3
Claremont Specl Sch BS9 18 C5
Claremont St BS5 . . . . . . .9 B6
Claremont Terr 10 BS5 . . . 9 D7
Clarence Ave BS16 . . . . . 20 E5
Clarence Ct
 Bristol BS15 . . . . 20 B1
 1 Cheltenham GL52 . . 193 C4
 2 Wotton-u-E GL12 . . . 68 B7
Clarence Gate GL50 . . . 193 B4
Clarence Gdns BS16 . . . . 20 E5
Clarence Ho BS15 . . . . . . 20 B1
Clarence Par GL50 . . . . 193 B3
Clarence Pl BS2 . . . . 194 C4
Clarence Rd
 Bristol BS1 . . . . 195 B1
 Bristol, Kingswood BS15 . . 20 B1
 Bristol, Newton BS2 . . . . .9 A7
 Bristol, Staple Hill BS16 . . 20 E5
 Cheltenham GL52 . . . . . 193 C4
 Tewkesbury GL20 . . . . . 192 C2
 Wotton-u-E GL12 . . . . . . 68 B7
Clarence Row GL1 . . . . . 196 C3
Clarence Sq GL50 . . . . . 193 C4
Clarence St
 Cheltenham GL50 . . . . . 193 B4
 Gloucester GL1 . . . . 196 B2
Clarence Wlk
 Cheltenham GL50 . . . . . 193 B3
 Gloucester GL1 . . . . 196 B2
Clarendon Cl NP16 . . . . . 61 A4
Clarendon Ct 6 GL5 . . . . 99 C7
Clarendon Rd
 Bristol BS6 . . . . 18 C2
 Winchcombe GL54 . . . . . 174 A8
Clare Pl GL53 . . . . 193 B1
Clare Rd
 Bristol, Cotham BS6 . . . . 18 D1
 Bristol, Kingswood BS15 . . 20 C2
 Bristol, Lower Easton BS5 . 19 B2
Clare St
 Bristol BS1 . . . . 195 A2
 Bristol, Moorfields BS5 . . . 9 C8
 Cheltenham GL53 . . . . . 193 B1
 Gloucester GL1 . . . . 196 A3
Clare Wlk BS35 . . . . 64 B2
Claridge Cl GL4 . . . . 119 D4
Clarington Mews GL50 . 133 B3
Clark Dr BS16 . . . . 19 F7
Clarke Ave GL56 . . . . . . 187 C3
Clarken Coombe BS41 . . . .7 B3
Clarkes Field SN16 . . . . . 142 D1
Clarke St BS3 . . . . 8 D4
Clarke Way GL50 . . . . . . 133 D3
Clarkia Cl GL3 . . . . 127 F7
Clark's Alley GL20 . . . . . 192 C5
Clark's Hay GL7 . . . . 142 F8
Clark's La
 Blakeney GL15 . . . . 156 D1
 Siddington GL7 . . . . 150 D2
Clark St BS5 . . . . 9 A8
Clarrie Rd 1 GL8 . . . . . 140 C4
Clattergrove GL6 . . . . . . 112 A2
Clatworthy Dr BS14 . . . . . 3 A7
Claudians Cl GL4 . . . . . . 119 D7
Claudius Way GL15 . . . . . 92 B4
Clavell Rd BS10 . . . . 27 F2
Claverham Rd BS16 . . . . . 20 A5
Claverton Rd BS31 . . . . . .5 E2
Claverton Rd W BS31 . . . . 5 D3
Clay Bottom BS5 . . . . 19 E2
Clayburn Cl GL2 . . . . . . 125 E5
Claydon Gn BS14 . . . . 3 A3
Clayfield BS37 . . . . 43 E5

Clayfield Rd BS4 . . . . 9 E3
Clayfurlong Gr GL7 . . . . 141 F8
Clay Hill BS5 . . . . 19 E2
Clay La
 Bitton BS30 . . . . 5 D8
 Bristol, Little Stoke BS34 . . 29 C4
 Bristol, Willsbridge BS30 . . 11 D1
 Thornbury BS35 . . . . 64 E1
Claymore Cres BS15 . . . . 20 B5
Claypatch Rd 5 NP25 . . . 154 A7
Claypiece Rd BS13 . . . . . .2 A4
Clay Pitch BS37 . . . . 45 E3
Claypit Hill BS37 . . . . . . 33 B7
Clay Pit Rd BS6 . . . . 18 A3
Claypits Hill GL2, GL10 . 100 D1
Claypits La GL6 . . . . 99 F5
Claypool Rd BS15 . . . . . . 10 E7
Clay Rd GL16 . . . . 155 B2
Clays Rd GL16 . . . . 155 B2
Clayton St
 Avonmouth BS11 . . . . . . 26 A1
 21 Bristol BS5 . . . . .9 B8
Clearview NP25 . . . . 154 A3
Clearwater Dr GL2 . . . . . 117 E1
Clearwell Caves★ GL16 . .155 A3
Clearwell CE Prim Sch
 GL16 . . . . 155 A2
Clearwell Gdns GL52 . . . 134 B2
Cleave St BS2 . . . . 19 A2
Clee Ho GL20 . . . . 192 C3
Cleeve Ave BS16 . . . . . . 20 E7
Cleeve Bsns Pk GL52 . . . 137 E1
Cleeve Cloud La GL52 . . 134 D3
Cleevecroft Ave GL52 . . 138 A3
Cleeve Ct
 Bishop's Cleeve GL52 . . . 137 E5
 Bristol BS16 . . . . 20 D7
Cleeve Gdns BS16 . . . . . 20 D7
Cleeve Gr BS31 . . . . .4 D5
Cleeve Hill BS16 . . . . . . 20 D7
Cleeve Hill Extension
 BS16 . . . . 20 E6
Cleeve Ho GL5 . . . . 99 F1
Cleeve La BS30 . . . . 22 D1
Cleeve Lake Ct GL52 . . . 137 E4
Cleevelands Ave GL50 . . 133 C4
Cleevelands Cl GL50 . . . 133 C5
Cleevelands Dr GL50 . . . 133 C5
Cleeveland St GL51 . . . . 133 C3
Cleeve Lawns BS16 . . . . . 20 D7
Cleeve Lodge Cl BS16 . . . 20 E6
Cleeve Lodge Rd BS16 . . . 20 E6
Cleeve Mill Bsns Pk
 GL18 . . . . 171 A5
Cleeve Mill La GL18 . . . . 171 A5
Cleevemont Cl GL52 . . . 133 E5
Cleevemont Rd GL52 . . . 133 F4
Cleeve Park Rd BS16 . . . . 20 E7
Cleeve Rd
 Bristol BS4 . . . . .9 B3
 Bristol, Frenchay BS16 . . . 20 D6
 Bristol, Mangotsfield BS16 . 20 E6
 Gloucester GL4 . . . . 119 B4
 Gotherington GL52 . . . . 138 A7
 Yate BS37 . . . . 43 E1
Cleeve Rise GL18 . . . . . . 171 A4
Cleeve Sch GL52 . . . . . . 138 A2
Cleeve View GL52 . . . . . 136 E5
Cleeve View Rd GL52 . . . 134 A2
Cleeve Wood Pk BS16 . . . 20 C8
Cleeve Wood Rd BS16 . . . 20 D7
Clegram Rd GL1 . . . . . . 118 D7
Clematis Ct GL52 . . . . . 137 E3
Clementles The GL56 . . . 186 C6
Clements End Rd GL16 . . 155 B2
Clement St
 Bristol BS2 . . . . 195 C4
 Gloucester GL1 . . . . 119 A8
Clencher's Mill La HR8 . .179 B7
Clent Cl GL52 . . . . 133 F1
Clermont Cl
 Bristol BS34 . . . . 28 F8
 Bristol BS34 . . . . 29 A8
Cleve Ct
 4 Bristol, Clifton Wood
  BS8 . . . . .7 F7
 Bristol, Filton BS34 . . . . . 29 A8
Clevedale BS16 . . . . 20 D7
Clevedale Ct BS16 . . . . . 20 D7
Clevedon Rd
 Bristol BS7 . . . . 18 D4
 Gloucester GL1 . . . . 118 F6
Clevedon Sq GL53 . . . . . 133 A2
Clevedon Terr BS6 . . . . . 195 A4
Cleve House Sch BS4 . . . . .9 B3
Cleveland Cl BS35 . . . . . . 51 E8
Cleveland Dr GL3 . . . . . . 120 C4
Cleve Rd BS34 . . . . 29 A4
Clevewood BS16 . . . . 20 C7
Clewson Rise BS14 . . . . . .2 F3
Cliff Court Dr BS16 . . . . . 20 B7
Clifford Ave GL20 . . . . . 192 E2
Clifford Cl GL7 . . . . 190 F3
Clifford Gdns BS11 . . . . . 16 E6
Clifford Rd BS16 . . . . 20 C4
Cliffords 8 SN6 . . . . 143 E4
Cliff View NP16 . . . . 61 B7
Clift House Rd BS3 . . . . . .8 A4
Clift House Spur BS3 . . . . .7 F4
Clifton Cath★ BS8 . . . . . 194 A4
Clifton Arc BS8 . . . . 194 A3
Clifton Cl
 1 Bristol BS8 . . . . .7 F7
 14 Stow-on-t-W GL54 . . 176 F4
Clifton Coll BS8 . . . . . . 194 A4

Clifton College Prep Sch
BS8 . . . . **17** F1
Clifton Down BS8 . . . .**7** F7
Clifton Down Rd BS8 . . **194** A3
Clifton Down Sh Ctr 11
BS8 . . . . **18** B1
Clifton Down Sta BS8 . . **18** B1
Clifton High Gr BS8 . . **17** E5
Clifton High Sch BS8.. **194** A4
Clifton Hill BS8 . . . . . . **194** A2
Clifton Metro 10 BS8.. **18** B1
Clifton Park Rd BS8....**7** F8
Clifton Pk BS8 . . . . . . **194** A3
Clifton Pl BS5 . . . . **9** A8
Clifton Rd
 Bristol BS8. . . . . **194** A2
 Gloucester GL1 . . **196** A1
Clifton St
 Bristol, Bedminster BS3 . . **8** C3
 Bristol, Upper Easton BS5...**9** A8
Clifton Suspension Bridge★
BS8 . . . . **7** E7
Clifton Vale BS8 . . . . . . **194** A2
Clifton Vale CI BS8 . . **194** A2
Clifton View 1 BS3....**8** F4
Cliftonwood Cres BS8.. **194** B2
Clifton Wood Ct BS8 . . **194** B2
Clifton Wood Rd BS8 . . **194** A2
Cliftonwood Terr BS8 . . **194** A2
Clift Pl BS1 . . . . **195** A1
Clift Rd BS3 . . . . **8** A4
Cliinton Ho GL7 . . . . . . **190** D5
Clingre Down GL11 . . . **87** C4
Clingre La GL11 . . . . **87** C4
Clinton Rd BS3 . . . . **8** C2
Clissold Ct GL6 . . . . **91** B3
Clive Rd BS14 . . . . **3** C8
Cloatley Rd SN16 . . **141** E1
Clock House Sq GL54.. **166** C6
Cloisters BS8 . . . . **7** F8
Cloisters Ct BS36 . . **30** E6
Cloisters Rd BS36 . . **30** F6
Cloisters The
 Bishop's Cleeve GL52 . . **137** E4
 Chepstow/Cas-Gwent NP16 **72** D2
Clomoney Way GL11.. **127** D5
Clonmel Rd BS4 . . . . **8** D1
Close Field GL54 . . **183** F1
Close Gdns
 Condicote GL54 . . **176** B7
 14 Tetbury GL8 . . . . . . **140** B4
Close The
 Bristol BS16. . . . . . . **29** F1
 Bristol, Henbury BS10 . . **28** A5
 Bristol, Little Stoke BS34.. **29** C6
 Bristol, Patchway BS32 . . . . **40** C1
 Bristol, Upper Soundwell
 BS16 . . . . **20** D3
 Cheltenham GL53.. **130** D4
 Coaley GL11 . . . . . . **88** E7
 Coalpit Heath BS36 . . **31** C6
 Coleford GL16 . . **155** C6
 Dursley GL11 . . . . **87** E4
 Lechlade on T GL7 . . **153** E3
 Siddington GL7 . . **150** E2
 Slimbridge GL2 . . **95** E3
 Southam GL52 . . **134** C4
 South Cerney GL7 . . **143** A8
 Thornbury BS35. . . **51** B8
 Whiteshill GL6 . . **102** F3
 Whitminster GL2 . . **100** F5
Clothier Rd BS4....**9** F2
Clouds Hill Ave BS5 . . .**9** E8
Clouds Hill Rd BS5 . . .**9** F8
Cloud The GL12 . . **68** B7
Clovelly CI BS5....**9** F8
Clovelly Rd BS5 . . . .**9** F8
Clover CI
 Cinderford GL14 . . **156** C6
 Milkwall GL16 . . **155** B4
Cloverdale Dr BS30 . . **11** A3
Clover Dr GL2 . . **109** E6
Clover Ground BS9.. **18** B7
Cloverlea Bsns Ctr BS36.. **31** C3
Cloverlea Rd BS30 . . **11** C5
Clover Leaze BS32 . . **29** D6
Clover Piece GL4 . . **119** D6
Clyde Ave BS31 . . . .**4** F4
Clyde Cres GL52 . . **134** A2
Clyde Ct 2 BS3. . . . . **8** C3
Clyde Gdns BS5. . . **10** B6
Clyde Gr BS34 . . . . **28** F2
Clyde Ho 7 BS35 . . **51** C8
Clyde La BS6 . . . . **18** C2
Clyde Mews 3 BS6 . . **18** C2
Clyde Rd
 Bristol, Redland BS6 . . **18** B2
 Bristol, Totterdown BS4.. **9** A3
 Brockworth GL3.. **120** F5
 Frampton Cotterell BS36.. **31** B8
Clydesdale CI BS14. . . **3** A6
Clyde Terr
 3 Bristol, Bedminster BS3.. **8** C3
 Bristol, Totterdown BS4.. **9** A3
Coach CI GL13 . . **85** E3
Coach Ho The
 Blockley GL56 . . . . . . **186** C7
 Tewkesbury GL20 . . **192** D4
Coach House Mews GL7 **190** D4
Coach Rd HR9 . . **164** D8
Coachworks The BS30.. **10** F4
Coaley CE Prim Sch GL11 **88** E6
Coaley Rd BS15 . . **16** D5
Coalsack La BS31 . . **31** B3
Coalville Rd BS36 . . **31** D7

Coalway Com Inf Sch
GL16 . . . . **155** B5
Coalway Jun Sch GL16.. **155** B5
Coalway Rd GL16 . . **155** B5
Coape Rd BS14 . . . .**3** F5
Coates Gdns GL10 . . **97** F8
Coates Ho 11 GL51 . . **132** E2
Coates La GL7 . . **149** F4
Coates Mill Cotts GL54 . . **139** F4
Coates The GL54 . . **139** F4
Coates Wlk BS4. . . . . **2** D6
Cobbler's CI The GL12.. **68** D8
Cobblestone Mews BS8.. **194** A4
Cobden Ctr The BS16.. **31** B2
Cobden St BS5. . . . . **9** C7
Coberley CE Prim Sch
GL53 . . . . **123** A5
Coberley Rd
 Cheltenham GL51.. **129** D8
 Gloucester GL4 . . **118** E3
Cobham Ct GL51 . . **133** B3
Cobham Rd GL51.. **133** B3
Cobhorn Dr BS13 . . . .**1** F4
Cobourg Rd BS6 . . **18** F2
Coburn Gdns GL51 . . **132** C1
Cochran Cl GL3 . . **128** C5
Cockadilly GL10 . . **89** D5
Cockatoos La HR9 . . **170** B5
Cock La SN14 . . **23** D5
Cock Rd BS15 . . **10** F6
Cockshoot Hill GL15.. **146** E7
Codrington Pl BS8 . . **194** A3
Codrington Rd BS7.. **18** D3
Cody Ct 2 BS15 . . **10** B5
Coed Barnet/Barnets Wood
 NP16 . . . . **60** C8
Coed Castell/Castle Wood
 NP16 . . . . **60** C8
Coed Cilfach/Alcove Wood
 NP16 . . . . **60** C8
Coed Fedw/Fedw Wood
 NP16 . . . . **60** C8
Coed Ffawydd/Beechwood
 Chepstow NP16 . . . . . . **61** A5
 Saltford BS31 . . . . **5** E2
Coed Ffwyth/Fryth Wood
 NP16 . . . . **60** C8
Coed Hale/Hale Wood
 NP16 . . . . **60** C8
Coed Maenor/Manor Wood
 NP16 . . . . **60** C8
Coed Wallwern/Wallwern
 Wood NP16 . . **72** C1
Coed Woolpitch/Woolpitch
 Wood NP16 . . **60** B8
Coffin CI SN6 . . **145** D3
Cogan Rd BS16 . . **20** E3
Cogsall Rd BS14 . . . .**3** F6
Colburn CI BS7 . . **18** F7
Colchester CI
 Mitcheldean GL17 . . **164** D5
 Westbury-on-S GL14 . . **165** C1
Colchester Cres BS4 . . **2** D7
Cold Aston CE Prim Sch
 GL54 . . . . **168** B6
Coldharbour La
 Bristol BS16. . . . . . . **19** E8
 Newent GL18 . . **170** F6
Coldharbour Rd
 Bristol BS6. . . . . . . **18** B4
 St Briavels GL15 . . **146** E6
Coldicott Leys GL55 . . **189** D2
Coldicotts CI 7 GL55.. **189** A2
Coldpark Gdns BS13 . . . .**1** E5
Coldpark Rd BS13....**1** E5
Cold Pool La
 CheltenhamBadgeworth
 GL51 . . . . **129** B5
 Cheltenham, Up Hatherley
 GL51 . . . . **129** C6
Coldray CI GL1. . . **127** B1
Coldrick CI BS14 . . **2** F3
Coldwell GL10 . . **98** B3
Coldwell CI GL10 . . **98** B3
Coldwell La GL10 . . **98** B3
Cole Ave GL2 . . **118** C3
Colebridge Ave GL2.. **127** C3
Colebrook Rd BS15 . . **10** C8
Coleford Rd
 Bream GL15 . . **147** C8
 Bristol BS16. . . . . . . **28** D1
 Tutshill NP16 . . **72** F2
Colemead BS13 . . . .**2** B5
Cole Rd BS2 . . . .**9** B6
Coleridge Ho BS34 . . **40** A1
Coleridge Rd BS5 . . **19** C3
Colerne Dr GL3 . . **120** B7
Colesborne CI BS37 . . **32** E8
Colesbourne Rd GL51.. **129** D8
Coleshill Dr BS13 . . . .**2** B5
Colethrop Wy GL2 . . **110** A5
Colin CI BS35 . . **64** C1
Colin Rd GL4 . . **127** D1
Collard Ho 2 BS16 . . **19** F4
College Ave BS16 . . **20** A5
College Baths Rd GL53.. **193** C2
College Ct
 Bristol, Clifton BS8 . . **194** A4
 Bristol, Fishponds BS16 . . **20** A5
 Gloucester GL1 . . **196** B3
College Farm Wkshps
 GL7 . . . . **150** B3
College Fields
 Bristol BS8. . . . . . . **7** F8
 Gloucester GL2 . . **127** D4
College Gate GL53 . . **193** C2

College Gn
 Bristol BS1. . . . . . . **194** C2
 Gloucester GL1 . . **196** B3
College La 8 BS1. . . **194** C2
College Lawn GL53.. **193** C1
College Mews BS9 . . **18** A7
College Park Dr BS10 . . **27** F1
College Rd
 Bredon GL20 . . **182** B7
 Bristol, Clifton BS8 . . . .**7** F8
 Bristol, Fishponds BS16 . . **20** A5
 Bristol, Westbury on Trym
 BS9 . . . . **18** A7
 Cheltenham GL53.. **193** C2
 Cinderford GL14 . . **191** C4
 Stroud GL5. . . . . **99** A8
College Row 22 GL54.. **168** A1
College Sq BS1 . . **194** C2
College St
 Bristol BS1. . . . . . . **194** C2
 Gloucester GL1 . . **196** B3
College View
 Cirencester GL7 . . **190** B1
 9 Stonehouse GL10 . . **97** F7
College Way BS34. . . **29** A4
College Yd GL1 . . **196** A3
Collett CI
 Bristol BS15. . . . . . . **10** B5
 Hardwicke GL2 . . **109** D7
Collett Ho BS36 . . **30** D4
Collett Pl SN6 . . **143** E6
Colletts Ct 2 GL54 . . **168** F7
Colletts Dr GL51 . . **133** B3
Colletts Fields WR12 . . **185** C8
Colletts Gdns 6 WR12 . . **185** C8
Collett Way GL37 . . **43** C3
Colliers Break BS16 . . **21** B5
Colliers Field GL14 . . **191** C5
Colliers Pitch GL15 . . **147** C5
Colliers Wood GL6 . . **91** A5
Collin CI WR12 . . **188** B2
Collingbourne Rd GL4.. **119** C1
Collingwood Ave BS15 . . **20** E1
Collingwood CI
 Chepstow NP16 . . . . . . **61** A5
 Saltford BS31 . . . . **5** E2
Collingwood Rd 4 BS6.. **18** B1
Collin La WR12 . . **188** A2
Collin Rd BS4. . . . . **9** D4
Collins Ave BS34 . . **29** C6
Collins CI GL19 . . **172** A8
Collins Dr BS35 . . **38** C3
Collinson Rd BS13 . . . .**2** B5
Collins St BS11 . . **16** B8
Collier Cres BS3 . . . .**8** B2
Collum End Rise GL53.. **130** D4
Collyberry Rd GL53 . . **138** B4
Colne Ave GL52 . . **134** A3
Colne BS31. . . . . **5** A4
Coln House Sch GL7 . . **152** D3
Coln Pk GL54 . . **166** D6
Coln Rise GL54 . . **166** D6
Coln Sq GL35 . . **51** C8
Colston Ave BS1 . . **195** A3
Colston CI
 Bristol BS16. . . . . . . **20** D3
 Winterbourne BS36 . . **30** E4
Colston Ct BS7. . . . . **18** D3
Colston Dale BS16 . . **19** E4
Colstone Ct 3 BS16 . . **19** E3
Colston Fort 2 BS2.. **195** A4
Colston Hall★ BS1 . . **195** A3
Colston Hill BS16 . . **19** D4
Colston Mews BS6 . . **18** E1
Colston Par BS1 . . **195** B1
Colston Rd BS5 . . **19** C1
Colston's Almshouses
 BS2 . . . . **195** A3
Colston's Lower Sch BS16 **19** D5
Colston's Prim Sch BS6.. **18** D1
Colston's Sch BS16 . . **19** C4
Colston St
 Bristol, Kingsdown BS1.. **195** A3
 Bristol, Upper Soundwell
 BS16 . . . . **20** D3
Colston Yd BS1 . . **195** A3
Colsty Mdw GL15 . . **156** D1
Coltham CI 7 GL52 . . **130** F8
Coltham Fields GL52 . . **130** F8
Coltham Rd GL52 . . **130** F8
Colthurst Dr BS15 . . **10** E5
Coltman CI GL1 . . **127** B1
Colts Gn BS37 . . **33** E8
Columbia CI GL1 . . **196** C3
Columbia St GL52 . . **193** C4
Columbine Rd GL20 . . **192** E1
Colville Ho 7 . . **190** D5
Colwell Ave GL3 . . **128** A8
Colwell School CI GL1.. **127** A1
Colwyn Dr GL51 . . **129** E6
Colwyn Rd 2 BS5. . . **19** C1
Colyton Ct BS3 . . . . **8** D1
Combe Ho GL8 . . **140** B4
Combermere BS35 . . **51** D8
Combfactory La 13 BS5...**9** B8
Comb Paddock BS9 . . **18** B7
Combrook CI GL4 . . **119** E4
Commerce Rd GL2.. **173** E1
Commercial Rd
 Bristol BS1. . . . . . . **195** A1
 Chalford GL6 . . **148** C5
 Gloucester GL1 . . **196** A2
Commercial St
 Cheltenham GL50.. **193** B1
 Cinderford GL14 . . **191** D4
Common (East) The BS32 **40** C1

Commonfield Rd BS11 . . **27** B1
Common Hill SN6 . . **143** E4
Common Rd BS20 . . **16** B2
Commonlead La BS37.. **33** F8
Common Mead La BS16 . . **30** A1
Common Rd
 Bristol BS15. . . . . . . **10** B3
 Minchinhampton GL6 . . **91** E6
 Winterbourne BS36 . . **30** F7
Common The
 Berkeley Heath GL13.. **86** C3
 Bristol, Frenchay BS16 . . **20** B7
 Bristol, Patchway BS32 . . **40** C1
 Minety SN16 . . **142** E1
 Olveston BS35 . . **49** F3
 Siddington GL7 . . **150** E2
Compton CI
 Churchdown GL3 . . **128** A8
 Corse GL19 . . **172** A7
Compton Dr BS9. . . **17** C7
Compton Gn BS35. . . . .**4** E4
Compton Lodge 3 BS6.. **18** B1
Compton Rd GL51 . . **133** B4
Compton Rise GL54 . . **166** E2
Compton's Alley GL20 . . **192** C4
Compton St BS5 . . . . **9** C7
Comyn Wlk BS16 . . **20** A5
Concord CI GL4 . . **91** A3
Concorde Dr BS10 . . **28** B1
Concorde Ho BS34 . . **28** F2
Concorde Rd BS34 . . **28** E7
Concorde Way GL4. . . **119** B7
Conderton Pottery★
 GL20 . . . . **183** A8
Condicote La GL54 . . **176** B5
Condor Ho BS7. . . . . **19** C7
Condover Rd BS4 . . **10** A3
Conduit CI GL55 . . **188** F1
Conduit PI 2 BS2. . . **19** A1
Conduit Rd BS2 . . **19** A1
Conduit St GL1 . . **196** C1
Condurrow St 18 GL54 . . **176** F4
Cone The BS10, BS34 . . **28** C6
Coneygar Rd GL7 . . **152** C7
Coneygree BS13 . . . .**1** F6
Coneygree La WR12 . . **185** B7
Coney Hill Com Prim Sch
 GL4 . . . . **119** C7
Coney Hill Par GL4. . . **119** C7
Coney Hill Rd GL4. . . **119** C7
Congleton Rd BS5 . . . . **9** D8
Conham Hill BS15 . . **10** A5
Conham Rd BS4, BS5, BS15 ...**9** F5
Conifer CI
 Bristol BS16. . . . . . . **20** D6
 Frampton Cotterell BS36 . . **42** A1
Conifers The
 2 Cheltenham GL52 . . **134** A2
 Gloucester GL1 . . **119** A7
 Minety SN16 . . **142** D1
Conigree La GL20 . . **192** C2
Coniston Ave BS9 . . **17** E6
Coniston CI BS30 . . **11** D6
Coniston Prim Sch BS34 . . **39** F1
Coniston Rd
 Bristol BS34. . . . . . . **39** F1
 Cheltenham GL51.. **129** E7
 Gloucester GL2 . . **127** C4
Connaught Rd BS4. . . . .**2** E8
Consell Gn BS34 . . **184** C3
Constable CI BS31 . . . .**4** F6
Constable Rd BS7. . . **19** B6
Constance CI GL5 . . **98** F5
Constantine Ave BS34 . . **29** E5
Constitution Hill BS8.. **194** B2
Contemporis BS8 . . **194** A3
Convent CI BS10 . . **27** D3
Convent La GL5 . . **90** F7
Convent The OX7 . . **169** E7
Conway Ct 4 GL16.. **155** A7
Conway Gn BS31 . . . . **5** A3
Conway Rd
 Bristol BS4. . . . . . . **9** C4
 Gloucester GL3 . . **120** A8
Conygar Rd GL8 . . **140** C4
Conygre Gr BS34. . . **29** C3
Conygre Rd BS34 . . **29** B3
Cook CI BS30 . . **11** C4
Cooke's Dr BS35 . . **39** A1
Cook La GL2. . . **173** B3
Cooks CI BS32 . . **40** D3
Cook's Folly Rd BS9.. **17** D3
Cook's Hill GL19 . . **172** C4
Cooks La BS36 . . **31** D3
Cook's La GL19 . . **179** F4
Cooksley Rd BS5 . . . . **9** C8
Cookson Terr GL15 . . **84** B8
Cooks Orch GL1 . . **127** A3
Cookspool 2 GL8. . . **140** C4
Cook St BS11 . . **16** C8
Cookworthy CI 2 BS5. . . **9** B6
Coomb Dr GL14 . . **191** C1
Coombe Ave BS35 . . **64** B2
Coombe Bridge Ave BS9 . . **17** D6
Coombe Brook CI BS15.. **20** B1
Coombe CI BS10 . . **27** D3
Coombe Dale BS9. . . **17** C6
Coombe Gdns
 Bristol BS9. . . . . . . **17** E6
 Stinchcombe GL11 . . **87** C3
Coombe Glen La GL51.. **129** D6
Coombe Ho BS15 . . **10** E8
Coombe La
 Bristol BS9. . . . . . . **17** E6
 Easton-in-G BS8. . . **16** A1
 King's Stanley GL10.. **98** C2

Coombe La continued
 Wotton-u-E GL12 . . **68** D8
Coombe Lea NP16 . . **146** A5
Coombe Mead GL52.. **138** B3
Coombe Rd
 Bristol BS5. . . . . . . **19** C2
 Wotton-u-E GL12 . . **68** C8
Coombes Way BS30.. **11** D4
Coombe Terr GL12 . . **68** C8
Coombe Way BS10 . . **27** F1
Coomb Rocke BS9 . . **17** D6
Coombs Rd GL16.. **155** A6
Cooperage La BS3 . . **194** B1
Cooperage Rd BS5 . . . . **9** D7
Co-operation Rd BS5 . . **19** C1
Cooper Rd
 Bristol BS9. . . . . . . **17** F7
 Thornbury BS35. . . **51** B7
Cooper's Ct
 Brockworth GL3.. **120** E5
 Charlton Kings GL53 . . **131** B5
Coopers Dr BS37. . . **43** F5
Coopers Edge Sch GL3.. **120** B4
Coopers Elm GL2 . . **117** F2
Cooper's Hill★ GL3 . . **120** E2
Coopers Mill GL6 . . **91** A6
Coopers Rd GL16 . . **155** A8
Cooper's View GL3 . . **120** C5
Coopers Way 27 GL18 . . **171** A4
Coots The BS14. . . . . **3** E6
Copeland Dr BS14. . . **3** B5
Copenacre SN16 . . **142** B1
Cope Pk BS32. . . **40** C5
Copford La BS41....**7** B1
Copley Ct BS15 . . **10** E5
Copley Di 10 GL16.. **155** A5
Copley Gdns BS7. . . **19** B6
Copperas Rd BS5 . . **19** A3
Copper Beeches SN6.. **145** C3
Copper Beech Gr GL2 . . **117** E1
Copperfield CI GL4. . . **119** B4
Coppice Daw Pitch GL19 **165** D5
Coppice Gate GL51. . . **132** F5
Coppice Hill GL6. . . **148** D5
Coppice La SN16 . . **141** F4
Coppice The
 Bristol, Bradley Stoke
 BS32 . . . . **29** E7
 Bristol, Highridge BS13 . . . . **1** E4
Copsehill Rd GL54 . . **176** C1
Copse Rd
 Bristol BS4. . . . . . . **9** B3
 Keynsham BS31. . . **5** C4
Copse The
 Broad Blunsdon SN26 . . **144** D1
 Gloucester GL4 . . **119** E7
Copt Elm CI GL53 . . **131** A6
Copt Elm Rd GL53 . . **131** A6
Copthorne CI BS14 . . . .**3** B5
Coral CI GL4 . . **118** B3
Corbet CI BS11 . . **27** C2
Corbett CI BS37 . . **43** F4
Corbett Ho 11 BS5 . . . . **9** C7
Corders CI 5 GL56 . . **187** A3
Corder's La 3 GL56.. **187** A3
Cordingley CI GL3. . . **128** C5
Cordwell Wlk BS10 . . **18** D7
Corey CI 6 BS5. . . . . **18** F1
Corfe CI GL52. . . **134** C4
Corfe Cres BS31 . . . .**4** E4
Corfe PI BS30. . . **11** B1
Corfe Rd BS4 . . . . **2** D7
Coriander Dr
 Bristol BS34. . . . . . . **30** A7
 Innsworth GL3. . . **127** C7
Coriander Wlk BS5. . . **19** C2
Corinium Ave GL4.. **127** D2
Corinium Bsns Pk GL14 . . **191** B7
Corinium Cntr GL7.. **190** D1
Corinium Gate GL7.. **190** D5
Corinium Ho GL7 . . **190** B3
Corinium Mus★ GL7 . . **190** C5
Corinthian Ct 9 BS1.. **195** B1
Corinum CI BS16 . . **21** C6
Corker's Hill 9 BS5....**9** F6
Cormorant Ave GL4 . . **192** E2
Corncroft La GL4 . . **119** D2
Corndean La GL54 . . **174** A5
Corner Farm Dr WR11.. **188** C3
Corner Rd GL15 . . **155** F1
Cornfield CI BS32 . . **40** C1
Cornfield Dr
 Bishop's Cleeve GL52 . . **137** E4
 Hardwicke GL2 . . **109** E7
Cornfields The GL52 . . **137** E4
Cornflower La GL20 . . **192** E1
Cornflower Rd GL4. . . **119** E5
Cornhill GL5 . . **99** C7
Cornhill Dr BS14. . . **3** A7
Cornish Gr BS14 . . . .**3** E6
Cornish Hos
 Cinderford GL14 . . **156** C6
 9 Moreton-in-M GL56 . . **187** B3
Cornish Rd BS14 . . . .**3** E6
Cornish Wlk BS14 . . . .**3** E6
Cornleaze BS13. . . . . **2** A5
Cornmeadow Dr GL51.. **132** D5
Corn St BS1 . . **195** A3
Cornwall Ave GL51 . . **133** A2
Cornwall Cres BS37 . . **43** F3
Cornwallis Ave BS8 . . **194** A2
Cornwallis Cres 8 BS8....**7** F6
Cornwallis Ho BS8 . . **194** A2

Cornwallis Ho BS8 . . . . **194** A2
Cornwall Rd BS7 . . . . **18** D4
Corolin Rd GL2 . . . . **118** B4
Coronation Ave
  Bristol BS16 . . . . **20** A4
  Keynsham BS31 . . . . **4** D4
Coronation Cl
  Bristol BS30 . . . . **11** A5
  Chipping Campden GL55 . . **188** F2
Coronation Flats GL52 . . **131** A7
Coronation Gr GL2 . . . . . . **127** B2
Coronation Pl BS1 . . . . . . **195** A2
Coronation Rd
  Bristol, Cadbury Heath
   BS30 . . . . **11** B5
  Bristol, Mangotsfield BS16 . **20** E5
  Bristol, Southville BS3 . . . **194** C1
  Bristol, Warmley BS15 . . . . **11** A7
  Cheltenham GL52 . . . . . . **134** B4
  Cinderford GL14 . . . . . . **191** D3
  Stroud GL5 . . . . **99** B6
  Tetbury GL8 . . . . **140** B5
Coronation Sq GL51 . . . . **132** E2
Coronation St GL7 . . . . . . **152** D4
Corpus St BS2 . . . . **193** C2
Corriett The GL11 . . . . **88** A5
Corse Ind Est GL19 . . . . **172** B7
Corsend Rd GL19 . . . . . . **172** B4
Corsley Wlk BS4 . . . . **2** F8
Corston Wlk BS11 . . . . . . **16** D7
Cosford Cl **3** GL2 . . . . . . **118** A1
Cossham St BS35 . . . . **64** C2
Cossham Memorial Hospl
 BS16 . . . . **20** C2
Cossham Rd BS5 . . . . **9** D7
Cossham St BS16 . . . . **21** B5
Cossham Wlk BS5 . . . . . . **20** A1
Cossington Rd BS4 . . . . **2** F8
Cossins Rd BS6 . . . . **18** B3
Costers Cl BS35 . . . . **51** A5
Costiland Dr BS13 . . . . **1** F6
Cote Bank Ho BS9 . . . . . . **18** B7
Cote Dr BS9 . . . . **18** A4
Cote House La BS9 . . . . . . **18** A5
Cote La BS9 . . . . **18** A5
Cote Lea Pk BS9 . . . . **18** B7
Cote Paddock BS9 . . . . . . **17** F4
Cote Pk BS9 . . . . **17** E6
Cote Rd BS9 . . . . **18** A4
Cotham Brow BS6 . . . . . . **18** D1
Cotham Gdns **15** BS6 . . . . **18** B1
Cotham Gr BS6 . . . . **18** D1
Cotham Gram Sch
(Charnwood Annex)
 BS6 . . . . **18** C1
Cotham Hill BS6 . . . . . . **194** C4
Cotham Lawn Ho BS6 . . . **194** C4
Cotham Lawn Rd BS6 . . . . **18** C1
Cotham Pk BS6 . . . . **18** C1
Cotham Pk N BS6 . . . . . . **18** C1
Cotham Pl BS6 . . . . **194** C4
Cotham Rd BS6 . . . . **194** C4
Cotham Rd S BS6 . . . . . . **195** A4
Cotham Sch BS6 . . . . **194** C4
Cotham Side BS6 . . . . **18** D1
Cotham Vale BS6 . . . . **18** C1
Cothar's Pitch HR9 . . . . . **170** A5
Cothers Ct GL56 . . . . **186** C6
Cotman Wlk BS7 . . . . **19** B6
Cotrith Gr BS10 . . . . **27** E3
Cotsmore Cl GL56 . . . . . . **187** B3
Cotswold Acad The GL54 **168** F8
Cotswold Ave
  Cirencester GL7 . . . . . . **190** C4
  Eastington GL10 . . . . **96** F7
Cotswold Bsns Village
 GL56 . . . . **187** B3
Cotswold Chine Home Specl
Sch GL6 . . . . **91** D5
Cotswold Cl
  Bredon GL20 . . . . **182** C7
  Brimscombe GL5 . . . . . . **148** A5
  Cirencester GL7 . . . . . . **190** B3
  5 Tetbury GL8 . . . . **140** C5
Cotswold Community
 GL7 . . . . **142** E6
Cotswold Cotts
  Eastcombe GL6 . . . . **148** C7
  Nailsworth GL6 . . . . **90** F3
Cotswold Court Pk GL51 . **173** F1
Cotswold Ct BS37 . . . . **44** B1
Cotswold Ed Ctr The BS34 **28** F2
Cotswold Edge GL55 . . . . **189** A6
Cotswold Edge Bsns Pk
 GL2 . . . . **118** C8
Cotswold Falconry Ctr★
 GL56 . . . . **186** E4
Cotswold Farm Pk★
 GL54 . . . . **175** D5
Cotswold Gdns
  Gloucester GL2 . . . . . . **127** D5
  25 Moreton-in-M GL56 . **187** A3
  Tewkesbury GL20 . . . . . **192** D5
  Wotton-u-E GL12 . . . . . . **68** C7
Cotswold Gn GL10 . . . . . . **98** A8
Cotswold La BS37 . . . . **34** A8
Cotswold Link GL55 . . . . **187** B3
Cotswold Lo **11** GL52 . . . **133** F2
Cotswold Mdws GL54 . . . **169** C4
Cotswold Mead GL6 . . . . **103** D7
Cotswold Mill GL7 . . . . . **190** C4
Cotswold Pl GL20 . . . . . . **192** D5

Cotswold Rd
  Bristol BS3 . . . . **8** D3
  Cheltenham GL52 . . . . . . **134** B3
  Chipping Sodbury BS37 . . **33** B8
  Stroud GL5 . . . . **98** E8
Cotswolds Countryside
 Mus★ GL54 . . . . **167** F2
Cotswolds Motoring Mus &
 Toy Collection The★
 GL54 . . . . **168** F7
Cotswolds Water Pk★
 GL7 . . . . **153** A2
Cotswold Terr GL10 . . . . . . **89** D5
Cotswold View
  Bristol, Filton BS34 . . . . . **29** A3
  Bristol, Kingswood BS15 . . **20** D2
  Charfield GL12 . . . . **67** B5
  Tirley GL19 . . . . **172** F7
  Wickwar GL12 . . . . **54** B6
  Woodmancote GL52 . . . . **138** B3
Cotswold Water Pk★
 GL7 . . . . **142** D5
Cotswold Way
  Cold Ashton SN14 . . . . . . **14** A6
  Highworth SN6 . . . . **145** C3
Cottage Field GL2 . . . . . . **125** D5
Cottage Gdns BS5 . . . . **10** A7
Cottage Pitch GL18 . . . . . **171** A5
Cottage Pl BS2 . . . . **195** A4
Cottage Rake Ave GL50 . . **133** C5
Cottage The GL5 . . . . **98** C7
Cottesmore Cl GL4 . . . . . . **110** C8
Cotteswold Rd
  Gloucester GL4 . . . . **119** B5
  Tewkesbury GL20 . . . . . **192** D5
Cotteswold Rise GL5 . . . . . **99** D7
Cottington Ct BS15 . . . . . . **10** E5
Cottisford Rd BS5 . . . . **19** B4
Cottle Gdns BS14 . . . . **3** F6
Cottle Rd BS14 . . . . **3** F6
Cotton Cl GL4 . . . . **119** F5
Cotton's La GL8 . . . . **140** B3
Cottonwood Dr BS30 . . . . **11** A3
Cottrell Ave BS15 . . . . **20** C2
Cottrell Rd BS5 . . . . **19** C3
Cotts The GL56 . . . . **186** F6
Coughton Pl HR9 . . . . **163** C8
Coulson Ho **2** BS7 . . . . . . **18** F4
Coulson's Cl BS14 . . . . **3** A3
Coulson's Rd BS14 . . . . **3** A3
Coulson Wlk BS15 . . . . . . **20** C2
Council Hos
  Cold Aston GL54 . . . . . . **168** B6
  Eastnor HR8 . . . . **179** C7
  Ledbury HR8 . . . . **178** A8
  Stow-on-t-W GL54 . . . . . **176** F5
Council Villas
  Clearwell GL16 . . . . **154** F3
  Edge End GL16 . . . . **155** C8
  English Bicknor GL16 . . . **163** B1
  Sling GL16 . . . . **155** B3
Counterpool Rd BS15 . . . . **10** C7
Countership BS1 . . . . **195** B2
Countership Gdns BS14 . . . **3** C6
Countess Lilias Rd GL7 . . **190** C2
Countess Wlk BS16 . . . . . . **19** D6
Country Choice Cvn Pk
 GL20 . . . . **180** E9
Country Vw GL4 . . . . **119** B5
County Court Rd GL50 . . . **193** B3
County Cres **5** GL1 . . . . . **127** A1
County St BS4 . . . . **9** A4
County Way BS34 . . . . **30** A4
Court Ave BS34 . . . . **29** F5
Courtbrook GL7 . . . . **152** E3
Court Cl BS7 . . . . **18** E7
Court Cotts BS37 . . . . **45** D6
Court Dr GL19 . . . . **173** B6
Courtenay Cres BS4 . . . . . . **2** D7
Courtenay Rd BS31 . . . . **5** B2
Courtenay St GL50 . . . . . **133** D3
Court Farm
  Oaksey SN16 . . . . **142** A4
  Tibberton GL19 . . . . . . **124** B8
Court Farm La
  Beckford GL20 . . . . **183** B6
  Mitcheldean GL17 . . . . . **164** D5
Court Farm Mews GL10 . . **97** D7
Court Farm Rd
  Bristol, Longwell Green
   BS30 . . . . **10** E2
  Bristol, Whitchurch BS14 . . **2** F3
Court Field **11** GL8 . . . . . **140** B4
Courtfield Dr **6** GL52 . . . **131** B6
Courtfield Gr BS16 . . . . . . **20** A4
Courtfield Rd GL2 . . . . . . **109** F8
Courtfields SN6 . . . . **143** E6
Court Gdn GL11 . . . . **89** B1
Court Gdns
  Gloucester GL2 . . . . . . **118** B6
  St Arvans NP16 . . . . **72** B6
  Westbury-on-S GL14 . . . **157** C8
  Yate BS37 . . . . **32** E8
Court Gdns The GL2 . . . . **157** B5
Court Hay BS20 . . . . **16** A4
Courthouse Gdns GL11 . . . **87** F6
Courtiers Dr GL52 . . . . . . **138** A3
Court La
  8 Newent GL18 . . . . . **171** A4
  Wick BS30 . . . . **12** B6
  Woolaston GL15 . . . . . . **147** D3
Courtlands
  Bristol BS32 . . . . **40** C1
  Keynsham BS31 . . . . **4** E5
Courtlands La BS3 . . . . **7** E4

Court Mdw
  Stone GL13 . . . . **77** E3
  Wotton-u-E GL12 . . . . . . **68** C7
Court Mead GL13 . . . . **77** E3
Court Mews GL52 . . . . . . **131** A7
Courtney Cl GL20 . . . . . . **192** D1
Courtney Pl BS15 . . . . **10** E7
Courtney Prim Sch BS15 . **10** E7
Courtney Rd BS15 . . . . **10** E7
Courtney Vw BS15 . . . . . . **10** E7
Courtney Way BS15 . . . . . **11** A7
Court Orch GL12 . . . . **68** C7
Court Orchard GL54 . . . . **183** E1
Court Pl GL4 . . . . **119** D7
Court Rd
  Bristol, Horfield BS7 . . . . **18** F6
  Bristol, Kingswood BS15 . . **10** D7
  Bristol, Oldland Common
   BS30 . . . . **11** C3
  Brockworth GL3 . . . . . . **120** E6
  Frampton Cotterell BS36 . . **30** F8
  Frocester GL10 . . . . **97** B3
  Lydney GL15 . . . . **92** B5
  Newent GL18 . . . . **171** A5
  Upper Strensham WR8 . . **180** A10
Courtside Mews BS6 . . . . . **18** C1
Court St SN16 . . . . **58** C1
Court View
  Chalford GL6 . . . . **148** D5
  Stonehouse GL10 . . . . . . **97** D7
  Wick BS30 . . . . **12** C6
Court View CI BS32 . . . . . . **40** A5
Court Way GL5 . . . . **99** A5
Courtyard The
  Bourton-on-t-W GL54 . . **168** F8
  Cheltenham GL50 . . . . . **193** A2
  Gloucester GL1 . . . . **127** A2
  Stow-on-t-W GL54 . . . . . **176** F5
  Tewkesbury GL20 . . . . . **182** B5
Courville Cl BS35 . . . . **51** A4
Cousins Cl BS10 . . . . **27** D3
Cousins La BS5 . . . . **9** F8
Cousins Mews BS4 . . . . **9** F6
Cousins Way BS16 . . . . . . **21** B8
Cousley Cl GL3 . . . . **120** A7
Couzens Cl BS37 . . . . **44** B2
Couzens Pl BS34 . . . . **29** F5
Cove House Gdns **3**
 SN6 . . . . **142** F5
Coventry Cl GL20 . . . . . . **192** D2
Coventry Wlk BS4 . . . . **9** F6
Coverham Cl **10** GL16 . . . **155** A4
Coverham Rd GL16 . . . . . **155** A4
Cow Barton **1** BS7 . . . . . **19** C8
Cowcombe Hill GL6 . . . . . **148** C5
Cowdray Rd BS4 . . . . **2** D7
Cowhorn Hill BS30 . . . . . . **11** C4
Cow La GL5 . . . . **91** A6
Cowler Wlk BS13 . . . . **1** F4
Cowley Cl GL51 . . . . **129** E7
Cowley La HR9 . . . . **170** C2
Cowley Rd GL4 . . . . **118** E3
Cowling Dr BS14 . . . . **3** C5
Cowling Rd BS14 . . . . **3** D5
Cowl La GL54 . . . . **174** A7
Cowlsmead GL51 . . . . . . **129** E2
Cowper Rd
  Bristol BS6 . . . . **18** C1
  Cheltenham GL51 . . . . . **132** E1
Cowper St BS5 . . . . **9** C7
Cowship La GL12 . . . . **53** D6
Cowsley Dr GL3 . . . . **120** C6
Cowslip Dr GL52 . . . . **137** F5
Cowslip Mdw GL52 . . . . . **138** B3
Cowslip Mead BS32 . . . . . **40** D5
Cow St SN5 . . . . **143** D1
Cowslade La GL6 . . . . . . **148** B6
Coxbury & Wyegate La
 GL15 . . . . **154** D2
Cox Ct BS30 . . . . **10** F4
Coxgrove Hill BS16 . . . . . **21** F7
Coxmoor Cl OX7 . . . . **177** F2
Coxmore Cl GL3 . . . . **120** A7
Cox's Hill SN6 . . . . **142** F5
Coxs Mdws HR9 . . . . **164** C8
Cox's Way
  Bream GL15 . . . . **155** D1
  Gloucester GL4 . . . . **120** A6
Coxwell Ct GL7 . . . . **190** C5
Coxwell St GL7 . . . . **190** C5
Cozens La OX7 . . . . **177** F2
Crabtree Cl BS41 . . . . **1** D1
Crabtree La
  Cirencester GL7 . . . . . . **190** F3
  Dundry BS41 . . . . **1** D2
  Duntisbourne Abbots GL7 . **107** B3
Crabtree Pk GL7 . . . . **152** E4
Crab Tree Pl GL50 . . . . . . **133** C3
Crabtree Rd GL14 . . . . . . **191** B5
Crabtree Wlk BS5 . . . . **19** D2
Craddock Ct GL6 . . . . **90** F5
Craddock Rd **7** GL18 . . . **171** A4
Cradock Cl BS30 . . . . **11** B4
Craftes Ct BS5 . . . . **19** E1
Craig Yr Afon NP16 . . . . . . **60** E7
Crail View GL54 . . . . **168** A1
Cranberry Wlk BS9 . . . . . . **17** C8
Cranbourne GL12 . . . . **68** C7
Cranbourne Rd BS34 . . . . . **28** F7
Cranbrook Rd BS6 . . . . . . **18** C3
Crandell Cl BS10 . . . . **27** F4
Crane Cl BS15 . . . . **11** B8
Crane Furlong SN6 . . . . . **145** D4
Cranford Cl GL52 . . . . . . **138** C3
Cranford Ct **1** BS9 . . . . . . **18** B6

Cranham BS37 . . . . **32** C7
Cranham CE Prim Sch
 GL4 . . . . **112** E6
Cranham Cl
  Bristol BS15 . . . . **20** F2
  6 Gloucester GL4 . . . . **119** E5
Cranham Dr BS34 . . . . **40** C1
Cranham La GL3 . . . . **128** D3
Cranham Rd
  Bristol BS10 . . . . **18** C8
  Cheltenham GL52 . . . . . **133** F1
Cranhams La GL7 . . . . . . **190** B2
Cranleigh Court Rd BS37 . **43** D2
Cranleigh Gdns BS9 . . . . . **17** E4
Cranleigh Rd BS14 . . . . **3** B5
Cranley GL50 . . . . **133** E3
Cranmoor Gn BS35 . . . . . **38** D6
Cranmore Ave BS31 . . . . . . **4** E6
Cranmore Cres BS10 . . . . . **28** D1
Cranside Ave BS6 . . . . **18** C4
Cransley Cres BS9 . . . . . . **18** C7
Crantock Ave BS13 . . . . . . **28** B8
Crantock Dr BS32 . . . . **40** B5
Crantock Rd BS37 . . . . . . **43** D1
Cranwell Cl GL4 . . . . **119** C4
Cranwell Gr BS14 . . . . **3** A5
Crapen The GL11 . . . . **87** E4
Crashmore La GL20 . . . . . **182** F7
Crates Cl BS15 . . . . **10** E8
Craven Cl BS30 . . . . **10** F5
Craven Dr GL3 . . . . **128** B6
Craven Way BS30 . . . . **10** F5
Crawley Hill GL11 . . . . . . **89** B3
Crawley La GL11 . . . . **89** B3
Crawshay Pl GL14 . . . . . . **191** C4
Craydon Gr BS14 . . . . **3** D4
Craydon Rd BS14 . . . . **3** D5
Craydon Wlk BS14 . . . . **3** D5
Crease The **16** GL18 . . . . **171** A4
Crediton Cres BS4 . . . . **8** F1
Credon Rd GL3 . . . . **127** C1
Crescent Cl
  Coleford GL16 . . . . **155** A6
  Stonehouse GL10 . . . . . . **97** E6
Crescentdale GL2 . . . . . . **127** A5
Crescent Pl GL50 . . . . . . **193** B3
Crescent Rd
  Bristol BS16 . . . . **20** C6
  Stonehouse GL10 . . . . . . **97** E6
Crescent Terr GL50 . . . . . **193** B3
Crescent The
  8 Berry Hill GL16 . . . . **155** A4
  Bristol BS16 . . . . **29** F1
  Bristol, Frenchay BS16 . . . **29** F1
  Bristol, Henleaze BS9 . . . **18** C6
  Bristol, Sea Mills BS9 . . . . **17** C6
  Bristol, Upper Soundwell
   BS16 . . . . **20** D3
  Brockworth GL3 . . . . . . **120** D6
  Chalford GL6 . . . . **148** E6
  Coleford, Baker's Hill
   GL16 . . . . **155** A6
  Coleford GL16 . . . . **155** A5
  Dursley GL11 . . . . **87** F4
  Gloucester GL1 . . . . **127** A2
  Mitcheldean GL17 . . . . . **164** D6
  Newton GL13 . . . . **85** D8
  Northwood Green GL14 . . **165** D3
  Olveston BS35 . . . . **50** D4
  Wick BS30 . . . . **12** C7
Crest The
  Bristol BS4 . . . . **9** C2
  West Kington SN14 . . . . . **25** F3
Crest Way GL4 . . . . **127** F1
Creswicke Ave BS15 . . . . . **10** C5
Creswicke Rd BS4 . . . . **2** E7
Crew's Hole Rd BS5 . . . . . . **9** E7
Cribbs Causeway Ctr
 BS34 . . . . **28** A6
Cribbs Cswy BS10 . . . . . . **28** A6
Cricket La BS10 . . . . **18** A8
Cricklade Mus★ SN6 . . . . **143** E4
Cricklade Rd
  Bristol BS7 . . . . **18** E4
  Cirencester GL7 . . . . . . **190** E2
  Highworth SN6 . . . . **145** C3
  Purton Stoke SN5 . . . . . **143** D1
Cricklade St
  Cirencester GL7 . . . . . . **190** C4
  Poulton GL7 . . . . **151** E3
Crickley Hill Ctry Pk★
 GL4 . . . . **122** A5
Crickley Hill Ctry Pk Visitor
 Ctr★ GL4 . . . . **121** F5
Criftycraft La GL3 . . . . . . **128** C3
Crippetts La GL51 . . . . . . **130** E3
Cripps Rd
  Bristol BS3 . . . . **8** C3
  Cirencester GL7 . . . . . . **190** C4
Crispin Cl
  Gloucester GL4 . . . . **127** C5
  1 Winchcombe GL54 . . **174** A7
Crispin La **4** BS35 . . . . . . **64** B1
Crispin Rd GL54 . . . . **174** A7
Crispin Way BS15 . . . . **20** F2
Critchford La GL54 . . . . . **175** A5
Crockerne CE Prim Sch
 BS20 . . . . **16** C4
Crockerne Dr BS20 . . . . . . **16** C3
Crockerne Ho BS20 . . . . . **16** D4
Crock Mead GL4 . . . . **119** E6
Croft Ave
  Bristol BS16 . . . . **19** C4
  Charlton Kings GL53 . . . **131** B5
Croft Cl
  Bitton BS30 . . . . **5** D8

Croft Cl continued
  Churchdown GL3 . . . . . **128** D4
  Latton SN6 . . . . **143** E6
  Newent GL18 . . . . **171** A5
Croft Cotts GL7 . . . . **142** C5
Croft Ct GL53 . . . . **131** A5
Croft Dr GL53 . . . . **131** A5
Croft Farm Leisure & Water
 Pk★ GL20 . . . . **182** A2
Croft Gdns
  8 Broadway WR12 . . . **185** B8
  Charlton Kings GL53 . . . **131** B4
Croft Holm GL56 . . . . . . **187** B3
Croft La
  12 Fairford GL7 . . . . . **152** E4
  Latton SN6 . . . . **143** E6
  Winstone GL7 . . . . **107** A7
Croftlands The GL20 . . . . **182** C7
Crofton Ave BS7 . . . . **18** F6
Crofton Fields BS36 . . . . . **30** E6
Crofton Mews BS15 . . . . . **10** E7
Croft Par GL53 . . . . **131** B5
Croft Rd
  Charlton Kings GL53 . . . **131** A5
  Newent GL18 . . . . **171** A5
Croft Sch The GL6 . . . . . . **103** E8
Crofts End Ind Est BS5 . . . **19** E1
Crofts End Rd BS5 . . . . . . **19** E1
Crofts Field GL20 . . . . . . **181** D5
Croft St GL53 . . . . **130** D6
Crofts The GL18 . . . . **171** A5
Croft The
  Bristol, Mangotsfield BS16 . **20** F1
  Bristol, Oldland Common
   BS30 . . . . **11** C3
  Cirencester GL7 . . . . . . **190** C4
  Dursley GL11 . . . . **88** A4
  14 Fairford GL7 . . . . . **152** E4
  Lydney GL15 . . . . **92** B6
  Painswick GL6 . . . . **111** F1
Croft Thorne Cl GL51 . . . . **129** F5
Croft View BS9 . . . . **18** C6
Crokeswood Wlk BS11 . . . **27** A1
Crome Rd BS7 . . . . **19** B7
Cromer Rd BS5 . . . . **19** C2
Cromers Cl GL20 . . . . . . **182** C5
Cromhall La GL12 . . . . . . **65** D1
Cromwell Cl GL13 . . . . . . **85** C8
Cromwell Ct
  Bristol BS15 . . . . **10** E5
  Olveston BS35 . . . . **50** A3
Cromwell Rd
  Bristol, Montpelier BS6 . . **18** E2
  Bristol, St George BS5 . . . **10** A8
  Cheltenham GL52 . . . . . **134** A3
  Chepstow/Cas-Gwent NP16 **60** E5
Cromwells Hide BS16 . . . . **19** E5
Cromwell St
  Bristol BS3 . . . . **8** C3
  Gloucester GL1 . . . . **196** B2
Cromwell View BS6 . . . . . . **18** E2
Crooked End Pl GL17 . . . . **163** F4
Crooks Ind Est GL53 . . . . **130** D6
Croome Gdns GL54 . . . . . **168** F8
Croomes Hill BS16 . . . . . . **20** D6
Cropthorne Rd BS7 . . . . . . **29** A3
Cropthorne Road S BS7 . . **19** A8
Crosby Cl GL3 . . . . **120** B6
Crosby Row BS8 . . . . **194** A2
Cross Barn GL16 . . . . **163** B2
Cross Chambers GL15 . . . **147** B5
Cross Cl GL7 . . . . **190** E3
Cross Combe Dr BS13 . . . . . **2** C3
Cross Combe Wlk BS13 . . . **2** B3
Cross Cotts GL13 . . . . **76** C3
Cross Elms La BS9 . . . . . . **17** E5
Cross Farm Cl GL15 . . . . . **147** E4
Crossfield Rd BS16 . . . . . . **20** E3
Crossfields GL15 . . . . **166** D6
Cross Hands GL15 . . . . . . **92** C4
Cross Hands Rd BS35 . . . . **38** D7
Cross Keys GL15 . . . . **146** F7
Cross Keys La GL1 . . . . . . **196** B3
Cross Keys Rdbt GL2 . . . . **109** E4
Cross Lanes BS20 . . . . **16** C4
Crossleaze Rd BS15 . . . . . **10** C3
Crossley Cl BS36 . . . . **30** F8
Crossling La SN16 . . . . . . **142** C2
Crossman Ave BS36 . . . . . **30** E5
Cross St
  Bristol BS15 . . . . **20** D1
  Keynsham BS31 . . . . **4** F7
Cross The
  Bromesberrow Heath
   HR8 . . . . **179** B4
  Horsley GL6 . . . . **90** F1
  Nympsfield GL10 . . . . . . **89** E6
  Ripple GL20 . . . . **181** D8
Cross Tree Cres GL7 . . . . **144** E8
Cross Tree Flats GL7 . . . . **144** E7
Cross Tree Gr BS32 . . . . . . **29** D8
Cross Vane NP25 . . . . **154** B3
Crossways
  Coleford GL16 . . . . **154** F6
  Lower Wick GL11 . . . . . . **78** F8
Crossways Inf Sch BS35 . . **64** C1
Crossways La BS35 . . . . . . **64** E2
Crossways Rd
  Bristol BS4 . . . . **9** A1
  Thornbury BS35 . . . . **64** D1
Cross Wlk BS14 . . . . **3** A6
Crouch Cl GL20 . . . . **192** C3
Crow Ash **9** GL16 . . . . . . **155** A4
Crow Ash Rd GL16 . . . . . **155** A7
Crowfield GL52 . . . . **138** B4

Crowfield La GL18 . . . . 178 E2
Crowgate La GL14 . . . . . . 157 F8
Crow La
  Bristol BS1 . . . . 195 A2
  Henbury BS10 . . . . 27 F2
Crowley Way BS11 . . . . . . 26 B1
Crow Mdw GL12 . . . . 67 F4
Crown Cl
  Bishop's Cleeve GL52 . . . 137 F3
  Dymock GL18 . . . . 178 D2
Crown Cotts GL5 . . . . 98 B4
Crown Ct GL10 . . . . 98 A3
Crowndale Rd BS4 . . . . 9 A3
Crown Dr GL52 . . . . 137 F2
Crown Gdns BS30 . . . . 11 B7
Crown Hill BS5 . . . . 9 B8
Crown Hill Wlk BS5 . . . . . . 19 F1
Crown Ind Est BS30 . . . . . . 11 C7
Crown La
  Bristol BS16 . . . . 20 D1
  Parkend GL15 . . . . 155 E2
  St Briavels GL15 . . . . 146 E2
  Yorkley GL15 . . . . 156 A1
Crownleaze BS16 . . . . 20 D3
Crown Mdw [13] GL16 . . . . 155 B5
Crown Rd
  Bristol, Upper Soundwell
    BS15 . . . . 20 D2
  Bristol, Warmley BS30 . . . 11 C6
Crown Way BS30 . . . . 11 C7
Crows Gr BS32 . . . . 40 D3
Crowther Pk BS7 . . . . 19 A4
Crowther Rd BS7 . . . . 19 A4
Crowthers Ave BS37 . . . . . 43 E3
Crowther St [4] BS3 . . . . 8 B3
Croydon Ho [1] BS5 . . . . 9 B8
Croydon St BS5 . . . . 9 B8
Crucible Cl GL16 . . . . 155 A5
Crucible Ct GL16 . . . . 155 A5
Crudwell CE Prim Sch
  SN16 . . . . 141 C3
Crudwell La GL8 . . . . 140 F3
Crump Pl GL15 . . . . 92 C2
Crumps Cotts GL20 . . . . . 183 B6
Crunnis The BS32 . . . . 29 E6
Crusty La BS20 . . . . 16 C5
Crypt Ct GL4 . . . . 118 C3
Crypt Sch The GL2 . . . . . . 118 D4
Crypt The GL18 . . . . 178 D2
Crystal Way BS32 . . . . 29 E8
Crythan Wlk [4] GL51 . . . . 129 F5
Cuckoo Cl [4] GL6 . . . . . . 148 C6
Cuckoo La BS36 . . . . 30 F3
Cuckoo Row GL6 . . . . 91 F6
Cud La GL6 . . . . 103 B8
Cudnall St GL53 . . . . 131 A7
Cuffington Ave BS4 . . . . 9 D4
Culkerton GL8 . . . . 140 F6
Cullerns The SN6 . . . . 145 D3
Culleysgate La BS30 . . . . . 12 F6
Cullimore View GL14 . . . . 191 C1
Cullingham Cl GL19 . . . . . 172 A8
Cullis La GL16 . . . . 155 B6
Culls Mdw GL54 . . . . 184 A4
Culross Cl GL50 . . . . 133 E4
Culverhay
  [11] Cricklade SN6 . . . . . . 143 F4
  Wotton-u-E GL12 . . . . 68 B7
Culver Hill GL5 . . . . 91 A8
Culverhill Rd BS37 . . . . . . 44 A1
Culverin Cl [16] GL4 . . . . . 119 C4
Culvers Cl BS31 . . . . 4 E6
Culvers Rd BS31 . . . . 4 E6
Culver St
  Bristol BS1 . . . . 194 C2
  Newent GL18 . . . . 171 A4
Culvert Ave BS37 . . . . 43 B1
Culvert The BS32 . . . . 29 D8
Culverwell Rd BS13 . . . . 2 A4
Cumberland Basin Rd BS8 . . 7 D7
Cumberland Cl BS1 . . . . . . 194 A1
Cumberland Cres BS1 . . . 133 A2
Cumberland Gr [5] BS6 . . . 18 F2
Cumberland Pl [7] BS8 . . . . 7 F6
Cumberland Rd BS1 . . . . . 194 B1
Cumberland St BS2 . . . . . . 195 B4
Cumbria Cl BS35 . . . . 64 E1
Cumming Ct GL52 . . . . . . 134 A4
Cunningham Gdns BS16 . . 20 B5
Cunnington Cl BS30 . . . . . 11 B1
Cupola Cl GL16 . . . . 155 A5
Curland Gr BS14 . . . . 3 B5
Curlew Cl
  Bristol BS16 . . . . 19 F6
  Northway GL20 . . . . 182 B5
Curlew Rd GL4 . . . . 119 C6
Cursey La GL51 . . . . 136 B5
Cursey Lane Cvn Site
  GL51 . . . . 173 F7
Cursus The GL7 . . . . 153 E3
Curtis Hayward Dr GL2 . . 117 E1
Curtis La BS34 . . . . 30 A4
Custom Cl BS14 . . . . 3 A7
Custom Ho The BS1 . . . . . 195 A1
Cut & Fry Rd GL15 . . . . . . 156 B1
Cutham La GL12 . . . . 158 C1
Cuthwine Pl GL7 . . . . 153 E3
Cutler Rd
  Bristol BS13 . . . . 1 F6
  Stroud GL5 . . . . 99 D8
Cutsdean Cl GL52 . . . . 137 D4
Cutsheath Rd GL12 . . . . . . 52 C8
Cutters Row GL5 . . . . 8 E4
Cut Throat La HR9 . . . . . . 170 A2
Cutwell GL8 . . . . 140 B3
Cylde Pk BS6 . . . . 18 B2

Cynder Way BS16 . . . . 31 A1
Cypress Ct BS9 . . . . 17 D3
Cypress Gdns
  Bristol BS8 . . . . 7 E6
  Gloucester GL2 . . . . 127 D5
Cypress Gr BS9 . . . . 18 C6
Cypress Rd GL20 . . . . 192 E2
Cypress Wlk SN14 . . . . 15 F6
Cyrus Ct BS16 . . . . 21 B7

D

Daffodil Cl GL4 . . . . 119 E5
Daffodil Leaze GL10 . . . . . . 98 B3
Daffodil St GL50 . . . . 193 B2
Daffodils The GL10 . . . . . . 98 B3
Daglingworth Path GL7 . . 149 E6
Dagmar Rd GL50 . . . . 193 A1
Daines St [4] BS16 . . . . 19 E3
Dainty St GL1 . . . . 118 F7
Dairycroft BS2 . . . . 195 B4
Dairy Farm SN6 . . . . 142 F4
Dairy La WR11 . . . . 183 F6
Daisy Bank GL5 . . . . 99 E6
Daisybank Rd GL53 . . . . . . 130 E2
Daisy Green Cl GL12 . . . . . 79 D2
Daisy Rd BS5 . . . . 19 C2
Dakin Cl BS4 . . . . 8 E1
Dakota Dr BS14 . . . . 3 A4
Dalby Ave BS3 . . . . 8 D4
Dalby Ave BS3 . . . . 8 D4
Daldry Gdns BS35 . . . . 50 A3
Dale Cl GL4 . . . . 118 F5
Dale St
  Bristol, St George BS5 . . . . 9 F8
  Bristol, St Pauls BS2 . . . . 195 C4
  Temple Guiting GL54 . . . . 175 D2
Dale Wlk GL52 . . . . 138 A3
Dalkeith Ave BS15 . . . . 20 C1
Dallaway BS37 . . . . 99 E2
Dalrymple Rd [10] BS2 . . . . 18 E1
Dalston Rd BS3 . . . . 8 B4
Dalton Sq BS2 . . . . 195 B4
Damery La
  Stone GL13 . . . . 77 F3
  Woodford GL13 . . . . 78 A4
Damery Works GL13 . . . . . . 78 B3
Dampier Rd BS3 . . . . 8 A3
Damsells The [9] GL8 . . . . 140 C4
Damson Cl GL4 . . . . 119 E4
Danbury Cres BS10 . . . . . . 28 C1
Danbury Wlk BS10 . . . . . . 28 C1
Danby Cl
  Cinderford GL14 . . . . 191 B6
  Yorkley GL15 . . . . 156 B2
Danby Ho BS7 . . . . 19 A5
Danby Rd GL15 . . . . 156 B2
Danby St BS7 . . . . 19 C8
Dancers Hill GL4 . . . . 119 E6
Dancey Mead BS13 . . . . 1 F6
Dancey Rd GL3 . . . . 127 F6
Dancing Gn HR9 . . . . 164 A7
Dane La GL7 . . . . 149 B6
Danes Cl NP16 . . . . 60 D8
Danes Hill NP16 . . . . 61 B7
Danford Cl GL2 . . . . 172 B3
Danford Villas GL19 . . . . . 172 B3
Dangerfield Ave BS13 . . . . . 1 F6
Daniels Ind Est GL5 . . . . . 98 F5
Daniels Rd GL5 . . . . 99 F7
Danwood Ct GL1 . . . . 118 D7
Dapps Hill BS31 . . . . 4 F5
Dapwell La BS14, BS31 . . . 4 A1
Darell Cl GL2 . . . . 109 F7
Darell Gdns GL2 . . . . 157 F3
Darken La GL15 . . . . 147 E4
Dark La
  Chalford GL6 . . . . 148 C5
  Nailsworth GL6 . . . . 91 A4
  North Cerney GL7 . . . . . . 158 E3
  Stroud GL5 . . . . 99 B5
  Swindon GL51 . . . . 133 A7
Dark Ride GL7 . . . . 149 C8
Darks Rd GL18 . . . . 170 C3
Darley Cl BS10 . . . . 27 D3
Darleydale Cl GL2 . . . . . . 109 D8
Darnell's La HR9 . . . . 170 B4
Darnley Ave BS7 . . . . 18 F6
Darren Rd [13] GL16 . . . . . 155 A7
Dart Cl
  Quedgeley GL2 . . . . 117 F2
  Thornbury BS35 . . . . 51 B8
Darters Cl GL15 . . . . 92 A2
Dartmoor St BS3 . . . . 8 B3
Dartmouth Wlk BS31 . . . . . 4 D4
Dart Rd GL52 . . . . 134 B3
Darwin Cl
  Bristol BS30 . . . . 11 A4
  Cheltenham GL51 . . . . . . 129 C8
Darwin Rd GL4 . . . . 119 A5
Daston Cl [2] WR12 . . . . . 185 C8
Daubeny Cl BS16 . . . . 20 B5
Daubeny Ct BS1 . . . . 195 A1
Daunt Rd GL3 . . . . 120 B4
Davallia Dr GL51 . . . . 129 F5
Daventry Rd BS4 . . . . 8 F1
Daventry Terr GL1 . . . . . . 196 C1
Davey Cl GL2 . . . . 109 F6
Davey Rd GL20 . . . . 182 C4
Davey St BS2 . . . . 18 F1
Davey Terr [8] BS2 . . . . . . 18 F1
David French Ct GL51 . . . 130 A5
David Hook Wy GL2 . . . . . 118 A6
Davids Ct BS35 . . . . 51 A4

David's La BS35 . . . . 51 A4
Davidson Rd BS10 . . . . 28 D2
David's Rd BS14 . . . . 3 C6
David St BS2 . . . . 195 C3
David Thomas Ho BS6 . . . 18 E2
Davies Dr BS4 . . . . 9 F5
Davies Rd [1] GL56 . . . . . 187 B3
Davillian Ct GL2 . . . . 118 A3
Davin Cres BS20 . . . . 16 C3
Davis Cl BS30 . . . . 10 F5
Davis Ct BS35 . . . . 64 C2
Davis St BS11 . . . . 16 B8
Davron Ct BS3 . . . . 8 E4
Dawes Cl
  Meysey Hampton GL7 . . . 152 A3
  Southrop GL7 . . . . 153 C6
Dawes Ct [3] BS8 . . . . 7 F6
Dawes The GL2 . . . . 109 F8
Dawley Cl GL3 . . . . 30 E7
Dawlish Rd BS3 . . . . 8 D2
Dawn Dr GL2 . . . . 127 A6
Dawneys The SN16 . . . . . . 141 D3
Dawn Rise BS15 . . . . 21 A1
Daws Cl BS16 . . . . 20 B4
Day House La GL12 . . . . . . 55 C8
Daylesford Ct GL51 . . . . . 129 D8
Days Ct SN16 . . . . 141 C3
Day's La GL56 . . . . 186 C5
Day's Rd BS2 . . . . 9 A6
Days Road Commercial Ctr
  BS2 . . . . 9 A7
Deacon Cl
  Cheltenham GL51 . . . . . . 129 F7
  Winterbourne BS36 . . . . . 30 E5
Deacons Cl GL10 . . . . 98 A4
Deacons Pl GL52 . . . . 137 E2
Deakin Cl GL51 . . . . 133 B7
Deakin's Ho GL15 . . . . . . 155 E2
Dean Acad The GL15 . . . . . 92 A2
Dean Ave BS35 . . . . 64 C2
Dean Cl BS15 . . . . 10 B4
Dean Close Prep Sch
  GL51 . . . . 130 A8
Dean Close Sch GL51 . . . 129 F8
Dean Cres
  [8] Bristol BS3 . . . . 8 C4
  [1] Bristol BS3 . . . . 8 D4
  Littledean GL14 . . . . 156 E8
Dean Ct
  Lydney GL15 . . . . 92 B5
  Yate BS37 . . . . 43 C3
Deanery Cl BS15 . . . . 11 B8
Deanery Rd
  Bristol, Brandon Hill BS1 . 194 C2
  Bristol, Warmley BS15 . . . 11 B8
Deanery Rd Rdbt BS15 . . . 11 B8
Dean Farm Cotts GL7 . . . 160 F2
Dean Forest Railway Mus ★
  GL15 . . . . 147 F7
Dean Forest Rly ★ GL15 . . 92 A2
Dean Heritage Mus ★
  GL14 . . . . 156 D5
Deanhill La BA1 . . . . 6 F7
Dean La
  Bristol BS3 . . . . 8 C4
  Stoke Orchard GL52 . . . . 136 E5
Dean Mdws GL17 . . . . . . 164 D5
Deanna Ct BS16 . . . . 20 E6
Dean Rd
  Avonmouth BS11 . . . . 26 C5
  Newnham GL14 . . . . 156 C6
  Yate BS37 . . . . 43 C3
Dean Rise GL14 . . . . 156 C6
Deans Ct
  Bishop's Cleeve GL52 . . . 137 F5
  [3] Cheltenham GL51 . . . 129 F7
Dean's Ct BS1 . . . . 194 C2
Dean's Dr BS5 . . . . 20 A2
Deansfield SN6 . . . . 143 E4
Deans Gdns NP16 . . . . 72 D1
Deans Hill NP16 . . . . 60 D8
Deans Mead BS11 . . . . 17 A8
Dean's Quarry GL5 . . . . . . 91 F7
Deans Row GL1 . . . . 126 A2
Dean St
  Bristol, St Pauls BS2 . . . . 195 B4
  Bristol, Southville BS3 . . . . 8 C4
Dean's Terr GL1 . . . . 196 B4
Deans Way GL52 . . . . 137 F3
Dean's Way GL1 . . . . 196 B4
Deansway Rd GL17 . . . . . 164 D6
Dean Swift Cl HR9 . . . . . . 162 F6
Dean's Wlk GL1 . . . . 196 B4
Dean's Wlk GL17 . . . . 164 B4
Dean The HR9 . . . . 163 E6
Dean View GL14 . . . . 191 C1
Debecca's La BS20 . . . . . . 16 B4
De Clifford Rd BS11 . . . . . . 27 C2
Deep Coombe Rd BS3 . . . . . 8 A2
Deep Dean HR9 . . . . 163 E6
Deep Pit Rd BS5 . . . . 19 F2
Deep St GL52 . . . . 134 B4
Deerhurst
  Bristol BS15 . . . . 20 E3
  Yate BS37 . . . . 32 C8
Deerhurst & Apperley CE
  Prim Sch GL19 . . . . 173 C7
Deerhurst Cl
  Gloucester GL4 . . . . 119 E4
  Little Compton GL56 . . . . 187 F1
Deerhurst Pl GL2 . . . . 117 E1
Deering Cl BS11 . . . . 27 B1
Deer Park Rd GL3 . . . . 128 A1
Deer Pk GL15 . . . . 156 A2
Deerswood BS15 . . . . 21 A4

De Ferrieres Wlk [12]
  GL51 . . . . 132 D2
De Havilland Rd GL54 . . . 169 D7
Delabere Ave BS16 . . . . . . 20 B5
Delabere Rd GL52 . . . . . . 138 A2
Delancey Cres GL53 . . . . . 130 D5
Delavale Rd GL54 . . . . . . 174 A7
De La Warre Ct [11] BS4 . . 9 F6
Deleware Rd GL7 . . . . 152 E2
Delkin The GL11 . . . . 87 F4
Delkin The GL11 . . . . 87 F4
Dell Prim Sch The NP16 . . 72 E1
Dell The
  Blockley GL56 . . . . 186 C6
  Bredon GL20 . . . . 186 A4
  Bristol, Bradley Stoke BS32 29 E7
  Bristol, Oldland Common
    BS30 . . . . 11 C5
  Bristol, Westbury on Trym
    BS9 . . . . 17 F5
  Gloucester GL4 . . . . 119 E7
Dell View NP16 . . . . 60 E8
Delmont Gr GL5 . . . . 99 C8
Delphinium Dr GL52 . . . . 137 E3
Delta Dr GL20 . . . . 182 B4
Delta Way GL3 . . . . 120 C6
Delvin Rd BS10 . . . . 18 C8
Denbigh Dr NP16 . . . . 61 A5
Denbigh Rd GL51 . . . . 129 E6
Denbigh St BS2 . . . . 18 F1
Dene Cl BS31 . . . . 4 F3
Dene Magna Sch GL17 . . . 164 D4
Dene Rd BS14 . . . . 3 C4
Denfurlong Farm Trail ★
  GL54 . . . . 159 B5
Denham Cl
  Gloucester GL4 . . . . 118 C1
  Woodmancote GL52 . . . . 138 C3
Denleigh Cl BS14 . . . . 3 A4
Denley Cl GL52 . . . . 137 F2
Denman Ave GL50, GL51 . . 133 C4
Denmark Ave [2] BS1 . . . . 194 C2
Denmark Ct GL1 . . . . 127 A3
Denmark Dr NP16 . . . . 61 B7
Denmark Pl BS7 . . . . 18 E3
Denmark Rd GL1 . . . . 196 C4
Denmark St BS1 . . . . 194 C2
Denmark Villas GL14 . . . . 165 F1
Denning Ct GL50 . . . . 193 A1
Dennisworth BS16 . . . . . . 22 B5
Dennor Pk BS14 . . . . 3 B7
Denny Isle Dr BS35 . . . . . . 38 A6
Denston Wlk BS13 . . . . 2 A7
Denton Patch BS16 . . . . . . 21 B7
Dent's La GL19 . . . . 172 B2
Dent's Terr [24] GL54 . . . . 174 A7
Dentwood Gr BS9 . . . . 17 B8
Denvale Trad Pk BS4 . . . . . 2 E7
Denys St BS35 . . . . 50 A3
Derby Cl GL1 . . . . 127 A1
Derby Rd
  Bristol BS7 . . . . 18 E3
  Gloucester GL1 . . . . 127 A1
Derby St BS5 . . . . 9 D7
Derham Rd BS13 . . . . 2 A5
Dermot St [11] BS2 . . . . . . 18 F1
Derricke Rd BS14 . . . . 3 F6
Derrick Rd BS15 . . . . 10 D8
Derry Pk SN16 . . . . 142 E1
Derry Rd BS3 . . . . 8 B2
Derry The SN6 . . . . 142 F4
Derwent Cl
  Bristol BS34 . . . . 29 A8
  Brockworth GL3 . . . . 120 E5
Derwent Cts BS35 . . . . 51 D8
Derwent Dr GL20 . . . . 192 E6
Derwent Gr BS31 . . . . 5 A5
Derwent Rd BS5 . . . . 19 F1
Derwent Wlk [1] GL51 . . . 129 F7
Desert Orchid Rd GL52 . . 134 D4
Desford Cl GL4 . . . . 119 F5
Despenser Rd GL20 . . . . . 192 C2
Detmore Cl GL53 . . . . 131 D5
Devaney Cl BS34 . . . . 9 F5
Devauden Rd NP16 . . . . . . 72 B7
Devereaux Cres GL5 . . . . . 98 C7
Devereaux Rd GL5 . . . . . . 98 C7
Deveron Dr GL51 . . . . 5 A4
De Verose Ct BS15 . . . . . . 10 E4
Devil's Chimney ★ GL53 . . 130 D1
Devil's Elbow The GL6 . . . 91 E4
Devil's La GL12 . . . . 67 A2
Devon Ave GL51 . . . . 133 A2
Devon Gr BS5 . . . . 9 C8
Devon Rd BS5 . . . . 19 C1
Devon Road Trad Est [1]
  BS5 . . . . 19 C1
Devonshire Bldgs BS3 . . . . 8 E4
Devonshire Pl GL20 . . . . . 192 D2
Devonshire Rd BS6 . . . . . . 18 B4
Devonshire St GL50 . . . . . 193 A4
Devonshire Terr [2] GL56 . 187 A3
Dewey Cl GL52 . . . . 138 D2
Dewfalls Dr BS32 . . . . 40 D1
Dexter Wy GL1 . . . . 126 D4
Dial La BS16 . . . . 20 D6
Diamond Jubilee Cl GL1 . . 119 A7
Diamond Rd BS5 . . . . 9 F7
Diamond St BS3 . . . . 8 C3
Diamonite Ind Pk BS16 . . . 20 A3
Diana Gdns BS32 . . . . 29 E8
Dianas Ct GL4 . . . . 119 F6
Dibden Cl BS16 . . . . 21 A8

Dibden La
  Alderton GL24 . . . . 183 E4
  Bristol BS16 . . . . 21 B7
Dibden Rd BS16 . . . . 21 A7
Dickens Cl
  Bristol BS7 . . . . 19 A8
  Gloucester GL4 . . . . 118 F5
Dickens Mews GL4 . . . . . . 118 F5
Didbrook Mews GL4 . . . . . 119 E4
Didsbury Cl BS10 . . . . 27 F1
Digbeth St [10] GL54 . . . . 176 F4
Digby Dr GL20 . . . . 192 E6
Dighton Ct [3] BS2 . . . . . . 195 A4
Dighton Gate BS34 . . . . . . 29 E5
Dighton St BS2 . . . . 195 A4
Dikler Cl GL54 . . . . 169 A6
Dilke Memorial Hospl
  GL14 . . . . 191 A2
Dill Ave GL51 . . . . 132 E4
Dillon Ct [18] BS5 . . . . 9 D7
Dimore Cl GL2 . . . . 109 E7
Dinas Cl GL51 . . . . 129 F6
Dinas Rd GL51 . . . . 129 F6
Dinely St GL1 . . . . 196 C1
Dingle Bglws GL53 . . . . . 158 A8
Dingle Cl BS9 . . . . 17 C6
Dingle Ct BS13 . . . . 1 F7
Dingle La GL20 . . . . 182 A8
Dingle Rd BS9 . . . . 17 D7
Dingle The
  Bristol BS9 . . . . 17 D7
  Winterbourne BS36 . . . . . 30 F3
  Yate BS37 . . . . 43 F4
Dingle View BS9 . . . . 17 C7
Dinglewell [3] 119 F7
Dinglewell Inf Sch GL3 . . . 119 F7
Dinglewood Cl BS9 . . . . . . 17 D7
Dings Wlk [4] BS2 . . . . 9 A6
Dirac Rd BS7 . . . . 18 F4
Discovery Rd GL4 . . . . 119 F6
Dishforth Dr [7] GL2 . . . . 110 B8
Distel Cl GL50 . . . . 133 C5
District Ctr BS32 . . . . 29 E8
Ditch La GL7 . . . . 159 E3
Dixon Bsns Ctr BS4 . . . . . . 9 F2
Dixon Rd BS4 . . . . 9 F2
Dixton Cl NP25 . . . . 154 A8
Dixton Rd NP25 . . . . 154 A8
Dockham Rd GL14 . . . . . . 191 D4
Dockins Hill Way GL17 . . . 164 D4
Dock La GL20 . . . . 182 C8
Dock Rd GL13 . . . . 93 B1
Doctors La [20] GL54 . . . . 168 A1
Dodington Ash BS37 . . . . . 34 B2
Dodington Cl GL4 . . . . 119 D7
Dodington La BS37 . . . . . . 33 D5
Dodington Rd BS37 . . . . . . 33 B7
Dodisham Wlk BS16 . . . . . 20 B6
Dog La
  Hallen BS10 . . . . 27 C4
  Little Shurdington GL3 . . 121 D5
Dog Trap La SN16 . . . . 142 C1
Dogwood Rd BS32 . . . . . . 40 D5
Dollar St GL7 . . . . 190 C5
Dolman Cl BS10 . . . . 27 F3
Dolphin Sch The BS6 . . . . . . 1 F7
Domby Ct [18] GL16 . . . . . 155 A5
Domestic Fowl Trust ★
  WR11 . . . . 188 C7
Dominion Rd BS16 . . . . . . 19 F3
Donald Rd BS13 . . . . 1 F7
Doncaster Rd BS10 . . . . . . 18 C8
Doncombe Hill SN14 . . . . . 15 F7
Doncombe La SN14 . . . . . . 15 F7
Donegal Rd BS4 . . . . 8 D1
Dongola Ave BS7 . . . . 18 E4
Dongola Rd BS7 . . . . 18 E4
Donkey Field The GL7 . . . 151 C5
Donkey La GL56 . . . . 186 C5
Donnington Wlk BS31 . . . . 4 D4
Donns Cl BS34 . . . . 29 A7
Donside GL7 . . . . 190 A7
Doone Rd BS7 . . . . 18 F8
Dora Wlk [6] GL1 . . . . 118 F7
Dorcas Ave BS34 . . . . 29 F5
Dorchester Ct GL50 . . . . . 130 C6
Dorchester Rd BS7 . . . . . . 19 A7
Dorester Cl BS10 . . . . 28 C4
Dorian Cl BS7 . . . . 18 E7
Dorian Rd BS7 . . . . 18 E7
Dorian Way BS7 . . . . 18 E8
Dorington Ct [6] GL6 . . . . 148 C6
Dorington Wlk [13] GL51 . 132 D2
Dormer Cl BS36 . . . . 31 D6
Dormer House Sch GL56 . 187 A3
Dormer Rd
  Bristol BS7 . . . . 19 B3
  Cheltenham GL51 . . . . . . 132 F4
Dormers The SN6 . . . . 145 D3
Dorn GL56 . . . . 187 A5
Dorney Rd GL1 . . . . 118 E7
Dorrit Cl GL1 . . . . 118 F6
Dorset Ave GL51 . . . . 133 A2
Dorset Gr [9] BS2 . . . . 19 A2
Dorset Ho [2] GL50 . . . . . 193 B4
Dorset Rd
  Bristol, Kingswood BS15 . . 20 D1
  Bristol, Westbury on Trym
    BS9 . . . . 18 B6
Dorset St [6] BS3 . . . . 8 B3
Dorset Way BS37 . . . . 44 A3
Doubledays [7] SN6 . . . . . 143 E4

Double View GL14 ... 191 D3
Doudney Ct BS3 ... 8 E4
Doughmeadow Cotts
WR12 ... 184 F6
Douglas Ho GL50 ... 193 B2
Douglas Rd
Bristol, Horfield BS7 ... 18 F7
Bristol, Kingswood BS15 ... 10 D7
Douglas Road Ind Pk
BS15 ... 10 D7
Doulton Way BS14 ... 3 B5
Douro Lo GL50 ... 193 A2
Douro Rd GL50 ... 133 B1
Dovecote BS37 ... 32 E7
Dovedale BS35 ... 51 D8
Dovedale Cl GL2 ... 109 D8
Dove La
Bristol, Russell Town BS5 ... 9 C7
Bristol, St Pauls BS2 ... 195 C4
Dovercourt Rd BS7 ... 19 A6
Doverdale Dr GL2 ... 127 D4
Dover Hay GL51 ... 129 F5
Dover Pl BS8 ... 194 B3
Dover's View GL55 ... 188 D4
Dove St S BS2 ... 195 A4
Dove St BS2 ... 195 A4
Doveswell Gr BS13 ... 2 A4
Dovey Ct BS30 ... 11 C5
Dowdeswell Cl BS10 ... 27 F3
Dowding Cl BS37 ... 44 C2
Dowding Way GL3 ... 128 C5
Dowers' La GL7 ... 150 A8
Dowland Gr BS4 ... 2 D6
Dowling Rd BS13 ... 2 D3
Down Ampney CE Prim Sch
GL7 ... 143 F8
Down Ampney Rd GL7 ... 143 D7
Downend Park Rd BS16 ... 20 D5
Downend Pk BS7 ... 18 F5
Downend Rd
Bristol, Fishponds BS16 ... 20 C5
Bristol, Horfield BS7 ... 18 F5
Bristol, Kingswood BS15 ... 20 D1
Downend Sch BS16 ... 20 F7
Down Farm Ho BS36 ... 30 D6
Downfield
Bristol BS9 ... 17 C7
Keynsham BS31 ... 4 D5
Stroud GL5 ... 98 F7
Downfield Cl 1 BS35 ... 51 A5
Downfield Dr BS36 ... 31 B8
Downfield Ho GL51 ... 129 D2
Downfield La GL20 ... 182 A8
Downfield Lodge BS8 ... 18 A1
Downfield Rd
Bristol BS8 ... 18 A1
Stroud GL5 ... 98 F7
Downham Ct GL11 ... 80 D8
Downhams The 14 NP25 ... 154 A7
Downham View GL11 ... 80 D8
Downham Wlk GL11 ... 80 D8
Down Hatherley La GL2 ... 173 C1
Downleaze
Bristol, Downend BS16 ... 20 D8
Bristol, Stoke Bishop BS9 ... 17 F3
Down Leaze 2 BS35 ... 51 A5
Downleaze Dr BS37 ... 33 B8
Downman Rd BS7 ... 19 A5
Down Rd
Alveston BS35 ... 51 A5
Marshfield SN14 ... 25 C2
Winterbourne BS36 ... 30 F4
Downs Cl 3 BS35 ... 51 A5
Downs Cote Ave BS9 ... 17 F6
Downs Cote Dr BS9 ... 17 F6
Downs Cote Gdns BS9 ... 18 A6
Downs Cote Pk BS9 ... 18 A6
Downs Cote View BS9 ... 18 A6
Downs Ct BS9 ... 18 B6
Downside Cl BS30 ... 10 F5
Downside Rd BS8 ... 18 A1
Downs Mill GL6 ... 148 E4
Downs Pk E BS6 ... 18 A4
Downs Pk W BS6 ... 18 A4
Downs Rd
Bristol BS9 ... 18 A6
Dundry BS41 ... 1 D2
Downs The GL12 ... 53 F7
Downs View SN6 ... 145 D3
Downsview Ct BS8 ... 18 A1
Downs Way GL7 ... 150 D7
Down The
Alveston BS35 ... 50 F5
Tockington BS32 ... 50 D3
Downton Rd
Bristol BS4 ... 8 D1
Stonehouse GL10 ... 97 E6
Down View
Bristol BS7 ... 18 F3
Chalford GL6 ... 148 C6
Downy Cl GL2 ... 117 E2
Dowry Mews BS8 ... 194 A2
Dowry Pl 8 BS8 ... 7 F5
Dowry Rd BS8 ... 194 A2
Dowry Sq BS8 ... 194 A2
Dowty Rd GL51 ... 132 E2
Doynton La SN14, BS30 ... 23 B3
Dozule Cl GL10 ... 97 F3
Dragon Ct BS5 ... 19 E1
Dragonfly Cl BS15 ... 10 D7
Dragon Rd BS36 ... 30 D5
Dragons Hill Cl BS31 ... 4 F5
Dragons Hill Ct BS31 ... 4 F5
Dragons Hill Gdns BS31 ... 4 F5
Dragonswell Rd BS10 ... 28 A2
Dragon Wlk BS5 ... 19 F1
Drag Rd HR9 ... 162 E3
Drake Cl
Innsworth GL3 ... 127 F7
Saltford BS31 ... 5 D2
Drake Ho BS1 ... 195 A3
Drake La GL11 ... 88 C2
Drake Rd BS3 ... 8 A3
Drakes Pl GL50 ... 193 A3
Dram La BS5 ... 10 A6
Dramway Rdbt BS16 ... 21 D6
Draper Ct 3 BS5 ... 9 C7
Drapers Ct GL52 ... 138 B3
Draper's La GL19 ... 172 D6
Draycot Pl BS1 ... 195 A1
Draycott GL11 ... 87 F7
Draycott Bsns Pk GL11 ... 87 F7
Draycott Cres GL11 ... 87 F7
Draycott Ind Est GL56 ... 186 D6
Draycott Rd BS7 ... 18 F5
Draydon Rd BS4 ... 2 D8
Drayton Cl
Bristol BS14 ... 3 B8
Cheltenham GL51 ... 133 B6
1 Gloucester GL4 ... 119 C4
Drayton Rd
Bristol BS9 ... 17 C8
Cheltenham GL51 ... 129 E8
Drayton Way GL4 ... 119 C5
Dr Brown's Cl GL6 ... 91 F6
Dr Brown's Rd GL6 ... 91 F7
Dr Crawfords Way GL6 ... 91 F6
Dr. Crouch's Rd GL6 ... 148 B7
Drews Cl GL3 ... 128 C4
Drews Ct GL3 ... 128 C4
Driffield Cross Rds GL7 ... 151 B1
Driffield Rd GL15 ... 92 C5
Drift Cl GL7 ... 190 A2
Drifton Hill SN14 ... 25 F7
Drift Way GL7 ... 190 A2
Drivemoor GL4 ... 119 D3
Drive The
Bristol, Hengrove BS14 ... 3 C6
Bristol, Henleaze BS9 ... 18 B5
Dursley GL11 ... 87 F4
Keynsham BS31 ... 4 E6
Tetbury GL8 ... 140 D2
Dr Middletons Rd GL6 ... 148 C5
Dr Newton's Way GL5 ... 99 C6
Drovers Wy 31 GL18 ... 171 A4
Druetts Cl BS10 ... 18 E6
Drugger's End La WR13 ... 180 C8
Druid Cl BS9 ... 17 E5
Druid Hill BS9 ... 17 E5
Druid Rd BS9 ... 17 D4
Druids Cl 1 GL4 ... 119 C7
Druids La GL4 ... 119 C7
Druids Oak GL2 ... 109 F8
Druid Stoke Ave BS9 ... 17 D5
Druid Woods BS9 ... 17 C5
Drummond Ct BS30 ... 10 F4
Drummond Rd
Bristol, Fishponds BS16 ... 19 F3
Bristol, St Pauls BS2 ... 18 E1
Drury La GL19 ... 179 D2
Dr White's Cl BS1 ... 195 B1
Drybrook Prim Sch GL17 ... 164 B4
Drybrook Rd GL17 ... 164 B4
Drydock Wy GL2 ... 118 C7
Dryland Mews GL3 ... 120 B6
Dryleaze
Keynsham BS31 ... 4 E7
Wotton-u-E GL12 ... 68 A7
Yate BS37 ... 43 E5
Dryleaze Ct GL12 ... 68 A7
Dryleaze Gdns GL12 ... 68 A7
Dryleaze Ho GL12 ... 68 A7
Dryleaze Rd BS16 ... 19 F6
Dry Meadow La GL3 ... 127 C7
Dubbers La BS5 ... 19 E2
Dublin Cres BS9 ... 18 B6
Duchess Rd BS8 ... 18 A1
Duchess Way BS16 ... 19 D6
Ducie Cl GL12 ... 66 B2
Ducie Ct BS16 ... 20 E4
Ducie Rd
Bristol, Russell Town BS5 ... 9 B7
Bristol, Staple Hill BS16 ... 20 E5
Ducie Rd Bsns Pk 6 BS5 ... 9 B7
Ducie St GL1 ... 118 F7
Duckmoor Rd BS3 ... 8 A3
Duckmoor Road Ind Est
BS3 ... 8 A4
Duck St GL12 ... 52 C5
Duckworth Cl GL53 ... 130 D5
Dudbridge Hill GL5 ... 98 F6
Dudbridge Mdw GL5 ... 98 F5
Dudbridge Rd GL5 ... 98 F5
Duderstadt Cl GL5 ... 98 F8
Dudley Cl BS31 ... 4 E4
Dudley Cnr GL7 ... 151 C5
Dudley Ct 3 BS30 ... 10 F4
Dudley Farm GL7 ... 151 C5
Dudley Gr BS7 ... 19 A8
Dudley Rd WR11 ... 188 C7
Duffield's La NP25 ... 154 C5
Dugar Wlk BS6 ... 18 C3
Dugdale Rd GL7 ... 190 C5
Duglynch La GL54 ... 183 E1
Duke of Beaufort Ct GL1 ... 118 D5
Duke Of York Rd GL16 ... 154 C7
Dukeries The GL1 ... 196 A3
Dukes Field GL7 ... 143 F8
Duke St GL52 ... 133 F1
Dukes Way GL20 ... 192 D1
Dulverton Ct GL51 ... 132 D3
Dulverton Pl GL56 ... 187 B3
Dulverton Rd BS7 ... 18 D4
Dumaine Ave BS34 ... 29 E5
Dumbleton Gr GL51 ... 129 B6
Dunalley Par GL50 ... 133 D3
Dunalley Prim Sch GL50 ... 133 E3
Dunalley St GL50 ... 193 B4
Dunbar Cl GL51 ... 132 D4
Duncombe La BS15 ... 20 B2
Duncombe Rd BS15 ... 20 B1
Duncroft Rd GL3 ... 127 F1
Dundas Cl BS10 ... 27 E2
Dundee Dr BS16 ... 20 C5
Dundonald Rd BS6 ... 18 B3
Dundridge Gdns BS5 ... 10 A6
Dundridge La BS5 ... 10 A6
Dundry CE Prim Sch BS41 ... 1 D2
Dundry Cl BS15 ... 10 D6
Dundry La BS41 ... 1 C3
Dundry View BS4 ... 9 A1
Dunelm Cl GL51 ... 132 F4
Dunford Rd BS3 ... 8 D3
Dunkeld Ave BS34 ... 28 F2
Dunkerry Rd BS3 ... 8 D3
Dunkirk Cotts GL9 ... 56 C1
Dunkirk Rd BS16 ... 19 F3
Dunlin Cl GL2 ... 117 D1
Dunmail Rd BS10 ... 28 C2
Dunmore St 3 BS2 ... 8 F4
Dunmurry BS9 ... 17 D3
Dunns Copse 15 HR8 ... 178 F8
Dunsdown La SN14 ... 24 B5
Dunsmore Gn GL19 ... 181 B3
Dunstall Ho 19 GL56 ... 187 A3
Dunstan Glen GL3 ... 128 D4
Dunster Cl
Cheltenham GL51 ... 132 D3
Gloucester GL4 ... 118 B1
Dunster Gdns
Bristol BS30 ... 11 B2
Cheltenham GL51 ... 132 D3
Dunster Gr GL51 ... 132 D3
Dunster Rd
Bristol BS4 ... 2 F8
Cheltenham GL51 ... 132 D3
Keynsham BS31 ... 4 E4
Dunstone Pl GL17 ... 164 D5
Durand Cl GL2 ... 127 C6
Durand Ct GL12 ... 68 A7
Durban Ho 4 GL51 ... 132 F4
Durban Rd BS34 ... 28 F8
Durbin Wlk BS5 ... 9 A8
Durbridge Rd GL19 ... 179 C1
Durdham Ct BS6 ... 18 A3
Durdham Pk BS6 ... 18 A3
Durham Cl GL51 ... 130 A5
Durham Gr BS31 ... 4 D4
Durham Rd
10 Bristol BS2 ... 19 A2
Charfield GL12 ... 67 A5
Gloucester GL4 ... 119 C8
Durleigh Cl BS13 ... 2 A7
Durley Hill BS31 ... 4 C7
Durley La BS31 ... 4 D7
Durncourt Cotts GL7 ... 151 C5
Durnford Ave BS3 ... 8 A4
Durnford St BS3 ... 8 A4
Durn's Rd GL12 ... 68 C7
Dursley CE Prim Acad
GL11 ... 80 C8
Dursley Cl BS37 ... 43 E1
Dursley Ct GL11 ... 88 A1
Dursley Rd
Bristol BS11 ... 16 E5
Dursley GL11 ... 87 E3
Slimbridge GL2 ... 95 F3
Durville Rd BS13 ... 2 B6
Durweston Wlk BS14 ... 3 C8
Dutton Cl BS14 ... 3 D6
Dutton Leys GL54 ... 168 A1
Dutton Rd BS14 ... 3 D6
Duttons La GL17 ... 163 F3
Dutton Wlk BS14 ... 3 D6
Dye House Rd GL12 ... 67 F5
Dyersbrook GL12 ... 68 B7
Dyers Cl BS13 ... 2 D4
Dyer's La
Chipping Campden GL55 ... 188 F2
Yate BS37 ... 43 A4
Dyer St GL7 ... 190 D4
Dyke House La GL18 ... 179 B4
Dylan Thomas Ct 4 BS30 ... 11 A5
Dymock Rd
Ledbury HR8 ... 178 E7
Much Marcle HR8 ... 178 A3
Dymock Wlk GL52 ... 134 B2
Dynevor St GL1 ... 118 F7
Dynevor Terr GL7 ... 152 D4
Dyrham BS16 ... 30 C1
Dyrham Cl
Bristol, Henleaze BS9 ... 18 D6
Bristol, Kingswood BS15 ... 10 F8
Pucklechurch BS16 ... 22 C4
Thornbury BS35 ... 64 C3
Dyrham Par BS34 ... 29 C8
Dyrham Park★ SN14 ... 23 F5
Dyrham Rd BS15 ... 10 F8

E

Eagar Ho GL53 ... 131 B4
Eagle Cl GL6 ... 148 B6
Eagle Cres BS16 ... 22 C5
Eagle Dr BS34 ... 28 E8
Eagle Mill Cl GL5 ... 99 D5
Eagle Rd BS4 ... 9 D2
Eagles Wood BS32 ... 40 D3
Eagles Wood Bsns Pk
BS32 ... 40 C3
Eagle Way GL4 ... 119 C5
Ealy Hill GL7 ... 107 C5
Eardisland Rd GL4 ... 118 E2
Earl Russell Way BS5 ... 9 B7
Earls Cnr SN16 ... 141 F4
Earlsmead BS16 ... 19 E4
Earl St BS1 ... 195 A4
Earlstone Cl BS30 ... 11 A4
Earlstone Cres BS30 ... 11 A4
Early Way BS7 ... 18 E8
Earthcott Rd BS35 ... 51 F1
Easedale Cl BS10 ... 28 D2
East Allcourt GL7 ... 153 E2
East Approach Dr GL52 ... 133 F4
Eastbourne Rd 9 BS5 ... 9 B8
Eastbourne Terr GL7 ... 152 E3
Eastbrook Rd GL4 ... 119 C8
Eastbury Cl BS35 ... 64 C1
Eastbury Rd
Bristol BS16 ... 20 A4
Thornbury BS35 ... 64 C1
Eastcombe Prim Sch
GL6 ... 148 B7
Eastcote Pk BS14 ... 3 B5
Eastcott Way GL3 ... 128 A6
East Court Mews GL52 ... 131 C5
East Croft BS9 ... 18 C7
East Ct BS3 ... 7 F3
East Dr GL5 ... 98 C7
East Dundry La BS41 ... 2 A1
East Dundry Rd BS13, BS14 ... 2 F2
East End GL54 ... 168 A1
East End Flats GL53 ... 131 C5
East End Rd GL52, GL53 ... 131 C5
Easter Ct BS37 ... 43 B1
Eastern Ave
Gloucester GL4 ... 119 B8
Mitcheldean GL17 ... 164 D5
Eastern Way GL14 ... 156 C6
Eastfield
Ashton Keynes SN6 ... 142 F5
Bristol BS9 ... 18 B7
Eastfield Dr BS37 ... 43 E4
Eastfield Mews GL4 ... 118 F5
Eastfield Rd
Bristol, Eastfield BS9 ... 18 B7
Bristol, Montpelier BS6 ... 18 D2
Bristol, Westbury on Trym
BS9 ... 18 A7
Minchinhampton GL6 ... 148 A3
East Fields Rd 4 BS16 ... 19 D8
Eastfield Terr BS9 ... 18 B6
East Gable GL52 ... 138 B3
Eastgate Ho GL1 ... 196 C2
Eastgate Office Ctr BS5 ... 19 B3
Eastgate Ret Pk BS5 ... 19 B3
Eastgate Sh Ctr GL1 ... 196 B2
Eastgate St GL1 ... 196 B2
East Gr BS6 ... 18 F1
East Hill BS9 ... 18 B7
Eastholm Lawns GL3 ... 128 C5
Eastington Prim Sch
GL10 ... 97 A8
Eastington Rd GL54 ... 168 A1
Eastington Trad Est
GL10 ... 100 F1
Eastlake Cl BS7 ... 19 B7
Eastland Ave BS35 ... 64 C2
Eastland Rd BS35 ... 64 C2
Eastleigh Cl BS16 ... 20 E4
Eastleigh Rd
Bristol, Brentry BS10 ... 28 D1
Bristol, Staple Hill BS16 ... 20 E3
Eastley Cl GL12 ... 65 E7
East Link GL17 ... 164 D5
Eastlyn Rd BS13 ... 2 B8
Eastmead Ct BS9 ... 17 E4
Eastmead La BS9 ... 17 E4
Eastnor Castle★ HR8 ... 179 B7
Eastnor Ho 14 GL51 ... 132 E2
Eastnor Parochial Prim Sch
HR8 ... 179 B8
Eastnor Rd BS14 ... 3 A3
Easton Bsns Ctr BS5 ... 9 B8
Easton CE Prim Sch BS5 ... 9 A8
Easton Hill Rd BS35 ... 64 D1
Easton Rd
Bristol, Newton BS5 ... 9 A7
Bristol, Upper Easton BS5 ... 9 B8
Pill BS20 ... 16 C4
Easton Sq SN16 ... 58 D1
Easton Town SN16 ... 58 D1
Easton Way BS5 ... 9 A8
Eastover Cl BS9 ... 18 A8
East Par BS9 ... 17 C6
East Park Dr BS5 ... 19 C2
Eastpark Trad Est BS5 ... 19 D1
East Pk BS5 ... 19 C2
East Priory Cl BS9 ... 18 A7
East Ridge Dr BS13 ... 1 F5
Eastrop SN6 ... 145 D3
Eastrop Inf Sch SN6 ... 145 D3
East Shrubbery 3 BS6 ... 18 B2
East St
Avonmouth BS11 ... 26 A1
Bristol, Southville BS3 ... 8 D4
Moreton-in-M GL56 ... 187 A3
St Briavels GL15 ... 146 F7
Tewkesbury GL20 ... 192 C4
East Tucker St BS1 ... 195 B2
East View
Bristol BS16 ... 20 F6
Newnham GL14 ... 156 F7
Eastville Cl GL4 ... 119 B8
East Wlk BS37 ... 43 E1
Eastwood Cres BS4 ... 9 F3
Eastwood Rd
Bristol BS4 ... 9 F4
Harrow Hill GL17 ... 164 B3
Eaton Cl
Bristol, Fishponds BS16 ... 20 B4
Bristol, Stockwood BS14 ... 3 E5
Eaton Cres BS8 ... 194 A4
Eaton Pl GL53 ... 193 B2
Eaton St 15 BS3 ... 8 C3
Ebenezer La BS9 ... 17 E5
Ebenezer St BS5 ... 9 D7
Ebley Ind Pk GL5 ... 98 D6
Ebley Rd GL10 ... 98 B6
Ebor Rd GL2 ... 127 C1
Ebrington GL55 ... 189 D3
Ebrington CE Prim Sch
GL55 ... 189 D3
Ebrington Cl GL4 ... 119 D8
Eccles Ct 11 GL8 ... 140 C4
Eccleston Ho 1 BS5 ... 9 B6
Echo La GL11 ... 87 B2
Eclipse Ct 1 BS16 ... 20 C4
Eclipse Office Pk 2 BS16 ... 20 C4
Eddys La GL17 ... 163 E3
Edencroft SN6 ... 145 D4
Edendale App 2 GL51 ... 129 C8
Edendale Rd GL51 ... 132 C1
Eden Gr BS7 ... 29 A1
Eden Office Pk BS20 ... 16 E4
Eden's Hill GL18 ... 171 D6
Edenwall GL16 ... 155 B5
Edenwall Rd GL16 ... 155 B4
Edgecombe Cl BS15 ... 20 F1
Edgecorner La SN14 ... 36 A3
Edgecumbe Rd BS6 ... 18 D2
Edge End Rd 1 GL16 ... 155 B6
Edgefield Cl BS14 ... 2 F3
Edgefield Rd BS14 ... 2 F3
Edge Hills Cl GL14 ... 191 D5
Edge Hills Rd GL14 ... 191 D5
Edge La GL6 ... 103 C8
Edge Rd GL6 ... 103 E8
Edgeware Rd
Bristol, Southville BS3 ... 8 C4
Bristol, Staple Hill BS16 ... 20 D4
Edgewood Cl
Bristol, Hengrove BS14 ... 3 B8
Bristol, Longwell Green
BS30 ... 11 A3
Edgeworth BS37 ... 32 C6
Edgeworth Cl
Cirencester GL7 ... 190 B2
5 Gloucester GL4 ... 119 E5
Edinburgh Pl
Cheltenham GL51 ... 132 E2
3 Coleford GL16 ... 155 B5
Edinburgh Rd BS31 ... 4 E4
Edington Gr BS10 ... 28 A2
Edison Cl
Hardwicke GL2 ... 109 F7
Quedgeley GL2 ... 110 A7
Edmond Rd NP16 ... 61 B8
Edmund Cl BS16 ... 20 D6
Edmund Ct BS16 ... 22 B6
Edmunds Wy GL14 ... 191 C2
Edna Ave BS4 ... 9 E3
Edward Bird Ho BS7 ... 19 B6
Edward Ct BS31 ... 4 F4
Edward Jenner Mus★
GL13 ... 85 E3
Edward Jenner Sch GL1 ... 196 B3
Edward Massey Gdns
GL4 ... 119 C3
Edward Pl GL20 ... 192 D1
Edward Rd
Bristol, Kingswood BS15 ... 10 E8
Bristol, Totterdown BS4 ... 9 B4
Edwards Cl
Joy's Green GL17 ... 163 D3
Poulton GL7 ... 151 E3
Edwards' Coll GL7 ... 142 F8
Edwards Ct 17 BS5 ... 9 D7
Edward St
Bristol, Eastville BS5 ... 19 D2
Bristol, Moorfields BS5 ... 9 C7
Cheltenham GL53 ... 193 B1
Edward Wilson Ho 2
GL51 ... 132 E3
Edward Wilson Villas 2
GL50 ... 130 B6
Edwin Short Cl BS30 ... 5 E8
Edwy Par GL1 ... 196 B4
Effingham Rd BS6 ... 18 E2
Egdon Cres GL51 ... 129 C6
Egerton Brow BS7 ... 18 D4
Egerton Rd BS7 ... 18 D4
Eggshill La BS37 ... 43 D1
Eglin Croft BS13 ... 2 B4
Egypt Ho GL6 ... 91 B4
Eighteen Acre Dr BS34 ... 29 A7
Eighth Ave
Bristol, Filton BS7 ... 29 B1
Bristol, Hengrove BS14 ... 3 A7

Eirene Terr BS20 . . . . 16 D4
Elberton BS15 . . . . 11 A8
Elberton Rd
  Bristol BS9 . . . . 17 B7
  Elberton BS35 . . . . 49 F5
Elbridge Ho **4** BS2 . . . . 195 C3
Elbury Ave BS15 . . . . 20 C2
Elbury View GL12 . . . . . . 67 B5
Elcombe GL11 . . . . 81 A7
Elderberry Mews GL3 . . 127 F6
Elderberry Wlk BS10 . . . . 28 C3
Elderberry Wy BS32 . . . . 40 E5
Eldersfield Cl
  Quedgeley GL2 . . . . 117 E2
  Winchcombe GL54 . . . . . 174 A8
Eldersfield Lawn CE Prim
  Sch GL19 . . . . 180 F1
Elderwood Dr BS30 . . . . . 11 A3
Elderwood Rd BS14 . . . . . . 3 B7
Elderwood Way GL4 . . . . 118 C2
Eldon Ave GL52 . . . . 134 A1
Eldon Rd GL52 . . . . 133 F1
Eldon Terr BS3 . . . . 8 D3
Eldonwall Trad Est BS4 . . 9 C5
Eldon Way BS3 . . . . 9 C5
Eldorado Cres GL50 . . . . 133 B1
Eldorado Rd GL50 . . . . . 133 B1
Eldred Cl BS9 . . . . 17 D5
Eleventh Ave BS7 . . . . . . 29 B1
Elfin Rd BS16 . . . . 20 A5
Elf Mdw GL7 . . . . 151 F4
Elgar Cl
  Bristol BS4 . . . . 2 D6
  Ledbury HR8 . . . . 178 E8
Elgar Ho GL51 . . . . 132 E2
Elgin Ave BS7 . . . . 28 F1
Elgin Hall GL10 . . . . 97 F7
Elgin Pk BS16 . . . . 18 B2
Elgin Rd BS16 . . . . 20 B2
Eliot Cl
  Bristol BS7 . . . . 29 A1
  Gloucester GL2 . . . . 118 C4
Elizabeth Cl BS35 . . . . . . 51 D8
Elizabeth Cres BS34 . . . . 29 E4
Elizabeth Gdns
  Meysey Hampton GL7 . . 152 B3
  5 Tetbury GL8 . . . . 140 B4
Elizabeths Mews **12** BS4 . . . 9 F6
Elizabeth Way
  Bristol BS16 . . . . 21 B3
  Siddington GL7 . . . . 150 E2
Elkstone Wlk BS30 . . . . . 11 C2
Ella Cl BS16 . . . . 20 C6
Ellacombe Rd BS30 . . . . . 10 F2
Ellan Hay Rd BS34 . . . . . . 30 A6
Ellbridge Cl BS9 . . . . 17 D5
Ellenborough Ho BS8 . . 194 A2
Ellenborough Rd GL52 . . 138 A2
Ellendene Dr GL20 . . . . . 182 E4
Ellenor Dr GL20 . . . . 183 E4
Ellerncroft Rd
  Kingswood GL12 . . . . 67 A8
  Wotton-u-E GL12 . . . . . . 68 A8
Ellesmere BS35 . . . . 51 C8
Ellesmere Cl GL3 . . . . . . 119 F8
Ellesmere Gr **5** GL50 . . 130 B6
Ellesmere Rd **1** BS4 . . . . . 9 D1
Ellfield Cl BS13 . . . . 1 F6
Ellicks Cl BS32 . . . . 40 E2
Ellicott Rd BS7 . . . . 18 F5
Ellingham Cl GL52 . . . . . 133 E3
Ellinghurst Cl BS10 . . . . . 28 A2
Elliott Ave BS16 . . . . 30 C1
Elliott Ct **5** GL20 . . . . . . 192 C4
Elliott Ho BS7 . . . . 19 A3
Elliott Pl GL51 . . . . 129 F7
Elliott Rd GL7 . . . . 190 E1
Ellis Ave BS13 . . . . 2 A8
Ellison Cl GL4 . . . . 120 A6
Ellison Rd GL51 . . . . 132 E2
Elliston La BS6 . . . . 18 C2
Elliston Rd BS6 . . . . 18 C2
Ellsbridge Cl BS31 . . . . 5 B1
Ellsworth Rd BS10 . . . . . 27 F2
Ellwood Prim Sch GL16 . 155 B3
Ellwood Rd GL16 . . . . . . 155 B3
Ellyott Ct **5** BS16 . . . . . 19 E3
Elmbridge Inf Sch GL2 . . 127 C2
Elmbridge Jun Sch GL2 . 127 C2
Elmbridge Rd GL2 . . . . . 127 C3
Elmbury Dr GL20 . . . . . . 192 F5
Elm Cl
  Avonmouth BS11 . . . . . . 26 F1
  Bristol BS34 . . . . 29 D7
  Cheltenham, Prestbury
    GL52 . . . . 134 A5
  Cheltenham, St Peter's
    GL51 . . . . 133 B3
  Chipping Sodbury BS37 . . 44 A1
  King's Stanley GL10 . . . . . 98 A4
  Tutshill NP16 . . . . 73 A2
Elmcroft Cres BS7 . . . . . . 19 A4
Elm Ct
  Bristol, Hengrove BS14 . . . 3 A6
  Bristol, Redland BS6 . . . . 18 B2
  Cheltenham GL53 . . . . . . 133 F4
  Keynsham BS31 . . . . 4 C4
  Woolaston GL15 . . . . 147 C3
Elmdale GL14 . . . . 191 C5
Elmdale NP16 . . . . 72 E1
Elmdale Cotts NP16 . . . . 72 E1
Elmdale Cres BS35 . . . . . 64 C1
Elmdale Gdns **4** BS16 . . 20 A4
Elmdale Rd
  Bristol, Bedminster BS3 . . . 8 B2
  Bristol, Tyndall's Park BS8 194 B3

Elm Dr GL3 . . . . 120 D7
Elm Farm Cl SN16 . . . . . 142 B1
Elmfield
  Bristol BS15 . . . . 10 E6
  Cheltenham GL50 . . . . . . 193 A3
Elmfield Ave GL51 . . . . . 133 C4
Elmfield Cl BS15 . . . . 10 E6
Elmfield Rd
  Bristol BS9 . . . . 18 A8
  Cheltenham GL51 . . . . . . 133 C4
Elmfield Sch for Deaf
  Children BS16 . . . . 18 B8
Elm Garden Dr GL51 . . . 129 A7
Elm Gr
  Dursley GL11 . . . . 87 F4
  Ebrington GL55 . . . . 189 D3
  Huntley GL19 . . . . 165 D6
Elmgrove Ave **10** BS5 . . . . 9 B8
Elmgrove Dr BS37 . . . . . . 43 F2
Elmgrove Est GL2 . . . . . . 109 E7
Elmgrove Pk **1** BS6 . . . . 18 D1
Elmgrove Rd
  Bristol, Fishponds BS16 . . 19 E3
  Bristol, Redland BS6 . . . . 18 D1
  Gloucester GL3 . . . . 120 A6
Elmgrove Rd E GL2 . . . . 109 E7
Elmgrove Rd W GL2 . . . 109 D7
Elm Hayes BS13 . . . . 1 F6
Elmhirst Gdns BS37 . . . . 44 A2
Elmhurst Ave BS5 . . . . . . 19 D3
Elming Down Cl BS32 . . . 29 D6
Elmira Rd GL4 . . . . 118 F4
Elm La BS6 . . . . 18 B2
Elmlea Ave BS9 . . . . 17 F5
Elmlea Jun & Inf Schs
  BS9 . . . . 17 F5
Elmlea Rd GL10 . . . . 98 A4
Elmleaze GL2 . . . . 127 D3
Elmleigh Ave BS16 . . . . . 21 B5
Elmleigh Cl BS16 . . . . 21 B5
Elmleigh Rd BS16 . . . . . . 21 B5
Elmley Rd WR11 . . . . . . 183 D8
Elm Lodge GL11 . . . . 88 B4
Elmore
  Bristol BS15 . . . . 20 F2
  Yate BS37 . . . . 32 D8
Elmore Lane E GL2 . . . . 117 F3
Elmore Lane W GL2 . . . . 117 D2
Elmore Rd
  Bristol BS34 . . . . 39 F1
  Bristol, Horfield BS7 . . . . 19 A6
Elm Park Prim Sch BS36 . 30 A2
Elm Pk BS34 . . . . 29 A2
Elm Rd
  Bristol, Horfield BS7 . . . . 18 E5
  Bristol, Kingswood BS15 . . 10 E6
  Northway GL20 . . . . 182 C4
  Stroud GL5 . . . . 98 E8
  Tutshill NP16 . . . . 73 A2
Elms Gr BS34 . . . . 40 B1
Elm Side GL2 . . . . 173 B3
Elms Rd GL10 . . . . 97 E8
Elm St GL51 . . . . 133 B4
Elms The
  Bristol, Frenchay BS16 . . . 30 C1
  Bristol, Henbury BS10 . . . 27 F2
  14 Bristol, Upper Soundwell
    BS16 . . . . 20 D3
  Gloucester GL2 . . . . 127 C4
  Highworth SN6 . . . . 145 C3
  Tockington BS32 . . . . 50 B2
Elm Terr **1** GL5 . . . . 98 D6
Elmtree Ave BS16 . . . . . . 21 A7
Elmtree Cl BS15 . . . . 20 D1
Elmtree Cotts GL3 . . . . . . 68 D3
Elmtree Dr BS13 . . . . 1 F5
Elmtree Way BS15 . . . . . . 20 D1
Elm View GL7 . . . . 142 C6
Elmvil Rd **1** GL20 . . . . . 182 B4
Elm Wood BS37 . . . . 32 E8
Elphick Rd GL7 . . . . 190 B8
Elr Gr BS9 . . . . 17 E8
Elsbert Dr BS13 . . . . 1 E6
Elstree Rd BS5 . . . . 19 E1
Elstub La BS11 . . . . 87 E5
Eltham Lawn **5** GL50 . . 130 B8
Elton Ho
  3 Bristol BS2 . . . . 195 C3
  Huntley GL19 . . . . 165 D7
Elton La BS7 . . . . 18 D2
Elton Mans **5** BS7 . . . . 18 D2
Elton Rd
  Bristol, Bishopston BS7 . . 18 D2
  Bristol, Kingswood BS15 . . 20 C1
  Bristol, Tyndall's Park BS8 194 C3
  Elton GL14 . . . . 157 A8
  Littledean GL14 . . . . 156 E8
Elton St BS2 . . . . 195 C4
Elvard Cl BS13 . . . . 2 A4
Elvard Rd BS13 . . . . 2 A4
Elvaston Rd BS3 . . . . 8 E3
Elwell La BS40, BS41 . . . . . 1 A1
Embassy La BS5 . . . . 19 E1
Embassy Rd BS5 . . . . 19 E1
Embassy Wlk BS5 . . . . . . 19 E1
Embleton Rd BS10 . . . . . 28 C2
Embrook GL56 . . . . 177 C4
Emerald Cl GL4 . . . . 118 C3
Emerald Pk BS16 . . . . 31 B2
Emersons Green La BS16 . 21 B6
Emersons Green Prim Sch
  BS16 . . . . 21 B7
Emerson Sq BS7 . . . . 19 A8
Emerson Way BS16 . . . . . 21 C7
Emery Rd BS4 . . . . 9 F1

Emet Gr BS16 . . . . 21 B6
Emet La BS16 . . . . 21 B6
Emlyn Rd BS5 . . . . 19 C2
Emma-Chris Way BS34 . . 29 C2
Emmanuel Ct BS8 . . . . . 194 A4
Emmanuel Gdns GL53 . . 130 D6
Emmerson La GL6 . . . . . 149 A4
Emmett Wood BS14 . . . . . 3 B3
Emperor Ho **7** GL51 . . . 132 D2
Emperor Ct GL50 . . . . . . 193 A4
Empire Cres BS15 . . . . . . 10 E4
Empire Way GL2 . . . . 118 C5
Emra Cl BS5 . . . . 19 F1
Emra Ho BS5 . . . . 9 B8
Enborne Cl GL4 . . . . 118 D1
Enfield Rd BS16 . . . . 20 A3
Enfield Villas GL54 . . . . . 139 F5
Engine Common La BS37 . 43 C5
England's Cres BS36 . . . . 30 E7
English Bicknor CE Prim Sch
  GL16 . . . . 163 B2
Englishcombe Rd BS13 . . . 2 C3
Ennerdale Ave GL2 . . . . . 127 D5
Ennerdale Rd
  Bristol BS10 . . . . 28 D2
  Cheltenham GL51 . . . . . . 129 E7
Enoch's Row GL54 . . . . . 176 A1
Enstone Cvn Pk GL51 . . . 129 C7
Enterprise Way GL51 . . . 133 B3
Epney Cl BS34 . . . . 39 F1
Epney Rd GL4 . . . . 118 C3
Epsom Cl BS16 . . . . 30 F1
Epworth Rd BS10 . . . . . . 28 A3
Equinox BS32 . . . . 40 C3
Erin Pk GL5 . . . . 99 A5
Erin Wlk BS4 . . . . 2 D8
Ermine Par GL3 . . . . 120 D6
Ermine Way BS11 . . . . . . 16 C7
Ermin Pk GL3 . . . . 120 D6
Ermin Pl GL7 . . . . 190 E2
Ermin St
  Broad Blunsdon SN26 . . . 144 D1
  Brockworth GL3 . . . . 120 E5
Erminster Dr GL3 . . . . . . 120 A7
Ermleet Rd **1** BS6 . . . . . 18 C2
Ernest Barker Cl **15** BS5 . . 9 B7
Ernest Ct BS34 . . . . 29 B1
Ernestville Rd BS16 . . . . . 19 F3
Eros Cl GL5 . . . . 99 A5
Errington **2** GL56 . . . . . 187 B3
Ervine Terr BS2 . . . . 195 C4
Eskdale Cl BS35 . . . . 51 D7
Esland Pl GL7 . . . . 190 C2
Essery Rd BS5 . . . . 19 C2
Essex Ave GL51 . . . . 133 A2
Essex Cl GL3 . . . . 128 A8
Essex Pl BS34 . . . . 168 F8
Esson Cl BS15 . . . . 20 B1
Estate Rd GL14 . . . . 191 B6
Estcote Rd GL7 . . . . 190 C2
Estcourt Cl GL1 . . . . 127 A4
Estcourt Gdns BS16 . . . . 19 D5
Estcourt Rd GL1 . . . . 127 A3
Estoril BS37 . . . . 43 F1
Estune Wlk BS41 . . . . 7 A2
Etheldene Rd GL5 . . . . . . 98 D8
Etheridge Pl GL11 . . . . . 127 B1
Etloe Rd BS6 . . . . 18 A4
Eton Rd BS4 . . . . 9 D3
Ettington Cl GL51 . . . . . . 132 C3
Ettricke Dr BS16 . . . . 20 B5
Eugene Flats **7** BS2 . . . 195 A4
Eugene St
  Bristol, Kingsdown BS2 . . 195 A4
  Bristol, St Pauls BS2, BS5 195 C4
Eunice Saunders Way
  HR9 . . . . 164 A7
Evans Cl BS4 . . . . 9 F5
Evans Rd BS6 . . . . 18 B2
Eva Turner Cl BS14 . . . . . 3 C6
Evelyn Cl GL53 . . . . 130 F5
Evelyn Ct GL50 . . . . 193 A3
Evelyn La BS11 . . . . 26 B1
Evelyn Rd BS10 . . . . 18 C2
Evenlode Ave GL52 . . . . 134 A2
Evenlode Gdns
  Bristol BS11 . . . . 16 F5
  Moreton-in-M GL56 . . . . 187 B3
Evenlode Rd
  Gloucester GL4 . . . . 118 D1
  Moreton-in-M GL56 . . . . 187 B3
Evenlode Way BS31 . . . . . . 5 A3
Evercreech Rd BS14 . . . . . 3 B4
Eve Rd BS5 . . . . 19 B1
Everest Ave BS16 . . . . . . 19 E4
Everest Cl GL6 . . . . 91 C6
Everest Rd
  Bristol BS16 . . . . 19 E4
  Cheltenham GL53 . . . . . . 130 E4
Evergreen Ind Pk GL7 . . 142 F7
Evergreen Wlk GL2 . . . . 127 D5
Everlands GL11 . . . . 88 A4
Everside Cl GL11 . . . . 87 F6
Everside La GL11 . . . . 87 F6
Everyman Theatre The★
  GL50 . . . . 193 B3
Evesham Rd
  Bishop's Cleeve GL52 . . . 137 F5
  Cheltenham GL50, GL52 . . 133 E5
  Greet GL54 . . . . 184 A1
  Stow-on-t-W GL54 . . . . . 176 D5
Evington Ct **7** GL51 . . . 132 E2
Evington Rd **8** GL51 . . . 132 E2
Ewell Rd BS14 . . . . 3 B6
Ewens Rd GL52 . . . . 131 A8
Ewlyn Rd GL53 . . . . 130 D6

Ewlyn Terr GL53 . . . . . . 130 D6
Exchange Ave BS1 . . . . . 195 A2
Exchange Ct **8** BS15 . . . 10 D8
Exell Cl GL11 . . . . 87 F4
Exemouth Pl **14** NP16 . . 60 E8
Exeter Bldgs BS6 . . . . . . 18 B2
Exeter Rd BS3 . . . . 8 B4
Exley Cl BS30 . . . . 11 D5
Exmoor St BS3 . . . . 8 B3
Exmouth Ct GL53 . . . . . 193 B1
Exmouth Rd BS4 . . . . 8 F1
Exmouth St GL53 . . . . . . 193 B1
Exton Cl BS14 . . . . 3 B5
Eyer's La BS2 . . . . 195 C3
Eyford Cotts GL54 . . . . . 176 A3
Eynon Cl GL53 . . . . 130 C5

F

Faber Gr BS13 . . . . 2 C4
Fabian Dr BS34 . . . . 29 E5
Factory Rd BS36 . . . . 30 F7
Failand Cres BS9 . . . . 17 C5
Failand La BS20 . . . . 16 A1
Failand Wlk BS9 . . . . 17 C6
Fairacre Cl BS7 . . . . 19 B5
Fairacres BS31 . . . . 4 F5
Fairfax Cl GL7 . . . . 190 D3
Fairfax Rd GL7 . . . . 190 D3
Fairfax St BS1 . . . . 195 B3
Fairfield
  14 Cricklade SN6 . . . . 143 E4
  Minety SN16 . . . . 142 E1
Fairfield Ave GL53 . . . . . 130 D6
Fairfield Cl
  21 Coleford GL16 . . . . 155 A5
  Marshfield SN14 . . . . 15 A8
Fairfield Ct **15** GL4 . . . . 119 C4
Fairfield High Sch
  Bristol BS6 . . . . 18 F2
  Bristol BS7 . . . . 19 A3
Fairfield Par GL53 . . . . . 130 D6
Fairfield Park Rd GL53 . . 130 D6
Fairfield Pl BS3 . . . . 8 B4
Fairfield Rd
  Bristol, Montpelier BS6 . . 18 F2
  Bristol, Southville BS3 . . . . 8 A4
  Cheltenham GL53 . . . . . . 130 D6
Fairfields BS14 . . . . 191 C4
Fairfields Rd **13** HR8 . . . 178 E8
Fairfield St GL53 . . . . . . 130 D6
Fairfield Wlk GL53 . . . . . 130 D6
Fairfoot Rd BS4 . . . . 9 A3
Fairford CE Prim Sch
  GL7 . . . . 152 E4
Fairford Cl BS15 . . . . 20 F2
Fairford Cres BS34 . . . . . 29 C8
Fairford Hospl GL7 . . . . 152 E4
Fairford Rd
  Bristol BS11 . . . . 16 D7
  Quenington GL7 . . . . 152 D7
Fairford Way GL4 . . . . . . 119 D7
Fair Furlong **1** BS41 . . . . 2 A4
Fair Furlong Prim Sch
  BS13 . . . . 2 B4
Fairhaven BS37 . . . . 43 F1
Fairhaven Ave GL3 . . . . . 120 E6
Fairhaven Park Cvn Pk
  GL51 . . . . 129 B6
Fairhaven Rd
  Bristol BS6 . . . . 18 C4
  Cheltenham GL53 . . . . . . 130 D6
Fairhavens Ct **9** GL52 . . 133 C4
Fairhaven St GL53 . . . . . 130 D6
Fairlawn BS16 . . . . 20 D4
Fairlawn Ave BS34 . . . . . 29 A3
Fairlawn Rd BS6 . . . . 18 F2
Fairlyn Dr BS15 . . . . 20 F3
Fairmead GL11 . . . . 87 F5
Fairmile Gdns GL2 . . . . . 126 F5
Fairmoor Cl GL15 . . . . . . 155 E2
Fairmount Rd GL51 . . . . 132 F1
Fairoaks BS30 . . . . 11 A3
Fair View
  Chepstow/Cas-Gwent
    NP16 . . . . 60 D6
  Highworth SN6 . . . . 145 C3
Fairview
  Cheltenham GL52 . . . . . . 193 C3
  Monmouth/Trefynwy
    NP25 . . . . 154 A7
Fair View Ct BS15 . . . . . . 10 D6
Fair View Cvn Pk GL1 . . . 126 C3
Fair View Dr BS6 . . . . 18 C2
Fairview Ho BS9 . . . . 17 F8
Fairview Rd
  Bristol BS15 . . . . 10 F8
  Cheltenham GL53 . . . . . . 193 C4
Fairview St GL52 . . . . . . 193 C4
Fairwater Pk GL4 . . . . . . 127 D1
Fairway
  Bristol BS4 . . . . 9 D1
  Northway GL20 . . . . 182 C4
Fairway Cl BS30 . . . . 11 B4
Fairway Ind Ctr BS34 . . . 28 F3
Fairways BS31 . . . . 5 E2
Fairways Ave GL16 . . . . . 155 A5
Falcon Cl
  Bristol, Patchway BS34 . . 28 E8
  Bristol, Westbury on Trym
    BS9 . . . . 17 F8

Falcon Cl continued
  Innsworth GL3 . . . . 127 C6
  Quedgeley GL2 . . . . 117 F3
Falcon Ct BS9 . . . . 18 A7
Falcondale Rd BS9 . . . . . 17 F7
Falcondale Wlk BS9 . . . . 18 A8
Falcon Dr BS34 . . . . 28 E8
Falcon La HR8 . . . . 178 C8
Falcons Gate BS37 . . . . . 43 C3
Falcon Way BS35 . . . . 64 D2
Falcon Wlk BS34 . . . . 39 E1
Faldo Cl GL4 . . . . 119 F5
Falfield Rd
  Bristol BS4 . . . . 9 C3
  Gloucester GL4 . . . . 118 D3
Falfield Wlk BS10 . . . . . . 18 C8
Falkland Pl GL51 . . . . . . 132 D3
Falkland Rd **4** BS6 . . . . 18 F2
Falkner St GL1 . . . . 196 C1
Faller Fields GL15 . . . . . . 92 C2
Fallodon Ct BS9 . . . . 18 B5
Fallodon Way BS9 . . . . . . 18 B5
Fallowfield BS30 . . . . 11 D5
Fallows Rd GL54 . . . . . . 168 A1
Falmouth Rd BS7 . . . . . . 18 E4
Fancy Hill GL15 . . . . 155 E3
Fancy Rd GL15 . . . . 155 E3
Fane Cl BS10 . . . . 28 A3
Fanshawe Rd BS14 . . . . . . 3 A7
Fantasia Dr GL51 . . . . . . 129 C6
Faraday Cl **4** GL1 . . . . . 118 F7
Faraday Rd **2** BS8 . . . . . . 7 F5
Farendell Rd BS16 . . . . . . 31 B1
Far Handstones BS30 . . . 11 A4
Faringdon Rd GL51 . . . . 129 D7
Farington Rd BS10 . . . . . 18 D7
Farlands BS16 . . . . 22 B6
Far Leazes GL15 . . . . 99 D7
Farleigh Cl GL52 . . . . . . 131 C6
Farleigh La GL12 . . . . 66 C2
Farleigh Rd BS31 . . . . 4 D4
Farleigh Wlk BS13 . . . . . . 2 A8
Farley Cl BS34 . . . . 29 C7
Farman Cres GL54 . . . . . 169 D6
Farm Cl
  Bristol BS16 . . . . 21 B6
  Cheltenham GL51 . . . . . . 132 E3
  Northway GL20 . . . . 182 C5
Farmcote GL12 . . . . 55 D8
Farmcote Cl GL14 . . . . . . 148 B6
Farmcote Gdns GL54 . . . 139 F5
Farm Ct
  Bristol BS16 . . . . 20 E7
  Willersey WR12 . . . . 188 B2
  Woodchester GL5 . . . . . . 90 F8
Farmer Rd BS13 . . . . 1 E4
Farmfield Rd GL51 . . . . . 130 A5
Farm Hill GL8 . . . . 140 A8
Farmhill Cres GL5 . . . . . . 98 F8
Farmhill La GL5 . . . . 102 F1
Farmhouse Mews NP25 . 146 B7
Farmington Cl **4** GL4 . . 119 E5
Farmington Rd
  Cheltenham GL51 . . . . . . 129 E8
  Northleach GL54 . . . . . . 168 A1
Farmington Rise **13**
  GL54 . . . . 168 A1
Farm La
  Bredon GL20 . . . . 182 C7
  Cheltenham GL51, GL53 . . 130 B4
  Easter Compton BS35 . . . 38 E2
  Leighterton GL8 . . . . 70 C3
  Llangrove HR9 . . . . 162 B5
  Shurdington GL51 . . . . . 129 E1
  Westmancote GL20 . . . . 182 E8
Farm Lees GL12 . . . . 67 A6
Farm Mews GL1 . . . . 196 B1
Farmor's Sch GL7 . . . . . 152 E4
Farm Rd
  Bristol BS16 . . . . 20 E7
  Edgeworth GL6 . . . . 106 C1
  Ruardean Woodside GL17 . 163 F3
Farm St GL1 . . . . 196 B1
Farmwell Cl BS13 . . . . 2 B5
Farnaby Cl BS4 . . . . 2 C7
Farnborough Cl **2** GL4 . . 110 C3
Farndale BS5 . . . . 10 A6
Farne Cl BS9 . . . . 18 B5
Farrant Ave GL3 . . . . 128 A6
Farrant Cl BS4 . . . . 2 D6
Farrell Cl GL7 . . . . 190 C4
Farriers Croft **9** GL6 . . . 148 C6
Farriers Ct
  Bristol BS16 . . . . 21 A7
  10 Coleford GL16 . . . . 155 A6
Farriers End GL2 . . . . . . 117 F1
Farriers Reach GL52 . . . 137 D4
Farriers The GL7 . . . . . . 153 C6
Farringford Ho BS5 . . . . . 19 D2
Farr's La
  Bristol BS1 . . . . 195 A2
  Stroud GL5 . . . . 99 C7
Farr St BS11 . . . . 16 B8
Far Sandfield GL3 . . . . . . 128 C5
Farthing Croft GL2 . . . . . 125 D4
Farthings WR13 . . . . 180 C5
Farthings The GL54 . . . . 166 E2
Far View Cotts **7** GL10 . . 97 F7
Far Wells Rd GL6 . . . . . . 148 C8
Far Westrip GL6 . . . . 98 C8
Fauconberg Rd GL50 . . . 193 A3
Faulkner's La GL7 . . . . . . 152 E3

Fawkes Cl BS15......... 11 B8
Fawkes Pl **7** GL5....... 99 C7
Fawley Dr GL52........134 C4
Featherbed La BS35.... 63 B6
Feathers Dr GL15........ 92 C1
Featherstone Rd **4** BS16. 19 F4
Fedw Wood/Coed Fedw
  NP16................ 60 C8
Feeder Rd BS2........... 9 A5
Felix Rd BS5............9 B8
Felstead Rd BS10....... 28 E1
Feltham Ct BS34....... 28 F2
Feltham Rd BS16...... 22 C6
Felton Gr BS13.......... 2 A8
Fenbrook Cl BS16...... 30 B1
Fenhill Cl BS56.......186 D3
Fennel Cl GL4......... 119 D4
Fennel Dr BS34........ 30 A7
Fennell Gr BS10....... 28 A2
Fennell's View GL5.....103 E1
Fenshurst Gdns BS41..... 1 A8
Fenton Cl BS31.......... 5 D3
Fenton Ct BS7......... 18 D4
Fenton Rd BS7........ 18 D4
Fermaine Ave BS4....... 9 F3
Fernbank Ct **2** BS6.... 18 C2
Fernbank Rd BS6...... 18 C2
Fernbrook Cl BS16..... 30 B1
Fern Cl BS10........... 28 B3
Fern Cl NP16.......... 60 F5
Ferndale Ave BS30.... 11 A3
Ferndale Cl
  Cinderford GL14......191 D5
  Gloucester GL2.......127 B5
  Woodhouse Down BS32.. 40 D7
Ferndale Rd
  Bristol BS34......... 29 A2
  Whiteshill GL6........103 A3
Ferndales Cl **2** GL51..129 F5
Ferndene BS32........ 40 C2
Ferndown BS11........ 17 A7
Ferndown Cl BS11..... 17 A7
Ferndown Grange BS9.. 18 B6
Ferndown Rd **7** HR8...178 E2
Ferney GL11........... 80 C8
Fern Gr BS32......... 29 D8
Fernhill BS32......... 40 C7
Fernhill Ct
  Bristol BS11......... 27 B1
  Tockington BS32..... 40 C7
Fernhill La BS11...... 27 B1
Fernhurst Rd BS5...... 19 F1
Fernihough Ave WR11..188 C7
Fern Lawn GL4........119 D2
Fernlea Gdns BS20.... 16 B4
Fernleaze BS36....... 31 C6
Fernleigh Cres GL51..129 E6
Fernleigh Ct **1** BS6... 18 B2
Fern Rd
  Bristol BS16......... 20 D5
  Ellwood GL16........155 C3
Fern St BS2........... 18 F1
Fernstead Rd BS13....... 1 F6
Ferns The GL8........140 B4
Ferrie La HR9........162 E3
Ferris Court View **9**
  GL6................148 B6
Ferry Gdns GL2.......117 D1
Ferry La GL20........181 C8
Ferryman's Ct BS2....195 B2
Ferry Rd BS15........ 10 D1
Ferry St BS1..........195 B2
Ferry Steps Ind Est BS2.. 9 A4
Ferry Way NP16....... 61 B4
Festival Ho GL3......193 C3
Festival Rd GL10...... 97 E7
Fewster Rd GL4....... 91 B4
Fewster Sq GL6....... 91 B4
Fiddes Rd BS6........ 18 C4
Fiddler'S Gn La **3** GL51.129 C8
Fiddler's Green La GL51..132 C2
Fiddlers Wood La BS37.. 29 E8
Fiddle The SN6.......143 E4
Fidges La GL6........148 C7
Field Cl GL7..........143 A8
Fieldcote Dr GL3......120 A7
Field Court CE Inf Sch
  GL2................109 F8
Field Court Dr GL2....109 E7
Fieldcourt Farmhouse
  GL2................109 E8
Field Court Gdns GL2..109 E8
Fielden GL4...........119 D3
Field End GL3........128 A7
Fieldfare
  Bristol BS16......... 31 A2
  Gloucester GL4.......119 D5
Field Farm Ct BS34... 29 F4
Fieldgate Rd GL52....138 A4
Field House Gdns GL5.. 99 D6
Field La
  Bristol BS30......... 10 F3
  Coaley GL11......... 88 E7
  Dyrham SN14........ 87 D5
  Littleton-u-S BS35... 50 A8
  Tytherington BS35.... 51 E3
Field Marshal Slim Ct **1**
  BS2................195 C3
Field Pl GL5.......... 98 F8
Field Rd
  Bristol BS15......... 20 C1
  Kingham OX7........177 F2

Field Rd continued
  Stroud, Bowbridge GL5... 99 D6
  Stroud, Rodborough GL5... 99 B6
  Whiteshill GL6........103 A3
Fields La WR12.......188 B2
Fields Rd GL54.......159 B5
Fieldview GL13........ 85 E4
Field View BS5......... 9 A8
Field View Dr BS16.... 20 C6
Fieldways GL6........ 91 A4
Fiennes Cl BS16...... 20 E4
Fiery La GL11........ 89 C2

Fifth Ave
  Bristol, Filton BS7.... 29 A1
  Bristol, Hengrove BS14.. 3 B7
Fifth Way BS11....... 26 E2
Filbert Cl GL4........119 D3
Filby Dr BS34........ 29 C8
Filton Abbey Wood Sta
  BS34................ 29 B1
Filton Ave
  Bristol, Filton BS34.... 29 B3
  Bristol, Horfield BS7, BS34. 19 A7
Filton Ave Inf Sch BS7.. 19 A7
Filton Coll North BS34.. 29 A4
Filton Gr BS7......... 18 F6
Filton Hill Prim Sch BS34. 29 B4
Filton La BS34........ 29 D2
Filton Rd
  Bristol, Frenchay BS16.. 29 F2
  Bristol, Harry Stoke BS34. 29 D2
  Bristol, Horfield BS7... 18 F8
Filton Rdbt BS34...... 29 A2
Filton Way GL4.......119 B7
Filwood Broadway BS4...2 E8
Filwood Dr BS15...... 20 B3
Filwood Ho BS15...... 10 F8
Filwood Rd BS16...... 20 A3
Finch Cl BS35........ 64 C2
Finchcroft Ct GL52...134 D4
Finchcroft La GL52...134 C4
Finchmoor Mews GL2.126 F6
Finch Rd
  Chipping Sodbury BS37... 33 A8
  Innsworth GL3........127 D7
Finlay Com Sch GL4...119 A6
Finlay Pl GL4.........118 F5
Finlay Rd GL4........118 F5
Finstock Cl GL51.....129 F8
Fircroft Cl GL3.......119 F8
Fircroft Rd GL4......126 F5
Fire Engine La BS36... 31 D7
Fire Service Coll The
  GL56................187 C3
Fire Station La GL2... 26 B2
Firethorne Cl GL2....127 B5
Firework Cl BS15..... 11 B8
Firfield St BS4........ 9 A4
Firgrove Cres BS37... 44 A2
Firgrove Wlk **3** GL51..129 C7
Fir Rd SN14.......... 15 F6
Firs Cl OX7..........177 E1
Firs Ct BS31........... 4 C4
Firs Rd GL5.......... 91 C5
First Ave
  Bristol, Hengrove BS14... 3 A7
  Bristol, St Anne's BS4.... 9 E5
  Dursley GL11......... 80 C8
Firs The
  Bristol BS16......... 20 E6
  Gloucester GL1.......196 C4
  Kemble GL7..........141 D6
  Swindon GL51........133 B7
First Way BS11....... 26 C1
Firth Ave GL56.......187 C3
Fir Tree Cl
  Bristol BS16......... 28 F7
  Cheltenham GL52.....134 A4
Fir Tree La BS5....... 10 A7
Fir View Rd GL14.....156 C6
Firwood Dr GL4......118 E3
Fish Alley **13** GL20....192 C4
Fisher Ave BS15...... 21 A1
Fisher Cl **30** GL54....176 F4
Fisher Rd BS15....... 21 A1
Fishers La GL52......193 C4
Fishers Rd GL13...... 85 E4
Fishers Way GL5...... 99 A4
Fish Hill WR12.......185 D8
Fishponds CE Acad BS16. 20 A4
Fishponds Rd BS5..... 19 D3
Fishponds Trad Est BS5.. 19 E2
Fishpool Hill BS10.... 28 B4
Fitchett Wlk BS10.... 27 F3
Fitzgerald Rd BS3.......8 F3
Fitzgerold Ave SN6...145 C4
Fitzhamon Pk GL20...182 C4
Fitzharding Ho BS1...195 A3
Fitzharding Rd BS20.. 16 E3
Fitzosborn Cl NP16.... 60 D7
Fitzroy Rd BS16...... 20 B2
Fitzroy St BS4........ 9 A4
Fitzroy Terr **7** BS6.... 18 B2
Five Acre Dr BS16.... 20 A7
Five Acres GL11...... 80 A8
Five Lanes SN16......141 B1
Five Mile Dr GL7.....186 C5
Five Trees Cl **8** GL8... 140 B4
Flaxley Ho GL1.......127 A2
Flaxley Rd GL4.......118 E3
Flaxley St GL14.......191 D4
Flaxman GL7.......... 19 B6
Flaxpits La BS36...... 30 E5

Flecker's Dr GL51.....129 F7
Fleece Alley **24** GL54...176 F4
Fleece Inn * WR11....188 A6
Fleece Rd WR12......188 A1
Fleet Close Cvn Site
  GL20................182 A7
Fleet La GL20........182 A7
Fleet Rd GL20........182 A7
Fleming Cl GL2.......127 C6
Fletchers Alley **11** GL20..192 C4
Flint Rd GL51........129 E6
Flisteridge Rd SN16...142 B2
Florence Brown Com Sch
  The BS4............. 2 D8
Florence Pk
  Almondsbury BS32.... 40 C5
  Bristol BS6.......... 18 B4
Florence Rd BS16..... 20 E3
Florence Terr SN16...142 E1
Florida Bvd GL7......152 E3
Florida Dr GL52......134 C4
Flowers Hill BS4.......9 E1
Flowers Hill Cl BS4.....9 E1
Flowers Hill Trad Est BS4...9 E1
Flower Way GL2......127 B4
Flowerwell Rd BS13.....2 B5
Focus Sch - Gloucester
  Campus GL4.........119 C8
Focus School - Berkeley
  Campus GL13........ 85 E7
Folders The GL15..... 92 B3
Foley Cl GL4.........118 D3
Foley Rd GL18........171 A4
Foley Rise GL19......172 C4
Folk Mus * GL1.......196 A3
Folland Ave GL3......120 B6
Folleigh Cl BS41.......7 B2
Folleigh Dr BS41.......7 B2
Folleigh La BS41.......7 B2
Folliot Cl BS16....... 20 A7
Folly Bridge Cl BS37.. 43 D2
Folly Brook Rd BS16... 31 B1
Folly Cl SN6.........145 D4
Folly Cres SN6.......145 D4
Folly Dr SN6.........145 D4
Follyfield SN16.......141 E1
Folly Field GL54......169 A8
Folly Gdns GL20......192 D4
Folly La
  Bristol BS2.......... 9 A6
  Cheltenham GL50.....133 D3
  English Bicknor GL16..163 A1
  Huntley GL17........165 B7
  Stroud GL5, GL6.....103 C2
Folly Rd BS37........ 42 A5
Folly Rise GL5.......103 D1
Folly The
  Bristol BS16......... 20 F7
  Cold Ashton SN14.... 13 F6
  Longborough GL56...176 E8
  Saltford BS31.......... 5 F2
Folly Way SN6.......145 D4
Fontana Cl BS30..... 11 B3
Fonthill Prim Sch BS10.. 28 E2
Fonthill Rd BS10..... 28 D2
Fonthill Way BS30.... 11 C2
Fontmell Ct BS14...... 3 D7
Fontwell Dr BS16..... 30 F1
Footes La BS36....... 31 B7
Footshill Cl BS15..... 10 C6
Footshill Dr BS15..... 10 C7
Footshill Rd BS15..... 10 C6
Fop St GL11.......... 89 A1
Forbes Cl GL4........119 F6
Forde Cl BS30........ 10 F5
Fordell Pl BS4......... 9 A3
Ford House Rd GL18..171 B6
Ford La
  Bristol BS16......... 21 B6
  Gorsley BS18........170 D4
Ford St BS5........... 9 C6
Fordwich Cl NP16..... 72 B5
Fore St SN6..........142 F5
Forest Ave BS16...... 20 B3
Forest Cl GL16.......154 E7
Forest Dr BS10....... 28 C3
Forest E-ACT Acad GL14 191 B6
Forest Edge BS15.... 10 C4
Foresters Rd GL20...192 C2
Forest Hills BS32.... 40 B5
Forest of Dean Sculpture
  Trail * GL16.........155 E7
Forest Par **4** GL15.... 92 A3
Forest Park Camping Site
  GL16................154 F7
Forest Patch **6** GL16...155 A7
Forest Rd
  Bream GL15.........147 D8
  Bristol, Fishponds BS16.. 20 B4
  Bristol, Kingswood BS15... 10 D7
  Cinderford GL14......191 D4
  Lydney GL15........ 92 A3
  Mile End GL16.......155 B7
  Milkwall GL16.......155 B4
  Ruardean Woodside GL17. 163 F3
Forest Rise
  Cinderford GL14......191 E5
  Nailsworth GL6...... 90 F4
  Upper Lydbrook GL17..163 D2
Forest Vale Ind Est GL14. 191 B5
Forest View
  Cinderford GL14......191 C1
  Narth The NP25......154 B1
Forest View Cvn Site
  GL14................191 C3

Forest View Prim Sch
  GL14................191 E5
Forest View Rd
  Berkeley GL13........ 85 E4
  Gloucester GL4......118 E1
Forest Wlk
  Bristol, Fishponds BS16... 20 B2
  Bristol, Kingswood BS15... 10 C7
Forge Cotts GL18.....171 D6
Forge Gdns NP16..... 72 B6
Forge Hill GL17......163 C3
Forge La GL18........171 D6
Forge Rd GL11........ 88 B1
Forge The
  Gloucester GL2......118 B6
  Lower Lydbrook GL17..163 C1
Forsdene Wlk GL16...155 B5
Forstall Wy GL7......190 F5
Forsyte Way GL4.....119 B7
Forsythia Cl **8** GL3...128 A2
Fortey Rd GL54......168 A1
Fortfield Rd BS14......3 B5
Fortfields **5** GL11.... 80 B8
Fortina Cl GL50......133 C5
Fort La GL11......... 80 B8
Fort Leney Wlk **3** GL51. 133 C4
Fortress The GL11.... 80 B8
Fort View Terr GL5.... 98 E6
Forty Acre La
  Alveston BS35....... 51 B3
  Stroud GL6..........148 A8
Forty's Pitch HR9....170 B5
Forty The SN6.......143 E4
Forum The GL1.......196 B2
Foscombe La GL19...172 C5
Fosscross La GL54, GL7..159 C3
Foss Ct **8** BS5........9 F8
Fosse Cl
  Cirencester GL7......190 E5
  Gloucester GL4......119 E6
Fossedale Ave BS14.... 3 C5
Fosse Folly GL54.....176 F5
Fosse La GL54........176 F5
Fosseway Ave GL56...187 A2
Fosseway Cl **7** GL56...187 A2
Fosseway Ct
  Bristol BS8..........194 A2
  Lechlade on T GL7....153 E3
Fosseway Dr **6** GL56..187 A2
Fosseway Ho GL54....176 F5
Fosseway The BS8....194 A3
Foss Field GL7.......107 A8
Foss La BS35......... 63 E6
Foster Cl GL2.........138 A5
Foster Ct **3** GL52....134 A3
Foster Dr WR12......188 A2
Foster's Almshouses
  BS1................195 A3
Foundry La BS5...... 19 F2
Foundry Rd GL14.....191 D5
Foundry Wood Forest
  Trails * GL14........156 D5
Foundry Yd BS5...... 19 F2
Fountain Cres GL12... 68 C6
Fountain Ct
  Bristol BS32......... 40 C3
  2 Yate BS37....... 32 D7
Fountaine Ct **3** BS5... 19 C2
Fountains Dr BS30.... 10 F6
Fountain Sq GL11....196 A3
Fountain St GL6...... 91 C4
Fountain Way NP16... 60 F4
Four Acre Ave BS16... 20 E8
Four Acre Cl SN6....143 A4
Four Acre Cres BS16... 30 E1
Four Acre Rd BS16.... 20 E8
Four Acres BS13.......1 F4
Four Acres Cl BS13.....1 F4
Four Acres Prim Sch BS13. 1 F4
Four Acres View GL7..190 B3
Four Seasons Sq BS37. 43 E1
Fourth Ave
  Bristol, Filton BS7.... 29 A1
  Bristol, Hengrove BS14.. 3 B7
  Dursley GL11........ 80 C8
Fourth Way BS11..... 26 E1
Fowbridge Gdns HR9..163 C8
Fowler's Hill GL7.....152 D7
Foxborough Gdns BS32. 40 D2
Fox Cl
  Bristol BS4..........9 F5
  Gloucester GL4......119 E5
  Hawkesbury Upton GL9... 55 F3
Foxcombe Rd BS14..... 3 B4
Foxcote
  Bristol BS15........ 10 F7
  Gloucester GL2......127 B5
Foxcote Hill CV36....189 F5
Foxcott SN6.........143 E6
Foxcroft Cl BS32..... 29 F6
Foxcroft Rd BS5....... 9 D8
Fox Ct BS30.......... 10 F3
Fox Den Rd BS34..... 29 D3
Fox Dr GL54.........176 D4
Fox Elms Rd GL4.....118 E2
Foxe Rd BS36........ 31 B8
Foxes Bank Dr GL14..191 B5
Foxes Cl
  3 Bourton-on-t-W GL54. 168 F7
  6 Chalford GL6.....148 C6
Foxes Dell GL6....... 91 A5

Foxes Row GL56.....177 A6
Foxfield Ave BS32.... 40 D3
Foxglove Cl
  Bristol BS16......... 19 E5
  Cirencester GL7......190 E2
  Gloucester GL4......119 E5
  Thornbury BS35...... 64 D2
Foxglove Way GL16...155 B4
Foxgrove Dr GL52....134 A1
Fox Hill GL8.........140 C3
Fox Ho BS4............9 E3
Foxholes La BS32.... 50 C4
Fox & Hounds La BS31...4 F5
Fox La **7** GL54.......176 F4
Foxleaze SN6........143 E5
Foxleigh Cres GL2....127 E5
Foxmoor GL52........137 E4
Foxmoor La GL5...... 98 C7
Foxmoor Prim Sch GL5.. 98 D7
Fox Rd BS5........... 19 B1
Fox Run GL2.........118 A2
Fox's La GL16........155 B5
Foxtail Cl GL4.......119 A5
Foxwell Dr GL3.......120 A8
Foye Ho BS8...........7 E6
Fraley Rd BS9........ 18 A7
Framlington Ct GL51..133 A1
Frampton Cotterell CE Prim
  Sch BS36........... 31 A8
Frampton Cotts GL20..183 E3
Frampton Cres BS16.. 20 C4
Frampton Ct
  8 Bristol, Longwell Green
  BS30................ 10 F4
  16 Bristol, Pile Marsh BS5.. 9 D7
Frampton End Rd BS37.. 42 D2
Frampton Mews GL51..129 B7
Frampton Rd GL11....118 D7
France La GL9........ 56 B2
Frances Ct GL52......133 F1
Frances Greeves Ct BS10. 27 F1
Francis Ct BS5.........9 F7
Francis Ho BS2.......195 A4
Francis Pl BS30...... 10 F4
Francis Rd
  Bristol, Bedminster BS3... 8 C2
  Bristol, Westbury on Trym
  BS10................ 18 C3
Francis St GL53......193 B1
Francis Way BS30.... 11 D6
Francis Woodcock Trad Est
  5 GL1.............119 A8
Francombe Gr BS10... 18 E6
Francombe Ho BS1...195 A1
Frank Brookes Rd GL51. 133 A4
Franklin Ct BS1......195 B1
Franklyn Ct
  6 Bristol BS16..... 19 E3
  6 Cheltenham GL51..132 E2
Franklyn La **10** BS2... 18 F1
Franklyn St BS2...... 18 F1
Fraser St BS3.......... 8 D3
Frayne Rd BS3........ 8 A4
Frazier's Folly GL7...150 E2
Freame Cl GL6.......148 B6
Frederick Pl BS8.....194 B3
Fredericks Way SN14.. 36 B3
Frederick Thomas Rd
  GL11................ 87 C3
Fredrick St BS4........ 9 B4
Freeland Bldgs **1** BS5.. 19 C2
Freeland Pl BS8.......7 F6
Freeling Ho BS1......195 B1
Freemans Cl GL20....181 F8
Freemans Orch **30** GL14. 171 A4
Freemantle Gdns BS5.. 19 C3
Freemantle Ho BS2...195 A4
Freemantle Rd BS5... 19 C3
Freeminers Way GL14..191 D5
Freestone Rd BS2......9 A6
Free Tank BS2.......195 C2
Freezinghill La BS30... 13 B4
Fremantle La **8** BS6... 18 D1
Fremantle Rd BS6.... 18 D1
Fremantle Sq BS6.... 18 D1
Frenchay CE Prim Sch
  BS16................ 20 D7
Frenchay Cl BS16.... 20 D7
Frenchay Hill BS16... 20 C7
Frenchay Hospl BS16.. 20 D8
Frenchay Park Rd BS16. 19 F6
Frenchay Rd BS16.... 20 C6
French La
  Lower Redbrook NP25..154 C1
  Newland GL16.......154 D4
Freshland Way BS15.. 10 B8
Fretherne Rd GL4....118 D3
Frewin Cl GL51.......132 D2
Frewins La GL14......165 D3
Friars Cl GL51.......130 B5
Friars Ho **4** BS37.... 32 D7
Friar's Wlk GL18.....171 A5
Friary BS1...........195 C2
Friary Grange Pk BS36. 30 E6
Friary Rd
  Bristol BS7.......... 18 D4
  Gloucester GL4......119 E6
Fridays Ham La SN6..143 A5
Friday St
  Arlingham GL2.......157 C2
  Minchinhampton GL6..148 A3
  Painswick GL6.......103 F8
Friendly Row BS20... 16 C5
Friendship Rd BS4....9 A2
Friezewood Rd BS3....8 A4

Fripp Cl BS5 . . . . .9 B6
Frith La GL12 . . . . 53 F3
Frith The GL6 . . . . 148 B6
Frithwood GL6 . . . . 148 B6
Frithwood Cl GL6 . . . . . . 148 B6
Frithwood Pk GL6 . . . . . 148 B6
Frobisher Mews GL3 . . . 127 F8
Frobisher Rd BS3 . . . . 8 A3
Frocester Hill GL10 . . . . 89 C8
Frog Furlong La GL2,
GL3 . . . . 127 E8
Frog La
  Bristol BS1 . . . . 194 C2
  Coalpit Heath BS36 . . . . 31 E7
  Frocester GL10 . . . . 97 A3
  Huntley GL19 . . . . 165 D6
  Ilmington CV36 . . . . . . 189 F6
  North Nibley GL11 . . . . . 79 C5
Frogmarsh La GL5 . . . . . 91 A8
Frogmore Rd GL19 . . . . . 165 D6
Frogmore St BS1 . . . . . . 194 C2
Frome Ave GL5 . . . . 99 A6
Frome Ct BS35 . . . . 51 C8
Frome Gdns GL5 . . . . . . 98 E6
Frome Glen BS36 . . . . . . 30 E4
Frome Park Rd GL5 . . . . 99 A6
Frome Pl 1 BS16 . . . . . . 19 E5
Frome Rd BS37 . . . . 44 C1
Fromeside GL5 . . . . 99 C6
Fromeside Dr GL5 . . . . . 98 D6
Fromeside Ind Est GL5 . . 99 C6
Fromeside Pk BS16 . . . . 20 B7
Frome Terr GL5 . . . . 19 E5
Frome Vale Acad BS16 . . 20 C7
Frome Valley Rd BS16 . . . 19 F6
Frome View BS36 . . . . . . 31 B7
Frome Villas BS16 . . . . . 20 C7
Frome Way BS36 . . . . . . 30 E5
Front La SN26 . . . . 144 D2
Front St
  Ilmington CV36 . . . . . . 189 F6
  Nympsfield GL10 . . . . . . 89 E5
Froomshaw Rd BS16 . . . . 20 A7
Frost & Reed Ho 3 BS5 . .9 F8
Frowens La HR9 . . . . 170 B4
Fry Cl GL7 . . . . 190 E3
Fry Ct 2 BS3 . . . . 8 C4
Fry's Cl BS16 . . . . 19 D4
Frys Hill BS15 . . . . 20 E2
Fry's Hill BS4 . . . . .9 D2
Frys House of Mercy
  BS1 . . . . 195 B1
Fryth Wood/Coed Ffwyth
  NP16 . . . . 60 C8
Fulbrook Cl GL51 . . . . . 132 D5
Fulford Ctr BS13 . . . . . . .2 C4
Fulford Rd BS13 . . . . 2 C5
Fulford Wlk BS13 . . . . . . .2 B5
Fullers Ave 10 SN6 . . . . 143 E4
Fullers Ct GL1 . . . . 196 A3
Fuller's La GL19 . . . . . . 172 B4
Fulmar BS35 . . . . 64 D2
Furber Ct BS5 . . . . 10 B6
Furber Rd BS5 . . . . 10 B6
Furber Ridge BS5 . . . . . . 10 B6
Furber Vale BS5 . . . . 10 B6
Furlong Ct 3 HR8 . . . . . 178 E7
Furlong La GL52 . . . . . . 137 F3
Furlong Rd GL1 . . . . 118 E7
Furlongs The GL12 . . . . . 69 C3
Furlong The BS6 . . . . . . 18 D6
Furnace Cl GL14 . . . . . . 191 C4
Furnace La GL18 . . . . . . 171 A5
Furnace Valley GL15 . . . 156 D1
Furnwood BS5 . . . . 10 A6
Furrowfield Pk 5 GL20 . 182 B4
Furze La GL55 . . . . 189 B4
Furze Rd BS16 . . . . 20 C5
Furze The GL4 . . . . 119 A4
Furzewood Rd BS15 . . . . 10 F8
Fussell Ct BS15 . . . . 10 F8
Fylingdales Gdn GL2 . . . 110 C7
Fylton Croft BS14 . . . . . .3 B3

G

Gabb La GL19 . . . . 173 B7
Gable Cl BS35 . . . . 39 A2
Gable Cotts GL7 . . . . . . 152 E3
Gable Point GL52 . . . . . 138 B3
Gable Rd 7 BS5 . . . . . . 19 A1
Gable Row BS20 . . . . . . 182 F8
Gabriel Cl BS30 . . . . 11 B5
Gadshill Dr BS34 . . . . . . 29 E5
Gadshill Rd
  Bristol BS5 . . . . 19 C2
  Charlton Kings GL53 . . . 131 B3
Gadwell Rd GL20 . . . . . 192 E3
Gages Cl BS15 . . . . 10 F7
Gages Rd BS15 . . . . 10 F7
Gaineys Well GL5 . . . . . . 99 D7
Gainsborough Dr GL4 . . 118 C2
Gainsborough Ho GL55 . 189 B2
Gainsborough Mews
  BS10 . . . . 28 B2
Gainsborough Rd BS31 . . .4 F5
Gainsborough Sq BS7 . . 19 B7
Gainsborough Terr GL55 189 A1
Gales Ct GL7 . . . . 153 E2
Galileo Gdns GL51 . . . . 132 C1
Gallagher Ret Pk
  Bristol BS30 . . . . 10 E4
  Cheltenham GL51 . . . . . 132 F5
Galleries The BS1 . . . . . 195 B3

Galley Orch SN6 . . . . . . 143 F4
Gallivan Cl BS34 . . . . . . 29 B8
Gallops Cl GL52 . . . . . . 134 D4
Gallops The GL2 . . . . . . 118 B6
Gallows Pound La GL7 . . 190 B8
Galway Rd BS4 . . . . .8 E1
Gambet Rd GL3 . . . . . . 120 B4
Gambier Parry Gdns GL2 126 F4
Gambles La GL52 . . . . . 138 D2
Gambril La GL12 . . . . . . 65 F5
Gamecock Cl GL4 . . . . . 120 B4
Ganborough Rd GL56 . . . 176 D8
Gander Cl BS13 . . . . .2 B5
Gander La
  Teddington GL20 . . . . . 183 A4
  Tewkesbury GL20 . . . . . 192 C3
Gannaway La GL20 . . . . 192 F5
Gannet Cl GL3 . . . . 120 E5
Gannicox Rd GL5 . . . . . . 99 A7
Ganzell La GL11 . . . . 80 C7
Gara Cl GL51 . . . . 132 F5
Garamond Ct BS1 . . . . . 195 B1
Garden City Way 12 NP16. 60 E8
Garden Cl
  Bristol BS9 . . . . 17 C5
  Cirencester GL7 . . . . . . 190 C3
  Dumbleton WR11 . . . . . 183 F7
  Mickleton GL55 . . . . . . 189 A6
Garden Cotts GL19 . . . . 172 A2
Garden Ct BS8 . . . . 194 A4
Gardeners Way
  King's Stanley GL10 . . . . 98 A4
  Newent GL18 . . . . 170 F4
Gardeners Wlk BS41 . . . . .7 B1
Gardenia Gr GL51 . . . . . 129 F5
Garden Rd GL53 . . . . . . 131 B4
Gardens The
  Bristol, Frenchay BS16 . . 29 F1
  4 Bristol, Upper Soundwell
    BS16 . . . . 20 D3
  Cheltenham GL50 . . . . . 133 C4
  Monmouth/Trefynwy
    NP25 . . . . 154 A8
Garden Suburb GL11 . . . 88 A1
Garden The GL5 . . . . 99 A2
Garden Way GL2 . . . . . . 127 B4
Gardiner Cl GL6 . . . . . . 148 C6
Gardiners Cl GL3 . . . . . 128 A6
Gardner Ave BS13 . . . . . .1 F7
Gardner Ct GL7 . . . . . . 190 D3
Gardner's La GL51 . . . . 133 C4
Gardners Lane Prim Sch
  GL51 . . . . 133 C4
Garfield Ct BS5 . . . . .9 F8
Garfield Rd BS5 . . . . . . 10 A8
Garland Ct GL7 . . . . 190 C3
Garlands Rd GL15 . . . . . 147 D3
Garlandstone Wlk GL2 . . 118 C6
Garnalls Rd GL4 . . . . . . 119 C4
Garnet St BS3 . . . . .8 B3
Garnett Pl BS16 . . . . . . 20 F7
Garns Cl GL11 . . . . 89 B1
Garren View HR9 . . . . . 162 C7
Garrett Dr BS32 . . . . . . 29 D7
Garretts The GL7 . . . . . 152 D4
Garth Rd BS13 . . . . .2 B3
Garton Ho 3 BS16 . . . . 20 D5
Garvey Cl NP16 . . . . . . 60 F4
Garvey Ho 14 BS5 . . . . . .9 C7
Gascoigns Wy BS34 . . . . 29 A7
Gasferry Rd BS1 . . . . . . 194 B1
Gaskins The BS7 . . . . . . 19 A5
Gas La
  Bristol BS2 . . . . 9 A6
  Cricklade SN6 . . . . 143 F4
Gassons Rd GL7 . . . . . . 153 E3
Gassons Way GL7 . . . . . 153 E2
Gaston La SN16 . . . . 58 D1
Gastons The BS11 . . . . . 17 A8
Gastrells Com Prim Sch
  GL5 . . . . 99 A4
Gatcombe Ct BS13 . . . . . 2 A5
Gatcombe Dr BS34 . . . . 29 E4
Gatcombe Rd BS13 . . . . .2 B5
Gatcombe GL52 . . . . . . 137 E3
Gatehouse Ave BS13 . . . 2 A5
Gatehouse Cl BS13 . . . . 2 A5
Gatehouse Ct BS13 . . . . .2 B5
Gatehouse Ctr The BS13 . . 2 A5
Gatesby Mead BS34 . . . . 29 E5
Gathorne Cres BS37 . . . 43 D2
Gathorne Rd BS3 . . . . . .8 B4
Gatmeres Rd GL4 . . . . . 119 C3
Gatton Rd BS2 . . . . 19 A1
Gatton Way GL3 . . . . . . 127 F1
Gatwick Cl GL14 . . . . . 157 E8
Gauntlet Rd GL4 . . . . . . 119 C4
Gaunt's Earthcott La BS32 41 B5
Gaunt's La 7 BS1 . . . . . 194 C2
Gaunts Rd BS37 . . . . . . 33 B8
Gavel Wy GL1 . . . . 196 A4
Gay Elms Rd BS13 . . . . . 2 A4
Gayner Rd BS7 . . . . 29 A1
Gays Rd BS15 . . . . 10 B4
Gaywood Ho 7 BS3 . . . . .8 B3
Gazelle Cl GL2 . . . . 117 F2
Gazzard Rd BS36 . . . . . 30 E7
Gazzard Rd BS36 . . . . . 30 E7
Gee Moors BS15 . . . . . . 10 F7
Gefle Cl BS1 . . . . 194 B1
Gegg Cl GL7 . . . . 190 F3

Gemini Cl
  4 Cheltenham GL51 . . . . 129 C8
  Cheltenham GL51 . . . . . 132 C1
Genista Way 3 GL51 . . . 129 F5
Geoffrey Cl BS13 . . . . . . .1 E6
George Ct
  12 Bristol BS6 . . . . 18 B1
  Painswick GL6 . . . . 103 F8
George Dowty Dr GL20 . 182 C5
George & Dragon La 11
  BS5 . . . . 9 D7
George Jones Rd BS2 . . . 9 A6
George La
  Chipping Campden GL55 . 189 A1
  Cinderford GL14 . . . . . . 164 E1
  Littledean GL14 . . . . . . 191 F4
  Marshfield SN14 . . . . . . 24 E1
George Naisey Ho 6
  GL52 . . . . 134 A3
George Pl 14 GL16 . . . . 155 A7
George Rd GL15 . . . . . . 156 A2
George Readings Way
  GL51 . . . . 133 A4
George St
  Bisley GL6 . . . . 105 A1
  Bristol BS5 . . . . .9 C8
  Gloucester GL1 . . . . . . 196 C3
  Nailsworth GL6 . . . . . . 91 C4
  5 Stroud GL5 . . . . 99 C7
George The GL54 . . . . . 174 A7
George Whitefield Cl 5
  GL4 . . . . 119 C4
Georgian Cl GL4 . . . . . . 119 E3
Georgian House Mus ★
  BS1 . . . . 194 C2
Georgia Rd GL7 . . . . . . 152 E2
Gerald Rd BS3 . . . . 8 A3
Geralds Way GL6 . . . . . 148 C6
Gere Cl GL4 . . . . 118 D2
Gerrard Cl BS4 . . . . 2 D7
Gerrish Ave
  Bristol, Moorfields BS5 . . . 9 C8
  Bristol, Staple Hill BS16 . . 20 F5
Gervase Cl GL54 . . . . . . 174 A4
Gibbet La BS14 . . . . 3 D1
Gibbs Ct 15 BS5 . . . . . . .9 D7
Gibbsfold Rd BS13 . . . . . 2 C4
Gibraltar Way NP16 . . . . 61 B4
Gibson Cl GL5 . . . . 99 F7
Gibson Ct GL7 . . . . 190 D3
Gibson Rd
  Bristol BS6 . . . . 18 D1
  Innsworth GL3 . . . . 127 E7
Giffard Rd BS34 . . . . . . 29 D6
Giffard Way GL53 . . . . . 130 D4
Gifford Cl
  Gloucester GL2 . . . . . . 127 C5
  Rangeworthy BS37 . . . . . 43 A8
Gifford Cres BS34 . . . . . 29 C6
Gifford Ct BS34 . . . . . . 29 D2
Gifford Rd BS10 . . . . . . 27 F4
Giffords Pl BS13 . . . . 2 A7
Gilbert Hill GL13 . . . . . . 85 E4
Gilbert Rd
  Bristol, Kingswood BS15 . . 20 D1
  Bristol, Moorfields BS5 . . . 9 C8
  Gloucester GL2 . . . . . . 127 C5
Gilberts La GL4 . . . . 110 F6
Gilda Cl BS14 . . . . 3 C5
Gilda Cres BS14 . . . . . . .3 B6
Gilda Par BS14 . . . . 3 C5
Gilda Sq W BS14 . . . . . . 3 B5
Gilder Rd GL52 . . . . 138 A2
Gilders Paddock GL52 . . 137 F4
Giles Ave SN6 . . . . 143 E3
Giles Cox GL2 . . . . 109 F8
Giles Ct GL14 . . . . 191 D4
Gillard Cl BS15 . . . . 10 D8
Gillard Rd BS15 . . . . . . 10 B8
Gill Ave BS16 . . . . 20 B6
Gillebank Cl BS14 . . . . . 3 D5
Gillett Cl GL14 . . . . 191 D5
Gillham Ho 4 BS7 . . . . . 18 D2
Gillingham Hill 7 BS15 . 10 B5
Gillingstool BS35 . . . . . 51 C8
Gillingstool Prim Sch
  BS35 . . . . 51 B8
Gillman Cl GL7 . . . . 190 E3
Gillray Cl BS7 . . . . 19 B6
Gilpin Ave GL3 . . . . 127 F1
Gilpin Cl BS15 . . . . 20 F1
Gilroy Cl BS30 . . . . 11 B3
Gilslake Ave BS10 . . . . . 28 B3
Gilton Ho BS4 . . . . .9 E2
Gimson Cl GL4 . . . . 118 D2
Gingell's Gn 4 BS5 . . . . 10 A8
Gipsy La
  Chalford GL6 . . . . 148 C4
  Leonard Stanley GL10 . . . 97 C2
Gipsy Patch La BS34 . . . 29 C6
Glades The BS5 . . . . 19 E2
Glade The GL7 . . . . 190 E2
Gladfield Gdns GL5 . . . . 98 E6
Gladfield Sq GL5 . . . . . . 98 E6
Gladiator Cl GL3 . . . . . . 120 E5
Gladstone Ct BS16 . . . . 20 E4
Gladstone Dr BS16 . . . . 20 E3
Gladstone La BS36 . . . . 31 C7
Gladstone Rd
  Bristol, Hengrove BS14 . . .3 B6
  2 Bristol, Kingswood BS15 20 D1
  Charlton Kings GL53 . . . 131 A5
  Gloucester GL52 . . . . . 118 D6
Gladstone St
  Bristol, Bedminster BS3 . . .8 B3
  Bristol, Kingswood BS15 . 20 D3

Gladstone St continued
  13 Bristol, Pile Marsh BS5 . . 9 D7
Glaisdale Rd BS16 . . . . . 20 A5
Glamorgan Rd GL51 . . . 129 E6
Glanville Gdns BS15 . . . 10 E7
Glasshouse Hill GL17 . . 165 B7
Glass House La BS2 . . . . .9 B5
Glasshouse The GL50 . . 193 A3
Glastonbury Cl BS30 . . . 10 F5
Glebe Cl
  Frampton on Severn GL2 . 157 F1
  Long Ashton BS41 . . . . . 7 C2
  Mitcheldean GL17 . . . . . 164 D6
  Newent GL18 . . . . 170 F5
  11 Stow-on-t-W GL54 . . . 176 F4
  Stratton GL7 . . . . 190 B8
Glebe Ct GL18 . . . . 170 F5
Glebe Farm Ct GL51 . . . 129 F5
Glebe Field BS32 . . . . . . 40 A5
Glebe Fold 10 GL55 . . . 189 A6
Glebeland Dr GL20 . . . . 182 C7
Glebelands GL11 . . . . . . 87 F5
Glebelands Rd BS34 . . . . 29 A3
Glebe Orch HR8 . . . . . . 178 A3
Glebe Pl SN6 . . . . 145 D3
Glebe Rd
  Bristol BS5 . . . . .9 E8
  Cheltenham GL52 . . . . . 134 B4
  Long Ashton BS41 . . . . . 7 C2
  Minchinhampton GL6 . . . 148 A3
  Newent GL18 . . . . 170 F4
Glebes The BS5 . . . . .9 E8
Glebe The
  Pilning BS35 . . . . 38 C7
  Sapperton GL7 . . . . 149 B6
Glebe View GL17 . . . . . 158 C4
Glebe Way GL18 . . . . . . 170 F4
Glebe Wlk BS31 . . . . 4 C4
Gledemoor Dr BS36 . . . . 31 D7
Glena Ave BS4 . . . . .9 B2
Glenarm Rd BS4 . . . . . . .9 B2
Glenarm Wlk BS4 . . . . . .9 B2
Glenavon Ct BS9 . . . . . . 17 C4
Glenavon Pk BS9 . . . . . . 17 C4
Glenburn Rd BS15 . . . . . 20 B1
Glencairn Ave GL4 . . . . 118 C1
Glencairn Cl GL50 . . . . . 130 A8
Glencairn Park Rd GL50 130 A8
Glencarn Pl 13 GL16 . . . 155 A7
Glencoe La GL17 . . . . . . 164 D4
Glencoyne Ct 1 BS10 . . 28 C2
Glencoyne Sq BS10 . . . . 28 C2
Glen Ct GL10 . . . . 97 F8
Glendale
  17 Bristol BS8 . . . . .7 F6
  Bristol, Downend BS16 . . 20 E8
  Bristol, Hillfields BS16 . . . 20 C3
Glendare St BS5 . . . . 9 C6
Glendevon Rd BS14 . . . . 3 A3
Glendower Cl GL3 . . . . . 127 F8
Glendower Ho 5 BS8 . . . .7 F7
Glen Dr BS9 . . . . 17 D5
Gleneagles BS37 . . . . . . 43 E1
Gleneagles Dr BS10 . . . . 27 D3
Gleneagles Rd BS30 . . . 11 B6
Glenfall BS37 . . . . 32 D7
Glenfall Com Prim Sch
  GL52 . . . . 131 C6
Glenfall St GL52 . . . . . . 133 F2
Glenfall Way GL52 . . . . 131 B6
Glenfrome Prim Sch BS5 . 19 B4
Glenfrome Rd BS2 . . . . . 19 B3
Glen La BS4 . . . . .9 D2
Glenlea Gr GL51 . . . . . . 129 F5
Glen Park Cres GL5 . . . . 99 A4
Glen Park Gdns BS5 . . . . 10 A8
Glen Pk
  Bristol, Eastville BS5 . . . 19 C2
  Bristol, St George BS5 . . . 10 A8
Glenroy Ave BS15 . . . . . 20 B1
Glensanda Ct GL50 . . . . 26 C7
Glenside Cl BS16 . . . . . . 20 C7
Glenside Hospl Mus ★
  BS16 . . . . 19 E5
Glenside Pk 3 BS16 . . . 19 E5
Glen The
  Bristol, Hanham BS15 . . . 10 B4
  Bristol, Redland BS6 . . . . 18 B3
  Saltford BS31 . . . . .5 F1
  Yate BS37 . . . . 43 E2
Glenthorne Cl GL10 . . . 101 F1
Glentworth Rd
  Bristol, Clifton Wood
    BS8 . . . . 194 B2
  Bristol, Redland BS6 . . . . 18 C2
Glenview Rd BS4 . . . . . . .9 D2
Glenville Par GL3 . . . . . 120 A7
Glenwood BS30 . . . . . . 11 B4
Glenwood Rd BS10 . . . . 18 C7
Glevum Cl
  Bristol BS16 . . . . 21 C7
  Gloucester GL2 . . . . . . 127 B4
Glevum Ct 11 GL51 . . . . 132 D2
Glevum Sh Ctr GL4 . . . . 119 C4
Glevum Way GL4 . . . . . 119 E4
Glevum Works Trad Est
  GL1 . . . . 118 F7
Glevum Works (Trad Est)
  GL1 . . . . 119 A7
Gloster Ades Rd WR11 . . 188 B6
Gloster Ave BS5 . . . . . . 19 D3
Gloucester Acad GL14 . 191 B5
Gloucester Bsns Pk GL3 . 120 B6

Gloucester Cl BS34 . . . . . 29 D5
Gloucester Cotts 5
  GL50 . . . . 133 B2
Gloucester Ho 12 BS2 . . 195 C3
Gloucester House Mews
  GL12 . . . . 68 A8
Gloucester La
  20 Bristol BS2 . . . . 195 C3
  Mickleton GL55 . . . . . . 189 A6
Gloucester Mus & Art Gal ★
  GL1 . . . . 196 B2
Gloucester Pl GL52 . . . . 193 C4
Gloucester Prison Mus ★
  GL1 . . . . 196 A3
Gloucester Quays GL2 . . 196 A1
Gloucester Rd
  Almondsbury BS32, BS35 . 40 C6
  Andoversford GL54 . . . . 166 D6
  Avonmouth BS11 . . . . . 26 A1
  Bristol, Bishopston BS7 . . 18 E4
  Bristol, Patchway BS34 . . 28 B7
  Bristol, Staple Hill BS16 . . 20 E3
  Cheltenham GL51 . . . . . 132 C1
  Cirencester GL7 . . . . . . 190 B6
  Coleford GL16 . . . . 155 A5
  Corse GL19 . . . . 172 B8
  Mitcheldean GL17 . . . . . 164 D5
  Newton BS13 . . . . 85 C8
  Painswick GL6 . . . . 111 F1
  Stone GL13 . . . . 77 F3
  Stonehouse GL10 . . . . . 101 F1
  Tadwick BA1 . . . . 13 F2
  Tewkesbury GL20 . . . . . 181 F1
  Thornbury BS35 . . . . . . 64 C3
  Tutshill NP16 . . . . 73 A2
  Upleadon GL18 . . . . . . 171 D5
Gloucester Rd N BS7,
  BS34 . . . . 29 A4
Gloucester Retail Pk
  GL4 . . . . 119 C8
Gloucester Road Prim Sch
  GL51 . . . . 133 B2
Gloucester Row
  7 Bristol BS8 . . . . .7 F1
  Kingswood GL12 . . . . . . 67 F8
Gloucester Royal Hospl
  GL1 . . . . 196 C3
Gloucester Rugby Football
  Gd GL1 . . . . 196 B4
Gloucestershire Airport
  GL51 . . . . 128 D8
Gloucestershire Coll
  GL2 . . . . 126 C1
Gloucestershire Coll of Art &
  Tech GL51 . . . . 132 D2
Gloucestershire Cty Cricket
  Club ★ BS7 . . . . 18 F4
Gloucestershire Royal Hospl
  GL1 . . . . 127 A2
Gloucestershire
  Warwickshire Rly ★
  GL54 . . . . 183 D1
Gloucestershire &
  Warwickshire Rly ★
  Bishop's Cleeve GL52 . . . 138 B5
  Toddington GL54 . . . . . 184 C1
  Winchcombe GL54 . . . . 174 B8
Gloucester Ski Ctr ★ GL4 119 B3
Gloucester St
  12 Bristol, Clifton BS8 . . . .7 F7
  Bristol, Eastville BS5 . . . 19 D3
  5 Bristol, St Pauls BS2 . . 195 B4
  Cirencester GL7 . . . . . . 190 B6
  Newent GL18 . . . . 171 A4
  Painswick GL6 . . . . 103 F8
  2 Stroud GL5 . . . . 99 C7
  Winchcombe GL54 . . . . 174 A7
  Wotton-u-E GL12 . . . . . 68 A7
Gloucester Sta GL1 . . . . 196 A2
Gloucester Waterways Mus ★
  GL1 . . . . 196 A2
Glynbridge Ct 3 GL1 . . 118 F7
Glynbridge Gdns GL51 . . 132 F5
Glyndthorpe Gr 12 GL51 129 E5
Glynfield Rise GL5 . . . . . 98 C2
Glynrosa Rd GL53 . . . . . 131 B5
Glyn Terr GL5 . . . . 99 E3
Glyn Vale BS3 . . . . .8 E1
Goddard Way
  Bristol BS10 . . . . 28 A1
  Gloucester GL4 . . . . . . 118 D2
Godfrey Cl GL51 . . . . . . 130 A7
Godfrey Ct 7 BS30 . . . . 10 F4
Godwin Cl 15 GL52 . . . 133 F2
Godwin Rd GL54 . . . . . 174 A8
Goffenton Dr BS16 . . . . 20 B6
Goldcrest Ct 6 GL10 . . . 97 F8
Goldcrest Rd BS37 . . . . 32 F7
Goldcrest Wy BS35 . . . . 38 C3
Golden Arrow Wy GL4 . . 120 A4
Golden Cl GL4 . . . . 118 C2
Golden Farm Rd GL7 . . . 190 E4
Golden Hay WR11 . . . . . 183 F7
Golden Hill BS6 . . . . 18 C5
Golden Jubilee Way GL5 . 98 E6
Golden La GL12 . . . . 67 F4
Golden Lion Ct BS1 . . . . 195 B2
Golden Miller Rd GL50 . 133 C5
Golden Vale GL3 . . . . . . 128 B6
Golden Valley
  Brimscombe GL5 . . . . . 148 A5
  Newent GL18 . . . . 171 D4
Golden Valley La BS30 . . 11 F2

Goldfinch Way BS16 . . . . . 22 C4
Goldfoot Ho GL51 . . . . . . 132 F1
Goldney Ave
　Bristol, Clifton Wood
　　BS8 . . . . 194 A2
　Bristol, Warmley BS30 . . . . 11 C7
Goldney Ct 7 BS16 . . . . . . 19 E3
Goldney Rd BS8 . . . . 194 A2
Goldsborough Cl GL4 . . . . 119 B6
Goldsbury Wlk BS11 . . . . . 27 A1
Goldsmith Cl GL51 . . . . . . 132 E2
Goldsmith Rd GL51 . . . . . . 132 E2
Goldsmiths Ho BS2 . . . . . 195 C2
Golf Club La
　Saltford BS31 . . . . 5 E2
　Watermead GL3 . . . . 120 C5
Golf Course La BS34 . . . . . 28 F3
Golf Course Rd GL6 . . . . . 111 F2
Gooch Cl WR11 . . . . 188 C2
Gooch Ct BS30 . . . . 11 C3
Goode Cl 2 GL13 . . . . 92 A3
Goodeve Pk BS9 . . . . 17 D3
Goodeve Rd BS9 . . . . 17 D3
Goodhind St BS5 . . . . 9 A8
Goodier's La GL20 . . . . . . 182 A7
Goodmans Terr 5 GL7 . . . 152 E4
Goodmoor Cres GL3 . . . . 128 A6
Good Neighbours La
　NP25 . . . . 154 B7
Goodneston Rd BS16 . . . . . 20 A3
Goodrich Castle★ HR9 . . . 163 A6
Goodrich CE Prim Sch
　HR9 . . . . 163 A6
Goodrich Cl BS37 . . . . 43 B1
Goodrich Hill GL19 . . . . . 172 D4
Goodrich Rd GL52 . . . . . . 134 C2
Goodridge Ave GL2 . . . . . 118 B3
Goodridge Trad Est GL2 . . 118 A4
Goodring Hill BS11 . . . . . . 27 A1
Good Shepherd Cl BS7 . . . 18 C4
Goodwin Ct GL1 . . . . 118 E7
Goodwin Dr BS14 . . . . 2 F4
Goodwood Gdns BS16 . . . . 30 F1
Goodyere St GL1 . . . . 196 C1
Goolden St BS4 . . . . 9 A3
Goose Acre BS32 . . . . 29 F6
Gooseacre Ct GL7 . . . . . . 190 C6
Gooseacre La GL7 . . . . . . 190 C6
Goosebay Dr GL2 . . . . . . 110 C7
Goose Gn
　Bristol BS30 . . . . 11 C5
　Frampton Cotterell BS36 . . 31 C8
　Yate BS37 . . . . 43 E3
Goose Green Way BS37 . . . 43 E4
Goose La GL14 . . . . 157 F8
Gooseland Cl BS14 . . . . 2 F3
Gooselands SN16 . . . . 141 B3
Gopshill La GL54 . . . . 183 E1
Gordano Gdns BS20 . . . . . 16 B4
Gordon Ave BS5 . . . . 19 E1
Gordon Cl
　Bristol BS5 . . . . 19 E1
　Broadway WR12 . . . . 185 B8
　Higham GL2 . . . . 125 E5
Gordon Rd
　14 Bristol, St Pauls BS2 . . 18 F1
　Bristol, Victoria Park BS8 . 194 B2
　Bristol, Whitehall BS5 . . . . 19 D1
　Cheltenham GL53 . . . . . . 130 C5
Gordon Terr
　Brimscombe GL5 . . . . 99 F1
　Stroud GL5 . . . . 99 D7
Gore Rd BS3 . . . . 8 A3
Gore's Marsh Rd BS3 . . . . . 8 A2
Gorham Cl BS11 . . . . 27 C2
Gorlands Rd BS37 . . . . 44 C1
Gorlangton Cl BS14 . . . . . . 3 A7
Gorse Bglws GL16 . . . . . . 155 A6
Gorse Cl
　Bourton-on-t-W GL54 . . . 169 A7
　Gloucester GL4 . . . . 119 F4
Gorse Cover Rd BS35 . . . . 38 A7
Gorse Hill BS16 . . . . 20 C3
Gorse La
　Bristol BS8 . . . . 194 B2
　Cold Ashton BS30, SN14 . . 13 D7
　Sling GL16 . . . . 155 B3
Gorse Mdw GL54 . . . . 169 A6
Gorse Rd GL52 . . . . 137 F5
Gorse The GL54 . . . . 169 A7
Gorsley Bglws HR9 . . . . . . 170 B4
Gorsley Goffs Prim Sch
　HR9 . . . . 170 B5
Gosditch
　Ashton Keynes SN6 . . . . . 142 F4
　Latton SN6 . . . . 143 E6
Gosditch Cl GL50 . . . . 133 D3
Gosditch St GL7 . . . . 190 C5
Gosforth Cl BS10 . . . . 28 B1
Gosforth Rd BS10 . . . . 28 B1
Goshawk Rd GL2 . . . . 117 F3
Goslet Rd BS14 . . . . 3 E5
Goss Wood Cnr GL2 . . . . . 109 E8
Gotherington Fields
　GL52 . . . . 137 E8
Gotherington La GL52 . . . 138 A5
Gotherington Prim Sch
　GL52 . . . . 138 B7
Gotherington Sta★
　GL52 . . . . 138 D8
Gothic Cotts GL1 . . . . 196 C2
Gotley Rd BS4 . . . . 9 D2
Gott Dr BS4 . . . . 9 D5

Gouda Way GL1 . . . . 196 B4
Gould Cl BS13 . . . . 2 C5
Gould Dr GL20 . . . . 182 C5
Goulston Rd BS13 . . . . 2 A5
Goulston Wlk BS13 . . . . . . 2 A5
Goulter St BS5 . . . . 9 B6
Gourney Cl BS11 . . . . 27 B2
Gover Rd BS15 . . . . 10 C3
Govier Way BS35 . . . . 38 C4
Gower Cotts NP16 . . . . 72 F2
Gowle Rd GL5 . . . . 99 D6
Grace Cl BS37 . . . . 44 C1
Grace Ct BS16 . . . . 20 D6
Grace Dr
　Bristol BS15 . . . . 11 A8
　1 Northleach GL54 . . . . . 168 A1
Gracefield Sch BS16 . . . . . 20 C5
Grace Gdns GL51 . . . . 129 D7
Grace Park Rd BS4 . . . . 9 D1
Grace Rd BS16 . . . . 20 C5
Graces Field GL5 . . . . 99 A8
Graces Pitch 15 GL18 . . . . 171 A4
Graeme Cl BS16 . . . . 20 A4
Grafton Cl GL50 . . . . 193 B1
Grafton La GL19 . . . . 180 B3
Grafton Rd
　Cheltenham GL50 . . . . . . 193 A1
　Gloucester GL2 . . . . 127 B3
Graham Cl GL20 . . . . 192 D5
Graham Gdns GL2 . . . . . . 127 B3
Graham Pl GL51 . . . . 132 D3
Graham Rd
　4 Bristol, Bedminster BS3 . . 8 C3
　Bristol, Downend BS16 . . . 20 F6
　21 Bristol, Upper Easton
　　BS5 . . . . 19 B1
Grahamstown Gr NP16 . . . . 61 B8
Grahamstown Rd NP16 . . . . 61 B8
Grainger Ct BS11 . . . . 16 E7
Grampian Cl BS30 . . . . 11 C4
Granary The
　Blockley GL56 . . . . 186 C7
　Bristol BS1 . . . . 195 A2
Granbrook La GL55 . . . . . 189 B7
Granby Hill BS8 . . . . 7 F6
Grandmother's Rock La
　BS30 . . . . 12 D2
Grange Ave
　Bristol, Hanham BS15 . . . . 10 D5
　Bristol, Little Stoke BS34 . . 29 C6
Grange Cl
　Bristol, Patchway BS32 . . . 40 C2
　Highworth SN6 . . . . 145 D3
　Minchinhampton GL6 . . . . 91 F6
Grange Cl N BS9 . . . . 18 B6
Grange Cotts GL8 . . . . 140 C3
Grange Court La GL19 . . . 165 D6
Grange Court Rd
　Bristol BS9 . . . . 18 A6
　Westbury-on-S GL14 . . . . 165 D2
Grange Ct
　Bristol BS15 . . . . 10 D5
　Bristol, Henleaze BS9 . . . . 18 B6
　Bristol, Westbury on Trym
　　BS9 . . . . 18 A8
　Northway GL20 . . . . 182 C5
Grange Dr
　Bishop's Cleeve GL52 . . . 137 F3
　Bristol BS16 . . . . 20 C6
Grangefield Prim Sch
　GL52 . . . . 137 E3
Grangefield Rd GL20 . . . . 182 C7
Grange La GL8 . . . . 140 B3
Grange Pk
　Bristol, Frenchay BS16 . . . 20 C8
　Bristol, Westbury on Trym
　　BS9 . . . . 18 B6
　St Arvans NP16 . . . . 72 A6
　Whitchurch HR9 . . . . 162 D4
Grange Prim Sch GL4 . . . 118 C3
Grange Rd
　Bristol, Bishopsworth BS13 . 2 A5
　Bristol, Victoria Park BS8 . 194 A3
　Gloucester GL4 . . . . 118 D1
　Northway GL20 . . . . 182 C5
　Saltford BS31 . . . . 5 C3
　St Arvans NP16 . . . . 72 A6
Grange Sch & Sports Coll
　The BS30 . . . . 11 B7
Grange The
　Bristol, Coombe Dingle
　　BS9 . . . . 17 D7
　Bristol, Sneyd Park BS9 . . . 17 F3
　Cheltenham GL51 . . . . . . 129 B6
　Gloucester GL2 . . . . 127 B2
　8 Moreton-in-M GL56 . . . 187 A3
Grange View GL5 . . . . 99 C8
Grangeville Cl BS30 . . . . . 11 B3
Grangewood Cl 4 BS16 . . . 20 C6
Granley Cl GL51 . . . . 129 E8
Granley Ct GL1 . . . . 118 D6
Granley Dr GL51 . . . . 129 F8
Granley Gdns GL51 . . . . . 129 E8
Granley Rd GL51 . . . . 129 F8
Granna La GL52 . . . . 138 D8
Granny's La BS15 . . . . 10 E6
Gransmoor Grange GL3 . . 120 B7
Grantham Cl 1 BS15 . . . . . 10 C8
Grantham Ho BS15 . . . . . . 20 C1
Grantham La BS15 . . . . . . 10 C8
Grantham Rd BS15 . . . . . . 20 C1
Grantley Cres GL7 . . . . . . 190 C3
Grantson Cl BS4 . . . . 9 E2
Granville Cl BS15 . . . . 10 B3

Granville St
　Bristol BS5 . . . . 9 C6
　Cheltenham GL50 . . . . . . 133 C3
　Gloucester GL1 . . . . 118 D6
　21 Monmouth/Trefynwy
　　NP25 . . . . 154 A7
Grasby Cl GL4 . . . . 119 E7
Grasmere Cl BS10 . . . . 18 A8
Grasmere Rd
　Cheltenham GL51 . . . . . . 129 F7
　Gloucester GL2 . . . . 127 C4
Grasmere Way NP16 . . . . . 61 A4
Grassington Dr BS37 . . . . . 33 A8
Grass Meers Dr BS14 . . . . . 3 A4
Grassmere Gdns BS30 . . . . 11 D6
Gratitude Rd BS5 . . . . 19 C1
Gratton Rd GL50 . . . . 193 A1
Gratton St GL50 . . . . 193 B1
Gravel Hill Rd N BS37 . . . . 44 A5
Gravel Pit Cotts GL52 . . . . 131 C6
Gravel Pit La GL52 . . . . . . 134 C5
Gravel Pits Cl GL20 . . . . . 182 C7
Gravel Wlk
　Southam GL52 . . . . 134 C8
　Tewkesbury GL20 . . . . . . 192 D5
Graveney Cl BS4 . . . . 9 D1
Graveney Rd GL54 . . . . . . 168 A1
Gravney Ct GL51 . . . . 132 E4
Gray Cl
　Bristol BS10 . . . . 27 E2
　Innsworth GL3 . . . . 127 E7
Grayle Rd BS10 . . . . 28 A2
Grayling Cl 7 GL4 . . . . . . 119 E5
Grayling Ho BS9 . . . . 17 F7
Gray Rd GL7 . . . . 151 A2
Gray's La 20 GL56 . . . . . . 187 A3
Grayston Cl GL20 . . . . 192 E6
Great Ann St BS2 . . . . 195 C3
Great Brockeridge BS9 . . . . 17 F6
Great Copsie Way 4 BS37 . 19 C8
Great Dowles BS30 . . . . . . 11 A4
Greatfield Dr GL53 . . . . . . 130 F5
Greatfield La
　Cheltenham, Hatherley
　　GL51 . . . . 129 E5
　Cheltenham, Warden Hill
　　GL51 . . . . 129 E5
Greatfield Park Prim Sch
　GL51 . . . . 129 F5
Great George St
　Bristol, Brandon Hill BS1 . 194 C2
　Bristol, St Pauls BS2 . . . . 195 C3
Great Gr GL4 . . . . 119 D7
Great Hayes Rd BS14 . . . . . 3 A6
Great Leaze BS30 . . . . 11 A4
Great Mdw BS34 . . . . 30 A6
Great Meadow Rd BS32 . . . 29 F6
Great Norwood St GL50 . 193 B1
Great Orch GL5 . . . . 99 E3
Great Park Rd BS32 . . . . . . 40 C3
Great Rissington Prim Sch
　GL54 . . . . 169 D4
Great Rose La SN26 . . . . . 144 D3
Great Stoke Way
　Bristol, Great Stoke BS34 . 30 A5
　Bristol, Harry Stoke BS34 . 29 D3
Great Western Bsns Pk
　BS37 . . . . 43 B3
Great Western Ct
　Bristol BS34 . . . . 29 F4
　3 Gloucester GL1 . . . . . . 127 A1
Great Western La BS5 . . . . . 9 C6
Great Western Railway Mus★
　GL16 . . . . 155 A5
Great Western Rd
　Cheltenham GL50 . . . . . . 193 A4
　Gloucester GL1 . . . . 196 C3
　Sharpness GL13 . . . . 93 B1
Great Western Terr
　GL50 . . . . 193 A4
Great Witcombe Roman
　Villa★ GL3 . . . . 120 F1
Great Wood Cl BS13 . . . . . 2 C4
Grebe Cl GL4 . . . . 119 D5
Grebe Gdns GL3 . . . . 120 B4
Grebe Sq GL54 . . . . 169 D6
Green Acre
　Bream GL15 . . . . 147 D8
　Watermead GL3 . . . . 120 C5
Green Acre Rd BS14 . . . . . . 3 A3
Greenacres
　Bristol BS9 . . . . 17 E7
　Twyning GL20 . . . . 181 F8
Greenacres Park Homes
　BS36 . . . . 31 E5
Greenacres Pk GL7 . . . . . . 152 A3
Greenacre Wy GL52 . . . . . 137 F5
Greenaways
　Newent GL18 . . . . 170 F5
　Stroud GL5 . . . . 98 D6
Green Bank GL3 . . . . 120 E4
Greenbank Avenue E BS5 . 19 C1
Greenbank Avenue W
　BS5 . . . . 19 C1
Greenbank Cl GL17 . . . . . 164 B3
Greenbank Rd
　Bristol, Hanham BS15 . . . . 10 D5
　Bristol, Lower Easton BS5 . 19 D2
　Bristol, Southville BS3 . . . . 8 A4
Greenbanks NP25 . . . . 146 B7
Greenbank View BS5 . . . . . 19 D2
Green Cl
　Bristol BS7 . . . . 19 A8
　Honeybourne WR11 . . . . 188 C6
　Uley GL11 . . . . 89 C2
　Watermead GL3 . . . . 120 E4

Green Colley Cl HR9 . . . . 163 B6
Green Cres BS36 . . . . 31 B6
Green Croft BS5 . . . . 20 A1
Green Ct BS35 . . . . 50 A2
Greendale Rd
　Bristol, Lower Knowle BS3 . 8 E2
　Bristol, Redland BS6 . . . . . 18 B3
Green Dell Cl BS10 . . . . . . 27 D3
Green Dragon Rd BS36 . . . 30 D5
Greendown BS5 . . . . 10 A7
Greenfield Ave BS10 . . . . . 18 D8
Greenfield Cl GL17 . . . . . . 163 D3
Greenfield E-Act Prim Acad
　. . . . . 2 C7
Greenfield Rd
　Bristol BS10 . . . . 28 D1
　Coleford GL16 . . . . 155 A6
　Joy's Green GL17 . . . . . . 163 D3
Greenfield Vw SN6 . . . . . . 142 C3
Greenfinch Lodge BS16 . . . 19 E6
Green Gdns BS30 . . . . 11 D6
Greenhaven 6 BS5 . . . . . . 19 C1
Green Hayes BS37 . . . . 33 C8
Greenhill BS35 . . . . 51 A4
Green Hill BS35 . . . . 51 A4
Greenhill Cl GL14 . . . . . . 191 E5
Greenhill Ct GL4 . . . . 118 B2
Greenhill Down BS35 . . . . 51 A5
Greenhill Dr GL2 . . . . 118 A3
Greenhill Flats GL5 . . . . . . 99 E3
Greenhill Gdns BS35 . . . . 51 A4
Greenhill Gr BS3 . . . . 8 A2
Greenhill Ho GL52 . . . . . . 137 F3
Greenhill La
　Alveston BS35 . . . . 50 F4
　Bristol BS11 . . . . 27 C1
Greenhill Par 5 BS35 . . . . 51 A5
Greenhill Rd BS35 . . . . . . 51 A5
Greenhills Cl GL53 . . . . . . 130 E5
Greenhills Rd GL53 . . . . . 130 F5
Greenhouse La GL6 . . . . . 104 A7
Greenings The GL51 . . . . . 129 F5
Green La
　Avonmouth BS11 . . . . 26 B1
　Chedworth GL54 . . . . . . 159 B6
　Churchdown GL3 . . . . . . 128 C4
　Easter Compton BS35 . . . . 38 C1
　Evenlode GL56 . . . . 177 C7
　Gloucester GL3 . . . . 120 A6
　Hardwicke GL2 . . . . 109 E6
　Little Witcombe GL3 . . . . 121 C3
　Marshfield SN14 . . . . 14 E8
　Moreton Valence GL2 . . . 101 A6
　Naunton WR8 . . . . 180 D10
　Rangeworthy BS37, GL12 . 53 B2
　Severn Beach BS35 . . . . . . 38 B8
　Sherston SN16 . . . . 58 C1
　Tewkesbury GL20 . . . . . . 182 B4
　Tytherington GL12 . . . . . 52 B8
　Winterbourne BS36 . . . . . 30 C7
　Winterbourne BS36 . . . . . 30 D7
Green Lake Cl GL54 . . . . . 168 F8
Greenlands 12 NP25 . . . . . 154 A7
Greenlands Way BS10 . . . . 27 F4
Greenleaze
　Bristol BS4 . . . . 9 B1
　Marston Meysey SN6 . . . . 144 B8
Greenleaze Ave BS16 . . . . . 30 D1
Greenleaze Cl BS16 . . . . . . 30 D1
Green Meadow Bank
　GL52 . . . . 137 E3
Greenmeadows Pk GL51 . 128 F8
Greenmeadow Park Cvn Site
　GL51 . . . . 129 D5
Greenmore Rd BS4 . . . . . . 9 B2
Greenore BS15 . . . . 10 C7
Greenpark Rd BS10 . . . . . . 28 E1
Green Pastures NP25 . . . . 154 A3
Green Pippin Cl GL2 . . . . 127 C2
Green Pk
　Bristol BS30 . . . . 11 D6
　Hardwicke GL2 . . . . 109 E6
Greenridge Cl BS13 . . . . . . 1 E4
Green's Cl GL54 . . . . 169 C4
Greenside Cl BS10 . . . . 27 D3
Greensplott Rd BS11 . . . . . 26 E7
Green St
　Bristol BS3 . . . . 8 F4
　Bushley GL19, GL20 . . . . 181 B5
　Chepstow/Cas-Gwent NP16 60 B8
　Dursley GL11 . . . . 88 C6
　Watermead GL3 . . . . 120 D3
Greenstreet GL10 . . . . 97 F8
Green The
　Bishop's Cleeve GL52 . . . 137 F3
　Bledington OX7 . . . . 177 E1
　Bristol, New Cheltenham
　　BS15 . . . . 20 E2
　Bristol, Stoke Gifford BS34 . 29 E4
　6 Broadway WR12 . . . . . 185 B8
　Chepstow/Cas-Gwent NP16 60 B5
　Chipping Campden GL55 . 189 A1
　Chipping Sodbury BS37 . . 34 A8
　Churchdown GL3 . . . . . . 128 C3
　Cirencester, Siddington
　　GL7 . . . . 190 D4
　Cirencester, The Beeches
　　GL7 . . . . 190 E5
　Cromhall GL12 . . . . 53 B8
　Fairford GL7 . . . . 152 D4
　Frampton on Severn GL2 . 157 F2
　Great Wolford CV36 . . . . 187 E5

Green The continued
　Highworth SN6 . . . . 145 C3
　Honeybourne WR11 . . . . 188 C6
　Iron Acton BS37 . . . . 42 D4
　Luckington SN14 . . . . . . 47 E4
　10 Moreton-in-M GL56 . . 187 A3
　Newnham GL14 . . . . 156 F6
　18 Northleach GL54 . . . . 168 A1
　Oaksey SN16 . . . . 141 F4
　Olveston BS35 . . . . 50 A2
　Pill BS20 . . . . 16 D4
　Tetbury GL8 . . . . 140 C4
　Uckington GL51 . . . . 132 D6
　Uley GL11 . . . . 89 C2
　Woodmancote GL52 . . . . 138 C3
Greenview
　Bristol BS30 . . . . 11 A2
　Quenington GL7 . . . . 152 D7
Greenway GL52 . . . . 138 B3
Green Way GL3 . . . . 120 E5
Greenway Bush La BS3 . . . . 8 B4
Greenway Cl GL51 . . . . . . 129 D1
Greenway Dr BS10 . . . . . . 18 B8
Greenway Ho 10 BS6 . . . . 18 B2
Greenway La
　Bristol BS10 . . . . 28 D1
　Charlton Kings GL52 . . . . 131 C2
　Cheltenham GL53 . . . . . . 122 B4
　Cold Ashton SN14 . . . . . . 13 D5
　Gretton GL54 . . . . 183 F1
　Little Shurdington GL51,
　　GL53 . . . . 121 E8
　Llandogo NP25 . . . . 146 A8
　Shurdington GL51 . . . . . . 129 D1
Greenway Pk BS10 . . . . . . 18 B8
Greenway Rd
　Blockley GL56 . . . . 186 C5
　Bristol BS6 . . . . 18 B2
　Cinderford GL14 . . . . . . 191 C5
Greenways
　Bristol BS15 . . . . 21 A3
　Gloucester GL4 . . . . 119 E8
　Gloucester GL4 . . . . 127 E1
　Lydney GL15 . . . . 147 F5
　Winchcombe GL54 . . . . . 174 A8
Greenways Dr GL16 . . . . . 155 B4
Greenways Rd BS37 . . . . . 43 E3
Greenway The
　Bristol BS16 . . . . 20 C5
　Gloucester GL1 . . . . 118 D6
Greenwich Apartments
　BS6 . . . . 18 C3
Green Wlk BS4 . . . . 9 A1
Greenwood Cl
　Bristol BS7 . . . . 18 E7
　Gloucester GL3 . . . . 120 B6
Greenwood Dr BS35 . . . . . 50 F4
Greenwood Rd BS4 . . . . . . 9 A1
Greet Rd GL54 . . . . 174 A8
Gregory Ct BS30 . . . . 11 A4
Grenadier Cl GL4 . . . . 119 F6
Grenadier Rd GL51 . . . . . 132 E4
Grenville Chapel 5 BS8 . . . 7 F5
Grenville Cl
　Bristol BS5 . . . . 9 F5
　Innsworth GL3 . . . . 127 F8
Grenville Pl 7 BS1 . . . . . . 7 F5
Grenville Rd BS6 . . . . 18 E3
Gresham Ct 5 GL51 . . . . . 132 E2
Gretton Prim Sch GL54 . . 183 F1
Gretton Rd
　Gotherington GL52 . . . . 138 D5
　Winchcombe GL54 . . . . . 174 A8
Gretton View GL20 . . . . . 183 E4
Greve Ct 5 BS30 . . . . 10 F4
Grevel La GL55 . . . . 189 A4
Greville Cl GL2 . . . . 126 E4
Greville Ct GL51 . . . . 129 F8
Greville Rd BS3 . . . . 8 C4
Greville St BS3 . . . . 8 C4
Grevil Rd 3 GL51 . . . . . . 132 E4
Greyfriars GL1 . . . . 196 B2
Greyfriars Church★ GL1 . . 196 B2
Greyfriars Wlk GL7 . . . . . 190 B2
Grey Gables BS35 . . . . 50 A3
Greyhound Gdns GL2 . . . . 127 B4
Greylag Cres GL20 . . . . . . 192 E3
Greylands Rd BS13 . . . . . . 1 F7
Greyrick Ct GL55 . . . . 189 A6
Greys Cl 5 GL6 . . . . 148 B6
Greystoke Ave BS10 . . . . . 28 C1
Greystoke Gdns BS10 . . . . 18 A8
Greystone Lodge GL3 . . . . 120 B7
Greystones BS16 . . . . 30 E1
Greystones La GL54 . . . . . 169 A4
Grierson Cl GL3 . . . . 120 B6
Griffin Cl GL54 . . . . 177 A4
Griffin Ct GL54 . . . . 177 A4
Griffiths Ave GL51 . . . . . . 132 F1
Griffon Cl GL2 . . . . 117 F3
Griggfield Wlk BS14 . . . . . . 3 A7
Griggs Cl 3 GL55 . . . . . . 189 A4
Grimsbury Rd BS15 . . . . . 11 A7
Grimwade Cl GL51 . . . . . . 132 F1
Grindell Rd BS5 . . . . 9 D7
Grinfield Ave BS13 . . . . . . 2 C4
Grinfield Ct BS13 . . . . 2 C4
Grisedale Cl GL2 . . . . 127 D5
Grist Mill Cl GL51 . . . . . . 132 D5
Grittleton Rd BS7 . . . . 18 E8
Groaten The WR11 . . . . . . 183 D8
Grosvenor Ct 2 BS6 . . . . . 18 B1
Grosvenor Ho GL1 . . . . . . 196 B3
Grosvenor Pl S GL52 . . . . 193 C4
Grosvenor Rd
　Bristol BS2 . . . . 18 F1

Grosvenor Rd *continued*
Gloucester GL2 127 B2
Stonehouse GL10 101 F1
Grosvenor St GL52 193 C3
Grosvenor Terr GL52 193 C3
Grouse Gdns GL3 120 B4
Grove Ave
Bristol BS1 195 A1
Bristol, Coombe Dingle BS9 17 C7
3 Bristol, Fishponds BS16 19 F4
Honeybourne WR11 188 C7
Grove Bank BS16 30 C1
Grove Cotts GL5 98 F8
Grove Cres
7 Coleford GL16 155 A6
Gloucester GL4 127 D1
Grove Ct BS9 17 E5
Grovefield GL19 180 A4
Grovefield Way GL51 129 B7
Grove Gdns GL8 140 B5
Grove Hall BS4 9 D2
Grove Hill SN6 145 C4
Grove Ind Est The BS34 29 B8
Grove La
Cirencester GL7 190 D5
Hinton SN14 23 C6
Lydney GL15 92 B6
Whitminster GL2 100 F4
Grovelands GL4 127 E1
Grovelands Cl 1 GL53 131 B6
Grove Leaze BS11 16 D6
Grove Orch SN6 145 C4
Grove Park Ave BS4 9 D2
Grove Park Rd
Bristol BS4 9 D2
Stroud GL5 99 C8
Grove Park Terr BS16 19 F4
Grove Pk
Bristol, Brislington BS4 9 D2
Bristol, Redland BS6 18 C2
Whitecroft GL15 155 F1
Grove Rd
Berry Hill GL16 155 A7
Bristol, Coombe Dingle BS9 17 D8
Bristol, Fishponds BS16 19 F4
Bristol, Redland BS6 18 A2
Innsworth GL3 127 F6
Lydney GL15 147 F6
Whitecroft GL15 155 F1
Grovesend Rd BS35 51 D8
Groves Pl GL7 152 E3
Grove St
Cheltenham GL50 193 A4
Gloucester GL1 196 C1
Groves The BS13 2 D4
Grove The
Avening GL8 140 B8
Bristol, Canon's Marsh BS1 195 A1
Bristol, Oldland BS30 11 A4
Bristol, Patchway BS34 29 B7
Cheltenham, Battledown GL52 134 A1
Cheltenham, Lansdown GL50 130 B8
Chelworth SN16 141 E5
Kempsford GL7 144 E7
5 Moreton-in-M GL56 187 B3
Rangeworthy BS37 43 A8
Selsley GL5 98 E4
Stonehouse GL10 98 A6
Stroud GL5 98 D6
Grove View
Bristol BS16 19 E6
Greet GL54 184 A1
Grump St CV36 189 F6
Gryphons The 16 GL52 133 F2
Guan Rd GL3 120 B4
Guardian Ct
10 Bristol BS8 7 F7
Cheltenham GL53 130 F6
Guernsey Ave BS4 9 F4
Guest Ave BS16 21 B7
Guestriss Cotts GL50 133 C5
Guggle La 7 GL54 168 A1
Guild Ct BS1 195 B2
Guildford Rd BS4 9 E6
Guildings Way GL10 98 A4
Guinea La
Bristol BS16 20 A4
Bristol BS16 20 A5
Guinea St
Bristol BS1 195 A1
Gloucester GL1 196 C4
Guinevere Rd GL51 132 F1
Guise Ave GL3 120 F4
Guise Cl GL2 109 F8
Gullimores Gdns BS13 2 B4
Gullivers Pl BS37 33 A8
Gullons Cl BS13 2 A6
Gullon Wlk BS13 1 F5
Gullybrook La 3 BS5 9 B7
Gully La BS35 64 E7
Gully The BS36 30 F7
Gumstool Hill 13 GL8 140 C4
Gunhouse La GL5 99 D5
Gunning Cl BS15 10 D6
Gunter's Hill BS5 10 A6
Gupshill Cl GL20 192 C2
Gurney Ave GL4 118 D2
Gustav Holst Birthplace Mus★ GL52 193 C4
Guthrie Rd BS8 194 A4
Gwentlands Cl NP16 60 E7
Gwernant Rd GL51 129 F6
Gwilliam St BS3 8 D3
Gwilym Cl GL11 80 C8
Gwinnett Ct GL51 129 E2
Gwy Ct NP16 72 F1
Gwyn St BS2 18 E1
Gyde Ho GL6 111 F1
Gyde Rd GL6 111 F1
Gydynap La GL5 91 A7
Gypsy La
Gorsley GL18 170 C3
Marshfield SN14 14 F7
Gypsy Patch North Ind Est BS34 29 B6

H

Haberdashers' Agincourt Sch NP25 154 A8
Haberdashers Monmouth Sch for Grils NP25 154 A8
Haberfield Hill BS8 16 E2
Haberfield Ho 1 BS8 7 F6
Hacket Hill BS35 51 F8
Hacket La BS35 51 F8
Haddrell Ct BS35 50 F5
Hadfield Cl GL19 172 A8
Hadley Ct BS30 11 B6
Hadley Rd GL11 87 E4
Hadnock Rd NP25 154 A8
Hadnock Road Ind Est 5 NP25 154 A8
Hadow Way GL2 109 F8
Hadrian Cl
Bristol BS9 17 C4
Lydney GL15 92 B4
Hadrians Way GL4 119 F7
Hadrians Wlk BS16 21 C6
Hadwells Rd BS34 28 F7
Hague Ave GL11 87 F4
Haig Cl BS9 17 B7
Hailes Abbey & Mus★ GL54 184 D1
Hailes Green Barns GL54 174 C8
Hailes Rd GL4 119 D7
Hailes St 28 GL54 174 A7
Hakeburn Rd GL7 190 C5
Halbrow Cres BS16 20 C5
Haldon Cl BS3 8 D1
Hale Cl BS15 10 D4
Hale La GL6 103 F8
Hales Cl GL52 134 A1
Hales Horn Cl BS32 29 D6
Hale's Rd GL52 134 A1
Hale Wood/Coed Hale NP16 60 C8
Halfacre Cl BS14 3 A3
Halfacre La BS14 3 B4
Halford Ho GL2 118 C4
Halfway Pitch GL6 103 B4
Halifax Rd BS37 43 D4
Halifax Wy 13 GL56 187 B3
Halland Rd GL53 130 D5
Hallards Cl BS11 16 F8
Hallen Cl
Bristol, Emerson's Green BS16 21 C6
Bristol, Henbury BS10 27 D3
Hall End La BS37 53 D2
Hallen Dr BS9 17 C7
Hallen Ind Est BS10 27 A7
Hallen Rd BS10 27 D4
Hall La
Cold Ashton BA1, SN14 13 E2
Horton BS37 45 E5
Lower Hamswell BA1 13 B3
Hallmead Cl GL51 132 D5
Hall Rd GL53 130 D4
Hallsfield SN6 143 E5
Halls Gdns BS34 30 A4
Halls Rd BS15 10 D8
Hall St BS3 8 C2
Hallwood Dr HR8 178 D8
Halmore La GL13 86 A8
Halsbury Rd BS6 18 B4
Halstock Ave BS16 19 F3
Halston Dr BS2 195 C4
Halswell Gdns BS13 2 B4
Halt End BS14 3 C3
Halton Wy
6 Gloucester GL2 118 A1
Quedgeley GL2 110 A8
Halwyn Cl BS9 17 D5
Hambidge La GL7 153 E3
Hamble Cl BS35 51 C8
Hambledon Cl GL7 150 F2
Hamblins Cotts GL53 123 A5
Hambrook La BS34 30 A3
Hambrook Prim Sch BS16 30 D3
Hambrook St GL52 131 B7
Hambutts Dr GL6 103 E8
Hambutts Mead GL6 103 E8
Ham Cl GL52 131 C7
Hamer St GL1 127 B1
Hamfallow Ct GL13 85 D8
Ham Farm La BS16 21 B6
Hamfield La GL13 85 D3
Ham Gn BS20 16 D3
Hamilton Croft GL7 152 A2
Hamilton Ct GL51 132 D3
Hamilton Rd
Bristol, Southville BS3 8 B4
Bristol, Upper Easton BS5 9 B8
Hamilton St GL53 131 A7
Ham La
Bristol BS16 19 E6
Ham La *continued*
Charlton Kings GL52 131 D7
Doynton BS30 22 E1
Dundry BS41 1 D3
Kempsford GL7 144 F7
Oldbury-on-S BS35 63 C7
South Cerney GL7 142 F7
Hamlen Cl GL19 165 D6
Hamlet Cl GL51 132 E2
Hammersmith Bottom GL7 153 B7
Hammersmith Rd BS5 9 D8
Hammett Ct NP25 154 B7
Ham Mill La GL5 99 E3
Hammond Cl BS4 9 E1
Hammond Ct GL53 193 C1
Hammond Dr 3 GL54 168 A1
Hammond Gdns BS9 17 E7
Hammond Rd BS34 28 F7
Hammonds SN6 143 F4
Hammond Way
Cirencester GL7 190 C4
Gloucester GL4 127 D1
Hampden Cl BS37 43 D4
Hampden Rd BS4 9 B3
Hampden Way GL1 196 B2
Hampen Cotts GL54 167 A7
Hampshire Gdns GL16 155 A5
Hampshire Way BS37 43 F4
Hampstead Rd BS4 9 C3
Hampton Cl
Bristol BS30 11 A5
Cheltenham GL51 130 A5
Gloucester GL3 120 B7
Hampton Cnr BS11 16 E6
Hampton Ct
Bristol BS6 18 B1
Gloucester GL1 127 A3
Hampton Fields GL6 148 B2
Hampton Gr GL7 152 A3
Hampton Hill GL6, GL8 148 B1
Hampton La 17 BS6 18 B1
Hampton Mews GL15 92 B3
Hampton Pk BS6 18 B1
Hampton Pl GL3 128 A8
Hampton Rd BS6 18 B1
Hampton St
Bristol BS15 20 D1
Tetbury GL8 140 B4
Hampton Street Ind Est GL8 140 B5
Ham Rd
Andoversford GL54 166 A8
Ashleworth GL19 172 E5
Charlton Kings GL52, GL54 131 E7
Hamshill GL11 88 E6
Ham Sq GL52 131 C7
Hams Rd
Keynsham BS31 4 F7
Lydney GL15 92 B3
Ham The GL11 89 A6
Hanbury Cl BS15 10 D5
Hanbury Ct BS8 194 A4
Hanbury Ho NP16 60 C8
Hanbury Rd BS8 194 A4
Handel Ave 2 BS5 9 D7
Handel Cossham Ct 3 BS15 20 C1
Handel Rd BS31 4 E5
Handford Way BS30 11 B3
Handley La HR9 164 A8
Hanford Ct BS14 3 D7
Hangar Wy BS14 2 F5
Hangerberry New Rd GL17 163 D1
Hang Hill Rd GL15 155 D1
Hanham Abbots Jun Sch BS15 10 C4
Hanham Bsns Pk BS15 10 B5
Hanham Hall Hospl BS15 10 D4
Hanham Lodge BS15 10 D7
Hanham Mills BS15 10 D1
Hanham Rd BS15 10 D7
Hanham Woods Acad BS15 10 C4
Hankerton Rd SN16 142 B1
Hanley La NP16 73 E6
Hanman Rd GL1 118 F7
Hanman Villas GL2 124 C8
Hanna Ct GL50 193 B4
Hannah Boote Ho 8 GL52 134 A3
Hannah Cres
Siddington GL7 150 F2
South Cerney GL7 151 A2
Hannah More Prim Sch BS1 195 C2
Hannah Pl GL3 127 E7
Hannam Cl GL53 130 E4
Hanover Cl NP16 72 D1
Hanover Ct
Bristol, Filton BS34 29 A3
Bristol, St Pauls BS1 195 B3
14 Cheltenham GL51 130 B8
Cirencester GL7 190 D4
2 Tewkesbury GL20 192 C4
Tutshill NP16 61 A8
Hanover Gdns 2 GL6 91 B4
Hanover Ho
Bristol BS2 9 A7
Highworth SN6 145 C3
Hanover Lodge GL5 98 D7
Hanover Pl BS1 194 B1
Hanover St
9 Bristol, Brandon Hill BS1 194 C2
Hanover St *continued*
2 Bristol BS1 195 A2
Bristol, Russell Town BS5 9 C7
Cheltenham GL50 133 D3
Hanover Way 1 GL3 128 A7
Hanson Gdns GL52 137 D4
Hanstone Cl GL7 190 B2
Happerton La BS20 16 D2
Happy Land SN6 142 F4
Harbour Rd GL15 84 B8
Harbourside GL20 192 D5
Harbour View GL20 192 D5
Harbour Wall BS9 17 B4
Harbour Way BS1 194 C1
Harbour Wlk BS1 194 C1
Harbour Wy BS3 194 C1
Harbury Mews GL1 119 A8
Harbury Rd BS9 18 C7
Harcombe Hill BS36 30 E4
Harcombe Rd BS36 30 D5
Harcourt Ave BS5 10 A6
Harcourt Cl BS31 5 E2
Harcourt Hill BS6 18 C3
Harcourt Rd BS6 18 B3
Hardenhuish Rd BS4 9 D5
Harden Rd BS14 3 E5
Harding Pl BS31 5 B5
Harding Rd BS16 29 F2
Hardings Cl GL11 88 A1
Harding's Dr GL11 88 A1
Hardington Dr BS31 5 A2
Hardwick Ave NP16 60 E7
Hardwick Bank Rd GL20 182 B5
Hardwick Cl
Bristol, Broom Hill BS4 9 E3
Bristol, North Common BS30 11 D5
Hardwicke BS37 32 C7
Hardwicke Prim Sch GL2 109 E6
Hardwick Hill NP16 60 E7
Hardwick Hill La NP16 60 E8
Hardwick Rd BS20 16 C5
Hardy Ave BS3 8 A4
Hardy Ct BS30 10 F5
Hardy La BS32 50 A1
Hardy Rd
Bishop's Cleeve GL52 138 A4
Bristol BS3 8 B2
Harebell Pl GL4 119 E5
Hareclive Acad BS13 2 C4
Hareclive Rd BS13 2 C4
Harefield Cl BS15 10 C2
Harefield Gr GL50 130 C6
Hare La GL1 196 B3
Harescombe BS37 32 E7
Harescombe Dr GL1 127 A1
Haresdown Hill GL7 141 C8
Haresfield GL7 190 B8
Haresfield CE Prim Sch GL10 110 B1
Haresfield Ct GL10 110 A1
Haresfield La GL2, GL10 109 F5
Haresfield Lodge GL4 119 B4
Harewood Cl GL4 118 C1
Harewood Ho BS6 18 A3
Harewood Jun Sch GL4 118 C1
Harewood Rd BS5 20 A1
Harford Cl BS9 17 C7
Harford Dr BS16 30 C1
Harlech Way BS30 11 B2
Harleston St 1 BS5 9 A8
Harley Ct 3 BS8 7 F7
Harley Mews 2 BS8 7 F7
Harley Pl 4 BS8 7 F7
Harleys Field GL4 119 D7
Harling Ct 12 HR8 178 E8
Harmer Cl BS10 27 F3
Harness Cl GL2 118 B6
Harnham La GL54 166 E2
Harnhill Cl BS13 2 B4
Harnwood Sq BS7 18 E5
Harold Rd GL15 156 B2
Harolds Way BS15 10 C6
Harper Rd GL5 98 E8
Harpfield Cl GL52 137 F3
Harpfield Rd GL52 137 F2
Harp Hill GL52 134 B1
Harptree Ct 5 BS30 11 A4
Harptree Gr BS3 8 B2
Harptree Way GL17 164 D6
Harrier Cl GL20 192 E2
Harrington Ave BS14 3 E6
Harrington Cl BS30 5 E8
Harrington Dr GL51 129 F7
Harrington Gr BS14 3 E6
Harrington Rd BS14 3 E6
Harrington Wlk BS14 3 E6
Harris Barton BS36 31 B7
Harris Cl GL3 128 C5
Harris Ct BS30 10 F4
Harris Gdns GL54 169 D6
Harris Gr BS13 2 B3
Harrison Cl
Bristol BS16 21 B6
Newnham GL14 156 F6
Harrison Rd GL51 129 D2
Harrison Way GL15 92 C2
Harris Rd SN6 143 A5
Harrolds Cl 11 GL11 80 B8
Harrowdene Rd BS4 9 B3
Harrow Rd BS4 9 D3
Harry Stoke Rd BS34 29 E2
Harry Yates Way GL51 132 D4
Hartbury Cl GL51 132 C3
Hart Cl BS20 16 E4
Hartcliffe Rd BS4 2 E8
Hartcliffe Way BS3, BS4, BS13 2 C7
Hartcliffe Wlk BS4 2 F8
Hartfield Ave BS6 194 C4
Hartgill Cl BS13 2 B3
Hart Gn GL14 191 C2
Harthurstfield Pk GL51 132 B1
Hartington Pk BS6 18 C2
Hartington Rd GL1 118 C6
Hart La GL17 163 F4
Hartland Ho BS5 9 C6
Hartland Rd GL1 118 F6
Hartlands 22 GL18 171 A4
Hartlebury Way GL52 131 C6
Hartley Bridge Hill GL6 82 F8
Hartley Cl
Cheltenham GL53 130 F4
Chipping Sodbury BS37 44 C1
Hartley Gdns GL4 119 C7
Hartley La GL53 122 E8
Hartpury CE Prim Sch GL19 172 C3
Hartpury Coll
Blaisdon GL17 165 A4
Hartpury GL19 172 A1
Harts Barn Flower & Craft Ctr★ GL17 164 E5
Harts Cotts GL2 157 F2
Harts Croft BS37 43 F4
Harvard Ave WR11 188 C7
Harvard Cl 3 GL56 187 B3
Harvest Cl BS32 40 D1
Harvesters View GL52 137 D4
Harvest Gr GL51 132 D5
Harvest Way GL2 109 F7
Harvey Cl GL2 118 C5
Harveys La GL15 156 A2
Harvey's La
6 Bristol BS5 9 F8
Winchcombe GL54 139 F5
Harwell Cl GL4 118 D1
Harwood Ho 14 BS5 9 B7
Haselbury Gr BS31 5 E2
Hasfield Cl GL2 117 E1
Hasfield Rd GL19 172 C6
Haskins Ct 4 BS30 11 A4
Haslemere Ct GL3 120 F5
Haslemere Ind Est BS11 26 C2
Haslette Way GL51 129 E5
Hasnett Rd HR8 178 E8
Hassell Dr BS2 9 A7
Hastings Cl BS3 8 C1
Hastings Pl GL20 192 C2
Hastings Rd
Bristol BS3 8 C1
Cinderford GL14 191 C4
Hatcher's Cres SN26 144 D1
Hatchet La BS34 29 E4
Hatchet Rd BS34 29 E5
Hatchmere BS35 51 D8
Hatfield Rd GL1 119 A7
Hathaway Cl GL2 118 C4
Hathaway Ho BS2 195 A4
Hatherley BS37 32 E7
Hatherley Brake GL51 129 E7
Hatherley Court Rd GL51 130 B7
Hatherley Ct GL51 130 B7
Hatherley Gate GL51 130 B8
Hatherley Hall GL51 130 A7
Hatherley Ho 12 GL51 130 B8
Hatherley Inf Sch GL1 119 A7
Hatherley La GL51 129 D7
Hatherley Mews GL51 129 D7
Hatherley Rd
Bristol BS7 18 E4
Cheltenham GL51 129 F7
Gloucester GL1 119 A7
Hatherley St GL50 130 B7
Hatherop Castle Sch GL7 152 E8
Hatherop CE Prim Sch GL7 152 E8
Hatherop Rd GL7 152 E4
Hathorn Rd GL3 120 B6
Hathway Wlk BS5 9 A8
Hatters Cl BS36 30 E7
Hatters' La BS37 44 C1
Hatton Cl GL17 163 D1
Hatton Rd BS7 19 C8
Havelock Rd GL3 120 A8
Haven Ave GL10 97 E6
Haven Ct GL2 127 C3
Haven Park Mobile Home Site GL51 129 C5
Haven The BS15 20 E1
Haverstock Rd BS4 9 A3
Haviland Ho 8 BS2 195 C3
Hawburn Cl BS4 9 D2
Hawcombe Mews 1 GL51 129 F5
Haweswater BS10 28 B2
Haweswater Cl BS30 11 D6
Haweswater Rd GL51 129 F6
Hawk Cl
5 Chalford GL6 148 C6
Gloucester GL4 119 D5
Hawker Hill GL17 164 D5
Hawker Rd GL51 133 E8
Hawkers Hill GL7 160 A1
Hawker Sq GL54 169 D6
Hawkesbury CE Prim Sch GL9 55 F3

Hawkesbury Rd
Bristol BS16 . . . . 19 E3
Hillesley GL12 . . . . 55 D6
Hawkesley Dr BS34 . . . 29 D6
Hawkesworth Rd BS37 . . 43 C3
Hawkfield Bsns Pk BS14 . . 2 D5
Hawkfield Ind Est BS14 . . . . 2 D5
Hawkfield Rd BS13 . . . . . . 2 D5
Hawkfield Way BS14 . . . . 2 D5
Hawkins Cl BS30 . . . . . . 11 C5
Hawkins Cres BS32 . . . . 29 E8
Hawkins La GL14 . . . . . 157 A7
Hawkins St BS2 . . . . . . 195 C3
Hawkley Dr BS32 . . . . . . 40 D3
Hawkmoth Cl GL20 . . . . 192 E6
Hawkridge Dr BS16 . . . . 22 C5
Hawksmoor Cl BS14 . . . . 3 A6
Hawksmoor La BS16 . . . . 19 E8
Hawkswood Rd GL51 . . . 130 B5
Hawksworth Dr BS15 . . . 10 B5
Hawkwell Cotts GL17 . . . 164 B3
Haw La BS35 . . . . 50 B3
Haworth Cl GL2 . . . . . . 117 F2
Haw Rd GL16 . . . . 155 C8
Haw St
Coaley GL11 . . . . 88 F7
Wotton-u-E GL12 . . . . 68 A7
Hawthorn Ave BS15 . . . 10 B5
Hawthorn Cl
Bristol BS34 . . . . 28 E7
Charfield GL12 . . . . 67 A4
Chepstow/Cas-Gwent NP16 60 E4
Quedgeley GL2 . . . . 110 A5
Hawthorn Cres BS35 . . . 64 C2
Hawthorn Ct GL15 . . . . 92 B3
Hawthorn Dr
Innsworth GL3 . . . . . 127 F6
Sling GL16 . . . . 155 B2
Woodmancote GL52 . . . 138 B3
Hawthorne Ave GL4 . . . 119 C6
Hawthorne Ct BS16 . . . 22 C5
Hawthorne Gdns BS16 . . . 20 F4
Hawthorne Hill GL18 . . . 170 D5
Hawthorne Rise BS10 . . . 28 C3
Hawthorne St BS4 . . . . . 9 A3
Hawthornes The
Bristol BS16 . . . . 20 F4
4 Cheltenham GL51 . . . 129 D6
Hawthorn Rd GL51 . . . 132 B3
Hawthorn Ridge GL6 . . . 90 F5
Hawthorn Rise GL5 . . . 98 D8
Hawthorns La BS31 . . . . 4 E5
Hawthorns Rd GL17 . . . 164 B5
Hawthorns The
Bishop's Cleeve GL52 . . 137 E4
Bussage GL6 . . . . . . 148 B6
Dursley GL11 . . . . 87 F5
Lydney GL15 . . . . 92 B3
Hawthorn Way
Bristol BS34 . . . . 29 E5
Northway GL20 . . . . . 182 C5
Haycombe BS14 . . . . 2 F6
Haycroft GL52 . . . . . . 137 E4
Haycroft Dr GL42 . . . . . 119 D3
Haycroft La GL13 . . . . . 78 C6
Haycroft Rd
Bristol BS34 . . . . 29 A3
Northleach GL54 . . . . 168 F2
Haydale Gdns GL2 . . . 127 C5
Hayden Court Cvn Pk
GL51 . . . . 132 A1
Hayden Gn GL51 . . . . . 132 A3
Hayden La GL51 . . . . . 132 A3
Hayden Rd GL51 . . . . . 132 F5
Haydock Cl BS16 . . . . . 30 F1
Haydon Ct 12 BS8 . . . . . 18 A2
Haydon Gdns BS7 . . . . . 19 B5
Haydons Cl GL55 . . . . 189 A2
Hayeley Dr BS32 . . . . . 29 E6
Hayes Cl BS2 . . . . 9 A7
Hayes Ct
Bristol BS34 . . . . 29 A7
Cheltenham GL52 . . . 134 C4
Gloucester GL2 . . . . . 126 F6
Hayes Knoll Sta SN5 . . 143 F1
Hayes La GL7 . . . . . . 158 B4
Haye's La GL9 . . . . 46 F2
Hayes Rd
Cheltenham GL52 . . . 134 A2
Nailsworth GL6 . . . . . 91 A5
Hayes The NP16 . . . . . . 61 B8
Hayes Wy
Bristol BS34 . . . . 29 A6
Bristol, Filton BS34 . . . 28 E6
Hayfield SN14 . . . . 15 A8
Hayfield La BS6 . . . . . . 18 C1
Hayfield Way GL52 . . . 137 E5
Haygarth Cl GL7 . . . . . 190 B2
Hayhedge La GL6 . . . . 148 D8
Hay La
Ablington GL7 . . . . . 159 E1
Horsley GL6 . . . . 83 A7
Haylea Rd GL52 . . . . . 137 D4
Hay Leaze BS37 . . . . . . 43 D4
Hayleigh Ho BS13 . . . . . . 2 C4
Haymans Cl GL53 . . . . 130 E5
Haymarket The BS1 . . . 195 A3
Haymarket Wlk 9 BS1 . . 195 A4
Haymead La GL8 . . . . . . 70 D5
Haymes Dr GL52 . . . . 138 C1
Haymes Rd GL52 . . . . 138 C1
Haynes Ho 2 BS16 . . . . 20 D4
Haynes La BS16 . . . . . . 20 D5

Hays Cl WR12 . . . . . . 188 B2
Hay's Cotts GL53 . . . . 130 E6
Hay St SN14 . . . . 15 A8
Haysum's Cl GL55 . . . 189 A1
Hayter Ct BS10 . . . . . . 28 D3
Haythorn Ct BS16 . . . . 20 F5
Haythorne Ct 8 BS16 . . . 19 E3
Haytor Pk BS9 . . . . . . 17 D6
Hayward Cl GL4 . . . . . 119 D7
Hayward Ind Est 1 BS16 . 20 D3
Hayward Rd
Bristol, Russell Town BS5 . . . 9 C7
Bristol, Staple Hill BS16 . . . 20 D3
Haywards GL7 . . . . . . 144 F7
Haywards La GL52 . . . . 131 A8
Hayward's Rd GL52 . . . 131 A8
Haywood Pitch HR9 . . . 170 C5
Hazebrouck Cl GL51 . . . 129 E7
Hazel Ave
Bristol BS6 . . . . 18 B2
Tewkesbury GL20 . . . 192 F1
Hazel Brook Gdns BS10 . . 28 A5
Hazelbury Dr BS30 . . . . 11 C6
Hazelbury Rd BS14 . . . . 3 C7
Hazel Cl GL2 . . . . 127 B5
Hazel Cote Rd BS14 . . . 3 B4
Hazel Cres BS35 . . . . . . 64 D1
Hazelcroft GL3 . . . . . . 128 B6
Hazel Ct GL4 . . . . 127 D1
Hazeldean GL14 . . . . . 191 C5
Hazeldene GL7 . . . . . . 153 E3
Hazeldene Rd BS34 . . . . 29 A7
Hazel Field GL17 . . . . 164 B5
Hazel Gdns BS35 . . . . . 51 A4
Hazel Gr BS7 . . . . 19 A8
Hazelgrove BS36 . . . . . . 30 E5
Hazelhurst Bglws HR7 . . 163 B5
Hazel La
Alveston BS35 . . . . . . 50 F2
Tockington BS32 . . . . 50 E3
Hazel Rd GL17 . . . . . . 164 B4
Hazels The GL4 . . . . . 119 E7
Hazelton Cl GL4 . . . . . 118 F6
Hazelton Rd BS7 . . . . . 18 D3
Hazelwood 1 GL10 . . . 97 F7
Hazelwood Cl BS16 . . . 20 F5
Hazelwood Ct BS9 . . . . 17 D3
Hazelwood Rd BS9 . . . . 17 D3
Hazel Wy GL4 . . . . . . 120 A5
Hazle Cl HR8 . . . . 178 E2
Hazlecote La GL6, GL8 . . 82 F6
Hazledean Rd GL51 . . . 132 D4
Hazlewood Cl GL51 . . . 130 B5
Hazlitt Croft GL51 . . . 132 B4
Headford Ave BS5 . . . . 10 B7
Headford Rd BS4 . . . . . . 8 D1
Headington Cl BS15 . . . 10 D4
Headlam Cl GL4 . . . . . 118 D1
Headlands The GL5 . . . 98 F2
Headland The NP16 . . . 61 A4
Headley Ct
Bristol BS13 . . . . 2 B6
4 Gloucester GL2 . . . . . 118 A1
Headley La BS13 . . . . . . 2 B7
Headley Park Ave BS13 . . 2 B7
Headley Park Prim Sch
BS13 . . . . 2 B6
Headley Park Rd BS13 . . . 2 A7
Headley Rd BS13 . . . . . . 2 A6
Headley Wlk BS13 . . . . . 2 B7
Healey Dr SN14 . . . . . . 23 C6
Healey Mews SN14 . . . 127 A4
Heapey Cl 8 GL51 . . . 132 D2
Hearne Cl GL53 . . . . . 131 B6
Hearne Rd GL53 . . . . . 131 B6
Heart Meers BS13 . . . . . 3 D7
Heart of the Forest Com
Specl Sch GL16 . . . . . 155 E6
Heath Cl BS36 . . . . 30 E6
Heathcote Dr BS36 . . . . 31 D7
Heathcote La BS36 . . . . 31 D7
Heathcote Rd
Bristol, Chester Park
BS16 . . . . 20 B2
Bristol, Staple Hill BS16 . . 20 E5
Heathcote Wlk BS16 . . . 20 C2
Heath Ct
Bristol BS16 . . . . 20 D7
Dursley GL11 . . . . 80 C8
Heathdean Rd GL3 . . . . 127 F6
Heather Ave
Frampton Cotterell BS36 . . 31 B6
Gloucester GL4 . . . . . 119 F4
Heather Cl
Bristol BS15 . . . . 10 B8
Chepstow/Cas-Gwent NP16 60 F5
Stroud GL5 . . . . 99 A4
Heatherdene BS14 . . . . . 2 F7
Heathfield Cl BS31 . . . . 4 C5
Heathfield Cres BS14 . . . 3 B4
Heathfield Rd GL5 . . . 103 A1
Heathfields BS16 . . . . . 20 D8
Heath Gdns
Bristol BS16 . . . . 20 D8
Coalpit Heath BS36 . . . 31 C5
Heath House Priory Hospl
BS16 . . . . 19 B4
Heath Lo 6 GL52 . . . . 133 F2
Heath Rd
Bristol, Downend BS16 . . 20 D8
Bristol, Eastville BS5 . . . 19 B3
Bristol, Hanham BS15 . . 10 B4
Heath Ridge BS41 . . . . . . 7 A2
Heath Rise BS30 . . . . . 11 B5

Heath St
Bristol BS5 . . . . 19 C3
11 Monmouth/Trefynwy
NP25 . . . . 154 A7
Heath The BS9 . . . . . . 17 E3
Heathville Rd GL1 . . . 127 A3
Heath Wlk BS16 . . . . . . 20 D7
Heazle Pl GL5 . . . . 99 C8
Hebden Cl GL3 . . . . . . 120 F5
Heberden Ho 6 SN6 . . . 143 E4
Heber St BS5 . . . . 9 C7
Hebron Ct BS3 . . . . 8 C3
Hebron Rd 10 BS3 . . . . . 8 C3
Hedgeditch La GL8 . . . . 59 D7
Hedgemead Cl BS16 . . . 19 D5
Hedgemead View BS16 . . 19 E5
Hedgerows The 3 BS32 . . 40 D1
Hedgerow The GL2 . . . 127 B4
Hedwick Ave BS5 . . . . . . 9 E7
Hedwick St BS5 . . . . 9 E7
Heggard Cl BS13 . . . . . . 2 A5
Helens Cl GL53 . . . . . 132 D3
Hellier Wlk BS13 . . . . . . 2 C3
Hembury Cl GL2 . . . . . 109 D7
Hemmingsdale Rd GL2 . . 126 C1
Hemmings Par 4 BS5 . . . 9 B7
Hemming Way GL52 . . . 137 F3
Hemplands The GL54 . . 159 B5
Hemplow Cl BS14 . . . . . . 3 D7
Hempsted CE Prim Sch
GL2 . . . . 118 A7
Hempsted La GL2 . . . . 118 B7
Hempton Field Dr BS34 . . 29 A7
Hempton La BS32 . . . . . 40 B2
Henacre Rd BS11 . . . . . 16 F8
Henbury Court Prim Acad
BS10 . . . . 27 F3
Henbury Ct BS10 . . . . . 27 F3
Henbury Gdns BS10 . . . . 27 E2
Henbury Hill BS9 . . . . . 27 F1
Henbury Rd
Bristol, Hanham BS15 . . 10 B5
Bristol, Henbury BS10 . . 27 F2
Bristol, Westbury on Trym
BS9 . . . . 18 A8
Henbury Road Henbury Hill
BS9 . . . . 17 F8
Henbury Sch BS10 . . . 27 E3
Hencliffe Ho 3 D7
Hencliffe Way BS15 . . . 10 B3
Henderson Ho 1 BS2 . . 195 B4
Henderson Rd BS15 . . . 10 B5
Hendingham Cl GL4 . . . 118 B2
Hendre Mews GL50 . . . 193 A3
Hendre Rd BS3 . . . . 8 A2
Hendrick Dr NP16 . . . . 61 A8
Heneage La GL12 . . . . . 65 D1
Henfield Cres BS30 . . . 11 B3
Henfield Rd BS36 . . . . 31 C4
Hengaston St BS3 . . . . . . 8 B2
Hengrove Ave BS14 . . . . 3 A8
Hengrove Farm La BS14 . . 3 A8
Hengrove La BS14 . . . . . 3 B8
Hengrove Prom BS14 . . . 2 E5
Hengrove Rd BS4 . . . . . . 9 A2
Hengrove Way BS14 . . . 2 E6
Henleaze Ave BS9 . . . . 18 A5
Henleaze Gdns BS9 . . . 18 A5
Henleaze Jun Sch BS9 . . 18 C5
Henleaze Park BS9 . . . 18 C5
Henleaze Park Dr BS9 . . 18 C5
Henleaze Pk BS9 . . . . . 18 C5
Henleaze Rd BS9 . . . . . 18 B6
Henleaze Terr BS9 . . . . 18 B7
Henley Dr SN6 . . . . . . 145 D4
Henley Gr BS9 . . . . 18 B5
Henley Grove Ct BS9 . . . 18 B5
Henley Pl GL1 . . . . . . 118 D5
Henley Rd
Bream GL15 . . . . 155 D1
Cheltenham GL51 . . . 132 C4
Henley Villas GL5 . . . . 99 C8
Henlow Dr GL11 . . . . . . 80 B8
Hennessy Cl BS14 . . . . . 2 F3
Henrietta St
Bristol, Kingsdown BS2 . . 195 A4
5 Bristol, Lower Easton
BS5 . . . . 19 B1
Cheltenham GL50 . . . . 193 B4
Henry Cres GL20 . . . . 192 F2
Henry Ryder Cl GL4 . . . 119 F6
Henry St
Bristol BS3 . . . . 8 F4
Gloucester GL1 . . . . . 196 C3
Henry Williamson Ct 1
BS30 . . . . 11 A5
Henry Withers Pl GL2 . . 100 F5
Henshaw Cl BS15 . . . . 20 C2
Henshaw Rd BS15 . . . . 20 C2
Henshaw Wlk BS15 . . . 20 C2
Hensman's Hill BS8 . . . 194 A2
Hentley Tor GL12 . . . . 68 C6
**Heol Merthyr Tewdrig/
Mathern Rd** NP16 . . . 60 D5
Hepburn Rd BS2 . . . . 195 B4
Herald Cl BS9 . . . . 17 D5
Herapath St BS5 . . . . . . 9 C6
Herbert Cres BS5 . . . . . 19 D3
Herbert Howells Cl GL15 . . 92 A2
Herbert's Hill HR9 . . . 162 B8
Herbert St
Bristol, Moorfields BS5 . . . 9 C8
Bristol, Southville BS3 . . . 8 D4
Gloucester GL1 . . . . . 119 A8
Herbert Stark Cl GL7 . . 190 E4

Herberts Way GL15 . . . 156 B1
Hercules Cl BS34 . . . . 29 D6
Herd La GL8 . . . . 140 C4
Hereford Ct 1 GL50 . . . 193 B4
Hereford Pl GL50 . . . . 193 A4
Hereford Rd BS2 . . . . . 19 A2
Hereford St BS3 . . . . . . 8 D3
Hereward Rd GL7 . . . 190 C5
Herkomer Cl BS7 . . . . . 19 B7
Hermes Cl BS31 . . . . . . 5 D2
Hermitage Cl BS11 . . . 16 E7
Hermitage Dr GL11 . . . 80 B7
Hermitage Rd BS16 . . . 20 E5
Hermitage St GL53 . . . 193 B1
Hermitage Wood Rd 2
BS7 . . . . 19 C8
Heron Cl GL51 . . . . . 129 E7
Heron Prim Sch GL4 . . . 119 D5
Heron Rd BS5 . . . . 19 B1
Heron Way
Chipping Sodbury BS37 . . 33 A8
Gloucester GL4 . . . . . 119 C5
Herrick Cl GL51 . . . . . 173 F1
Herrick Way GL51 . . . 173 F1
Herridge Cl BS13 . . . . . 2 B4
Herridge Rd BS13 . . . . . 2 B4
Hersey Gdns BS13 . . . . . 1 E3
Hersta Cl GL7 . . . . . . 190 E4
Hertford Rd GL52 . . . 138 A4
Hesding Cl BS15 . . . . . 10 C3
Hestercombe Rd BS13 . . 2 B6
Hester's Way La GL51 . . 132 D4
Hester's Way Prim Sch
GL51 . . . . 132 E4
Hester's Way Rd GL51 . . 132 B3
Hester Wood GL51 . . . . 43 F4
Hethersett Rd GL1 . . . 119 A8
Hetton Gdns GL53 . . . 131 A7
Hever Cl GL20 . . . . . . 192 E2
Hewelsfield La GL15 . . . 146 F7
Hewelsfield Rd GL15 . . . 147 A4
Hewland Ct BS11 . . . . . 27 C2
Hewlett Pl GL52 . . . . 193 C3
Hewlett Rd GL52 . . . . 133 F1
Hewlett Way GL14 . . . 156 C6
Hewlins La HR9 . . . . . 162 D3
Heyford Ave BS5 . . . . . 19 B4
Heyron Wlk BS13 . . . . . 2 B1
Heywood Rd
Cinderford GL14 . . . . 191 D5
Pill BS20 . . . . 16 C4
Heywood Terr BS20 . . . 16 C4
Hiam's La GL19 . . . . . 172 C2
Hiatt Rd GL6 . . . . 91 F7
Hibbs Cl SN14 . . . . 14 F8
Hicking Ct 8 BS15 . . . 20 D1
Hickley Gdns GL3 . . . . 120 E6
Hickory La
Bristol BS32 . . . . 40 D5
Bristol BS32 . . . . 40 D5
Hicks Ave
Bristol BS16 . . . . 21 B8
Dursley GL11 . . . . 87 F4
Hicks Beach Rd GL51 . . 132 D2
Hicks Common Rd BS36 . . 30 E5
Hicks Ct BS30 . . . . 10 F4
Hidcote Ave GL51 . . . 130 A5
Hidcote Boyce GL55 . . . 189 C4
Hidcote Cl BS14 . . . . . 148 B6
Hidcote Manor Gdns
GL55 . . . . 189 C5
Hidcote Rd GL55 . . . . 189 C3
Hide Mkt BS2 . . . . . . 195 C3
Higham St 4 BS2 . . . . . . 8 F4
Highbank Pk GL2 . . . 126 F5
High Beech Ave GL15 . . . 155 C7
**High Beech La/Lon
Ffawyoden Uchel** NP16 . . 60 D6
Highbeech Rd
Bream GL15 . . . . 147 D8
Upper Lybrook GL17 . . 163 E3
Highbury La GL52 . . . 193 C3
Highbury Rd
Bream GL15 . . . . 147 D8
Bristol, Bedminster BS3 . . . 8 C2
Bristol, Horfield BS7 . . . 18 F7
Lower Redbrook NP25 . . 154 C4
Highbury Terr NP25 . . . 154 C4
Highbury Villas BS2 . . 194 C4
Highclere Rd GL2 . . . 117 E2
High Cnr BS10 . . . . . . 27 F1
Highcroft
3 Bristol BS30 . . . . . . 11 C6
Minchinhampton GL6 . . 91 F7
High Cross GL53 . . . . 115 B7
Highdale Cl BS14 . . . . . 3 B4
High Delt Ct 9 GL16 . . . 155 B5
High Delt Way GL15 . . . 155 F1
High Elm BS15 . . . . . . 10 E6
Higher Newmarket Rd
GL6 . . . . 90 F4
Highett Dr BS5 . . . . . . 19 A1
Highfield
Blakeney GL15 . . . . . 156 D1
Whiteshill GL6 . . . . . 103 A3
Highfield Ave BS15 . . . 10 D5
Highfield Bsns Pk GL19 . . 173 F7
Highfield Cl GL15 . . . 155 D1
Highfield Gdns BS30 . . . 11 C2
Highfield Gr BS7 . . . . . 18 D5
Highfield La
Cirencester GL7 . . . . 190 C2
Horton BS37 . . . . 45 E7
Lydney GL15 . . . . 92 C5
Highfield Pl
4 Coleford GL16 . . . 155 B5

Highfield Pl *continued*
Gloucester GL4 . . . . . 119 B7
Highfield Rd
Bream GL15 . . . . 155 D1
Chipping Sodbury BS37 . . 44 A1
Gloucester GL4 . . . . . 119 B7
Keynsham BS31 . . . . . . 4 F2
Lydney GL15 . . . . 92 B4
Lydney GL15 . . . . 92 C4
Ruardean GL17 . . . . 163 F4
Stroud GL5 . . . . 99 E6
Tetbury GL8 . . . . 140 B5
Whiteshill GL6 . . . . . 103 A3
Highfield Rise GL15 . . . 92 B3
Highfields
Frampton Mansell GL6 . . 148 F5
Hawkesbury Upton GL9 . . 55 F5
Twyning GL20 . . . . . 182 A7
Highfields App GL11 . . . 80 C8
Highfields Cl BS34 . . . . 29 F3
Highfield Villas GL14 . . . 156 F6
Highfield Way GL6 . . . 148 D6
High Furlong GL11 . . . . 87 F5
Highgate Ct WR12 . . . 185 B8
High Gr BS9 . . . . 17 B7
Highgrove Cotts GL8 . . . 140 A2
Highgrove St BS4 . . . . . . 9 A4
Highgrove The GL52 . . . 137 E3
Highgrove Way GL3 . . . 127 F8
High La BS36 . . . . 30 C8
Highland Cres 3 BS8 . . . 18 A2
Highland Ho GL10 . . . . 89 E5
Highland Pl 13 BS8 . . . 18 A2
Highland Rd GL53 . . . 130 F4
Highlands Dr GL11 . . . 79 E4
Highland Sq 4 BS8 . . . 18 A2
Highlands Rd BS41 . . . . . 7 A2
Highleaze BS30 . . . . . . 11 C4
Highliffe Dr GL2 . . . . 118 A1
High Mdw GL4 . . . . . . 119 D4
Highmead Gdns BS13 . . . 1 E4
Highmore Ct BS7 . . . . . 19 B7
Highmore Gdns BS7 . . . 19 C4
Highnam Bsns Ctr GL2 . . 125 C5
Highnam CE Prim Acad
GL2 . . . . 125 D5
Highnam Cl BS34 . . . . . 40 B1
Highnam Gn GL2 . . . 125 C5
**Highnam Woods (Nature
Reserve)** GL2 . . . . . . 124 F4
High Nash GL16 . . . . . 155 B5
High Orchard St GL2 . . 196 A1
High Pk BS14 . . . . 9 B1
High Point GL50 . . . . 193 A3
High Point Ho 1 BS15 . . 20 C1
High Rd
Ashton Keynes SN6 . . 142 F4
Mitcheldean GL17 . . . 164 D5
Highridge Cres BS13 . . . 1 F5
Highridge Gn BS13 . . . . 1 F6
Highridge Pk BS13 . . . . 1 F6
Highridge Rd
Bristol, Bedminster BS3 . . . . 8 B2
Bristol, Withywood BS13,
BS41 . . . . 1 E4
Highridge Wlk BS13 . . . 1 F1
High Row GL17 . . . . . 163 C3
High Sch for Girls GL1 . . 196 C4
High St
Arlingham GL2 . . . . . 157 B6
Avening GL8 . . . . 148 A1
Aylburton GL15 . . . . 147 E4
Badminton GL9 . . . . . . 46 E2
Berkeley GL13 . . . . . . 85 E3
Bisley GL6 . . . . 148 D8
Bitton BS30 . . . . 5 E8
Blakeney GL15 . . . . . 156 E1
Blockley GL56 . . . . . 186 C6
Bourton-on-t-W GL54 . . 168 F4
Bream GL15 . . . . 147 D8
Bredon GL20 . . . . . . 182 C7
Brierley GL17 . . . . . . 163 F2
Bristol BS1 . . . . 195 A2
Bristol, Clifton BS8 . . . 18 A2
Bristol, Jefferies Hill BS15 . . 10 C5
Bristol, Kingswood BS15 . . 10 E8
Bristol, Lower Easton BS5 . . . 19 B1
Bristol, Oldland Common
BS30 . . . . 11 B4
Bristol, Shirehampton BS11 . . 16 E6
Bristol, Staple Hill BS16 . . 20 D4
Bristol, Warmley BS15 . . 11 B8
Bristol, Westbury on Trym
BS9 . . . . 18 A4
Broad Blunsdon SN26 . . 144 B3
Broadway WR12 . . . . 185 B8
Chalford GL6 . . . . . . 148 C8
Cheltenham, Prestbury
GL52 . . . . 134 C4
Cheltenham, St Paul's GL50,
GL52 . . . . 193 B4
Chepstow/Cas-Gwent NP16 . . 60 E4
Chipping Campden GL55 . . 189 A2
Chipping Sodbury BS37 . . 44 B1
Cinderford GL14 . . . . 191 D5
Clearwell GL16 . . . . . 155 A3
11 Coleford GL16 . . . 155 A5
Cricklade SN6 . . . . . . 143 F4
Doynton BS30 . . . . . . 22 F1
Drybrook GL17 . . . . 164 B4
Dursley GL11 . . . . 87 F6
Fairford GL7 . . . . . . 152 E4
Gloucester GL1 . . . . 118 F7
Hawkesbury Upton GL9 . . 55 F7
Highworth SN6 . . . . 145 D3

High St *continued*
Hillesley GL12 . . . . 55 D8
Honeybourne WR11 . . . . . . 188 C6
Huntley GL19 . . . . 165 D6
Iron Acton BS37 . . . . 42 D4
Kemerton GL20 . . . . 182 E8
Kempsford GL7 . . . . 144 E7
Keynsham BS31 . . . . 4 E6
King's Stanley GL10 . . . . 98 A3
Kingswood GL12 . . . . 67 F4
Lechlade on T GL7 . . . . 153 E2
Ledbury HR8 . . . . 178 F8
Littledean GL14 . . . . 191 F4
Longborough GL56 . . . . 176 D8
Lydney GL15 . . . . 92 A3
Marshfield SN14 . . . . 14 F8
Meysey Hampton GL7 . . . . 152 A2
Mickleton GL55 . . . . 189 B6
Minchinhampton GL6 . . . . . 148 A3
Mitcheldean GL17 . . . . 164 D5
Moreton-in-M GL56 . . . . . . 187 A3
Newent GL18 . . . . 171 A4
Newnham GL14 . . . . 157 A7
Northleach GL54 . . . . 168 A1
Ruardean GL17 . . . . 163 F4
Saltford BS31 . . . . 5 F3
Saul GL2 . . . . 157 F4
South Cerney GL7 . . . . 142 F7
Stanton WR12 . . . . 184 F5
St Briavels GL15 . . . . 146 E7
Stonehouse GL10 . . . . 97 F7
Stow-on-t-W GL54 . . . . 176 F5
Stroud GL5 . . . . 99 C7
Tewkesbury GL20 . . . . 192 C4
Thornbury BS35 . . . . 51 B8
Tormarton GL9 . . . . 34 D2
Upper Lydbrook GL17 . . . . . 163 E3
Upton St Leonards GL4 . . . . 119 E1
Westbury-on-S GL14 . . . . . 165 C1
Wick BS30 . . . . 12 D6
Wickwar GL12 . . . . 54 A5
Winchcombe GL54 . . . . 174 A7
Winterbourne BS36 . . . . 30 D6
Withington GL54 . . . . 166 D2
Woodchester GL5 . . . . 98 F1
Wotton-u-E GL12 . . . . 68 B7
High View Lodge 14 GL5 . . 99 C7
High View
Chepstow/Cas-Gwent NP16 . . . . 60 E8
Gloucester GL2 . . . . 118 A6
Highview Rd
Bristol BS15 . . . . 20 F2
Cinderford GL14 . . . . 191 E4
Ruardean Hill GL17 . . . . . . 164 A3
Yorkley GL15 . . . . 156 A2
Highview Way GL15 . . . . . 147 D8
Highwall La BS14, BS31 . . . . . 3 F1
Highway BS37 . . . . 43 F2
Highwood Ave GL53 . . . . . 130 C5
Highwood Bsns Pk BS34 . 28 E7
Highwood Ct GL6 . . . . 90 F5
Highwood Dr GL6 . . . . 90 F5
Highwood La BS10, BS34 . . 28 D7
Highwood Pk Cvn Site BS34 . . . . 28 E6
Highwood Rd BS34 . . . . 28 F7
Highworth Cres BS37 . . . . 32 D8
Highworth Rd
Bristol BS4 . . . . 9 D6
Gloucester GL1 . . . . 118 F6
Highworth SN6 . . . . 145 F1
Stanton Fitzwarren SN6 . . 145 B1
Highworth Warneford Sch SN6 . . . . 145 D3
Hilcote Dr GL54 . . . . 169 A6
Hildyard Cl GL2 . . . . 109 E7
Hilhouse BS9 . . . . 17 C6
Hillands Dr GL53 . . . . 130 D4
Hillary Rd GL53 . . . . 130 E4
Hill Ash Mdw GL18 . . . . . . 178 E3
Hill Ave BS3 . . . . 8 E3
Hillborough Rd GL4 . . . . . 118 E3
Hillbrook Rd 5 BS35 . . . . . 51 D8
Hill Burn BS9 . . . . 18 C6
Hillburn Rd BS5 . . . . 10 A8
Hill Cl
Bristol BS16 . . . . 21 B8
Dursley GL11 . . . . 87 F4
Westmancote GL20 . . . . . . 182 D8
Hillclose Est GL5 . . . . 99 A4
Hillcot Cl GL2 . . . . 117 E1
Hill Court Rd GL52 . . . . . . 133 E4
Hillcrest
Berkeley GL13 . . . . 85 F4
Thornbury BS35 . . . . 64 B1
Hill Crest
Bristol BS4 . . . . 9 B1
Highnam GL2 . . . . 125 E5
Hillcrest Cl 15 NP25 . . . . . 154 A7
Hillcrest La GL16 . . . . 155 B6
Hillcrest Prim Sch BS4 . . . . 9 A3
Hillcrest Rd
Berry Hill GL16 . . . . 155 A7
Monmouth/Trefynwy NP25 . . . . 154 A7
Stroud GL5 . . . . 98 E8
Hillcroft Cl BS15 . . . . 10 E4
Hill Ct GL52 . . . . 133 E4
Hill End Cl GL20 . . . . 181 F7
Hill End Dr BS10 . . . . 27 D3
Hill End Rd GL20 . . . . 181 F8
Hillersland La GL16 . . . . . 155 A8
Hillesley CE Prim Sch GL12 . . . . 55 E8
Hillesley Rd GL12 . . . . 67 F4
Hillfield
Cheltenham GL51 . . . . 132 F1
Stroud GL5 . . . . 98 F7
Hillfield Court Rd GL1 . . . 127 A3
Hillfield Ct GL1 . . . . 127 A3
Hillfields Ave BS16 . . . . 20 C3
Hill Gr BS9 . . . . 18 C6
Hillgrove St BS2 . . . . 195 B4
Hill Hay Rd GL4 . . . . 119 C3
Hill Ho GL7 . . . . 190 D5
Hill House Rd BS16 . . . . . . 20 F5
Hillier Cl GL5 . . . . 103 D1
Hillier Dr 8 GL51 . . . . 129 F5
Hill La
Chipping Sodbury BS37 . . . . 34 B7
Thornbury BS35 . . . . 76 A2
Hill Lawn BS4 . . . . 9 D3
Hill Mead GL4 . . . . 110 F5
Hillmill La GL12 . . . . 69 B5
Hill Paul GL5 . . . . 99 B7
Hill Pk GL15 . . . . 156 A2
Hill Rd
Dundry BS41 . . . . 1 D2
Dursley GL11 . . . . 88 A1
Gloucester GL4 . . . . 118 F4
Wotton-u-E GL12 . . . . 68 C6
Hillrise GL15 . . . . 155 D1
Hill's Barton BS13 . . . . 8 A1
Hillsborough BS8 . . . . 194 A2
Hillsborough Rd BS4 . . . . . . 9 C4
Hills Cl BS31 . . . . 5 A5
Hillsdon Rd BS9 . . . . 17 F8
Hillside
Bristol, Mangotsfield BS16 . . . . 21 A5
Bristol, Tyndall's Park BS6 194 C4
Burton SN14 . . . . 36 A4
Chalford GL6 . . . . 148 D6
Leigh SN6 . . . . 143 B3
Hillside Ave BS15 . . . . 10 C8
Hillside Cl
10 Bream GL15 . . . . 155 D1
Cheltenham GL51 . . . . 130 A7
Frampton Cotterell BS36 . . . 31 C7
Woodmancote GL52 . . . . . . 138 C3
Hillside Ct
Bristol BS5 . . . . 10 B7
6 Dursley GL11 . . . . 80 B8
Hillside Est 11 GL15 . . . . . 155 D1
Hillside Gdns GL52 . . . . . . 138 C3
Hillside Ho 5 BS6 . . . . 18 D1
Hillside La BS36 . . . . 31 C7
Hillside Rd
Bristol BS5 . . . . 10 A7
Drybrook GL17 . . . . 164 B5
Long Ashton BS41 . . . . 7 B2
Mitcheldean GL17 . . . . 164 D5
Hillside St BS4 . . . . 9 A4
Hillside Terr GL17 . . . . 163 D3
Hillside Villas GL5 . . . . 99 D5
Hillside Way SN26 . . . . . . 144 D1
Hill Sq GL11 . . . . 88 A3
Hill St
Bristol, Brandon Hill BS1 . . 194 C2
Bristol, Kingswood BS15 . . . 10 F8
Bristol, St George BS5 . . . . . . 9 F8
Bristol, Windmill Hill BS3 . . . . 8 F4
Lydney GL15 . . . . 92 A3
Hills View 17 GL18 . . . . . . 171 A4
Hill The
Almondsbury BS32 . . . . 40 B4
Randwick GL6 . . . . 102 E2
Stroud GL5 . . . . 99 B7
Westwell OX18 . . . . 161 F5
Hilltop 8 GL15 . . . . 147 D8
Hill Top NP16 . . . . 60 D7
Hill Top Cl GL5 . . . . 99 F7
Hilltop Gdns
Bristol, St George BS5 . . . . . 10 A7
Bristol, Upper Soundwell BS16 . . . . 20 D2
Hill Top La GL18 . . . . 171 B5
Hilltop Rd BS16 . . . . 20 D2
Hill Top Rd GL50 . . . . 133 D5
Hilltop View
Bristol BS5 . . . . 10 A7
Dursley GL11 . . . . 87 F4
Hill Top View GL6 . . . . 148 B6
Hillview GL7 . . . . 158 D3
Hill View
Bristol, Blackhorse BS16 . . . 21 A8
Bristol, Clifton Wood BS8 . 194 B2
Bristol, Filton BS34 . . . . 29 A3
Bristol, Henleaze BS9 . . . . . 18 C6
Bristol, Upper Soundwell BS16 . . . . 20 D2
Elkstone GL53 . . . . 115 B6
Lydney GL15 . . . . 92 A3
Naunton GL54 . . . . 175 E2
Sandhurst GL2 . . . . 172 E1
Hillview Ave GL3 . . . . 120 D6
Hill View Cl BS30 . . . . 11 C4
Hill View Cotts GL4 . . . . . . 118 E2
Hill View Ct BS16 . . . . 20 C5
Hillview Dr GL3 . . . . 120 A8
Hillview Gdns GL51 . . . . . . 129 D1
Hill View Ho 2 BS15 . . . . . . 20 C1
Hillview House Pk (Mobile Home Pk) 1 GL3 . . . . . 120 A8
Hillview La GL20 . . . . 181 F8
Hill View La GL18 . . . . 170 C4
Hillview Prim Sch GL3 . . 120 A8
Hillview Rd
Cheltenham GL52 . . . . 134 B2
Gloucester GL3 . . . . 120 A8
Pucklechurch BS16 . . . . 22 C5
Hill View Rd
Bristol BS13 . . . . 2 A8
Upper Strensham WR8 . . 180 A10
Hillview Rise GL16 . . . . . . 155 A7
Hill View Villas 2 GL5 . . . . 98 D6
Hillwell SN16 . . . . 141 E1
Hillyfield Rd BS13 . . . . 2 A6
Hilly Orch GL5 . . . . 98 E6
Hilton Cl GL2 . . . . 118 B6
Hilton Ct 5 BS5 . . . . 9 B8
Hinders La GL17, GL19 . . . 165 B5
Hine Gdns GL52 . . . . 133 F3
Hinton Cl BS31 . . . . 5 E3
Hinton Ct GL13 . . . . 85 C8
Hinton Dr BS30 . . . . 11 C6
Hinton La 13 BS8 . . . . 7 F6
Hinton Rd
Bristol, Fishponds BS16 . . . 20 A4
Bristol, Lower Easton BS5 . . 19 C1
Gloucester GL1 . . . . 126 F4
Hisnams Field GL52 . . . . . 137 F3
Historic Gloucester Docks★ GL1 . . . . 196 A2
Hitchen Cl SN14 . . . . 14 F8
Hitchen Hollow NP16 . . . . . 61 B4
Hitchings GL15 . . . . 156 D2
Hither Bath Bridge BS4 . . . 9 C1
Hither Mead BS36 . . . . 31 B6
Hithe The GL5 . . . . 99 C3
Hive The GL54 . . . . 166 E5
Hobart Ho GL51 . . . . 132 E2
Hobbs La
Bristol BS30 . . . . 21 B1
Longhope GL17 . . . . 165 A6
Woodmancote GL7 . . . . 158 B4
Hobb's La 4 BS1 . . . . 194 C2
Hobby Cl GL53 . . . . 130 C5
Hobhouse Cl BS9 . . . . 18 C7
Hobwell La BS41 . . . . 7 C2
Hocker Hill St 4 NP16 . . . . 60 E8
Hockeys La BS16 . . . . 20 A4
Hoddon La BS16 . . . . 22 D5
Hodges Way GL14 . . . . 191 C3
Hodges Yd 7 HR8 . . . . 178 E8
Hogarth Wlk BS7 . . . . 19 C7
Hogues Wlk BS13 . . . . 2 B4
Holbeach Dr GL2 . . . . 118 A1
Holbeach Way BS14 . . . . 3 A2
Holbrook GL17 . . . . 163 D2
Holbrook Cres BS13 . . . . 2 D4
Holbrook La BS30 . . . . 12 B7
Holbury Cres GL2 . . . . 100 E5
Holcombe BS14 . . . . 3 A5
Holcombe Gr BS31 . . . . 4 D5
Holcot Cl 8 GL16 . . . . 155 B5
Holcot Rd GL16 . . . . 155 B5
Holdcroft Cl SN26 . . . . 144 E1
Holdenhurst Rd BS15 . . . . . 20 C1
Holder Cl 13 GL8 . . . . 140 B4
Holder Rd GL52 . . . . 137 F2
Holders La GL18 . . . . 170 E6
Holford Cres GL7 . . . . 144 F7
Holford Ct BS14 . . . . 3 B5
Hollams Rd GL20 . . . . 192 D5
Holland Ct GL1 . . . . 127 A3
Hollidge Gdns 3 BS3 . . . . . . 8 D4
Hollies Hill GL6 . . . . 91 C4
Hollies The BS15 . . . . 10 E6
Hollingham La GL6 . . . . 90 E1
Hollins Cl NP16 . . . . 72 F1
Hollis Cl
Long Ashton BS41 . . . . 1 A8
Long Ashton BS41 . . . . 7 A1
Hollis Gdns
Cheltenham GL51 . . . . 129 D6
Luckington SN14 . . . . 47 E4
Hollis Rd GL51 . . . . 129 D6
Hollister's Dr BS13 . . . . 2 D4
Holloway Hill SN14 . . . . 25 F7
Holloway Rd
Bisley GL6 . . . . 148 D8
Severn Beach BS35 . . . . 38 C4
Hollow La GL5 . . . . 99 D7
Hollow Rd
Almondsbury BS32 . . . . 40 A4
Bristol BS15 . . . . 10 E8
Hollows The BS36 . . . . 31 D2
Hollow The GL17 . . . . 164 A4
Hollway Cl BS14 . . . . 3 E5
Hollway Rd BS14 . . . . 3 E5
Hollybrook Mews 5 BS37 . . . . 32 D8
Hollybush Cl GL9 . . . . 36 A6
Hollybush La
Bristol BS9 . . . . 17 E5
Bristol BS9 . . . . 17 F4
Holly Cl
Alveston BS35 . . . . 50 F4
Bretforton WR11 . . . . 188 A7
Bristol BS5 . . . . 20 A2
Chepstow/Cas-Gwent NP16 60 E5
Innsworth GL3 . . . . 127 F6
Pucklechurch BS16 . . . . 22 C5
Holly Cres BS15 . . . . 20 E1
Holly Ct BS2 . . . . 194 C4
Hollydean GL14 . . . . 191 C5
Holly Dr SN14 . . . . 15 F6
Holly End GL2 . . . . 109 F8
Holly Gn BS15 . . . . 21 A1
Holly Gr BS16 . . . . 20 C3
Holly Gr The GL2 . . . . 109 F8
Hollyguest Rd BS15 . . . . . . 10 E6
Holly Hill BS37 . . . . 42 E3
Hollyhill Pk GL14 . . . . 191 B5
Hollyhill Rd GL14 . . . . 191 B5
Holly Hill Rd BS15 . . . . 20 F1
Holly Ho BS11 . . . . 27 C2
Hollyhock La GL6 . . . . 103 F8
Holly La GL16 . . . . 155 C3
Hollyleigh Ave BS34 . . . . . . 28 F2
Holly Lodge Cl BS5 . . . . 20 A2
Holly Lodge Rd BS5 . . . . . . 19 F2
Hollymead La BS9 . . . . 17 E4
Hollyridge BS14 . . . . 3 C6
Holly Tree Gdn GL5 . . . . . . 98 D6
Holly Tree Pl GL15 . . . . . . 156 B1
Hollywell Rd GL17 . . . . 164 D6
Holly Wlk BS31 . . . . 4 D4
Hollywood La BS10, BS35 . . 28 A7
Hollywood Rd BS4 . . . . 9 D2
Holmdale Rd BS34 . . . . 29 C3
Holmer Cres GL51 . . . . 129 D6
Holme Rd GL20 . . . . 192 D1
Holmes Ct BS9 . . . . 18 B5
Holmesdale Rd BS3 . . . . 8 E3
Holmes Gr BS9 . . . . 18 B5
Holmes Hill Rd BS5 . . . . 9 F8
Holmes St BS5 . . . . 9 B6
Holmfield Dr NP25 . . . . . . 146 B7
Holm La BS35 . . . . 49 B2
Holmleigh Par GL4 . . . . . . 118 C2
Holmleigh Rd GL4 . . . . . . 118 C3
Holm-Mead La BS30 . . . . . . 5 C7
Holmoak Cl GL20 . . . . 192 E2
Holmoak Rd BS31 . . . . 4 C4
Holmwood BS15 . . . . 10 C5
Holmwood Cl
Gloucester GL4 . . . . 118 D2
Winterbourne BS36 . . . . 30 D6
Holmwood Dr GL4 . . . . 118 D2
Holmwood Gdns BS9 . . . . . 18 B8
Holroyd Ho BS3 . . . . 8 D3
Holsom Cl BS14 . . . . 3 F6
Holsom Rd BS14 . . . . 3 F6
Holst Gdns BS4 . . . . 2 D7
Holst Gr GL51 . . . . 129 C6
Holst Way GL4 . . . . 118 D3
Holtham Ave GL3 . . . . 128 B7
Holton Rd BS7 . . . . 19 A6
Holts Rd GL18 . . . . 170 F4
Holt The
Bishop's Cleeve GL52 . . . . 137 E2
Gloucester GL4 . . . . 119 E7
Holy Apostles CE Prim Sch GL52 . . . . 131 A8
Holy Cross RC Prim Sch BS3 . . . . 8 C4
Holy Family RC Prim Sch BS34 . . . . 29 B8
Holymead Prim Sch BS4 . . 9 D2
Holyrood Cl BS34 . . . . 29 D4
Holy Trinity CE Prim Sch GL52 . . . . 193 C4
Holy Trinity Prim Sch BS32 . . . . 40 C2
Holy Well Cl BS4 . . . . 9 E6
Holywell Rd
Dursley GL11 . . . . 88 A4
Wotton-u-E GL12 . . . . 68 C8
Homeabbey Ho GL20 . . . . . 192 C5
Homeapple Hill BS30 . . . . . 11 F6
Homeavon Ho BS31 . . . . 4 F5
Homeberry Ho GL7 . . . . . . 190 C4
Home Cl
Bristol BS10 . . . . 28 E2
Cheltenham GL51 . . . . 132 E3
Lower Oddington GL56 . . . 177 C5
Homecroft Dr GL51 . . . . . . 132 E6
Homefarm SN6 . . . . 145 C3
Home Farm Ct GL52 . . . . . 131 A7
Home Farm Rd BS8 . . . . 7 B8
Home Farm Way BS35 . . . . 39 A1
Homefield
Nailsworth GL6 . . . . 91 A3
Thornbury BS35 . . . . 51 D8
Yate BS37 . . . . 43 E3
Homefield Cl BS31 . . . . 5 E3
Home Field Cl BS16 . . . . . . 21 B6
Homefield Dr BS16 . . . . 20 A5
Homefield Rd
Pucklechurch BS16 . . . . 22 B5
Saltford BS31 . . . . 5 F3
Homeground BS16 . . . . 21 B6
Home Ground
Bristol, Eastfield BS9 . . . . . 18 B7
Bristol, Shirehampton BS11 16 D7
Cricklade SN6 . . . . 143 E4
Homeground La GL7 . . . . . 152 F4
Home Leas Cl 6 BS7 . . . . . . 19 C8
Homeleaze Rd BS10 . . . . 28 D3
Homemead BS30 . . . . 11 A4
Home Mead BS4 . . . . 2 E7
Homemead Dr BS4 . . . . 9 D1
Homend Cres 2 HR8 . . . . . 178 F8
Homend The 16 HR8 . . . . . 178 F8
Home Orch
Stroud GL5 . . . . 98 D6
Yate BS37 . . . . 43 D2
Homepiece WR12 . . . . 185 B4
Home Piece GL7 . . . . 149 E3
Homespa Ho 2 GL50 . . . . . 133 B1
Homespring Ho GL52 . . . . . 134 A2
Homestead Cl
Bredon GL20 . . . . 182 C7
Frampton Cotterell BS36 . . . 31 D7
Homestead Ct GL4 . . . . . . 119 F5
Homestead Gdns BS16 . . . . 20 B8
Homestead Rd BS34 . . . . . . 29 A3
Homestead The BS31 . . . . . . 4 F2
Hone Ct 18 GL20 . . . . 192 C4
Honeyborne Way GL12 . . . . 54 B5
Honeybourne Airfield Ind Est WR11 . . . . 188 C5
Honeybourne Dr GL51 . . . 132 D4
Honeybourne Fst Sch WR11 . . . . 188 C6
Honeybourne Pottery★ WR11 . . . . 188 C6
Honeybourne Rd WR11 . . 188 D4
Honeybourne Sta WR11 . 188 C7
Honeybourne Way GL50 . 193 A4
Honey Garston Cl BS13 . . . . 2 B4
Honey Garston Rd BS13 . . . 2 B4
Honey Hill Rd BS15 . . . . . . 10 F8
Honeymead BS14 . . . . 3 C6
Honeysuckle Cl
Bristol BS32 . . . . 40 E2
Cheltenham GL52 . . . . 134 C3
Honeysuckle Dr GL4 . . . . 119 E5
Honey Suckle La BS16 . . . . 19 E5
Honeysuckle Way GL52 . . 137 F5
Honeythorn Cl GL2 . . . . . . 118 B7
Honey Way BS15 . . . . 10 F8
Honeywick Cl BS3 . . . . 8 C2
Honister Ho BS34 . . . . 29 A8
Honiton Rd BS16 . . . . 20 A3
Honyatt Rd GL1 . . . . 196 C4
Hookshouse La
Doughton GL8 . . . . 71 E4
Tetbury GL8 . . . . 140 A3
Hook's La GL18 . . . . 171 D5
Hoo La
Chipping Campden GL55 . . 188 F2
Tewkesbury GL20 . . . . 173 E8
Hooper Cl GL4 . . . . 119 B6
Hooper Rd BS14 . . . . 3 D5
Hoopers Yd GL5 . . . . 98 C6
Hoovers La HR9 . . . . 164 B8
Hoover's La BS36 . . . . 42 B3
Hope Brook CE Prim Sch GL17 . . . . 164 F6
Hopechapel Hill 11 BS8 . . . . 7 F6
Hope Cotts GL5 . . . . 99 D6
Hope Ct BS1 . . . . 194 B1
Hopelands Prep Sch GL10 97 F7
Hope Mill La GL5 . . . . 99 E2
Hope Mills Bsns Ctr GL5 . 99 E2
Hope Orch GL51 . . . . 132 D4
Hope Rd
Bristol BS3 . . . . 8 C2
Yate BS37 . . . . 43 A2
Hopes Cl GL15 . . . . 92 C2
Hope Sq BS8 . . . . 7 F6
Hope St GL51 . . . . 133 B3
Hopetoun Rd BS2 . . . . 18 F3
Hope Villas GL5 . . . . 99 C8
Hopewell GL14 . . . . 191 E5
Hopewell Cl NP16 . . . . 61 A4
Hopewell Colliery Mus★ GL16 . . . . 155 D6
Hopewell Gdns BS11 . . . . . 16 F7
Hopewell St GL1 . . . . 196 C1
Hop Gdn The NP16 . . . . 60 F4
Hopkin Cl BS35 . . . . 51 D7
Hopkins Ct 13 BS6 . . . . 18 B1
Hopkins Orch 1 SN6 . . . . . 143 E4
Hopland Cl BS30 . . . . 11 B3
Hopp's Rd BS15 . . . . 10 D7
Hopton Rd GL11 . . . . 88 B4
Hopwood Gr 1 GL52 . . . . . 134 A1
Hopyard La GL18 . . . . 171 A5
Hopyard The GL20 . . . . 182 B5
Horcott Ind Est GL7 . . . . . 152 D3
Horcott Rd GL7 . . . . 152 D3
Horesham Gr BS13 . . . . 2 C5
Horfield CE Prim Sch BS10 . . . . 18 D7
Horfield Ct BS7 . . . . 18 E4
Horfield Rd BS2 . . . . 195 A4
Horley Rd BS2 . . . . 19 A2
Hornbeam Cl BS32 . . . . 29 D8
Hornbeam Ho 5 BS16 . . . . . 20 C6
Hornbeam Mews GL2 . . . . 127 B5
Hornbeams The BS16 . . . . . 30 B1
Hornbeam Wlk BS31 . . . . 4 C3
Hornbury Cl SN16 . . . . 142 D1
Hornbury Hill SN16 . . . . . . 142 D1
Horn La GL56 . . . . 177 C7
Horns Rd GL5 . . . . 99 D6
Horsbere Rd GL3 . . . . 120 B8
Horsecroft Gdns BS30 . . . . . 11 A6
Horsefair Cl GL53 . . . . 131 A5
Horsefair La GL18 . . . . 170 F5
Horse Fair La SN6 . . . . 143 F4
Horsefair St GL53 . . . . 131 A5
Horsefair The BS1 . . . . 195 B3
Horse La BS35 . . . . 64 D5
Horse Lane Orch HR8 . . . . 178 F8
Horse Leaze Rd BS7 . . . . . . 19 C8
Horsemarling La GL10 . . . 101 F1
Horsepool La
Doynton BS30 . . . . 12 F8
St Briavels GL15 . . . . 146 E6
Horse Pool La HR9 . . . . . . 162 E2
Horsepool Rd BS13 . . . . 1 E3
Horsepool The 3 GL16 . . . 155 A7
Horseshoe Ct BS36 . . . . 31 D7
Horseshoe Dr
Bristol BS9 . . . . 17 C4
Over GL2 . . . . 126 B4
Horseshoe La BS37 . . . . 44 B1
Horseshoe Way GL2 . . . . . . 118 B6
Horse St BS37 . . . . 44 C1
Horsetrough Rdbt GL10 . . . 97 F6

Horsford Rd GL12......67 B5
Horslea GL17......163 D3
Horsley CE Prim Sch GL6. 90 F1
Horsley Cl GL4......119 E5
Horsley Hill GL6......91 A1
Horsley Rd GL6......91 A2
Hortham La BS32......40 E5
Horton CE Prim Sch BS37 45 C5
Horton Court* BS37......45 D7
Horton Hill BS37......45 C5
Horton Rd
  Chipping Sodbury BS37..44 C2
  Chipping Sodbury, Little Sodbury
    End BS37......44 D4
  Gloucester GL1......127 A4
Horton St BS2......195 C3
Horwood Ct 3 BS30......11 A4
Horwood La GL12......54 B4
Hosey Wlk BS13......2 A5
Hospital Rd (West St)
  GL56......187 A4
Hossil La SN6......145 A1
Host St BS1......195 A3
Hottom Gdns BS7......19 A7
Hot Water La BS15......21 A3
Hotwell Rd BS8......194 B1
Hotwells Ho BS8......194 A2
Hotwells Prim Sch BS8....7 F6
Houlton St BS2......195 C4
Hounds Cl BS37......44 B1
Hounds Rd BS37......44 B1
Howard Ave BS5......9 E8
Howard Cl
  Northway GL20......182 C4
  Saltford BS31......5 D3
Howard Ho GL54......139 F5
Howard Pl GL3......120 A7
Howard Rd
  Bristol, Southville BS3......8 C4
  Bristol, Staple Hill BS16...20 D4
  Bristol, Westbury Park BS6. 18 B4
  5 Coleford GL16......155 B6
  Northway GL20......182 C4
  Thornbury BS35......64 C2
Howard St
  Bristol BS5......19 E1
  Gloucester GL1......118 F7
Howard Wlk BS30......11 D7
Howcroft GL3......128 C4
Howcroft Ct BS9......17 E4
Howecroft Gdns BS9......17 E4
Howell Rd
  Cheltenham GL51......132 E4
  Cheltenham GL51......132 F4
Howell's La GL15......156 E3
Howells Mead BS16......21 B7
Howells Rd GL20......192 D4
Howells Row NP16......72 F1
Howes Cl BS30......11 A6
Howett 16 BS5......9 C7
Howgate Cl 1 GL4......119 F5
Howmead GL13......85 E4
Howsmoor La
  Bristol, Lyde Green BS16...21 C8
  Bristol, New England BS16. 21 B8
Hoylake BS37......32 E8
Hoylake Dr BS30......11 B6
Hubble Rd GL51......132 D1
Hucclecote La GL3......128 D2
Hucclecote Mews GL3...119 F7
Hucclecote Rd GL3......120 B7
Huckford La BS36......31 A4
Huckford Rd BS36......30 E5
Huckley Way BS32......29 F6
Huddleston Rd GL54......174 A8
Hudd's Hill Rd BS5......9 F8
Hudd's Vale Rd BS5......9 E8
Hudman's Cl GL20......182 A7
Hudnalls View NP25......146 B7
Hudson Cl
  Chipping Sodbury BS37....32 F8
  Honeybourne WR11......188 C7
Hudson La GL14......191 C1
Hudson St GL50......133 D3
Hudsons View GL14......191 C1
Hughenden Rd
  Bristol, Clifton BS8......18 A2
  Bristol, Horfield BS7......18 E5
Hughes Cl GL20......182 C5
Hughes Cres NP16......60 E7
Hughes Gdn BS7......19 A8
Hughes Terr GL15......155 E3
Hulbert Cl
  Bristol BS4......10 A2
  Swindon GL51......133 A7
Hulbert Cres GL51......129 F5
Hulse Rd BS4......9 D1
Humber Pl GL3......120 F5
Humber Rd GL52......134 A2
Humberstan Wlk BS11...16 E8
Humber Way BS11......26 D5
Humphreys Cl BS4......98 E8
Humphry Davy Way 6 BS8 .7 F6
Humphrys Barton BS4......9 F5
Hungerford Cl BS4......3 E8
Hungerford Cres BS4......9 E1
Hungerford Gdns BS4......3 E8
Hungerford Rd BS4......3 E8
Hungerford St GL50......133 D3
Hungerford Wlk BS4......9 E1
Hunger Hill GL11......80 A8
Hung Rd BS11......16 E5

Hunters Cl
  Bristol BS15......10 C5
  Stroud GL5......98 D7
Hunters Dr BS15......20 F1
Huntersfield SN16......58 D1
Hunters Gate GL4......119 D4
Hunters Mead GL9......56 A2
Hunters Rd
  Bishop's Cleeve GL52....137 E4
  Bristol BS15......10 C5
Hunters Rd E BS15......10 C4
Hunters Way GL5......98 D7
Hunter's Way
  Andoversford GL54......166 C6
  Bristol BS34......29 B3
Hunters Wy GL2......110 A5
Huntfield Rd NP16......60 D8
Hunthill GL14......165 E1
Huntingdon Cl GL5......98 D6
Huntingham Rd BS13......1 F4
Huntings The 7 WR12......185 B8
Huntley CE Prim School
  GL19......165 C6
Huntley Cl GL4......119 E5
Huntlowe Cl GL52......138 A5
Huntscote Rd GL51......133 A5
Huntsfield Cl GL50......133 E4
Hunts Ground Rd BS34......29 F4
Hunts Grove Dr
  Quedgeley GL2......110 A5
  Quedgeley GL2......110 B5
Hunts Grove View GL2...110 B7
Hunts Hill SN26......144 D1
Hunts La BS7......18 E6
Huntsmans Cl GL52......138 A4
Huntsmans Meet GL54...166 D6
Hurcombe Way GL3......120 E6
Hurle Cres BS8......18 B1
Hurle Rd BS8......18 B1
Hurlingham Rd BS7......18 F2
Hurn La BS31......5 A3
Hurricane Rd GL3......120 C5
Hursley Hill BS14......3 D1
Hursley La BS14......3 E1
Hurst Cl GL2......127 D5
Hurston Rd BS4......2 D7
Hurst Rd BS4......2 F8
Hurst Wlk BS4......2 F8
Hurstwood Rd BS16......20 D5
Hutton Cl
  Bristol BS9......17 E3
  Keynsham BS31......5 A2
Hutton Raufe GL51......132 F1
Huxley Cl GL7......143 A8
Huxley Rd GL1......118 F7
Huxley Way GL52......137 D4
Huyton Rd BS5......19 E3
Hyatts Way GL52......138 A3
Hyde Apartments BS6...18 C3
Hyde Ave BS35......64 B3
Hyde Bank GL14......156 F7
Hyde Cl
  Cirencester GL7......190 F6
  Gloucester GL1......127 A4
Hyde Cotts GL54......139 F4
Hyde La
  Gloucester GL1......127 A2
  Newnham GL14......156 F7
  Swindon GL50, GL51......133 D7
  Whitminster GL2......100 F6
Hyde Park Cnr GL19......179 D2
Hyde's La SN14......14 A6
Hydes The BS31......4 F5
Hyde The GL54......139 F5
Hyde View GL16......154 F3
Hyett Cl GL6......103 F8
Hyett Orch GL6......103 F8
Hyett Rd GL5......98 E7
Hygrove La GL2......125 B1
Hyland Gr BS9......17 F8

I

Ibis Wlk GL2......117 D1
Icehouse La GL56......186 D1
Icombe Cl GL52......137 F3
Idaho St GL7......152 E2
Ida Rd 2 BS5......9 C8
Iddesleigh Rd BS6......18 B3
Idsall Dr GL52......134 C4
Idstone Rd BS16......20 B4
Iford Cl BS31......5 E3
Ilchester Cres BS13......8 B1
Ilchester Rd BS13......2 B8
Iles Cl BS15......10 D4
Ilex Cl BS13......1 F6
Ilmington CE Prim Sch
  CV36......189 F6
Ilminster Ave BS4......2 F8
Ilminster Ave E-ACT Acad
  BS4......3 A8
Ilminster Avenue Prim Sch
  BS4......3 A8
Ilsom Cotts GL8......140 D5
Ilsyn Gr BS14......3 D7
Imber Court Cl BS14......3 E8
Imjin Rd GL52......134 B2
Immanuel Christian Sch
  BS37......32 B5
Imperial Arc 11 BS3......8 D4
Imperial Cir GL50......193 B3
Imperial Cl GL50......193 B3
Imperial Gate GL50......193 B3
Imperial Gate Bsns Pk
  GL4......127 D2

Imperial La GL50......193 B3
Imperial Pk BS13......2 C6
Imperial Rd
  8 Bristol, Clifton BS6......18 B1
  Bristol, Knowle BS14......3 C8
Imperial Sq GL50......193 B2
Imperial Wlk BS14......9 B1
Ince Castle Way GL1......119 A8
Inchbrook Cl GL5......90 F6
Inchbrook Hill GL5......91 A6
Inchbrook Trad Est GL5...91 A7
Inchbrook Way GL5......90 F6
India Ho 2 GL51......132 E2
India Rd GL1......119 A8
Industrial Ctr BS15......10 D8
Inglecote GL52......131 B6
Ingleside Rd BS15......20 C1
Ingleside Sch GL7......190 D4
Inglestone Rd GL12......54 B5
Ingmire Rd BS5......19 B3
Ingram Ct CV36......187 E5
Ingst Hill BS35......49 B3
Ingst Rd BS35......49 D4
Inkerman St BS7......18 E7
Inkerman La 16 GL50......130 B8
Inn Cotts BS11......17 A7
Inner Ctyd GL7......190 D7
Inner Down The BS12......50 D3
Inner Loop Rd NP16......61 B6
Innerstone La GL19......171 D4
Innocks Est GL11......79 D4
Innox Gdns BS13......2 A5
Inns Court Ave BS4......2 D7
Inns Court Dr BS4......2 D6
Inns Court Gn BS4......2 D7
Innsworth Jun Sch GL3..127 D6
Innsworth La GL3......127 D7
Innsworth Tech Pk GL3...127 C6
Insley Gdns BS13......119 F8
Instow Rd BS4......2 E8
Instow Wlk BS4......2 E8
International Centre of Birds
  of Prey* GL18......170 E2
International Dr 3 GL20 182 B4
International Trad Est
  BS11......26 B2
  Interplex 16 BS32......40 C3
Inverlea Ct GL55......189 A6
IO Ctr BS11......26 F5
Ipswich Dr BS4......9 E6
Irby Rd BS3......8 A3
Irena Rd BS16......19 F3
Ireton Rd BS3......8 B1
Iron Acton CE Prim Sch
  BS37......42 E4
Iron Acton Way BS37......43 B3
Ironchurch Rd BS11......26 C5
Iron Hogg La GL12......65 C3
Iron Mills GL6......91 E3
Ironmonger's La GL13......86 B4
Ironmould La BS4......10 A1
Ironstone Cl 2 GL15......147 D8
Irving Cl BS16......20 E4
Irving Cl GL52......193 C3
Irving Ho
  Bristol BS1......194 C3
  14 Cheltenham GL52......133 F2
Isambard Wlk BS1......195 C2
Isbourne Rd GL52......134 B2
Isbourne Valley Sch
  GL54......184 D2
Isbourne Way GL54......174 B8
I.S.F. Rd BS11......26 C3
Island Gdns BS16......19 C4
Island Trad Pk BS11......26 C1
Islay Cres SN6......145 C4
Isle Of Rhé GL11......79 C5
Isleys Ct BS30......10 F3
Islington Rd BS3......8 C4
Ismay Rd GL51......132 F4
Ison Hill Rd BS10......27 D3
Itchington Rd
  Alveston BS35......51 F4
  Tytherington GL12......52 B4
Itlay GL7......150 A8
Itton Rd NP16......72 B2
Ivanhoe Rd GL2......118 C4
Ivor Rd BS5......9 C8
Ivory Cl GL4......118 C2
Ivy Bank GL52......134 C3
Ivy Cotts NP16......73 B1
Ivy House Est HR9......170 B5
Ivy House La HR9......170 B5
Ivy La
  Bristol BS16......20 A3
  Broad Blunsdon SN26...144 D1
Ivy Lodge 4 BS9......18 A7
Ivy Lodge Barns GL4......121 F1
Ivy Mews GL1......118 F5
Ivy Terr BS37......32 B4
Ivywell Rd BS9......17 E3
Izod's Cl GL55......188 F1

J

Jackbarrow Rd GL7......107 A8
Jack Knight Ho BS7......18 F5
Jack Price Cl BS13......2 C3
Jack Russell Cl GL5......99 A8
Jackson Cl BS35......38 D7
Jackson Cres GL3......127 E6
Jackson Rd
  Bledington OX7......177 E1
  Siddington GL7......150 F2
Jacobs Cl 4 GL8......140 C5

Jacob's Ct BS1......194 B2
Jacobs Piece GL7......152 D3
Jacob St BS2......195 B3
Jacob's Wells Rd BS8......194 B2
Jamaica St BS2......195 B4
James Ave 10 GL2......117 D1
James Cl
  Bristol BS16......20 E4
  12 Quedgeley GL2......117 D1
James Counsell Wy BS16..29 F2
James Ct
  Cheltenham GL51......132 F1
  Yorkley GL15......156 B1
James Donovan Ct GL52. 134 A2
James Dr 9 GL2......117 D1
James Grieve Rd GL4......119 F6
Jameson Cl 24 GL56......187 A3
James Orch GL13......85 E3
James Pl 8 GL2......117 D1
James Rd BS16......20 E3
James Row 13 GL2......117 D1
James St
  Bristol, Baptist Mills BS2...19 A2
  Bristol, St Pauls BS5......19 A2
James Stephens Wy NP16 60 F4
James Way
  Gloucester GL3......120 C6
  Quedgeley GL2......117 E1
James Wlk
  Pillowell GL15......155 F1
  11 Quedgeley GL2......117 D1
Jane St BS5......9 B7
Japonica Cl 5 GL3......128 A7
Japonica Dr GL51......130 A5
Jardine Dr GL52......137 E4
Jarratts Rd BS10......28 D2
Jarvis St BS5......9 B6
Jasmine Cl GL4......119 D4
Jasmine Gr BS11......27 C2
Jasmin Way GL51......130 A5
Jasper Dr GL20......192 F2
Jasper St BS3......8 B3
Javelin Pk GL10......109 E1
Javelin Way GL3......120 F5
Jay's Gn HR9......170 A5
Jay's Mead GL12......68 C7
Jays The GL12......52 B6
Jaythorpe GL4......119 D3
Jean Rd BS4......9 E2
Jefferies Cl 7 GL52......152 E4
Jefferies Hill Bottom
  BS15......10 B5
Jeffery Ct BS30......11 B6
Jeffreys Ct 9 BS16......19 E3
Jeffries Ct GL7......190 D4
Jellicoe Ave BS16......19 E8
Jena Ct BS31......5 D3
Jenkin's La GL6......103 C7
Jenner Bvd BS16......31 B1
Jenner Ct
  Chipping Sodbury BS37....33 D8
  Gloucester GL3......119 F8
Jenner Ct GL13......85 E3
Jenner Wlk BS10......193 B4
Jennings Ct 1 BS3......8 A4
Jennings Orch GL52......138 B4
Jersey Ave
  Bristol BS4......9 F4
  Cheltenham GL52......133 F2
Jersey Rd GL1......119 A8
Jersey St BS2......193 C4
Jesse Mary Chambers
  Almshouses GL51......132 F1
Jesson Rd GL52......138 A3
Jessop Ave GL50......193 A3
Jessop Cres BS10......28 A1
Jessop Ct
  Bristol BS1......195 B2
  Quedgeley GL2......110 B5
Jessop Dr 2 GL52......168 A1
Jessop Underpass BS3......7 F4
Jet Age Air Mus* GL2..128 C8
Jetty Rd GL2......118 C7
Jewson Cl GL4......118 D2
Jeynes Bldgs GL20......192 D5
Jeynes Row GL20......192 D5
Jim O'Neil Ho BS11......16 D7
Jinty La BS15......21 B2
Joan Hawley Mews
  GL52......131 A7
Jobbins Ct GL7......190 C4
Job's La GL20......182 E8
Jocelyn Rd BS7......18 F7
Jockey La BS5......10 A7
Jockey Stable Cotts
  GL56......186 A4
John Bevan Cl GL5......99 D8
John Buck Ho 8 GL52..193 C4
John Cabot Acad BS15...10 C7
John Carr's Terr BS8......194 B2
John Chiddy Cl BS15......10 C2
John Cozens Ho 7 BS2. 195 C3
John Daniels Way GL3...128 B4
John Hall Cl BS14......3 B7
John James Ct BS7......19 B7
John Lamb Ho GL51......129 D2
John Masefield High Sch
  HR8......178 F8
John Moore Countryside
  Mus* GL20......192 C4
John Moore Gdns 4
  GL50......130 B6
John Moore Prim Sch The
  GL20......192 E1
John of Gaunt Rd GL7...144 E8

John Rastrick Rise/Rhodfa
  John Rastrick NP16......60 F4
John Repton Gdns BS10...28 B2
John Rushout Ct GL56...186 C7
John St Quinton Cl BS34..29 C2
Johnson Dr BS30......10 F5
Johnson Rd BS16......21 C5
Johnsons La BS5......19 C1
Johnsons Rd
  Bristol BS5......19 C1
  1 Bristol, Moorfields BS5...9 C8
Johnsons Way GL15......156 B2
John St
  Bristol, Baptist Mills BS2...19 A2
  Bristol BS5......19 C1
  Bristol, Two Mile Hill BS15..10 C8
  Stroud GL5......99 C7
Johnstone Cl GL19......172 A1
Johnstone Rd 3 GL18...171 A4
John Tame Cl 4 GL7......152 E4
John Wesley Ct 9 BS16...20 D5
John Wesley Rd BS5......10 B6
John Wesleys Chapel*
  BS1......195 B3
John Woolfe Ct GL56...186 C7
Joiners La GL6......148 D9
Jones Ho 3 NP25......154 A8
Jordans Cl WR12......188 B2
Jordans Way GL2......126 F5
Jordan Wlk BS32......29 D8
Jorrocks Ind Est BS37....32 C4
Josend Cres GL19......172 F7
Joyce Cl BS7......19 A4
Joyford Hill GL16......155 A8
Joyford Pas GL52......134 B2
Joy Hill BS8......7 F6
Joyner Rd GL51......133 A4
Joys Green Prim Sch
  GL17......163 D3
Joys Green Rd GL17......163 D3
Jubilee Ave GL11......87 F6
Jubilee Cl
  Chipping Campden GL55. 188 F2
  Dursley GL11......87 F6
  Ledbury HR8......178 F7
  12 Stow-on-t-W GL54......176 F4
Jubilee Cotts GL6......148 B5
Jubilee Cres BS16......21 A6
Jubilee Ct
  Bristol BS4......9 C4
  Cheltenham GL50......193 B1
Jubilee Dr
  Bredon GL20......182 C7
  Thornbury BS35......64 D1
Jubilee Flats GL7......150 E2
Jubilee Gdns
  South Cerney GL7......142 F7
  Yate BS37......44 A2
Jubilee Gn GL7......190 D3
Jubilee Ho BS34......29 C8
Jubilee La
  Bream GL15......147 D8
  Cromhall GL12......53 B7
Jubilee Park* HR9......162 E4
Jubilee Pl
  Bristol BS1......195 A1
  Bristol, Woodstock BS15...10 F7
  Corse GL19......172 A7
Jubilee Rd
  Bristol, Baptist Mills BS2...19 A1
  Bristol, Crew's Hole BS5...9 F7
  Bristol, Staple Hill BS15...20 E3
  Bristol, Upper Knowle BS4..9 C2
  Dursley GL11......88 A2
  Lydney GL15......92 C3
  Mitcheldean GL17......164 D3
  Nailsworth GL6......91 A3
Jubilee St BS2......195 C2
Jubilee Way
  Avonmouth BS11......26 B2
  Newton GL13......85 D8
Judge's La
  Longhope GL18......170 F1
  Taynton GL18......171 A7
Julian Cl
  Bristol BS9......17 E3
  Gloucester GL4......119 D8
Julian Ct BS9......17 E3
Julian Rd BS9......17 E3
Julius Cl BS16......21 C6
Julius Rd BS7......18 D3
Julius Way GL15......92 B4
Jumpers La GL13......85 E3
Junction Rd BS4......9 C4
Junction Wy BS15......21 A3
Juniper Ave GL4......119 B4
Juniper Cotts GL6......103 C5
Juniper Ct
  2 Bristol BS5......19 C2
  Cheltenham GL51......132 C2
Juniper Way
  Bristol BS34......30 A7
  Stonehouse GL10......97 F8
Juniper Wy GL3......120 B4
Juno Dr GL15......92 B5
Jupiter Cl GL2......128 C8
Jupiter Rd BS34......28 E7
Jupiter Way GL4......119 F6
Justice Ave BS31......5 E3
Justice Rd BS16......20 A3
Justicia Wy GL51......129 F5
Justin's Hill NP25......154 A7
Jutland Rd BS11......26 B1

Kansas Dr GL7 . . . . 152 E2
Karelean Ct BS10 . . . . 28 D3
Kaskelot Way GL2. . . . . . 118 C6
Katharine Ct GL51. . . . . . 130 A5
Katharine Lady Berkeley
Mews GL12 . . . . 68 B7
Katharine Lady Berkeley's
Sch GL12 . . . . 67 F6
Kathdene Gdns BS7 . . . . 18 F3
Katherine Cl
  Charfield GL12. . . . . . . 67 A5
  Innsworth GL3. . . . . . .127 F8
Katherine's Wlk
  Lechlade on T GL7 . . . . 153 E2
  5 Ledbury HR8 . . . . . . 178 E7
Kaybourne Cres GL3 . . . 128 D5
Kayte Cl GL52. . . . . 137 F2
Kayte La GL52 . . . . 138 A2
Keats Ave GL2 . . . . 118 C4
Keats Ct BS7. . . . . 19 A8
Keats Gdns GL5 . . . . 103 A1
Keble Ave BS13. . . . . 1 F5
Keble Cl
  Cirencester GL7 . . . . . . 190 B1
  Lechlade on T GL7 . . . . 153 E2
Keble Lawns GL7 . . . . . . 152 E3
Keble Rd
  Chalford GL6. . . . . 148 D6
  Moreton-in-M GL56 . . . 187 A2
Keel Cl BS5. . . . . 9 F6
Keelings The GL14 . . . . . 191 C5
Keels SN6 . . . . 143 E5
Keen's Gr BS35 . . . . 38 C7
Keepers La BS7. . . . . 18 F3
Keepers Mill GL52 . . . . . 138 B3
Keep The BS30 . . . . 11 D5
Keg Store The BS1. . . . . 195 B2
Keil Cl **5** WR12. . . . . 185 B8
Keinton Wlk BS10. . . . . . . 28 A2
Keirle Wlk GL51. . . . . 133 A4
Kelbra Cres BS36. . . . . 31 B6
Kellaway Ave BS7. . . . . . . 18 D5
Kellaway Cres BS9 . . . . . . 18 D6
Kellaway Ct BS6 . . . . 18 D5
Kells Meend GL16. . . . . . 155 A4
Kells Rd GL16. . . . . 155 A7
Kellys La NP16 . . . . 146 F1
Kelston Cl
  Saltford BS31 . . . . 5 D4
  Yate BS37 . . . . 32 D7
Kelston Gdns BS10. . . . . . 18 D8
Kelston Gr BS15 . . . . 10 E6
Kelston Rd
  Bristol BS10. . . . . 18 D8
  Kelston BA1. . . . . 6 E1
  Keynsham BS31 . . . . 4 D5
Kelston Wlk BS16 . . . . . . 20 C4
Kemble Bsns Pk SN16. . . 141 D6
Kemble Cl
  Bristol BS15. . . . . 10 E6
  Gloucester GL4 . . . . . . 118 D2
Kemble Dr GL7 . . . . 190 B2
Kemble Gdns BS11. . . . . . 16 F5
Kemble Gr GL51 . . . . 129 B7
Kemble Ho BS34 . . . . 39 F1
Kemble Pk GL7 . . . . 141 F7
Kemble Prim Sch GL7. . . 141 F8
Kemble Rd GL4 . . . . 118 E2
Kemble Sta GL7. . . . . 141 F8
Kemerton Rd
  Bredon GL20 . . . . 182 C7
  Cheltenham GL50. . . . . 130 B6
  Westmancote GL20 . . . 182 D8
Kemperleye Way BS32 . . 29 D7
Kempe's Cl BS37. . . . . 7 A2
Kempley Cl GL52. . . . . . . 134 B2
Kempley Rd GL18 . . . . . . 178 C1
Kempsford Acre GL52 . . . 138 B3
Kempsford CE Prim Sch
  GL7. . . . . 144 B8
Kemps La GL6 . . . . 103 F8
Kempton Cl
  2 Bristol BS16. . . . . . . 30 F1
  Thornbury BS35. . . . . . . 64 B3
Kempton Gr GL51 . . . . . . 132 D2
Kencot Wlk BS13 . . . . 2 B3
Kencourt Cl **2** GL2 . . . . . 127 B2
Kendall Gdns BS16. . . . . . 20 D4
Kendall Rd BS16 . . . . 20 D4
Kendal Rd
  Bristol BS7. . . . . 19 A7
  Gloucester GL2 . . . . . . 127 C4
Kendon Dr BS10 . . . . 18 D7
Kendon Way BS10. . . . . . . 18 D8
Kendrick La **11** GL5 . . . . . . 99 C7
Kendrick St **9** GL5. . . . . . . 99 C7
Kenelm Dr GL53 . . . . 130 C6
Kenelm Gdns GL53 . . . . . 130 B6
Kenelm Rise GL54. . . . . . 174 A8
Kenilworth BS37 . . . . 32 F8
Kenilworth Ave GL2. . . . 127 B3
Kenilworth Cl BS31 . . . . . . 4 D4
Kenilworth Dr BS30 . . . . . 11 B2
Kenilworth Ho **3** GL51. . 132 E3
Kenilworth Rd BS6. . . . . . 18 C1
Kenmare Rd BS4. . . . . 8 E1
Kenmore Cres BS7. . . . . . 28 E1
Kenmore Dr BS7. . . . . 28 E1
Kenmore Gr BS7. . . . . 28 E1
Kennard Cl BS15. . . . . 10 C7
Kennard Rd BS15. . . . . . . 10 C8
Kennard Rise BS15. . . . . . 10 C8

Kenn Court Bsns Pk BS4 . . .2 E7
Kennedy Cl GL3. . . . . 127 F1
Kennedy Ho BS37. . . . . . . 43 F1
Kennedy Way BS37. . . . . . 43 F1
Kennel Dr GL9 . . . . 46 E2
Kennel La
  10 Broadway WR12. . . . . 185 B8
  Broadwell GL56 . . . . . . 177 A6
  Watermead GL3. . . . . . 127 B6
Kennel Lodge Rd BS3. . . . .7 E4
Kennerwell La GL12. . . . . 68 E3
Kennet Cl GL20 . . . . 182 B4
Kennet Ct GL55 . . . . 130 E4
Kenneth Rd BS4. . . . . 9 D2
Kennet Rd BS31. . . . . 5 A4
Kennett Gdns GL4. . . . . . 119 F4
Kennett Way **4** BS35 . . . . . 51 D8
Kennington Ave
  Bristol, Bishopston BS7. . . 18 F4
  3 Bristol, Two Mile Hill
  BS15. . . . . 20 D1
Kennion Rd BS5 . . . . 10 A7
Kennmoor Cl BS30 . . . . . . 11 A6
Kenn Rd BS5. . . . . 10 A7
Kensal Ave BS3. . . . . 8 E3
Kensal Rd BS3 . . . . 8 E3
Kensington Apartments
  BS6 . . . . 18 C3
Kensington Ave GL50. . . 130 A8
Kensington Cl BS35. . . . . 64 B2
Kensington Ct BS8 . . . . . 194 A3
Kensington Ho **5** BS5. . . . . 10 A8
Kensington Park Rd BS4 . . 9 C2
Kensington Pk **12** BS5. . . . . 19 A1
Kensington Pl BS8 . . . . . 194 A3
Kensington Rd
  Bristol, Redland BS6 . . . . 18 C1
  3 Bristol, St George BS5. . 10 A8
  Bristol, Staple Hill BS16. . 20 D4
Kent Ave BS37 . . . . 43 F3
Kent Cl
  Bristol BS34. . . . . 29 D4
  Churchdown GL3. . . . . 128 D5
Kent End SN6. . . . . 143 A5
Kent End Cl SN6 . . . . 143 A5
Kentmere Rd BS16 . . . . . . 19 E7
Kent Mews BS16. . . . . 19 E7
Kenton Dr GL2. . . . . 127 C5
Kenton Ho BS34 . . . . 39 F1
Kenton Mews BS9 . . . . . . 18 C5
Kent Rd BS7. . . . . 18 E4
Kents Gn BS15. . . . . 20 E2
Kent St BS3. . . . . 8 C3
Kenulf Rd **29** GL54 . . . . . . 174 A7
Kenwood Cl BS15. . . . . . . 20 F1
Keppel Cl BS31 . . . . 5 D2
Keriston Ave GL3 . . . . . . 128 A6
Kerrin La GL15 . . . . 147 C2
Kerris Ct **9** GL3 . . . . 128 A7
Kerr Way GL56. . . . . 187 C3
Kerry Rd BS4 . . . . .8 E1
Kersteman Rd BS6 . . . . . . 18 C3
Kerstin Cl GL50 . . . . 133 C5
Kestrel Cl
  Bristol BS34. . . . . 28 E8
  Cheltenham GL53. . . . . 130 C5
  Chipping Sodbury BS37. . 32 F8
  Thornbury BS35. . . . . . . 64 D2
Kestrel Ct **8** GL10 . . . . 97 F8
Kestrel Dr BS16. . . . . 22 C4
Kestrel Gdns GL2. . . . . . 117 F3
Kestrel Par GL3. . . . . 127 D6
Kestrel Way GL20 . . . . . . 182 B5
Keswick Cl GL2 . . . . 127 B3
Keswick Rd GL51. . . . . . . 129 E7
Keswick Wlk BS10 . . . . . . 28 C2
Ketch Rd BS3. . . . . .8 F3
Kevin Cl GL4. . . . . 127 D1
Kew Pl GL53 . . . . 193 B1
Kews La GL18. . . . . 170 D4
Kewstoke Rd BS9 . . . . 17 E4
Kew Wlk BS4 . . . . 3 C8
Keynes Ctry Pk★ GL7 . . . 142 D6
Keynsham Bank GL52 . . 130 F8
Keynshambury Rd GL52 . 193 C2
Keynsham By-Pass BS31 . . 4 E7
Keynsham La GL15 . . . . . 147 B2
Keynsham Rd
  Bitton BS30, BS31 . . . . . . 5 A8
  Cheltenham GL53. . . . . 193 C2
Keynsham St GL52 . . . . . 130 F8
Keynsham Sta BS31. . . . . . .4 F6
Keys Ave BS7 . . . . 18 F7
Keytes Acre GL55 . . . . . . 189 D3
Kibble's La GL14. . . . . . . 191 C1
Kidnalls Dr GL15 . . . . . . 155 F1
Kidnalls Rd GL15. . . . . . . 155 F1
Kidnams Wlk GL4. . . . . . 100 F5
Kidnappers La GL53. . . . 130 B4
Kidney Hill BS37 . . . . 32 A3
Kiftsgate Court Gdns★
  GL55. . . . . 189 C6
Kilbirnie Rd BS14 . . . . 3 A3
Kilburn Ct **17** BS5 . . . . .9 B8
Kilburn St **18** BS5 . . . . .9 B8
Kilda Rd SN6 . . . . 145 C4
Kildare Rd BS4. . . . . 8 D1
Kilham La GL54. . . . . 166 E5
Kilkenny St BS2. . . . . 195 C4
Killcott Rd GL12 . . . . 55 E8
Kilmersdon Rd BS13 . . . . . .2 B4
Kilminster Cl BS34 . . . . . . 29 D7
Kilminster Ct **10** GL3 . . . . 128 A7
Kilminster Rd BS11 . . . . . 16 D7
Kilmore La GL20 . . . . 181 F7

Kiln Cl BS15 . . . . 20 B2
Kiln Ct BS5. . . . . .9 B8
Kilnhurst Cl BS30 . . . . . . 10 F2
Kilvert Cl BS4. . . . . 9 D5
Kimberland Way GL4. . . 119 E6
Kimberley Ave BS16. . . . . 20 C5
Kimberley Cl
  Bristol BS16. . . . . 20 F7
  Gloucester GL2 . . . . . . 127 D4
  Lydney GL15. . . . . 92 B3
Kimberley Cres BS16. . . . 20 C5
Kimberley Dr GL15. . . . . . 92 B3
Kimberley Rd
  Bristol, Fishponds BS16. . 20 C5
  Bristol, Kingswood BS15. . 20 D1
Kimberley Wlk GL52. . . . 134 C2
Kimbrose GL1 . . . . 196 A2
Kimbrose Way GL1. . . . . 196 A2
Kimmins Rd GL10 . . . . . . 98 A8
Kinder Ho GL52. . . . . 134 B4
Kinema Ho BS4. . . . . 9 C4
King Alfreds Rd NP16 . . . 61 A8
King Alfred Way GL52. . . 130 F8
Kingcomb La GL55 . . . . . 188 F2
King Arthur Cl GL53. . . . 130 F7
King Dick's La **7** BS5. . . . . .9 F8
King Edward Cl BS14. . . . . 3 A6
King Edward's Ave GL1. . 118 C4
Kingfisher Bsns Pk GL5 . . . 99 C3
Kingfisher Cl
  Bristol BS10. . . . . 28 B4
  Bristol BS32. . . . . 40 E2
  Thornbury BS35. . . . . . . 64 D2
Kingfisher Ct GL51 . . . . . 132 E5
Kingfisher Dr
  Bristol BS16. . . . . 19 E6
  Cheltenham GL51. . . . . 132 E5
Kingfisher Pl GL7 . . . . . . 143 A8
Kingfisher Rise **6** GL2 . . . 117 D1
Kingfisher Sch The BS4 . . . 2 F8
King George Cl GL53 . . . 130 F6
King Georges Field BS14. . 176 F4
King George's Rd BS13. . . . 1 F5
King George V Pl **6**
  BS1 . . . . 195 A2
King Henry Cl GL53 . . . . 130 F6
King John's Cotts GL20. . 192 C5
King Johns Ct GL20 . . . . 192 C5
King John's Rd BS15. . . . . 20 B2
King La BS37. . . . . 45 A7
Kingley Rd GL5 . . . . 98 E7
King Rd BS4 . . . . 9 C1
King Road Ave BS11. . . . . 26 B2
Kingrove Cres BS37. . . . . 33 C8
Kingrove La BS37 . . . . 33 C7
Kings Ave
  Bristol BS15. . . . . 10 B4
  Highworth SN6 . . . . 145 D3
King's Ave BS6, BS7 . . . . . 18 C4
King's Barton St GL1 . . . 196 C2
Kingsbridge Mews GL51 132 D3
Kings Chase BS15. . . . . . . 10 D8
Kingsclere Dr GL52 . . . . . 137 E3
Kingscote BS37 . . . . 32 D6
Kingscote Ave GL51 . . . . 129 D7
Kingscote Cl
  Cheltenham GL51. . . . . 129 D7
  Churchdown GL3. . . . . 128 D4
Kingscote Dr GL4 . . . . . . 119 E5
Kingscote Gr GL51 . . . . . 129 D7
Kingscote Pk BS5. . . . . . . 10 B6
Kingscote Rd W GL51 . . . 129 D6
Kingscourt BS14 . . . . 3 A4
Kingscourt La GL5 . . . . . . 99 A4
Kingscroft Rd GL3 . . . . . 120 A7
Kings Ct
  Bristol BS13. . . . . 1 F4
  Bristol, Canon's Marsh
  BS1. . . . . 195 A2
  Bristol, Kingsdown BS1. . 195 A4
  Bristol, Little Stoke BS34. . 29 C6
Kingsdale Ct WR12. . . . . 185 C8
Kingsdown Gr BS6 . . . . . 195 A4
Kingsdown Par BS6 . . . . 195 A4
Kings Dr
  Bristol, Hanham BS15 . . . 10 B4
  Bristol, Stoke Gifford BS34. . 30 B4
  Dursley GL11. . . . . 88 A2
King's Dr BS7. . . . . 18 C4
Kings Elm GL2. . . . . 173 B3
Kings Field BS37 . . . . 43 A8
Kingsfield Cl BS30 . . . . . . 12 D6
Kingsfield La
  Bristol, Longwell Green
  BS15. . . . . 10 E5
  Bristol, Mount Hill BS30 . . 10 F5
Kingsfield Rdbt BS15. . . . 10 E5
Kingsfield Sch BS15. . . . . 11 A8
Kings' Forest Prim Sch
  BS15. . . . . 21 A2
Kings Gate GL20 . . . . . . 192 F4
Kingsgate Ct BS37. . . . . . 32 E8
Kings Head La BS13. . . . . 166 F2
King's Head La **1** F7
Kingshill Ho BS4. . . . . .9 B1
Kingshill La
  Cirencester GL7. . . . . . 150 F4
  Dursley GL11. . . . . 88 A2
Kingshill Pk GL11 . . . . . . 88 A3

Kingshill Rd
  Bristol BS4. . . . . 9 B1
  Dursley GL11. . . . . 88 A2
Kingsholm CE Prim Sch
  GL1. . . . . 196 C4
Kingsholm Ct GL1. . . . . . 126 E4
Kingsholme Rd BS15. . . . 20 D1
Kingsholm Rd
  Bristol BS10. . . . . 18 D8
  Gloucester GL1 . . . . . . 196 B4
Kingsholm Sq GL1. . . . . 196 B4
Kingsland Cl **1** BS2. . . . . . . 9 A6
Kingsland Rd BS2. . . . . 9 A6
Kingsland Road Bridge **3**
  BS2. . . . . 9 A6
Kingsland Trad Est BS2. . . . 9 A7
Kingsleigh Ct BS15. . . . . 10 F7
Kingsleigh Gdns BS15. . . 10 F7
Kingsleigh Pk BS15. . . . . 10 F7
Kingsley Gdns GL51 . . . . 129 E8
Kingsley Ho
  Bristol BS2. . . . . 195 C2
  Bristol, Westbury on Trym
  BS9. . . . . 18 A8
Kingsley Pl **1** BS3. . . . . 8 C4
Kingsley Rd
  Bristol, Lower Easton BS5. . 19 C1
  Bristol, Montpelier BS6 . . 18 D2
  Gloucester GL4 . . . . . . 119 A5
Kingsmark La/Lon Cyn Farch
  NP16 . . . . 72 D1
Kingsmarsh Ho **3** BS5 . . . .9 B7
Kings Mdw
  Bourton-on-t-W GL54 . . . 168 F8
  Charfield GL12. . . . . . . 67 B5
  Crudwell SN16 . . . . 141 B3
Kingsmead
  Cirencester GL7. . . . . . 190 E2
  Gloucester GL4 . . . . . . 119 F4
  Lechlade on T GL7 . . . . 153 E3
  Painswick GL6. . . . . . . 103 E8
Kings Mead GL14 . . . . . . 156 F6
Kingsmead Ave GL51. . . 132 F4
Kingsmead Ind Est GL51 . 133 A4
Kingsmead Rd
  Bristol BS5. . . . . 20 A1
  Cheltenham GL51. . . . . 132 F4
Kingsmead Wlk BS5. . . . . 20 A1
Kingsmill BS9 . . . . 17 D5
King's Mill La GL6. . . . . . 102 F3
King's Parade Ave BS8 . . 18 B1
King's Parade Mews BS8 . 18 A1
Kings Park Ave BS2 . . . . . . 9 C6
King Sq BS2. . . . . 195 A4
King Square Ave BS2. . . 195 A4
King's Rd
  Bristol, Kensington Park
  BS4. . . . . 9 C3
  Bristol, Victoria Park BS8 . 194 A3
  Cheltenham GL52. . . . . 133 F1
  Stonehouse GL10. . . . . 101 F1
  Stroud GL5. . . . . 99 B6
King's Sch The GL1 . . . . . 196 B3
Kings Sq BS30 . . . . 5 D8
King's Sq GL1. . . . . 196 B3
King's Stanley CE Jun Sch
  GL10. . . . . 98 A4
King's Stanley CE Prim Sch
  GL10. . . . . 98 A3
King St
  Avonmouth BS11 . . . . . . 26 A1
  Bristol BS1. . . . . 195 A2
  Bristol, Lower Easton BS5. . 19 C1
  Bristol, St George BS15. . . 10 B8
  Cheltenham GL50. . . . . 193 B4
  Cirencester GL7. . . . . . 190 D3
  Minchinhampton GL6. . 148 A3
  Stroud GL5. . . . . 99 C7
Kings Terr GL9. . . . . 57 B3
Kingston Ave BS31. . . . . . . 5 C3
Kingston Cl BS16 . . . . 21 A7
Kingston Dr
  Bristol BS16. . . . . 21 A7
  Cheltenham GL51. . . . . 132 C1
Kingstone Ave GL3. . . . . 127 F1
Kingston Rd
  Bristol BS3. . . . . 8 C4
  Northway GL20 . . . . . . 182 C4
  Slimbridge GL2 . . . . 95 C4
Kingstree St BS4. . . . . 9 A4
King Street Par **4** GL5 . . . 99 C7
Kingsville BS37. . . . . 133 A5
Kings Walk Sh Ctr GL1 . . 196 B2
Kingsway
  Bristol, Little Stoke BS34. . 29 C6
  Bristol, St George BS5. . . 10 B7
  Coleford GL16. . . . . . . 155 B6
  Dursley GL11. . . . . 88 A3
  Gloucester GL2 . . . . . . 110 A8
  Preston GL7. . . . . 150 F3
Kingsway Ave BS15 . . . . . 10 B8
Kingsway Bsns Pk GL2 . . 110 A7
Kingsway Cres BS15 . . . . 10 C8
Kingsway La GL17. . . . . . 163 C4
Kingsway Pk BS30 . . . . . . 11 B8
Kingsway Prim Sch GL2 . . 110 B7
Kingsway Sh Prec GL2. . . 110 B7
Kingswear Rd BS3 . . . . 8 D2
Kings Well La GL54 . . . . . 176 C1
Kings Weston Ave BS11. . 16 E6
Kingsweston Down Nature
  Res★ BS9, BS11. . . . . . . 27 C1

Kings Weston La
  Avonmouth BS11 . . . . . . 26 E3
  Bristol BS11. . . . . 17 A8
Kings Weston Rd BS11,
  BS10 . . . . 27 C1
Kingsweston Sch BS11 . . . 17 A8
Kings Wlk
  Bristol BS13. . . . . 1 E7
  Gloucester GL1 . . . . . . 196 B3
Kingswood Abbey
  Gatehouse★ GL12. . . . . 67 F5
Kingswood Cl GL52 . . . . 137 F3
Kingswood Foundation Est
  BS15. . . . . 10 C7
Kingswood Hertitage Mus★
  BS30. . . . . 11 B6
Kingswood Hts BS15 . . . . 20 D1
Kingswood Prim Sch
  GL12. . . . . 67 F5
Kingswood Rd GL12. . . . . 55 D8
Kingswood Trad Est BS15. . 20 D1
Kington La BS35. . . . . 63 E1
Kington Rd BS35. . . . . 63 E3
King William Ave BS1 . . 195 A2
King William Dr GL53 . . 130 F6
Kinloss Dr GL2. . . . . 118 C4
Kinmoor GL4. . . . . 119 D3
Kinsale Rd BS14 . . . . 3 C7
Kinsale Wlk BS4. . . . . 8 E1
Kinsham La GL20 . . . . . . 182 E7
Kinvara Rd
  1 Bristol BS4. . . . . 2 E8
  Bristol BS4. . . . . 2 E8
Kipling Cl GL2 . . . . 118 C4
Kipling Rd
  Bristol BS7. . . . . 29 B1
  Cheltenham GL51. . . . . 132 E1
  Dursley GL11. . . . . 80 C7
Kirby Rd GL54 . . . . 169 E6
Kirkby Rd BS11 . . . . 27 A1
Kirkstone Gdns BS10 . . . 28 C2
Kirkstone Ho BS34 . . . . . 29 A8
Kirtlington Rd BS5 . . . . . . 19 B3
Kitchener Ave GL51 . . . . 118 E6
Kitebrook House GL56 . . . 187 E2
Kitefield **15** SN6 . . . . 143 E4
Kite Hay Cl BS16. . . . . 19 E5
Kites Cl BS32 . . . . 40 C2
Kitesnest GL6. . . . . 102 F3
Kitesnest La GL5 . . . . 99 A4
Klondyke Ave GL15. . . . . 92 B3
Knap La GL6. . . . . 103 F7
Knapp Cl HR9. . . . . 163 A6
Knapp Cotts GL18. . . . . . 179 B3
Knapp La
  Brimscombe GL5. . . . . . 148 A4
  Cheltenham GL50. . . . . 193 A4
  Coaley GL11. . . . . 89 B5
  Cromhall GL12. . . . . . . 66 B3
  Dursley GL11. . . . . 87 F6
  Stroud GL6. . . . . 104 B2
  Woolaston GL15 . . . . . . 147 D3
Knapp Rd
  Cheltenham GL50. . . . . 193 A4
  Thornbury BS35. . . . . . . 64 D1
  Wotton-u-E GL12. . . . . . 68 C7
Knapps Cres GL52. . . . . . 138 B4
Knapps La BS5. . . . . 19 E2
Knapp The
  Dursley GL11. . . . . 88 B1
  Yate BS37 . . . . 43 F5
Kneller Cl BS11. . . . . 17 A8
Knighton Rd BS10. . . . . . . 28 E1
Knightsbridge Bsns Ctr
  GL51. . . . . 173 F5
Knightsbridge Cres GL53 130 F7
Knightsbridge Gn GL51. . 173 F5
Knightsbridge Pk BS13. . . .2 E4
Knights Cl BS9. . . . . 18 B6
Knights Cres GL18 . . . . . 170 F4
Knightshill HR9. . . . . 164 D8
Knightstone Ct BS5 . . . . . 19 D2
Knightstone Ho **1** BS4. . . 195 A4
Knightstone Lodge BS6. . 18 D1
Knightstone Mount BS5 . . 10 A6
Knightstone Rise **5** BS5. . .9 F8
Knightstone Sq BS14 . . . . 3 C5
Knightstone Wlk BS2. . . 194 C4
Knights Way
  Newent GL18 . . . . 170 E4
  Tewkesbury GL20 . . . . 192 E4
Knightwood Rd BS34. . . . 29 F5
Knockdown Rd SN16. . . . 58 C1
Knockley Patch GL15. . . . 155 D1
Knole Cl BS32. . . . . 39 F4
Knole La BS10 . . . . 28 B3
Knole Pk BS32. . . . . 39 F3
Knoll Ct BS9. . . . . 17 D3
Knoll Hill BS9. . . . . 17 D3
Knoll The
  Kempsford GL7 . . . . . . 144 E8
  Stroud GL5. . . . . 99 D7
  Uley GL11. . . . . 89 C1
Knolls End GL2. . . . . 109 F8
Knottes Cl GL54. . . . . 139 F6
Knovill Cl BS11. . . . . 27 B2
Knowesend SN6. . . . . 145 D4
Knowle DGE School 2 D8
Knowle Park Prim Sch BS4 9 A1
Knowle Rd BS2. . . . . 8 F3
Knowles Rd GL1. . . . . 118 F7

Knowsley Rd BS16 . . . . . . 19 E3
Knox Rd GL15 . . . . 147 E8
Kydderminster Rd GL54 . . 174 A8
Kyght Cl BS15 . . . . 11 A8
Kylross Ave BS14 . . . . 3 B5
Kymin Lea NP25 . . . . . . 154 A7
Kymin Rd NP25 . . . . 154 B7
Kynges Mill Cl BS16 . . . . . 20 A7
Kyngstone Ct **10** BS16 . . . . 19 E3

L

Labbott The BS31 . . . . .4 E5
Laburnum Cres GL6 . . . . . 102 F2
Laburnum Ct GL51 . . . . . 132 C2
Laburnum Gdns GL2 . . . . 117 F2
Laburnum Gr BS16 . . . . . . 20 B4
Laburnum Mews GL10 . . . . 97 E7
Laburnum Rd
 Bristol BS15 . . . . 10 C5
 Gloucester GL1 . . . . . . 118 D5
Laburnum Way NP16 . . . . . 60 E5
Laburnum Wlk
 Keynsham BS31 . . . . .4 C3
 Stonehouse GL10 . . . . . . 97 E7
Lacca Cl GL2 . . . . 127 D5
Lacey Rd BS14 . . . . .3 F6
Lacock Dr BS30 . . . . 10 F5
Lacy Cl GL2 . . . . 127 C6
Ladbarrow Cotts GL54 . . 161 A4
Ladd Cl BS15 . . . . 10 F7
Ladden Ct BS35 . . . . 51 C8
Ladder The GL6 . . . . 91 C4
Ladies Mile BS8 . . . . 17 F1
Ladman Gr BS14 . . . . .3 E6
Ladman Rd BS14 . . . . .3 E5
Ladybellegate St GL1 . . . 196 A2
Lady Chapel Rd GL4 . . . . 119 E6
Lady Downe Cl GL4 . . . . . 119 E6
Ladygrove Bsns Pk GL17 164 E5
Lady La SN25 . . . . 144 D1
Lady Margaret Ct NP16 . . . 60 F4
Lady Mead SN6 . . . . 143 E4
Ladysmith Rd
 Bristol BS6 . . . . 18 B4
 Cheltenham GL52 . . . . . 134 B2
 Gloucester GL1 . . . . . . 118 E6
Ladywell Cl GL2 . . . . 118 B7
Laggar La GL5 . . . . 98 F1
Laines Est The GL54 . . . . 158 F6
Lake Cl GL2 . . . . 124 B3
Lakefield CE Prim Sch
 GL2 . . . . 100 A6
Lake La
 Churcham GL2 . . . . 124 B3
 Frampton on Severn GL2 . 157 F3
Lake Louise SN6 . . . . 143 E6
Lakemead Gdns BS13 . . . . .1 F4
Lakemead Gr BS13 . . . . . . 1 F6
Lakenheath GL2 . . . . 110 B8
Lake Rd BS10 . . . . 18 C8
Lakers Rd GL16 . . . . 155 A4
Lakers Sch GL16 . . . . . . 155 B7
Lakeside
 Bristol BS16 . . . . 19 E3
 Fairford GL7 . . . . 152 D3
 South Cerney GL7 . . . . . 143 A8
Lake Side GL18 . . . . 171 A5
Lakeside Ave GL15 . . . . . . 92 C2
Lakeside Ct GL52 . . . . . . 133 F4
Lakeside Dr GL15 . . . . . . 92 C2
Lakeside Gdns GL15 . . . . . 92 B2
Lakeside Prim Sch GL51 . 129 E7
Lake St
 Cheltenham GL52 . . . . . 134 B5
 Quedgeley GL2 . . . . . . 116 D4
Lake View BS16 . . . . 19 F3
Lake View Rd BS5 . . . . 9 D8
Lakewood Cres BS10 . . . . 18 B8
Lakewood Rd BS10 . . . . . . 18 B8
La Maison BS5 . . . . 20 A2
Lambe Cl GL7 . . . . 152 D3
Lambert Ave GL51 . . . . . 129 D1
Lambert Cl GL51 . . . . . . 129 D1
Lambert Dr GL51 . . . . . . 129 D1
Lambert Gdns GL51 . . . . 129 D1
Lambert Pl BS4 . . . . .2 D6
Lamberts Field GL54 . . . . 169 A7
Lambert Terr GL51 . . . . . 129 D2
Lamb Hill BS5 . . . . .9 F7
Lamb La GL14 . . . . 191 D4
Lambley Rd BS5 . . . . 9 E8
Lambourn Cl
 Bristol BS3 . . . . .8 D3
 Gloucester GL2 . . . . . . 127 C3
Lambourne Ave GL19 . . . . 165 D6
Lambourne Cl **14** HR8 . . . 178 F8
Lambourn Rd BS3 . . . . 5 A4
Lambrook Rd BS16 . . . . . . 20 A4
Lambs Barn Pitch GL18 . . 171 A5
Lambs Cross HR9 . . . . . . 170 B4
Lambsdowne GL11 . . . . . . 87 F3
Lambsquay Rd GL16 . . . . 155 A3
Lamb St BS2 . . . . 195 C3
Lamington Cl BS13 . . . . . . 1 F6
Lamord Gate BS34 . . . . . . 29 E5
Lampern View GL11 . . . . . 89 B1
Lampeter Rd BS9 . . . . 18 A7
Lampreys The GL4 . . . . . 119 B6
Lampton Ave BS13 . . . . . . .2 E3
Lampton Gr BS13 . . . . 2 E3
Lampton Rd BS41 . . . . 7 A1

Lanaway Rd BS16 . . . . 20 B6
Lancashire Rd BS7 . . . . . . 18 E3
Lancaster Cl BS34 . . . . . . 29 D4
Lancaster Ct
 2 Cheltenham GL50 . . 130 B8
 Lydney GL15 . . . . 92 B5
Lancaster Dr
 Lydney GL15 . . . . 92 B5
 Upper Rissington GL54 . . 169 D6
Lancaster Gr GL4 . . . . . . 119 A6
Lancaster Rd
 Bristol BS2 . . . . 19 A2
 Gloucester GL3 . . . . . . 120 B4
 Kempsford GL7 . . . . . . 144 F7
 Tewkesbury GL20 . . . . . 192 D2
 Yate BS37 . . . . 43 E3
Lancaster St **10** BS5 . . . . . 9 C7
Lancaster Terr GL18 . . . . 171 A5
Lancaster Way NP16 . . . . . 60 D8
Lancaut La NP16 . . . . 72 F6
Lancelot Ct GL2 . . . . 95 D4
Lancelot Rd BS16 . . . . 19 E8
Landgate Yard **2** GL54 . . 176 F4
Landing Lights BS14 . . . . . .2 E5
Landmark Ct BS1 . . . . . . 194 C1
Landor Gdns **20** GL52 . . . 133 F2
Landseer Ave BS7 . . . . . . 19 B7
Land The BS36 . . . . 31 C7
Lane End
 Fairford GL7 . . . . 152 F2
 Great Rissington GL54 . . 169 C4
Lanercost Rd BS10 . . . . . . 28 C2
Lanesborough Rise BS14 . . 3 D7
Lanescourt GL20 . . . . . . 192 D3
Lanes Ct BS37 . . . . 192 C3
Lanes Dairy BS34 . . . . . . 29 A3
Lanes End BS4 . . . . 9 C1
Lanes The
 Cheltenham GL53 . . . . . 130 B4
 Gorsley HR9 . . . . 170 B4
Lane The
 Broadway WR12 . . . . . . 184 F7
 Chaselton GL56 . . . . . . 177 E8
 Easter Compton BS35 . . . 38 E7
 Randwick GL6 . . . . 102 D2
Langdale Ct BS34 . . . . 29 A8
Langdale Gdns GL2 . . . . . 127 C5
Langdale Rd
 Bristol BS16 . . . . 19 F4
 Cheltenham GL51 . . . . . 129 F6
Langdon Rd GL53 . . . . . . 130 D6
Langdown Ct BS14 . . . . . . .3 E5
Langet GL7 . . . . 142 F7
Langetts Rd **4** GL16 . . . . 155 A5
Langfield Cl BS10 . . . . 27 E3
Langford Rd BS13 . . . . 1 F8
Langford Way BS15 . . . . . . 10 E7
Langham Rd BS4 . . . . .9 B2
Langhill Ave BS4 . . . . .2 D7
Langley Cl GL54 . . . . 139 F5
Langley Cres BS3 . . . . 7 E1
Langley Mow BS16 . . . . . . 21 B7
Langley Rd
 Gloucester GL4 . . . . . . 119 B5
 Winchcombe GL54 . . . . 139 D5
Langsdown Ho **7** BS2 . . . . 18 F1
Langston Priory Workshops
 OX7 . . . . 177 F1
Langthorn Cl BS36 . . . . . . 31 C7
Langtoft Rd GL5 . . . . 99 E7
Langton Cl GL4 . . . . 119 E8
Langton Court Rd BS4 . . . . 9 D5
Langton Ct **11** BS16 . . . . . 19 E3
Langton Grove Rd GL52 . . 131 A7
Langton Ho **10** BS2 . . . . . 195 C3
Langton Pk BS3 . . . . 8 C4
Langton Pl GL53 . . . . . . 131 A7
Langton Rd BS4 . . . . 9 D5
Langton Way BS4 . . . . .9 F6
Lanham Gdns GL2 . . . . . . 109 F7
Lannett Rd GL1 . . . . 118 E6
Lansdown
 Stroud GL5 . . . . 99 C7
 Yate BS37 . . . . 32 E8
Lansdown Castle Dr
 GL51 . . . . 129 F8
Lansdown Cl
 Bristol BS15 . . . . 20 D2
 Cheltenham GL51 . . . . . 130 A8
Lansdown Cotts GL54 . . . 168 F8
Lansdown Cres GL51 . . . . 193 A2
Lansdown Crescent La
 GL50 . . . . 193 A2
Lansdown Ct GL50 . . . . . 193 A2
Lansdowne BS16 . . . . 30 C1
Lansdowne Ct **2** BS5 . . . . .9 B8
Lansdown Ho BS15 . . . . . . 20 D2
Lansdown Ind Est GL51 . . 133 A1
Lansdown La BS30 . . . . . . 12 C1
Lansdown Lodge Dr
 GL51 . . . . 130 A8
Lansdown Par GL50 . . . . 130 B8
Lansdown Pl
 Bristol BS8 . . . . 194 A3
 Cheltenham GL50 . . . . . 193 A2
Lansdown Place La
 GL50 . . . . 193 A2
Lansdown Rd
 Bristol, Kingswood BS15 . . 20 D2
 Bristol, Redland BS6 . . . . 18 B1
 6 Bristol, Upper Easton BS5 .9 B8
 Bristol, Victoria Park BS8 . 194 A3
 Cheltenham GL51 . . . . . 130 A8
 Gloucester GL1 . . . . . . 127 A3
 Pucklechurch BS16 . . . . . 22 C6

Lansdown Rd continued
 Saltford BS31 . . . . 5 E3
Lansdown Terr
 Bristol BS6 . . . . 18 D5
 Cheltenham GL50 . . . . . 193 A2
Lansdown Terrace La
 GL50 . . . . 193 A2
Lansdown View BS15 . . . . 10 F8
Lansdown Wlk
 11 Bream GL15 . . . . . . 147 D8
 Cheltenham GL50 . . . . . 193 A2
Lanson Roberts Rd BS35 . 38 D5
Lantern Cl
 Berkeley BS13 . . . . 85 E3
 Cinderford GL14 . . . . . . 191 C4
Lapdown La GL9 . . . . 34 D1
Lapwing Cl
 Bristol BS32 . . . . 40 D2
 Northway GL20 . . . . . . 182 B5
Lapwing Ct **10** GL6 . . . . . 148 C6
Lapwing Gdns BS16 . . . . . 19 F6
Larch Cl GL53 . . . . 131 C5
Larches The GL4 . . . . 119 E6
Larchmere Gr **8** GL51 . . . 129 E5
Larch Rd
 Bristol BS15 . . . . 20 E3
 Colerne SN14 . . . . 15 F6
Larch Rise GL53 . . . . 130 B4
Larch Way BS34 . . . . 28 E7
Larchwood Dr GL4 . . . . . . 118 E3
Larkfield BS36 . . . . 31 D7
Larkfield Ave NP16 . . . . . . 60 E7
Larkfield Gr NP16 . . . . 60 D7
Larkfield Ho NP16 . . . . 60 D7
Larkfield Inf Sch GL3 . . . . 127 E6
Larkfield Pk NP16 . . . . 60 D7
Larkham Cl GL4 . . . . 119 B3
Larkham Pl GL4 . . . . 119 B3
Larkhay Rd GL3 . . . . 120 A8
Larkhill Rd NP16 . . . . 60 E7
Larkin Pl BS7 . . . . 29 A1
Larkrise GL11 . . . . 87 F5
Lark Rise
 Chalford GL6 . . . . 148 C6
 Coleford GL16 . . . . 155 A6
 Yate BS37 . . . . 43 F4
Larks Field BS16 . . . . 19 E5
Larksfield Rd
 Harrow Hill GL17 . . . . . 164 B4
 Stroud GL5 . . . . 99 A4
Lark's La BS37 . . . . 42 B7
Larksleaze Rd BS30 . . . . . 10 F2
Larkspear Cl GL1 . . . . . . 118 E5
Larkspur Cl BS35 . . . . 64 D1
Larput Pl GL50 . . . . 133 D3
Lasborough Dr **2** GL2 . . 118 A1
Lasbury Gr BS13 . . . . 2 C5
Lasne Cres GL3 . . . . 120 F4
Lassington Gr GL2 . . . . . 125 C5
Lassington La GL2 . . . . . 125 D6
Lassington Wood (Nature
 Reserve)★ GL2 . . . . . . 125 E5
Latchen GL17 . . . . 164 F5
Latchen Orch GL17 . . . . . 164 F5
Latchmoor Ho BS13 . . . . . 2 A8
Latimer Cl
 Bristol BS4 . . . . 9 E4
 Minchinhampton GL6 . . . 148 A3
Latimer Ct GL54 . . . . 175 B3
Latimer Rd
 Cinderford GL14 . . . . . . 191 E5
 Stonehouse GL10 . . . . . 101 D1
Latteridge La
 Latteridge BS37 . . . . 42 A7
 Tytherington BS35 . . . . . 51 F1
Latteridge Rd BS37 . . . . . . 42 D4
Latton Rd BS7 . . . . 18 F8
Latymer Croft GL3 . . . . . 128 B5
Launceston Ave BS15 . . . . 10 B5
Launceston Rd BS15 . . . . . 20 B1
Laundry Cotts GL56 . . . . 177 E5
Laundry Rd GL16 . . . . . . 154 E4
Laura Cl GL2 . . . . 127 B4
Laurel Ave GL20 . . . . 192 E2
Laurel Cotts GL20 . . . . . . 192 E2
Laureldene GL16 . . . . 155 B3
Laurel Dr
 Cheltenham GL52 . . . . . 134 B4
 Colerne SN14 . . . . 15 F6
 Gloucester GL3 . . . . . . 120 B4
Laurel Farm Cl GL4 . . . . . 118 F4
Laurel Gate GL4 . . . . 119 F5
Laurel Pk NP16 . . . . 72 B6
Laurel St BS15 . . . . 10 D8
Laurels The
 Bristol, Catbrain BS10 . . . 28 A6
 Bristol, Mangotsfield BS16 . 21 A6
 Castle Eaton SN6 . . . . . 144 D6
 Gloucester GL1 . . . . . . 118 F7
 South Cerney GL7 . . . . . 142 F8
Laurence Cl GL11 . . . . . . 129 D2
Laurie Cres BS9 . . . . 18 D6
Laurie Lee Ct **3** BS30 . . . . 11 A5
Lauriston Pk GL50 . . . . . 130 B6
Lavender Cl BS35 . . . . 64 D1
Lavender Ct BS55 . . . . 19 F1
Lavender La GL7 . . . . 190 C3
Lavender Mews GL52 . . . . 137 E3
Lavender Rd GL51 . . . . . . 129 F5
Lavender View GL4 . . . . . 119 F4
Lavender Way BS32 . . . . . . 29 F7
Lavenham Rd BS37 . . . . . . 43 B2
Lavers Cl BS15 . . . . 10 E6
Lavington Dr GL2 . . . . . . 127 E4
Lavington Rd BS5 . . . . 10 B6

Lawford Ave BS34 . . . . 29 C6
Lawfords Gate BS2 . . . . . 195 C3
Lawfords Gate Ho **19**
 BS2 . . . . 195 C3
Lawford St BS2 . . . . 195 C3
Lawn Ave BS16 . . . . 20 B5
Lawn Cl BS7 . . . . 19 C8
Lawn Cres GL51 . . . . 129 E2
Lawn Rd
 Ashleworth GL19 . . . . . 172 D4
 Bristol BS16 . . . . 20 B5
Lawnside GL6 . . . . 91 A4
Lawnside Rd **6** HR8 . . . . 178 E8
Lawns Pk GL5 . . . . 98 F2
Lawns Rd BS37 . . . . 43 F2
Lawns The
 Bristol BS11 . . . . 16 E7
 Gloucester GL4 . . . . . . 119 D3
 Gotherington GL52 . . . . 138 B7
 Stonehouse GL10 . . . . . . 97 E8
Lawnwood Ind Units **14**
 BS5 . . . . .9 B8
Lawnwood Rd **15** BS5 . . . .9 B8
Lawrence Ave BS5 . . . . . . 19 B1
Lawrence Cl
 Bristol BS15 . . . . 21 A2
 Charlton Kings GL52 . . . 131 B6
Lawrence Dr BS37 . . . . . . 43 B2
Lawrence Gr
 Bristol BS9 . . . . 18 B5
 Dursley GL11 . . . . 88 A2
Lawrence Hill BS5 . . . . . . .9 B7
Lawrence Hill Ind Pk BS5 . .9 B8
Lawrence Hill Rdbt BS5 . . . 9 A7
Lawrence Hill Sta BS5 . . . .9 B7
Lawrence Rd
 Avening GL8 . . . . 148 B1
 Cirencester GL7 . . . . . . 190 B8
Lawrence's Mdw GL52 . . . 138 A8
Lawrence Way N GL1 . . . 126 E4
Lawrence Weston Rd
 Avonmouth BS11 . . . . . . 26 F4
 Bristol BS11 . . . . 27 A2
Lawrence Wy GL1 . . . . . . 196 B4
Lawson Cl BS31 . . . . 5 C2
Lawson Glade GL53 . . . . . 131 A4
Laxey Rd BS7 . . . . 18 F7
Laxton Cl BS35 . . . . 50 A3
Laxton Dr GL12 . . . . 67 F4
Laxton Rd
 Cheltenham GL51 . . . . . 132 E2
 Gloucester GL4 . . . . . . 120 A6
Laymore Rd GL14 . . . . . . 191 B5
Laynes Rd GL3 . . . . 120 A7
Lays Dr BS31 . . . . 4 C5
Lays Farm Bsns Ctr BS31 . . 4 C4
Lays Farm Trad Est BS31 . . 4 C4
Lazenby Ct GL51 . . . . 132 C1
Lea CE Prim Sch HR9 . . . 164 C8
Leacey Ct GL3 . . . . 128 A7
Leacey Mews GL3 . . . . . . 128 A7
Lea Cres GL2 . . . . 127 C5
Lea Croft BS13 . . . . 2 A4
Lea Ct GL10 . . . . 96 E7
Leader St BS7 . . . . 19 C7
Leading Edge The BS8 . . 194 B2
Leadon Cl GL3 . . . . 120 F5
Leadon Pl **9** HR8 . . . . . . 178 E7
Leadon Way HR8 . . . . . . 178 E7
Leafield Rd GL7 . . . . 152 E4
Leaholes Ct GL7 . . . . 190 D4
Leaholme Gdns BS14 . . . . . 3 A3
Leaman Cl BS37 . . . . 44 B1
Leamington Rd WR12 . . . 188 A1
Leaping Stocks Rd HR9 . . 162 D3
Leap Vale BS16 . . . . 21 A8
Leap Valley Cres BS16 . . . . 21 A8
Lear Cl BS30 . . . . 11 B5
Lea Rd GL3 . . . . 120 F5
Lears Dr GL52 . . . . 138 A3
Leasbrook La/Lon Leasbrook
 NP25 . . . . 154 A8
Leaside Cl GL11 . . . . 88 A4
Leasow La GL54 . . . . 169 B5
Leasows The
 Broadwell GL56 . . . . . . 177 A6
 Chipping Campden GL55 . 188 F1
 Mickleton GL55 . . . . . . 189 B6
Lea The GL52 . . . . 137 F5
Leaze Cl
 Berkeley BS13 . . . . 85 E3
 Thornbury BS35 . . . . 51 B8
Leaze Ct GL15 . . . . 92 C2
Leaze The
 2 Ashton Keynes SN6 . . 142 F5
 South Cerney GL7 . . . . . 142 F7
 Yate BS37 . . . . 43 D2
Lechlade Rd
 Highworth SN6 . . . . . . 145 D4
 Lechlade on T GL7 . . . . 153 F1
 Southrop GL7 . . . . 153 C6
 Upper Inglesham SN6 . . 145 D7
Lechmere Rd **1** GL51 . . . 132 E3
Leckhampton CE Prim Sch
 GL53 . . . . 130 D4
Leckhampton Farm Ct
 GL51 . . . . 130 B3
Leckhampton Gate GL51 . 130 A4
Leckhampton Hill GL53 . . 130 D2
Leckhampton Ind Est
 GL53 . . . . 130 D4
Leckhampton La GL51,
 GL53 . . . . 130 A2
Leckhampton Pl GL53 . . . 130 D5
Leckhampton Rd GL53 . . 130 D5
Leckhampton View GL51 . 129 F2

Leconfield Dr **9** GL2 . . . 110 B8
Leda Ave BS14 . . . . 3 A7
Ledbury Heritage Ctr★
 HR8 . . . . 178 F8
Ledbury Pk **9** HR8 . . . . . 178 E8
Ledbury Prim Sch HR8 . . 178 E8
Ledbury Rd
 Bristol BS16 . . . . 20 C4
 Dymock GL18 . . . . 178 A3
 Eastnor HR8 . . . . 179 B8
Ledbury Road Cres GL19 172 A8
Leddington Ct HR8 . . . . . 178 D7
Ledmore Rd GL53 . . . . . . 131 B6
Leechpool Way BS37 . . . . 43 E5
Lee Cl
 Bristol BS34 . . . . 28 F8
 Cheltenham GL51 . . . . . 132 F3
Leeming Way BS11 . . . . . . 16 C8
Lee Rd GL20 . . . . 182 C4
Lees Ct BS15 . . . . 20 E1
Lees Hill BS15 . . . . 20 E2
Lees La BS30 . . . . 11 D5
Lee Villa Cvn Pk HR9 . . . 164 E6
Lefroy Ct GL51 . . . . 130 A4
Leicester Sq BS16 . . . . . . 20 D3
Leicester St **6** BS3 . . . . . 8 D4
Leicester Wlk BS4 . . . . . . .9 F5
Leigh Court Bsns Ctr BS8 17 A2
Leigh Ct BS9 . . . . 17 D3
Leigh La
 Cold Ashton BA1 . . . . . . 14 B3
 Westerleigh BS37 . . . . . . 32 B1
Leigh Rd BS8 . . . . 194 B4
Leigh St BS3 . . . . 8 A3
Leighterton Prim Sch
 GL8 . . . . 70 C3
Leighton Rd
 Bristol, Southville BS3 . . . 8 B4
 Bristol, Upper Knowle BS4 . 9 B2
 Cheltenham GL52 . . . . . 133 F1
Leigh Woods Forest Walks★
 BS8 . . . . 17 C1
Leinster Ave BS4 . . . . 2 D8
Leinster Cl GL51 . . . . 132 C4
Leisure Rd BS15 . . . . 10 E5
Lemon La BS2 . . . . 195 C4
Lena Ave **3** BS5 . . . . 19 C1
Lena St BS5 . . . . 19 C1
Lennards The GL7 . . . . . . 143 E4
Lennox Ho BS11 . . . . 26 B1
Lenover Gdns BS13 . . . . . .2 B1
Lensbrook GL15 . . . . 93 A8
Leonard La BS1 . . . . 195 A3
Leonard Rd
 Bristol BS5 . . . . 9 D7
 Gloucester GL1 . . . . . . 118 F6
Leonards Ave BS5 . . . . . . 19 C1
Leonard Stanley CE Prim Sch
 GL10 . . . . 97 F4
Leopold Rd BS6 . . . . 18 E2
Lesanne Ct GL1 . . . . 196 B2
Les Brown Ct BS2 . . . . . . 195 C2
Lescren Way BS11 . . . . . . 26 D1
Letch Hill Dr GL54 . . . . . 168 F7
Letch La GL54 . . . . 168 F7
Leuchars Cl GL2 . . . . 110 A7
Leven Cl GL2 . . . . 127 D4
Lever's Hill GL11 . . . . 89 B7
Lewington Rd BS16 . . . . . 20 C4
Lewins Mead BS1 . . . . . . 195 A3
Lewin St **9** BS5 . . . . .9 D7
Lewis Ave BS5 . . . . 126 F6
Lewis Cl
 Bristol, Emerson's Green
 BS16 . . . . 21 C5
 Bristol, North Common
 BS30 . . . . 11 D5
Lewis Glade **2** GL16 . . . 155 B5
Lewisham Rd GL1 . . . . . . 118 E5
Lewisham Terr GL13 . . . . . 85 C8
Lewis La GL7 . . . . 190 D4
Lewis Rd
 Bristol BS13 . . . . .2 A8
 Cheltenham GL51 . . . . . 132 D2
Lewis St BS2 . . . . .9 B5
Lewiston Cl GL5 . . . . 148 A5
Lewiston Rd GL5 . . . . 148 A5
Lewis Way NP16 . . . . 60 F4
Lewton La BS36 . . . . 30 C7
Lexington Cl GL20 . . . . . 192 E2
Lexington Sq GL52 . . . . . 133 E5
Ley La BS35 . . . . 49 F3
Leyland Wlk BS13 . . . . . . .1 F4
Ley Mary Farm OX18 . . . 161 C8
Ley Orch WR12 . . . . 188 B2
Ley Rd GL2 . . . . 116 A5
Leysbourne GL55 . . . . . . 189 A2
Leyson Rd GL51 . . . . 129 C6
Leys The GL13 . . . . 85 E4
Leyton Villas BS6 . . . . . . 18 B2
Libby's Dr GL5 . . . . 99 D8
Libertus Cl GL51 . . . . 133 A1
Libertus Mews GL51 . . . . 133 A1
Libertus Rd GL51 . . . . . . 133 A1
Liberty Gdns BS1 . . . . . . 194 C1
Liberty Ind Pk BS3 . . . . . . 8 A1
Library Pl **2** NP16 . . . . . 60 E8
Lichfield Dr GL51 . . . . . . 130 A5
Lichfield Rd
 Bristol BS4 . . . . 9 E6
 Gloucester GL4 . . . . . . 119 D8
Lidderdale Rd GL54 . . . . 169 D6
Liddington Rd GL53 . . . . 130 D4
Liddington Rd
 Cheltenham GL53 . . . . . 130 D4
 Gloucester GL2 . . . . . . 127 E3

Liddington Trad Est GL53 130 D5
Lifford Gdns WR12 185 B8
Lightenbrook La GL2 95 C3
Lightfoot 21 GL18 171 A4
Lightpill Trad Est GL5 99 A6
Lightwood La GL6 102 E3
Lilac Cl
Bristol BS10 28 C1
Cheltenham GL51 130 A5
Lilac Ct BS31 4 C4
Lilac Way
Gloucester GL4 118 C3
Quedgeley GL2 117 F1
Lilley's Alley 9 GL20 192 C4
Lillian St 5 BS5 9 C8
Lilliesfield Ave GL3 119 F8
Lilliput Ave BS37 33 A8
Lilliput Ct BS37 33 B8
Lilly Hall La HR8 178 C7
Lilstock Ave 4 BS7 18 F4
Lilton Wlk BS13 8 A1
Lilymead Ave BS4 9 A3
Limber Hill GL50 133 C5
Limbury Hostels GL19 172 A2
Lime Ave GL9 35 B8
Lime Cl
Brentry BS10 28 B3
Cheltenham GL52 134 A5
Lime Croft BS37 43 F4
Lime Ct
Innsworth GL3 127 F6
Keynsham BS31 4 C4
Lime Gr
Alveston BS35 50 F4
Stroud GL5 99 C7
Limekiln Cl GL14 191 D3
Lime Kiln Cl BS34 29 D3
Lime Kiln Gdns BS32 40 D2
Limekiln Gr GL2 125 D5
Limekiln La GL6 148 E8
Limekiln Rd BS37, GL12 53 C2
Lime Kiln Rd BS1 194 B2
Limekilns Cl BS31 4 F5
Lime Rd
Bristol, Hanham BS15 10 A5
Bristol, Southville BS3 8 B4
Tewkesbury GL20 192 E1
Limerick Rd BS6 18 C2
Limes Cl GL7 190 C3
Limes Pl SN6 143 E6
Limes Rd GL7 141 F8
Lime St GL19 180 D1
Limes The
Badminton GL9 46 E2
Bristol BS16 30 B1
Gloucester, Barnwood GL4 127 C1
Gloucester, Kingsholm GL2 126 E5
South Cerney GL7 142 F7
Limetree Ave 9 NP25 154 A7
Lime Tree Ave
3 Broadway WR12 185 C8
Quedgeley GL2 110 A5
Lime Tree Cotts GL7 152 D7
Lime Tree Ct GL1 118 E5
Lime Tree Gr BS20 16 D3
Lime Trees Rd BS9 18 D6
Lime Way GL15 92 B4
Linacre Cres GL7 190 B2
Lincoln Ave GL51 130 A5
Lincoln Cl
Keynsham BS31 4 C4
Tewkesbury GL20 192 B2
Upper Rissington GL54 169 D6
Lincoln Ct BS16 19 D6
Lincoln Green La GL20 192 B2
Lincoln St BS5 9 B7
Lincombe Ave BS16 20 D6
Lincombe Rd BS16 20 C6
Linden Ave GL52 134 A5
Linden Cl
Bristol, Mayfield Park BS16 20 A2
Bristol, Stockwood BS14 3 E6
Cheltenham GL52 134 B5
Chepstow/Cas-Gwent NP16 60 E5
Colerne SN14 15 F6
Gloucester GL3 120 B4
Winterbourne BS36 30 E6
Linden Dr BS32 29 E8
Linden Grange BS6 18 C3
Linden Ho BS16 19 C5
Linden Lea GL7 143 F8
Linden Prim Sch GL1 118 D6
Linden Rd
Bristol BS6 18 B4
Gloucester GL1 118 D6
Lindon Ct BS15 20 B1
Lindon Ho BS4 9 E3
Lindrea St 3 BS3 8 B3
Lindsay Rd BS7 19 A4
Linegar Wood Rd GL14 191 C1
Lines Way BS14 3 C3
Line The HR9 170 A3
Linfoot Rd GL8 140 B4
Lingfield Pk BS16 30 F2
Lining Wood GL17 164 D6
Linkend Rd GL19 180 F2
Link Rd
Bristol BS34 28 F3
Pillowell GL15 155 F1
Tewkesbury GL20 192 D4
Yate BS37 43 F1
Links The GL16 155 A5
Links View GL7 150 C7
Linley Rd SN26 144 E1
Linnell Cl BS7 19 B6
Linnet Cl
Bristol BS34 28 E8
Gloucester GL4 119 C5
Linsley Way GL4 118 D1
Lintern Cres BS30 11 B6
Lintham Dr BS15 10 F6
Linton Ave
Quedgeley GL2 110 B8
Quedgeley GL2 110 B8
Quedgeley GL4 110 C8
Linton Ct GL53 193 C1
Linton Rd HR9 170 B4
Linton's Wlk BS14 3 A7
Linwell Cl GL50 133 B5
Linworth Rd GL52 138 A3
Lion Cl
Bristol BS7 19 B7
Quedgeley GL2 117 F2
Lipson Rd GL51 132 E4
Lipson Villas GL51 132 E4
Lisburn Rd BS4 8 E1
Lisle Pl GL12 68 A7
Lismore Rd SN6 145 C4
Lister Rd
Dursley GL11 88 B1
Dursley GL11 88 B3
Listers Pl GL14 191 C4
Litfield Pl BS8 7 F7
Litfield Rd BS8 7 F8
Lithgow Rd GL54 169 D6
Little Acorns GL52 137 E5
Little Acre GL12 68 A8
Little Ann St BS2, BS5 195 C4
Little Ashley Ct GL52 131 B7
Little Bayshill Terr GL50 193 B3
Little Birch Croft BS14 3 A3
Little Bishop St BS2 195 B4
Little Bristol Cl GL12 67 B4
Little Bristol La GL12 67 B4
Little Caroline Pl 4 BS8 7 F5
Little Cleevemount GL52 133 F3
Little Compton Jun and Inf Sch GL56 177 F8
Littlecote Cl GL52 137 E3
Littlecross Ho BS3 8 B4
Littledean BS37 32 E7
Littledean CE Prim Sch GL14 156 E8
Littledean Hall★ GL14 156 E8
Littledean Hill Rd GL14 191 E4
Little Dowles BS30 11 A4
Littledown Rd GL53 130 F4
Little Elmbridge GL2 127 E3
Littlefield GL2 117 E2
Little Field GL4 119 D7
Little Fishers GL5 99 A4
Little George St BS2 195 C4
Little Gn
4 Bristol BS32 40 D1
Redmarley D'Abitot GL19 179 D2
Little Green La BS35 38 A7
Little Hayes BS16 20 B6
Little Headley Cl BS13 2 B7
Little Herbert's Cl GL53 131 B5
Little Herbert's Rd GL53 131 B4
Little Holbury GL2 100 E5
Little Horcott La GL7 152 E3
Little King St BS1 195 A2
Little Lancarridge GL2 125 D4
Little Locky Cl BS34, BS7 29 C1
Little Marcle Court Rd HR8 178 A7
Little Marcle Rd HR8 178 E8
Little Mdw BS34 30 A6
Little Mead BS11 27 B1
Little Mead Prim Acad BS10 28 C2
Little Mill Ct GL5 99 D8
Little Normans GL2 127 C5
Little Oaks GL18 179 B4
Little Orch GL52 137 E4
Little Paradise BS3 8 D3
Little Parr Cl BS16 19 C5
Little Paul St BS2 194 C4
Little Pheasants GL53 131 A5
Little Quillet Ct GL11 87 F4
Little Rd WR11 188 B8
Little Rose La SN26 144 C3
Little Stoke La BS34 29 D6
Little Stoke Prim Sch BS34 29 D6
Little Stoke Rd BS9 17 E4
Little Stony Leas 5 BS16, BS34 19 D8
Little Thatch Cl BS14 3 C6
Little Thomas La BS1 195 B2
Littleton Ct BS34 39 F1
Littleton Drew La GL9 36 A6
Littleton La BS41 1 C1
Littleton Rd BS3 8 D2
Littleton St 4 BS5 19 C1
Little Trewen La HR9 162 C5
Little Witcombe Ct GL3 121 C3
Little Withey Mead BS9 17 F5
Little Wlk GL2 127 C5
Littlewood Cl BS14 3 B3
Littleworth GL55 188 F2
Livia Way GL15 92 B4
Livingstone Mews BS3 8 C3
Llanarth Villas 3 BS6 18 D1
Llandilo St 1 GL1 118 F7
Llandogo Prim Sch NP25 146 B7
Llangarron Bsns Ctr HR9 162 B7
Llangrove CE Prim Sch HR9 162 B6
Llangrove Rd HR9 162 D5
Llanthony Cotts GL20 136 B7
Llanthony Ind Est GL2 126 C1
Llanthony Rd GL2 126 C1
Llanthony Secunda Priory★ GL2 126 C1
Llanwrithy HR9 162 C5
Llewellyn Ct BS9 18 A8
Lloyd Baker Ct GL2 109 E7
Lloyd Cl GL51 132 D2
Lobb Ct 4 GL1 127 A1
Lobleys Dr GL4 120 A5
Lockemor Rd BS13 2 F4
Lock Gdns BS13 1 E7
Locking Hill 3 GL5 99 C7
Lockingwell Rd BS31 4 D5
Lockleaze Rd BS7 19 A6
Lock's Acre BS35 51 B6
Lock's La BS37 41 E4
Locombe Hill GL7 153 D8
Locombe Pl GL12 68 C6
Lodersfield GL7 153 E2
Lodge Causeway Trad Ctr BS16 19 F3
Lodge Cswy BS16 20 A3
Lodge Ct BS9 17 E4
Lodge Dr
Bristol BS30 11 C2
Long Ashton BS41 7 B2
Lodge Gdns GL15 146 E7
Lodge Hill BS15 20 C2
Lodge La GL15 147 D6
Lodgemore Cl GL5 99 A7
Lodgemore La GL5 99 A7
Lodge Park & Sherborne Estate★ GL54 160 D7
Lodge Pl BS1 194 C3
Lodge Rd
Bristol BS15 20 C1
Wick BS30 22 B1
Yate BS37 43 A3
Lodgeside Ave BS15 20 C1
Lodgeside Gdns BS15 20 C1
Lodge St BS1 194 C3
Lodge Wlk BS16 20 D6
Lodore Rd BS16 19 F3
Lodway BS20 16 C4
Lodway Cl BS20 16 C5
Lodway Gdns BS20 16 C4
Lodway Rd BS4 9 C2
Logan Rd BS7 18 D3
Logus Ct 14 BS30 10 F4
Loiterpin GL15 156 D2
Lombard St BS3 8 D4
Lomond Rd BS7 28 F1
Lon Cyn Farch/Kingsmark La NP16 72 D1
Londonderry Farm BS30 5 A8
London La SN16 142 E1
London Pl GL7 190 D4
London Rd
Brimscombe GL5, GL6 148 B5
Bristol, St Pauls BS2 18 F1
Bristol, Warmley BS30 11 D7
Charlton Kings GL52, GL53 131 C5
Cheltenham GL52 130 F8
Fairford GL7 152 F4
Gloucester GL1, GL2 127 A2
Moreton-in-M GL56 187 B3
Stroud GL5 99 C6
10 Tetbury GL8 140 C4
Thrupp GL5 99 E3
Wick BS30 12 E6
London Road Terr 6 GL56 187 B3
London St
Bristol BS15 10 D8
Fairford GL7 152 E3
Lone La NP25 154 C4
Lon Ffawyoden Uchel/High Beech La NP16 60 D6
Long Acre Rd BS14 3 A3
Long Acres 5 HR8 178 E8
Long Acres Cl BS9 17 D7
Long Ashton Rd BS41 7 B2
Longaston Cl GL2 95 D4
Longaston La GL2 95 D5
Long Beach Rd BS30 11 B3
Longborough CE Prim Sch GL56 176 D8
Longborough Dr GL4 119 E4
Long Cl
Bristol, Fishponds BS16 20 C6
Bristol, Little Stoke BS32 29 E6
Long Croft BS37 43 D4
Longcross GL12 66 B1
Long Cross BS11 27 B2
Longden Rd BS16 20 F6
Longdon St Mary's CE Prim Sch GL20 180 F7
Long Down Ave
Bristol BS7, BS16 19 C8
Bristol BS34 29 C1
Long Dr GL16 155 B6
Long Eaton Dr BS14 3 B7
Long Eights GL20 182 C5
Longfield GL2 117 E2
Long Field GL2 125 D6
Longfield Rd BS7 18 E3
Longford BS37 32 C8
Longford Ave BS10 18 D8
Longford Ct GL50 193 A1
Longford La GL2 127 A5
Longford Mews GL2 126 F6
Long Fox Manor BS4 10 A1
Long Furlong GL52 137 F7
Long Furlong La GL8 140 B3
Long Ground Rd BS34 29 A7
Long Handstones BS30 11 A4
Longhill Rd GL7 149 E8
Longhope Cl 3 GL4 119 E5
Longhope Rd GL19 165 C6
Longhorn Ave
Gloucester GL1 126 D4
Gloucester GL1 196 A4
Longland Ct GL2 127 B4
Longland Gdns GL2 127 B4
Longlands Cl GL52 138 B4
Longlands Ho 13 BS5 9 C7
Longlands Rd GL52 138 B4
Long Lease SN14 36 C1
Longleat GL53 131 A5
Longleat Ave GL4 118 C1
Longleat Cl BS9 18 C5
Longlength La GL6 83 C8
Longlevens Inf Sch GL2 127 D4
Longlevens Jun Sch GL2 127 C4
Long Marston Rd CV37, GL55 189 A8
Long Mdw BS16 19 D6
Long Mead
Bristol BS34 19 C8
Bristol BS34 29 C1
Yate BS37 43 E5
Longmead Ave BS7 18 D5
Longmead Croft BS13 1 F4
Longmeadow Rd BS31 4 C4
Longmead Rd BS16 31 B1
Longmoor Ct BS3 8 A2
Longmoor Rd BS3 8 A2
Longmore Ave GL54 169 D6
Long Mynd Ave GL51 129 E6
Longney CE Prim Sch GL2 108 C5
Longney Pl BS34 39 F1
Longney Rd GL4 118 D3
Long Rd BS16 21 A5
Longreach Gr BS14 3 D6
Longridge La GL19 172 C3
Long Row
Bristol BS1 195 B2
Castle Eaton SN6 144 D6
Longs Dr BS37 43 C2
Longsmith St GL1 196 B3
Long St
Dursley GL11 88 B1
Tetbury GL8 140 B4
Wotton-u-E GL12 68 B7
Longs View GL12 67 A5
Longtown Rd GL20 192 E2
Longtree Cl GL8 140 B5
Longville Cl GL4 119 F5
Longway Ave
Bristol BS13, BS14 2 F4
Charlton Kings GL53 131 A4
Longwell Ho BS30 10 F3
Longwood BS4 10 A2
Longwood Leys GL52 138 B4
Longwood Mdws BS7 19 C7
Long Wood Rd BS7 19 C8
Lonk The GL16 155 A7
Lon Leasbrook/Leasbrook La NP25 154 A8
Lons Ct BS30 11 C1
Lonsdale Bsns Ctr BS15 20 C2
Lonsdale Cl SN26 144 E1
Lonsdale Rd GL2 127 C2
Loop Rd
Beachley NP16 61 B5
Bristol BS15 21 A3
Lorain Wlk BS10 27 F2
Lord Eldon Dr NP16 60 F4
Lords Gate GL16 155 A5
Lords Gn GL52 138 C3
Lord's Hill GL16 155 A5
Lord's Hill Cl 5 GL16 155 A5
Loriners Cl GL2 117 F2
Lorton Cl BS10 28 B1
Lorton Rd BS10 28 B1
Lossiemouth Rd GL2 110 B7
Lotts The 6 SN6 142 F5
Loughman Cl 2 BS15 10 E8
Louisa St BS2 195 C2
Louise Ave BS16 21 A5
Lovage Cl GL3 127 F6
Lovedays Mead GL5 99 C8
Love La
Chipping Sodbury BS37 33 A8
Cirencester GL7 190 D2
Yate BS37 44 A4
Love Lane Ind Est GL7 190 D2
Lovell Ave BS30 11 D4
Lovell's Hill BS15 10 B5
Lovells The BS20 16 B4
Loveridge Ct BS36 31 B7
Loveringe Cl BS10 27 F4
Lovers Wlk HR9 170 B4
Lovett Cl GL19 172 A8
Lowbourne BS14 2 F6
Lowdilow La GL51 136 E1
Lower Ashley Rd
Bristol, Baptist Mills BS2, BS5 19 A1
13 Bristol, St Pauls BS2 18 F1
Lower Berrycroft GL13 85 E3
Lower Castle St BS1 195 B3
Lower Chapel La BS36 31 C7
Lower Chapel Rd BS15 10 C5
Lower Cheltenham Pl BS6 18 F1
Lower Churchfield Rd GL5 99 D6
Lower Church La BS2 195 A3
Lower Church St NP16 72 F1
Lower Clifton Hill BS8 194 B2
Lower Cock Rd BS15 10 F7
Lower College St BS1 194 C2
Lower Comm GL15 147 D5
Lower Conham Vale BS15 10 A5
Lower Court Rd BS32 40 A5
Lower Croft GL7 152 E4
Lower Cross GL16 154 F3
Lower Fallow Cl BS14 2 F3
Lower Farm Cotts GL7 151 C3
Lower Gay St BS2 195 A4
Lower Grove Rd BS16 19 F4
Lower Guinea St BS1 195 A1
Lower Hanham Rd BS15 10 C6
Lower High St
Bristol BS11 16 D7
Chipping Campden GL55 189 A2
Lower House Cres BS34 29 B4
Lowerhouse La GL11 79 D5
Lower Kitesnest La GL6 103 A3
Lower Knole La BS10 28 A3
Lower Lamb St BS1 194 C2
Lower Leazes GL5 99 D7
Lower Lode La GL20 192 A2
Lower Maudlin St BS1 195 A3
Lower Mdw GL2 109 F7
Lower Mill St GL51 133 B3
Lower Moor Rd BS37 43 E4
Lower Newmarket Rd GL6 90 F4
Lower Park Row BS1 195 A3
Lower Park St 27 GL54 176 F4
Lower Poole Cl 9 GL11 80 B8
Lower Poole Rd 8 GL11 80 B8
Lower Quay St GL1 196 A3
Lower Rd
Berry Hill GL16 155 A7
Ledbury HR8 178 E8
St Briavels GL15 146 E7
Upper Soudley GL14 156 C5
Yorkley GL15 156 A2
Lower Redland Mews 2 BS6 18 B2
Lower Redland Rd BS6 18 B2
Lower Road Trad Est HR8 178 E8
Lower Sidney St BS3 8 A4
Lower Spillman's GL5 99 A6
Lower St
Blockley GL56 186 C5
Dyrham SN14 23 D4
Stroud GL5 99 D6
Whiteshill GL6 102 F3
Lower Station Rd
6 Bristol, Ridgeway BS16 20 A4
Bristol, Staple Hill BS16 20 C4
Lower Stone Cl BS36 31 C7
Lower Terr 7 GL56 186 C5
Lower Thirlmere Rd BS34 29 A8
Lower Tockington Rd BS32 50 B1
Lower Tuffley La GL2 118 B4
Lower Tuffley Lane Ind Pk GL2 118 B4
Lower Washwell La GL6 104 A8
Lower Wharf Ind Est GL5 99 B7
Lower Wyndcliff Nature Trail★ NP16 72 D7
Loweswater Cl GL51 129 F7
Loweswater Rd GL51 129 F7
Lowfield Rd GL8 140 B5
Lowlis Cl BS10 27 F3
Lowry Gr 6 BS7 19 D8
Lowther Rd BS10 28 C2
Loxton Sq BS14 3 A6
Lucas Cl BS4 9 D1
Luccombe Hill BS6 18 B2
Lucinia Mews GL51 132 F3
Luckington Com Sch SN14 47 E5
Luckington Court Gdns★ SN14 47 F5
Luckington Rd BS7 18 E8
Luckley Ave BS13 2 C5
Luckwell Prim Sch BS3 8 A3
Luckwell Rd BS3 8 B3
Lucky La BS3 8 D4
Lucy Ct GL16 163 B2
Ludgate Hill GL12 68 B7
Ludlow Cl
Bristol, St Pauls BS2 18 F1
Bristol, Willsbridge BS30 11 B2
Keynsham BS31 4 D5
Ludlow Ct BS30 11 B1
Ludlow Gn GL6 102 F3
Ludlow Rd BS7 19 A7
Ludwell Cl BS36 30 D5
Luggs The GL10 98 A3
Luke La GL3 127 E6
Lullington Rd BS4 9 B2
Lulsgate Rd BS13 2 A8
Lulworth Cres BS16 20 F8
Lulworth Rd BS31 4 E4
Lurgan Wlk BS4 8 D1
Lurks La GL6 103 B4
Lushill Cotts SN6 144 E5
Luther Challis Bsns Ctr The GL4 127 D2
Lutyens Cl BS16 19 E8

Lux Furlong BS9 . . . . 17 B7
Luxton St BS5 . . . . .9 B8
Lych Gate Mews GL15 . . . 92 A1
Lych Vale Cvn Pk GL13 . . 85 D4
Lydbrook Cl **6** BS37 . . . . 32 D8
Lydbrook Prim Sch
  GL17 . . . . .163 D2
Lyddington Rd BS7 . . . . . . 18 F8
Lyde Green Rdbt BS16 . . 21 B8
Lydfield Rd GL15 . . . . 92 B3
Lydford Wlk BS3 . . . . 8 C2
Lydiard Croft BS15 . . . . . 10 C4
Lydney CE Com Sch GL15 92 A3
Lydney & District Hospl
  GL15 . . . . .147 F6
Lydney Ind Est GL15 . . . . 84 C8
Lydney Junc Sta* GL15 . . 92 A1
Lydney Park Blvd GL15 . . 92 C1
Lydney Park Gdns*
  GL15 . . . . .147 E5
Lydney Rd
  Bream GL15 . . . . .147 D8
  Bristol, Southmead BS10 . . 28 D1
  Bristol, Staple Hill BS16 . . 20 E4
Lydney Sta GL15 . . . . 84 A8
Lydney Town Sta* GL15 . . 92 A3
Lydstep Terr BS3 . . . . 8 C4
Lyefield Cl GL52 . . . . 131 B6
Lyefield Rd E GL53 . . . . 131 B6
Lyefield Rd W GL53 . . . . 131 A6
Lye La GL52 . . . . 138 D1
Lygon Ct GL7 . . . . 152 E3
Lygon Wlk **3** GL51 . . . . . 132 F3
Lyley Ho GL12 . . . . 68 A7
Lynch Ct BS30 . . . . 10 F4
Lynch Rd
  Berkeley GL13 . . . . 85 D3
  Chalford GL6 . . . . .148 D6
Lynch Road Ind Est GL13 . 85 C3
Lyncombe Wlk BS16 . . . . 20 B2
Lyncroft GL2 . . . . 116 F7
Lyncroft Farm Wkshps
  GL7 . . . . .150 C8
Lyndale Ave BS9 . . . . 17 D5
Lyndale Rd
  Bristol BS5 . . . . 9 D8
  Yate BS37 . . . . 43 D1
Lyndale Terr
  Cheltenham GL51 . . . . . .133 A2
  Norton GL2 . . . . .173 B3
Lynde Cl BS13 . . . . .2 B4
Lyndhurst Cl GL52 . . . . . 138 B3
Lyndhurst Gdns GL51 . . 129 E2
Lyndhurst Rd
  Bristol BS9 . . . . 17 F7
  Keynsham BS31 . . . . .4 F3
Lyndley Chase GL52 . . . 137 D4
Lyneham Dr GL2 . . . . . . 110 A8
Lyng Cl GL4 . . . . 119 E8
Lynmouth Rd
  3 Bristol BS2 . . . . 19 A2
  Gloucester GL3 . . . . . . 119 F7
Lynn Rd BS16 . . . . 19 D5
Lynt Farm Cotts SN6 . . 145 D7
Lynton **3** BS15 . . . . 11 A8
Lynton Pl **9** BS5 . . . . . . 9 C8
Lynton Rd
  Bristol BS3 . . . . 8 D2
  Gloucester GL3 . . . . . . 119 F7
Lynton Way BS16 . . . . . . 30 B1
Lynt Rd SN6 . . . . 145 D7
Lynwood Rd
  Bristol BS3 . . . . 8 B2
  Lydney GL15 . . . . 92 A5
Lynworth Ct **5** GL52 . . 134 A3
Lynworth Exchange **9**
  GL52 . . . . .134 A3
Lynworth La GL20 . . . . . 181 F8
Lynworth Orch GL20 . . . 181 F8
Lynworth Pl GL52 . . . . . 134 A3
Lynworth Prim Sch GL52 134 B3
Lynworth Terr GL52 . . . 134 B4
Lyons Court Rd BS14 . . . . 3 D7
Lypiatt Dr GL50 . . . . 193 A2
Lypiatt La GL50 . . . . 193 A2
Lypiatt Mews GL50 . . . . 193 A2
Lypiatt Rd GL50 . . . . 193 A2
Lypiatt St GL50 . . . . 193 A1
Lypiatt View GL6 . . . . . . 148 B6
Lyppiatt Rd BS5 . . . . 9 D8
Lyppincourt Rd BS10 . . . 28 A3
Lysander Ct GL3 . . . . 128 C5
Lysander Rd BS10, BS34 . . 28 C6
Lysander Wlk BS34 . . . . . 29 E5
Lysander Wy GL56 . . . . . 187 B3
Lysons Ave GL1 . . . . 118 D7
Lytchet Dr BS16 . . . . 20 F8
Lytes Cary Rd BS31 . . . . . 5 A3
Lytham Ho BS4 . . . . 9 D1
Lytton Gr
  Bristol BS7 . . . . 19 A8
  Keynsham BS31 . . . . 5 A5
Lyveden Gdns BS13 . . . . . .2 B5
Lyvedon Way BS41 . . . . . .7 B1

M

Mabberley Cl BS16 . . . . . . 21 C5
Mabel's Furlong **12** HR8 . 178 E8
McAdam Way BS1 . . . . . . .7 F5
Macaroni Wood GL7 . . . 153 A7
Macarthur Rd GL54 . . . . 168 A1

Macauley Rd BS7 . . . . 19 A8
Macdonald Wlk **3** BS15 . . 10 D8
Macey's Rd BS13 . . . . .2 D3
Machen Rd GL16 . . . . . . 155 B6
Machin Cl BS10 . . . . 27 F3
Machine Ct **1** GL20 . . . 192 C4
Machin Gdns BS10 . . . . . 28 A3
Machin Rd BS10 . . . . 28 A3
MacKenzie Way GL51 . . 133 A5
Mackie Ave BS34 . . . . . . 29 B2
Mackie Gr BS34 . . . . 29 B2
Mackie Rd BS34 . . . . 29 B2
McLaren Rd BS11 . . . . . . 26 B1
Macrae Ct BS15 . . . . 10 E8
Macrae Rd BS20 . . . . 16 E4
Madeline Rd BS16 . . . . . 19 F2
Madison Cl BS37 . . . . . . 43 D2
Madleaze Ind Est GL1 . . 196 A1
Madleaze Rd GL1 . . . . . 196 A1
Madocke Rd NP16 . . . . . . 61 A7
Maesbury BS15 . . . . 10 E6
Maesbury Rd BS31 . . . . . .5 A2
Maesknoll La BS14 . . . . . .3 B1
Maesknoll Rd BS4 . . . . . . 9 A2
Magdalana Ct BS1 . . . . . 195 B1
Magdala Rd **1** GL1 . . . . 127 A1
Magdalene Pl BS2 . . . . . 18 F1
Magdalen Rd GL8 . . . . . 140 B4
Maggs Cl BS10 . . . . 28 C3
Maggs La
  Bristol BS5 . . . . 19 E2
  Whitchurch BS14 . . . . . . .3 C4
Magnolia Cl NP16 . . . . . . 60 F5
Magnolia Ct **1** GL51 . . 132 D2
Magnolia Gdns BS32 . . . 40 E5
Magnolia Wlk GL2 . . . . . 117 E1
Magpie Bottom La
  Bristol BS5 . . . . 10 B6
  Bristol BS15 . . . . 10 C6
Magpie Ct GL10 . . . . 97 F8
Maida Vale Rd GL53 . . . 130 D6
Maidencroft La GL7 . . . . 144 F7
Maidenhall GL2 . . . . 125 D5
Maidenhead Rd BS13 . . . .2 D3
Maidenhill Sch GL10 . . . 101 F1
Maiden Way BS11 . . . . . . 16 C8
Maidstone St BS3 . . . . . . .8 F3
Mainard Sq GL2 . . . . . . 127 C5
Main Dr GL8 . . . . 58 C8
Maine St GL7 . . . . 152 E2
Main Rd
  Bristol BS16 . . . . 21 D5
  Easter Compton BS35 . . 39 A1
  Mile End GL16 . . . . 155 B6
  Pillowell GL15 . . . . 155 F1
  Tintern Parva NP16 . . . . 146 B3
  Whiteshill GL6 . . . . 102 F3
  Woolaston, Alvington
    GL15 . . . . .147 D3
  Woolaston, Brookend
    GL15 . . . . .147 C2
Mainsail La GL2 . . . . 118 C7
Main St
  Adlestrop GL56 . . . . . . 177 E6
  Beckford GL20 . . . . . . 183 B6
  Bledington OX7 . . . . . . 177 E1
  Bretforton WR11 . . . . . 188 A6
  Willersey WR12 . . . . . . 188 B2
Main View BS36 . . . . 31 D7
Maisemore BS37 . . . . . . 32 E6
Maisemore Ave BS34 . . . 40 B1
Maitlands GL4 . . . . 110 F5
Makin Cl BS30 . . . . 11 C5
Malago Rd BS3 . . . . 8 D3
Malago Vale Est BS3 . . . . 8 D3
Malago Wlk BS13 . . . . . . .1 E4
Malden Mead BS14 . . . . . 3 A5
Malden Rd GL52 . . . . . . 133 E3
Maldon Gdns GL1 . . . . . 118 F7
Maldowers La **2** BS5 . . 10 A8
Malet Cl GL2 . . . . 127 C5
Mallard Cl
  Bristol BS32 . . . . 40 D2
  Bristol, Crofts End BS5 . . 19 F1
  Cheltenham GL51 . . . . . 132 E5
  Chipping Sodbury BS37 . . 33 A8
  1 Quedgeley GL2 . . . 117 D1
Mallards The GL7 . . . . . 143 A7
Malleson Rd GL52 . . . . . 137 F8
Mallow Cl BS35 . . . . 64 D2
Mall The BS8 . . . . .7 F7
Mall The BS8 . . . . 28 D6
Malmains Dr BS16 . . . . . 30 B1
Malmesbury Cl
  Bristol, Bishopston BS6 . . 18 C4
  Bristol, Longwell Green
    BS30 . . . . 10 F5
Malmesbury Rd
  Cheltenham GL51 . . . . . 133 A5
  Gloucester GL4 . . . . . . 119 B7
  Leigh SN6 . . . . 143 C3
Malmsey Cl GL20 . . . . . 192 D1
Malthouse Cl SN26 . . . . 144 E1
Malt House Cl GL15 . . . 147 D3
Malthouse La
  Cheltenham GL50 . . . . . 133 D3
  Lower Slaughter GL54 . . 176 C1
  17 Winchcombe GL54 . . 174 A7
Malthouse Wlk **9** GL8 . . 140 B4
Maltings The GL17 . . . . 163 E4
Malvern Cl BS5 . . . . .9 F7
Malvern Dr
  Bristol BS30 . . . . 11 C5
  Thornbury BS35 . . . . . . 51 D8
Malvern Gdns GL5 . . . . . 98 E7
Malvern Pl GL50 . . . . . . 193 A3

Malvern Rd
  Bristol, Crew's Hole BS5 . . .9 F7
  Bristol, Kensington Park BS4 . 9 D3
  Cheltenham GL50 . . . . . 133 B1
  Corse GL19 . . . . 172 B8
  Gloucester GL1 . . . . . . 126 F4
Malvern St GL51 . . . . . . 133 B4
Malverns The GL4 . . . . . 119 D6
Malvern View Bsns Pk
  GL52 . . . . .137 C4
Malvern Way GL16 . . . . . 155 C8
Manchester Ct **4** GL56 . 187 A4
Manchester Rd GL1 . . . 133 B4
Manchester Way **1**
  GL50 . . . . .193 A4
Mancroft Ave BS11 . . . . . 16 F7
Mandalay Dr GL2 . . . . . . 173 B3
Mandara Gr GL4 . . . . . . 119 D4
Mandarin Way GL50 . . . 133 C5
Mandeville Cl GL2 . . . . . 127 C6
Mangotsfield CE Prim Sch
  BS16 . . . . 21 B6
Mangotsfield Rd BS16 . . 21 A5
Mangotsfield Sch BS16 . . 21 B4
Manilla Rd BS8 . . . . 194 A3
Mankley Rd GL10 . . . . . . 97 F4
Manley Gdns GL2 . . . . . 127 C5
Mannings Rd GL17 . . . . 164 B4
Manor Ave
  Dursley GL11 . . . . 87 F5
  Lechlade on T GL7 . . . . 153 F2
Manor Barn GL53 . . . . . 122 C6
Manorbrook Prim Sch
  BS35 . . . . 64 C2
Manor Cl
  Broad Blunsdon SN26 . . 144 E1
  Coalpit Heath BS36 . . . . 31 C6
  Dursley GL11 . . . . 87 F6
  Easton-in-G BS20 . . . . . 16 A4
  8 Fairford GL7 . . . . . 152 E4
  Honeybourne WR11 . . . 188 C6
  Minchinhampton GL6 . . . 91 F6
  Sherston SN16 . . . . 58 C1
  Stratton GL7 . . . . 150 C7
  Teddington GL20 . . . . . 183 A3
  Tockington BS32 . . . . . . 50 C1
Manor Cl The BS8 . . . . . . 7 A8
Manor Coalpit Heath Prim
  Sch The BS36 . . . . 31 D6
Manor Cott SN16 . . . . . 141 B4
Manor Cotts
  Pitt Court GL11 . . . . 79 F5
  Sopworth SN14 . . . . . . 57 D1
Manor Court Dr BS7 . . . . 18 E7
Manor Ct
  Bristol, Fishponds BS16 . . 19 E4
  9 Bristol, Upper Easton
    BS5 . . . . 19 B1
  15 Fairford GL7 . . . . . 152 E4
  Gloucester GL4 . . . . . . 119 B4
  Lydney GL15 . . . . 92 C3
  Swindon GL51 . . . . 133 A6
  Whitminster GL2 . . . . . 100 F5
Manor Dr **5** GL51 . . . . . 99 A1
Manor End **2** GL51 . . . 129 D6
Manor Farm
  Bristol BS32 . . . . 29 D8
  Little Rissington GL54 . . 169 C6
Manor Farm Barns GL54 166 D6
Manor Farm Cotts GL8 . 141 A6
Manor Farm Dr **1** GL51 . 129 D6
Manor Fields GL54 . . . . 183 F1
Manor Gardens Ho BS16 . 19 F5
Manor Gdns
  Gloucester GL4 . . . . . . 119 E8
  Lechlade on T GL7 . . . . 153 E2
  Newnham GL14 . . . . . . 156 F6
  Woodchester GL5 . . . . . 99 A2
Manor Gr
  Bristol BS34 . . . . 40 B2
  Bristol, Mangotsfield BS16 . 21 A4
Manor Ho
  6 Bristol BS5 . . . . 19 B1
  Bristol, Kingsdown BS2 . . 194 C3
Manor La
  Bretforton WR11 . . . . . 188 A6
  Charfield GL12 . . . . 67 A4
  Gotherington GL52 . . . . 138 B7
  Winterbourne BS36 . . . . 30 F7
  Wotton-u-E GL12 . . . . . 68 C7
Manor Orch SN6 . . . . . . 143 F4
Manor Park Bsns Ctr
  GL51 . . . . .133 A5
Manor Pk
  Bristol BS6 . . . . 18 B3
  Cheltenham GL51 . . . . . 129 D5
  Gloucester GL2 . . . . . . 127 E4
  Tewkesbury GL20 . . . . . 192 E6
  Tockington BS32 . . . . . . 50 C1
Manor Pl
  Bristol, Frenchay BS16 . . 30 C1
  Bristol, Stoke Gifford BS34 . 30 A4
  Tewkesbury GL20 . . . . . 192 D1
Manor Rd
  Abbots Leigh BS8 . . . . . . 7 A8
  Bristol, Bishopston BS7 . . 18 E4
  Bristol, Bishopsworth BS13 . 2 A6
  Bristol, Fishponds BS16 . . 20 A5
  Bristol, Mangotsfield BS16 . 21 A4
  Cheltenham GL51 . . . . . 133 A6
  Lydney GL15 . . . . 92 C3
  Rangeworthy BS37 . . . . 43 A7
  Saltford BS31 . . . . 5 C2
  Wick BS30 . . . . 12 C5
Manor St GL6 . . . . 105 A1

Manor The
  Churchdown GL3 . . . . . 128 C4
  4 Newnham GL14 . . . 157 A6
Manor View
  St Arvans NP16 . . . . . . 72 B5
  Stroud GL5 . . . . 98 E4
Manor Way BS37 . . . . . . 44 C2
Manor Wlk BS35 . . . . 64 B3
Manor Wood/Coed Maenor
  NP16 . . . . 60 C8
Manor Wood Forest Trail*
  NP25 . . . . .146 B8
Manse Gdns **4** GL51 . . 129 F7
Manse La The HR9 . . . . 170 B5
Mansel Cl BS31 . . . . 5 C3
Mansell Cl GL2 . . . . 118 C5
Manse Rd GL17 . . . . 164 B4
Manser St GL50 . . . . . . 133 B3
Mansfield Mews GL2 . . . 109 F7
Mansfield St BS3 . . . . 8 C2
Manson's La NP25 . . . . . 162 A1
Manston Cl BS14 . . . . 3 C7
Manston Wy **8** GL2 . . . 110 B8
Manworthy Rd BS4 . . . . . 9 D3
Manx Rd BS7 . . . . 18 F8
Maple Ave
  Bristol BS16 . . . . 20 C3
  Chepstow/Cas-Gwent NP16 60 E5
  Thornbury BS35 . . . . . . 64 C1
Maple Cl
  Bristol, Little Stoke BS34 . . 29 C7
  Bristol, Oldland BS30 . . . 11 B4
  Bristol, Stockwood BS14 . . 3 D5
  Dursley GL11 . . . . 88 A3
  Hardwicke GL2 . . . . . . 109 E8
Maple Ct
  Bristol BS9 . . . . 17 F8
  5 Bristol BS15 . . . . . . 20 D1
  Gloucester GL2 . . . . . . 127 E4
Mapledean GL14 . . . . . . 191 C5
Maple Dr
  Brockworth GL3 . . . . . . 120 D7
  Charlton Kings GL53 . . . 131 B5
  Stroud GL5 . . . . 103 A1
Maplefield GL15 . . . . . . 147 E5
Maple Ho BS2 . . . . 195 A4
Maple Leaf Ct BS8 . . . . 194 A3
Mapleleaze BS4 . . . . 9 D3
Maplemeade BS7 . . . . . . 18 C4
Maple Rd
  Bristol, Horfield BS7 . . . 18 E5
  Bristol, St Anne's BS4 . . . 9 D5
Mapleridge La BS37 . . . . 44 D7
Maples The
  Cirencester GL7 . . . . . . 190 B1
  Gloucester GL4 . . . . . . 119 E6
Maplestone Rd **3** BS14 . . 3 A3
Maple Wlk
  Keynsham BS31 . . . . 4 D4
  Pucklechurch BS16 . . . . 22 C5
Mapstone Cl BS16 . . . . . 30 B3
Marbeck Rd BS10 . . . . . . 28 B1
Marchant Cl GL51 . . . . . 132 F3
Mardale Cl BS10 . . . . . . 28 C2
Marden Rd BS31 . . . . 5 A4
Mardon Rd BS4 . . . . 9 D6
Mardyke Ferry Rd BS1 . . 194 B1
Marefield Cl GL4 . . . . . . 119 E7
Marells Way GL17 . . . . . 163 F3
Margaret Rd
  Bristol BS13 . . . . .1 F4
  3 Ledbury HR8 . . . . . 178 E8
  Tewkesbury GL20 . . . . . 192 D3
Margate St BS3 . . . . .8 F3
Margery Rd GL15 . . . . . 154 F2
Margrett Rd GL50 . . . . . 133 D3
Marguerite Rd BS13 . . . . .1 F7
Marham Dr
  Gloucester GL2 . . . . . . 118 B1
  1 Quedgeley GL2 . . . 110 B8
Marian Ct GL1 . . . . 196 A3
Marian La GL16 . . . . 155 A7
Marians Wlk GL16 . . . . . 155 A7
Marigold Wlk BS3 . . . . . . 8 A2
Marina Bsns Pk GL15 . . 84 C8
Marina Gdns BS16 . . . . . 19 E3
Marina The GL15 . . . . . . 84 B8
Marine Gdns GL16 . . . . 155 A5
Marine Par BS20 . . . . . . 16 C5
Mariners Dr BS9 . . . . . . 17 D4
Mariners' Path BS9 . . . . 17 E3
Mariners Reach NP16 . . . 61 A4
Mariner's Way BS20 . . . . 16 C5
Marion Rd BS15 . . . . 10 B3
Marion Wlk BS5 . . . . 10 A7
Marissal Cl BS10 . . . . . . 27 E3
Marissal Rd BS10 . . . . . . 27 E3
Mariston Way BS30 . . . . 11 C6
Maritime Ct GL2 . . . . . . 118 C7
Marjoram Cl **2** GL4 . . . 119 F5
Marjoram Pl BS32 . . . . . 29 F7
Market Cl GL54 . . . . 168 F8
Market Gate BS1 . . . . . . 195 C3
Market La GL54 . . . . 184 A1
Market Par GL1 . . . . 196 B3
Market Pl
  Berkeley GL13 . . . . 85 E3
  Cirencester GL7 . . . . . . 190 C5
  Coleford GL16 . . . . 155 A5
  Dursley GL11 . . . . 88 B1
  11 Fairford GL7 . . . . . 152 E4
  Lechlade on T GL7 . . . . 153 E2
  Marshfield SN14 . . . . . . 15 A8
  Northleach GL54 . . . . . 168 A1
  14 Tetbury GL8 . . . . . 140 C4
Marketside BS2 . . . . .9 B4

Market Sq
  Bristol BS16 . . . . 20 C3
  Minchinhampton GL6 . . . 148 A3
  14 Newent GL18 . . . . 171 A4
  Stow-on-t-W GL54 . . . . 176 F4
Market St
  Cheltenham GL50 . . . . . 193 A4
  Cinderford GL14 . . . . . 191 D5
  Ledbury HR8 . . . . 178 E8
  Nailsworth GL6 . . . . . . 91 B3
  Wotton-u-E GL12 . . . . . 68 B7
Market Way GL1 . . . . . . 196 B2
Mark La BS1 . . . . 194 C2
Marklands BS9 . . . . 17 E3
Marksbury Rd BS3 . . . . . 8 B3
Marlborough Ave **13** BS16 19 E3
Marlborough Cl
  Bishop's Cleeve GL52 . . 137 E3
  Cheltenham GL53 . . . . . 130 F6
Marlborough Cres GL4 . . 119 A7
Marlborough Dr BS16 . . . 30 B1
Marlborough Flats **8**
  BS2 . . . . .195 A4
Marlborough Hill BS2 . . 195 A4
Marlborough Hill Pl BS2 195 A4
Marlborough Ho BS2 . . . 195 A4
Marlborough Pl GL52 . . 133 F1
Marlborough Rd GL4 . . . 119 A7
Marlborough St
  Bristol, Eastville BS5 . . . 19 E3
  Bristol, Kingsdown BS2 . . 195 A4
Marle Hill GL6 . . . . 148 C5
Marle Hill Par GL50 . . . 133 F2
Marle Hill Rd GL50 . . . . 133 D3
Marlepit Gr BS13 . . . . . . .1 E6
Marle Rise GL52 . . . . . . 133 E4
Marleyfield Cl **3** GL3 . . 128 A7
Marleyfield Way GL3 . . . 128 A7
Marley La GL6 . . . . 148 D5
Marlfield Wlk BS13 . . . . . .1 E7
Marling Cl GL5 . . . . 91 C8
Marling Cres GL5 . . . . . . 98 F7
Marling Rd BS5 . . . . .9 F8
Marling Sch GL5 . . . . . . 98 F7
Marlstone Dr GL3 . . . . . 128 A6
Marlstone Rd GL11 . . . . . 88 A4
Marlwood Dr BS10 . . . . . 28 A3
Marlwood Sch BS32 . . . . 50 F5
Marmaduke St BS3 . . . . . .8 F3
Marment Rd GL11 . . . . . . 87 E4
Marmion Cres BS10 . . . . 27 F3
Marne Cl BS14 . . . . 3 D5
Marram Cl GL4 . . . . 119 F5
Marshacre La BS35 . . . . 49 F6
Marshall Ho **1** BS16 . . . 19 F4
Marshall's La GL14 . . . . 191 D5
Marshall Wlk BS4 . . . . . . 2 D7
Marsham Way BS30 . . . . 10 F4
Marsh Cl
  Cheltenham GL51 . . . . . 133 C3
  Winterbourne BS36 . . . . 30 C5
Marsh Common Rd BS35 . 38 E3
Marsh Ct **1** GL56 . . . . . 187 A4
Marsh Dr GL51 . . . . 133 C4
Marshfield CE VC Prim Sch
  SN14 . . . . 15 B3
Marshfield La BS30 . . . . 12 D1
Marshfield Pk BS16 . . . . 20 C8
Marshfield Rd
  Bristol, Frenchay BS16 . . 20 C8
  Bristol, Hillfields BS16 . . 20 C4
  Tormarton BS30 . . . . . . 34 C4
Marsh Gdns GL51 . . . . . 133 C3
Marsh La
  Bristol, Ashton Vale BS3 . . 8 B2
  Bristol, Barton Hill BS5 . . 9 C6
  Burton SN14, GL9 . . . . . 36 C4
  Cheltenham GL51 . . . . . 133 C3
  Easton-in-G BS20 . . . . . 16 A4
  Frampton on Severn GL2 . 157 F1
  Leonard Stanley GL10 . . 97 F3
Marsh Mews GL10 . . . . . 97 F3
Marshmouth La GL54 . . 169 A4
Marsh Rd
  Bristol BS3 . . . . .7 F3
  Chepstow/Cas-Gwent NP16 60 E5
  Leonard Stanley GL10 . . 97 F4
Marsh St
  Avonmouth BS11 . . . . . . 16 C8
  4 Bristol BS1 . . . . 195 A2
Marsh Terr GL51 . . . . . . 129 D2
Marshwall La BS32 . . . . . 39 E6
Marsh Way GL16 . . . . . . 155 B3
Marsland Rd GL51 . . . . . 132 D2
Marston Hill GL7 . . . . . . 152 C2
Marston Rd
  Bristol BS4 . . . . 9 B3
  Cheltenham GL52 . . . . . 133 F3
Martcombe Rd BS20 . . . 16 C2
Marten Cl GL4 . . . . 120 A5
Marten Rd NP16 . . . . 60 E6
Martha's Orch BS13 . . . . .1 E7
Martin Cl
  Bristol BS34 . . . . 28 E8
  Cirencester GL7 . . . . . . 190 C3
Martin Ct **12** BS16 . . . . 19 E3
Martindale Rd GL3 . . . . 128 A6
Martingale Rd BS4 . . . . . 9 D4
Martins Cl BS15 . . . . 10 C5
Martin's Rd BS15 . . . . . . 10 C5
Martin St **2** BS3 . . . . . . .8 B3
Martins The
  Stroud GL5 . . . . 98 C8
  Tutshill NP16 . . . . 73 A1
Martins Way HR8 . . . . . 178 E7
Martlock Cres BS3 . . . . . 8 C1

Martock Cres BS3 8 C1
Martock Rd
Bristol BS3 8 C2
Keynsham BS31 5 A3
Martor Ind Est SN14 25 A2
Marwood Rd BS4 2 E8
Marybrook St GL13 85 E3
Marybush La BS2 195 B3
Mary Carpenter Pl 15 BS2 18 F1
Mary Ct BS5 9 D8
Mary Godwin Ct GL51 132 F4
Marygold Leaze BS30 11 A4
Mary Gr GL2 125 D5
Mary Rose Ave GL3 127 F7
Mary's La GL16 154 F6
Mary St BS5 9 D8
Mascot Rd BS3 8 D3
Masefield Ave GL2 118 C4
Masefield Cl 8 HR8 178 E8
Masefield Rd GL7 190 B2
Masefield Way BS7 19 A6
Maskelyne Ave BS10 18 D7
Mason Ct GL13 85 E3
Mason Rd GL5 99 F7
Masons View BS36 30 F7
Massey Par 5 GL1 118 F7
Massey Rd GL1 119 A7
Massey Sham Ave GL56 187 C3
Matchells Cl BS4 9 E6
Materman Rd BS14 3 E5
Matford Cl
Bristol BS10 28 D4
Winterbourne BS36 30 E5
Matford La GL13 77 F4
Mathern Cres NP16 60 B4
Mathern Rd/Heol Merthyr Tewdrig NP16 60 D5
Mathern Way NP16 60 E5
Mathews Way GL5 99 A8
Matson Ave
Gloucester GL4 119 B2
Gloucester GL4 119 C3
Matson La GL4 119 B3
Matson Lodge 13 GL4 119 C4
Matson Pl GL1 119 A7
Matthew Ho BS1 195 A3
Matthews Cl BS14 3 F6
Matthew's Rd 17 BS5 9 C7
Mattishall Cl GL2 110 B7
Maud's Elm Ho GL51 133 B4
Maugersbury Cl GL54 176 F4
Maugersbury Pk GL54 176 F4
Maules Gdns BS16 29 F2
Maules La BS16 29 F2
Maunsell Rd BS11 27 B2
Maurice Rd BS6 18 E3
Mautravers Cl BS32 29 D7
Maverdine Ct GL1 196 A3
Mawdeley Ho 11 BS3 8 C4
Mawley Rd GL7 152 D7
Maxse Rd BS4 9 B2
Maxstone Cl GL20 192 E2
Mayall Ct GL4 119 C3
Mayalls Cl GL19 172 F7
Mayalls The GL20 182 A7
Maybank Rd BS37 43 D1
Maybec Gdns BS5 10 A6
Maybourne BS4 10 A2
May Bush La HR9 162 E2
Maycliffe Pk BS6 18 F2
May Evans Cl GL11 87 F5
Mayfair Cl GL2 118 C8
Mayfield Ave BS16 20 A2
Mayfield Cl GL52 137 F2
Mayfield Ct BS16 20 A3
Mayfield Dr GL3 119 F8
Mayfield Ho 8 GL50 130 B8
Mayfield Pk BS16 20 A2
Mayfield Pk (Mobile Home Ctr) GL7 150 C8
Mayfield Pk N BS16 20 A2
Mayfield Pk S BS16 20 A2
Mayfields BS31 4 E5
Mayflower Ct BS16 20 E5
May Gr GL12 67 B5
MAY HILL 165 C8
Mayhill Ind Est 24 NP25 154 A7
May Hill Vw 32 GL18 171 A4
Mayhill Way GL1 127 A2
May La
Dursley GL11 88 A1
Ebrington GL55 189 D2
May Meadow La GL17 164 D5
Maynard Cl BS13 2 C5
Maynard Rd BS13 2 C5
Mayors Bldgs BS16 20 B5
May Park Prim Sch BS5 19 C2
Maypole Cl GL9 56 A2
Maypole Ct 1 BS15 10 B5
Maypole Gn 3 GL15 147 D8
Maypole Rd GL15 147 D8
Maypole Terr GL5 98 F8
Mays Cl BS36 31 D7
May's Cres 6 GL54 168 A1
Mays Hill
Coalpit Heath BS36 31 F8
Mayshill BS36 42 F1
Mays La GL8 140 B8
May St BS15 20 C1
Maythorn Dr GL51 132 D4
Maytree Ave BS13 2 B7
Maytree Cl BS13 2 B7
May Tree Cl GL7 149 E3
Maytrees BS5 19 C2
May Trees GL50 193 A2
May Tree Sq GL4 119 C7
May Tree Wlk BS31 4 C3
Mayville Ave BS34 29 A3
Maywood Ave 3 BS16 20 B4
Maywood Cres BS16 20 B4
Maywood Rd BS16 20 C4
Maze St BS5 9 B6
Maze Wlk GL16 155 A7
Mead Cl
Bristol BS11 16 E6
Cheltenham GL53 130 E5
22 Moreton-in-M GL56 187 A3
Mead Ct Bsns Pk BS35 51 B8
Meade-King Gr GL52 138 B3
Meadgate BS16 21 B7
Mead La
Aylburton GL15 147 F4
Ingst BS35 49 D2
Lydney GL15 84 A8
Saltford BS31 5 F4
Mead Lane Ind Est GL15 147 F4
Meadoway GL52 137 E2
Meadowbank GL15 92 C3
Meadowbrook Prim Sch BS32 29 E8
Meadow Cl
Bristol BS16 20 F7
Cheltenham GL51 132 C1
Cirencester GL7 190 C3
Tewkesbury GL20 192 E6
Viney Hill GL15 156 C1
Meadow Cotts WR12 184 F6
Meadow Court Dr BS30 11 C3
Meadowcroft
Bristol BS16 21 A8
Gloucester GL4 119 E5
Meadow Ct 2 GL10 97 F8
Meadow Gr BS11 16 D7
Meadow La 9 GL51 129 E5
Meadowland Rd BS10 27 E4
Meadow La W GL5 98 E6
Meadow Lea GL52 137 E2
Meadowleaze GL2 127 D3
Meadow Mead
Frampton Cotterell BS36 31 B8
Yate BS37 43 E5
Meadow Orch 4 WR12 185 B8
Meadowpark Sch SN6 143 F4
Meadow Rd
Chipping Sodbury BS37 44 A1
Cinderford GL14 191 E5
Cirencester GL7 190 C3
Honeybourne WR11 188 A8
Leyhill GL12 66 B4
Stonehouse GL10 97 F8
Meadow Rise GL17 164 F6
Meadows End GL17 164 F6
Meadowside 2 BS35 51 D8
Meadowside Dr BS14 3 A3
Meadowside Prim Sch GL2 117 F2
Meadows Prim Sch The BS30 5 D8
Meadow St
Avonmouth BS11 26 A1
Bristol BS2 195 C4
Meadows The
Bristol BS15 10 D4
Luckington SN14 47 F4
Minety SN16 142 D1
Meadowsweet Ave BS34 29 B3
Meadowsweet Wlk 1 GL2 118 A1
Meadow Vale
Bristol BS5 20 A1
Dursley GL11 87 F4
Meadow View
Baunton GL7 150 D7
Frampton Cotterell BS36 31 D7
Kempsford GL7 144 E8
Meadowview Cotts GL6 148 C5
Meadow Vw
Frampton on Severn GL2 157 F1
Lydney GL15 92 C3
Meadow Way
Bristol BS32 29 E7
Churchdown GL3 128 B7
Kingham OX7 177 F2
South Cerney GL7 142 F8
Stroud GL5 98 E6
Meadow Wlk
Chepstow/Cas-Gwent NP16 60 D8
Sling GL16 155 B2
Mead Rd
Bristol BS34 29 F5
Cheltenham GL53 130 E5
Chipping Sodbury BS37 44 C1
Gloucester GL4 119 E5
Mead Rise BS3 8 F4
Meads Cl
Bishop's Cleeve GL52 138 A3
4 Coleford GL16 155 A6
Meads Ct NP16 60 E6
Mead St BS3 195 C1
Meads The
Bristol BS16 20 F7
Burton SN14 36 B3
Leighterton GL8 70 C3
Mead The
Alveston BS35 51 A5
3 Ashton Keynes SN6 142 F4
Bristol BS34 29 B4
Cirencester GL7 190 B5
Dundry BS41 1 D2
Keynsham BS31 4 E3
Meadvale Cl GL2 126 F6
Mead Vw Cl SN14 14 F8
Meadway BS9 17 C6
Mead Way BS35 51 B7
Meadway Rd GL10 97 E6
Meardon Rd BS14 3 E6
Mechanical Organ Mus* GL17 164 B5
Mede Cl BS1 195 B1
Media Ho BS8 194 B3
Medical Ave BS2, BS8 194 C3
Medina Cl BS35 51 C7
Medlar Cl BS10 28 B6
Medoc Cl GL50 133 C5
Medway Cl BS31 5 A3
Medway Cres GL3 120 F5
Medway Ct
Cheltenham GL52 134 A2
Thornbury BS35 51 D8
Medway Dr
Frampton Cotterell BS36 31 B7
Keynsham BS31 5 A3
Meeks Hill NP25 154 B1
Meeks Well La HR9 162 E3
Meend Gardens Terr GL14 191 D3
Meendhurst Rd GL14 191 C4
Meend La GL17 163 F4
Meerbrook Way GL2 109 F7
Meere Bank BS11 27 B1
Meerstone Way GL4 119 D3
Meg Thatcher's Gdns BS5 10 B7
Meg Thatchers Gn BS5 10 B7
Melbourne Cl
Cheltenham GL53 130 C6
Stonehouse GL10 101 F1
Melbourne Dr
Chipping Sodbury BS37 44 C1
Stonehouse GL10 101 E1
Melbourne Rd BS7 18 D4
Melbourne St E
Gloucester GL1 118 F7
Gloucester GL1 119 A7
Melbourne St W GL1 118 F7
Melbury Rd BS4 9 A2
Meldon Terr GL5 99 B7
Melick Cl GL4 119 A5
Melita Rd BS6 18 E3
Mellent Ave BS13 2 C3
Mellersh Ho GL50 193 A1
Mells Cl BS31 5 A2
Melmore Gdns GL7 190 E2
Melody Way GL2 127 E5
Melrose Ave
Bristol BS8 194 B4
Yate BS37 44 A2
Melrose Cl BS37 44 A2
Melrose Pl BS8 194 B4
Melton Cres BS7 19 A7
Melville GL54 168 F8
Melville Rd
Bristol BS6 18 B1
Churchdown GL3 128 B5
Melville Terr BS3 8 C3
Melvin Sq BS4 8 E1
Memorial Cl BS15 10 B4
Memorial Cotts
Coln St Aldwyns GL7 152 D8
Tetbury GL8 140 A2
Memorial Rd BS15 10 B4
Memorial Stadium (Bristol Rovers FC)* BS7 18 F6
Mendip Cl
Cheltenham GL52 134 A3
Keynsham BS31 4 D5
Quedgeley GL2 109 E8
Mendip Cres BS16 21 A8
Mendip Ho 7 GL52 134 A3
Mendip Rd
Bristol BS3 8 D3
Cheltenham GL52 134 A3
Mendip View BS30 12 C7
Mendip View Ave BS16 20 A3
Menhyr Gr BS10 28 B3
Meon Rd GL55 189 B7
Mercer Ct BS14 3 B8
Merchants' Acad BS13 2 A5
Merchants Almshouses 5 BS1 195 A2
Merchants Ct BS8 194 A1
Merchants Mead 5 GL2 117 D1
Merchants Quay BS1 195 A1
Merchants Rd
Bristol, Hotwells BS8 194 A1
Bristol, Victoria Park BS8 194 A3
Merchants' Rd GL2 196 A2
Merchants Row BS1 194 C1
Merchant St BS1 195 B3
Merchants The SN14 47 E4
Merchants Trad Pk BS2 9 C6
Mercia Dr BS2 19 A2
Mercian Cl GL7 190 D3
Mercian Ct GL50 193 A1
Mercian Way NP16 61 A7
Mercia Rd
Gloucester GL1 196 B4
Winchcombe GL54 139 F6
Mercier Cl BS37 43 F2
Mercury Way GL4 119 F6
Meredith Ct BS1 194 A1
Meredith Ind Est GL17 163 C3
Merestones Cl GL50 130 B6
Merestones Dr GL50 130 B6
Merestones Rd GL50 130 B6
Merevale Rd GL2 127 C3
Merfield Rd BS4 9 B2
Meridian Pl BS8 194 B3
Meridian Rd BS6 18 C1
Meridian Vale BS8 194 B3
Meriet Ave BS13 2 B4
Merioneth St BS3 8 F3
Meriton St BS2 9 B5
Merlin Cl
Bristol BS9 17 F8
Cheltenham GL53 130 C5
Gloucester GL4 120 A4
Gloucester GL4 120 A4
Merlin Ct BS10 18 B7
Merlin Dr GL2 117 F2
Merlin Haven GL12 68 A7
Merlin Rd BS10, BS34 28 C6
Merlin Ridge BS16 22 C4
Merlin Way
Cheltenham GL53 130 C5
Chipping Sodbury BS37 32 F8
Merret Cl GL20 182 C5
Merrett Ct BS7 19 B6
Merrett's Orch GL2 95 D3
Merrick Ct BS1 195 A1
Merricks La NP16 146 D4
Merrimans Rd BS11 16 D8
Merrin St GL17 164 D5
Merrin The GL17 164 D5
Merritt Rd BS15 21 A3
Merriville Gdns GL51 133 A3
Merriville Rd GL51 133 A3
Merryfields GL10 110 B1
Merrywalks GL5 99 B7
Merrywalks Sh Ctr 1 GL5 99 C7
Merryweather Cl BS32 29 D8
Merryweathers BS4 9 E2
Merrywood Cl 5 BS3 8 C4
Merrywood Ct BS4 9 B2
Merrywood Rd BS3 8 C4
Mersey Rd GL52 134 A2
Merstham Rd 12 BS2 19 A2
Merthyr Terr GL17 163 D2
Merton Cl GL10 98 B6
Merton Cotts GL6 90 F3
Merton Rd BS7 18 E5
Mertons The GL14 156 F6
Mervyn Rd BS7 18 E4
Meryl Ct BS6 18 B1
Messenger Wy GL51 129 C6
Meteor Way GL3 120 E5
Metford Gr BS6 18 B3
Metford Pl BS6 18 C3
Metford Rd BS6 18 C3
Metropolitan The BS1 195 B1
Metz Way GL1, GL4 119 B8
Mews Enterprise Workshops GL17 164 D5
Mews The
Highworth SN6 145 D3
6 Tewkesbury GL20 192 C4
Meysey Cl GL7 152 B3
Meysey Hampton CE Prim Sch GL7 152 A3
Michaelmas Ct GL1 127 A3
Michaels Mead GL7 190 B2
Michaels Way GL16 155 B2
Mickle Mead
Gloucester GL4 119 E6
Highnam GL2 125 D5
Mickleton Prim Sch GL55 189 A6
Mickleton Rd
Honeybourne WR11 188 D7
Ilmington CV36 189 F7
Middi Haines Ct SN6 145 D3
Middle Ave BS1 195 A2
Middlecroft GL10 96 F7
Middle Croft GL4 119 D7
Middledown Rd SN14 24 C1
Middle Farm Ct GL7 144 E8
Middleford Ho BS13 2 C4
Middle Ground SN6 143 E4
Middlehay Ct GL52 137 E3
Middle Hill
Chalford GL6 148 C6
Stroud GL5 99 E7
Middle Hill Cres GL6 148 C6
Middle Leazes GL5 99 D7
Middle Mead GL7 190 E3
Middlemead La SN6 145 A5
Middlemoor Mill GL5 91 A6
Middle Orch OX7 177 E1
Middle Rd
Bristol BS15 20 F3
Little Barrington OX18 161 D7
Thrupp GL5 99 E3
Middle Spillman's GL5 99 A6
Middle Spring GL6 102 F3
Middle St
7 Chepstow/Cas-Gwent NP16 60 E8
Stroud, Bowbridge GL5 99 D7
Stroud, Uplands GL5 99 C8
Middleton Lawn GL3 127 E6
Middleton Rd BS11 16 F8
Middle Tynings GL6 91 A4
Middle Way NP16 60 F5
Midenhall Wy
4 Gloucester GL2 118 B1
Quedgeley GL2 110 B8
Midland Ct GL7 190 D3
Midland Mews 14 BS2 195 C3
Midland Rd
Bristol, Newton BS2 195 C3
Bristol, Staple Hill BS16 20 D4
Cirencester GL7 190 D2
Gloucester GL1 196 B1
Stonehouse GL10 97 E8
Midland Road Bsns Pk BS16 20 D4
Midland St BS2 195 C2
Midland Terr BS16 19 F3
Midland Way BS35 51 C7
Midnight Ct GL52 134 D4
Midsummer Wlk GL2 118 C6
Midway GL6 148 C6
Midwinter Ave GL51 133 C3
Midwinter Gdns GL50 133 C5
Midwinter Rd 4 GL54 168 A1
Mildred's Farm Barns GL7 150 F3
Mildred St BS5 9 C7
Mile End Rd GL16 155 B6
Miles Cl BS20 16 E3
Miles Cotts GL16 155 A3
Miles Ct
Bristol, Cadbury Heath BS30 10 F4
Bristol, Clifton BS8 18 A1
Miles Rd
Bishop's Cleeve GL52 137 E1
Bristol BS8 18 A1
Milestone Sch The GL2 127 B5
Milestone Wlk GL16 155 B2
Mile Wlk BS14 3 A6
Milford Ave BS30 12 B7
Milford Cl GL2 127 B5
Milford St BS3 8 C4
Millard Cl BS10 28 D2
Millar Ho BS8 194 A2
Mill Ave
Bristol BS1 195 A2
Broadway WR12 185 A8
Millbank GL11 88 A4
Mill Bank GL20 192 B4
Millbank Cl BS4 9 E3
Millbook Ct 3 BS6 18 E1
Millbridge Rd GL3 120 A7
Millbrook GL5 148 A5
Millbrook Acad GL3 120 F6
Millbrook Ave BS4 9 F3
Millbrook Cl
Bristol BS30 11 C6
6 Gloucester GL1 127 A1
Millbrook Ct GL50 193 A4
Millbrook Gdns
Cheltenham GL50 133 B2
Lea HR9 164 D8
Millbrook Gn GL15 147 E5
Millbrook Ley GL56 177 A6
Millbrook Pl GL5 99 D7
Millbrook Rd BS37 43 B2
Millbrook Rdbt GL50 193 A4
Millbrook St
Cheltenham GL50 193 A4
Gloucester GL1 127 A1
Millbrook Wlk GL5 90 F6
Mill Cl
8 Blockley GL56 186 C5
Brimscombe GL5 99 F2
Frampton Cotterell BS36 31 C7
South Cerney GL7 143 A8
Wotton-u-E GL12 68 C6
Mill Cotts
Saltford BS31 5 F2
Upper Redbrook NP25 154 C5
Mill Cres BS37 32 B4
Mill Ct 11 GL18 171 A4
Mill Dene Garden* GL56 186 C5
Millend GL15 156 E1
Mill End GL17 164 D5
Millend La GL10 97 A7
Millend Row GL10 97 A7
Millennium Cl
Frampton Cotterell BS36 31 D7
Tewkesbury GL20 192 E2
Millennium Cotts GL19 172 A7
Millennium Park Ctr* GL7 142 D6
Millennium Sq BS1 194 C1
Millennium Way GL7 190 F5
Miller Cl
Ashleworth GL19 172 D4
Gloucester GL2 127 D5
Miller Craddock Way 1 HR8 178 E7
Miller Ct GL52 136 E5
Millers Cl BS20 16 C4
Millers Dr BS30 11 D5
Millers Dyke GL2 117 D1
Millers Gn
Drybrook GL17 164 A4
Gloucester GL1 196 B3
Millers Way GL14 191 C4
Mill Farm Dr GL5 98 E8
Millfield BS35 64 C2
Millfield Dr BS30 11 C6
Millfields GL3 120 A8
Mill Gr GL2 117 D1
Millground Rd BS13 1 F5
Millgrove St N BS2 195 A4
Millham Rd GL52 138 A4
Mill Hill NP16 146 D4
Millhill La GL16 154 F3
Mill Ho
10 Bristol, Baptist Mills BS5 19 A1
Bristol BS1 195 A2
Millhouse Dr GL50 133 C5
Milliman Cl BS13 2 C5

Millin Ave GL4 . . . . 118 D2
Milling Cl SN6 . . . . 143 A5
Milling Cres GL15 . . . . . . 147 E5
Mill La
 Avening GL8 . . . . 140 B8
 Bitton BS30 . . . . 5 E8
 Bristol, Southville BS3. . . . . 8 D4
 Bristol, Warmley BS30. . . . 11 C5
 Brockworth GL3. . . . . 120 F6
 Castle Eaton SN6 . . . . . . 144 D6
 Charlton Kings GL54 . . . . 131 D8
 Cheltenham GL52. . . . . . . 134 D4
 Chipping Sodbury BS37 . . . 33 E6
 Cranham GL4 . . . . 112 D6
 Doynton BS30 . . . . 22 F1
 Fairford GL7 . . . . 152 D4
 Falfield GL12 . . . . 65 F7
 Frampton Cotterell BS36. . . 42 B1
 Gorsley GL18 . . . . 170 C3
 Greet GL54 . . . . 184 A1
 Lechlade on T GL7 . . . . . 153 F2
 Longhope GL17 . . . . 165 A5
 Lower Slaughter GL54 . . . 176 C1
 Lower Swell GL54 . . . . . . 176 D4
 Mickleton GL55 . . . . 189 A6
 Redmarley D'Abitot GL19 . 179 F2
 Stanton Fitzwarren SN6 . . 145 A1
 Staunton GL19 . . . . 179 F1
 Stoke Orchard GL52 . . . . . 136 D5
 Tockington BS32 . . . . 50 B1
 Upper Strensham WR8 . . 180 B10
 Upton Cheyney BS30 . . . . . 11 F1
 Winchcombe GL54 . . . . . . 174 A7
Millmead Ho BS13 . . . . 2 C4
Millpill Cl BS9 . . . . 17 D5
Mill Pl
 Cirencester GL7. . . . . 190 B5
 Gloucester GL1 . . . . 119 A7
Mill Place Trad Est GL1. . 118 D7
Millpond End GL5. . . . . 99 A2
Millpond St **9** BS5. . . . . . . 19 A1
Millpool Ct BS9 . . . . 18 B8
Mill Rd BS36 . . . . 30 D4
Mill Reef Dr GL52 . . . . 134 C4
Mill Row
 Blockley GL56 . . . . 186 D6
 King's Stanley GL10 . . . . . . 98 A5
 Lower Lydbrook GL17 . . . . 163 C3
Mills Cl **2** WR12 . . . . 185 B8
Mill St
 Cheltenham GL52. . . . . . . 134 C5
 Gloucester GL1 . . . . 127 A1
 Tewkesbury GL20 . . . . . . 192 B4
Mill Steps BS36 . . . . 30 E4
Millview GL56. . . . . 186 C6
Mill View
 Baunton GL7 . . . . 150 D7
 25 Northleach GL54 . . . . 168 A1
Millward Gr BS16 . . . . 20 C4
Mill Way GL11 . . . . 87 F4
Milne Pastures **2** GL20 . 182 B4
Milner Rd BS7 . . . . 18 F5
Milne Wlk GL51 . . . . 132 E4
Milo Pl GL1. . . . . 118 E6
Milsom St
 Bristol BS5. . . . . 9 A8
 Cheltenham GL50. . . . . . . 193 B4
Milton Ave
 Cheltenham GL51. . . . . . . 129 F8
 Gloucester GL2 . . . . 118 C5
Milton Cl BS37 . . . . 43 D2
Milton Gr GL5 . . . . 99 E7
Milton Pk **1** BS5. . . . . 9 C7
Milton Pl GL7 . . . . 152 D3
Milton Rd
 Bristol BS7. . . . . 18 E6
 Cheltenham GL51. . . . . . . 132 F1
 Yate BS37 . . . . 43 D2
Miltons Cl BS13. . . . . 2 D4
Milton St GL7 . . . . 152 D3
Milverton Gdns BS6 . . . . . 18 F2
Milward Rd BS31. . . . . 4 E6
Mimosa Ave GL3. . . . . 130 A4
Mimosa Ct **6** GL3. . . . . . . 128 A7
Mina Rd BS2. . . . . 19 A2
Minchinhampton Sch
 GL6 . . . . 148 A3
Minehead Rd BS4. . . . . 8 F1
Mine Pitts La HR9 . . . . . . 162 E3
Miners Wlk GL14. . . . . . . 191 C4
Minerva Cl GL4 . . . . 119 F6
Minerva Ct GL7 . . . . 190 D4
Minerva Prim Acad BS16 . 20 C2
Minerva Wlk GL15. . . . . . . 92 B5
Minetts Ave GL3 . . . . 128 A3
Minety CE Prim Sch
 SN16. . . . . 142 D1
Minety Crossroads SN16 142 D1
Minety La SN16 . . . . 142 A3
Minnow La OX18 . . . . 161 D7
Minor's La BS10 . . . . 27 A8
Minsmere Rd BS31. . . . . . . 5 A4
Minster Cl GL52. . . . . 137 E4
Minster Ct **1** BS37 . . . . . . 32 D7
Minster Gdns GL4. . . . . . 119 F6
Minsterworth CE Prim Sch
 GL2 . . . . 116 F7
Minstrel Way GL3 . . . . . . 127 F8
Minton Cl BS14 . . . . 3 B5
Minto Rd BS2. . . . . 19 A2
Minto Road Ind Ctr **8**
 BS2. . . . . 19 A2

Misarden Park Gdns★
 GL6 . . . . 106 B6
Misarden Park Woodland
 Trail★ GL6 . . . . 106 B6
Miserden CE Prim Sch
 GL6. . . . . 106 A6
Miserden Rd GL51 . . . . . . 132 D1
Miss Grace's La NP16 . . . 146 E2
Mission Rd BS37 . . . . 43 B4
Mistletoe Mews GL3 . . . . 127 F6
Mitcheldean Endowed Prim
 Sch GL17. . . . . 164 D5
Mitchell Ct BS1. . . . . 195 B2
Mitchell La BS1. . . . . 195 B2
Mitchell Wlk BS30 . . . . . . 11 D7
Mitford Cotts OX18. . . . . 161 F5
Mitford Villas GL56. . . . . 187 A3
Mitre Gdns GL51. . . . . . . 129 E2
Mitre Pitch GL12. . . . . 68 C7
Mitre St GL3 . . . . 193 C2
Mitton Ct GL20. . . . . 192 E6
Mitton Manor Prim Sch
 GL20. . . . . 192 E6
Mitton Way GL20. . . . . . . 192 E6
Mivart St BS5. . . . . 19 B2
Moat Bank GL20 . . . . 180 F7
Moat Ho GL4 . . . . 119 B4
Moat La
 Corse GL19 . . . . 172 A8
 Huntley GL19 . . . . 165 E8
 Uckington GL51 . . . . 132 D6
Moat Prim Sch GL4 . . . . . 119 B4
Moat The
 Kingham OX7 . . . . 177 F3
 Quedgeley GL2 . . . . 117 F1
Mobley GL13. . . . . 86 A3
Modecombe Gr BS10. . . . . 27 F3
Model Village The★
 GL54 . . . . 169 A7
Moffatt Rd GL6 . . . . 91 A4
Mogg St BS2 . . . . 19 A2
Mogridge Cl GL3. . . . . . . 120 A7
Mohair Countryside Ctr★
 GL17 . . . . 165 A5
Molesworth Cl BS13. . . . . . 2 A4
Molesworth Dr BS13 . . . . . 2 A4
Mona Ave **3** GL4 . . . . 110 C8
Monarch Cl GL4 . . . . 119 E4
Monarch Ct BS16. . . . . . . 31 A1
Monica Dr GL50. . . . . 133 E4
Monkey Mdw GL20. . . . . 182 C5
Monkey Puzzle Cl GL5. . . . 98 E6
Monk Rd BS7 . . . . 18 D4
Monks Ave BS15 . . . . 10 B8
Monks Croft GL51. . . . . . 132 E1
Monks Field Wy GL20 . . . 192 C3
Monks Ho **3** BS37 . . . . . . 32 D7
Monks La GL20 . . . . 182 C2
Monk's Park Ave BS7 . . . . 18 E8
Monks Park Way BS7 . . . . 18 E8
Monkswell Cl **2** NP25. . . 154 A8
Monkswell Rd **1** NP25 . . 154 A8
Monks Wlk GL7 . . . . 153 F2
Monkton Rd BS15. . . . . . . 10 B5
Monmouth Comp Sch
 NP25. . . . . 154 A8
Monmouth Cl BS20 . . . . . 16 C5
Monmouth Hill BS32 . . . . 39 E4
Monmouth Rd
 Bristol BS7. . . . . 18 D4
 Edge End GL16. . . . . 155 C8
 Keynsham BS31. . . . . 4 D5
 Pill BS20 . . . . 16 C5
Monmouthshire Pupil
 Referral Service BS34. . . 30 A7
Monmouth St BS3 . . . . 8 F3
Monsdale Cl BS10. . . . . . . 28 A3
Monsdale Dr BS10 . . . . . . 28 A2
Monson Ave GL50. . . . . . 193 B4
Montague Cl BS34 . . . . . . 29 E5
Montague Ct **2** BS2 . . . . 195 A4
Montague Flats **6** BS2. . 195 A4
Montague Hill BS2. . . . . . 195 A4
Montague Hill S **5** BS2. . 195 A4
Montague Pl BS2. . . . . . . 195 A4
Montague Rd BS31. . . . . . . 5 D2
Montague St BS1 . . . . 195 A4
Monterey Rd GL20 . . . . . 192 E1
Montfort Rd GL2. . . . . . . 127 B5
Montgomery Cl GL3. . . . . 120 B6
Montgomery Rd GL51 . . . 129 D6
Montgomery St BS3. . . . . . 8 F3
Montpelier Central **1**
 BS6 . . . . 18 E1
Montpelier St BS6 . . . . . . 18 E2
Montpelier Sta BS6 . . . . . 18 E2
Montpellier GL1 . . . . 196 B1
Montpellier Arc GL50 . . . 193 B2
Montpellier Ave GL50 . . . 193 A4
Montpellier Ct GL50. . . . . 193 A2
Montpellier Dr GL50 . . . . 193 B2
Montpellier Gr GL50. . . . . 193 B2
Montpellier Ho GL50 . . . . 193 A4
Montpellier Mews GL1 . . 196 B2
Montpellier Par GL50 . . . 193 B2
Montpellier Rd GL15 . . . . 155 E1
Montpellier Retreat
 GL50. . . . . 193 B2
Montpellier Spa Rd
 GL50. . . . . 193 B2
Montpellier St GL50. . . . . 193 B3
Montpellier Terr GL50. . . 193 B2
Montpellier Villas GL50 . . 193 B3
Montpellier Wlk GL50 . . . 193 A2
Montreal Ave BS7. . . . . . . 19 A8

Montreal Dr GL51 . . . . . . 132 E3
Montreaux Ct **10** BS16. . . 20 D3
Montreaux Ho **2** BS5 . . . 10 A7
Montrose Ave BS6 . . . . . . 18 C1
Montrose Dr BS30 . . . . . . 11 B6
Montrose Pk BS4. . . . . 9 D2
Montroy Cl BS9. . . . . 18 C6
Montserrat BS5. . . . . 99 D3
Mont The **2** BS6. . . . . 18 E1
Moon's La GL6. . . . . 148 E7
Moon St BS2 . . . . 195 B4
Moor Court Dr GL52. . . . . 133 F2
Moor Croft Dr BS30 . . . . . 10 F3
Moor Ct
 Amberley GL5 . . . . 91 C8
 Amberley GL5 . . . . 99 C1
Moordell Cl BS37 . . . . 43 D1
Moorend Cres GL53 . . . . . 130 C6
Moorend Gdns BS11 . . . . . 16 F7
Moorend Glade GL53. . . . 130 F6
Moorend Gr GL53 . . . . . . 130 C5
Moorend La GL2 . . . . 95 C2
Moorend Park Rd GL53. . 130 C6
Moorend Rd
 Cheltenham, Charlton Park
  GL53. . . . . 130 F6
 Cheltenham, Leckhampton
  GL53. . . . . 130 C5
 Hambrook BS16. . . . . 30 D3
 Staunton GL19. . . . . 180 C1
Moorend St GL53. . . . . . . 130 C6
Moorend Terr GL53 . . . . . 130 C6
Moore Rd GL54 . . . . 168 F7
Moores Ground GL19. . . . 173 C6
Moorfield Ave GL15 . . . . . 156 D1
Moorfield Rd GL3. . . . . . . 120 F5
Moorfields Ho BS5. . . . . . . 9 C7
Moorgate GL7 . . . . 153 D2
Moor Gr BS11. . . . . 17 A8
Moorgrove Ho BS9. . . . . . 17 C7
Moor Hall Pl GL5. . . . . 98 E8
Moorhen Ct GL2 . . . . 117 D1
Moorhill St **17** BS5 . . . . . 19 B1
Moor House Cvn Pk BS10. 27 A4
Moorhouse La BS10. . . . . 27 B4
Moorings The BS20 . . . . . 16 C4
Moor La
 Bourton-on-t-W GL54 . . . 169 A8
 Fairford GL7 . . . . 152 E3
 Tockington BS32 . . . . 40 A8
Moorland Cl GL14. . . . . . . 191 D5
Moorland Rd BS37. . . . . . . 43 D1
Moorlands Rd
 Bristol, Mayfield Park
  BS16. . . . . 20 A2
 Bristol, Ridgeway BS16. . . 19 F3
Moor Lane Ct GL7. . . . . . . 152 E3
Moorpark Ave BS37. . . . . . 43 D1
Moors Ave GL1 . . . . 133 A4
Moorslade La GL12. . . . . . 77 D1
Moor St
 Chepstow/Cas-Gwent
  NP16. . . . . 60 E8
 Gloucester GL1 . . . . 118 F7
 Saul GL2 . . . . 157 F4
Moor The SN16 . . . . 142 D2
Moor Wood Cotts GL7. . . 158 B3
Mop Hale GL5. . . . . 186 C6
Mopla Rd NP16 . . . . 72 F2
Moravian Ct **4** BS15 . . . . 10 D8
Moravian Rd BS15 . . . . . . 10 D8
Morcroft Pl GL15. . . . . . . 155 F1
Morden Wlk BS14. . . . . 3 D7
More Hall Pk GL5 . . . . . . 102 D1
Morelands GL1 . . . . 118 E5
Morelands Trad Est GL1 . 196 A1
Morestall Dr GL7. . . . . . . 190 B2
Moreton Cl
 Bishop's Cleeve GL52 . . . 138 A2
 Bristol BS34 . . . . 3 A4
Moreton-in-Marsh Sta
 GL56. . . . . 187 A3
Moreton La GL20. . . . . . . 182 C6
Morgan Cl BS31. . . . . 5 D2
Morgans Dr GL50 . . . . . . 193 A1
Morgans La GL17 . . . . . . 164 A3
Morgan St BS2 . . . . 18 F1
Morgans Terr GL7 . . . . . . 142 F7
Morgan's Way GL14 . . . . 156 C6
Mork La GL15 . . . . 146 E7
Mork Rd GL15 . . . . 146 E7
Morlands Dr GL53. . . . . . 131 B4
Morley Ave
 Bristol BS16. . . . . 21 A4
 Churchdown GL3. . . . . . . 128 A6
Morley Cl
 Bristol, Little Stoke BS34. . 29 C7
 Bristol, Staple Hill BS16 . . 20 D4
Morley Pl **13** BS16. . . . . . 20 D3
Morley Rd
 Bristol, Southville BS3. . . . 8 C4
 Bristol, Staple Hill BS16 . . 20 D4
Morley Sq BS7 . . . . 18 E4
Morley St
 Bristol, Baptist Mills BS2. . 18 F1
 Bristol, Russell Town BS5 . . 9 B7
Morley Terr **5** 20 D1
Morman Cl GL17 . . . . 164 B4
Morningside Cl GL52. . . . 134 C4
Morningside Ctyd GL52. . 134 C4
Mornington Dr GL53 . . . . 130 D6
Mornington Rd **14** BS8 . . 18 A2
Mornington Terr **6**
 GL14. . . . . 157 A6
Morpeth Rd BS4 . . . . 2 D8
Morpeth St GL1. . . . . 118 F7

Morris Cl GL15. . . . . 156 B2
Morris Ct **7** GL51. . . . . . . 129 F7
Morris Hill Cl GL51 . . . . . 133 B6
Morris Orch GL11. . . . . . . 87 F6
Morris Rd
 Bristol BS7. . . . . 19 A5
 Broadway WR12 . . . . 185 B8
Morse La GL17. . . . . 164 A4
Morse Rd
 Bristol BS5. . . . . 9 C7
 Drybrook GL17. . . . . 164 B4
Mortimer Rd
 Bristol, Filton BS34 . . . . . 29 B2
 Bristol, Victoria Park BS8 . 194 A3
 Gloucester GL2 . . . . 127 C5
Morton Mill BS35. . . . . . . 64 C3
Morton St
 Bristol BS5. . . . . 9 B7
 Gloucester GL1 . . . . 118 F7
 Thornbury BS35 . . . . 64 C4
Morton Way BS35. . . . . . . 64 D1
Morwent Cl GL4 . . . . 119 E6
Mosedale **12** GL56. . . . . . 187 B3
Moselle Dr GL3 . . . . 128 A6
Mosley Cres GL5. . . . . 98 E7
Mosley Rd GL5. . . . . 98 E7
Moss Wy GL7 . . . . 190 F5
Mostham Pl GL3 . . . . 120 D6
Motor Museum (The Bugatti
 Trust)★ GL52. . . . . 138 E8
Motorway Distribution Ctr
 BS11. . . . . 26 C2
Mottershead Dr GL3 . . . . 127 E6
Mottershead Rd GL17 . . . 150 F2
Moulder Rd GL20 . . . . . . 192 E4
Mountain Mews **5** BS5 . . 10 A7
Mountain View 117 F4
Mountbatten Cl BS37. . . . 43 D3
Mount Cl
 Cirencester GL7. . . . . 190 C3
 Frampton Cotterell BS36. . 30 F8
 Harrow Hill GL17. . . . . . . 164 B4
Mount Craig Hall HR9 . . . 162 F8
Mount Cres BS36 . . . . 30 E5
Mounteney's La GL12 . . . . 54 D7
Mount Gdns GL53 . . . . . . 10 D6
Mount Hill Rd BS15. . . . . 10 D6
Mountjoy's La GL14 . . . . . 191 D5
Mountjoy's Lane End
 GL14. . . . . 191 D5
Mounton Chambers NP16 60 D7
Mounton Cl NP16. . . . . . . 60 D7
Mounton Dr NP16. . . . . . . 60 D7
Mounton Rd NP16. . . . . . . 60 D7
Mount Pleasant
 Bisley GL6 . . . . 148 D8
 Blockley GL56 . . . . 186 C6
 Chepstow/Cas-Gwent NP16 60 E8
 Fairford GL7 . . . . 152 E4
 Hallen BS10. . . . . 27 C4
 Lechlade on T GL7 . . . . . 153 E2
 Lydney BS11. . . . . 92 C2
 Parkend GL15 . . . . 155 E3
 Pill BS20 . . . . 16 D4
 Stroud GL5 . . . . 99 E7
 Tirley GL19 . . . . 172 F7
 Wotton-u-E GL12 . . . . 68 C7
Mount Pleasant Cl
 Lydney BS11. . . . . 92 C2
 17 Stow-on-t W GL54 . . 176 F4
Mount Pleasant Rd
 Cinderford GL14 . . . . 191 D3
 Tewkesbury GL20 . . . . . . 192 F4
Mount Pleasant Terr BS3. . 8 C4
Mount St
 Cirencester GL7. . . . . 190 C3
 Gloucester GL1 . . . . 196 A3
Mount Way
 Chepstow/Cas-Gwent
  NP16. . . . . 60 D8
 Chepstow/Cas-Gwent NP16 72 D1
Mousell La GL14 . . . . 191 D4
Mousetrap La GL54 . . . . . 168 F8
Mow Barton
 Bristol BS13. . . . . 1 F6
 Yate BS37 . . . . 43 D2
Mowberry Cl GL2 . . . . . . 127 C5
Mowbray Ave GL20. . . . . 192 D1
Mowbray Rd BS14. . . . . . . 3 C7
Mowcroft Rd BS13 . . . . . . 2 D4
Moxham Dr BS13. . . . . 2 C4
Moyle Old School La
 NP16. . . . . 73 A4
M Shed★ BS1 . . . . 195 A1
Muirfield
 Bristol BS30. . . . . 11 A6
 Yate BS37 . . . . 32 E8
Mulberry Cl
 1 Bristol BS15 . . . . 10 E8
 Hardwicke GL2 . . . . 109 E8
Mulberry Ct **2** GL51 . . . . 132 D2
Mulberry Dr BS15. . . . . . . 20 F1
Mulberry Gdns
 11 Bristol BS16. . . . . . . 20 D3
 Gloucester GL4 . . . . 119 B4
Mulberry Gn GL56. . . . . . 177 C4
Mulberry Gr **12** BS16. . . . 20 D3
Mulberry Rd GL3 . . . . 120 B4
Mulberry Tree Steiner Sch
 GL12 . . . . 66 C2
Mulberry Wlk BS9 . . . . . . 17 C8
Mule St GL13 . . . . 78 B3
Muller Ave BS7 . . . . 18 F4
Muller Rd BS5, BS7 . . . . . 19 B3
Mullings Ct GL7. . . . . 190 C5
Mulready Cl BS7 . . . . 19 C6

Mumbleys Hill BS35. . . . . 50 E7
Mumbleys La
 Thornbury, Alveston Down
  BS35. . . . . 50 E6
 Thornbury, Kington BS35. . . 50 E8
Munday Cl **8** GL6. . . . . . . 148 B6
Munsley Gr GL4. . . . . 119 C3
Murdoch Sq BS7. . . . . 18 F8
Murford Ave BS13. . . . . 2 B4
Murford Wlk BS13 . . . . 2 B4
Murray Cl GL52 . . . . 137 F5
Murray St **9** BS3 . . . . 8 C4
Murrell Dr GL3. . . . . 120 E4
Murrells Rd GL16 . . . . . . 163 A2
Murvagh GL53 . . . . 193 C1
Murvagh Cl GL53. . . . . . . 193 C1
Muscroft Rd GL52. . . . . . 134 D4
Musgrove Cl BS11. . . . . . . 27 C2
Mushet Ind Pk GL16. . . . . 155 B5
Mushet Pl GL16. . . . . 155 A5
Musket Cl
 Gloucester GL4 . . . . 119 C4
 Tewkesbury GL20 . . . . . . 192 E2
Mutsilver Mews GL2 . . . . 127 E5
Muzzle Patch GL2. . . . . . . 124 C4
Myers Rd GL1. . . . . 127 A1
Myrtle Cl GL4 . . . . 119 A5
Myrtle Dr BS11. . . . . 16 C5
Myrtle Hill BS20 . . . . 16 C5
Myrtle Pl NP16. . . . . 72 F1
Myrtle Rd BS2 . . . . 194 C4
Myrtle St BS3. . . . . 8 B3
Myrtles The NP16 . . . . 73 A4
Mystic Cnr GL51 . . . . 129 C6
Mythe Rd GL20. . . . . 192 C5
Mythe Terr **3** GL14 . . . . . 157 A6

N

Naas La
 Lydney GL15. . . . . 92 C3
 Quedgeley GL2, GL4 . . . . 110 C6
Naas La Rdbt GL2. . . . . . . 109 F7
Nags Head Hill BS5 . . . . . 10 A7
Nagshead Nature Reserve★
 GL15 . . . . 155 C5
Nagshead Nature Trails★
 GL15 . . . . 155 D3
Nailers La GL18. . . . . 170 D3
Nailsea BS13 . . . . 2 A7
Nailsworth Ave BS37. . . . . 43 C3
Nailsworth CE Prim Sch
 GL6 . . . . 90 F5
Nailsworth Mills Est GL6 . 91 C4
Nailsworth Terr **2** GL50. 193 A4
Naishcombe Hill BS30. . . . 12 C7
Naite The BS35. . . . . 63 D6
Nanfan and Dobyn Pl
 GL18. . . . . 171 A3
Napier Ct BS1. . . . . 194 B1
Napier Dr GL3 . . . . 120 B4
Napier Ho BS6 . . . . 18 B2
Napier Miles Rd BS11 . . . . 17 A8
Napier Rd
 Avonmouth BS11 . . . . 26 B1
 Bristol, Baptist Mills BS5. . 19 B2
 Bristol, Redland BS6 . . . . 18 B2
Napier Sq BS11 . . . . 26 A1
Napier St
 Bristol BS5. . . . . 9 B6
 Gloucester GL1 . . . . 196 C2
Napping La GL17. . . . . . . 164 F6
Napping The GL17. . . . . . 164 F6
Narles Rd GL2 . . . . 96 A3
Narroways Rd BS2 . . . . . . 19 A3
Narrowcut La GL6. . . . . . . 90 F1
Narrow La BS15. . . . . 20 E4
Narrow Plain BS2. . . . . . . 195 B2
Narrow Quay BS1. . . . . . . 195 A2
Narrows The GL55 . . . . . . 188 E1
Narth La NP25 . . . . 154 B1
NAS Anderson Sch The
 BS35. . . . . 39 A6
Naseby Ho **4** GL52. . . . . 134 A3
Naseby Wlk BS5 . . . . 19 F1
Nash Cl BS31 . . . . 5 A5
Nash Dr BS7 . . . . 19 C7
Nash's La GL55 . . . . 189 D3
Nash Way GL16 . . . . 155 A5
Nasse Ct GL11 . . . . 87 F5
Nastend La GL10. . . . . . . 101 C1
National Star Coll The
 GL53. . . . . 122 C6
Nature Cl GL3. . . . . 120 E5
Naunton Cres GL53. . . . . 130 D6
Naunton La GL53. . . . . . . 130 D6
Naunton Par GL53 . . . . . . 130 D6
Naunton Park Cl GL53. . . 130 E6
Naunton Park Ind Est
 GL53. . . . . 130 E6
Naunton Park Prim Sch
 GL53. . . . . 130 E6
Naunton Park Rd GL53 . . 130 E6
Naunton Rd GL4. . . . . 119 D7
Naunton Terr GL53. . . . . 193 B1
Naunton Way GL53. . . . . 130 D6
Naval Temple★ NP25 . . . 154 B7
Neads Dr BS30. . . . . 11 C5
Neale Way BS11. . . . . 26 C1
Neata Farm GL54 . . . . . . 184 A1
Neate Ct BS34 . . . . 29 C8
Neath Rd BS5. . . . . 9 D8
Neatishead Rd **2** GL2. . . 110 B8
Nebraska Circle GL7 . . . . 152 E1
Nebsworth La CV36 . . . . . 189 E5

Needham Ave GL2 . . . . . 110 B6
Neigh Bridge Ctry Pk★
GL7 . . . . 142 C5
Nell Hill SN6 . . . . 145 A4
Nelmes Row GL53 . . . . . . 131 C5
Nelson Ho
Bristol BS1 . . . . 195 A3
■8 Bristol, Staple Hill BS16 . 20 D5
Nelson Par ■10 BS3 . . . . . . 8 D4
Nelson Rd
■3 Bristol BS16 . . . . 20 D5
Bristol BS16 . . . . 20 D5
Nelsons Pl HR9 . . . . 163 B7
Nelson St
Bristol, Ashton Vale BS3 . . 8 A2
Bristol BS1 . . . . 195 A3
Chepstow/Cas-Gwent NP16 . 60 F8
Gloucester GL1 . . . . 118 F6
Stroud GL5 . . . . 99 C7
Tewkesbury GL20 . . . . . . 192 C4
Nene Cl GL2 . . . . 117 E2
Neptune Bsns Ctr GL51 . 133 B3
Neptune Business Ctr
GL51 . . . . 133 B3
Neptune Cl GL4 . . . . 119 F6
Nero Cl GL15 . . . . 92 C4
Neston Wlk BS4 . . . . 2 F8
Netham Gdns BS5 . . . . 9 D7
Netham Park Ind Est BS5. . 9 D6
Netham Rd BS5 . . . . 9 D6
Netham View Ind Pk BS5 . . 9 D7
Nethercote CV36 . . . . . . 187 F5
Nethercote Dr GL54 . . . . 169 A7
Nethercote Farm Dr
GL54 . . . . 169 A6
Netherend La GL15 . . . . . 147 C3
Netherend Cres GL15 . . . 147 C3
Netherhope La NP16 . . . . 73 B5
Netheridge Cl GL2 . . . . . 118 A4
Netherley La GL19 . . . . . 180 A4
Nether-Swell Manor
GL54 . . . . 176 E3
Netherwood Cl GL51 . . . . 133 A3
Netherwood Gdns GL51 . 133 A3
Netting La GL2 . . . . 157 B6
Nettlestone Cl BS10 . . . . 27 E4
Nettleton Rd
Burton SN14 . . . . 36 B2
Cheltenham GL51 . . . . . . 129 E7
Gloucester GL1 . . . . 196 C2
Nevalan Dr BS5 . . . . 10 A6
Neville Rd
Bristol BS15 . . . . 20 E2
Tewkesbury GL20 . . . . . . 192 D3
Nevil Rd BS7 . . . . 18 E4
Newark Ho GL2 . . . . 118 B7
Newark Pk★ GL12 . . . . . . 69 A4
Newark Rd GL1 . . . . 118 C6
New Barn Ave GL52 . . . . 134 A4
New Barn Cl GL52 . . . . . 134 A4
New Barn La GL52 . . . . . 134 A4
New Bldgs BS16 . . . . 19 F4
Newbridge Cl BS4 . . . . 9 D5
Newbridge Farm Pk★
HR8 . . . . 178 A8
Newbridge Ho BS9 . . . . . 17 C4
Newbridge Rd BS4 . . . . . . .9 E6
Newbridge Trad Est BS4 . . 9 D5
New Brunswick Ave BS5 . 10 B7
Newburgh Ho SN6 . . . . . 145 C3
Newburgh Pl SN6 . . . . . . 145 C3
Newbury Rd BS7 . . . . 19 A7
New Charlotte St BS3 . . . . 8 D4
New Charlton Wy BS10 . . 28 A6
New Cheltenham Rd BS15 . 20 E1
New Church St GL8 . . . . . 140 B4
Newcombe Ave GL4 . . . . 114 B5
Newcombe Ct GL7 . . . . . 190 D4
Newcombe Dr BS9 . . . . . . 17 C4
Newcombe Rd BS9 . . . . . . 17 F7
Newcourt Pk GL53 . . . . . 131 A6
Newcourt Rd GL53 . . . . . 131 A5
New Cut GL11 . . . . 89 B1
New Dawn Cl GL52 . . . . . 137 F3
Newent Ave BS15 . . . . . . 10 B7
Newent Bsns Pk GL18 . . 171 B4
Newent Com Sch & Sixth
Form Ctr GL18 . . . . 170 F4
Newent La GL19 . . . . 165 C6
Newerne St GL15 . . . . . . 92 B3
New Fancy View★ GL15 . 155 F4
New Fosseway Rd BS14 . . 3 B6
New Fosseway Sch BS13 . . 2 E4
Newfoundland St BS2 . . 195 C4
Newfoundland Rd
■6 Bristol, Baptist Mills
BS2 . . . . 19 A1
Bristol, St Pauls BS2 . . . 195 C4
Newfoundland St BS2 . . 195 C4
Newfoundland Way BS2 . 195 C4
Newgate BS1 . . . . 195 B3
Newgrounds La GL2 . . . . 95 B6
New Horizons Learning Ctr
BS15 . . . . 20 F1
Newhouse Farm Ind Est
NP16 . . . . 60 F3
New Inn La
Avening GL8 . . . . 140 B8
Gloucester GL1 . . . . 196 B3
New John St ■1 BS3 . . . . . . 8 C3
New Kings Ct BS7 . . . . . . 18 C4
New Kingsley Rd BS2 . . . 195 C2
New La BS35 . . . . 51 C3
Newland Ct GL52 . . . . . . 134 B3
Newland Dr BS13 . . . . 2 A4

Newland Pl GL20 . . . . . . 192 D4
Newland Rd BS13 . . . . 2 A3
Newlands Ave BS36 . . . . . 31 C7
Newlands Ct
■20 Newent GL18 . . . . . . 171 A4
Stow-on-t-W GL54 . . . . . 176 E5
Newlands Rd BS31 . . . . 4 D4
Newland St
Coleford GL16 . . . . 155 A5
Gloucester GL1 . . . . 196 C3
Newlands The BS16 . . . . . 20 B7
Newland View GL51 . . . . 132 F5
Newland Way ■1 NP25 . . 154 A7
Newland Wlk BS13 . . . . 2 A3
Newleaze BS34 . . . . 29 A2
New Leaze BS32 . . . . 40 C3
Newleaze Gdns GL8 . . . . 140 B4
Newleaze Rd BS34 . . . . . . 29 B2
Newlyn Ave BS9 . . . . 17 D5
Newlyn Way BS37 . . . . . . 43 F2
Newlyn Wlk BS4 . . . . .9 B1
Newman Cl BS37 . . . . 32 B4
Newmarket Ave BS1 . . . . 195 A3
Newmarket Rd GL6 . . . . . 91 A4
New Mdws BS14 . . . . .3 B6
New Mills GL15 . . . . 92 A6
Newmills Hill HR9. . . . . . . 64 D2
New mills Ind Est HR8 . . 178 E8
New Mills La GL12 . . . . . . 16 E5
New Mills Trad Est GL5 . . 99 D8
New Mills Way ■1 HR8 . . 178 E8
Newnham Cl BS34 . . . . 3 D7
Newnham Pl BS34 . . . . . . 39 F1
Newnham St Peter's CE Prim
Sch GL14 . . . . 157 A7
Newnton Hill GL8 . . . . . . 140 D5
Newnton Rd GL8 . . . . 140 C3
Newpit La BS30 . . . . 11 F2
Newport Rd
Chepstow/Cas-Gwent
NP16 . . . . 60 D7
Pill BS20 . . . . 16 C5
Newport St BS3 . . . . .8 E3
Newquay Rd BS4 . . . . 8 F1
New Queen St
Bristol, St George BS15 . . 10 B8
Bristol, Windmill Hill BS3 . . 8 E4
New Rd
Aylburton GL15 . . . . 147 D5
Blakeney GL15 . . . . 156 D1
Bledington OX7 . . . . 177 E1
Bream GL15 . . . . 147 D8
Bristol, Filton BS34 . . . . . 28 F2
Bristol, Harry Stoke BS34 . . 29 D3
Coleford, Cannop GL15,
GL16 . . . . 155 D6
Coleford GL16 . . . . 155 B5
Dursley GL11 . . . . 87 E4
Ebrington GL55 . . . . 189 D3
Kingham OX7 . . . . 177 F2
Kingswood GL12 . . . . 67 F6
Lydney GL15 . . . . 147 F7
Minchinhampton GL6 . . . 91 F5
Mitcheldean GL17 . . . . . . 24 F7
■9 Moreton-in-M GL56 . . 187 A3
North Nibley GL11 . . . . . . 79 E4
Olveston BS35 . . . . 50 A2
Parkend GL15 . . . . 155 E2
Pendock WR13 . . . . 180 A8
Pill BS20 . . . . 16 C4
Rangeworthy BS37 . . . . . 43 A8
Rangeworthy, Hall End
BS37 . . . . 53 C1
Stroud GL5 . . . . 98 E5
Tytherington GL12 . . . . . 52 C6
Woodmancote GL52 . . . . 138 C2
Yorkley GL15 . . . . 156 A1
New Row
Aldsworth GL54 . . . . 160 E5
Brockhampton GL54 . . . 174 B1
New Rutland Ct GL50 . . . 193 B4
Newry Wlk BS4 . . . . 8 E1
New Siblands Sch BS35 . . 64 B7
Newsome Ave BS20 . . . . . 16 C4
New St
Bretforton WR11 . . . . . . 188 A6
Bristol BS2 . . . . 195 C3
Charfield GL12 . . . . 67 A6
Charlton Kings GL53 . . . 131 B5
Cheltenham GL50 . . . . . 193 A4
Gloucester GL1 . . . . 196 B3
King's Stanley GL10 . . . . 98 A3
Ledbury HR8 . . . . 178 E8
Mitcheldean GL17 . . . . . 164 D5
Newton GL13 . . . . 85 C8
Painswick GL6 . . . . 103 F8
New Stadium Rd BS5. . . . 19 B2
New Station Rd BS16 . . . 20 A4
New Station Wy BS16 . . . 20 A4
Newstead Rd GL4 . . . . . . 119 E8
New Street Flats ■5 BS2 . 195 C3
New Thomas St BS2 . . . . 195 C2
Newth's La SN5 . . . . 143 C1
Newton Ave GL4 . . . . 119 C7
Newton Cl
Bristol BS15 . . . . 21 A1
Cheltenham GL51 . . . . . . 132 E2
Huntley GL19 . . . . 165 D6
■2 Ledbury HR8 . . . . 178 F7
Newton Court La NP25 . . 162 B1
Newton Dr BS30 . . . . 11 A5
Newton Rd
Bristol BS30 . . . . 11 A5
Cheltenham GL51 . . . . . . 132 E2
Newton St BS5 . . . . 9 A8
Newtown GL12 . . . . 67 A5

New Town
Cinderford GL14 . . . . . . 191 B7
New Town GL54 . . . . 184 C3
Toddington GL54 . . . . . . 184 C3
Newtown La GL20 . . . . . . 192 F5
Newtown Rd GL14 . . . . . 191 B7
New Villa SN14 . . . . 57 D1
New Walls BS41 . . . . 8 F4
New Wlk BS15 . . . . 10 B5
New Zealand Ho ■2 GL51 132 F3
Niblett Cl BS15 . . . . 10 F6
Niblett's Hill BS5 . . . . . . 10 A6
Nibley La BS37 . . . . 42 F3
Nibley Rd BS11 . . . . 16 E5
Nicholas La BS5 . . . . 10 A6
Nicholas Rd BS5 . . . . 19 B1
Nicholas St BS3 . . . . 8 E4
Nicholettes BS30 . . . . 11 D5
Nicholls Ct BS36 . . . . 30 E7
Nicholls La BS36 . . . . 30 E6
Nicolson Cl GL3 . . . . 127 E6
Nigel Pk BS11 . . . . 16 E7
Nightingale Cl
Bristol BS5 . . . . .9 E6
Frampton Cotterell BS36 . 31 A6
Thornbury BS35 . . . . 64 D2
Nightingale Croft GL3 . . 127 D6
Nightingale Ct BS4 . . . . . . .9 D3
Nightingale Ho GL4 . . . . 119 D4
Nightingale La BS36 . . . . 31 A8
Nightingale Wy
South Cerney GL7 . . . . . 143 A7
Tewkesbury GL20 . . . . . 192 F1
Nind La GL12 . . . . 68 B4
Nine Elms Rd GL2 . . . . . 127 E4
Nine Tree Hill ■16 BS1 . . 18 E1
Nine Wells Cl ■16 GL16 . 155 A7
Ninewells Forest Wlk★
NP25 . . . . 146 B6
Nine Wells Rd GL16 . . . . 155 B7
Ninth Ave BS7 . . . . 29 B1
Niven Ctyd GL51 . . . . . . 132 C1
Noake Rd GL3 . . . . 120 A8
Noble Ave BS30 . . . . 11 C4
Noden Cl HR9 . . . . 164 C8
Nodens Way GL15 . . . . . . 92 C4
Noel Ct ■8 GL55 . . . . . . 189 A2
Noel Lee Way GL11 . . . . . 87 F5
Norbury Ave GL4 . . . . . . 119 B4
Norchard Gdns GL15 . . . 155 F1
Nordown Cl GL11 . . . . 87 F4
Nordown Rd ■2 GL11 . . . 87 F4
Norfolk Ave
Bristol, Montpelier BS6 . . 18 E2
Bristol, St Pauls BS2 . . . 195 B4
Cheltenham GL51 . . . . . . 132 F2
Norfolk Gr BS31 . . . . .4 C4
Norfolk Hts BS2 . . . . 195 B4
Norfolk Mews GL51 . . . . 132 F2
Norfolk Pl BS3 . . . . 8 C3
Norfolk St GL1 . . . . 196 A2
Norland Rd BS8 . . . . 7 F8
Norley La GL9 . . . . 34 D2
Norley Rd BS7 . . . . 18 F7
Normal Terr GL50 . . . . . 193 B4
Norman Ball Way GL1 . . 127 B1
Normanby Rd ■20 BS5 . . 19 B1
Normandy Way NP16 . . . 72 D1
Norman Cl GL20 . . . . 181 F7
Normandy Way BS37 . . . . 43 A8
Norman Gr BS15 . . . . 20 D2
Norman Hill GL11 . . . . . . 87 F4
Norman Rd
Bristol, Baptist Mills BS2 . 19 A2
Bristol, Warmley BS30 . . 11 B8
Saltford BS31 . . . . 5 E3
Norman's Cotts BS36 . . . 30 D7
Normanton Rd ■16 BS8 . . 18 A2
Norman Way GL7 . . . . . . 163 F4
Norrisville Rd ■8 BS6 . . . 18 E1
Norrland Pl HR9 . . . . 163 C8
Norse Way NP16 . . . . 61 B7
Nortenham Cl GL52 . . . . 137 D4
North Ave
Ashchurch GL20 . . . . . . 182 D4
Drybrook GL17 . . . . 164 B4
Northavon Bsns Ctr BS37 . 43 C3
Northbank GL51 . . . . 129 B7
Northbook Rd GL4 . . . . . 127 C1
North Cerney CE Prim Sch
GL7 . . . . 158 D3
North Circular Rd GL56 . 187 C4
Northcote Ho ■2 BS8 . . . 194 A1
Northcote Rd
Bristol, Clifton BS8 . . . . . 17 F1
Bristol, Crew's Hole BS5 . . .9 E7
Bristol, Mangotsfield BS16 . 20 F6
Northcote St ■18 BS5 . . . 19 B1
Northcot La GL50 . . . . . . 186 D6
North Cotswolds Hospl
GL56 . . . . 187 A2
Northcroft GL50 . . . . 130 B7
North Croft BS30 . . . . 11 D4
North Ct BS32 . . . . 40 D3
North Devon Rd BS16 . . . 20 A5
North East Rd BS35 . . . . 64 C2
North East Terr GL20 . . . 192 D4
Northen Cl GL7 . . . . 144 F7
Northend Ave BS15 . . . . 20 D2
Northend Gdns BS15 . . . 20 D2
North End Gdns SN16 . . 58 C1
Northend Rd BS15 . . . . . . 20 E1
Northern Way GL17 . . . . 164 D5
North Farm Cotts GL8 . . 141 A6

Northfield BS37 . . . . 32 D8
Northfield Ave BS15 . . . . 10 D5
Northfield Cl GL8 . . . . . . 140 C4
Northfield Ho ■10 BS3. . . . . 8 C4
Northfield La SN14 . . . . . . 24 F1
Northfield Pas GL50 . . . . 193 C4
Northfield Rd
Bristol BS5 . . . . 10 B7
Gloucester GL4 . . . . 118 F5
Tetbury GL8 . . . . 140 C4
Northfields GL5 . . . . 99 D8
Northfield Sq GL4 . . . . . . 118 F5
Northfields Rd GL6. . . . . . 91 A5
Northfield Terr GL50 . . . 193 C4
Northgate St GL1 . . . . . . 196 B3
North Gr BS20 . . . . 16 C4
North Green St ■12 BS8 . . . 7 F6
North Hall Mews GL52. . . 133 F2
North Hill Rd GL7 . . . . . . 190 E2
North Home Rd GL7 . . . . 190 E2
Northington La GL14 . . . 157 B3
Northlands Way GL8 . . . . 140 C5
Northleach CE Prim Sch
GL54 . . . . 168 A1
Northleach Wlk BS11. . . . 16 F5
Northleaze GL8 . . . . 140 C4
North Leaze BS41 . . . . .7 B2
Northleaze CE Prim Sch
BS41 . . . . 7 B2
Northmead La BS37 . . . . 42 F6
North Meadow (Nature
Reserve)★ SN6 . . . . 143 E5
North Meadow Rd SN6 . . 143 E5
Northmoor La GL7 . . . . . 151 A1
North Nibley CE Prim Sch
GL11 . . . . 79 D5
Northolt Wy GL2 . . . . 110 B7
Northover Ct BS35 . . . . . . 38 E6
Northover Rd BS9 . . . . . . 28 A1
North Par BS37 . . . . 43 E2
North Pk BS15 . . . . 20 E1
North Pl GL50 . . . . 193 C4
North Pole La HR9 . . . . . 170 C5
North Rd
■7 Bristol BS3 . . . . 8 A4
Bristol, Montpelier BS6 . . 18 E2
Bristol, Stoke Gifford BS34 . 29 F4
Coleford GL16 . . . . 155 B6
Engine Common BS37 . . . 43 B5
Gloucester GL1 . . . . 126 F4
Huntley GL19 . . . . 165 D6
Leigh Woods BS8 . . . . 7 D7
Thornbury BS35 . . . . 64 C2
Winterbourne BS36 . . . . 30 F7
Yate BS37 . . . . 43 B3
North Rd E GL51 . . . . 129 C7
North Rd W GL51 . . . . . . 129 B7
Northridge Bsns Ctr BS37 43 C2
North Road Com Prim Sch
BS37 . . . . 43 B4
North Somerset Junc BS5 . .9 B6
North St
Bristol, Downend BS16 . . . 20 E5
Bristol, Oldland Common
BS30 . . . . 11 C4
Bristol, St Pauls BS1 . . . 195 B4
Bristol, Southville BS3 . . . .8 A3
Cheltenham GL50 . . . . . 193 B4
Wickwar GL12 . . . . 54 A6
Winchcombe GL54 . . . . . 174 A4
North Stoke La BS30 . . . . .6 B8
Northumberland Rd BS6 . 18 E4
Northumbria Dr BS9 . . . . 18 B4
North Upton La GL4 . . . . 119 E8
North View
Bristol BS6 . . . . 18 A4
Bristol, Mangotsfield BS16 . 20 E5
Bristol, Upper Soundwell
BS16 . . . . 20 D4
Highworth SN6 . . . . 145 C3
North View Bglws GL7 . . 151 F3
North Wall SN6 . . . . 143 F4
North Way
Bristol BS34 . . . . 29 B4
Cirencester GL7 . . . . 190 C4
Northway Inf Sch GL20 . 182 C4
Northway Rd GL20 . . . . . 182 B4
Northway Trad Est GL20 182 C4
Northwick Bsns Ctr
GL56 . . . . 186 C8
Northwick Rd
Bristol BS7 . . . . 18 F8
Northwick BS35 . . . . 48 E1
Northwick Terr GL56 . . . 186 C6
North Wlk BS37 . . . . 43 E1
Northwood Cl GL14 . . . . 191 D5
Northwood Dr GL2 . . . . . 110 B8
Northwoods Wlk BS10 . . 28 D3
Norton CE Prim Sch GL2 173 B2
Norton Cl
Bristol BS15 . . . . 10 F7
Whitchurch HR9 . . . . 162 D4
Winchcombe GL54 . . . . . 174 A8
Norton Ct GL6 . . . . 90 F5
Norton Farm Rd BS10 . . . 27 D3
Norton Ho
■7 Bristol BS1 . . . . 195 B1
Bristol, Patchway BS34 . . 39 F1
Cheltenham GL51 . . . . . . 133 C1
Norton La BS14 . . . . 3 C2
Norton Rd BS4 . . . . 9 A3
Norton Ridge GL6 . . . . . . 91 A5
Norton View GL55 . . . . . 189 A6
Nortonwood GL6 . . . . 90 F5
Norval Rd WR11 . . . . 188 A8

Nee–Oak 225

Norwich Dr
Bristol BS4 . . . . 9 E6
Cheltenham GL50 . . . . . 130 A6
Norwood Rd GL50 . . . . . 193 B1
Nostle Rd GL14 . . . . 168 A1
Notch Rd GL7, GL53 . . . . 107 C8
Notgrove Cl
Cheltenham GL51 . . . . . . 129 E8
Gloucester GL4 . . . . 118 C2
Notgrove Long Barrow★
GL54 . . . . 167 E8
Notley Pl GL3 . . . . 120 A7
Nottingham Rd
Bishop's Cleeve GL52 . . 137 F5
Bristol BS7 . . . . 18 E3
Nottingham St BS3 . . . . . . 8 F3
Nouncells Cross GL5 . . . . 99 D7
Nourse Cl GL53 . . . . 130 B4
Nourse Pl GL17 . . . . 164 D5
Nova Distribution Ctr
BS11 . . . . 26 B1
Nova Scotia Pl BS1 . . . . 194 A1
Nova Way BS11 . . . . 26 B1
Novers Cres BS4 . . . . 2 C8
Novers Hill BS4 . . . . 2 C8
Novers Hill Trad Est BS3 . 8 C1
Novers La BS4 . . . . 2 D7
Novers Park Dr BS4 . . . . . 2 C8
Novers Park Rd BS4 . . . . . 2 D8
Novers Rd BS4 . . . . 2 C8
Noverton Ave GL52 . . . . 134 D4
Noverton La GL52 . . . . . 134 D4
Nugent Hill BS6 . . . . 18 D1
Nunnery La GL11 . . . . 80 B7
Nunney Cl BS31 . . . . 5 A2
Nunny Cl GL51 . . . . 132 C1
Nupdown Rd BS35 . . . . . 75 E5
Nup End GL19 . . . . 172 D4
Nupend Gdns GL17 . . . . 164 F5
Nupend La GL17 . . . . 164 F5
Nup End La GL19 . . . . . . 172 D4
Nurseries The
Bishop's Cleeve GL52 . . 137 E2
Tytherington GL12 . . . . . 52 B5
Nursery Cl
Cirencester GL7 . . . . 190 E2
Mickleton GL55 . . . . 189 B7
Moreton-in-M GL56 . . . . 187 A4
Stroud GL5 . . . . 99 D6
Nursery Cott GL7 . . . . . . 190 D3
Nursery Dr GL5 . . . . 148 A5
Nursery Gdns BS10 . . . . . 28 A3
Nursery La GL54 . . . . . . 184 B3
Nursery Rd GL7 . . . . 190 E2
Nursery The
Bristol BS3 . . . . 8 B3
King's Stanley GL10 . . . . 98 A4
Nursery View GL7 . . . . . 150 E2
Nutbridge Cotts GL52 . . 138 C3
Nut Croft GL4 . . . . 119 B7
Nutfield Gr BS34 . . . . 29 B2
Nutfield Ho BS34 . . . . 29 B1
Nutgrove Ave BS3 . . . . . . .8 E3
Nuthatch Dr
Bishop's Cleeve GL52 . . 138 A5
Bristol BS16 . . . . 19 F6
Nuthatch Gdns BS16 . . . . 20 A6
Nuthill GL4 . . . . 120 B2
Nutley Ave GL4 . . . . 119 D4
Nutmeg GL4 . . . . 119 D4
Nut Orchard La GL20 . . . 181 F8
Nympsfield BS15 . . . . 20 E2
Nympsfield Long Barrow★
GL11 . . . . 89 C7
Nympsfield Rd
Gloucester GL4 . . . . 118 D3
Nailsworth GL6 . . . . 90 E5

O

Oak Ave
Cheltenham GL52 . . . . . 131 A7
Knockdown GL8 . . . . 57 F7
Oakbank GL4 . . . . 118 F4
Oakbrook Dr GL51 . . . . . 129 C7
Oak Cl
Bristol BS34 . . . . 29 D7
Chepstow/Cas-Gwent NP16 . 60 E5
Yate BS37 . . . . 43 D3
Oak Cres/Cilgant Defiw★
NP25 . . . . 154 A7
Oakcroft Cl GL4 . . . . 119 D3
Oak Ct
Bristol BS14 . . . . 3 A5
Cheltenham GL52 . . . . . 134 A1
Oakdale Ave BS16 . . . . . 20 D8
Oakdale Cl BS16 . . . . 20 E8
Oakdale Ct BS16 . . . . 20 D7
Oakdale Rd
Bristol, Downend BS16 . . 20 E8
Bristol, Hengrove BS14 . . 3 A8
Oakdean GL14 . . . . 191 C5
Oakdene
■11 Cheltenham, Lansdown
GL51 . . . . 130 B8
■2 Cheltenham, Whaddon
GL52 . . . . 134 A1
Oakdene Ave BS5 . . . . . . 19 D3
Oak Dr
Brockworth GL3 . . . . 120 D6
Dursley GL11 . . . . 88 A3

Oak Dr *continued*
Highworth SN6 . . . . 145 C3
Northway GL20 . . . . 182 B4
Stroud GL5 . . . . 99 B6
Oakenhill Rd BS4 . . . . 9 E2
Oakenhill Wlk BS4 . . . . 9 E2
Oakes La GL9 . . . . 35 B5
Oakeys Cl 20 GL54 . . . . 176 F4
Oakfield Ave NP16 . . . . 72 D1
Oakfield Bsns Pk BS15 . . . 10 D7
Oakfield Gr BS8 . . . . 194 B4
Oakfield Pl BS8 . . . . 194 B4
Oakfield Rd
Bishop's Cleeve GL52 . . . . 138 A4
Bristol, Kingswood BS15 . . . 10 D7
Bristol, Victoria Park BS8 . 194 B4
Keynsham BS31 . . . . 4 F2
Oakfields GL16 . . . . 155 A6
Oakfield St GL50 . . . . 130 B7
Oak Field The GL14 . . . . . 191 E5
Oakfield Way GL13 . . . . 93 D1
Oakford La SN14 . . . . 15 B2
Oak Gdns GL20 . . . . 182 C7
Oak Gr BS20 . . . . 16 C5
Oakhanger La GL2 . . . . 110 B7
Oakhill Ave BS30 . . . . 11 C2
Oak Hill CE Prim Sch (Inf)
WR11 . . . . 183 F7
Oak Hill CE Prim Sch (Jun)
GL20 . . . . 183 E4
Oakhill La BS10 . . . . 27 C4
Oakhill Pitch GL15 . . . . . . 146 F3
Oakhill Rd GL17 . . . . 164 D5
Oak Ho
Bristol BS13 . . . . 2 D4
Brockworth GL3 . . . . 120 D6
Oakhunger La GL13 . . . . . . 85 C4
Oakhurst Cl GL3 . . . . 128 A5
Oakhurst Rd BS9 . . . . 17 F5
Oakhurst Rise GL52 . . . . . 131 A8
Oak Inn GL1 . . . . 119 A7
Oak La
Bredon GL20 . . . . 182 C7
Bristol BS5 . . . . 19 F2
Whitecroft GL15 . . . . 155 F1
Oakland Ave GL52 . . . . 133 F3
Oakland Bsns Pk BS37 . . . 43 A3
Oakland Dr HR8 . . . . 178 E8
Oakland Rd
Bristol, Crew's Hole BS5 . . . . 9 E8
6 Bristol, Redland BS6 . . . 18 B1
Harrow Hill GL17 . . . . 164 B3
Oaklands
Cirencester GL7 . . . . 190 C2
Sling GL16 . . . . 155 B2
Oaklands Cl BS16 . . . . 21 B5
Oaklands Dr
Almondsbury BS32 . . . . . . 40 A4
Bristol, Frenchay BS16 . . . 20 A7
Bristol, Oldland Common
BS30 . . . . 11 C2
Oaklands Pk GL15 . . . . . . 155 E1
Oaklands Rd BS16 . . . . 21 A5
Oakland St GL53 . . . . 131 A7
Oaklea Rd GL15 . . . . 156 B2
Oakleaze
Coalpit Heath BS36 . . . . . . 31 D7
Gloucester GL2 . . . . 127 D3
Minety SN16 . . . . 142 D1
Oak Leaze BS34 . . . . 28 F6
Oakleaze Rd BS35 . . . . 64 C1
Oakleigh Ave BS5 . . . . 19 D1
Oakleigh Gdns BS30 . . . . . 11 C2
Oakley Flats GL7 . . . . 144 E7
Oakley Rd
Bristol BS7 . . . . 18 F7
Cheltenham GL52 . . . . 134 B1
Cirencester GL7 . . . . 190 C2
Oakley Way 1 GL15 . . . . . 147 D8
Oak Lodge 2 BS37 . . . . 32 D8
Oak Manor 3 GL52 . . . . . . 134 A1
Oak Manor Dr GL52 . . . . . 134 A1
Oak Mdw GL15 . . . . 92 B6
Oakmeade Pk BS4 . . . . 9 B2
Oak Rd
Bristol BS7 . . . . 18 E5
Colerne SN14 . . . . 15 F5
Down Ampney GL7 . . . . . 143 F7
Marston Meysey SN6 . . . . 144 A6
Oakridge GL2 . . . . 125 E5
Oakridge Cl
Bristol BS15 . . . . 11 A7
Gloucester GL4 . . . . 119 E5
Oakridge Parochial Sch
GL6 . . . . 148 E6
Oaksey CE Prim Sch
SN16 . . . . 141 F4
Oaksey Rd SN16 . . . . 142 B2
Oaks La GL18 . . . . 170 D2
Oak St GL7 . . . . 153 E2
Oaks The
Berry Hill GL16 . . . . 155 A8
Bristol BS7 . . . . 18 E4
Cheltenham GL51 . . . . 129 D6
Cinderford GL14 . . . . 191 C5
Gloucester GL4 . . . . 119 E7
Kemble GL7 . . . . 141 F8
Oak The BS9 . . . . 17 D3
Oak Tree Ave BS16 . . . . . . 22 B4
Oak Tree Cl
Bristol BS15 . . . . 10 C3
Hardwicke GL2 . . . . 109 E7

Oaktree Cres BS32 . . . . . . 40 C2
Oaktree Ct BS11 . . . . 16 E7
Oaktree Gdn GL4 . . . . 119 C3
Oaktree Gdns BS13 . . . . 1 E5
Oak Tree View GL4 . . . . . . 119 C3
Oak Tree Wlk BS31 . . . . 4 D3
Oak Tree Wy 33 GL18 . . . . 171 A4
Oak Vw GL2 . . . . 110 A5
Oak Way
Huntley GL19 . . . . 165 D6
Littledean GL14 . . . . 156 E8
South Cerney GL7 . . . . . . 142 F7
Stonehouse GL10 . . . . 97 F7
Oakwood Ave BS9 . . . . 18 C6
Oakwood Cl
Bream GL15 . . . . 155 D1
Cinderford GL14 . . . . 191 D5
Oakwood Dr GL3 . . . . 119 F6
Oakwood Gdns BS36 . . . . . 31 E7
Oakwood Pk BS16 . . . . 20 A3
Oakwood Rd
Bream GL15 . . . . 155 D1
Bristol BS9 . . . . 18 B6
Sling GL16 . . . . 155 B3
Oasis Acad Bank Leaze
BS11 . . . . 27 B2
Oasis Academy Brightstowe
BS11 . . . . 16 E7
Oasis Academy Connaught
BS4 . . . . 2 E8
Oasis Academy John
Williams BS14 . . . . 3 B7
Oasis Academy Long Cross
BS11 . . . . 16 F8
Oasis Academy New Oak
BS14 . . . . 3 A7
Oatfield GL2 . . . . 117 E2
Oatfield Rd GL2 . . . . 100 A6
Oatground GL12 . . . . 68 C7
Oathill La GL7 . . . . 141 A8
Oatlands Ave BS14 . . . . 3 A6
Oatley Ho BS9 . . . . 18 A5
Oatleys Cres 11 HR8 . . . . 178 E8
Oatleys Rd HR8 . . . . 178 E8
Oatleys Terr 10 HR8 . . . . 178 E8
Oatley Trad Est 6 BS15 . . 20 D1
Oberon Ave BS5 . . . . 19 E2
O'Brien Rd GL51 . . . . 133 A4
Ocker Hill GL6 . . . . 102 E2
Octagon The NP16 . . . . 60 F5
Octavia Pl GL15 . . . . 92 B4
October La BS37 . . . . 27 F2
Odda's Chapel ★ GL19 . . . 173 C8
Oddfellows Row 3 GL54 . 176 F4
Oddfellows Terr 18 GL54 . 174 A7
Oddfellows' Terr 14
GL56 . . . . 187 A3
Oddington Rd GL54 . . . . . 176 F4
Odessa Rd GL20 . . . . 173 F8
Offas Cl NP16 . . . . 61 A7
Offa's Mead Acad NP16 . . 61 A8
Office Rd GL14 . . . . 191 C3
Ogbourne Cl GL2 . . . . 127 E3
Ohio Ave GL7 . . . . 152 E2
Okebourne Cl BS10 . . . . . . 28 B4
Okebourne Rd BS10 . . . . . . 28 B4
Okus Rd GL53 . . . . 131 A5
Oldacre Dr GL52 . . . . 138 A4
Old Acre Rd BS14 . . . . 3 A3
Old All Saints Sch 12
GL50 . . . . 193 C4
Old Ashley Hill BS6 . . . . . 18 F2
Old Aust Rd BS32 . . . . 40 C6
Old Barns The WR8 . . . . . 180 A10
Old Barrow Hill BS11 . . . . 16 D7
Old Bath Rd GL53 . . . . . . 130 E5
Old Bell Chambers 3
NP16 . . . . 60 E8
Old Bread St BS2 . . . . 195 C2
Old Brewery La 16 GL8 . . 140 B4
Oldbridge Rd BS14 . . . . 3 C3
Old Bristol Rd GL6 . . . . . . 91 B3
Old Bulwark Rd NP16 . . . . 60 E7
Old Burford Rd OX7 . . . . . 177 E1
Oldbury Chase BS30 . . . . . 11 A2
Oldbury Court Dr BS16 . . 20 B6
Oldbury Court Rd BS16 . . 20 A5
Oldbury Ho GL20 . . . . 192 D5
Oldbury La
Thornbury BS35 . . . . 64 B4
Wick BS30 . . . . 12 E5
Oldbury-on-Severn Prim Sch
BS35 . . . . 63 B5
Oldbury Orch GL3 . . . . . . 128 D4
Oldbury Power Station
Visitor Ctr ★ BS35 . . . . . . 75 B1
Oldbury Rd
Cheltenham GL51 . . . . 132 E3
Tewkesbury GL20 . . . . 192 C5
Old Cheltenham Rd GL2 . . 127 D4
Old Coach Cl NP16 . . . . . . 61 C2
Old Coach Rd NP16 . . . . . . 61 C3
Old Coach The WR12 . . . . 185 C8
Old Coalyard Farm Est
GL54 . . . . 168 A2
Old Common GL6 . . . . 148 A4
Old Common The GL6 . . . . 148 B6
Old Comm The GL6 . . . . . . 148 C6
Old Co-op The GL15 . . . . . 156 A2
Old Court Dr GL19 . . . . . . 171 D1
Oldcroft Rd GL15 . . . . 156 B1
Old Dam Rd GL15 . . . . 92 D7
Old Dean Rd GL17 . . . . . . 164 D6
Old Dixton Rd NP25 . . . . . 154 A8
Old Down Hill BS32 . . . . . . 50 B2

Old Down Rd GL9 . . . . 35 C8
Olde La GL54 . . . . 184 B3
Old Elmore La GL2 . . . . . . 117 F2
Old Estate Yd The GL7 . . . 143 E8
Old Farm Cl SN16 . . . . . . 141 E1
Old Farm Dr 3 GL51 . . . . 129 D6
Old Farm La BS5 . . . . 10 B6
Oldfield GL20 . . . . 192 D4
Oldfield Cres GL51 . . . . . 129 F8
Oldfield Girls Sch BA1 . . . . 6 F1
Oldfield Pl BS8 . . . . 7 F5
Oldfield Rd
Bristol, Hotwells BS8 . . . . 194 A1
Watermead GL3 . . . . 120 C4
Oldfields La BS35 . . . . 41 D7
Old Forge Cl OX7 . . . . 177 E1
Old Forge Cotts
Didbrook GL54 . . . . 184 D2
Stoke Orchard GL52 . . . . 136 E5
Old Forge The GL15 . . . . . 147 D3
Old Furnace Ct GL15 . . . . 147 F5
Old George The GL6 . . . . . 91 C4
Old Gloucester Rd
Alveston BS35 . . . . 51 B5
Bourton-on-t-W GL54 . . . . 168 E7
Bristol, Hambrook BS16 . . 30 B2
Bristol, Stoke Gifford BS16 . 30 B4
North Corner BS36 . . . . . . 41 D3
Staverton GL51 . . . . 173 F1
Thornbury BS35 . . . . 65 B2
Uckington GL51 . . . . 132 B5
Old Grammar School Mews
The 9 GL55 . . . . 189 A2
Oldhill GL5 . . . . 98 D8
Old Hill
Avening GL8 . . . . 148 B1
Longhope GL17 . . . . 165 A5
Oldhill La GL11 . . . . 87 C4
Old Horsley Rd GL6 . . . . . . 91 B3
Old Hospital La GL2 . . . . . 192 D5
Old Hospital Lawn GL5 . . . 98 F7
Old Hundred La GL3 . . . . . 34 D2
Old King Street Ct BS1 . . . 195 B3
Old La BS16 . . . . 21 C6
Oldland Common Sta ★
BS30 . . . . 11 C3
Oldlands Ave BS36 . . . . . . 31 C6
Old La (Simmonds La) HR9,
GL18 . . . . 170 C4
Old Lodge Ct GL50 . . . . . . 133 E3
Old London Rd GL12 . . . . . 80 C1
Old Malt Ho BS2 . . . . 195 C4
Old Manor Cl GL12 . . . . . . 67 A5
Old Manor Gdns GL55 . . . 189 B6
Old Manor La GL20 . . . . . 192 E6
Old Mansion The GL52 . . . 134 C4
Old Market GL6 . . . . 91 B4
Old Market Rdbt BS2 . . . . 195 C3
Old Market St BS2 . . . . . . 195 C3
Old Market Way 12 GL56 . 187 A3
Oldmead Wlk BS13 . . . . 1 E7
Old Millbrook Terr 4
GL50 . . . . 133 B2
Old Mill Cl BS37 . . . . 32 B4
Old Mill Mus The ★ GL54 . 176 C1
Old Mill The WR12 . . . . . . 185 B8
Oldminster Rd GL13 . . . . . 93 D1
Old Moat Ctyd GL2 . . . . . . 172 F1
Old Monmouth Rd GL17 . . 165 A5
Old Neighbourhood GL6 . . 148 C6
Old Oak Cl NP16 . . . . 60 F5
Old Orchard Ct GL7 . . . . . 152 D7
Old Orchard The GL55 . . . 189 D3
Old Painswick Cl GL4 . . . . 119 B6
Old Painswick Rd GL4 . . . . 119 B6
Old Park Hill BS2 . . . . 194 C3
Old Park Rd BS11 . . . . 16 D7
Old Pk BS2 . . . . 194 C3
Old Police Sta The BS4 . . . . 9 A3
Old Pooles Yd BS4 . . . . 9 E2
Old Post Office Alley 15
GL20 . . . . 192 C4
Old Priory Rd BS20 . . . . . . 16 B4
Old Quarry Gdns BS16 . . . 20 F4
Old Quarry Ind Units The
GL8 . . . . 140 C3
Old Quarry Rd BS11 . . . . . 16 E7
Old Quarry Rise BS11 . . . . 16 E7
Old Rd
Coleford GL16 . . . . 155 B5
Maisemore GL2 . . . . 126 A4
Southam GL52 . . . . 134 C8
Old Rd The/Yr Hen Heol 22
NP25 . . . . 154 A7
Old Rectory Cl GL5 . . . . . . 99 A5
Old Rectory Gdns GL56 . . 176 B8
Old Rectory Rd GL12 . . . . . 67 F4
Old Rectory The
Longborough GL56 . . . . . . 176 D8
Staunton GL16 . . . . 154 E7
Old Reddings Cl GL51 . . . . 129 C7
Old Reddings Rd GL51 . . . 129 C7
Old Ross Rd HR9 . . . . 162 E4
Old Row GL4 . . . . 196 C1
Old School Cl
Bristol BS30 . . . . 11 D7
Nailsworth GL6 . . . . 91 B4
Old School Ct SN14 . . . . . . 15 A8
Old School Ct The 18
GL8 . . . . 140 B4
Old School Ho
Bristol BS4 . . . . 9 B2
3 Cheltenham GL50 . . . . 193 A4

Old School Mews The 4
GL53 . . . . 131 B6
Old Silk Mill The GL6 . . . 148 B5
Old Sneed Ave BS9 . . . . . . 17 D4
Old Sneed Cotts BS9 . . . . . 17 E4
Old Sneed Pk BS9 . . . . 17 D4
Old Sneed Rd BS9 . . . . 17 D4
Old Sodbury CE Prim Sch
BS37 . . . . 34 B8
Old Station Dr GL53 . . . . . 130 D5
Old Station Rd GL18 . . . . . 171 A5
Old Station Way GL16 . . . 155 A5
Old Tannery The BS2 . . . . 195 C3
Old Town
26 Moreton-in-M GL56 . . 187 A3
Wotton-u-E GL12 . . . . 68 B7
Old Town Mews GL15 . . . . 147 F5
Old Tram Rd GL1 . . . . 196 A2
Old Vicarage Ct
6 Coleford GL16 . . . . 155 A5
Whitchurch BS14 . . . . 3 C4
Old Vicarage Gn BS31 . . . . 4 E6
Old Vicarage La GL7 . . . . . 141 F7
Old Vicarage Pl BS8 . . . . . 18 A1
Old Vicarage The
Bristol, Highridge BS13 . . . . 1 F6
Bristol, Montpelier BS6 . . . 18 E1
Old Wesleyan Chapel The
BS30 . . . . 11 B5
Old Wharf Ind Est HR8 . . . 178 E2
Old Wharf La HR9 . . . . . . 162 E4
Old White Hart GL13 . . . . . 85 E3
Old Winding Wheel The
GL15 . . . . 147 C8
Oldwood La BS37 . . . . 43 B8
Olio La GL3 . . . . 193 C2
Olive Gdns BS35 . . . . 50 F4
Olive Gr GL11 . . . . 88 A2
Oliver Cl GL4 . . . . 118 D2
Ollney Rd GL6 . . . . 91 F6
Olveston CE Prim Sch
BS35 . . . . 50 A3
Olveston Rd BS7 . . . . 18 E5
Olympic Pk Bsns Ctr
GL2 . . . . 118 A2
Olympus Cl BS34 . . . . 29 D6
Olympus Pk GL2 . . . . 118 A2
Olympus Rd BS34 . . . . 28 D7
Onslow Rd GL18 . . . . 171 A4
Oram Ct BS30 . . . . 10 F4
Orange Cl SN6 . . . . 145 D3
Orangery The GL4 . . . . . . 119 E7
Orange St BS2 . . . . 195 C4
Orchard Ave
3 Bristol BS1 . . . . 194 C2
Broadway WR12 . . . . 185 C8
Cheltenham BS35 . . . . 132 F2
Chepstow/Cas-Gwent NP16 60 E5
Thornbury BS35 . . . . 64 D1
Orchard Bank
2 Blockley GL56 . . . . 186 C5
Great Rissington GL54 . . . 169 C4
Orchard Bvd BS30 . . . . 11 B4
Orchard Cl
Almondsbury BS32 . . . . . . 40 B5
Aylburton GL15 . . . . 147 E4
Bredon GL20 . . . . 182 D7
Bretforton WR11 . . . . 188 A6
Bristol, Kingswood BS15 . . 10 E8
Bristol, Westbury on Trym
BS9 . . . . 17 F5
Charfield GL12 . . . . 67 A5
Clearwell GL16 . . . . 154 F3
Dursley GL11 . . . . 87 F5
English Bicknor GL16 . . . . 163 A2
Gloucester GL2 . . . . 126 E5
Hardwicke GL2 . . . . 109 D7
Kemble GL7 . . . . 141 F8
Keynsham BS31 . . . . 4 D6
King's Stanley GL10 . . . . . 98 B3
Lea HR9 . . . . 164 C8
Lechlade on T GL7 . . . . . . 153 D2
Leonard Stanley GL10 . . . . 97 F4
Mickleton GL55 . . . . 189 B7
Mitcheldean GL17 . . . . . . 164 D5
Winterbourne BS36 . . . . . . 30 E5
Woodcroft NP16 . . . . 73 A4
Yate BS37 . . . . 43 F2
Orchard Cotts
10 Bristol BS16 . . . . 20 D5
Chipping Campden GL55 . 189 C2
Orchard Cres BS11 . . . . . . 16 D7
Orchard Ct
Bristol BS9 . . . . 17 C3
Bristol, Filton BS34 . . . . . . 29 A4
19 Bristol, Pile Marsh BS5 . 9 D7
3 Monmouth/Trefynwy
NP25 . . . . 154 A7
Orchard Dr
Aust BS35 . . . . 49 A7
Bristol BS13 . . . . 2 A6
Churchdown GL3 . . . . 128 D4
Twyning GL20 . . . . 182 A7
Orchard End
Apperley GL19 . . . . 173 C7
Monmouth/Trefynwy
NP25 . . . . 154 A7
Orchard Farm Cl NP16 . . . 61 B7
Orchard Field GL8 . . . . . . 140 B4
Orchard Gate
Blakeney GL15 . . . . 156 D2
Bristol BS32 . . . . 40 C2

Orchard Gdns BS15 . . . . . 10 F8
Orchard Grange BS35 . . . . 64 B2
Orchard Gr The GL51 . . . . 129 D1
Orchard Ho
2 Bristol BS5 . . . . 9 E4
Cirencester GL7 . . . . 190 D5
Orchard Ind Est GL54 . . . 184 A3
Orchard La
Brimscombe GL5 . . . . 99 F1
6 Bristol BS1 . . . . 194 C2
Ledbury HR8 . . . . 178 E8
Orchard Lea
6 Alveston BS35 . . . . 51 A5
Pill BS20 . . . . 16 D4
Orchard Leaze GL11 . . . . . 87 D4
Orchard Mead
Nailsworth GL6 . . . . 91 B4
Painswick GL6 . . . . 103 F7
Orchard Pk
Cheltenham GL51 . . . . 132 F5
Gloucester GL3 . . . . 120 A6
Twigworth GL2 . . . . 173 A1
Orchard Pk The GL19 . . . . 173 C6
Orchard Pl
4 Ledbury HR8 . . . . 178 F7
Stonehouse GL10 . . . . 97 E7
Orchard Rd
Alderton GL20 . . . . 183 E4
Bishop's Cleeve, Brockhampton
GL52 . . . . 137 E1
Bishop's Cleeve GL52 . . . . 137 F3
Bristol, Ashley Down BS7 . 18 E4
Bristol, Crew's Hole BS5 . . . 9 F8
Bristol, Kingswood BS15 . . 10 E8
Coalpit Heath BS36 . . . . . . 31 D7
Coleford GL16 . . . . 155 A6
Gloucester GL2 . . . . 127 E4
Joy's Green GL17 . . . . 163 D3
Lydney GL15 . . . . 92 B2
Newent GL18 . . . . 171 A7
Pucklechurch BS16 . . . . . . 22 B5
Stroud GL5 . . . . 98 C6
Winchcombe GL54 . . . . . . 139 F6
Orchard Ridge GL20 . . . . . 180 F7
Orchard Rise
Chepstow/Cas-Gwent
NP16 . . . . 60 E5
Dursley GL11 . . . . 87 F3
Longborough GL56 . . . . . . 176 D8
Newnham GL14 . . . . 156 F6
Olveston BS35 . . . . 50 A3
Tibberton GL19 . . . . 171 E1
Orchard Sch Bristol BS7 . . 28 F5
Orchard Springs GL6 . . . . . 91 A4
Orchard Sq BS5 . . . . 9 D7
Orchard St
Bristol BS1 . . . . 194 C2
Wotton-u-E GL12 . . . . 68 B7
Orchards The
Bristol, Kingswood BS15 . . 10 F7
Bristol, Shirehampton BS11 16 E6
Charlton Kings GL52 . . . . 131 C6
Gloucester GL3 . . . . 120 A6
Longhope GL17 . . . . 164 F6
Lydney GL15 . . . . 92 A3
Orchard The
Bristol BS34 . . . . 29 F5
Clapton-on-t-H GL54 . . . . 168 F4
13 Bristol GL17 . . . . 152 E4
Frampton Cotterell BS36 . . 31 C8
North Cerney GL7 . . . . . . 158 D3
Oaksey GL7 . . . . 141 F4
Pill BS20 . . . . 16 C4
Tewkesbury GL20 . . . . 192 D5
Tytherington GL12 . . . . . . 52 B5
Uckington GL51 . . . . 132 D7
Uley GL11 . . . . 89 B1
Woolaston GL15 . . . . 147 C3
Orchard Vale BS15 . . . . . . 10 F7
Orchard View
Draycott GL56 . . . . 186 E6
Stroud GL5 . . . . 99 A4
Orchard Villas GL10 . . . . . 98 C3
Orchard Vw GL11 . . . . 87 F3
Orchard Way
17 Berry Hill GL16 . . . . . 155 A6
Cheltenham GL51 . . . . 132 F5
Churchdown GL3 . . . . 128 B7
Huntley GL19 . . . . 165 D6
Kingham OX7 . . . . 177 F2
Maisemore GL2 . . . . 126 A4
Orchard Wlk GL12 . . . . . . 67 F4
Orchid Dr BS31 . . . . 4 E3
Orchid Mdw NP16 . . . . 60 E5
Organ's Alley GL1 . . . . . . 196 B2
Oridge St GL19 . . . . 172 A6
Oriel Gr GL56 . . . . 187 A2
Oriel Rd GL50 . . . . 193 B3
Oriole Way GL4 . . . . 119 C6
Orion Dr BS34 . . . . 29 D6
Orland Way BS30 . . . . 11 A3
Orlebar Gdns BS11 . . . . . . 27 B2
Orlham La HR8 . . . . 178 C6
Ormand Cl GL7 . . . . 190 F5
Ormerod Rd
Bristol BS9 . . . . 17 E5
Sedbury NP16 . . . . 61 B7
Ormond Pl GL50 . . . . 193 B3
Ormonds Cl BS32 . . . . 40 E1
Ormond Terr GL50 . . . . . . 193 B3
Ormsley Cl BS34 . . . . 29 C8
Orpen Gdns BS7 . . . . 19 B5
Orpen Pk BS32 . . . . 40 B3
Orpet Cl GL7 . . . . 190 E3
Orpheus Ave BS34 . . . . 29 C6
Orrisdale Terr GL53 . . . . . 193 C2

Orwell Dr BS31 . . . . 5 A4
Orwell St BS3. . . . . .8 E3
Osborne Ave
  Bristol BS7. . . . . 18 F3
  Gloucester GL4 . . . . .118 C1
Osborne Cl BS34. . . . . 29 D4
Osborne Gdns GL20 . . . . 192 D4
Osborne Rd
  Bristol, Clifton BS8 . . . . . 18 A1
  Bristol, Southville BS3. . . . 8 C4
  Severn Beach BS35 . . . . . . 38 A7
Osborne Terr
  10 Bristol BS3. . . . . 8 B2
  Thrupp GL5. . . . . .99 E3
Osborne Villas BS2. . . . . 194 C4
Osbourne Wallis Ho BS8. 194 A1
Osbourne Ho 6 GL50 . . 130 B8
Osier Cl GL4. . . . . .119 A4
Osprey Cl GL4. . . . . 119 D5
Osprey Ct BS14 . . . . 2 D5
Osprey Dr GL10 . . . . 97 F8
Osprey Rd BS35. . . . . 64 D3
Osprey Rd
  15 Bristol BS5. . . . . 9 C7
  Cheltenham GL53. . . . . . .130 C5
Osric Rd GL1. . . . . 118 F6
Ossage GL54. . . . . 166 C6
Othello Cl GL51 . . . . 132 E2
Otterburn Ho GL2. . . . . . 118 C4
Otterford Cl BS14 . . . . .3 B5
Otter Rd GL4 . . . . .120 A5
Otters Field GL4 . . . . 174 A8
Ottery Cl BS11. . . . . 27 A1
Ottrells Mead BS32 . . . . . . 40 C3
Our Lady of Lourdes RC Prim
  Sch BS15. . . . . 10 E7
Our Lady of the Rosary Cath
  Prim Sch BS11. . . . . 17 A8
Our Lady of the Rosary Prim
  Sch BS11. . . . . 27 A1
Oval App GL2. . . . . 157 F3
Oval The
  Frampton on Severn GL2. .100 A3
  Gloucester GL50 . . . . . . .118 D6
Ovens Cl BS7. . . . . 190 F3
Over Bridge★ GL2 . . . . . . 126 B4
Overbrook Cl GL4. . . . . . .127 C1
Overbrook Dr GL52. . . . . 133 F3
Overbrook Rd GL2 . . . . . .109 E7
Overbury CE Fst Sch
  GL20. . . . . 182 F8
Overbury Rd GL1. . . . . . . 119 A8
Overbury St GL53 . . . . . . 131 A7
Over Cswy GL1. . . . . 126 C3
Over Dr BS34. . . . . 28 F7
Overhill GL20. . . . . 16 D4
Overhill Rd GL7. . . . . 190 B8
Over La BS35 . . . . 39 D2
Overley Rd GL7 . . . . 149 E7
Overndale Rd BS16. . . . . . 20 C6
Overndale Sch BS37 . . . . 34 A7
Overnhill Ct BS16 . . . . 20 D5
Overnhill Rd BS16. . . . . . . 20 D5
Overnhurst Ct 2 BS16 . . . 20 D5
Over Old Rd GL19, GL2 . .172 C3
Overstreet Gn GL15 . . . . . 92 C1
Overton Ct GL50 . . . . 193 A3
Overton Cl GL2. . . . . 157 E5
Overton La GL2. . . . . 157 E5
Overton Park Rd GL50. . 193 A3
Overton Rd
  Bristol BS6. . . . . 18 E2
  Cheltenham GL50. . . . . . .193 A3
Owen Gdns 1 GL16. . . . . 155 A6
Owen Gr BS9. . . . . 18 B5
Owen Henry Ho BS2. . . . 19 A1
Owen St 18 BS5. . . . . .9 B8
Owl Cl GL4. . . . . .119 D5
Owlpen Manor & Gardens★
  GL11. . . . . 89 E1
Owls End Rd GL52. . . . . . 138 A4
Owls Eye Cl 4 GL16. . . . 155 B6
Owls Head Rd BS15 . . . . . 10 E6
Oxbarton BS34. . . . . 29 F5
Oxbutts Cvn Pk GL52 . . 138 B4
Oxbutts Ind Est GL52 . . 138 B4
Oxebode The GL1 . . . . . . 196 B3
Oxenham Ct BS5. . . . . .9 D8
Oxen Leaze BS32. . . . . 40 E2
Oxford Cl 1 GL52. . . . . . 130 F8
Oxford Ho GL7. . . . . 190 D4
Oxford Pas GL50 . . . . 193 B4
Oxford Pl
  19 Bristol, Clifton BS8. . . . . .7 F4
  14 Bristol, Upper Easton
    BS5. . . . . 19 B1
Oxford Rd GL1 . . . . .196 C4
Oxford St
  Bristol BS2. . . . . 195 C2
  7 Bristol, Redfield BS5 . . . 9 C7
  Bristol, The Dings BS2. . . 194 A6
  Bristol, Tyndall's Park BS2 194 C4
  Bristol, Windmill Hill BS3. . .8 F4
  Cheltenham GL50. . . . . . .130 F8
  10 Chepstow/Cas-Gwent
    NP16. . . . . 60 E8
  Gloucester GL1. . . . . 196 C3
  Lydney GL15. . . . . 92 A2
  Moreton-in-M GL56 . . . . . 187 A3
Oxford Terr
  Gloucester GL1 . . . . 196 C3
  Stroud GL5. . . . . .99 C8
Oxford Way GL51 . . . . . . 130 A6
Oxford Wlk 2 GL52 . . . . 130 F8
Oxhouse Gdns BS10. . . . . 27 C3
Oxleaze BS13. . . . . 2 D4

Oxleaze Cl 4 GL8. . . . . . 140 B4
Oxleaze Farm Workshops
  GL7. . . . . 153 E8
Oxleaze La BS41. . . . . .1 E3
Oxleaze Rd
  Culkerton GL8. . . . . 140 F6
  7 Tetbury GL8. . . . . 140 B4
Oxleigh Wy BS34, BS16. . . 29 F3
Oxmead Cl GL52 . . . . 138 B4
Oxmoor GL4. . . . . 119 E3
Oxpens GL54. . . . . 167 D1
Oxstalls Dr GL2 . . . . 127 A5
Oxstalls La GL2 . . . . 127 B4
Oxstalls Way GL2 . . . . . . 127 B4
Ox Yd
  Rodmarton GL7 . . . . 141 B8
  Rodmarton GL7 . . . . 149 B1
Ozleworth BS15. . . . . 11 A8

P

Packer's Rd GL14 . . . . . . 191 D4
Packhorse La GL7. . . . . . . 160 A1
Pacquet Ho BS20 . . . . 16 D5
Paddock Cl
  Bristol BS32. . . . . 40 E2
  Bristol, Emerson's Green
    BS16. . . . . 21 C6
Paddock Gdn BS14. . . . . . . .2 F4
Paddock Gdns
  Alveston BS35 . . . . 51 A5
  Gloucester GL2 . . . . 127 D5
Paddock Rise GL10. . . . . . 97 F8
Paddocks La GL50 . . . . . . 133 D5
Paddocks The
  Baunton GL7. . . . . .150 D7
  Bristol BS16. . . . . 31 A1
  Highnam GL2 . . . . .125 D5
  Thornbury BS35. . . . . 64 D1
Paddock The
  Chepstow/Cas-Gwent
    NP16. . . . . 60 D6
  Cirencester GL7. . . . . 190 E4
  Coleford GL16 . . . . 155 B6
  Highworth SN6 . . . . 145 D3
  17 Ledbury HR8. . . . . 178 E8
  South Cerney GL7 . . . . . . 142 F7
Padin Cl 3 GL6. . . . . 148 C6
Padmore Ct 7 BS5. . . . . . . 9 D7
Padstow Rd BS4 . . . . .2 F8
Pady Ct GL7 . . . . 190 C3
Paganhill Est GL5. . . . . . . 98 F8
Paganhill La GL5. . . . . 98 F7
Page Ct BS16. . . . . 20 F4
Page Rd BS16. . . . . 20 D4
Page's La GL20 . . . . 181 F7
Pages Mead BS11. . . . . . . 16 C8
Paget Ho GL7. . . . . 190 D5
Pagets Rd GL52. . . . . 138 A2
Painswick Ave BS34. . . . . . 29 B8
Painswick Dr BS37 . . . . . . 43 E1
Painswick Hts GL6. . . . . . 104 A6
Painswick Lodge 2 GL4. 119 C4
Painswick Old Rd GL6. . . 103 C1
Painswick Rd
  Cheltenham GL50. . . . . . .193 A1
  Gloucester GL4 . . . . 119 C4
  Stroud GL5. . . . . .103 B2
  Watermead GL3. . . . . 120 D3
Painswick Rococo Garden★
  GL6. . . . . 111 C2
Painters Field GL7. . . . . . 152 D7
Pakistan Ho 1 GL51 . . . . 132 E2
Palestra Lo GL7 . . . . 190 C5
Palmdale Cl BS30. . . . . . . 11 A3
Palmer Ave
  Gloucester GL4 . . . . 119 F5
  Severn Beach BS35. . . . . . 38 C3
Palmers Cl BS30. . . . . 11 A6
Palmers Leaze BS34. . . . . 30 A6
Palmerston Rd BS6 . . . . . . 18 C4
Palmerston St 6 BS3 . . . . 8 C3
Palm Rd GL20. . . . . 192 E2
Palmyra Rd BS3 . . . . .8 B2
Pancake La GL19. . . . . 173 E5
Panoramic The BS1. . . . . 194 C3
Pantile The 8 BS5. . . . . . . 8 C3
Paper Mill Cotts OX18. . . 161 E7
Parabola Cl GL50 . . . . . . 193 A3
Parabola La GL50 . . . . . . 193 A3
Parabola Rd GL50. . . . . . 193 A3
Parade Ct BS5. . . . . 19 F2
Parade The
  Bristol, Bishopsworth BS13. . 2 A6
  Bristol BS34. . . . . 39 F1
  Bristol, Shirehampton BS11 16 E6
  Brockworth GL3. . . . . 120 C5
  Chipping Sodbury BS37. . . 44 A1
  Gloucester GL2 . . . . 127 E4
Paradise Row GL54 . . . . . 167 E2
Paragon Terr GL53. . . . . . 193 B2
Paragon The BS8 . . . . .7 F6
Parawell La GL15 . . . . 147 C8
Parbrook Ct BS14. . . . . . . .3 B5
Parfitt's Hill 8 BS5 . . . . . . 9 F6
Par Four La GL15 . . . . 92 C1
Parish The BS3. . . . . 194 B1
Park Ave
  Bristol BS32. . . . . 40 A2
  Bristol, Eastville BS5. . . . . 19 D1
  Bristol, Rose Green BS5 . . . 9 E8
  Bristol, Windmill Hill BS3. . 8 E3
  Frampton Cotterell BS36. . . 31 B6

Park Ave continued
  Gloucester GL2 . . . . 127 C5
  Highworth SN6 . . . . 145 D3
  Winterbourne BS36. . . . . . 30 E7
Park Brake GL2. . . . . 125 D4
Parkbury Cl GL51 . . . . . . 133 A2
Park Cl
  Bristol, Cadbury Heath
    BS30. . . . . 11 B5
  Bristol, Kingswood BS15 . . 10 E7
  Fairford GL7 . . . . 152 E4
  Keynsham BS31. . . . . 4 D5
  Northway GL20 . . . . 182 B5
  St Briavels GL15. . . . . . . 146 F7
  8 Tetbury GL8. . . . . 140 C4
Park Cres
  Bristol, Cadbury Heath
    BS30. . . . . 11 B5
  Bristol, Frenchay BS16 . . . 30 C1
  Bristol, Rose Green BS5 . . . 9 E8
Park Ct
  Lydney GL15. . . . . 92 A3
  Stroud GL5. . . . . .99 D6
Park Dr GL2 . . . . 117 F1
Park End 1 SN6. . . . . 142 F4
Parkend Rd
  Bream GL15. . . . . 155 D1
  Coleford GL16 . . . . 155 B5
  Yorkley GL15. . . . . 156 A2
Park End Rd GL16. . . . . . . 196 B1
Parkend Sta★ GL15 . . . . . 155 E3
Parkend Wlk
  Coleford GL16 . . . . 155 B5
  Sling GL16. . . . . 155 B3
Parker Pl 1 WR12. . . . . . 185 B8
Parkers Ave BS30. . . . . . . 12 C7
Parkers Barton BS5. . . . . . .9 B6
Parkers Cl BS10. . . . . 28 E4
Parkers La GL56 . . . . 187 A3
Parker St 5 BS3. . . . . 8 B3
Park Farm GL54. . . . . 168 F8
Park Farm Ct 18 BS30 . . . 10 F4
Park Farm Village Gn
  BS36. . . . . 31 B6
Parkfield Ave 3 BS5. . . . . 9 D7
Parkfield Cotts GL6. . . . . 112 A2
Parkfield Rank BS16 . . . . . 22 A7
Parkfield Rd BS16. . . . . . . 22 A6
Park Gate
  Cheltenham GL50. . . . . . .193 A1
  Redmarley D'Abitot GL19 . 179 E2
Park Glade NP16. . . . . . . 146 B4
Park Gr
  Bristol BS9. . . . . 18 C5
  Whitecroft GL15. . . . . 155 E1
Park Hill
  Bristol BS11. . . . . 16 F6
  Whitecroft BS15. . . . . 155 E1
Park Hill Comm GL15 . . . 147 A2
Park Hill La NP16, GL15 . . 146 E2
Park Hill Rd
  Tidenham Chase GL15. . . .146 F2
  Woolaston GL15 . . . . 147 A2
Park Ho GL50 . . . . 193 A1
Parkhouse La BS31 . . . . . . 4 C2
Parkhurst Ave 4 BS16 . . . 20 B4
Park Inf Sch The GL10. . . . 97 F8
Park Jun Sch GL10. . . . . . 97 E7
Park La
  Bristol BS2. . . . . 194 C3
  Brockhampton GL54 . . . . .174 A1
  Cheltenham GL52. . . . . . .134 B6
  Cirencester GL7. . . . . 190 C4
  Frampton Cotterell BS36. . . 31 B6
  Ilmington CV36 . . . . 189 E7
  North Nibley GL11 . . . . 79 E7
  Woodchester GL5 . . . . 90 F6
  Wotton-u-E GL12 . . . . 69 A8
Parkland Mews 26 GL54. . 176 E4
Parkland Rd
  Cheltenham GL53. . . . . . .130 F4
  Dursley GL11. . . . . 87 F4
Parklands
  Bristol, High Kingsdown
    BS8. . . . . 194 C4
  Bristol, Kingswood BS15 . . 10 E8
  Churchdown GL3. . . . . . . 128 A6
  Quedgeley GL2. . . . . 109 E8
  Quedgeley GL2. . . . . 117 F1
  Wotton-u-E GL12 . . . . 68 B8
Parklands Rd BS13 . . . . . . .7 E4
Parkland Sq GL7 . . . . 190 B2
Parklands Rd BS3. . . . . . . .7 E4
Parkland Way BS35 . . . . . . 64 C3
Park Leaze BS34. . . . . 39 E1
Park Mews GL50 . . . . 130 C6
Parkmill HR9 . . . . 162 C7
Park Par GL10 . . . . 97 E8
Park Pl
  5 Ashton Keynes SN6 . . . 142 F5
  Bristol, Tyndall's Park BS2 194 C3
  Bristol, Upper Eastville BS5 19 E3
  Bristol, Victoria Park BS8 . 194 A3
  Cheltenham GL50. . . . . . .193 A1
Park Prim Sch The
  Bristol BS15. . . . . 10 E8
  Bristol BS30. . . . . 10 F3
Park Rd
  Berry Hill GL16 . . . . 155 A7
  Blockley GL56 . . . . 186 C6
  Bristol, Brandon Hill BS3. .194 B1
  Bristol, Cadbury Heath BS30 11 A5
  Bristol, Kingswood BS15 . . 10 D8
  Bristol, Northville BS7. . . . 29 A1
  Bristol, Shirehampton BS11 16 F6

Park Rd continued
  Bristol, Staple Hill BS16 . . . 20 D5
  Bristol, Stapleton BS16 . . . 19 D5
  Chipping Campden GL55 . . 188 F1
  6 Coleford GL16 . . . . 155 A6
  Gloucester GL1. . . . . 196 B2
  Highleadon GL19 . . . . 171 F2
  Keynsham BS31. . . . . 4 E4
  Leyhill GL12. . . . . 66 B4
  Nailsworth GL6. . . . . 91 C3
  Stonehouse GL10. . . . . 97 E8
  Stroud GL5. . . . . .99 D6
  Thornbury BS35. . . . . 64 B2
Park Road Cres GL6. . . . . 91 C3
Park Row
  Aylburton GL15 . . . . 147 D4
  Bristol BS1. . . . . 194 C3
  Frampton Cotterell BS36. . . 31 A8
Parkside GL16. . . . . 155 A5
Parkside Ave BS16. . . . . . . 30 E6
Parkside Cl GL3. . . . . 127 F6
Parkside Dr GL3. . . . . 127 F6
Parkside Gdns BS5. . . . . . 19 B4
Parks Rd GL17. . . . . 164 D5
Park St
  Bristol, Brandon Hill BS1. .194 C3
  Bristol, Crew's Hole BS5 . . . 9 F8
  Bristol, Totterdown BS4. . . . 9 A3
  Cheltenham GL50. . . . . . .193 A4
  Cirencester GL7. . . . . 190 C5
  Fairford GL7 . . . . 152 E4
  Gloucester GL1. . . . . 196 B3
  Hawkesbury Upton GL9. . . . 56 A2
  Iron Acton BS37 . . . . 42 D4
  Stow-on-t-W GL54. . . . . . .176 F4
Park Street Ave BS1. . . . . 194 C3
Park Terr GL6. . . . . 91 F6
Park The
  Bristol BS32. . . . . 40 D1
  Bristol, Frenchay BS16 . . . 30 B1
  Bristol, Kingswood BS15 . . 10 E8
  Bristol, Willsbridge BS30. . . 11 B1
  Cheltenham GL50. . . . . . .130 B6
  Keynsham BS31. . . . . 4 E6
  Northway GL20 . . . . 182 B5
  Stow-on-t-W GL54. . . . . . .176 F4
Park View
  Bristol, Kingswood BS15 . . 10 E7
  Bristol, Southville BS3. . . . 8 C4
  Cheltenham GL51. . . . . . .132 E4
  Chepstow/Cas-Gwent NP16 72 C1
  4 Gloucester GL4 . . . . . . 119 C4
  Ruardean GL17 . . . . 163 F4
  Saul GL2. . . . . 157 F4
  Sedbury NP16. . . . . 61 B8
  Stratton GL7 . . . . 190 B8
  Yate BS37 . . . . 32 E8
Park View Ave BS35. . . . . 64 C2
Park View Ct BS16 . . . . . . 20 E5
Park View Dr GL5 . . . . 98 E8
Park View Rd GL13. . . . . . 85 D3
Park View Terr BS5. . . . . . .9 E8
Parkwall Cres BS30 . . . . . 10 F4
Parkwall Prim Sch BS30.. 11 A4
Parkwall Rd BS30 . . . . 11 A4
Parkway
  Bristol BS34. . . . . 30 A4
  Bristol BS34. . . . . 30 A4
  Siddington GL7 . . . . 150 D2
Parkway N BS34. . . . . 30 A4
Parkway Trad Est 10 BS2 . 30 A4
Park Way BS30 . . . . 11 B5
Park Wood Cl BS14. . . . . . .2 F4
Parkwood Cres GL3. . . . . 119 F6
Parkwood Gr GL53. . . . . . 131 A4
Parliament Cl GL5 . . . . . . 99 C7
Parliament Prim Sch GL5 99 F7
Parliament St
  Bristol BS5. . . . . 9 A4
  Gloucester GL1. . . . . 196 B3
  Stroud GL5. . . . . .99 C7
Parnall Cres BS37. . . . . . . 43 C2
Parnall Rd BS16. . . . . 20 A3
Parnall Road Ind Est
  BS16. . . . . 20 A3
Parnell Rd BS16 . . . . 19 E7
Parragate GL14 . . . . 191 D5
Parragate Rd GL14. . . . . . 191 C5
Parr Cl GL3. . . . . 127 F7
Parr Ho GL54 . . . . 139 F5
Parry Cl GL4 . . . . 190 F5
Parry Rd GL1 . . . . 118 F6
Parry's Cl BS9 . . . . 17 E5
Parry Rd GL1 . . . . 118 F6
Parry's Gr BS9 . . . . 17 E5
Parrys La BS9 . . . . 17 E5
Parslow Barton 4 BS5. . . 10 A7
Parsonage Farm 3 SN6. 143 E4
Parsonage Rd BS41. . . . . . 7 C2
Parsonage St GL11. . . . . . 88 A1
Parsons Ave BS34. . . . . . . 29 F5
Parsons Cl GL11 . . . . 80 C8
Parson's Cnr GL54 . . . . . . 176 F5
Parsons Cl GL6. . . . . 148 A3
Parsons La
  Redmarley D'Abitot GL19 . 179 F2
  Weston-s-E GL55. . . . . . . 188 D3
Parsons Paddock BS14. . . 3 A7
Parson St BS3. . . . . .8 B2
Parson Street Prim Sch
  BS3. . . . . 8 C2
Parson Street Sta BS3 . . .8 B2
Parsons Wlk BS30. . . . . . . 11 D7
Partition St BS1 . . . . 194 C2
Parton Dr GL3 . . . . 128 C5

Orw–Pea 227

Parton Manor Inf Sch
  GL3. . . . . 128 B6
Parton Mews GL3 . . . . 128 B6
Parton Rd GL3. . . . . 128 C6
Partridge Cl
  Gloucester GL2 . . . . 118 C5
  Stonehouse GL10. . . . . 97 F8
  Yate BS37. . . . . 43 F4
Partridge Dr BS16. . . . . . . 20 C6
Partridge Rd BS16 . . . . . . 22 C4
Partridge Way GL7. . . . . . 190 E4
Parva Springs NP16 . . . . . 146 B4
Passage Leaze BS11. . . . . 16 D6
Passage Rd
  Arlingham GL2. . . . . 157 B6
  Aust BS35 . . . . 48 F7
  Bristol, Brentry BS10. . . . . 27 F3
  Bristol, Westbury on Trym
    BS9. . . . . 18 A8
  Saul GL2. . . . . 157 F4
Passage Road Brentry Hill
  BS9, BS10 . . . . 28 A2
Passage St BS2. . . . . 195 B2
Pas Seul St 3 GL51 . . . . . 133 C4
Pastor's Hill GL15 . . . . . . 147 D8
Pasture La BS16. . . . . 186 C5
Pasture The 2 BS32. . . . . . 40 D1
Patch Cl BS16 . . . . 21 A8
Patch Elm La BS37. . . . . . 42 F7
Patches The GL17. . . . . . . 163 F3
Patch La BS37 . . . . 43 A8
Patchway BS34. . . . . 29 B8
Patchway Brook BS32 . . . 40 C2
Patchway Com Coll BS32. 40 B1
Patchway Sta BS34 . . . . . 29 C6
Patchway Trad Est BS34. . 28 E7
Paternoster Sch GL7. . . . 190 D3
Paterson Rd GL7. . . . . 190 E4
Pates Ave GL51. . . . . 133 B2
Pates Gram Sch GL51. . . 132 E3
Patseamur Mews GL2. . . 127 E5
Patterdale Cl GL51. . . . . . 132 F5
Patterson Ho 8 BS1. . . . . 195 B1
Paul Mead GL6. . . . . 111 B1
Pauls Croft SN6. . . . . 143 F4
Paul's Rise GL5. . . . . 99 A2
Paul St
  Bristol BS2. . . . . 194 C4
  Gloucester GL1. . . . . 118 F7
Pauls Wlk GL19 . . . . 165 D6
Paulton Dr BS7. . . . . 18 C4
Paultow Ave BS3. . . . . .8 E3
Paultow Rd BS3. . . . . .8 E3
Pauntley CE Prim Sch
  GL18. . . . . 171 B8
Pauntley Court Dr GL19 . 171 C7
Pavey Cl 3 BS13. . . . . 2 C4
Pavey Rd BS13. . . . . 2 C4
Pavilion Bsns Pk GL14.. . 191 B7
Pavilion Gdns GL50 . . . . . 130 C6
Pavilion Rd NP16 . . . . 61 C2
Pavilions The
  Bristol BS4. . . . . 9 C1
  Cheltenham GL53. . . . . . .193 B2
Pawlett Rd BS13. . . . . 2 C3
Pawlett Wlk BS13 . . . . 2 C3
Paxford Rd GL55. . . . . . . 189 B2
Paxhill La GL20 . . . . 182 A8
Paxton BS16. . . . . 19 E8
Paybridge Rd BS13. . . . . . .1 F4
Paygrove La GL2. . . . . 127 D5
Payne Dr BS5. . . . . .9 B7
Paynes Mdw GL2. . . . . . . 100 F5
Paynes Orchard Pk BS10. 28 D5
Paynes Pitch GL3 . . . . . . 128 D4
Peach Cl GL20 . . . . 192 E1
Peach Cotts GL20 . . . . . . 192 E1
Peache Ct BS16. . . . . 20 E6
Peache Rd BS16 . . . . 20 F6
Peacock Cl
  5 Cheltenham GL51. . . . . 132 D2
  Gloucester GL4. . . . . 119 E5
  5 Newent GL18 . . . . 171 A4
Peacock Gdns 6 GL18 . . 171 A4
Peacock La GL14. . . . . . . 191 C1
Peacocks La BS15. . . . . . . 10 C7
Peak Acad GL11 . . . . 88 C2
Peak La GL11 . . . . 89 A7
Peakstile Piece GL52. . . . 138 B3
Pearce Cl BS35. . . . . 51 C8
Pearces Hill BS16. . . . . . . 20 B7
Pearce Way GL2. . . . . 118 B4
Pearcroft Rd GL10. . . . . . 98 A6
Pearl St BS3. . . . . .8 B3
Pear Orch The GL20. . . . . 182 C5
Pearsall Rd BS30. . . . . 10 E2
Peart Cl
  Bristol BS13. . . . . 1 E5
  Gloucester GL1 . . . . 127 B1
Peart Dr BS13 . . . . .1 E4
Peartree Cl BS13. . . . . .2 B4
Pear Tree Cl
  Chipping Campden GL55 . . 189 A1
  Hardwicke GL2 . . . . 109 E7
  Lower Swell GL54 . . . . 176 D4
  32 Winchcombe GL54 . . . . 174 A7
  Woodmancote GL52. . . . . 138 C3
Pear Tree Hey BS37. . . . . . 43 E5
Peartree La
  Bristol, Lower Soundwell
    BS15. . . . . 20 F2
  Bristol, St George BS5. . . . 10 B6
Pear Tree Rd BS32. . . . . . . 40 C2

Pearwood Way GL4 . . . . . 118 C2
Peashill Cnr GL54 . . . . . 176 B2
Pecked La GL52. . . . . . 138 A3
Peel Cl GL53. . . . . . . 131 C5
Peel Ctr The GL1. . . . . . 196 A1
Peel St BS5. . . . . 195 C4
Peep The 24 GL54 . . . . . 168 A1
Pegasus Bldg GL2. . . . . . 118 A2
Pegasus Ct
  Bourton-on-t-W GL54 . . . . 169 A8
  12 Broadway WR12. . . . 185 B8
  Cheltenham GL51. . . . . 130 B7
  Gloucester GL4 . . . . . 127 E1
Pegasus Gdns GL2 . . . . . 117 F2
Pegasus Pk BS34 . . . . . . 29 C6
Pegasus Rd GL3 . . . . . . 28 D7
Peggotty Bglws 2 GL4 . . . 119 C7
Peg Hill BS37 . . . . 43 F4
Peghouse Cl GL5. . . . . . 103 D1
Peghouse Rise GL5 . . . . . 103 D1
Pelham Cres GL3 . . . . . . 128 A6
Pemberton Ct BS16 . . . . . 20 C5
Pembery Rd BS3. . . . . . . 8 B3
Pembridge Cl GL52 . . . . . 131 C6
Pembridge Ct GL50 . . . . . 193 A1
Pembroke Ave BS11. . . . . 16 E6
Pembroke Gate BS8. . . . . 18 A1
Pembroke Gr BS8 . . . . . . 194 A3
Pembroke Mans BS8 . . . . . 194 A4
Pembroke Pl
  Bristol, Hotwells BS8. . . . 194 A1
  Bristol, St Pauls BS1 . . . . 195 B4
Pembroke Rd
  Bristol, Clifton BS8 . . . . 194 A4
  Bristol, Kingswood BS15. . . 20 E2
  Bristol, Shirehampton BS11 16 E6
  Bristol, Southville BS3. . . . 8 C4
  Cheltenham GL51. . . . . 129 E6
  Chepstow/Cas-Gwent NP16 60 E6
Pembroke St
  Bristol BS2. . . . . . . 195 B4
  Cinderford GL14 . . . . . 191 D4
  Gloucester GL1. . . . . . 196 C1
Pembroke Vale BS8. . . . . 194 A4
Pembury GL50. . . . . . . 193 A2
Pembury Rd GL4 . . . . . . 118 E4
Penard Way BS15. . . . . . 10 F7
Penby Lawn GL14 . . . . . 156 F6
Penda Pl NP16. . . . . . . 61 A8
Pendennis Ave BS16 . . . . 20 D4
Pendennis Ho 5 BS16 . . . . 20 D5
Pendennis Pk BS4 . . . . . 9 D2
Pendennis Rd BS16 . . . . . 20 D5
Pendil Cl GL50. . . . . . . 133 B6
Pendock CE Prim Sch
  GL19. . . . . 180 A4
Pendock Cl
  Bristol BS30. . . . . . . 11 C1
  Quedgeley GL2. . . . . . 117 E1
Pendock Cross GL19. . . . . 180 A3
Pendock Ct BS16 . . . . . . 21 B7
Pendock Rd
  Bristol BS16. . . . . . . 20 C6
  Winterbourne BS36. . . . 30 E5
Penfield Ct BS2. . . . . . . 19 A2
Penfield Rd BS2. . . . . . . 19 A2
Penharva Cl GL51. . . . . . 133 A3
Penhill Hu GL4. . . . . . . 119 B5
Penhill Rd GL4. . . . . . . 119 B5
Penlea Ct BS11. . . . . . . 16 D7
Penlea Ho BS11. . . . . . . 16 D7
Pen-Moel Cotts NP16 . . . . 73 A4
Penmoel La NP16. . . . . . 73 A3
Penmoyle Gdns NP16. . . . 73 A4
Pennard Ct BS14. . . . . . 3 B5
Penn Dr BS16. . . . . 30 C1
Penngrove BS30 . . . . . . 11 A3
Pennine Cl GL2 . . . . . . 109 E8
Pennine Rd
  Bristol BS30. . . . . . . 11 C4
  Cheltenham GL52. . . . . 134 B3
Pennington Ct GL51. . . . . 132 E4
Penn La GL10. . . . . 98 B2
Pennlea BS13. . . . . 2 C7
Pennon Rise BS1 . . . . . . 194 C1
Penn St BS1. . . . . 195 B3
Pennsylvania Ave GL51. . . 132 F3
Pennsylvania Mews
  GL51. . . . . 132 F3
Penny Cl GL2. . . . . 127 D4
Penny La
  Bristol BS15. . . . . . . 20 F3
  Slimbridge GL2 . . . . . 95 B2
Pennylands Wy GL54 . . . . 174 A8
Pennyroyal Gr BS15. . . . . 19 E4
Pennywell Ct 3 BS5 . . . . 9 A8
Pennywell Rd BS5 . . . . . 9 A8
Pen Park Rd BS10. . . . . . 28 D2
Penpole Ave BS11. . . . . . 16 E6
Penpole Cl BS11. . . . . . . 16 D7
Penpole La BS11. . . . . . . 16 D7
Penpole Pk BS11. . . . . . . 16 E7
Penpole Pl BS11. . . . . . . 16 D7
Penrith Cl GL51. . . . . . . 129 F7
Penrith Gdns BS10. . . . . . 18 D8
Penrith Rd GL51. . . . . . . 129 F7
Penrose BS14. . . . . 2 F7
Penrose Ct GL6. . . . . . . 102 E3
Penrose Dr BS32. . . . . . . 29 D7
Penrose Rd GL3. . . . . . . 127 D6
Pensfield Pk BS10. . . . . . 28 D4
Pensford Ct BS14. . . . . . 3 D5
Pensile Rd GL6. . . . . . . 91 D4

Pentagon The BS9 . . . . . 17 B5
Pentathlon Way GL50 . . . 133 D5
Penterry La NP16 . . . . . 72 B7
Penterry Pk NP16 . . . . . 60 D8
Pentire Ave BS13 . . . . . 2 A6
Pentland Ave BS35 . . . . . 51 E8
Pentwyn Cl NP16 . . . . . 60 B6
Pentylands Cl SN6 . . . . . 145 C4
Pepys Cl BS31 . . . . 5 D2
Perch Dr GL16 . . . . 155 C6
Percival Rd
  Bishop's Cleeve GL52 . . . 137 E1
  Bristol BS8 . . . . 7 F8
Percy St
  8 Bristol BS3 . . . . . . 8 D4
  Gloucester GL1 . . . . . 118 F7
Percy Walker Ct BS16 . . . . 20 C6
Peregrine Cl GL2 . . . . . . 117 F3
Peregrine Rd GL53 . . . . . 130 C5
Perretts Cl GL14 . . . . . . 165 D3
Perrie Dr WR11 . . . . . . 188 C7
Perrinpit Rd BS36 . . . . . 41 E2
Perrinsfield GL7 . . . . . . 153 E3
Perrott Rd BS15 . . . . . . 21 A1
Perry Cl
  Charlton Kings GL53 . . . 131 B5
  28 Newent GL18 . . . . . 171 A4
  Winterbourne BS36. . . . 30 D4
Perry Court Prim Sch BS14 3 A6
Perrycroft Ave BS13. . . . . 2 A6
Perrycroft Rd BS13. . . . . 2 A6
Perry Ctr The GL2. . . . . . 109 F6
Perry Field GL15 . . . . . . 147 C3
Perryfield Ct 1 GL54. . . . 168 F7
Perrygrove Rd GL16. . . . . 155 A4
Perry Hill GL20 . . . . . . 192 C3
Perrymans Cl
  Bristol BS16. . . . . . . 20 A6
  Doynton BS30. . . . . . 13 A8
Perry Orch
  Stroud GL6. . . . . . . 98 D8
  Upton St Leonards GL4 . . . 119 E2
Perry Rd BS1. . . . . 195 A3
Perry's Court La GL17 . . . . 163 E4
Perrys Lea BS32. . . . . . . 40 D2
Perry St BS5. . . . . 9 A8
Perry Way GL2. . . . . . . 100 B3
Persh La GL2 . . . . 125 F6
Persh Way GL2 . . . . . . 126 A7
Persimmon Gdns GL51. . . 132 E4
Perth GL10. . . . . 101 E1
Perwell Cl GL20. . . . . . . 182 C8
Pesley Cl BS13. . . . . . . 2 A4
Petercole Dr BS13. . . . . . 2 A6
Peter Pennell Cl GL51. . . 132 E4
Peters Field GL2. . . . . . . 125 E5
Peterson Ave 2 BS13. . . . 2 C4
Peterson Sq BS13. . . . . . 2 C3
Peter's St GL10. . . . . . . 96 E3
Peter's Terr BS5. . . . . . . 9 B7
Petersway Gdns BS5 . . . . 10 A6
Pethera Cl GL7. . . . . . . 190 C6
Petherbridge Way BS7. . . 19 A5
Petherton Cl BS15. . . . . . 10 E7
Petherton Gdns BS14. . . . 3 B7
Petherton Rd BS14. . . . . 3 B7
Pethick Ho BS4. . . . . . . 2 F8
Pettigrove Gdns BS15. . . . 10 E7
Pettigrove Rd BS15. . . . . 10 E6
Pettycroft GL17. . . . . . . 163 F4
Petty La GL52. . . . . 138 F3
Petty Marsh GL15 . . . . . 146 E6
Petworth Ct GL4 . . . . . . 110 C8
Pevelands GL11. . . . . . . 87 F5
Pevensey Wlk BS4. . . . . . 2 D7
Peverell Cl BS10. . . . . . . 27 F3
Peverell Dr BS10. . . . . . . 27 F3
Peveril Ho GL2. . . . . . . 118 C4
Peymans Terr GL7. . . . . . 142 F7
Pheasant La GL51. . . . . . 132 B1
Pheasant Mead GL10. . . . 97 F8
Pheasant Rise HR9. . . . . 162 F7
Pheasantry The GL7. . . . 143 F8
Pheasant Way GL7. . . . . 190 F5
Phelps Mill Cl GL11 . . . . 88 B1
Phelps Way GL19 . . . . . 171 E1
Philippa Cl BS14. . . . . . . 3 A7
Philip's Cl GL15. . . . . . . 156 B1
Philips Ho 2 BS2 . . . . . 195 B4
Philip St
  Bristol, St Philip's Marsh
  BS2. . . . . 9 B5
  Bristol, Windmill Hill BS3. . . 8 B4
  Gloucester GL1. . . . . . 118 D7
Phillimore Gdns GL2 . . . 100 A5
Phillimore Rd GL11. . . . . 87 E4
Phillips La GL19. . . . . . . 179 F2
Phillips Rd WR12. . . . . . 188 A1
Phippen St 1 BS1. . . . . . 195 B1
Phipps Barton BS15. . . . . 10 B8
Phipps St BS3. . . . . 8 B4
Phoenix Bsns Pk BS3. . . . 8 A2
Phoenix Cl GL16. . . . . . . 155 A5
Phoenix Dr NP16. . . . . . 61 A4
Phoenix Gr
  Bristol BS6. . . . . 18 C5
  18 Bristol, Upper Soundwell
  BS16. . . . . 20 D3
Phoenix Ho BS5. . . . . . . 9 B6
Phoenix Trad Est GL5. . . 99 E3

Phoenix Way GL7 . . . . . 190 C4
Phoenix Way GL7 . . . . . 190 C4
Piccadilly
  Guiting Power GL54. . . . 175 B3
  Stroud GL5. . . . . . . 99 D7
Piccadilly Way GL52. . . . . 134 D4
Picked Acre GL2 . . . . . . 124 C2
Pickedmoor La BS35 . . . 63 E5
Pickering Cl GL53 . . . . . 130 C6
Pickering Rd GL53 . . . . . 130 C6
Picklenash Jun Sch
  GL18. . . . . 170 F5
Pickwick Cl GL2 . . . . . . 127 D3
Picton Ho GL7 . . . . 190 D5
Picton La BS6. . . . . 18 E1
Picton Mews 6 BS6 . . . . 18 E1
Picton St BS6. . . . . 18 E1
Piece Hedge GL54 . . . . . 168 F8
Piece The
  Churchdown GL3. . . . . 128 D4
  Hatherop GL7. . . . . . 152 E7
Piercefield Ave NP16. . . . 72 C1
Piercefield Terr NP16. . . . 72 B5
Piermont Dr NP16 . . . . . 73 A2
Pigeon House Dr BS13 . . . 2 D4
Pigeon La GL20 . . . . . . 183 A8
Pigott Ave BS13. . . . . . . 2 A4
Pigs Cross GL18. . . . . . . 170 C3
Pike Cnr WR12. . . . . . . 188 B2
Pike Hill Rise GL54. . . . . 167 B3
Pike House Cl 13 SN6 . . . 143 E4
Pike La GL6. . . . . 91 B3
Pike Rd
  9 Coleford GL16. . . . . 155 A6
  Winstone GL7, GL53. . . . 115 A1
Pilemarsh BS5. . . . . 9 D7
Pilford Ave GL53 . . . . . . 130 E4
Pilford Cl GL53 . . . . 130 E5
Pilford Ct GL53 . . . . 130 E5
Pilford Rd GL53 . . . . 130 E3
Pilgrim Cl 4 GL4 . . . . . . 119 E6
Pilgrims Way
  Avonmouth BS11. . . . . 16 C7
  Bristol BS16. . . . . . . 20 D8
Pilgrims Wharf BS4 . . . . 9 E7
Pilgrove Cl GL51 . . . . . . 132 D4
Pilgrove Way GL51 . . . . . 132 E5
Pilkington Cl BS34 . . . . . 29 C2
Pillcroft Cl GL3. . . . . . . 121 A4
Pillcroft Rd GL3. . . . . . . 121 A4
Pilley Cres GL53 . . . . . . 130 D4
Pilley La GL53 . . . . 130 D4
Pillingers Gdns BS6. . . . . 18 B2
Pillingers Rd BS15 . . . . . 10 C7
Pill La GL56. . . . . 187 F1
Pillowell Cl GL52. . . . . . 134 B2
Pillowell Com Prim Sch
  GL15. . . . . 155 F1
Pillowell Dr GL11 . . . . . . 127 A2
Pillowell Rd GL15 . . . . . . 155 F1
Pillows Green Rd GL19 . . . 172 B8
Pill Rd
  Abbots Leigh BS8. . . . . 7 A8
  Abbots Leigh BS8. . . . . 16 F1
  Pill BS20. . . . . 16 E2
Pill St BS20. . . . . 16 D4
Pilning St BS35 . . . . . . 39 C8
Pilning Sta BS35. . . . . . . 38 F5
Pimpernel Mead BS32. . . 29 E7
Pincoate GL2. . . . . 125 D6
Pincot La GL6. . . . . 103 D5
Pincots La GL12. . . . . . . 54 B3
Pine Bank GL52. . . . . . . 138 B4
Pine Cl
  Bishop's Cleeve GL52 . . . 138 B4
  Cheltenham GL52. . . . . 131 A8
  Thornbury BS35. . . . . 64 C1
Pine Crest Way 5 GL15 . . . 147 D8
Pinecroft BS14. . . . . . . 2 F7
Pine Ct BS31. . . . . 4 F2
Pinedale GL15 . . . . 147 B3
Pinefield BS9. . . . . 18 B7
Pine Gr BS7 . . . . 29 A1
Pine Grove Pl BS7 . . . . . 18 D3
Pine Halt GL54. . . . . . . 166 C6
Pineholt Gate GL3 . . . . . 120 B7
Pinemount Rd GL3 . . . . . 120 A7
Pine Rd BS10. . . . . 28 B3
Pine Ridge Cl BS9. . . . . . 17 C4
Pinery Rd GL4 . . . . 119 E7
Pines La BS35 . . . . 50 D3
Pines Rd BS30 . . . . 11 C1
Pines The
  Brimscombe GL6 . . . . 148 B5
  Bristol BS15. . . . . . . 21 A3
  Cheltenham GL50. . . . . 193 A3
  Greet GL54. . . . . . . 174 A8
Pine Tree Dr GL4 . . . . . . 119 E8
Pinetrees GL53 . . . . 130 F5
Pine Tree Way GL15. . . . . 156 C1
Pinetum Dr GL2. . . . . . . 125 A3
Pineway GL4 . . . . 119 B6
Pinewood BS15. . . . . . . 20 F1
Pinewood Cl
  Bristol BS9. . . . . 18 B7
  Cinderford GL14 . . . . . 191 E5
Pinewood Dr GL51 . . . . . 132 D1
Pinewood Rd GL2 . . . . . 109 E8
Pinewood Way SN14 . . . . 15 F7
Pingry La GL15. . . . . . . 155 A4
Pinhay Rd BS13. . . . . . . 2 B1
Pinkers Mead BS16 . . . . 21 C6
Pinkhams Twist BS14 . . . 3 A5
Pinlocks GL15 . . . . 119 E3
Pinnell Gr BS16 . . . . . . 21 C7
Pinnells End La GL11. . . . 88 D8

Pintail Cl GL2. . . . . 117 D1
Pioneer Ave GL3 . . . . . . 120 B6
Pioneer Pk BS4. . . . . . . 9 C5
Pioneer Pk BS4 . . . . . . 9 C5
Pipe La BS1 . . . . 194 C2
Piper Rd BS37 . . . . 43 E3
Pipers Gr GL2. . . . . 125 D5
Pippin Cl
  Gloucester GL4 . . . . . 120 A6
  35 Newent GL18 . . . . . 171 A4
Pippin Ct 4 BS30 . . . . . 10 F4
Pippins Rd GL20 . . . . . . 182 C7
Pips Field Wy GL7. . . . . . 152 D3
Pirton Cres GL3. . . . . . . 128 B5
Pirton La GL3. . . . . 128 B5
Pirton La GL3. . . . . 128 B5
Pirton Mdw GL3. . . . . . . 128 B5
Pitchcombe BS37 . . . . . 32 C7
Pitchcombe Gdns BS9. . . 17 D7
Pitching Gn GL15 . . . . . 156 C2
Pitch La BS6. . . . . 18 D1
Pitch & Pay La BS9. . . . . 17 E3
Pitch & Pay Pk BS9 . . . . 17 E3
Pitch The GL6. . . . . 148 B5
Pithay GL51. . . . . 195 A3
Pithay The BS1. . . . . . . 195 A3
Pitlochry Cl BS7 . . . . . . 28 F1
Pitman Pl GL12. . . . . . . 68 C6
Pitman Rd GL51. . . . . . . 132 E1
Pitt Ho GL52. . . . . 133 F1
Pitt Mill Gdns GL3. . . . . 120 A8
Pitt Rd BS7. . . . . 18 E5
Pittsfield SN6. . . . . 143 E4
Pitt St GL1. . . . . 196 B3
Pittville Cir GL52. . . . . . 133 F2
Pittville Circus Rd GL52 . 133 F2
Pittville Cl BS35. . . . . . . 64 C3
Pittville Cres GL52. . . . . . 133 F3
Pittville Crescent La
  GL52. . . . . 133 F3
Pittville Ct GL52. . . . . . . 133 F4
Pittville Lawn GL52 . . . . 133 F3
Pittville Mews GL52. . . . . 193 C4
Pittville Pump Room & Mus*
  GL52. . . . . 133 F4
Pittville Sch GL52. . . . . . 133 F4
Pittville St GL52. . . . . . . 193 C4
Pitville Pl 16 BS6. . . . . . 18 B1
Pixash Bsns Ctr BS31 . . . 5 B5
Pixash La BS31. . . . . . . 5 C5
Place Hill GL18. . . . . . . 170 C4
Plain The
  Stroud GL6. . . . . . . 103 A2
  Thornbury BS35. . . . . 64 B1
Planets La GL51. . . . . . . 129 C6
Plantation Cres GL20. . . 182 C7
Plantation The
  Gloucester GL4 . . . . . 119 E6
  Hardwicke GL2. . . . . . 109 D7
Platts Row GL17 . . . . . . 164 D5
Platts Wood BS16, BS34. . 19 D8
Players Cl BS16. . . . . . . 30 B3
Playford Gdns BS11. . . . . 16 E8
Playhouse Ct GL53 . . . . . 193 C3
Playhouse The* 7 GL50 . . 193 B3
Pleasant Ho 4 BS16 . . . . 20 D5
Pleasant Rd BS16 . . . . . 20 D5
Pleasant Stile GL14 . . . . 156 E7
Pleydells 16 SN6 . . . . . 143 E4
Pleydells The GL7. . . . . . 151 B5
Plies The GL7. . . . . 152 E3
Plimsoll Ho
  3 Bristol BS1. . . . . . . 195 B1
  5 Bristol, Woolcott Park
  BS6. . . . . 18 B1
Plock Ct GL2. . . . . 126 F5
Plough La HR9. . . . . . . 162 B5
Ploughmans Way GL2 . . . 109 E6
Plover Cl BS37 . . . . 43 C2
Plowright Ho 8 BS15 . . . . 10 B5
Pludds Court Rd GL17 . . . 163 E3
Plummer's Hill BS5 . . . . 9 E8
Plumpton Ct BS16 . . . . . 30 F1
Plum Tree Cl
  Gloucester GL4 . . . . . 119 E4
  Longborough GL56. . . . 176 E8
Pochard Cl GL2. . . . . . . 117 D1
Pockhill La GL54. . . . . . . 168 F7
Poden Gl GL55. . . . . . . 188 E4
Podsmead Pl GL1. . . . . . 118 D5
Podsmead Rd GL1. . . . . . 118 D5
Poets' Cl BS5. . . . . 9 D8
Point Rd GL8. . . . . 140 B8
Polar Gdns SN14. . . . . . 47 E4
Polden Ho BS3. . . . . . . 8 D3
Polefield Gdns GL51 . . . . 130 B8
Polefield Ho 13 GL51. . . . 130 B8
Pollards La GL15. . . . . . 156 D1
Polly Barnes Cl 6 BS15 . . . 10 B5
Polly Barnes Hill BS15. . . 10 B5
Polygon Rd BS8. . . . . . . 194 A2
Polygon The
  Avonmouth BS11. . . . . 26 D1
  16 Bristol BS6. . . . . . 7 F6
Pomfrett Gdns BS14 . . . . 3 E5
Pomphrey Hill BS16. . . . 21 C4
Pond Cl BS34. . . . . 40 B1
Pond La SN5. . . . . 143 D1
Ponsford Rd BS4. . . . . . 9 B1
Ponting Cl BS5. . . . . . . 20 A1
Ponting's Cl SN26. . . . . . 144 E1
Pool Cl GL56. . . . . 187 F1
Pool Cnr BS32. . . . . 50 B2
Poole Cl
  12 Bream GL15. . . . . . 147 D8
  Bristol BS15. . . . . . . 2 C5
Poole Court Dr BS37 . . . . 43 E2

Poole Ground GL2 . . . . . 125 D6
Pooles La GL5 . . . . 98 E4
Poole St BS11 . . . . 16 B8
Pooles Wharf BS8 . . . . . 194 A1
Pooles Wharf Ct BS8. . . 194 A1
Poole Way GL50 . . . . . . 193 B4
Poolhay Cl GL19 . . . . . . 180 E1
Pool Ho BS34. . . . . 29 A8
Pool La NP25 . . . . 154 B1
Pool Meadow Cvn Pk
  GL1. . . . . 126 C3
Pool Rd BS15. . . . . 20 E3
Poolway Ct 1 GL16. . . . . 155 A5
Poolway Pl GL16. . . . . . 155 A5
Poolway Rd GL16. . . . . . 155 B6
Poolway Rise 8 GL16. . . . 155 A5
Popes Cl GL50. . . . . . . 133 D3
Pope's Ct GL7. . . . . 190 A4
Pope's Ct GL7. . . . . 153 A1
Popes Meade GL2. . . . . . 125 D6
Poplar Ave BS9 . . . . . . 17 B5
Poplar Cl
  Bristol BS30. . . . . . . 11 C6
  Gloucester GL4 . . . . . 118 D5
Poplar Cres GL52 . . . . . 138 B4
Poplar Dr
  Pucklechurch BS16 . . . . 22 B5
  Woodmancote GL52. . . . 138 C3
Poplar Fields BS30. . . . . 11 D6
Poplar Gardens Ho 3
  BS15. . . . . 10 E8
Poplar La GL12. . . . . . . 54 B4
Poplar Pl BS16. . . . . . . 20 A3
Poplar Rd
  Bristol, Hanham BS15 . . . 10 A5
  Bristol, Highridge BS35. . . 1 F7
  Bristol, North Common
  BS30. . . . . 11 D6
  Bristol, Speedwell BS5 . . . 19 F1
Poplar Rdbt BS11. . . . . . 26 E5
Poplars Cl GL55. . . . . . . 188 F1
Poplars Pk GL2. . . . . . . 95 F3
Poplars The
  Cheltenham GL51. . . . . 129 E6
  Easton-in-G BS20. . . . . 16 B4
Poplar Terr BS15. . . . . . 10 F8
Poplar Way
  Colerne SN14. . . . . . 15 F5
  Hardwicke GL2. . . . . . 109 E7
Poplar Way E BS11. . . . . 26 F5
Poplar Way W BS11. . . . 26 E5
Poppy Field GL2 . . . . . . 125 E6
Poppy Mead BS32. . . . . 29 E7
Porchester Rd GL3. . . . . 119 F7
Porlock Rd BS3. . . . . . . 8 D3
Portbury Gr BS11. . . . . . 16 D6
Portbury Wlk BS11. . . . . 16 D6
Port Elizabeth Ho BS10. . 28 B1
Port Ind Est GL5 . . . . . . 99 F1
Portishead Way BS3. . . . 7 E3
Port La GL5. . . . . 99 F1
Portland Ct
  Bristol BS1. . . . . 194 B1
  Bristol, Upper Soundwell
  BS16. . . . . 20 D3
Portland Lofts BS2 . . . . . 195 B4
Portland Mansions BS2 . 195 B4
Portland Pl
  Bristol BS16. . . . . . . 20 D3
  9 Cheltenham GL52. . . . 193 C4
Portland Sq
  Bristol BS2. . . . . 195 B4
  Cheltenham GL52. . . . . 193 C4
Portland St
  Bristol BS2. . . . . 195 A4
  Bristol, Clifton BS8 . . . . 7 F7
  Bristol, Staple Hill BS16 . . . 20 D3
  Cheltenham GL52. . . . . 193 C4
Portman Terr GL50. . . . . 193 B2
Portmeirion Cl BS14 . . . 3 B5
Portreath Wy 10 GL2 . . . 110 B8
Port Side Cl 6 BS5 . . . . 9 F6
Port Terr GL5. . . . . 99 F1
Porturet Way 2 GL53 . . . 131 C6
Port View BS20. . . . . . . 16 C5
Portview Rd BS11. . . . . . 16 B8
Port Wall* NP16. . . . . . 60 F8
Portwall La BS1. . . . . . . 195 B1
Portwall La E 10 BS1 . . . 195 B1
Portwall Rd NP16. . . . . . 60 E8
Portway
  Bristol, Shirehampton
  BS11. . . . . 16 C6
  Bristol, Sneyd Park BS8. . . 17 C3
  Upton St Leonards GL4 . . . 112 B7
Portway La BS37. . . . . . 44 E2
Portway Rdbt BS11. . . . . 16 C8
Portwall 4 SN6. . . . . . . 143 E4
Postlip Way GL51 . . . . . 129 D8
Post Office Cotts GL2 . . . 108 C6
Post Office La
  Cheltenham GL50. . . . . 193 B3
  Cleeve Hill GL52. . . . . . 138 E3
  Draycott GL56. . . . . . 186 D6
  Guiting Power GL54. . . . 175 B3
  Tewkesbury GL20. . . . . 192 C4
Post Office Row GL2. . . . 101 B2
Post Office Sq GL7. . . . . . 150 E2
Post Paddocks The
  GL15. . . . . 147 C3
Potlicker's La
  Ablington GL7. . . . . . 159 F2
  Coln Rogers GL54, GL7. . . 159 E4
Potters Croft NP16. . . . . 61 B4
Potters Field Rd GL52 . . . 138 C3
Potters Pond GL12. . . . . 68 C7

Pound Cl
Ledbury HR8 . . . . .178 E8
Siddington GL7 . . . . .150 E2
Twyning GL20 . . . . .181 F7
Watermead GL3 . . . . . . .120 E4
Pound Dr BS16 . . . . .19 F5
Pound Farm Ctyd GL3 . .120 E5
Pound Farm La HR9 . . . .170 B5
Pound Hill GL8 . . . . .140 B4
Pound La
Arlingham GL2 . . . . .157 B5
Bristol BS16 . . . . .19 F4
Hardwicke GL2 . . . . .109 D5
Little Rissington GL54 . . .169 C6
Mickleton GL55 . . . . .189 A6
Pound Mdw HR8 . . . . . .178 E8
Pound Rd
Bristol BS15 . . . . .20 F2
Highworth SN6 . . . . .145 C4
Pound The
Almondsbury BS32 . . . . . .40 A5
Ampney Crucis GL7 . . . . .151 B5
Little Rissington GL54 . . .169 C6
Oldbury-on-S BS35 . . . . . .63 B6
Pountney Dr BS5 . . . . .9 B8
Powell Ct BS30 . . . . .22 F2
Powell's CE Prim Sch
GL7 . . . . .190 C5
Powells Way GL8 . . . . . .140 D3
Powis La GL8 . . . . .148 B1
Pow's Rd BS15 . . . . .10 D7
Poyntz Ct BS30 . . . . .10 F3
Poyntz Rd BS4 . . . . .2 F8
Pratten's La ⬛ BS16 . . . . .20 D4
Preacher Cl BS5 . . . . .10 B6
Preddy's La BS5 . . . . .10 A6
Prescott BS37 . . . . .32 D8
Prescott Ave GL4 . . . . . .119 B4
Prescott Wlk GL52 . . . . .134 B4
Press Moor Dr BS30 . . . . .10 F4
Prestbury BS37 . . . . .32 D8
Prestbury Green Dr
GL52 . . . . .134 C4
Prestbury Manor House
GL52 . . . . .134 C5
Prestbury Rd GL52 . . . . .134 B4
Prestbury St Mary's CE Jun
Sch GL52 . . . . .134 B4
Preston Cl NP16 . . . . .60 F4
Preston Cross HR8 . . . . .178 B6
Preston Wlk BS4 . . . . .9 A1
Prestwick Cl BS3 . . . . .9 D1
Prestwick Rd ⬛ GL2 . . . .110 B8
Pretoria Rd BS34 . . . . . . .28 F8
Prewett St BS1 . . . . .195 B1
Prices Ground GL4 . . . . .119 D6
Price St GL1 . . . . .118 D7
Priddy Ct BS14 . . . . .3 B5
Priddy Dr BS14 . . . . .3 B5
Priestley Ct ⬛ GL20 . . . .192 C4
Priestwood Cl BS10 . . . . .28 A3
Primrose Cl
Bristol BS32 . . . . .40 D2
Bristol, St George BS15 . . .10 C8
Gloucester GL4 . . . . .119 A4
Primrose Ct GL56 . . . . . .187 A3
Primrose Dr
Milkwall GL16 . . . . .155 B4
Thornbury BS35 . . . . .64 D2
Primrose Hill CE Prim Acad
GL15 . . . . .92 B5
Primrose Hill Rd GL15 . . .92 A5
Primrose La BS15 . . . . . . .20 C1
Primrose Terr BS15 . . . . .20 C1
Primrose Way
Cirencester GL7 . . . . .190 E1
Lydney GL15 . . . . .92 B5
Prince Albert St BS3 . . . . .8 C3
Prince Charles Rd ⬛
GL7 . . . . .152 E4
Prince Cres GL19 . . . . . .172 A8
Prince Ct ⬛ GL4 . . . . . .140 B4
Prince Of Wales Row ⬛
GL8 . . . . .140 B4
Prince Regent Ave ⬛
GL51 . . . . .133 C4
Prince's Bldgs BS8 . . . . . .7 A4
Princes Ct BS30 . . . . .10 F4
Princes' La BS8 . . . . .7 F6
Princes Mews GL3 . . . . .127 F7
Princes' Pl BS7 . . . . .18 E3
Princes Rd GL5 . . . . .98 E8
Prince's Rd GL50 . . . . . .130 B7
Princess Cl BS31 . . . . .4 E4
Princess Elizabeth Way
GL51 . . . . .132 E3
Princess Gdns BS16 . . . . .19 D6
Princess Row BS2 . . . . . .195 A4
Princess Royal Ind Est
GL15 . . . . .155 E1
Princess Royal Rd ⬛
GL15 . . . . .155 D1
Princess St
Bristol, Newton BS2 . . . . . .9 A7
Bristol, Windmill Hill BS3 . . .8 E4
Prince's St
Bristol BS2 . . . . .195 C4
Cheltenham GL52 . . . . . .133 F1
Princess Victoria St BS8 . .7 F6
Prince St
Bristol BS1 . . . . .195 A1
Gloucester GL1 . . . . .196 C2
Prince Street Rdbt BS1 . .195 A2
Prinknash Abbey★ GL4. . .112 B8
Prinknash Bird and Deer
Pk★ GL4 . . . . .112 B8

Prinknash Cl ⬛ GL4. . . . .119 C4
Prinknash Ct ⬛ BS37 . . . .32 D7
Prinknash Pottery★ GL4 .112 C8
Prinknash Rd ⬛ GL4 . . . .119 C4
Prior Park Prep Sch SN6 .143 F4
Priors Ct
Baunton GL7 . . . . .150 D7
Cheltenham GL52 . . . . . .134 B3
⬛ Tewkesbury GL20 . . . .192 C4
Prior's Hill ⬛ BS6 . . . . . .18 D1
Priors Lea GL7 . . . . .43 E1
Priors Lo ⬛ GL52 . . . . . .133 F2
Priors Rd GL52 . . . . .134 B3
Priors Wlk GL7 . . . . .153 F2
Priory Ave BS9 . . . . .18 A7
Priory Cl
Chepstow/Cas-Gwent
NP16 . . . . .72 D1
Cirencester GL7 . . . . .190 C5
Dursley GL11 . . . . .88 B1
Priory Court Rd BS9 . . . . .18 A7
Priory Ct
Bristol, Hanham BS15 . . . .10 C3
Bristol, Upper Knowle BS4 . .9 B2
Churchdown GL3 . . . . . . .128 D5
Dursley GL11 . . . . .88 A3
Leonard Stanley GL10 . . . .97 E3
Priory Dene BS9 . . . . .18 A7
Priory Fields GL6 . . . . . . .82 F8
Priory Gdns
Bristol, Horfield BS7 . . . . .18 E8
Bristol, Shirehampton BS11 .16 D7
Easton-in-G BS20 . . . . . . .16 B4
Priory Gn SN6 . . . . .145 D3
Priory Ho GL1 . . . . .196 B2
Priory Ind Est GL4 . . . . .140 C4
Priory La
Bishop's Cleeve GL52 . . . .138 A4
Monmouth NP25 . . . . . . .162 A1
Priory Lea HR9 . . . . .163 C8
Priory Lea Ho HR9 . . . . .163 C8
Priory Mews GL52 . . . . .193 C3
Priory Pl
Cheltenham GL52 . . . . . .193 C2
Gloucester GL1 . . . . .196 B2
Priory Rd
Bristol, Shirehampton BS8 . .16 D6
Bristol, Tyndall's Park BS8 .194 C4
Bristol, Upper Knowle BS4 . .9 B2
Easton-in-G BS20 . . . . . . .16 B4
Gloucester GL1 . . . . .196 A3
Gloucester GL1 . . . . .196 B4
Keynsham BS31 . . . . .4 E7
Priory St GL52 . . . . .193 C3
Priory Terr GL52 . . . . . . .133 F1
Priory The SN6 . . . . .143 F5
Priory Way ⬛ GL8 . . . . . .140 C4
Priory Wlk GL7 . . . . .133 F1
Pritchard St BS2 . . . . . . .195 B4
Private Rd GL5. . . . . .99 C2
Probertsbarn La GL17 . . .163 C3
Probyn Cl BS16 . . . . .20 A7
Pro-Cathedral La BS8 . . .194 B3
Proctor Cl BS4 . . . . .9 D1
Proctor Ho BS1 . . . . .195 B1
Promenade GL1 . . . . .196 B2
Promenade The BS7 . . . . .18 D2
Prospect Ave
Bristol BS15 . . . . .20 B1
Bristol, Kingsdown BS2 . . .195 A4
Prospect Cl
Coleford GL16 . . . . .155 A5
Easter Compton BS35 . . . .26 C8
Frampton Cotterell BS36. . .30 F8
Winterbourne BS36. . . . . .30 E4
Prospect Cres BS15 . . . . .20 F2
Prospect La
Frampton Cotterell BS36. . .30 F8
Llangrove HR9 . . . . .162 B6
Prospect Pl
⬛ Bristol, Bedminster BS3. . .8 C3
⬛ Bristol, Montpelier BS6 . .18 D2
Bristol, Moorfields BS5 . . . .9 C8
Cirencester GL7 . . . . .190 D3
Dursley GL11 . . . . .88 A1
Prospect Rd
Cinderford GL14 . . . . .191 D4
Severn Beach BS35 . . . . . .38 A5
Prospect Row HR9 . . . . . .170 B4
Prospect Terr
Chalford GL6 . . . . .148 C5
⬛ Cheltenham GL52 . . . . .133 F2
Prosper La GL16 . . . . .155 B5
Protheroes Ho ⬛ BS1 . . .194 C2
Providence Ho BS41 . . . . . .7 A1
Providence Pk GL51 . . . . .133 A4
Providence Pl BS2 . . . . . .195 C4
Providence View BS41 . . . .7 A1
Prowse Cl BS35 . . . . .64 C1
Prudham St ⬛ BS5 . . . . . .19 C1
Pry La WR12 . . . . .185 A8
Pucklechurch CE Prim Sch
BS16 . . . . .22 C6
Pucklechurch Trad Est
BS16 . . . . .22 B4
Puck Pit La GL54. . . . . . . .174 A4
Puckrup GL20 . . . . .181 E7
Pudlicott La GL55 . . . . . .189 D1
Pullar Cl GL52 . . . . .137 F4
Pullar Ct GL52 . . . . .137 F4
Pullen Ct GL52 . . . . .138 A7
Pullen Ho GL52 . . . . .138 A7
Pullin Ct BS30 . . . . .11 D4
Pullins Gn ⬛ BS35 . . . . . .64 B1
Pullman Ct GL1 . . . . .196 C3

Pullnoggin Pool La HR9 .162 D3
Pumphreys Ct GL53 . . . . .131 A5
Pumphreys Rd GL53. . . . .131 A5
Pump La
Bristol BS1. . . . . .195 B1
Tetbury GL8 . . . . .140 E3
Tockington BS32 . . . . .50 D4
Pump Row GL6 . . . . .91 C5
Pump Sq BS20 . . . . .16 D5
Purbeck Way GL52 . . . . . .134 C4
Purcell Rd GL3. . . . . .128 A8
Purcell Wlk BS4 . . . . .2 D7
Purdown Rd BS7. . . . . .18 F5
Purdy Ct BS16 . . . . .20 A4
Purley Ave GL7 . . . . .190 D4
Purley Rd GL7 . . . . .190 D4
Pursey Dr BS32 . . . . .29 F6
Purslane Cl GL4. . . . . .119 B4
Purton Cl BS15 . . . . .10 E6
Purton Pl GL15 . . . . .92 C2
Purton Rd BS7. . . . . .18 D2
Puxley Cl BS14 . . . . .3 C6
Puzzle Cl ⬛ GL15 . . . . . .147 D8
Puzzle Wood★ GL16 . . . .155 A4
Pyart Ct GL16 . . . . .155 A5
Pye Croft BS32. . . . . .40 E3
Pyecroft Ave BS9 . . . . . . .18 C7
Pyghtell The
Luckington SN14 . . . . .47 E5
Stratton GL7 . . . . .190 B7
Pyke Rd GL20 . . . . .192 B7
Pylers Way GL15 . . . . .92 B2
Pylle Hill Cres BS3. . . . . . . .8 F4
Pynne Cl BS14 . . . . .3 F5
Pynne Rd BS14 . . . . .3 F5
Pyracantha Wlk BS14 . . . .3 A6
Pyrton Mews ⬛ GL51 . . .129 E5
Pystol La GL15. . . . . .146 E7

Q

Quabbs Rd GL17 . . . . . . .164 B4
Quadrangle The
Naunton GL54. . . . . .175 D2
Westerleigh BS37 . . . . . . .32 C4
Quadrant BS32. . . . . .40 B3
Quadrant E BS16. . . . . . . .20 C3
Quadrant The BS6 . . . . . . .18 B3
Quadrant W BS16 . . . . . . .20 C3
Quail Cl GL4 . . . . .119 E7
Quail Mdws GL8 . . . . .140 B4
Quaker Ct ⬛ BS35 . . . . . . .64 B1
Quaker La BS35 . . . . .64 B1
Quaker's Cl BS16 . . . . .20 D8
Quaker's Friars BS1. . . . .195 B3
Quaker's Rd BS16 . . . . . . .20 E8
Quakers Row GL7. . . . . . .149 E4
Quantock Cl BS30 . . . . . . .11 C5
Quantock Rd
Bristol BS3. . . . . .8 D3
Quedgeley GL2. . . . . .109 E8
Quarhouse La GL5. . . . . .148 A5
Quarries The BS32 . . . . . . .40 C6
Quarrington Rd BS7. . . . . .18 E5
Quarry Barton BS16 . . . . .30 C4
Quarry Cl
Hartpury GL19 . . . . .172 C3
Stratton GL7 . . . . .190 B8
Quarry Cres SN6 . . . . . . .145 C3
Quarry Gdns GL11. . . . . . .87 D4
Quarry La
Bristol BS11 . . . . .27 C1
Gorsley HR9. . . . . .170 A4
Winterbourne BS36. . . . . .30 E4
Quarry Mead BS35 . . . . . .50 F5
Quarry Rd
Alveston BS35 . . . . .50 F5
Bristol BS8. . . . . .18 A2
Bristol, Frenchay BS16 . . . .20 C7
Bristol, Kingswood BS15 . . .10 D6
Chipping Sodbury BS37 . . . .44 A1
Quarry Steps ⬛ BS8 . . . . .18 A2
Quarry The
Ablington GL7 . . . . .159 F1
Bristol BS11. . . . . .27 C1
Dursley GL11 . . . . .87 D4
⬛ Fairford GL7. . . . . .152 E4
Quarry View GL7. . . . . . .153 C6
Quarry Way
Bristol, Emerson's Green
BS16 . . . . .31 A1
Bristol, Fishponds BS16 . . . .19 E5
Quat Goose La GL51. . . . .133 B7
Quayside
Bristol BS8. . . . . .194 B2
Tintern Parva NP16 . . . . . .146 C4
Quayside La ⬛ BS5 . . . . . . .9 F6
Quayside Wy GL2 . . . . . . .118 C7
Quay St
Bristol BS1. . . . . .195 A3
Gloucester GL1 . . . . .196 A3
Tewkesbury GL20 . . . . . . .192 C4
Quays The BS1. . . . . .194 C1
Quay The GL1. . . . . .196 A3
Quebec Dr GL51 . . . . .132 E3
Quedgeley East Bsns Pk
GL10 . . . . .109 F3
Quedgeley West Bsns Pk
GL2. . . . . .109 D5
Quedgeley BS37 . . . . .43 B3
Quedgeley Distribution Ctr
GL2. . . . . .109 F5
Quedgeley Ent Ctr GL2. . .110 B8

Quedgeley Enterprise Ctr
GL2. . . . . .118 A1
Queen Ann Rd BS5. . . . . .190 E5
Queen Anne Rd BS5. . . . . . .9 B6
Queen Charlotte St BS1 . .195 A2
Queen Charlton La BS14. . . .3 E2
Queen Elizabeth Rd GL7. .190 E4
Queen Elizabeth's Hospital
Sch BS8. . . . . .194 B3
Queen Margaret Prim Sch
and Children's Ctr Com Sch
GL20 . . . . .192 C2
Queen Quay BS1. . . . . . . .195 A2
Queens Acre GL14 . . . . . .156 F6
Queens Ave SN6 . . . . . . .145 D3
Queen's Ave BS8. . . . . . . .194 B3
Queen's Cir GL50 . . . . . . .193 B2
Queens Cl GL3 . . . . .128 A1
Queens Ct
Cheltenham GL50. . . . . . .130 A8
⬛ Tewkesbury GL20 . . . .192 C4
Queen's Ct
Brimscombe GL5 . . . . . . .148 A5
Bristol BS8. . . . . .194 B3
Ledbury HR8 . . . . .178 C4
Queensdale Cres BS4 . . . . .9 A1
Queens Down Ct BS4. . . . . .9 A3
Queensdown Gdns BS4. . . .9 C2
Queens Down Gdns BS4. . . .9 C2
Queens Dr BS15 . . . . .10 B4
Queen's Dr
Bristol BS7. . . . . .18 C5
Stroud GL5. . . . . .98 E8
Queens Field GL7 . . . . . . .152 E4
Queens Gate BS9 . . . . . . .17 D5
Queenshill Rd BS4 . . . . . . .9 A1
Queensholm Ave BS16 . . . .30 E1
Queensholm Cl BS16. . . . . .30 E1
Queensholm Cres BS16. . . .30 E1
Queensholm Dr BS16. . . . . .30 E1
Queens La GL50. . . . . .193 A2
Queensmead
Bredon GL20 . . . . .182 D7
Painswick GL6 . . . . .103 E7
Queens Par
Bristol BS1. . . . . .194 C2
Cheltenham GL50. . . . . . .193 A2
Queen Sq
Bristol BS1. . . . . .195 A2
Saltford BS31 . . . . .5 F3
Queen Square Ave ⬛
BS1 . . . . .195 A2
Queens Rd
Bristol BS6. . . . . .9 C2
Hannington SN6 . . . . .145 A4
Keynsham BS31. . . . . .4 D4
Tewkesbury GL20 . . . . . . .192 D2
Queen's Rd
Bristol, Ashley Down BS7 . .18 F5
Bristol, Bishopsworth BS13,
BS41. . . . . .7 F4
Bristol, Cadbury Heath BS30 11 B4
Bristol, Crew's Hole BS5 . . . .9 F7
Bristol, Victoria Park BS8 . .194 A3
Cheltenham GL50. . . . . . .130 B8
Chepstow/Cas-Gwent NP16 .60 E6
Pucklechurch BS16 . . . . . .22 B5
Stonehouse GL10 . . . . . . .97 F7
Stroud GL5 . . . . .99 B6
Queen's Retreat GL51 . . .133 B2
Queens Sq
Stroud GL5 . . . . .99 D7
⬛ Winchcombe GL54 . . . .174 A7
Queen St
Avonmouth BS11 . . . . . . .26 A1
Bristol BS2. . . . . .195 B3
Bristol, Eastville BS5. . . . . .19 D3
Bristol, St George BS15. . . .10 B8
Chedworth GL54 . . . . . . .159 A7
Cheltenham GL51. . . . . . .133 F1
Cirencester GL7. . . . . . . .190 D3
Lydney GL15. . . . . .92 B4
Queensway
Bristol BS34. . . . . .29 D6
Coleford GL16 . . . . .155 B5
Queens Way GL12. . . . . . .68 B7
Queen's Way HR8. . . . . . .178 E8
Queens Wlk BS35 . . . . . . .64 B3
Queens Wood Forest Trails★
GL18 . . . . .170 B7
Queen Victoria Rd BS6 . . .18 A4
Queen Victoria St BS2. . . . .9 A6
Queenwood Gr GL52 . . . .134 D5
Quenneys Cl GL4. . . . . . . .119 C3
Querns La GL7. . . . . .190 C3
Querns Rd GL7. . . . . .190 C3
Querns Westonbirt Sch
GL8. . . . . .58 F8
Quickthorn Cl BS14. . . . . . .3 A6
Quietways GL10. . . . . .97 E8
Quilter Gr BS4 . . . . .2 D7
Quinton Cl GL3 . . . . .128 B6

R

Rackham Cl BS7 . . . . .19 B6
Rackhay BS1 . . . . .195 A2
Radburn Cl ⬛ GL56 . . . . .187 B3
Radley Rd BS16 . . . . .20 B4
Radnor Bsns Ctr BS7. . . . .18 E5
Radnor Rd
Bristol, Horfield BS7 . . . . .18 E5
Bristol, Westbury on Trym
BS9. . . . . .18 B5
Cheltenham GL51. . . . . . .129 E6

Pou–Rec 229

Raeburn Rd BS5 . . . . .10 B6
Rag La GL12 . . . . .53 D5
Raglan Gdns ⬛ GL15 . . . . .92 A3
Raglan La BS5 . . . . .10 A7
Raglan Pl
Bristol BS7. . . . . .18 D3
Thornbury BS35. . . . . .51 B8
Raglan Rd BS7. . . . . .18 D3
Raglan St GL1 . . . . .196 C2
Raglan Way
Chepstow/Cas-Gwent
NP16. . . . . .60 F5
Uley GL11 . . . . .89 B1
Raglan Wlk BS31. . . . . .4 D4
Ragnall GL12 . . . . .68 D8
Ragnal La GL6 . . . . .91 A3
Raikes Rd GL1 . . . . .118 D6
Railton Jones Cl BS34. . . . .29 E3
Railway Arches BS2. . . . . .195 C2
Railway Cotts BS37 . . . . . .33 E8
Railway Dr ⬛ GL16. . . . . .155 A5
Railway Rd GL14 . . . . . . .191 C1
Railway Terr
Bristol BS16. . . . . .20 C4
Kemble GL7 . . . . .141 F8
Lechlade on T GL7 . . . . . .153 C3
Lydney GL15. . . . . .84 A8
Railway View GL15 . . . . . .148 A5
Rainbow Ct BS37. . . . . . . .43 B3
Raleigh Cl
Innsworth GL3. . . . . .127 F8
Saltford BS31 . . . . .5 D2
Raleigh Rd BS3 . . . . .8 B4
Ralph Rd BS7. . . . . .18 F4
Ram Hill BS36 . . . . .31 D5
Ramsdale Rd GL2 . . . . . . .118 B4
Ramsey Rd BS7 . . . . .18 F7
Rams Leaze BS34 . . . . . . .29 A7
Rance Pitch GL4 . . . . .119 E2
Randall Cl BS15. . . . . .20 F2
Randall Rd
Bristol BS8. . . . . .194 B2
Upper Rissington GL54 . . .169 D6
Randalls Field GL6. . . . . . .103 F7
Randalls Gn GL6 . . . . . . .148 C5
Randolph Ave
Bristol BS13. . . . . .2 B5
Yate BS37 . . . . .43 D4
Randolph Cl
Bristol BS13. . . . . .2 B5
Cheltenham GL53. . . . . . .130 F6
Randwick CE Prim Sch
GL6. . . . . .102 D2
Randwick Rd GL4 . . . . . . .118 D3
Rangers Ave GL11. . . . . . .80 C7
Rangers The GL11. . . . . . .80 C7
Rangers Wlk BS15 . . . . . . .10 C4
Range The GL2 . . . . .125 D5
Rangeworthy CE Prim Sch
BS37. . . . . .52 F1
Ranmoor GL4. . . . . .119 D3
Rannoch Rd BS7. . . . . .28 F1
Raphael Ct BS1 . . . . .195 B1
Ratcliffe Dr BS34 . . . . . . .29 E5
Ratcliff Lawns GL52 . . . . .134 B8
Rathbone Cl BS36. . . . . . . .31 C5
Rathmore Ct ⬛ GL54. . . . .174 A7
Raven Cl GL4 . . . . .119 C4
Raven Ct BS9 . . . . .17 F8
Ravendale Dr BS30. . . . . . .11 B2
Ravenglass Cres BS10. . . . .28 D2
Ravenhead Dr BS14 . . . . . .3 B8
Ravenhill Rd BS3 . . . . .8 F2
Ravenscourt Rd BS34 . . . . .29 B7
Ravensgate Rd GL53 . . . . .131 B4
Ravens Wood BS30. . . . . . .11 B3
Ravenswood Rd BS6 . . . . .18 C1
Ravis Cl GL4 . . . . .119 B6
Rawnsley Ho ⬛ BS5 . . . . .19 A1
Rayleigh Rd BS9 . . . . .17 E7
Raymend Rd BS3 . . . . .8 E3
Raymend Wlk BS3 . . . . . . .8 E2
Raymill BS4 . . . . .10 A2
Raymond Ho BS16 . . . . . . .20 F4
Raynes Rd BS3. . . . . .8 A3
Raysfield Inf Sch BS37 . . . .32 F8
Reaburn Cl ⬛ GL52 . . . . .131 B6
Reade Cl BS15. . . . . .10 D4
Reades Piece WR11. . . . . .188 C6
Reade St ⬛ NP25 . . . . . . .154 A7
Reading Ct BS15. . . . . .10 B8
Read Way GL52 . . . . .137 F2
Ready Token GL7 . . . . . . .151 F7
Rea La GL2 . . . . .118 A6
Rea The GL2 . . . . .117 F5
Rectory Barns GL54 . . . . .176 D4
Rectory Cl
Lower Swell GL54 . . . . . . .176 D4
Upton St Leonards GL4 . . .119 E2
Yate BS37 . . . . .43 F3
Rectory Cotts GL54. . . . . .176 D4
Rectory Ct GL52. . . . . . . .138 A4
Rectory La
Avening GL8 . . . . .148 B1
⬛ Bourton-on-t-W GL54. .168 F7
Bristol BS34. . . . . .29 A3
Cricklade SN6 . . . . .143 F4
Cromhall GL12 . . . . .53 A8
Gloucester GL2 . . . . .118 A6
Rectory Mdw GL17 . . . . . .164 F6

Rectory Rd
Easton-in-G BS20......... 16 B3
Frampton Cotterell BS36... 31 A8
Gloucester GL4 .... 119 C4
Red Admiral Dr GL4.... 119 E4
Redbrook CE Prim Sch
NP25............154 C4
Redcar Ct BS16....... 30 F1
Redcatch Rd BS4 .....8 F2
Redcliff Backs BS1... 195 B2
Redcliff Cres BS3....8 E4
Redcliffe Coll GL1 ....127 A2
Redcliffe Par E BS1... 195 A1
Redcliffe Par W BS1... 195 A1
Redcliffe Way BS1.... 195 B1
Redcliff Hill BS1..... 195 B1
Redcliff Mead La BS1... 195 B1
Redcliff St BS1...... 195 B2
Redcross Mews 16 BS2.. 195 C3
Redcross St BS2..... 195 C3
Redding GL2....... 117 E1
Reddings Cl GL15..... 147 E4
Reddings La GL14..... 191 F4
Reddings Pk GL15.... 129 D7
Reddings Rd GL51.... 129 C7
Reddings The
Bristol BS15...... 20 F2
Cheltenham BS15.... 129 B6
Chepstow/Cas-Gwent NP16 60 F5
Pendock WR13...... 180 A8
Red Ditch La GL19.... 179 D1
Redesdale Mews 6
GL56........... 187 A3
Redesdale Pl GL56..... 187 A2
Redfield Edge Prim Sch
BS30........... 11 D4
Redfield Educate Together
Prim Acad BS5...... 9 D7
Redfield Hill BS30..... 11 E3
Redfield Rd BS34..... 29 B7
Redford Cres BS13....1 F3
Redford La BS16...... 22 D4
Redford Wlk BS13.....1 F3
Redgrove Cotts GL51... 129 C8
Redgrove Pk GL51.... 129 D8
Redgrove Rd GL51.... 132 F4
Redham La BS35...... 38 F8
Redhill Cl BS16...... 19 E3
Redhill Dr BS16...... 19 E3
Redhill Farm Bsns Pk
BS35........... 49 F6
Redhill La BS35...... 49 E6
Redhouse La
English Bicknor GL16... 163 A2
Stroud GL5, GL6..... 98 D8
Red House La
Almondsbury BS32.... 40 B4
Bristol BS9....... 17 E6
Red La GL20....... 192 C5
Redland Cl GL2...... 127 B4
Redland Court Rd BS6... 18 C2
Redland Gr BS6...... 18 C2
Redland Green Rd BS6... 18 B3
Redland Green Sch BS8.. 18 C3
Redland High Sch BS6... 18 C2
Redland Hill BS6..... 18 B2
Redland Pk BS6...... 18 B2
Redland Rd BS6...... 18 C2
Redlands Cl SN6..... 145 D2
Redland Sta BS6..... 18 C2
Redland Terr 8 BS6... 18 B2
Red Lion Ct 2 GL1.... 119 A8
Red Lion La SN14..... 143 F4
Red Lion Mews SN6.... 145 D3
Redlynch La BS31..... 4 D2
Red Maids Jun Sch The
BS9............ 18 A6
Red Maids Sch The BS9.. 18 A6
Redmarley CE Prim Sch
GL19........... 179 D2
Redmarley Rd
Cheltenham GL52..... 134 B2
Newent GL18....... 171 A6
Rednock Dr GL11..... 88 A2
Rednock Sch GL11.... 88 A2
Redpoll Way GL4..... 119 C6
Red Rower Cl GL50.... 133 C5
Redshank Wlk BS11.... 27 A1
Redshelf Wlk BS10.... 28 C3
Redstart Way GL4.... 119 C6
Redthorne Way GL51... 129 E5
Red Well Rd BS4..... 119 C3
Redwick Cl BS11..... 27 C2
Redwick Crossroads BS35 38 C7
Redwick Gdns BS35.... 38 C7
Redwick & Northwick CE
Prim Sch BS35...... 48 D2
Redwick Rd
Pilning BS35........ 38 C8
Redwick BS35....... 38 B8
Redwind Way GL2.... 127 D5
Redwing Gdns BS16.... 19 E6
Redwood Cl
Bristol BS30....... 11 A3
Chepstow/Cas-Gwent NP16 60 E5
Gloucester GL1...... 118 D5
Redwood Ct
4 Cheltenham GL51... 132 D2
Northway GL20...... 182 C5
Redwood Ho
Bristol BS13....... 2 D3
Brookthorpe GL4..... 110 F5
Reed Cl BS16....... 18 D6

Reed Ct BS30....... 10 F3
Reedley Rd BS9......... 17 F5
Reedling Cl BS16...... 19 E6
Reeds SN6......... 143 E4
Reed's Row GL12..... 55 D7
Reema Hos The SN6.... 145 D1
Reevers Rd 25 GL18... 171 A4
Reeves Cl GL7...... 190 A2
Regency Cl GL10..... 97 E7
Regency Dr BS4...... 10 A2
Regent Apartments BS6.. 18 C3
Regent Arc GL50..... 193 B3
Regent Chambers GL50.. 193 B3
Regent Cl GL4...... 120 A5
Regent Ct
Cheltenham GL51..... 130 B8
Gloucester GL3..... 120 B6
Regent Ho 9 GL50.... 130 B8
Regent Rd BS3......8 D4
Regents Cl BS35..... 64 B2
Regent St
Bristol, Clifton Wood
BS8........... 194 A2
Bristol, Kingswood BS15.. 10 D8
Cheltenham GL50..... 193 B3
Gloucester GL1..... 196 C1
Lydney GL15....... 92 B3
Stonehouse GL10..... 97 F7
Regents The BS31.....4 F6
Regents Wlk 5 GL15... 92 A3
Regent Way NP16.... 60 E8
Regis Cl GL53...... 131 A5
Reine Barnes Cl 7 GL11.. 80 B8
Remenham Dr BS9.... 18 B5
Remenham Pk BS9.... 18 B5
Remus Cl GL4...... 119 F6
Renard Rise GL5..... 98 C6
Rendcomb Cl GL4..... 119 E4
Rendcomb Coll GL7.... 158 C4
Rendcomb Dr GL7.... 190 B2
Rendle Ho BS16...... 20 F4
Rene Rd 12 BS5...... 19 B1
Repton Hall BS10.... 28 B2
Repton Rd BS4......9 D3
Reservoir Cl GL5..... 99 E7
Reservoir Rd
Gloucester GL4..... 118 F4
Stroud GL5........ 99 F7
Restway Wall 11 NP16.. 60 E8
Retort Rd BS11...... 26 C3
Retreat The
3 Broadway WR12.... 185 B8
Gloucester GL4..... 118 D2
Highworth SN6...... 145 C3
4 Tetbury GL8..... 140 C4
Reynolds Cl BS31..... 5 A5
Reynold's Wlk BS7.... 19 A7
Rhapsody Ct GL51.... 129 C6
Rhode Cl BS31...... 5 A3
Rhodesia Ho 1 GL51... 132 F4
Rhodfa John Rastrick/John
Rastrick Rise NP16.... 60 F4
Rhodfa Wyesham/Wyesham
Ave 4 NP25....... 154 A7
Ribble Cl GL43..... 120 F5
Ribblesdale BS35.... 51 D8
Ribston Hall GL1..... 196 A2
Ribston Hall High Sch
GL1........... 118 E5
Ribston Mews GL1.... 118 E5
Ricardo Dr GL11..... 88 B3
Ricardo Rd GL6...... 91 F7
Richard Pate Sch The
GL53........... 130 E4
Richard Pl GL20..... 192 D1
Richards Dr SN14.... 25 E1
Richards Rd GL51.... 133 B4
Richeson Cl BS10.... 27 F2
Richeson Wlk BS10.... 27 F2
Richmond Apartments
BS6........... 18 C3
Richmond Ave
Bristol, Montpelier BS6... 18 F2
Bristol, Stoke Gifford BS34.. 29 E5
Gloucester GL4..... 119 C6
Richmond Bldgs 4 BS5.. 98 D6
Richmond Cl BS31....4 D4
Richmond Ct
1 Ashton Keynes SN6.. 142 F5
Bristol BS34....... 39 F1
7 Bristol, Clifton BS8... 18 A2
2 Bristol, Windmill Hill BS3..8 F4
Richmond Dale 6 BS8.. 18 A2
Richmond Dr 4 GL52.. 134 A1
Richmond Gdns GL2.. 127 D5
Richmond Hill BS8.... 194 B3
Richmond Hill Ave BS8.. 194 B3
Richmond Hts BS8.... 194 B3
Richmond La BS8.... 194 B3
Richmond Mews BS8... 194 A3
Richmond Park Rd BS8.. 194 A3
Richmond Rd
Bristol, Mangotsfield
BS16........... 21 A5
Bristol, Montpelier BS6... 18 E1
Bristol, Pile Marsh BS5...9 E7
Tewkesbury GL20.... 192 E1
Richmond St BS3.....8 F4
Richmonds The GL4... 119 D4
Richmond Terr
Avonmouth BS11..... 26 B1
Bristol BS8....... 194 A3
Rickfield The NP25.... 162 A1
Rickyard Way GL2.... 100 E5
Riddle St GL13..... 94 B3
Ride The BS15...... 21 A2

Ridgehill BS9....... 18 C6
Ridge Jun Sch The BS37.. 43 F2
Ridgemeade BS14.....3 B4
Ridgemont Rd GL5.... 99 E6
Ridgemount Cl GL3.... 120 E5
Ridgemount Gdns BS14.. 3 B5
Ridge Pl GL17...... 163 D1
Ridge's La GL8..... 140 C7
Ridge The
Bristol BS11....... 47 D8
Broad Blunsdon SN26... 144 D1
Bussage GL6....... 148 B6
Coalpit Heath BS36... 31 D7
Ridgeway
Coalpit Heath BS36... 31 D7
Eastnor HR8...... 179 B8
Monmouth/Trefynwy
NP25........... 154 A7
Yate BS37........ 44 A2
Yorkley GL15...... 156 B2
Ridgeway Cres HR9... 162 D4
Ridgeway Ct
Bristol, Henbury BS10... 28 A1
Bristol, Hengrove BS14...3 C5
Ridgeway Gdns BS14... 3 C5
Ridgeway Ind Ctr BS5... 19 E2
Ridgeway La
Bristol BS14.......3 B5
Marston Meysey SN6... 144 B6
Ridgeway Par BS5.... 19 E3
Ridgeway Rd
Bristol BS16....... 19 F3
Long Ashton BS41.....7 A2
Ridgeways GL56..... 177 C8
Ridgeway The
Bristol BS10....... 28 A1
Bussage GL6....... 148 B6
Crudwell SN16...... 141 C3
Ridge Wlk GL17..... 164 A4
Ridgewood BS9...... 17 D3
Riding Barn Hill BS30... 12 A6
Ridingleaze BS11..... 27 A1
Ridings Cl BS37..... 44 D1
Ridings Federation
Winterbourne International
Acad The BS36..... 30 D6
Ridings Federation Yate Int
Acad The BS37..... 43 E1
Ridings Rd BS36..... 31 C6
Ridings The
Bristol BS13........1 E4
Coalpit Heath BS36... 31 C6
Maisemore GL2..... 126 A7
Nailsworth GL6..... 91 C3
Ridler Rd GL15...... 92 C2
Ridley Ave BS15..... 21 A3
Rigestate Ind Est G13... 85 F5
Rigsby's La SN16.... 142 D3
Ringer's Cl GL19.... 173 C7
Ring Fence GL15..... 147 B3
Ringfield Cl GL6..... 91 C3
Ringspit La BS14......3 E1
Ringswell SN14...... 15 A7
Ringwood Cres BS10... 28 D1
Ripley Rd BS5...... 20 A1
Ripon Ct BS16...... 30 F2
Ripon Rd BS4.......9 E6
Rippledale Cl GL51.... 129 E7
Risdale Rd BS3......7 F1
Risedale Ho BS15.... 10 D5
Rise The GL54...... 166 E5
Rising Sun La GL52... 138 E2
Rissington Cl GL51.... 129 E8
Rissington Rd
Bourton-on-t-W GL54.. 169 A6
Gloucester GL4..... 118 E3
Rivelands Rd GL51... 133 B7
Riverdale GL14..... 157 A6
Rivergate BS1...... 195 C2
Riverland Dr BS13.....1 F5
Riverleaze BS9..... 17 C5
River Leys GL51.... 132 F5
River Mead BS37.... 43 C3
Rivermead GL2...... 126 E4
River Rd BS37...... 44 A1
Riverside
Dursley GL11....... 88 A4
Winchcombe GL54.... 174 A7
Riverside Bsns Pk BS4...9 D6
Riverside Cl
Bristol BS11....... 16 F5
Charlton Kings GL52... 131 B6
Riverside Cotts
Bristol BS15...... 10 B1
Brockworth GL3.... 120 E5
Riverside Ct
2 Bristol BS4......9 F6
Tewkesbury GL20.... 192 C5
Riverside Dr BS16.... 20 C7
Riverside Mews BS4...9 F6
Riverside Pk
Eastington GL10..... 97 A8
23 Monmouth/Trefynwy
NP25........... 154 A7
Severn Beach BS35... 37 F6
Riverside Steps BS4....9 E7
Riverside Way BS15... 10 C3
Riverside Wlk 6 BS5...9 F6
Riversley Rd GL2.... 127 C2
Riversmeet GL3..... 120 F5
Riversmill GL11..... 80 D8
Riversmill Ct GL11.... 80 D8
Riversmill Wlk GL11... 80 D8
River St BS2....... 195 C3
Rivers Way SN6..... 145 C3

River Terr BS31......4 F5
River View
Bristol BS16....... 19 E5
Chepstow/Cas-Gwent NP16 60 E8
Riverview Way GL51... 133 A4
River Way GL7...... 142 F8
Riverwood Ho BS16.... 30 C1
Riverwood Rd BS16.... 30 C1
Riviera Cres BS16.... 20 E4
Riviera Way BS34.... 30 A4
Rixon Gate SN6..... 143 A5
Roach's La GL9..... 46 D2
Road Hill SN14...... 15 D1
Road Two BS10...... 38 A3
Robbers Rd GL6..... 102 C2
Robbins Cl
Bristol BS32....... 29 F6
Marshfield SN14..... 14 F8
Stroud GL5........ 98 C6
Robbins Ct BS16..... 21 B6
Robel Ave BS36..... 31 A8
Robert Burns Ave GL51.. 129 D7
Robert St
Bristol BS11....... 21 B7
Leigh Woods BS8.....7 D7
Robert Franklin Way
GL7........... 143 A8
Robert Harvey Ho 4
GL52........... 193 C4
Robert Raikes Ave
Gloucester GL4..... 118 D2
Gloucester GL4..... 118 E2
Roberts Cl
Bishop's Cleeve GL52... 137 F4
Stratton GL7....... 190 B8
Robertson Dr BS4.....9 F6
Robertson Rd
Bristol BS5....... 19 C2
Shurdington GL51.... 129 D2
Roberts Rd
Cheltenham GL52.... 134 D3
Innsworth GL3..... 127 E7
Robert St
Bristol, Baptist Mills BS5... 19 B2
16 Bristol, Russell Town BS5 9 B7
Robin Cl
Bristol, Brentry BS10.... 28 B2
Bristol, Stockwood BS14....3 D6
2 Chalford GL6.... 148 C6
Gloucester GL4..... 119 C5
Northway GL20..... 182 B5
Robin Ct GL10...... 97 F8
Robin Hood Junc GL16... 154 F6
Robinhood St GL1.... 118 D7
Robinia Cl GL53..... 131 B5
Robinia Wlk BS14.....3 A7
Robins Cl GL52..... 134 A2
Robins End GL3..... 127 D7
Robinson Cl GL18.... 171 A5
Robinson Dr BS5.....9 A8
Robinson La
Upper Lydbrook GL17... 163 D2
Woodmancote GL7.... 158 B4
Robinson Rd GL1.... 118 E7
Robinswood Gdns GL4.. 119 A4
Robinswood Hill Ctry Pk*
GL4........... 118 F3
Robins Wood Hill Ctry Pk*
GL4........... 119 A4
Robinswood Pl 11 GL4.. 119 C4
Robinswood Prim Sch
GL4........... 119 C3
Robin Way BS37..... 33 A7
Rochester Cl GL51.... 130 A5
Rochester Rd BS4.....9 F5
Rock Cl BS4.......9 E2
Rock Cotts
Pill BS20........ 16 E4
Stroud GL5........ 99 C8
Rockfield Business Pk
GL53........... 130 D5
Rock & Fountain La
GL14........... 157 E8
Rockhill Est BS31.....4 F4
Rockhill Ho BS31.....4 F4
Rock Ho BS10...... 28 C3
Rockingham Gdns BS11.. 17 A8
Rockingham Rdbt BS11.. 26 D6
Rock La
Bristol BS34....... 29 F4
Coleford GL16..... 155 A5
Northwood Green GL14.. 165 E1
Rockland Cl BS16.... 20 C7
Rockland Gr BS16.... 19 D5
Rockland Rd BS16.... 20 D7
Rockleaze
Bristol BS9....... 17 E2
9 Thornbury BS35.... 64 B1
Rockleaze Ave BS9.... 17 E3
Rockleaze Ct BS9.... 17 E3
Rockleaze Rd BS9.... 17 E3
Rockleigh Cl GL4.... 118 E3
Rockness Hill GL6.... 91 A2
Rock Rd
Dursley GL11....... 87 D4
Keynsham BS31.....4 E5
Wick BS30........ 12 D8
Rockside Ave BS16.... 20 F8
Rockside Dr BS9.... 18 C6
Rockside Gdns
Bristol BS16....... 20 F8
Frampton Cotterell BS36... 31 D3
Rocks Rd GL17..... 163 D3
Rock St
Chaceley GL19..... 181 B1

Rock St continued
Thornbury BS35...... 51 B8
Rocks The GL16..... 155 A3
Rockstowes Way BS10.. 28 D3
Rock The BS4.......9 E3
Rock Villa La NP16.... 72 F1
Rockwell Ave BS11.... 27 B5
Rockwood Ho BS37.... 44 A4
Rockwood Rd NP16... 60 E7
Rodborough BS37.... 32 C7
Rodborough Ave GL5... 99 B6
Rodborough Com Prim Sch
GL5........... 99 B6
Rodborough Hill GL5... 99 B6
Rodborough La GL5... 99 C5
Rodborough Terr GL5... 99 B5
Rodborough Way BS15.. 11 A7
Rodbourne Rd BS10.... 18 E6
Rodfords Mead BS14....3 A7
Rodford Way BS37.... 32 D6
Rodley Rd GL15..... 92 C3
Rodley Sq GL15..... 92 C3
Rodmarton Sch GL7... 149 E6
Rodmead Wlk BS13.....2 A4
Rodney Ave BS15.... 10 A3
Rodney Cl GL2...... 127 B4
Rodney Cres BS34.... 29 A4
Rodney Pl BS8..... 194 A3
Rodney Rd
Bristol BS15...... 10 A3
Cheltenham GL50.... 193 B3
Saltford BS31.......5 E2
Rodney Wlk BS15.... 20 A1
Rodway Ct BS16..... 21 B3
Rodway Hill BS16.... 21 B3
Rodway Hill Rd BS16... 21 A4
Rodway La BS19, GL2... 172 E3
Rodway Rd
Bristol BS34....... 29 A8
Bristol, Mangotsfield BS16.. 21 A5
Bristol, Patchway BS34... 28 F7
Rodway View BS15.... 20 F3
Roebuck Mdws GL17... 163 F3
Roegate Dr BS4.....9 F6
Roegate Ho BS5..... 20 A1
Roel Gate GL54..... 174 D3
Rogers Cl BS30...... 11 B5
Rogers Ct BS37..... 44 C1
Rogers Wlk BS30.... 11 D7
Rokeby Ave BS6..... 18 C1
Rollers The GL6..... 91 B4
Rolleston Way BS15... 129 F7
Rolling Stones 4 GL55.. 189 C4
Rolph Ct 8 GL56.... 187 A2
Roman Amphitheatre*
GL7........... 190 B4
Roman Farm Ct BS11... 27 C2
Roman Farm Rd BS4....2 F1
Roman Hackle Ave GL50.133 C5
Roman Rd
Bristol BS5....... 19 B1
Cheltenham GL51.... 133 D4
Gloucester GL4..... 119 E6
Roman Way
Bourton-on-t-W GL54... 169 A8
Bristol BS9....... 17 C4
Brockworth GL3.... 120 E6
Coleford GL16..... 155 A5
Highworth SN6...... 145 C3
Lechlade on T GL7.... 153 E3
Littledean GL14..... 191 F4
Roman Wlk
Bristol, Kensington Park
BS4........... 9 C3
Bristol, Stoke Gifford BS34.. 29 E5
Roman Wy BS15..... 10 C4
Romney Ave BS7.... 19 B6
Romney Cl GL1..... 118 E5
Romney Rd GL8..... 140 B4
Romo Ct BS16...... 20 C4
Ronald Rd BS16..... 19 F6
Ronayne Wlk BS16.... 20 C6
Ron Jones Ho 3 BS1... 195 B4
Rookery La
Newton GL13....... 85 E7
Pilning BS35....... 39 A6
Pucklechurch BS30, SN14.. 22 F4
St Briavels GL15.... 154 F2
Rookery Rd
Bristol BS4.......9 A3
Innsworth GL3..... 127 D6
Rookery The GL54.... 159 A6
Rookery Villas GL2.... 116 A3
Rookery Way SN14.....2 F4
Rooksmoor Hill GL5... 99 A3
Roosevelt Ave GL52... 131 A8
Ropewalk GL20..... 192 D4
Rope Walk Ho BS2... 195 C3
Rope Wlk 3 GL12.... 68 B7
Rope Wlk The GL5.... 99 B3
Rosary RC Prim Sch The
GL5........... 99 B7
Rosary Rdbt The BS16.. 21 D7
Rosary The
Bristol BS16....... 21 D7
Bristol BS16....... 29 F2
Chepstow/Cas-Gwent NP16 72 D1
Rose Acre BS10..... 28 A3
Rosebank BS5...... 19 D2
Rosebay Gdns GL51... 132 E5
Rosebay Mead BS16... 19 E5
Roseberry Pk BS5.....9 D8
Roseberry Rd BS5.....9 C7
Roseberry Terr GL6... 148 C5
Rosebery Ave
Bristol BS2....... 19 A1

Rosebery Ave *continued*
Gloucester GL1 . . . . 118 E6
Rosebery Mount GL11 . . . . 80 C8
Rosebery Pk GL11 . . . . 80 C8
Rosebery Rd GL11 . . . . 80 C8
Rosebery Terr BS8 . . . . . . 194 B2
Rose Cl BS36 . . . . 30 E4
Rose & Crown Ho GL50 . . 193 B4
Rose & Crown Pas GL50 . 193 B4
Rosedale Ave GL10 . . . . 98 A7
Rosedale Cl GL2 . . . . 109 D8
Rosedale Rd BS16 . . . . 20 C3
Rosefield Cres GL20 . . . . . 192 F4
Rose Green Cl BS5 . . . . 19 E2
Rose Green Rd BS5 . . . . . . 19 D2
Rosehill Ct GL7 . . . . 190 C7
Rosehill St GL52 . . . . 130 F8
Rosehill Terr 6 GL52 . . . . 130 F8
Rosehip Ct GL51 . . . . 130 A4
Rosehip Way GL52 . . . . . . 137 E4
Rose La BS36 . . . . 31 D6
Roselarge Gdns BS10 . . . . 28 A2
Roselle Dr GL3 . . . . 120 B4
Rosemary Cl
Bristol BS32 . . . . 29 F7
Gloucester GL4 . . . . 119 D4
Rosemary La
Bristol BS5 . . . . 19 C2
Stroat NP16 . . . . 146 F1
Rosemary Terr GL12 . . . . . 68 B7
Rose Mead BS7 . . . . 19 A7
Rose Meadow Vw BS3 . . . . . .7 E1
Rose Meare Gdns BS13 . . . . .1 E7
Rosemont Terr BS8 . . . . . 194 A2
Rosemount Ct BS15 . . . . . . 10 B8
Rose Oak Dr BS36 . . . . 31 D7
Rose Oak Gdns
Bristol BS15 . . . . 20 F3
Coalpit Heath BS36 . . . . 31 D7
Rose Oak La BS36 . . . . 31 D7
Rose Rd BS5 . . . . .9 E7
Rose Row GL54 . . . . 176 B2
Rosery Cl BS9 . . . . 18 A8
Rosery The BS16 . . . . 20 C3
Rose Terr BS8 . . . . 194 B3
Rose Tree Ho BS16 . . . . 20 F4
Rosevear BS2 . . . . 9 A7
Roseville Ave BS30 . . . . 11 A2
Rose Way GL7 . . . . 190 E2
Rose Willis Ct 10 GL18 . . . 171 A4
Rose Wlk BS16 . . . . 20 C3
Rosewood Ave BS35 . . . . . 50 F5
Rosewood Wlk GL52 . . . . . 138 B4
Roshni Gar E 16 BS5 . . . . . 19 B1
Roshni Gar W 15 BS5 . . . . . 19 B1
Rosling Rd BS7 . . . . 18 E6
Roslyn Rd BS6 . . . . 18 C1
Rossall Ave BS34 . . . . 29 C6
Rossall Rd BS4 . . . . 9 D3
Ross Cl BS37 . . . . 44 B1
Rossiter's La BS5 . . . . 10 A6
Rossiter Wood Ct BS11 . . . 27 B2
Rosslyn Way BS35 . . . . 64 C3
Ross Rd
Berry Hill GL16 . . . . 155 A8
Mitcheldean GL17 . . . . 164 D6
Newent GL18 . . . . 170 F5
Rothermere Cl GL51 . . . . . 129 F5
Rothleigh GL51 . . . . 129 E5
Rotunda Terr GL50 . . . . . . 193 A2
Rougemont Gr NP16 . . . . . 60 F4
Rounceval St BS37 . . . . 44 A1
Roundabouts The GL5 . . . . 99 F1
Roundhills Mead SN6 . . . 145 D4
Roundhouse Mews 7
GL56 . . . . 187 A3
Roundmoor Cl BS31 . . . . 5 D3
Roundmoor Gdns BS14 . . . . 3 D7
Roundways BS36 . . . . 31 D6
Rousham Rd BS5 . . . . 19 A3
Roves La SN6 . . . . 145 D1
Rowacres BS14 . . . . .2 F6
Rowan Cl BS16 . . . . 20 A2
Rowan Ct
10 Bristol BS5 . . . . 9 B7
Yate BS37 . . . . 43 C3
Rowandean GL14 . . . . 191 C5
Rowan Dr
Chepstow/Cas-Gwent
NP16 . . . . 60 E5
Tewkesbury GL20 . . . . 192 F1
Rowanfield Exchange
GL51 . . . . 133 A2
Rowanfield Inf & Jun Schs
GL51 . . . . 133 A2
Rowanfield Rd GL51 . . . . . 133 A1
Rowan Gdns GL3 . . . . 120 D6
Rowan Gr GL11 . . . . 88 A3
Rowan Ho BS13 . . . . 2 D4
Rowans The
Bristol BS16 . . . . 30 B1
Pontshill HR9 . . . . 164 B8
Woodmancote GL52 . . . . . 138 B3
Rowan Tree Ho BS16 . . . . . 20 F4
Rowan Way
Bristol BS15 . . . . 10 B3
15 Cheltenham GL51 . . . . . 129 E5
Nailsworth GL6 . . . . 90 F5
Rowan Wlk BS31 . . . . 4 C4
Rowberrow BS14 . . . . .2 F7
Rowcroft GL5 . . . . 99 B7
Rowcroft Retreat GL5 . . . . 99 B7
Rowe Ct GL50 . . . . 193 A3
Rowena Cade Ave GL50 . 130 B6
Rowland Ave BS16 . . . . 19 D4
Rowlandson Gdns BS7 . . . 19 B6
Rowley GL11 . . . . 88 A5
Rowley Mews GL11 . . . . . . 88 A5
Rowley St BS3 . . . . 8 C3
Rownham Cl BS3 . . . . .7 E4
Rownham Ct BS8 . . . . 194 A1
Rownham Hill BS8 . . . . .7 E6
Rownham Mead BS8 . . . . 194 A1
Rows The GL55 . . . . 188 D4
Row The
Aust BS35 . . . . 49 A7
Donnington GL56 . . . . 176 F7
Hawkesbury Upton GL9 . . . . 55 F3
Lechlade on T GL7 . . . . 153 F4
Southrop GL7 . . . . 153 C6
St Arvans NP16 . . . . 72 B6
Roxburgh BS8 . . . . .7 F8
Roxton Dr GL51 . . . . 129 C7
Royal Agricultural Coll
GL7 . . . . 150 B4
Royal Albert Rd BS6 . . . . . . 18 A4
Royal Cl BS10 . . . . 27 D3
Royal Cres GL50 . . . . 193 B3
Royal Ct 9 GL51 . . . . 132 D2
Royal Forest of Dean Coll
GL16 . . . . 155 B7
Royal Fort Rd BS2, BS8 . . 194 C3
Royal La GL1 . . . . 127 A2
Royal Oak Mews GL50 . . . 193 B4
Royal Oak Rd
Gloucester GL1 . . . . 196 A3
Upper Lydbrook GL17 . . . . 163 E3
Royal Oak Terr GL55 . . . . 188 F1
Royal Par BS8 . . . . 194 B3
Royal Parade Mews
GL50 . . . . 193 A2
Royal Park Mews 3
BS8 . . . . 194 A3
Royal Pk BS8 . . . . 194 A3
Royal Prom BS8 . . . . 194 B3
Royal Rd BS16 . . . . 21 A6
Royal Spring GL17 . . . . . . 165 A5
Royal Victoria Pk BS10 . . . 28 B2
Royal Well La GL50 . . . . . . 193 B3
Royal Well Pl GL50 . . . . . . 193 B3
Royal Well Rd GL50 . . . . . 193 B3
Royal West of England
Acad★ BS8 . . . . 194 B3
Royal York Cres BS8 . . . . . . .7 F6
Royal York Ho BS8 . . . . . . 194 A2
Royal York Mews BS8 . . . . 194 A2
Royal York Villas BS8 . . . 194 A2
Royate Hill BS5 . . . . 19 D2
Roycroft Rd BS34 . . . . 29 B2
Roy King Gdns BS30 . . . . . . 11 C6
Royston Wlk BS10 . . . . 28 D2
Rozel Rd BS7 . . . . 18 E5
Ruardean CE Prim Sch
GL17 . . . . 163 E4
Ruardean Dr GL4 . . . . 118 B2
Ruardean Garden Pottery★
GL17 . . . . 163 E4
Ruardean Rd GL17 . . . . . . 163 F3
Ruardean Wlk GL52 . . . . . 134 B2
Rubens Cl BS31 . . . . 5 A5
Ruby St BS3 . . . . 8 B3
Rudford Cl BS34 . . . . 40 B1
Rudge Cl BS15 . . . . 20 F2
Rudge The
Maisemore GL2 . . . . 126 B8
Yorkley GL15 . . . . 156 A1
Rudgeway Pk BS35 . . . . 50 F1
Rudgewood Cl BS13 . . . . 2 D4
Rudgleigh Ave BS20 . . . . . . 16 C4
Rudgleigh Rd BS20 . . . . 16 C4
Rudhall Ct GL1 . . . . 196 A3
Rudhall Gr BS10 . . . . 18 E7
Rudhall View HR9 . . . . 164 D8
Rudloe Dr GL2 . . . . 110 A7
Rudthorpe Rd BS7 . . . . 18 E5
Ruffet Cl GL16 . . . . 155 B4
Ruffet Rd BS36 . . . . 31 B4
Ruffet's Cl NP16 . . . . 60 D8
Ruffitt The GL14 . . . . 191 F5
Rugby Rd BS4 . . . . 9 D3
Rumsey Cl GL4 . . . . 119 E4
Runnings Rd GL51 . . . . . . 133 A5
Runnings The GL51 . . . . . 133 A6
Runnymead Ave BS4 . . . . . . 9 D2
Runnymede
Bristol BS15 . . . . 20 E1
Cheltenham GL51 . . . . 129 E5
Runswick Rd BS4 . . . . 9 C3
Rupert St
Bristol, Kingsdown BS1 . . . 195 A3
Bristol, Redfield BS5 . . . . 9 C7
Ruscombe Rd GL6 . . . . 102 E2
Rusham BS13 . . . . .1 F4
Rush Cl BS32 . . . . 40 D2
Rushes The GL2 . . . . 118 A2
Rushley La GL54 . . . . 174 A7
Rushmead La SN14 . . . . 24 F2
Rushton Dr BS36 . . . . 31 D7
Rushworth Cl GL51 . . . . . . 132 D2
Rushworth Ho GL51 . . . . . 132 D2
Rushy BS30 . . . . 11 A4
Rushy Ho GL52 . . . . 134 A4
Rushyleaze GL15 . . . . 92 B2
Rushy Leaze BS34 . . . . 29 A7
Rushy Mews GL52 . . . . 134 A4
Rushy Way BS16 . . . . 31 A1
Ruskin Gr BS7 . . . . 19 A8
Ruskin Ho BS34 . . . . 29 A8
Ruskin Mill Coll GL6 . . . . . 91 A2
Ruspidge Cl GL4 . . . . 119 E5
Ruspidge Rd GL14 . . . . 156 C6
Russell Almshouses
GL20 . . . . 192 C3
Russell Ave BS15 . . . . 10 E7
Russell Cl GL9 . . . . 57 B3
Russell Gr BS6 . . . . 18 C5
Russell Pl GL51 . . . . 133 C3
Russell Rd
Bristol, Chester Park
BS16 . . . . 20 B2
Bristol, Westbury Park BS6 . 18 B4
Russell St
Cheltenham GL51 . . . . 133 C3
Gloucester GL1 . . . . 196 B2
Stroud GL5 . . . . 99 C7
Russell Town Ave BS5 . . . . . .9 B8
Russell Town Ind Pk 18
BS5 . . . . 9 C7
Russet Ave GL7 . . . . 153 F2
Russet Cl
Bredon GL20 . . . . 182 C7
Gloucester GL4 . . . . 118 B3
2 Ledbury HR8 . . . . 178 E7
Olveston BS35 . . . . 50 A3
Russet Ct GL12 . . . . 67 F4
Russet Rd GL51 . . . . 132 F3
Russett Way 24 GL18 . . . . 171 A4
Russ St BS2 . . . . 195 C2
Rustic Cl GL4 . . . . 119 C4
Rustic Pk BS35 . . . . 38 A6
Rutherford Cl BS30 . . . . 11 A3
Rutherford Way GL51 . . . 133 A5
Ruthven Rd BS4 . . . . .2 E8
Rutland Ave BS30 . . . . 11 A2
Rutland Ct 4 GL50 . . . . . . 133 B1
Rutland Pl GL7 . . . . 190 C3
Rutland Rd BS7 . . . . 18 E3
Ryalls La GL2 . . . . 95 E5
Rydal Ho BS34 . . . . 29 A8
Rydal Rd GL2 . . . . 127 B4
Rydal Wlk GL51 . . . . 129 E7
Ryder Cl GL11 . . . . 88 A4
Ryde Rd BS4 . . . . .9 B2
Ryder Row GL3 . . . . 127 E6
Rye Ave GL51 . . . . 132 D5
Rye Cl BS13 . . . . .1 E6
Ryeclose GL54 . . . . 169 A7
Rye Close Bglws GL54 . . . 169 A7
Rye Cres GL54 . . . . 169 A7
Ryecroft Ct BS36 . . . . 31 C7
Ryecroft Rd BS36 . . . . 31 C8
Ryecroft Rise BS41 . . . . .7 B1
Ryecroft St GL1 . . . . 196 C1
Ryedown La BS30 . . . . 11 D2
Ryeford Ind Est GL10 . . . . . 98 A6
Ryelands GL4 . . . . 118 C3
Ryelands Cl GL10 . . . . 97 E8
Ryelands Rd
7 Bream GL15 . . . . 147 D8
Stonehouse GL10 . . . . 97 E8
Ryelands The
36 Newent GL18 . . . . 171 A4
Randwick GL6 . . . . 102 D1
Ryeleaze Cl GL5 . . . . 99 C7
Ryeleaze Rd GL5 . . . . 99 C7
Rye St WR13 . . . . 180 A6
Ryeworth Dr GL52 . . . . . . 131 B7
Ryeworth Rd GL52 . . . . . . 131 B7
Ryland Cl GL8 . . . . 140 C5
Ryland Pl 1 BS2 . . . . 19 A2
Rylestone Cl BS36 . . . . 30 F8
Rylestone Gr BS9 . . . . 17 F5
Rysdale Rd BS9 . . . . 17 F6

S

Sabis International School
UK SN14 . . . . 15 C4
Sabre Cl GL2 . . . . 118 A3
Sabrina Way
Bristol BS9 . . . . 17 C4
Lydney GL15 . . . . 92 B4
Sackville App GL50 . . . . . 133 D4
Saco Ho BS1 . . . . 195 B2
Saddlers La GL50 . . . . 193 A1
Saddlers Rd GL2 . . . . 117 F2
Sadlers Ct 8 GL52 . . . . . . 130 F8
Sadlers Edge GL54 . . . . . . 169 A7
Sadlers Field 4 SN6 . . . . . 142 F5
Sadlier Cl BS11 . . . . 17 A8
Saffron Cl GL4 . . . . 119 A5
Saffron Rd GL20 . . . . 192 C4
Sage Cl GL3 . . . . 127 F6
Sages Mead BS32 . . . . 29 E8
St Agnes Ave BS4 . . . . .8 F2
St Agnes Gdns BS4 . . . . .8 F2
St Agnes Wlk BS4 . . . . .8 F2
St Aidans Cl GL51 . . . . 132 E2
St Aidan's Cl BS5 . . . . 10 B6
St Aidan's Rd BS5 . . . . 10 B6
St Albans Cl GL51 . . . . 130 A5
St Albans Rd GL2 . . . . 118 C5
St Alban's Rd BS6 . . . . 18 B4
St Aldams Dr BS16 . . . . 22 B5
St Aldate St GL1 . . . . 196 B3
St Aldwyn Rd GL1 . . . . 118 F6
St Aldwyn's Cl BS7 . . . . 18 F8
St Andrews
Ashleworth GL19 . . . . 172 D4
Bristol BS30 . . . . 11 B6
Yate BS37 . . . . 43 F1
St Andrew's Ave NP16 . . . . 60 E7
St Andrew's CE Prim Sch
GL54 . . . . 159 A6
St Andrew's CE Prim Sch
GL12 . . . . 66 A1
St Andrews Cl GL20 . . . . . 182 C4
St Andrews Gate Rdbt
BS11 . . . . 26 B2
St Andrews Gn GL3 . . . . . 128 B5
Saint Andrews Mews BS6 18 E3
St Andrew's Rd
Avonmouth BS11 . . . . 26 B1
Avonmouth BS11 . . . . 26 B4
Bristol BS6 . . . . 18 E2
St Andrews Road Sta
BS11 . . . . 26 B4
St Andrews Trad Est
BS11 . . . . 26 C2
St Annal's Rd GL14 . . . . . . 191 E4
St Anne's 13 GL52 . . . . 133 F2
St Anne's Ave BS31 . . . . 4 D6
St Anne's CE Prim Sch
BS30 . . . . 11 C3
St Annes Cl
7 Bristol BS5 . . . . .9 F6
Brockworth GL3 . . . . 120 E6
St Anne's Cl
Bristol BS30 . . . . 11 B4
Cheltenham GL52 . . . . 133 F2
St Annes Ct BS4 . . . . 9 D5
St Anne's Ct BS31 . . . . 4 D6
St Annes Dr BS30 . . . . 11 C2
St Anne's Dr
Coalpit Heath BS36 . . . . 31 C5
Wick BS30 . . . . 12 B7
St Anne's Inf Sch BS4 . . . . . 9 D5
St Anne's Jun Sch BS4 . . . . 9 D5
St Anne's Park Rd BS4 . . . . .9 E5
St Anne's Rd
Bristol, St Anne's Park BS4 . . 9 D6
Bristol, St George BS5 . . . . . 10 B6
Cheltenham GL52 . . . . 193 C3
St Anne's Terr
Bristol BS4 . . . . 9 E5
Cheltenham GL52 . . . . 193 C3
St Annes Way GL15 . . . . . 146 E7
St Ann's Cross 10 GL15 . . 147 D8
St Ann St NP16 . . . . 72 F1
St Ann Way GL1 . . . . 196 A1
St Anthony's Dr BS30 . . . . . 12 B7
St Anthony's Sch GL14 . . 191 D4
St Arild's Rd GL9 . . . . 57 B4
St Athan Cl GL2 . . . . 110 C7
St Aubin's Ave BS4 . . . . .9 F3
St Augustines of Canterbury
RC Sch BS16 . . . . 20 F7
St Augustine's Par BS1 . . 195 A2
St Augustine's Pl 1 BS1 195 A2
St Augustine's Working
Farm★ GL2 . . . . 157 B6
St Barbara's Cl GL20 . . . . 182 D4
St Barnabas CE Prim Sch
Bristol, Mont Pelier BS6 . . . 18 F1
Bristol, North Common
BS30 . . . . 11 C6
St Barnabas Cl
Bristol, Lower Knowle BS4 . . .8 F1
Bristol, Warmley BS30 . . . . . 11 C7
Gloucester GL1 . . . . 118 E4
St Barnabas Ho BS30 . . . . . 11 C7
St Bartholomews 12
GL18 . . . . 171 A4
St Bartholomews Cl GL11 . 87 F5
St Bartholomew's Rd BS7 18 F3
St Bede's RC Coll BS11 . . . 27 B2
St Bede's Rd BS15 . . . . 20 D2
St Benedicts Cl GL20 . . . . 192 C2
St Bernadette RC Prim Sch
BS14 . . . . .3 B6
St Bernadette RC Sec Sch
BS14 . . . . .3 B6
St Bernard's Cath Prim Sch
BS11 . . . . 16 E6
St Bernard's Rd BS11 . . . . 16 E6
St Birinus Ct GL7 . . . . 153 E3
St Blaize Ct GL7 . . . . 190 C4
St Bonaventure's Cath Prim
Sch BS7 . . . . 18 D4
St Brelades Gr BS4 . . . . .9 F5
St Brendan's Rd GL5 . . . . . 99 E7
St Brendans Rdbt BS11 . . . 26 C1
St Brendan's Sixth Form Coll
BS4 . . . . 10 A1
St Brendan's Way BS11 . . . 26 B1
St Brenda's Ct 1 BS8 . . . 194 A3
St Briavels Castle★
GL15 . . . . 146 E7
St Briavels Cl GL4 . . . . 118 B2
St Briavels Dr BS37 . . . . . . 32 D8
St Briavels Parochial CE
Prim Sch GL15 . . . . 146 E7
St Briavels Rd GL15 . . . . . 147 B2
Saintbridge Cl GL4 . . . . . . 119 B5
Saintbridge Pl GL4 . . . . . . 119 B5
St Bruel's Cl GL15 . . . . 146 F7
St Cadoc Ho BS31 . . . . .4 F5
St Catharine's RC Prim Sch
GL55 . . . . 188 F2
St Catherine Ct GL1 . . . . . 118 E7
St Catherine's Ind Est BS3 . 8 D3
St Catherine's Mead BS20 16 D3
St Catherines Pl 7 BS3 . . . 8 D4
St Catherine St GL1 . . . . . 196 B4
St Catherine's Terr BS3 . . . 8 D3
St Chad's Patchway CE VC
Prim Sch BS34 . . . . 40 C1
St Chloe Mead GL5 . . . . 91 B8
St Christopher's Sch BS6 . 18 B4
St Clair Cotts GL51 . . . . . . 173 F2
St Clements Ct
6 Bristol BS16 . . . . 20 D3
St Clements Ct *continued*
Keynsham BS31 . . . . 4 E4
St Clements Rd BS31 . . . . . . .4 F4
St Clement's Wlk GL7 . . . 190 C5
St Cyril's Rd GL10 . . . . 97 F7
St David's Ave BS30 . . . . . . 11 B5
St David's CE Prim Sch
GL56 . . . . 187 A3
St Davids Cl GL51 . . . . 130 A6
St David's Cl
Chepstow/Cas-Gwent
NP16 . . . . 60 E7
Gloucester GL4 . . . . 118 D3
St David's Cres BS4 . . . . .9 F6
St David's Ct GL56 . . . . . . 187 A3
St Davids Rd GL20 . . . . . . 182 C4
St David's Rd BS35 . . . . 64 C1
St Dominics RC Prim Sch
GL5 . . . . 91 A7
St Dunstans Cl BS31 . . . . . . .4 E6
St Dunstan's Rd BS3 . . . . 8 C2
St Edwards Ct 2 GL56 . . 187 A2
St Edwards Dr GL54 . . . . . 176 F4
St Edward's Prep Sch
GL52 . . . . 131 B7
St Edwards Rd GL54 . . . . . 176 F4
St Edward's Rd BS8 . . . . . 194 B2
St Edward's Sch GL52 . . . 131 A7
St Edwards Wlk GL53 . . . . 131 A6
St Edyth's Rd BS9 . . . . 17 C6
SS Gt Britain★ BS1 . . . . . 194 B1
SS Peter & Paul RC Prim Sch
BS8 . . . . 194 C4
St Ewens Rd NP16 . . . . 60 E6
St Fagans Ct BS30 . . . . 11 B2
St Francis Dr
Wick BS30 . . . . 12 B7
Winterbourne BS36 . . . . 30 F6
St Francis Rd
6 Bristol BS3 . . . . 8 A4
Keynsham BS31 . . . . 4 D6
St Gabriel's Bsns Pk 24
BS5 . . . . .9 B8
St Gabriel's Rd BS5 . . . . .9 B8
St George CE Prim Sch
BS1 . . . . 194 B2
St George Pl BS1 . . . . 194 C2
St George Rd NP16 . . . . 60 E7
St George's GL50 . . . . 193 B4
St Georges Ave 10 BS5 . . . . .9 F6
St George's Ave GL10 . . . . 98 A4
St Georges Bsns Pk
GL51 . . . . 133 A2
St Georges Cl GL10 . . . . . . 97 F4
St George's Cl
2 Cheltenham GL51 . . . . . 133 B2
Dursley GL11 . . . . 88 B3
Gloucester GL4 . . . . 118 C3
21 Moreton-in-M GL56 . . . 187 A3
St George's Dr GL51 . . . . . 133 B2
St George's Hill BS20 . . . . 16 A3
St Georges Ho BS5 . . . . .9 E8
St George's Ho BS1 . . . . . 194 B2
St George's Hts 12 BS5 . . . . 9 D7
St Georges Ind Est BS11 . . 26 B3
St George's Pl GL50 . . . . . 193 B3
St Georges Rd
Ashchurch GL20 . . . . 182 C4
Bristol BS1 . . . . 194 C2
Watermead GL3 . . . . 120 E5
St George's Rd
Cheltenham GL50 . . . . 193 A3
Dursley GL11 . . . . 88 A3
Keynsham BS31 . . . . 4 D6
St George's Sq GL50 . . . . 193 B4
St George's St GL50 . . . . . 193 B4
St George's Terr GL56 . . . 186 C6
St Georges Twr 5 GL50 . 193 B4
St Georges Way NP16 . . . . 61 B4
St Giles Barton GL12 . . . . . 55 D8
St Giles's Rd GL20 . . . . 182 C7
St Gregory's Rd BS7 . . . . . . 18 F8
St Helena Rd BS6 . . . . 18 B4
St Helens CE Prim Sch
BS35 . . . . 51 A4
St Helens Dr
Bristol BS30 . . . . 11 C2
Wick BS30 . . . . 12 C7
St Helen's Wlk BS5 . . . . . . 20 A1
St Helier Ave BS4 . . . . .9 F3
St Hilary Cl BS9 . . . . 17 D5
St Ivel Way BS30 . . . . 11 C6
St Ives Ct GL52 . . . . 133 F4
St James' GL2 . . . . 117 F1
St James' Barton BS1 . . . 195 B4
St James' Barton Rdbt
BS1 . . . . 195 B4
St James CE Jun Sch
GL1 . . . . 119 A8
St James CE Prim Sch
GL50 . . . . 130 B6
St James Cl BS35 . . . . 64 C3
St James' Cl GL2 . . . . 117 F1
St James Ct
Bristol BS32 . . . . 40 C3
4 Cheltenham GL50 . . . . . 193 A4
1 Moreton-in-M GL56 . . . 187 A2
St James Cvn Pk GL16 . . . 155 B3
St James & Ebrington CE
Prim Schs GL55 . . . . 189 A1
St James Mews 3 GL1 . . 119 A8
St James Pl BS16 . . . . 21 A5
St James' Pl GL50 . . . . 193 A1

St James' Rdbt GL50 . . . . **193** A4
St James's Ct BS8 . . . . **18** B1
St James Sq GL15 . . . . . . **147** D8
St James's Sq
  Cheltenham GL50 . . . . **193** B3
  20 Monmouth/Trefynwy
  NP25 . . . . **154** A7
St James's St BS16 . . . . . . **21** A5
St James St
  Cheltenham GL52 . . . . **193** C3
  Gloucester GL1 . . . . **18** B1
St James' St 18 NP25 . . . . . **154** A7
St James' Terr GL50 . . . . . **193** B2
St James Trad Est 4
  GL1 . . . . **119** A8
St Johns Ave
  Cheltenham GL52 . . . . **193** C3
  Churchdown GL3 . . . . **128** A6
St John's Bridge BS1 . . . . **195** A3
St John's CE Acad GL16 **155** A5
St John's CE Prim Sch
  Bristol BS8 . . . . **18** A2
  Cheltenham BS52 . . . . **193** C3
St John's CE Prim Sch
  BS31 . . . . **4** E5
St John's Cl
  Bishop's Cleeve GL52 . . . . **137** F4
  Stratton GL7 . . . . **190** B7
St John's Cres BS3 . . . . **8** E2
St Johns Ct
  Bristol, Bedminster BS3 . . . **8** D2
  Bristol BS16 . . . . **20** A3
  7 Coleford GL16 . . . . **155** A5
  Keynsham BS31 . . . . **4** E6
St John's Ct 3 GL50 . . . **133** B2
St John's Ct GL20 . . . . . . **136** A8
St John's Gdns NP16 . . . . . **72** D1
St John's Ho BS5 . . . . **9** D8
St John's La
  Bristol BS3 . . . . **8** E2
  Gloucester GL1 . . . . **196** B3
St John's Mead CE Prim Sch
  BS37 . . . . **44** B1
St John's-on-the-Hill Sch
  NP16 . . . . **72** F2
St John's Rd
  Bristol, Bedminster BS3 . . . **8** C3
  Bristol BS8 . . . . **18** A1
  Cirencester GL7 . . . . **190** C6
  Ruardean GL17 . . . . **163** F4
  Slimbridge GL2 . . . . **95** E3
St Johns Sq GL14 . . . . . . **191** C2
St John's St
  Bristol BS3 . . . . **8** C3
  12 Coleford GL16 . . . . . . **155** A5
  Lechlade on T GL7 . . . . . . **153** E2
St John St
  Hawkesbury Upton GL9 . . . . **56** A3
  2 Thornbury BS35 . . . . . . **64** B1
St Johns Way BS37 . . . . . **44** C2
St Joseph's RC Prim Sch
  BS16 . . . . **20** B3
St Joseph's RC Prim Sch
  GL10 . . . . **89** E6
St Joseph's Rd BS10 . . . . . **28** B3
St Judes Wlk GL53 . . . . . **130** F6
St Katherine's Hospl The
  Alms Houses 7 HR8 . . **178** F8
St Katherine's Sch BS20 . . **16** E3
St Kenya Ct BS31 . . . . **4** F5
St Keyna Prim Sch BS31 . . . **4** D5
St Keyna Rd BS31 . . . . **4** E5
St Kilda Par GL1 . . . . **196** C2
St Kingsmark Ave NP16 . . . **72** D1
St Ladoc Rd BS31 . . . . **4** D6
St Laud Cl BS9 . . . . **17** D5
St Lawrence CE Prim Sch
  GL7 . . . . **153** E2
St Lawrence Cl
  Chepstow/Cas-Gwent
  NP16 . . . . **60** D7
  Cirencester GL7 . . . . **190** B5
  Sandhurst GL2 . . . . **172** F2
St Lawrence La NP16 . . . . . **60** C7
St Lawrence Pk NP16 . . . . **60** C8
St Lawrence Rd
  Chepstow/Cas-Gwent
  NP16 . . . . **60** C8
  Gloucester GL4 . . . . **119** D8
  Lechlade on T GL7 . . . . . . **153** E2
St Leonard's CE Prim Acad
  SN26 . . . . **144** E1
St Leonards Cl
  Upper Minety SN16 . . . . . **142** B2
  Upton St Leonards GL4 . . . **177** E1
St Leonard's Ct OX7 . . . . **177** E1
St Leonard's Rd
  Bristol, Horfield BS7 . . . . . **18** E5
  Bristol, Lower Easton BS5 . . **19** C2
St Leonard's Row SN16 . . **142** B2
St Loe Cl BS14 . . . . **2** E3
St Loes Pitch GL5 . . . . **91** A8
St Lucia Cl BS7 . . . . **18** E7
St Lucia Cres BS7 . . . . **18** E7
St Lukes Cl BS16 . . . . **21** C7
St Luke's Cres BS3 . . . . **8** F4
St Luke's Ct BS3 . . . . **8** E4
St Luke's Gdns BS4 . . . . **9** E2
St Luke's Mews BS4 . . . . **9** E2
St Luke's Pl GL53 . . . . **193** C2
St Luke's Rd
  Bristol BS3 . . . . **8** E4
  Cheltenham GL53 . . . . **193** C2

St Lukes St GL1 . . . . **196** A1
St Luke St 18 BS5 . . . . **9** B7
St Margarets GL1 . . . . **127** A2
St Margaret's Cl BS31 . . . . . **4** D6
St Margarets Dr GL20 . . . **183** E4
St Margaret's Dr BS9 . . . . . **18** C5
St Margaret's Par 6
  GL50 . . . . **193** B4
St Margaret's Rd
  Cheltenham GL50 . . . . **193** B4
  Ruardean GL17 . . . . **163** F4
St Margaret's Terr 2
  GL52 . . . . **193** C4
St Mark's Ave 1 BS5 . . . . . **19** B1
St Mark's CE Jun Sch
  GL51 . . . . **129** D7
St Marks Church Ho 4
  BS5 . . . . **19** B1
St Marks Cl BS31 . . . . **4** D4
St Mark's Ct GL1 . . . . **196** C4
St Mark's Gr 8 BS5 . . . . . . **19** B1
St Mark's Ho 13 BS5 . . . . . **19** B1
St Mark's Rd BS5 . . . . **19** B1
St Mark St GL1 . . . . **196** B4
St Mark's Terr 11 BS5 . . . . . **19** B1
St Martins BS4 . . . . **9** B1
St Martin's Gdns BS4 . . . . . . **9** B1
St Martin's La SN14 . . . . . . **14** F8
St Martin's Pk SN14 . . . . . . **14** F8
St Martin's Rd BS4 . . . . **9** B2
St Martins Terr GL50 . . . . **133** B4
St Martin's Wlk BS4 . . . . **9** B1
St Mary Redcliffe CE Prim
  Sch BS3 . . . . **8** E4
St Mary Redcliffe & Temple
  CE Sch BS1 . . . . **195** B1
St Mary's Abbey Church★
  GL20 . . . . **192** C3
St Mary's Cath Prim Sch
  NP16 . . . . **60** E7
St Mary's CE Inf Sch
  GL52 . . . . **134** B3
St Mary's CE Prim Sch
  BS35 . . . . **64** A2
St Mary's CE Prim Sch
  BS37 . . . . **43** E2
St Mary's CE VA Prim Sch
  GL8 . . . . **140** B4
St Marys Cl
  Bristol BS30 . . . . **11** B5
  Dymock GL18 . . . . **178** D2
St Mary's Cl GL1 . . . . **196** A3
St Mary's Cl
  Kempsford GL7 . . . . **144** F7
  Lower Swell GL54 . . . . . . **176** D4
St Marys Dr GL7 . . . . **152** E4
St Marys Field GL7 . . . . . . **152** A3
St Mary's Halt★ GL15 . . . . **92** A2
St Mary's La GL20 . . . . . . **192** C4
St Mary's Mead GL6 . . . . . **103** E7
St Marys RC Prim Sch
  GL3 . . . . **127** F6
St Mary's Rd
  Bristol BS11 . . . . **16** D7
  Cirencester GL7 . . . . **190** E4
  Leigh Woods BS8 . . . . **7** D6
  Tetbury GL8 . . . . **140** B4
  Tewkesbury GL20 . . . . . . **192** B4
St Mary's Sq
  Gloucester GL1 . . . . **196** A3
  Lydney GL15 . . . . **92** C3
St Mary's St
  Gloucester GL1 . . . . **196** B3
  Painswick GL6 . . . . **103** F8
St Mary St
  8 Chepstow/Cas-Gwent
  NP16 . . . . **60** E8
  Thornbury BS35 . . . . **51** B8
St Mary Street Arc 9
  NP16 . . . . **60** E8
St Marys Way 6 BS35 . . . . **64** B1
St Mary's Way BS37 . . . . . **43** F2
St Mary's Wlk BS11 . . . . . . **16** D6
St Matthew's Ave 10 BS6 . **18** D1
St Matthew's CE Prim Sch
  GL5 . . . . **98** E7
St Matthews Ct GL5 . . . . . . **98** E6
St Matthew's Rd BS6 . . . . **195** A4
St Matthias Ho BS2 . . . . . **195** C3
St Matthias Pk BS2 . . . . . **195** C3
St Maur Gdns NP16 . . . . . **72** D1
St Mawgan St GL2 . . . . . . **110** B7
St Michaels 3 HR8 . . . . . **178** F8
St Michaels Ave GL52 . . . **138** A3
St Michael's Ave SN6 . . . . **145** C3
St Michaels CE Prim Sch
  BS36 . . . . **30** E6
St Michael's CE Prim Sch
  BS34 . . . . **29** C5
St Michaels Cl
  Bristol BS7 . . . . **18** E4
  Charlton Kings GL53 . . . . **131** A6
St Michael's Cl GL17 . . . . **165** B4
St Michael's Cl
  Mitcheldean GL17 . . . . . **164** D5
  Winterbourne BS36 . . . . . . **30** E7
St Michaels Ct BS15 . . . . . **10** B8
St Michael's Ct GL1 . . . . . **196** B2
St Michael's Hill BS2 . . . . **194** A4
St Michael's Hospl BS2 . **194** C4
St Michael's on the Mount CE
  Prim Sch BS2 . . . . **194** C3

St Michaels Pk GL14 . . . **191** C1
St Michael's Pk BS2 . . . . **194** C4
St Michael's Pl GL5 . . . . . . **98** D7
St Michaels Rd
  Cheltenham GL51 . . . . **130** B5
  Cirencester GL7 . . . . **190** C3
St Michael's Sq GL1 . . . . **196** B2
St Monica Ct BS9 . . . . **18** A5
St Nicholas Cl GL20 . . . . . **183** A3
St Nicholas Ct
  Gloucester GL1 . . . . **196** A3
  Hardwicke GL2 . . . . **109** E7
St Nicholas Dr GL50 . . . . **133** D5
St Nicholas of Tolentine RC
  Prim Sch BS5 . . . . **9** A8
St Nicholas Pk 10 BS5 . . . . **19** B1
St Nicholas Rd BS14 . . . . . . **3** C4
St Nicholas' Rd BS2 . . . . . . **18** F1
St Nicholas Sq GL1 . . . . . **196** A3
St Nicholas St BS1 . . . . . . **195** A4
St Oswald's Ct BS13 . . . . . . **2** A8
St Oswald's Ct BS6 . . . . . . **18** B3
St Oswald's Rd
  Bristol BS6 . . . . **18** B3
  Gloucester GL1 . . . . **196** A4
St Oswalds Ret Pk GL1 . . **126** D4
St Patricks Ct BS31 . . . . **4** E5
St Patrick's Ct GL53 . . . . . **120** E5
St Patrick's RC Prim Sch
  BS5 . . . . **9** D7
St Patricks Rd GL20 . . . . . **182** C4
St Patricks Vw BS5 . . . . **9** D7
St Paul's Catholic Prim Sch
  BS37 . . . . **32** E8
St Pauls Ct 5 BS6 . . . . . . **187** A2
St Paul's Ct GL1 . . . . **118** E7
St Paul's La GL50 . . . . **133** D3
St Paul's Par GL20 . . . . . **133** D3
St Paul's Prim Sch GL1 . . **196** A1
St Paul's RC Prim Sch
  BS37 . . . . **32** E8
St Paul's Rd
  2 Bristol, Southville BS3 . . . **8** D4
  Bristol, Victoria Park BS8 . . **194** B4
  Cheltenham GL50 . . . . **133** D3
  Gloucester GL1 . . . . **118** E7
St Paul's St N GL50 . . . . . **133** D3
St Paul's St S GL50 . . . . . **193** B4
St Paul St BS2 . . . . **195** B4
St Paul's Terr GL50 . . . . . **193** B4
St Peter's Anglican /
  Methodist VC Prim Sch
  BS35 . . . . **38** E6
St Peter's CE Prim Sch
  BS13 . . . . **1** F6
St Peters Cl
  Cheltenham GL51 . . . . **133** B4
  Rodmarton GL7 . . . . **149** B1
St Peter's Cl 9 GL14 . . . **157** A6
St Peter's Cres BS36 . . . . . **31** B8
St Peters Ct 3 GL56 . . . . **187** A2
St Peter's Ct GL7 . . . . **190** C4
St Peter's Ho BS8 . . . . **194** B2
St Peters La WR11 . . . . . . **183** F6
St Peter's RC High Sch &
  Sixth Form Ctr GL4 . . . . **118** E1
St Peter's RC Prim Sch
  GL1 . . . . **127** B2
St Peters Rd GL7 . . . . **190** C4
St Peter's Rd GL4 . . . . **119** C3
St Peter's Rise BS13 . . . . **2** B7
St Peters Sq GL51 . . . . . . **133** A4
St Peters Way 12 GL54 . . **174** A7
St Peters Wlk 3 BS9 . . . . **18** B6
St Philips Central BS2 . . . . . **9** A5
St Philip's Cl GL3 . . . . **120** A8
St Philips Cswy BS2 . . . . **9** B5
St Philip's Ct GL1 . . . . **118** D7
St Philips Trad Pk BS2 . . . . . **9** A7
St Phillips Rd BS2 . . . . **9** A7
St Phillip's St GL50 . . . . . **193** B1
St Pierre Dr BS30 . . . . **11** B6
St Pius X RC Prim Sch
  BS13 . . . . **2** A5
St Ronan's Ave BS6 . . . . . . **18** C1
St Rose's Specl Sch GL5 . . **99** B7
St Sampson's CE Prim Sch
  Cricklade SN6 . . . . **143** E4
  Cricklade SN6 . . . . **143** E4
St Saviours Ho BS4 . . . . **8** F2
St Saviour's Rise BS36 . . . . **31** B6
St Stephen's Ave BS1 . . . . **195** A4
St Stephens Bsns Ctr
  BS30 . . . . **11** C5
St Stephen's CE Jun Sch
  BS15 . . . . **20** D2
St Stephens Cl
  2 Bristol, Brentry BS10 . . . **28** C2
  Bristol, Upper Soundwell
  BS16 . . . . **20** E3
  Cheltenham BS50 . . . . **130** B7
St Stephen's Ct GL1 . . . . . **118** D7
St Stephen's Manor
  GL51 . . . . **130** B7
St Stephen's Rd
  Bristol BS16 . . . . **20** D2
  Cheltenham GL51 . . . . **130** B7
St Stephen's St BS1 . . . . . **195** A2
St Swithin's GL10 . . . . **97** E4
St Swithins Rd GL15 . . . . . **156** B1
St Swithuns Rd GL2 . . . . . **118** A6
St Tecla Rd NP16 . . . . **60** E6
St Teresa's RC Prim Sch
  BS7 . . . . **28** E1
St Tewdric Rd NP16 . . . . . **60** E7
St Tewdrics Pl NP16 . . . . . **60** B4

St Thomas More RC Prim
  Sch GL51 . . . . **132** D2
St Thomas Pl BS1 . . . . **195** B2
St Thomas St E BS1 . . . . . **195** B2
St Thomas St BS1 . . . . **195** B2
St Ursula's E-ACT Acad
  BS9 . . . . **18** A6
St Vincent's Hill 1 BS6 . . **18** A2
St Vincent's Rd BS8 . . . . . **194** A2
St Vincents Trad Est BS2 . . . **9** D6
St Vincent Way GL3 . . . . . **128** A8
Saint Way BS34 . . . . **30** A4
St Werburgh's Pk BS2 . . . . **19** A2
St Werburgh's Prim Sch
  BS2 . . . . **19** A2
St Werburgh's Rd BS2 . . . . **18** F2
St Whites Ct GL14 . . . . . . **191** C2
St Whites Prim Sch
  GL14 . . . . **191** C2
St Whites Rd GL14 . . . . . **191** D3
St Whites Terr GL14 . . . . **191** C2
St Whytes Rd BS4 . . . . **2** D8
St Wulfstans Ave BS10 . . . . **18** A8
Salamanca Rd GL52 . . . . . **134** B2
Salcombe Rd BS4 . . . . **9** A1
Salem Rd BS36 . . . . **30** F7
Salisbury Ave
  Bristol BS15 . . . . **10** B8
  Cheltenham GL51 . . . . **130** A5
Salisbury Dr BS16 . . . . **20** E6
Salisbury Gdns BS16 . . . . . **20** E5
Salisbury Ho 1 GL1 . . . . . **119** A8
Salisbury Pk BS16 . . . . **20** E6
Salisbury Rd
  Bristol, Mangotsfield
  BS16 . . . . **20** E6
  Bristol, Redland BS6 . . . . . . **18** D2
  Bristol, St Anne's BS4 . . . . . . **9** B5
  Gloucester GL1 . . . . **119** A8
Salisbury St
  Bristol, Pile Marsh BS5 . . . . **9** E7
  Bristol, Russell Town BS5 . . . **9** B6
Salix Ct GL51 . . . . **130** A4
Sallis Cl GL20 . . . . **182** B5
Sallybarn Cl BS30 . . . . **10** E2
Sallysmead Cl BS13 . . . . **2** B4
Sallys Way BS36 . . . . **30** F7
Salmon Cl BS35 . . . . **38** A6
Salmonsbury Cotts GL54 **169** A8
Salmon's Spring Ind Est
  GL6 . . . . **103** B1
Salmons Way BS16 . . . . . . **21** B8
Salterley Grange GL53 . . **122** D7
Salter's La GL54 . . . . **174** C8
Salter St GL13 . . . . **85** E3
Saltford CE Prim Sch BS31 . **5** E2
Saltford Cl BS31 . . . . **5** E3
Salthouse Farm Pk BS35 . **38** A7
Salthrop Rd BS7 . . . . **18** E4
Saltmarsh Dr BS11 . . . . **27** A1
Salt Way
  Coln St Aldwyns GL7 . . . . **152** D8
  Compton Abdale GL54 . . . **167** D3
Saltwell Ave BS14 . . . . **3** C5
Salvia Cl GL3 . . . . **127** F6
Sambourne La BS20 . . . . . . **16** C4
Sambourne Rd SN16 . . . . **142** E1
Samian Way BS34 . . . . **29** E5
Sampson House Bsns Pk
  BS10 . . . . **27** D7
Sampsons Rd BS13 . . . . **2** D4
Sams La SN26 . . . . **144** E1
Samuel Barnett Cl BS4 . . . **2** E8
Samuel Rodgers Cres
  NP16 . . . . **60** F4
Samuel St 3 BS5 . . . . **9** C8
Samuel White Rd BS15 . . . . **10** C4
Samuel White's Inf Sch
  BS15 . . . . **10** C4
Samuel Wright Cl BS30 . . . **11** B8
San Andreas BS34 . . . . **28** E6
Sanctuary Gdns BS9 . . . . . **17** D3
Sandalwood Dr GL2 . . . . . **118** B7
Sandbach Rd BS4 . . . . **9** D4
Sandbed Rd BS2 . . . . **19** A2
Sandburrows Rd BS13 . . . . . **1** F6
Sandburrows Wlk BS13 . . . . **1** F6
Sandcroft BS14 . . . . **2** F6
Sanderling Wy GL52 . . . . . **138** A5
Sanders Cl BS3 . . . . **7** F2
Sanders Ct 19 GL20 . . . . . **192** C4
Sandfield Cres GL2 . . . . . . **100** A7
Sandfield Rd GL3 . . . . **128** D5
Sandfields GL18 . . . . **179** B3
Sandford Leaze GL8 . . . . . **148** B1
Sandford Mill Cl GL53 . . . **130** F7
Sandford Mill Rd GL53 . . . **130** F7
Sandford Park Pl GL52 . . . **193** C2
Sandford Pk Trade Est
  GL52 . . . . **193** C2
Sandford Rd
  Aylburton GL15 . . . . **147** D4
  Bristol BS8 . . . . **194** A1
  Cheltenham GL53 . . . . **193** C1
Sandford Sch GL53 . . . . . **123** B7
Sandford St GL53 . . . . **193** C2
Sandford Terr GL53 . . . . . **147** D4
Sandford Way GL4 . . . . . . **118** B1
Sandgate Rd BS4 . . . . **9** D3
Sandgrove GL6 . . . . **82** F8
Sand Hill BS4 . . . . **9** C4
Sandholme Cl BS16 . . . . . . **20** E8
Sandholme Rd BS4 . . . . **9** D4
Sandhurst BS37 . . . . **32** D8
Sandhurst Cl BS34 . . . . **40** B1

Sandhurst La
  Down Hatherley GL2 . . . . **173** A2
  Gloucester GL2 . . . . **126** E5
Sandhurst Rd
  Bristol BS6 . . . . **9** D4
  Charlton Kings GL52 . . . . **131** B6
  Gloucester GL1 . . . . **126** E4
Sandiway La HR9 . . . . **162** D3
Sandling Ave BS7 . . . . **19** A7
Sandown Cl BS16 . . . . **30** F1
Sandown Rd
  Bishop's Cleeve GL52 . . . . **137** F4
  Bristol, Filton BS34 . . . . . . **29** C3
  Bristol, Kensington Park BS4 . **9** D4
Sandpiper Cl 2 GL2 . . . . **117** D1
Sandpiper Dr GL51 . . . . . **132** E6
Sandpits La
  Hawkesbury Upton GL9 . . . . **56** A2
  Randwick GL6 . . . . **102** C1
  Sherston SN16 . . . . **58** C1
  Stroud GL6 . . . . **98** C8
Sandpool La GL7 . . . . **149** C2
Sandringham Ave
  Bristol BS16 . . . . **20** E8
  Gloucester GL4 . . . . **118** C1
Sandringham Ct GL53 . . . **130** F7
Sandringham Pk BS16 . . . . **20** E8
Sandringham Rd
  Bristol, Kensington Park
  BS4 . . . . **9** D4
  Bristol, Longwell Green
  BS30 . . . . **10** F2
  Bristol, Stoke Gifford BS34 . **29** D4
Sands Cl WR12 . . . . **188** D3
Sands Croft Ave WR12 . . . **188** B1
Sands Hill SN14 . . . . **23** E3
Sands La BS36 . . . . **41** F1
Sandstar Cl GL2 . . . . **127** D5
Sands The 11 WR12 . . . . . **185** B8
Sandstone Rise BS36 . . . . . **30** E4
Sandtumps GL15 . . . . **147** B4
Sandwich Rd BS4 . . . . **9** D4
Sandy Cl BS32 . . . . **29** E6
Sandycroft Rd GL3 . . . . . **128** A4
Sandy La
  Aust BS35 . . . . **49** A8
  Aust BS35 . . . . **49** A8
  Bristol BS5 . . . . **19** C3
  Cheltenham GL53 . . . . **130** F4
  Easton-in-G BS20 . . . . **16** A1
  Hewelsfield GL15 . . . . **146** E3
  Upper Rissington GL54 . . . **169** D6
Sandy Lane Ct GL54 . . . . . **169** D6
Sandy Lane Rd GL53 . . . . **130** F5
Sandyleaze
  Bristol BS9 . . . . **17** E7
  Gloucester GL2 . . . . **127** C8
Sandy Lodge BS37 . . . . **32** E4
Sandy Park Rd BS4 . . . . **9** C3
Sandy Pluck La GL51 . . . . **121** D8
Sandywell Pk GL54 . . . . . **166** C7
Saniger La
  Berkeley GL13 . . . . **85** D6
  Newton GL13 . . . . **85** C7
Sankey Gr 9 GL56 . . . . . **187** B6
San Remo GL1 . . . . **118** E6
Sappercombe La GL53 . . **131** B5
Sapperton CE Prim Sch
  GL7 . . . . **149** B6
Sapperton Rd GL4 . . . . . . **118** F5
Sapphire Cl GL4 . . . . **118** C2
Sapphire Wy GL4 . . . . . . **120** A4
Sarah Siddons Wlk 1
  GL50 . . . . **130** B6
Sarah St BS5 . . . . **9** B7
Sargent's La HR9, GL18 . . **170** B4
Sargent St BS3 . . . . **8** E4
Sark Cl BS4 . . . . **9** E4
Sarnedy Rd 3 GL16 . . . . . **155** A5
Sarn Hill Grange GL20 . . **181** C5
Sarum Cl BS16 . . . . **21** C6
Sarum Cres BS10 . . . . **28** C1
Sassoon Ct BS30 . . . . **10** F5
Satchfield Cl BS10 . . . . **27** F2
Satchfield Cres BS10 . . . . . **27** F2
Satellite Bsns Pk BS5 . . . . . . **9** D6
Sates Way BS9 . . . . **18** C6
Saturn Cl GL4 . . . . **119** F6
Saunders Cl
  Huntley GL17 . . . . **165** A7
  Lea HR9 . . . . **164** D8
Saunders Rd BS16 . . . . **20** E4
Saunton Wlk BS4 . . . . **2** E8
Savage Hill GL16 . . . . **154** E4
Savages Wood Rd BS32 . . . **29** D8
Savages Wood Rd BS32 . . **29** D8
Savernake Rd GL4 . . . . . . **119** A4
Saville Cl GL50 . . . . **133** E4
Saville Gate Cl BS9 . . . . . . **17** F4
Saville Mews BS6 . . . . **195** A4
Saville Pl BS8 . . . . **194** A2
Saville Rd BS9 . . . . **17** F3
Savory Wy GL7 . . . . **190** E5
Savoy Rd BS4 . . . . **9** D4
Savoy The BS11 . . . . **16** E6
Saw Mill La 5 BS35 . . . . . **64** B1
Saw Mills End GL4 . . . . . **127** D1
Sawpit La GL19 . . . . **173** C7
Sawpits La GL56 . . . . **177** D5
Sawpits La HR9 . . . . **162** E4
Sawyers Cl SN16 . . . . **142** D1
Sawyers Hill SN16 . . . . . . **142** D1
Sawyers Rise
  Ashleworth GL19 . . . . **172** D4
  Minety SN16 . . . . **142** D1

Saxon Cl
Cricklade SN6 . . . . 143 E4
Gloucester GL2 . . . . 127 C5
Sherston SN16 . . . . 58 C1
Saxon Pl NP16 . . . . 61 A7
Saxon Rd
Bristol BS2 . . . . 19 A2
Cirencester GL7 . . . . 190 E5
Saxon Way
Bristol BS32 . . . . 40 C1
Cheltenham GL52 . . . . 131 A8
Fairford GL7 . . . . 152 D4
Sayers Cres GL3 . . . . 120 E5
Saylittle Mews GL2 . . . . . 127 E5
Sayth Ho GL7 . . . . 190 D5
Say Wlk BS30 . . . . 11 D7
SBI Ctr BS15 . . . . 10 B5
Scandrett Cl BS10 . . . . 27 E2
Scantleberry Cl BS16 . . . . 20 D8
Scar Hill GL6 . . . . 91 D4
Scarr Rd GL18 . . . . 171 A7
Scarr The GL18 . . . . 171 A7
Scholars Ct GL51 . . . . 133 B2
Scholars Wlk GL2 . . . . . . 117 F1
School Cl
Bristol, Eastville BS5 . . . . . . 19 D2
Bristol, Patchway BS34 . . . . 29 C8
5 Coleford GL16 . . . . 155 B5
Dursley GL11 . . . . 87 E4
Hillesley GL12 . . . . 55 E8
School Cres
Corse GL19 . . . . 172 B7
Joy's Green GL17 . . . . 163 D5
Lydney GL15 . . . . 92 B5
School Ct BS34 . . . . 30 A5
Schooler's La GL56 . . . . . 177 E6
Schoolfield Cl GL2 . . . . . 100 E5
School Hill
Bourton-on-t-W GL54 . . . . 168 F7
Chepstow/Cas-Gwent NP16 . 60 E8
Stratton GL7 . . . . 190 A8
Winstone GL7 . . . . 107 A8
School Hill Ind Est **13**
NP16 . . . . 60 E8
School Ho GL50 . . . . 193 B4
School La
Ampney Crucis GL7 . . . . . . 151 C5
Badminton GL9 . . . . 46 E2
Berkeley GL13 . . . . 85 E3
3 Blockley GL56 . . . . 186 C5
Bretforton WR11 . . . . 188 A6
2 Bristol BS16 . . . . 19 E5
Castle Eaton SN6 . . . . 144 D6
Cirencester GL7 . . . . 190 D3
Edgeworth GL6 . . . . 106 D1
Hardwicke GL2 . . . . 109 E8
Longhope GL17 . . . . 164 F6
Meysey Hampton GL7 . . . . 152 A2
Narth The NP25 . . . . 154 B1
Overbury GL20 . . . . 182 F8
Ruardean GL17 . . . . 163 F4
Shipton GL54 . . . . 166 E5
Shurdington GL51 . . . . 129 E2
Southam GL52 . . . . 134 C8
South Cerney GL7 . . . . 142 F8
Whitminster GL2 . . . . 100 E5
School Mead GL51 . . . . . 133 A2
School Mews GL4 . . . . . . 119 B4
School of Christ The King
Cath Prim BS4 . . . . .2 E8
School Rd
Alderton GL20 . . . . 183 E4
Apperley GL19 . . . . 173 C6
Bishop's Cleeve GL52 . . . . 138 A4
Bisley GL6 . . . . 105 A1
Bristol, Broom Hill BS4 . . . . . 9 F4
Bristol BS15 . . . . 10 C8
Bristol, Cadbury Heath
BS30 . . . . 11 A4
Bristol, Oldland Common
BS30 . . . . 11 C3
Bristol, Totterdown BS4 . . . . . 9 A3
Charlton Kings GL53 . . . . . 131 B6
Dursley GL11 . . . . 80 C8
Frampton Cotterell BS36 . . . 31 A8
Joy's Green GL17 . . . . 163 D5
Kemble GL7 . . . . 141 F8
Minchinhampton GL6 . . . . . 148 A3
Ruardean GL17 . . . . 163 F4
Upper Lydbrook GL17 . . . . 163 D2
Wotton-u-E GL12 . . . . 68 B7
School Road Flats **3**
GL53 . . . . 131 B6
School Row GL7 . . . . 149 E3
School Sq GL5 . . . . 98 F5
School St WR11 . . . . 188 C6
School Terr GL5 . . . . 98 D6
School Way BS35 . . . . 38 A6
School Wlk
Bristol BS5 . . . . 19 D1
Yate BS37 . . . . 43 E2
Scop The BS32 . . . . 40 B5
Scotland La BS4, BS14 . . . . . 4 A7
Scott Ave GL2 . . . . 118 C4
Scott Ct BS30 . . . . 10 F5
Scott Ho GL51 . . . . 132 E3
Scott Lawrence Cl BS16 . . 20 A7
Scott Way BS37 . . . . 32 F8
Scott Wlk BS30 . . . . 11 D7
Scowles Rd GL16 . . . . 154 F6
Scrubbett's La GL8 . . . . . . 69 F8
Seabright Cl GL51 . . . . . . 132 E5
Seabroke Rd GL1 . . . . . . 196 C4

Seabrook Rd GL3 . . . . . . 120 E5
Seacome Rd GL51 . . . . . . 132 D2
Seagry Cl BS10 . . . . 28 E1
Sealand Wy GL2 . . . . 110 B7
Sea Mills La BS9 . . . . 17 C5
Sea Mills Prim Sch BS9 . . 17 B5
Sea Mills Sta BS9 . . . . 17 B4
Searle Court Ave BS4 . . . . . 9 E4
Seaton Ct BS3 . . . . 8 D1
Seaton Rd BS5 . . . . 19 C1
Seawalls BS9 . . . . 17 D2
Seawalls Rd BS9 . . . . 17 D2
Sebert St GL1 . . . . 196 C4
Second Ave
Bristol BS14 . . . . 3 B7
Dursley GL11 . . . . 80 C8
Second Chance Touring Pk
SN6 . . . . 144 C7
Second Crossing Rd
GL20 . . . . 192 F2
Second Way BS11 . . . . 26 D1
Secret Gdn The GL7 . . . . 142 F8
Secret La GL1 . . . . 196 B4
Secunda Way GL2 . . . . . . 117 A3
Sedbury Bsns Pk NP16 . . . 61 B8
Sedbury Chase NP16 . . . . . 73 A1
Sedbury La NP16 . . . . 73 A1
Seddon Rd **4** BS2 . . . . . . 19 A2
Sedgefield Gdns BS16 . . . 30 F1
Sedgewick Gdns GL51 . . . 129 D6
Sedgewick Ho BS11 . . . . . . 16 E7
Sedgley Ct GL4 . . . . 118 C2
Sedgley Rd GL52 . . . . 137 F4
Sedum Ho **1** GL50 . . . . . 133 B1
Sefton Park Jun Sch BS7 . . 18 F3
Sefton Park Rd BS7 . . . . . . 18 F3
Sefton Wlk **5** GL51 . . . . . 129 D6
Selborne Rd
Bishop's Cleeve GL52 . . . . 137 F4
Bristol BS7 . . . . 18 F5
Selbrooke Cres BS16 . . . . . 20 C6
Selby Rd BS5 . . . . 19 F1
Selden Rd BS14 . . . . 3 E5
Selkirk Cl **3** GL52 . . . . . 133 F2
Selkirk Ct **3** GL52 . . . . . 133 F2
Selkirk Gdns GL52 . . . . . . 133 F2
Selkirk Rd BS15 . . . . 20 C1
Selkirk St GL52 . . . . 133 F2
Sellars Rd GL2 . . . . 109 D7
Selley Wlk BS13 . . . . 2 A5
Selsey Rd GL5 . . . . 98 F2
Selsley Hill GL5 . . . . 98 E4
Selworthy
Bristol BS15 . . . . 10 E7
Cheltenham GL51 . . . . 129 E5
Selworthy Cl BS31 . . . . 4 D5
Selworthy Ho BS4 . . . . 9 B2
Selwyn Cl GL10 . . . . 98 A5
Selwyn Rd GL51 . . . . 118 F5
Seneca Pl **1** BS5 . . . . 9 D7
Seneca St BS5 . . . . 9 D7
Seneca Way GL50 . . . . . . 133 B5
Sentinel Wy GL3 . . . . 120 B4
Septimus Bldgs BS14 . . . . . 2 D5
Serlo Rd GL1 . . . . 196 B4
Serridge La BS36 . . . . 31 D4
Setts Row GL7 . . . . 149 E4
Sevastopol Rd BS10 . . . . . 18 E7
Sevelm **11** GL51 . . . . 129 E5
Seven Acres GL4 . . . . 119 D7
Sevenacres Rd GL6 . . . . . . 91 A4
Seven Bridges Cotts
SN6 . . . . 144 B3
Sevenfields SN6 . . . . 145 D4
Sevenleaze La
Edge GL6 . . . . 111 B2
Gloucester GL4, GL6 . . . . . 111 D5
Seven Stars Rd GL14 . . . . 191 C6
Seventh Ave
Bristol, Filton BS7 . . . . 29 B1
Bristol, Hengrove BS14 . . . . . 3 A7
Gloucester GL4 . . . . 118 D2
Seven Waters GL10 . . . . . . 97 D4
Severnbank Ave GL2 . . . . . 92 C3
Severnbanks Prim Sch
GL15 . . . . 92 C3
Severn Beach Prim Sch
BS35 . . . . 38 A6
Severn Beach Sta BS35 . . . 38 A6
Severn Bridge Pk NP16 . . . 61 B5
Severn Cl
Charfield GL12 . . . . 67 A4
Maisemore GL2 . . . . 126 B7
Severn Cres NP16 . . . . 60 F7
Severn Distribution Pk
GL13 . . . . 85 B8
Severn Dr
Berkeley GL13 . . . . 85 E4
Tewkesbury GL20 . . . . 182 B5
Thornbury BS35 . . . . 64 B2
Severn Grange BS10 . . . . . 27 D3
Severn Ho BS10 . . . . 27 D3
Severn La
Berkeley GL13 . . . . 84 E1
Bevington GL13 . . . . 76 F8
Severnleigh Gdns BS9 . . . . 17 F3
Severnleigh Ho BS9 . . . . . . 17 F3
Severn Lodge **3** GL4 . . . . 119 C4
Severn Oaks GL2 . . . . 109 C7
Severn Rd
Avonmouth BS11 . . . . 26 C4
Bristol BS11 . . . . 16 D6
Cheltenham GL52 . . . . 134 A3
Dursley GL11 . . . . 87 E4
Gloucester GL1 . . . . 196 A2

Severn Rd continued
Hallen BS10 . . . . 27 A7
Lydney GL15 . . . . 92 B2
Newton GL13 . . . . 85 B8
Pill BS20 . . . . 16 C5
Severn Beach BS35 . . . . 37 F3
Stonehouse GL10 . . . . 97 E8
Severnside Trad Est
Avonmouth BS11 . . . . 26 C5
Gloucester BS2 . . . . 126 C1
Severn St **7** GL14 . . . . . . 157 A6
Severn Terr **8** GL14 . . . . 157 A6
Severnvale Dr GL2 . . . . . . 117 E2
Severn Vale Sch GL2 . . . . 109 E8
Severn View
Bristol BS10 . . . . 27 C1
Cinderford GL14 . . . . 191 E5
Severn View Par GL13 . . . . 85 C8
Severn View Rd
Thornbury BS35 . . . . 64 C2
Woolaston GL15 . . . . 147 B3
Yorkley GL15 . . . . 156 B2
Severn Way
Apperley GL19 . . . . 173 C7
Bristol BS34 . . . . 39 F1
Keynsham BS31 . . . . 5 A5
Severnwood Gdns BS35 . . 38 A5
Severn Wy BS35 . . . . 63 B6
Sevier St BS2 . . . . 18 F2
Seymour Ave BS7 . . . . 18 E4
Seymour Cl **5** GL51 . . . . . 155 A7
Seymour Gate **5** GL55 . . . 189 A2
Seymour Pl
Frampton Cotterell BS36 . . . 31 B6
Tewkesbury GL20 . . . . 192 C3
10 Winchcombe GL54 . . . . 174 A7
Seymour Rd
Bristol, Ashley Down BS7 . . 18 E4
Bristol, Kingswood BS15 . . . 20 C1
Bristol, Staple Hill BS16 . . . 20 D4
Bristol, Upper Easton BS5 . . 19 A1
Gloucester GL1 . . . . 118 D7
Seyton Wlk BS34 . . . . 29 E5
Sezincote Cl GL6 . . . . 148 B6
Sezincote House &
Gardens ★ GL56 . . . . . . 186 D2
Shackel Hendy Mews
BS16 . . . . 21 B5
Shackleton Ave BS37 . . . . . 32 F8
Shackleton Cl GL3 . . . . . . 128 C5
Shadwell GL11 . . . . 81 A8
Shadwell Rd BS7 . . . . 18 D3
Shaftesbury Ave BS6 . . . . . 18 E1
Shaftesbury Hall **4**
GL50 . . . . 193 B4
Shaftesbury Ind Est
GL51 . . . . 133 B6
Shaftesbury Pl **10** GL51 . . 132 D2
Shaftesbury Terr **8** BS5 . . . 9 D7
Shaft Rd BS35 . . . . 38 A8
Shakespeare Ave
Bristol BS7 . . . . 19 A8
Gloucester GL2 . . . . 118 C4
Shakespeare Cotts GL51 . 129 B7
Shakespeare Ct GL20 . . . . 192 C4
Shakespeare Rd
Cheltenham GL51 . . . . 132 E1
Dursley GL11 . . . . 80 C7
Shaldon Rd BS7 . . . . 19 A4
Shalford Cl GL7 . . . . 190 B3
Shallowbrooks La SN14 . . 47 F8
Shallows The BS31 . . . . 5 F3
Shambles Museum The ★
GL18 . . . . 171 A4
Shambles The **12** GL5 . . . . 99 C7
Shamrock Cl GL3 . . . . 127 F6
Shamrock Rd BS5 . . . . 19 D3
Shanklin Dr BS34 . . . . 29 B3
Shannaways Cl BS16 . . . . . 19 F4
Shannon Ct BS35 . . . . 51 D8
Shannon Pl GL20 . . . . 182 B5
Shannon Way GL20 . . . . . 182 B4
Shapcott Cl BS4 . . . . 9 B1
Shaplands BS9 . . . . 17 F4
Shard The GL6 . . . . 102 F3
Sharland Cl BS9 . . . . 17 E3
Sharland Gr BS13 . . . . 2 C4
Sharman Pitch HR9 . . . . . 163 C7
Sharpness Prim Sch GL13 85 D8
Sharps Way NP16 . . . . 60 F5
Shawbury Ave GL2 . . . . . . 110 A8
Shaw Cl
Bristol BS16 . . . . 21 B3
3 Bristol, Upper Easton BS5 . 9 B8
Shaw Gdns BS14 . . . . 3 A8
Shaw Green La GL52 . . . . 134 C5
Shaymoor La BS35 . . . . 39 A4
Shear Ho **7** WR12 . . . . . . 185 C8
Shearmore Cl BS7 . . . . 19 A7
Shearwater Ct BS16 . . . . . . 19 F6
Shearwater Gr GL3 . . . . . . 127 E6
Sheaves Pk BS10 . . . . 28 D2
Sheene Ct **17** BS3 . . . . 8 C3
Sheene La BS3 . . . . 8 C3
Sheene Way BS3 . . . . 8 C3
Sheenhill Rd WR11 . . . . . . 188 B8
Sheens Mdw GL14 . . . . . . 156 F7
Sheepfair La SN14 . . . . 14 F8
Sheepscombe Cl GL51 . . . 129 E8
Sheepscombe Prim Sch
GL6 . . . . 112 E1
Sheeps Croft BS13 . . . . 2 A5
Sheep St
Cirencester GL7 . . . . 190 C4
Highworth SN6 . . . . 145 D3
Stow-on-t-W GL54 . . . . . . 176 F4

Sheepwash The BS35 . . . . . 63 D5
Sheepwood Cl BS10 . . . . . . 28 A2
Sheepwood Rd BS10 . . . . . . 28 A2
Sheevaun Cl GL2 . . . . 127 D5
Sheiling Sch BS35 . . . . 64 B2
Shelburne Rd GL51 . . . . . 129 F8
Sheldare Barton BS5 . . . . . 10 B7
Sheldon Av WR12 . . . . 188 B1
Sheldons Ct GL52 . . . . 193 C4
Sheldrake Dr BS16 . . . . 19 E6
Shelduck Rd GL2 . . . . 117 D1
Shellard Rd BS34 . . . . 29 A2
Shellards La BS35 . . . . 51 E2
Shellards Rd BS30 . . . . 10 F3
Shelley Ave
Cheltenham GL51 . . . . 132 E1
Gloucester GL2 . . . . 118 C4
Shelley Cl BS5 . . . . 9 F8
Shelley Ho BS34 . . . . 40 A1
Shelley Rd
Cheltenham GL51 . . . . 132 E1
Dursley GL11 . . . . 80 C7
Shelley Way BS7 . . . . 19 A8
Shellmor Ave BS34 . . . . . . 40 B1
Shellmor Cl BS32 . . . . 40 D1
Shephard Mead GL20 . . . 192 B3
Shepherdine Cl GL15 . . . . . 92 C3
Shepherd Rd GL2 . . . . 118 B3
Shepherds Cl
Bristol BS16 . . . . 20 E5
Cheltenham GL51 . . . . 132 D4
8 Ledbury HR8 . . . . 178 E7
Stroud GL5 . . . . 99 D8
Shepherd's Cl GL55 . . . . . 188 F1
Shepherds Croft GL5 . . . . . 99 D8
Shepherd's Leaze GL12 . . . 68 C6
Shepherds Mead **3** GL8 . 140 C5
Shepherds Row **4** GL54 . . 176 F4
Shepherds Way
Cirencester GL7 . . . . 190 C6
Innsworth GL3 . . . . 127 F7
Northleach GL54 . . . . 167 F1
19 Stow-on-t-W GL54 . . . 176 F4
Shepherds Well GL5 . . . . . 99 D1
Shepherds Wlk
Wotton-u-E GL12 . . . . 68 C6
1 Bristol BS32 . . . . 40 D1
Sheppard Rd BS16 . . . . 20 C6
Sheppard Way
Minchinhampton GL6 . . . . . 91 F7
Newent GL18 . . . . 171 A4
Shepperdine Rd BS35 . . . . 75 D2
Sheppey Cnr WR12 . . . . . 184 F5
Shepton WR8 . . . . 8 C2
Sherborne CE Prim Sch
GL54 . . . . 169 A1
Sherborne Cl BS10 . . . . 97 F8
Sherborne Ho
Gloucester GL1 . . . . 196 C3
1 Stonehouse GL10 . . . . . 97 F8
Sherborne La GL54 . . . . . . 169 C3
Sherborne Park Nature
Trail ★ GL54 . . . . 168 E1
Sherborne Pl GL52 . . . . . 193 C3
Sherborne St
Bourton-on-t-W GL54 . . . . 168 F7
Cheltenham GL52 . . . . 193 C4
Gloucester GL1 . . . . 196 C4
Lechlade on T GL7 . . . . . . 153 E2
Sherborne Stables GL54 . 168 F1
Sherborne Terr **4** GL54 . . 168 F7
Sherbourne Ave BS32 . . . . 29 E7
Sherbourne Cl BS15 . . . . . . 20 D2
Sherbourne's Brake BS32 . 29 E6
Sherbourne St BS5 . . . . 9 E7
Shergar Cl GL4 . . . . 119 D4
Sheridan Rd BS7 . . . . 19 A8
Sheridan Way BS30 . . . . . . 11 A2
Sherrings The BS34 . . . . . . 29 B8
Sherrin Way BS13 . . . . 1 E3
Sherry The GL54 . . . . 175 B7
Sherston Cl BS16 . . . . 20 B5
Sherston Rd
Bristol BS7 . . . . 18 E8
Luckington SN14 . . . . 47 F5
Sherwell Rd BS4 . . . . 9 E3
Sherwood Cl BS31 . . . . 4 E5
Sherwood Gn GL2 . . . . . . 126 F6
Sherwood Rd
Bristol BS15 . . . . 20 B1
Keynsham BS31 . . . . 4 E5
Tetbury GL8 . . . . 140 B4
Shetland Rd BS10 . . . . 28 D1
Shield Ret Ctr BS34 . . . . . . 29 A3
Shield Road Prim Sch
BS7 . . . . 29 A1
Shields Ave BS7 . . . . 29 A1
Shiels Dr BS32 . . . . 29 D7
Shilham Wy GL7 . . . . 190 F3
Shilton Cl BS15 . . . . 10 F7
Shimsey Cl **2** BS16 . . . . . . 20 C6
Shipham Cl BS14 . . . . 3 B5
Ship La BS1 . . . . 195 B1
Shipley Mow BS16 . . . . 21 B6
Shipley Rd BS9 . . . . 18 A8
Shipman Cl BS16 . . . . 20 E4
Shipton's Grave La GL6 . . . 91 C1
Shipway Ct GL2 . . . . 137 F4
Shire Gdns BS11 . . . . 16 D8
Shirehampton Prim Sch
BS11 . . . . 16 A6
Shirehampton Rd BS9 . . . . 17 C6
Shirehampton Sta BS11 . . 16 D5
Shire Hill SN14 . . . . 25 D7
Shire Way BS37 . . . . 32 D6
Shirreff Ct **14** BS6 . . . . 18 B1

Shooters End GL5 . . . . 99 C8
Shophouse Rd GL15,
GL16 . . . . 155 A2
Shop La
Badminton GL9 . . . . 46 E2
Bretforton WR11 . . . . 188 A7
Shorland Ho BS8 . . . . 18 A1
Shorn Brook Cl GL2 . . . . . 110 A5
Short Hedges Cl **16**
GL54 . . . . 168 A1
Shorthill Rd BS37 . . . . 32 C4
Short La BS41 . . . . 7 A2
Shortlands Rd BS11 . . . . . . 27 A1
Short St
Bristol BS2 . . . . 9 A5
Cheltenham GL53 . . . . 130 C6
Short Way BS35 . . . . 51 B7
Shortwood Hill BS16 . . . . . 21 E4
Shortwood Rd
Bristol BS13 . . . . 2 E3
Nailsworth GL6 . . . . 91 A3
Pucklechurch BS16 . . . . 22 A4
Shortwood View BS15 . . . . 10 F8
Shortwood Wlk BS13 . . . . . .2 E3
Shotts La GL18 . . . . 170 C3
Showering Cl BS14 . . . . 3 D5
Showering Rd BS14 . . . . 3 D5
Shrivenham Rd SN6 . . . . . 145 D2
Shrubberies Sch The
GL10 . . . . 97 E8
Shrubbery Cotts **4** BS6 . . 18 B2
Shrubbery Ct **6** BS16 . . . . 20 D5
Shrubbery Rd BS16 . . . . . . 20 D5
Shrublands GL53 . . . . 130 F5
Shubbery The GL7 . . . . . . 153 E2
Shurdington CE Prim Sch
GL51 . . . . 129 D1
Shurdington Rd
Cheltenham GL50, GL51,
GL53 . . . . 130 B5
Little Shurdington GL3,
GL51 . . . . 121 B7
Shurdington GL51 . . . . 129 E2
Shutehay Dr GL11 . . . . 87 F5
Shuter Rd BS13 . . . . 1 E5
Shute St GL10 . . . . 98 A3
Shuthonger Manor GL20 181 E6
Shutter La GL7 . . . . 137 F8
Sibland BS35 . . . . 51 D8
Sibland Cl **3** BS35 . . . . 51 D8
Sibland Rd BS35 . . . . 51 D8
Sibland Way BS35 . . . . 51 D8
Sibree Cl GL6 . . . . 148 B6
Sidcot BS4 . . . . 10 A2
Siddington CE Prim Sch
GL7 . . . . 190 D1
Siddington Hall GL7 . . . . . 150 E2
Sideland Cl BS14 . . . . 3 E6
Sidelands Rd BS16 . . . . 20 C6
Sidings The
Bristol BS15 . . . . 21 B2
Bristol BS34 . . . . 29 C2
Charfield GL12 . . . . 67 B5
Sidmouth Ct BS3 . . . . 8 D1
Sidmouth Gdns BS3 . . . . . . 8 D2
Sidmouth Rd BS3 . . . . .8 E2
Sidney St
Cheltenham GL52 . . . . 193 C3
Gloucester GL1 . . . . 127 A1
Sigma Cl **4** GL20 . . . . . . 182 B4
Signal Rd BS16 . . . . 20 F4
Silbury Rd BS3 . . . . .7 E2
Silbury Rise BS31 . . . . 5 A2
Silcock Cl GL3 . . . . 127 F7
Silcox Rd BS13 . . . . 2 C4
Silklands Gr BS9 . . . . 17 C6
Silk Mill St **31** GL54 . . . . 174 A7
Silk Mill La GL54 . . . . 174 A7
Silley's Pl **1** NP16 . . . . 72 F2
Silver Birch Cl
Bristol BS34 . . . . 29 D7
Quedgeley GL2 . . . . 117 C1
Silver Cl
Gloucester GL4 . . . . 118 C3
Minety SN16 . . . . 142 D1
Silverdale Par GL3 . . . . . . 119 F8
Silverhill Brake BS35 . . . . . 50 E1
Silverhill Rd BS10 . . . . 27 E4
Silverhill Sch BS36 . . . . 30 E7
Silver St
Arlingham GL2 . . . . 157 C6
Bristol BS1 . . . . 195 A3
Cirencester GL7 . . . . 190 C5
Coaley GL11 . . . . 89 A7
Dursley GL11 . . . . 88 B1
Littledean GL14 . . . . 156 E8
Minety SN16 . . . . 142 D1
Mitcheldean GL17 . . . . 164 D5
South Cerney GL7 . . . . 142 F8
15 Tetbury GL8 . . . . 140 C4
7 Thornbury BS35 . . . . 64 B1
Silverthorne Cl GL53 . . . . 130 B5
Silverthorne La BS2 . . . . 9 A6
Silverthorne Wharf BS2 . . . .9 B6
Silverton Ct BS4 . . . . .8 F1
Silvertree Gdns GL5 . . . . . . 99 E3
Silverwood Way GL51 . . . 129 E5
Simmonds Cl GL6 . . . . 148 A3
Simmonds Rd GL3 . . . . . . 119 F6
Simmonds View BS34 . . . . 29 F5
Simmons Bldgs BS16 . . . . . 30 C3
Simon Rd GL2 . . . . 127 C5
Simplex Ind Est The BS30 . 11 D4

Simpson'S Orch GL4 .... 119 E4
Sims La GL2 .... 117 F4
Sinclair Ho
  Bristol, Clifton Wood
    BS8 ....194 A2
  Bristol, Filton BS34 ..... 29 A2
Sinclair Rd GL51 ....129 D1
Sinderberry Dr GL20 ...182 C5
Sinope St GL1 ....196 C2
Sion Hill BS8 ....7 F7
Sion La BS8 ....7 F7
Sion Pl BS8 ....7 F7
Sion Rd 11 BS3 ....8 C3
Sir Bernard Lovell Sch
  BS30 ....11 C4
Sir Bevil Grenville's Mon★
  BA1 ....13 A1
Sir Charles Irving Cl 6 GL50,
  GL51 ....130 B6
Sir John's La
  Bristol BS7 .... 19 B5
  Bristol, Eastville BS5 .... 19 B4
Sir Thomas Rich's Sch
  GL2 ....127 D3
Sir Walter Montague
  Almshouses NP16 .... 72 E1
Sir William Romney's Sch
  GL8 ....140 C5
Siskin Dr GL51 ....132 E5
Siskin Rd GL54 ....169 D7
Sissinghurst Gr GL51 ...130 A5
Sisson End GL2 ....127 D2
Sisson Rd GL2 ....127 C1
Siston Cl BS15 .... 21 A2
Siston Comm BS15 ..... 21 B1
Siston Common BS30 ... 21 B1
Siston Ctr The BS15 ..... 21 A2
Siston Hill BS30 .... 21 B1
Siston Hill Rdbt BS15 .. 21 B2
Siston La BS30 .... 21 F2
Siston Pk BS15 .... 21 A2
Sivell Cl GL2 ....127 A6
Six Acres GL4 ....119 F3
Sixth Ave
  Bristol, Filton BS7 ...... 29 B1
  Bristol, Horfield BS14 .... 3 A7
Skillicorne Mews GL50 . 130 B8
Skinner's Cl SN6 ....145 A4
Skinners Croft BS34 .... 29 A7
Skinner St GL1 ....196 B4
Skippon Ct BS15 .... 10 E5
Skye Cl SN6 ....145 A4
Skylark Way GL4 ....119 B6
Slade Brook GL5 .... 99 E8
Slade Rd
  Woolaston GL15 ....147 A3
  Yorkley GL15 ....156 B2
Slade The 1 GL11 ..... 80 B8
Slad La GL5, GL6 ...... 99 F8
Slad Mill GL5 .... 99 D8
Slad Rd GL5 .... 99 D8
Slad The
  Longhope GL17 ....165 B5
  Popes Hill GL14 ....156 E8
  Thornbury BS35 .... 51 F6
Slaney St GL1 ....118 F7
Sleep La BS14 ....3 D3
Slimbridge Cl BS37 .... 32 F7
Slimbridge La GL13 .... 94 D2
Slimbridge Prim Sch GL2 95 E2
Slimbridge Rd GL4 .....118 D3
Sloan St BS5 ....9 D8
Sloe Wy BS34 .... 29 F3
Slough La SN14 .... 13 F5
Slymbridge Ave BS10 .. 28 A3
Smallbrook Rd WR12 ..188 A1
Small La BS16 .... 19 E5
Small St
  Bristol BS1 ....195 A3
  Bristol, St Philip's Marsh BS2 9 A5
Smarts Gn BS37 .... 33 C8
Smeaton Rd BS1 ....7 F5
Smith Barry Cir GL54 ..169 E6
Smith Barry Cres GL54 .169 D6
Smith Barry Rd GL54 ..169 D6
Smithcourt Dr BS34 .... 29 D6
Smithmead BS13 ....2 B5
Smiths Ct
  Bristol BS34 .... 29 A8
  7 Tewkesbury GL20 ...192 C4
Smith's Field GL7 ......190 A3
Smiths Hill GL16 ....155 C3
Smith's La GL20 ....192 C4
Smithville Cl GL15 .....146 F7
Smithville Pl GL15 .....146 F7
Smithwood Gr GL53 ....131 A4
Smithy Cl GL16 ....163 A2
Smithy La GL54 ....184 A1
Smithyman Ct 1 GL14 .157 A6
Smithy The
  Blakeney GL15 ....156 E2
  Cirencester GL7 ....190 E3
Smoke La BS11 .... 26 D6
Smooth Stones NP16 .. 60 A7
Smythe Croft BS14 ......3 A3
Smythe Mdw GL6 ......148 B5
Smythe Rd GL51 ....133 B6
Smyth Ho BS8 ....7 E6
Smyth Rd BS3 ....8 A3
Smyths Cl BS11 .... 26 B1
Smyth Terr 3 BS3 ....8 C4
Snake Dr GL7 ....152 D7
Snead Pk GL4 ....119 F5

Sneedhams Rd GL4 .....119 B2
Sneyd Park Ho BS9 .... 17 D3
Sneyd Wood Rd GL14 ..191 D3
Snipe Rd GL54 ....169 D6
Snowberry Cl BS32 .... 29 E8
Snowberry Wlk BS5 .... 19 E1
Snowden Ho BS16 ..... 19 F5
Snowden Cl BS16 ...... 19 F4
Snowdon Gdns GL3 ....128 A7
Snowdonia Rd GL20 ...192 E2
Snowdon Rd BS16 ..... 19 F4
Snowdrop Cl 1 GL4 ... 119 E5
Snowshill Cl GL4 ......119 D7
Snowshill Dr GL52 .....137 F3
Snowshill Manor★
  WR12 ....185 B4
Snowshill Rd
  Broadway WR12 ....185 B7
  Gloucester GL4 ....119 E2
Snowswick La SN7 .....145 F8
Soapers La BS35 .... 51 B8
Soaphouse Ind Est BS5...9 E8
Sochi Mews 17 GL51 ...132 E2
Sodbury Rd
  Acton Turville GL9 ..... 35 F7
  Wickwar GL12 .... 54 A4
Soldiers of Gloucester Mus★
  GL1 ....196 A2
Solent Way BS35 .... 51 D7
Solon Ct BS13 ....1 F5
Solway Rd BS13 ....132 D4
Somerby Cl BS32 ...... 29 D7
Somerdale Ave BS4 ......9 A4
Somerdale Rd BS31 ......4 F7
Somerdale Rd N BS30, BS31 4 F8
Somerford Cl BS10 .... 27 F1
Somerford Rd GL7 .....190 C2
Somergate Rd GL51 ...132 D4
Somermead BS3 ....8 C1
Somerset Ave
  Cheltenham GL51......133 A2
  Dursley GL11 .... 80 C7
  Yate BS37 .... 43 F3
Somerset Cl GL12 ...... 67 F4
Somerset Cres BS34 ... 29 F5
Somerset Ho
  13 Bristol BS2 ....195 C3
  3 Cheltenham GL50 ...193 B4
Somerset Pl
  Gloucester GL1, GL2 ...196 A1
  Tewkesbury GL20 .....192 D1
Somerset Rd
  Bristol BS4 .... 9 B3
  Cinderford GL14 ......191 C4
Somerset Sq BS1 ......195 B1
Somerset St
  Bristol BS1 ....195 B1
  Bristol, Kingsdown BS2 ...195 A4
Somerset Way NP16 ... 60 F4
Somerton Cl BS15 ..... 10 E7
Somerton Rd BS7 ..... 18 E6
Somerville Cl BS31 ......5 E2
Somerville Ct GL7 .....190 B2
Somerville Ho BS10 ... 18 A8
Somme Rd GL52 ....134 B2
Sommerville Rd BS7 ... 18 E3
Sommerville Rd S 1 BS6. 18 F2
Soper Gdns BS4 ....2 D7
Sopwith Rd GL51 ......169 D7
Sopworth Rd SN14 .... 47 E5
Sorbus Cl BS32 .... 40 E5
Soren Larsen Way GL2 .118 C6
Sorrel Cl
  Gloucester GL4 ....119 A4
  Thornbury BS35 ...... 64 D2
Sotherby Dr GL51 .....132 D1
Soudley La GL14.......156 D5
Soundwell Rd BS15, BS16 . 20 D2
South Africa Ho 2 GL51. 132 F4
Southall Terr GL18 .....170 E2
Southam La GL52 ......134 B8
Southampton Gdns BS7 . 18 F5
Southampton Mews BS7 . 18 F5
South Ave
  Ashchurch GL20.......182 D4
  Yate BS37 .... 43 B1
Southbank GL5 .... 99 A2
South Bank GL51 ......132 F3
Southbow Ho 2 BS3 .....8 A3
South Bristol Comm Hospl
  BS14 ....2 E5
South Bristol Ret Pk BS3.. 8 A3
South Bristol Trad Pk BS3 ..7 F3
Southbrook Rd GL4 ....127 C1
South Cerney GL7.......151 A2
South Cerney CE GL7 ..150 E2
South Cl GL2 ....127 B4
Southcourt Cl GL53 ....130 D5
Southcourt Dr GL53 ....130 D5
South Croft BS9 .... 18 C7
South Dene BS9 .... 17 E6
Southdown Rd BS9 .... 17 F8
Southend Ho GL12 .... 54 A5
Southend La GL18......171 A4
Southend The HR8 .....178 F8
Southern Ave GL4......118 E4
Southernhay
  Bristol, Clifton Wood
    BS8 ....194 B3
  Bristol, Staple Hill BS16 .. 20 D4
Southernhay Ave BS8 ..194 B3
Southernhay Cres BS8 .194 B3
Southern Rd GL53 .....130 E4
Southey Ave BS15 ..... 20 E1

Southey Ct BS15 .... 20 D1
Southey St BS2 .... 18 F2
South Farm Cotts GL7 ..153 B5
Southfield
  Minchinhampton GL6.... 91 F6
  Tetbury GL8 ....140 B3
Southfield App GL53 ...130 E4
Southfield Ave BS15 ... 20 E1
Southfield Cl GL53 .....130 E4
Southfield Ct
  Bristol BS9 .... 18 A7
  Churchdown BS3 ......128 A6
Southfield Jun Sch SN6 145 D3
Southfield Manor Pk
  GL53 ....130 F3
Southfield Rd
  Bristol, Cotham BS6.... 18 D1
  Bristol, Westbury on Trym
    BS9 .... 18 A7
  5 Coleford GL16 ......155 A6
  Gloucester GL4 ....118 F5
  Woodchester GL5 ..... 99 A2
Southfield Rise GL53 ..130 E4
Southfield Way BS37 ... 44 A4
Southgate Cres GL5 ... 99 A5
South Gate Ct GL54 ...169 D6
Southgate Dr GL53 ....130 F7
Southgate Gdns GL5 ... 99 A5
Southgate Mews GL7...190 D3
Southgate St GL1 ......196 A2
South Gr
  Bristol BS6 .... 18 C5
  Pill BS20 .... 16 C4
South Green St 9 BS8 ...7 F6
South Hayes BS5 ...... 19 B4
Southlands
  Bristol, Clifton BS8 .... 18 A1
  Bristol, Knowle Park BS4... 9 B1
  Tytherington GL12 .... 52 B4
Southleigh Mews BS8 ..194 B4
Southleigh Rd BS8 .....194 B4
South Liberty La
  Bristol BS3 .... 8 A1
  2 Bristol BS13 .... 8 B2
South Mdw La SN5 ....143 F2
South Meadow La SN5 ..144 A2
Southmead Hospl BS10 .. 18 E8
Southmead La GL6......105 B5
South Meadow La SN5 ..144 A2
Southmead Rd BS10, BS34 28 E1
Southmead Way BS10 ....18 D8
Southover Cl BS9 ...... 18 A8
South Par
  11 Ledbury HR8 ......178 F8
  Yate BS37 .... 43 E1
South Rd
  12 Bristol, Bedminster BS3.. 8 C3
  Bristol, Kingswood BS15 ... 10 D8
  Bristol, Redland BS6 ... 18 C2
  Coleford, Broadwell GL16. 155 B5
  3 Coleford GL16 ......155 A6
  Lydney GL15........... 92 A4
  Woodhouse Down BS32 ... 40 E6
Southrop CE Prim Sch
  GL7 ....153 D6
Southsea Rd BS34 ..... 29 A8
Southside GL8 .... 59 E7
Southside Cl BS9 ...... 17 B8
South St
  Bristol BS3 .... 8 B3
  Uley GL11 .... 89 C1
South Street Prim Sch BS3 8 B3
South Terr 6 BS6 ...... 18 B2
South View
  Blockley GL56 ....186 C6
  Bristol BS16 .... 20 E5
  Frampton Cotterell BS36... 31 B7
  Ripple GL20 ....181 D8
  Stroud GL5............ 98 C7
South View Bsns Pk BS16. 20 F5
South View Cotts GL5 .. 98 E8
South View Cres BS36... 31 D6
South View Rise BS36... 31 D6
South View Way GL52 ..134 C4
Southville Pl BS3 ....8 D4
Southville Prim Sch BS3 .. 8 C4
Southville Rd BS3 .... 8 C4
South Way GL7 ....190 C4
Southway Dr BS15 ..... 11 D5
Southwell St BS2 ......194 C4
South Wlk
  Mitcheldean GL17......164 D5
  Yate BS37 .... 43 E1
Southwood Ave BS9.... 17 C8
Southwood Cl GL14 ....191 D5
Southwood Dr BS9 .... 17 B8
Southwood Dr E BS9 ... 17 C8
Southwood La GL50 ....193 A2
Sovereign Chase GL19 .172 B8
Sovereign Ct GL1 ......196 C3
Space Business Ctr GL51 133 B3
Spa Cl SN6 ....145 D4
Spa Ct GL50 ....193 A3
Spa Gdns GL20 ....192 F4
Spalding Cl BS7 .... 19 A3
Spa Mews GL1 ....196 A2
Spa Rd GL1 ....196 B1
Spark Hill GL11 .... 87 F6

Spar Rd
  Avonmouth BS11 ...... 26 D4
  Yate BS37 .... 43 D2
Sparrowbill Wy BS34 ... 29 A7
Sparrow Cl 1 GL2 .....148 C6
Sparrow Hill GL16......155 A5
Sparrows La HR9, GL18 .170 B4
Spartan Cl 2 GL4 ......119 E6
Spartley Dr BS13 ....1 F6
Spartley Wlk BS13 ....1 F6
Spa Villas GL1 ....196 B1
Speculation Rd GL14 ..191 B7
Speech House Rd
  Cinderford GL14, GL16 ..156 A7
  Coleford GL16 ....155 D6
Speedwell 3 GL16 .....155 B6
Speedwell Ave 5 BS5 ...9 D7
Speedwell Cl
  Gloucester GL4 ....119 C6
  Thornbury BS35 ...... 64 D2
Speedwell Rd BS5, BS15 . 20 A1
Spencer Cl GL3 ....119 F7
Spencer Ct GL50 ......193 A4
Spencer Ho 6 BS1 .....195 B1
Spencer's Ct BS35 ..... 51 B5
Spenser Ave GL51 .....132 E1
Spenser Rd GL51 ......132 E1
Sperringate GL7 ....190 D3
Spey Cl
  Quedgeley GL2........117 F2
  Thornbury BS35 ...... 51 C8
Spider La GL5 .... 99 E6
Spillman's Pitch GL5 ... 99 A6
Spillman's Rd GL5 ..... 99 A6
Spindles The GL53 .....130 A4
Spine Rd W GL7 ....142 D5
Spine Road E GL7 .....143 B7
Spinnaker Ho GL2 .....118 C8
Spinnaker Rd GL2 .....118 C8
Spinners Cotts GL6 .... 91 F3
Spinners Ho 15 BS5 ... 99 C7
Spinney Croft BS13 ......1 F5
Spinney Ct GL5 .... 99 F1
Spinney Rd GL4 ....119 E7
Spinney The
  Bristol BS32.......... 29 E7
  Cheltenham GL52......133 E4
  Frampton Cotterell BS36... 31 B7
  Lechlade on T GL7 ....153 C2
  Stroud GL6............105 C7
Spinning Wheel Ct GL5. 98 E7
Spires View 4 BS16 ... 19 E5
Spire Way GL4 ....119 D8
Spitalgate La GL7 ......190 C5
Spital La GL54 ....143 F4
Spittle Leys 5 GL54 ...174 A7
Spoonbill Cl GL2 ......117 D1
Spot The BS36 .... 31 C7
Spout Hill GL15 ....147 C3
Spouthouse La GL11 ... 88 A5
Spout La GL17 ....164 A4
Spratsgate La GL7 .....142 D6
Spread Eagle Rd GL1 ..196 B3
Springbank Cl GL51 ...132 C3
Springbank Dr GL51 ...132 C3
Springbank Gr GL51 ...132 C3
Springbank Prim Acad
  GL51 ....132 D4
Springbank Rd GL51 ...132 C3
Springbank Way GL51 .132 D4
Spring Cotts
  Stonehouse GL10....... 98 A6
  Stroud GL6............104 A2
Springdale HR9 ....170 B4
Spring Dale GL2 ....165 F5
Springdale Cl GL2......109 D8
Springfield
  Blockley GL56 ....186 C6
  Bourton-on-W GL54 ...168 F7
  Dursley GL11 .... 87 E4
  Hardwicke GL2 ....109 E7
  Tewkesbury GL20 .....192 F5
  1 Thornbury BS35 .... 51 D8
Springfield Ave
  Bristol, Horfield BS7 ... 18 F5
  Bristol, Mangotsfield BS16... 21 A7
  Bristol, Shirehampton BS11 16 D6
Springfield Bsns Ctr GL10 97 C8
Springfield Cl
  Bristol BS16 .... 21 A7
  Cheltenham GL51......129 C7
  2 Coleford GL16 ......155 A5
Springfield Cotts 6 A8
Springfield Ct 12 GL10 .. 97 F7
Springfield Dr GL14 ...191 C6
Springfield Gr BS6..... 18 C5
Springfield Ho
  Bristol BS6............194 C4
  Cheltenham GL51......132 E4
Springfield La WR12 ...185 B8
Springfield Lawns BS11.. 16 D6
Springfield Pl GL4 .....121 F1
Springfield Rd
  Bristol, Cotham BS6..... 18 D1
  Bristol, Mangotsfield BS16. 21 A7
  Cirencester GL7 ....190 B2
  Lydney GL15........... 92 A4
  Pill BS20 .... 16 C4
  Quenington GL7.......152 D7
  Stroud GL5............ 99 C8
  Stroud, Westrip GL5 ... 98 D8
Springfields
  Bristol BS34 .... 29 A2
  Tetbury GL8 ....140 C4
Springfields Ct GL11 ... 87 E4

Springfield Terr 3 GL5 . 98 D6
Spring Field Terr GL5 .. 99 A6
Springfort BS9 .... 17 F3
Spring Gdns
  Bristol BS5............ 9 A1
  Lechlade on T GL7 ....153 E2
  Quenington GL7.......152 D7
  Tewkesbury GL20 .....192 D4
Spring Gr 6 HR8 ....178 F7
Springhill
  Dursley GL11 .... 88 C3
  Sandhurst GL2 ....172 F2
  Stroud GL5............ 99 C8
Spring Hill
  Bristol, Kingsdown BS2...195 A4
  Bristol, Upper Soundwell
    BS15 .... 20 E2
  Eastington GL10 ...... 97 A8
  Nailsworth GL6 .... 91 B4
Springhill Cl GL6....... 91 B4
Springhill Cotts WR12...185 B4
Springhill Cres GL6 .... 91 B4
Springhill Gt GL2 .....172 F1
Springhill (Old Court)
  GL11 .... 88 B3
Spring Ho 2 BS35 ..... 51 C8
Spring La
  Cheltenham GL52......134 B6
  Cleeve Hill GL52 ......138 E2
  Dundry BS41 ....2 A1
  Stroud GL5............ 99 C6
  Thrupp GL5 .... 99 E3
Springleaze
  Bristol, Knowle Park BS4... 9 A4
  Bristol, Mangotsfield BS16 . 21 A7
Springly Ct BS15 ...... 11 B8
Spring Meadow Rd GL15. 92 A4
Spring Mill Ind Est GL6.. 91 D3
Spring Pl GL17 ....163 E4
Spring St BS3 ....8 E4
Springs The GL15 ..... 92 A4
Spring Street Pl BS3 .... 8 E4
Springvale GL54 ....168 F8
Springville Cl BS30..... 11 A3
Springwater Cl GL20 ..182 C5
Springwater Pk Trad Est
  BS5....................9 E7
Springwell Gdns GL3...128 A8
Springwood Dr BS10 ... 27 D3
Spruce Cl GL20 ....182 C5
Spruce Rd GL16 ....155 C6
Spruce Ride
  Cinderford GL14, GL16 ..156 A5
  Coleford GL16 ....155 F6
Spruce Way BS34 ..... 28 F7
Square The
  Alveston BS35 .... 51 A4
  Bibury GL7............160 A1
  Bristol BS1............195 C2
  Bristol, Knowle Park BS4... 9 A4
  Bristol, Staple Hill BS16 .. 20 E4
  6 Chipping Campden
    GL55 ....189 A2
  Gloucester GL3 ....120 B6
  Goodrich HR9 ....163 A6
  Guiting Power GL54 ...175 B3
  Ruardean GL17 ....163 E4
  St Briavels GL15 ......146 E7
  3 Stonehouse GL10....97 F8
  Stroud GL5............ 99 C8
  Toddington GL54 .....184 B3
  Wotton-u-E GL12 ..... 68 C6
Squires Ct
  Bretforton WR11 ......188 A6
  Bristol BS30........... 10 F4
  Highworth SN6 ....145 C3
Squires Leaze BS35 ... 64 D2
Squirrel Cl GL2 ....109 E7
Squirrels The GL17 ....164 B4
Stable Cotts
  Adlestrop GL56 ....177 F3
  Bromesberrow Heath HR8 179 C5
Stables The
  Cheltenham GL52......134 C4
  Lechlade on T GL7 ....153 E3
  Stow-on-t-W GL54 ....176 F4
Stable Yd GL5 .... 99 C8
Stable Yd The GL9 ..... 46 B2
Stackpool Rd BS3 ....8 C4
Stadium Rd BS6 .... 18 C5
Stafford Cl
  8 Coleford GL16 ......155 B6
  Quedgeley GL2........110 B7
Stafford Cres BS35..... 64 B1
Stafford Mill Ind Est GL5. 99 D4
Stafford Rd BS2 .... 19 A2
Staffords Ct BS30 ..... 11 A6
Stafford St BS3 ....8 D4
Stag Hill GL15 ....156 A2
Stainer Cl BS4 ....2 D1
Staites Orch GL4.......119 E3
Stamage's La GL6......103 F7
Stambourne La GL13... 85 E8
Stambourne Villas GL13.. 85 E8
Stamp's Mdw GL2......126 F5
Stanborough La GL54 ..167 F8
Stanbridge Cl BS16 ... 20 F6
Stanbridge Prim Sch
  BS16 ....20 F6
Stanbridge Rd BS16.... 20 F6
Stanbury Ave BS16.... 20 C5
Stanbury Mews GL3...120 B6
Stanbury Rd BS3.........8 E3

Stancombe La
Bisley GL6 . . . . 104 F2
Winchcombe GL54 . . . . . . 174 B7
Stancombe View
North Nibley GL11 . . . . 79 D5
25 Winchcombe GL54 . . . . 174 A7
Standfast Rd BS10 . . . . . 27 F3
Standish Ave BS34 . . . . . 40 C1
Standish Cl BS10 . . . . 27 F1
Standish Ct GL10 . . . . . 101 E5
Standish La GL2, GL10 . . 101 C6
Standish Park Cotts
GL10 . . . . 102 C4
Standish Westridge Hospl
GL10 . . . . 102 B2
Standle La GL11 . . . . 87 A2
Standon Way BS10 . . . . . 28 C2
Stane Way BS11 . . . . 16 C7
Stanfield Cl BS7 . . . . 19 C6
Stanford Cl BS36 . . . . 30 F8
Stanford Pl BS4 . . . . 2 D7
Stanford Rd
Lydney GL15 . . . . 92 A3
Northway GL20 . . . . 182 C4
Stanhope Rd BS30 . . . . . . 10 F2
Stanhope St BS5 . . . . 9 A5
Stanier Rd BS16 . . . . 21 B3
Stank La GL2 . . . . 109 C6
Stanleigh Terr GL2 . . . . . 126 A7
Stanley Ave
Bristol, Bishopston BS7 . . . 18 E3
Bristol, Filton BS34 . . . . . . 29 B2
Stanley Chase BS5 . . . . . 19 E2
Stanley Cotts
Gloucester GL1 . . . . 196 C1
Gretton GL54 . . . . 183 E1
Stanley Cres BS34 . . . . . . 29 B2
Stanley Gdns BS30 . . . . . 11 B4
Stanley Hill BS4 . . . . 9 A4
Stanley Mead BS32 . . . . . 40 E2
Stanley Mills Cotts GL10 . . 98 A5
Stanley Park Rd BS16 . . . 20 E3
Stanley Pk
Bristol BS5 . . . . 19 C1
Stroud GL5 . . . . 98 E4
Stanley Pl GL51 . . . . 132 D3
Stanley Rd
Bristol, Cotham BS6 . . . . . 18 C1
Bristol, Warmley BS15 . . . . 11 B8
Cheltenham GL52 . . . . . . 134 B1
Gloucester GL1 . . . . 118 E6
Stanley St N 13 BS3 . . . . . 8 C3
Stanley St S BS3 . . . . 8 C2
Stanley St
5 Bristol, Bedminster BS3 . . 8 C3
Bristol, Upper Easton BS5 . . . 9 A8
Stanley Terr
Bristol BS3 . . . . 8 C2
Gloucester GL1 . . . . 118 E7
Stanley The GL4 . . . . 119 F2
Stanley View GL5 . . . . 98 F5
Stanley Wlk GL4 . . . . 119 F1
Stanmoor GL4 . . . . 119 E3
Stansby Cres GL3 . . . . . . 128 A6
Stansby Park Cvn Pk
GL51 . . . . 129 B6
Stansby Touring Pk
GL51 . . . . 129 B6
Stanshaw Cl BS16 . . . . . . 20 A7
Stanshaw Cres BS37 . . . . 43 E1
Stanshawes Court Dr
BS37 . . . . 32 E8
Stanshawes Dr
3 Yate BS37 . . . . 32 D8
Yate BS37 . . . . 43 D1
Stanshaw Rd BS16 . . . . . 20 A7
Stanshaws Cl BS32 . . . . . 40 C2
Stansted Ho GL1 . . . . . . 196 A3
Stanthill Dr GL11 . . . . 80 C8
Stanton Cl BS15 . . . . 20 F1
Stanton Rd
Bristol BS10 . . . . 28 E2
Stroud GL5 . . . . 98 E8
Tewkesbury GL20 . . . . . . 192 D5
Stantons Dr GL51 . . . . . . 133 A7
Stanton Way GL51 . . . . . 129 E8
Stantway La GL14 . . . . . . 157 E8
Stanway BS30 . . . . 11 C1
**Stanway House & Water
Gdns** ★ GL54 . . . . 184 E3
Stanway Rd
Cheltenham GL51 . . . . . . 129 D8
Gloucester GL4 . . . . 119 C7
Stanton WR12 . . . . 184 E5
Stanway Wood Dr GL52 . . 137 E3
Stanwick Cres GL51 . . . . 133 B5
Stanwick Dr GL51 . . . . . 133 B5
Stanwick Gdns GL51 . . . 133 B4
Staple Gr BS31 . . . . 4 D5
Staple Grove Cres BS5 . . . 10 A7
Staple Hill Prim Sch BS16 20 D4
Staple Hill Rd BS16 . . . . . 20 B4
Staples BS37 . . . . 43 D2
Stapleton Cl
Bristol BS16 . . . . 19 D5
Highworth SN6 . . . . 145 C3
Stapleton Rd
Bristol, Baptist Mills BS5 . . . 19 B1
Bristol, Eastville BS5 . . . . . 19 C3
Stapleton Road Sta BS5 . . 19 B1
Star Ave BS34 . . . . 30 A4
Star Barn Rd BS36 . . . . . . 30 E7
Star Beech Hill GL17,
HR9 . . . . 163 E6
Star Ct 10 GL52 . . . . 133 F2
Star Hill GL6 . . . . 91 A5

Star La
Avening GL8 . . . . 140 B8
Bristol BS16 . . . . 19 F3
Pill BS20 . . . . 16 D4
Starling Ct 7 GL10 . . . . . 97 F8
Starling Rd GL20 . . . . . . 192 F1
Stars Pitch GL17 . . . . . . 164 D5
Starveall Cl 3 BS5, BS15 . . 20 A1
Station App
Bristol BS1 . . . . 195 C1
Gloucester GL1 . . . . 196 C3
Minety SN16 . . . . 142 E1
Station Ave 3 BS16 . . . . . 20 A4
Station Avenue S 5 BS16 . 20 A4
Station Cl
Bristol BS15 . . . . 11 C8
Cheltenham GL53 . . . . . . 130 D5
Chipping Sodbury BS37 . . . 33 D8
Churchdown GL3 . . . . . . 128 D5
Station Cotts GL20 . . . . . 182 C7
Station Ct
Bristol BS15 . . . . 9 E8
Bristol BS15 . . . . 10 F8
Station Dr GL20 . . . . 182 C7
Station Ind Est NP16 . . . . 60 F8
Station La
Bristol BS7 . . . . 19 A4
Longhope GL17 . . . . 164 F5
Tewkesbury GL20 . . . . . . 192 D5
Station Mdw GL54 . . . . . 168 F8
Station Rd
Acton Turville GL9 . . . . 35 F8
Andoversford GL54 . . . . . 166 D6
Ashton under Hill WR11 . . 183 B8
Beckford GL20 . . . . 183 B6
Berkeley GL13 . . . . 85 E5
Bishop's Cleeve GL52 . . . 138 B4
Bledington OX7 . . . . 177 F1
Blockley GL56 . . . . 186 D6
Bourton-on-t-W GL54 . . . 168 F8
Bretforton WR11 . . . . . . 188 A7
Bristol, Ashley Down BS7 . . 18 F4
Bristol, Filton BS34 . . . . . . 29 A3
Bristol, Fishponds BS16 . . . 20 A4
Bristol, Henbury BS10 . . . . 27 F4
Bristol, Montpelier BS6 . . . 18 E2
Bristol, Newleaze BS34 . . . 29 B2
Bristol, Patchway BS34 . . . 29 C7
Bristol, Shirehampton BS11 16 D5
Bristol, Shirehampton BS11 16 E6
Bristol, Staple Hill BS15 . . . 20 F3
Bristol, Upper Knowle BS4 . . 9 D2
Bristol, Warmley BS30 . . . . 11 C7
Broadway WR12 . . . . 185 B8
Charfield GL12 . . . . 67 B5
Chepstow/Cas-Gwent NP16 60 F8
Chipping Campden GL55 . . 189 A2
Churchdown GL3 . . . . . . 128 C5
Coalpit Heath BS36 . . . . . . 31 C5
Dursley GL11 . . . . 88 A5
Gloucester GL1 . . . . 196 C2
Highworth SN6 . . . . 145 C3
Honeybourne WR11 . . . . 188 C7
Iron Acton BS37 . . . . 42 D3
Kemble GL7 . . . . 141 F8
Keynsham BS31 . . . . 4 E6
Kingham OX7 . . . . 177 F2
Lechlade on T GL7 . . . . . . 153 E3
Lydney GL15 . . . . 84 A8
Lydney GL15 . . . . 84 A8
Milkwall GL16 . . . . 155 B4
Minety SN16 . . . . 142 E1
11 Moreton-in-M GL56 . . 187 A3
Nailsworth GL6 . . . . 91 C4
Newnham GL14 . . . . 156 F7
Pill BS20 . . . . 16 C4
Pilning BS35 . . . . 38 F4
Ripple GL20 . . . . 181 D8
Severn Beach BS35 . . . . . . 38 A6
South Cerney GL7 . . . . . . 143 A7
Stroud GL5 . . . . 99 B7
Tewkesbury GL20 . . . . . . 192 D5
Wickwar GL12 . . . . 54 B7
Winterbourne BS36 . . . . . 30 E4
Woodchester GL5 . . . . 99 A1
Woolaston GL15 . . . . 147 C2
Yate BS37 . . . . 43 C2
Station Road Bsns Ctr
BS15 . . . . 21 A3
Station Road Link BS15 . . 21 A2
Station Road Workshops
BS15 . . . . 21 A3
Station St
Cheltenham GL50 . . . . . . 193 A4
Cinderford GL14 . . . . 191 C5
Tewkesbury GL20 . . . . . . 192 D4
Station Terr
Cinderford GL14 . . . . 191 C5
Dymock GL18 . . . . 178 D2
Staunton Cl GL4 . . . . 119 E4
**Staunton & Corse CE Prim
Sch** GL19 . . . . 172 B8
Staunton Ct Bsns Pk
GL19 . . . . 172 A8
Staunton Fields BS14 . . . . 3 C4
Staunton Ho GL16 . . . . . 154 D7
Staunton La
Watermead GL3 . . . . 120 E4
Whitchurch BS14 . . . . 3 D3
Staunton Rd
Coleford GL16 . . . . 154 F6
Monmouth/Trefynwy GL16,
NP25 . . . . 154 C7
Staunton Way BS14 . . . . . 3 D4
Staveley Cres BS10 . . . . . 28 C2
Staverton Cl BS32 . . . . . . 40 C1

Staverton Connection
GL51 . . . . 173 F1
Staverton Pk GL51 . . . . . 173 F1
Staverton Tech Pk GL51 . . 173 F1
Staverton Way BS15 . . . . 11 A7
Stavordale Gr BS14 . . . . . . 3 B6
Staynes Cres BS15 . . . . . . 10 E8
Steadings Bsns Ctr The
GL2 . . . . 126 A8
Steam Mills GL14 . . . . . . 191 B8
Steam Mills Prim Sch
GL14 . . . . 191 B8
Steam Mills Rd GL14 . . . 191 B7
Steanbridge BS32 . . . . . . 29 D6
Stean Bridge Rd BS32 . . . 29 E6
Stearman Rd GL3, GL4 . . 120 B4
Steel Ave GL15 . . . . 92 B3
Steel Ct BS30 . . . . 10 F3
Steel Mills BS31 . . . . 4 F4
Steeple Cl GL4 . . . . 119 D8
Steeple View GL15 . . . . . . 92 A2
Steep St NP16 . . . . 60 F8
Steevens Ho (almshouses) 15
BS2 . . . . 195 C3
Steiner Academy Bristol
BS16 . . . . 20 A5
Stella Gr BS3 . . . . 8 A2
Stella Way BS3 . . . . 137 D4
Stenders Bsns Pk GL17 . . 164 C5
Stenders Ct GL17 . . . . . . 164 D5
Stenders Rd GL17 . . . . . . 164 D5
Stenders The GL17 . . . . . 164 C5
Stepaside NP16 . . . . 60 C3
Stepbridge Rd GL16 . . . . 155 B4
Stephens Dr GL2 . . . . 110 B6
Stephenson Dr GL2 . . . . . 110 B6
Stephenson Way WR11 . . 188 C7
Stephens Pl GL16 . . . . . . 155 B5
Stephen St BS5 . . . . 9 C8
Stepney Rd BS5 . . . . 19 C1
Stepney Wlk BS5 . . . . 19 C1
Stepping Stone La GL6 . . 103 E6
Stepping Stones The BS4 . . 9 E6
Steps Cl GL11 . . . . 87 F6
Step's La GL6, GL8 . . . . . 148 B1
Stepstairs Ct GL7 . . . . . . 190 D3
Stepstairs La GL7 . . . . . . 190 D3
Sterling Ct GL54 . . . . 176 F4
Sterling Ct GL51 . . . . 133 B2
Sterncourt Rd BS16 . . . . . 20 A7
Sterrys Cnr HR9 . . . . 170 C4
Sterrys Rd HR9 . . . . 170 C4
Stevans Cl GL2 . . . . 127 A5
Stevens Cres BS3 . . . . 8 F4
Stevens Way GL6 . . . . 90 F1
Stevens Wlk BS32 . . . . . . 29 D8
Steward Rd GL20 . . . . . . 182 C4
Stewarts Mill La GL4 . . . 119 E4
Stibbs Ct BS30 . . . . 10 F4
Stibbs Hill BS5 . . . . 10 A7
Sticky La GL2 . . . . 109 E6
Stidcote La GL12 . . . . 52 E5
Stidcot La GL12 . . . . 52 D5
Stile Acres BS11 . . . . 27 A1
Stillhouse La BS3 . . . . 8 D4
Stillingfleet Rd BS13 . . . . . 2 C5
Stillman Cl BS13 . . . . 1 E4
Stinchcombe BS37 . . . . . . 43 E1
Stirling Cl BS37 . . . . 43 D4
Stirling Rd BS4 . . . . 9 C3
Stirling Way
Gloucester GL4 . . . . 118 B2
Keynsham BS31 . . . . 4 E4
Stirling Wy 11 GL56 . . . . 187 B3
Stirrup Cl GL2 . . . . 118 B6
Stirrup The GL5 . . . . 98 D7
Stockdale Cl GL2 . . . . . . 109 D8
Stocken Cl GL3 . . . . 120 B6
Stockham Cl SN6 . . . . . . 143 F4
Stockham Gdns SN6 . . . . 143 F4
Stock Hill BS35 . . . . 63 C1
Stockholm Pl HR9 . . . . . . 164 C8
Stock La GL13 . . . . 85 E3
Stockley Way GL4, GL6 . . 111 D6
Stocks The GL6 . . . . 102 D2
Stockton Cl
Bristol, Oldland BS30 . . . . 11 B3
Bristol, Whitchurch BS14 . . . 2 F4
Cheltenham GL53 . . . . . . 130 F4
Stockwell Ave BS16 . . . . . 21 A6
Stockwell Cl BS16 . . . . . . 20 F7
Stockwell Dr BS16 . . . . . . 21 A6
Stockwell Gn GL14 . . . . . 191 D3
Stockwell La
Aylburton GL15 . . . . 147 E4
Woodmancote GL52 . . . . 138 D3
Stockwells GL56 . . . . 187 A3
Stockwood Chambers BS5 . 9 C7
Stockwood Cres BS4 . . . . . 8 F4
Stockwood Hill BS31 . . . . 4 C7
Stockwood La SN5 . . . . . 143 D1
Stockwood Mews BS4 . . . . 9 F5
Stockwood Rd BS4 . . . . . . 9 F1
Stockyards The GL1 . . . . 126 E4
Stoke Bishop CE Prim Sch
BS9 . . . . 17 D5
Stoke Bridge Ave BS34 . . 29 D6
Stoke Common La SN5 . . 143 D1
Stoke Cotts BS9 . . . . 17 E4
Stokefield Cl BS35 . . . . . . 64 B1
Stoke Gr BS9 . . . . 17 E6
Stoke Hamlet BS9 . . . . . . 17 F6
Stoke Hill BS9 . . . . 17 E3
Stoke La
Bristol, Broomhill BS16 . . . 19 E7
Bristol, Patchway BS34 . . . 29 C8

Stoke La *continued*
Bristol, Westbury on Trym
BS9 . . . . 17 F6
Stokeleigh Wlk BS9 . . . . . 17 C5
Stoke Lodge Prim Sch
BS34 . . . . 29 C8
Stoke Mdws BS32 . . . . . . 40 D1
Stokemead BS34 . . . . 29 C8
Stoke Orchard Rd GL52 . . 137 D4
Stoke Paddock Rd BS9 . . . 17 D6
Stoke Park Cl GL52 . . . . . 137 F4
Stoke Park Ct GL52 . . . . . 137 F4
Stoke Park Prim Sch BS7 . 19 B6
Stoke Park Rd BS9 . . . . . . 17 F4
Stoke Park Rd S BS9 . . . . 17 E3
Stoke Rd
Bishop's Cleeve GL52 . . . 137 E4
Bristol BS8 . . . . 18 A2
Stoke Orchard GL52 . . . . 137 C4
Stokes Croft BS1 . . . . 195 B4
Stokes Ct
11 Bristol BS30 . . . . 11 A4
17 Tewkesbury GL20 . . . 192 C4
Stokes Rd GL20 . . . . 181 D5
Stoke View BS34 . . . . 29 A3
Stoke View Bsns Pk 6
BS16 . . . . 19 F4
Stoke View Rd BS16 . . . . . 19 F3
Stoneberrow Pl GL18 . . . . 178 D2
Stoneberry Rd BS14 . . . . . . 3 B3
Stonebrack Piece GL4 . . . 119 E6
Stone Bridge GL56 . . . . . 187 D7
Stonebridge Pk BS5 . . . . . 19 E2
Stonechat Ave GL4 . . . . . 119 C5
Stonechat Gdns BS16 . . . 19 E6
Stone Cl
Gloucester GL4 . . . . 119 E4
Winterbourne BS36 . . . . . 30 E4
Stone Cotts GL6 . . . . 91 B3
Stone Cres GL51 . . . . 132 F2
Stonecroft GL52 . . . . 137 E4
Stonedale Rd GL10 . . . . . . 97 D8
Stonefern 18 GL56 . . . . . 187 A3
Stonefield Dr SN6 . . . . . . 145 D2
Stoneford La WR11 . . . . . 188 A5
Stonehenge Rd GL4 . . . . . 119 B7
Stonehill BS15 . . . . 10 E4
Stonehill Ctr BS30 . . . . . . 10 E4
Stonehill Farm BS15 . . . . 10 E4
Stonehill La GL7 . . . . 141 B7
Stone Hill Vw BS15 . . . . . 10 C2
Stonehouse Ct GL54 . . . . 176 D4
Stone House Mews BS7 . . 44 B1
Stonehouse Sta GL10 . . . . 97 F7
Stone La BS36 . . . . 30 F3
Stonelea GL11 . . . . 87 E4
Stoneleigh Cl GL53 . . . . . 130 C3
Stoneleigh Cres BS4 . . . . . 9 A2
Stoneleigh Dr BS30 . . . . . 10 F5
Stoneleigh Ho BS8 . . . . . 194 B3
Stoneleigh Rd BS4 . . . . . . 9 A2
Stoneleigh Wlk BS4 . . . . . 9 A2
Stone Manor GL5 . . . . 99 E6
Stone Manor Ct GL5 . . . . . 99 E7
Stone Monolith BS34 . . . . 28 E6
Stone Rd The GL19 . . . . . 172 A7
Stone's Cotts BS10 . . . . . . 27 C4
Stones Ct BS6 . . . . 18 B2
Stonesfield Cl GL7 . . . . . . 153 C6
Stones La SN6 . . . . 143 D4
Stoneville St GL51 . . . . . 193 A4
**Stone with Woodford CE
Prim Sch** GL13 . . . . 77 E4
Stoney Bridge GL4 . . . . . 119 E6
Stoney Field GL2 . . . . 125 C5
Stoneyfield Cl BS20 . . . . . 16 B5
Stoneyfields BS20 . . . . . . 16 B4
Stoneyhills Ind Est HR9 . . 162 D4
Stoney Pool GL7 . . . . 151 E3
Stoney Stile Rd BS35 . . . . 51 A5
Stony Riding GL6 . . . . . . 148 C5
Stores Rd BS11 . . . . 26 C4
Storrington Gdns 11 GL10 97 F7
Storrington Pl 8 GL10 . . . 97 F7
Storrington Rd GL10 . . . . 97 F7
Stothard Rd BS7 . . . . 19 B7
Stottbury Rd BS7 . . . . 19 A3
Stoulgrove La NP16 . . . . . 73 A4
Stoulton Gr BS10 . . . . 28 A3
Stourden Cl BS16 . . . . 20 A7
Stourton Dr BS30 . . . . 10 F4
Stover Rd BS37 . . . . 43 B2
Stover Trad Est BS37 . . . . 43 B2
Stow Cl GL4 . . . . 118 F6
Stow Ct GL51 . . . . 133 A1
Stowe La GL15 . . . . 154 E1
Stowell Hill Rd GL12 . . . . 52 B6
Stowell Mews GL4 . . . . . . 119 D7
Stowell Pk GL54 . . . . 159 D8
Stowe Rd GL15 . . . . 146 D8
Stowfield Rd GL17 . . . . . . 163 C4
Stow Gn 15 GL54 . . . . . . 176 F4
Stow Hill Rd GL12 . . . . . . 52 B6
Stow Ho BS11 . . . . 16 E5
Stowick Gdns BS11 . . . . . 27 C2
Stow-on-the-Wold Prim Sch
GL54 . . . . 176 F4
Stow Rd
Baunton GL7 . . . . 150 E7
Bledington OX7 . . . . 177 E1
Moreton-in-M GL56 . . . . 187 A4
Strachans Cl GL5 . . . . 99 A7
Stradbrook Ave BS5 . . . . . 10 A6
Stradling Rd BS11 . . . . . . 27 C2

Stradlings Yd BS2 . . . . . . 194 C4
Straight La GL19 . . . . 172 B8
Straight St BS2 . . . . 195 C2
Straits Par BS16 . . . . 20 B5
Strand Ct GL53 . . . . 193 C3
Strand La GL14 . . . . 157 C8
Strand The GL50 . . . . 193 C3
Stranks Cl SN6 . . . . 145 D2
Stratford Bridge GL20 . . . 180 E9
Stratford Cl
Bristol BS14 . . . . 2 F3
Gloucester GL2 . . . . 118 C4
Stratford Ct BS9 . . . . 17 F8
Stratford Rd
Honeybourne WR11 . . . . 188 D7
Mickleton GL55 . . . . 189 A7
Stroud GL5 . . . . 99 A8
Strathearn Dr BS10 . . . . . 28 B2
Stratheden BS8 . . . . 194 A4
Strathmore Rd BS7 . . . . . 18 F5
Stratmore Est GL16 . . . . . 155 B3
Stratton Brook GL7 . . . . . 190 A7
Stratton CE Prim Sch
GL7 . . . . 190 A8
Stratton Cl BS34 . . . . 29 C7
Stratton Cnr GL1 . . . . 196 C1
Stratton Ct GL20 . . . . 192 D5
Stratton Hts GL7 . . . . 190 B8
Stratton Mills GL7 . . . . . . 190 C7
Stratton Rd
Gloucester GL1 . . . . 196 C1
Saltford BS31 . . . . 5 E3
Strawberry Field 2
GL16 . . . . 155 A7
Strawberry Hill GL18 . . . . 171 A6
Strawberry La
Bristol BS5 . . . . 9 E7
Dundry BS13, BS41 . . . . . . 1 E3
Meysey Hampton GL7 . . . 152 B2
Strawbridge Rd 11 BS5 . . . 9 B7
Stream BS10 . . . . 28 D3
Streamfield GL12 . . . . 68 B8
Stream La GL18 . . . . 171 B5
Streamleaze BS35 . . . . . . 51 C8
Streamleaze Ct BS35 . . . . 51 B8
Streamside
Bishop's Cleeve GL52 . . . 137 F4
Gloucester GL4 . . . . 118 A2
Stroud GL5 . . . . 99 C7
Stream Side BS16 . . . . 20 F6
Streamside Rd BS37 . . . . . 44 A1
Streamside Wlk BS4 . . . . . 9 E3
Stream The BS16 . . . . 30 B2
Street Cotts SN16 . . . . . . 142 A4
Street The
Acton Turville GL9 . . . . . . 35 F6
Alveston BS35 . . . . 51 B5
Burton SN14 . . . . 36 B4
Castle Eaton SN6 . . . . . . 144 D6
Coaley GL11 . . . . 88 E8
Crudwell SN16 . . . . 141 C3
Didmarton GL9 . . . . 57 C3
Frampton on Severn GL2 . 157 F2
Horsley GL6 . . . . 90 F1
Latton SN6 . . . . 143 E6
Leighterton GL8 . . . . 70 C3
Leonard Stanley GL10 . . . 97 E3
Luckington SN14 . . . . 47 E4
Marston Meysey SN6 . . . 144 B8
North Nibley GL11 . . . . . . 79 D4
Oaksey SN16 . . . . 142 A4
Olveston BS35 . . . . 50 A3
Shipton Moyne GL8 . . . . . 59 D8
Uley GL11 . . . . 89 B1
Woodchester GL5 . . . . 99 B3
Strensham Bsns Pk WR8 . 180 A9
Strensham Court Mews
WR8 . . . . 180 A10
Strensham Gate WR8 . . . 180 A10
Stretford Ave BS5 . . . . 9 D8
Stretford Rd BS5 . . . . 9 D8
Strickland Homes 5
GL52 . . . . 130 F8
Strickland Rd GL52 . . . . . 130 F8
Stride Cl BS35 . . . . 38 A6
Striguil Rd NP16 . . . . 60 E6
Stringer's Cl GL5 . . . . 99 A5
Stringer's Dr GL5 . . . . 99 A5
Strode Comm BS35 . . . . . 50 F5
Strode Gdns BS35 . . . . . . 50 F5
Stroma Way SN6 . . . . . . 145 C4
Strongbow Rd NP16 . . . . . 60 E6
Stroud Ent Ctr GL5 . . . . . 98 F4
Stroud General Hospl
GL5 . . . . 99 D6
Stroud High Sch GL5 . . . . 99 A7
Stroud Maternity Hospl
GL5 . . . . 99 D6
Stroud Rd
Bisley GL6 . . . . 105 A1
Bristol, Patchway BS34 . . . 28 F8
Bristol, Shirehampton BS11 16 E5
Cirencester GL7 . . . . 150 B4
Gloucester GL1, GL4 . . . . 118 E6
Nailsworth GL6 . . . . 91 B5
Painswick GL6 . . . . 103 D6
Stroud Sta GL5 . . . . 99 C6
Stroud Valley Com Prim Sch
Stroud GL5 . . . . 99 C6
Stroud GL5 . . . . 99 C7
Stroudwater Bsns Pk
GL10 . . . . 97 C8
Stuart Ave NP16 . . . . 72 D1

Stuart St BS5 . . . . 9 C7
Stubbs Wy **7** BS7 . . . . . 19 C8
Studland Ct BS9 . . . . 18 B6
Studland Dr GL52 . . . . 134 C4
Stump La GL3 . . . . 120 B8
Stumpwell La GL12 . . . . . 79 E2
Sturden La BS16 . . . . . . 30 C3
Sturdon Rd BS3 . . . . 8 A3
Sturmer Cl BS37 . . . . . . 43 E4
Sturmey Way BS20 . . . . 16 E3
Sturminster Cl BS3 . . . . . 3 D6
Sturminster Rd BS14 . . . . 3 D7
Sturmyes Rd GL6 . . . . . 148 D6
Sudbrook Trad Est GL2 . 196 A1
Sudbrook Way GL4 . . . . 119 C5
Sudeley Castle & Gardens★
  GL54 . . . . 174 B6
Sudeley Dr GL7 . . . . . . 142 F7
Sudeley Ho **5** GL51 . . . 132 E3
Sudeley View GL54 . . . . 139 F5
Sudeley Wy **3** GL4 . . . . 118 B1
Sudgrove Pk GL4 . . . . . 119 E5
Sudmeadow Rd GL2 . . . 126 C1
Suffolk Cl
  Bristol BS10 . . . . 28 C4
  2 Tetbury GL8 . . . . . . 140 C4
Suffolk Dr GL1 . . . . 126 E4
Suffolk Ho GL50 . . . . . . 193 A2
Suffolk Mews GL50 . . . . 193 B1
Suffolk Par GL50 . . . . . . 193 B2
Suffolk Pl GL7 . . . . 143 E8
Suffolk Rd GL50 . . . . . . 193 A1
Suffolk Sq GL50 . . . . . . 193 A2
Suffolk St GL50 . . . . . . 193 B1
Suffolk Villas GL50 . . . . 193 B1
Sugar Tump HR9 . . . . . . 170 B4
Sugley La GL6 . . . . 90 F2
Sulgrave Cl GL4 . . . . . . 118 C1
Sullivan Cl BS4 . . . . 2 D6
Summer Cl GL5 . . . . 99 E7
Summer Cres GL5 . . . . . . 99 E7
Summer Ct BS8 . . . . . . 194 B3
Summerfield Cl
  Blockley GL56 . . . . 186 C6
  Cheltenham GL51 . . . . . 132 F5
Summer Ground Dr BS13 . 2 A5
Summerhayes BS30 . . . . 11 D5
Summer Hill BS4 . . . . 9 A4
Summerhill Acad BS5 . . . 9 F8
Summerhill Infant Sch BS5 9 E8
Summerhill Rd BS5 . . . . . 9 F8
Summerhill Terr BS5 . . . . 9 F7
Summerhouse La NP16 . . 60 F4
Summer House Way BS30 11 B7
Summer La SN14 . . . . . . 36 F3
Summerland Dr GL3 . . . 128 C5
Summerleaze
  Bristol BS16 . . . . 20 C3
  Keynsham BS31 . . . . 4 E7
  Lydney GL15 . . . . 92 B2
Summerleaze Rd GL15 . . 92 B2
Summer Mdw GL4 . . . . 119 B4
Summers Dr BS30 . . . . . 23 A1
Summersfield Cl GL6 . . . 148 A3
Summersfield Rd GL6 . . 148 A4
Summers Mead BS37 . . . 43 E4
Summers Rd
  4 Bristol BS2 . . . . 19 A1
  13 Winchcombe GL54 . . 174 A7
Summer St
  4 Bristol BS3 . . . . 8 C4
  Stroud GL5 . . . . 99 E7
Summers Terr **3** BS2 . . 19 A1
Summers Wy GL56 . . . . 187 B3
Summit Cl BS15 . . . . . . 10 E8
Sundale HR9 . . . . 170 B4
Sundays Hill BS32 . . . . . 40 A4
Sundayshill La GL12 . . . . 65 D7
Sunderland Ct GL3 . . . . 128 C5
Sunderland Pl BS8 . . . . 194 B3
Sunderland Rd **16** GL56 . 187 B3
Sundridge Pk BS37 . . . . 32 E8
Sun Green Cl **2** GL15 . . 155 D1
Sun Green Rd **3** GL15 . 155 D1
Sunground The GL8 . . . 148 B1
Sun La GL16 . . . . 155 B6
Sunningdale
  Bristol BS8 . . . . 194 B4
  Yate BS37 . . . . 32 E8
Sunningdale Dr BS30 . . . 11 B6
Sunnybank
  Bristol BS16 . . . . 20 E6
  Westerleigh BS37 . . . . . 32 A3
Sunny Bank
  Bristol BS15 . . . . 20 B1
  14 Coleford GL16 . . . . 155 A5
  Wick BS30 . . . . 12 B7
Sunnybank Rd GL16 . . . 155 A6
Sunnybrook Terr GL13 . . 93 D2
Sunnycroft GL52 . . . . . 138 A2
Sunnycroft Mews GL11 . 118 E5
Sunnydene BS4 . . . . 9 D4
Sunnyfield La GL51 . . . . 129 C5
Sunnyfield Rd GL2 . . . . 109 D8
Sunnyhill GL5 . . . . 98 E8
Sunny Hill BS9 . . . . 17 C7
Sunnyhill Ho BS11 . . . . . 16 E6
Sunnyhill Ho E BS11 . . . 16 E6
Sunnyhill Ho W BS11 . . . 16 E6
Sunnymead
  Bristol BS30 . . . . 11 D6
  Keynsham BS31 . . . . 4 F3
Sunnymead Cl GL17 . . . 164 B4

Sunnyside
  Bristol BS9 . . . . 17 E5
  Frampton Cotterell BS36 . 31 B8
Sunnyside Farm Trad Est
  BS20 . . . . 16 C2
Sunnyside La
  Bristol BS16 . . . . 30 C2
  Yate BS37 . . . . 43 C1
Sunnyvale Dr BS30 . . . . 11 B3
Sunny View GL6 . . . . . . 90 F4
Sunny Wlk BS15 . . . . . . 20 B1
Sunridge BS16 . . . . 20 D6
Sunrise Ave
  Bishop's Cleeve GL52 . . 137 F5
  Bishop's Cleeve GL52 . . 138 A5
Sunrise Gr BS4 . . . . 9 D4
Sun Rise Rd **1** GL15 . . 155 D1
Sunset La GL52 . . . . . . 134 C8
Sunset Pl GL19 . . . . . . 165 D6
Sun St
  Cheltenham GL51 . . . . . 133 C3
  Tewkesbury GL20 . . . . . 192 C5
Sun Tump GL15 . . . . . . 147 D8
Surrey Ave GL51 . . . . . 132 F2
Surrey Mews GL51 . . . . 132 F2
Surrey Rd BS7 . . . . 18 E3
Surrey St BS2 . . . . 195 B4
Sussex Ave GL51 . . . . . 133 A2
Sussex Gdns GL3 . . . . . 120 B7
Sussex Pl BS2 . . . . 18 F1
Sussex St BS2 . . . . 9 A6
Sutherland Ave
  Bristol BS16 . . . . 20 E7
  Yate BS37 . . . . 43 D4
Sutherland Cl GL4 . . . . 119 A6
Sutherland Pl **9** BS8 . . 18 A2
Sutton Ave BS4 . . . . 9 D4
Sutton Cl **10** GL11 . . . . 80 B8
Sutton Pk SN26 . . . . . . 144 E1
Sutton Pl GL5 . . . . 99 D7
Sutton Rd
  Littledean GL14 . . . . . . 191 F3
  Upper Soudley GL14 . . . 156 C5
Swagwater La HR9 . . . . 170 C5
Swains Field GL15 . . . . 147 C3
Swainswick BS14 . . . . . . 2 F6
Swaish Dr **3** BS30 . . . . 11 A4
Swallow Cres GL3 . . . . 127 D6
Swallow Croft GL10 . . . 96 F7
Swallow Ct BS14 . . . . . . 3 F6
Swallow Dr BS34 . . . . . 28 E8
Swallow Pk BS35 . . . . . 64 D3
Swallows Ct BS34 . . . . . 29 E4
Swallowtail Cl **6** GL51 . 132 D2
Swan Cl
  Lechlade on T GL7 . . . . 153 E2
  Moreton-in-M GL56 . . . 187 A3
  South Cerney GL7 . . . . 143 A7
Swan Ct GL1 . . . . 196 A3
Swan Field BS37 . . . . . . 43 F2
Swangrove Gdns **2** GL4. 118 B1
Swan La
  Blakeney GL15 . . . . . . 156 E2
  Leigh SN6 . . . . 143 A3
  Stoke Orchard GL52 . . . 136 D5
  18 Stroud GL5 . . . . . . 99 C7
  Winterbourne BS36 . . . . 30 C8
Swanley La GL13 . . . . . . 78 B5
Swanmoor Cres BS10 . . 28 A4
Swan Rd
  Gloucester GL1 . . . . . . 196 C4
  Lydney GL15 . . . . 92 A3
Swanscombe Pl **14** GL51. 129 E5
Swansfield GL7 . . . . . . 153 E3
Swans Mdw GL7 . . . . . 153 F2
Swanswell Dr GL51 . . . . 129 E8
Swan Yd GL7 . . . . 190 C5
Sweden La GL20 . . . . . 183 B5
Sweetbriar Cl GL52 . . . 137 E4
Sweetbriar Ho GL3 . . . . 128 C4
Sweetbriar St GL1 . . . . 196 C4
Sweetman Pl BS2 . . . . . 195 C2
Sweetmore Cl GL56 . . . 177 C5
Sweets Cl BS15 . . . . . . 20 E2
Sweets Rd BS15 . . . . . . 20 E2
Swell CE Prim Sch GL54 176 D4
Swells Hill GL5 . . . . 99 E1
Swift Link GL7 . . . . 143 A7
Swift Rd GL4 . . . . 119 D5
Swifts Hill View GL5 . . . 103 E1
Swilgate Rd GL20 . . . . . 192 C4
Swindon Cl GL51 . . . . . 133 C3
Swindon & Cricklade Rly★
  SN5 . . . . 143 F1
Swindon La GL50 . . . . . 133 D5
Swindon Manor GL51 . . 133 A6
Swindon Rd
  Cheltenham GL50 . . . . . 193 B4
  Cheltenham, St Peter's
    GL51 . . . . 133 B4
  Cirencester GL7 . . . . . . 190 E3
  Cricklade SN6 . . . . 143 F4
  Highworth SN6 . . . . . . 145 C2
Swindon St
  Cheltenham GL51 . . . . . 133 C3
  Highworth SN6 . . . . . . 145 D3
Swindon Village Prim Sch
  GL51 . . . . 133 B7
Swinhay La GL12 . . . . . . 67 B8
Swish La GL17 . . . . 164 A4
Swiss Cl BS3 . . . . 7 F1
Swiss Dr BS3 . . . . 7 F2
Swiss Rd BS3 . . . . 7 F1
Swordfish Cl GL3 . . . . . 128 C5
Swynford Cl GL7 . . . . . 144 E7

Sybil Rd GL1 . . . . 119 A6
Sycamore Ave NP16 . . . 60 E5
Sycamore Cl
  Bristol, Hanham BS15 . . 10 B3
  Bristol, Whitehall BS5 . . 19 E1
  Gloucester GL1 . . . . . . 118 D5
  Tetbury GL8 . . . . 140 D2
Sycamore Cres GL52 . . 138 B4
Sycamore Ct
  Bristol BS7 . . . . 18 E3
  3 Cheltenham GL51 . . 132 D2
  St Arvans NP16 . . . . . . 72 B5
Sycamore Dr
  Bristol BS34 . . . . 28 F7
  Stroud GL5 . . . . 99 B8
  Thornbury BS35 . . . . . . 64 C1
Sycamore Ho **6** BS16 . . 20 C6
Sycamore Rd
  Harrow Hill GL17 . . . . . 164 B3
  Northway GL20 . . . . . . 182 D4
Sydenham Hill BS6 . . . . 18 D1
Sydenham La BS6 . . . . . 18 E1
Sydenham Pl **15** BS6 . . 18 E1
Sydenham Rd
  Bristol, Cotham BS6 . . . 18 E1
  Bristol, Totterdown BS4 . . 9 A3
  3 Cheltenham GL52 . . 130 F8
Sydenham Rd S GL52 . . 130 F8
Sydenham Terr GL51 . . 118 E7
Sydenham Villas Rd
  GL52 . . . . 130 F8
Sydenham Way BS15 . . . 10 C3
Sydney GL10 . . . . 101 E1
Sydney Row BS1 . . . . . 194 B1
Sylvan Cl **19** GL16 . . . . 155 A5
Sylvan View NP16 . . . . 146 B4
Sylvan Way BS9 . . . . . . 17 B7
Sylvia Ave BS3 . . . . 8 F3
Symes Ave BS13 . . . . 2 C4
Symington Rd BS16 . . . 20 B5
Symn La GL12 . . . . 68 B7
Symphony Rd GL51 . . . 129 C6
Symns Ave BS36 . . . . . . 31 B6
Synwell La GL12 . . . . . . 68 C7
Syon Rd GL6 . . . . 148 A3
Syston View BS15 . . . . . 11 A8
Syston Way BS15 . . . . . 20 D1

T

Tabernacle Pitch GL12 . . 68 B7
Tabernacle Rd
  Bristol BS15 . . . . 10 C6
  Wotton-u-E GL12 . . . . . 68 B8
Tabernacle Wlk GL5 . . . 99 B5
Tabrams Pitch GL6 . . . . 91 C4
Tackley Rd BS5 . . . . . . 19 B3
Tadwick La BA1 . . . . . . 13 E1
Taena Pottery★ GL4 . . . 120 B2
Tailor's Ct BS1 . . . . . . 195 A3
Tainmor Cl GL2 . . . . . . 127 E5
Tait's Hill GL11 . . . . 87 C4
Taits Hill Ind Est GL11 . . 87 C4
Tait's Hill Rd GL11 . . . . 87 D4
Talbot Ave BS15 . . . . . . 20 C1
Talbot Ct
  Bristol BS4 . . . . 9 C2
  Cheltenham GL51 . . . . . 130 A8
Talbot Mews GL1 . . . . . 118 D6
Talbot Pl GL17 . . . . . . 164 D5
Talbot Rd
  Bristol BS4 . . . . 9 C2
  Cheltenham GL51 . . . . . 130 A8
Talbot Sq GL54 . . . . . . 176 E4
Talboy's Wlk **6** GL8 . . 140 C5
Talgarth Rd BS7 . . . . . . 18 F4
Tall Elms Cl GL3 . . . . . 128 B5
Tallis Gr BS4 . . . . 2 D6
Tallis Rd GL3 . . . . 127 F8
Tall Trees GL7 . . . . 190 A8
Tally Ho La GL54 . . . . . 175 B3
Talybont La HR9 . . . . . . 162 C3
Tamar Cl BS35 . . . . 51 D7
Tamar Dr BS31 . . . . 5 A4
Tamarisk Cl GL51 . . . . 130 A4
Tamar Rd
  Bristol BS2 . . . . 9 C6
  Brockworth GL3 . . . . . 120 F5
  Cheltenham GL52 . . . . . 134 A2
Tamesis Dr GL7 . . . . . . 141 F8
Tame Wy GL7 . . . . 152 D3
Tamsin Ct BS31 . . . . 4 F5
Tamworth Rd BS31 . . . . . 4 F5
Tandey Wlk GL3 . . . . . 127 E6
Tanglewood Way GL6 . . 148 B6
Tanhouse La BS37 . . . . 43 D7
Tankard's Cl BS8 . . . . . 194 C3
Tanner Cl BS30 . . . . . . 10 F5
Tanner Ct BS30 . . . . . . 10 F5
Tanners Cl GL3 . . . . . . 120 E6
Tanners Ct
  Bristol, Frenchay BS16 . . 30 B1
  4 Bristol, Two Mile Hill
    BS15 . . . . 20 C1
  Marshfield SN14 . . . . . 14 F8
Tanners La SN14 . . . . . . 14 F8
Tanner's La GL51 . . . . . 132 F3
Tanner's Piece GL6 . . . . 91 C3
Tanner's Rd GL51 . . . . 132 F3
Tanners Wlk SN14 . . . . 14 F8
Tannery Cl GL10 . . . . . . 97 E3
Tannery Gdns GL16 . . . 154 F3
Tannery La **19** GL54 . . 168 A1
Tanorth Cl BS14 . . . . . . 3 A3
Tanorth Rd BS14 . . . . . . 2 F3

Tansy Cl GL4 . . . . 119 F5
Tanyard The BS30 . . . . . 11 B2
Tapscott Ct GL12 . . . . . 68 A7
Tapsters BS30 . . . . 11 A4
Tara Cl BS36 . . . . 41 F1
Target Cl GL5 . . . . 99 F7
Tarlton Cl GL4 . . . . 119 E4
Tarn Ho BS34 . . . . 29 A8
Tarnock Ave BS14 . . . . . 3 A7
Tarragon Pl BS32 . . . . . 29 F7
Tarrington Rd **7** GL1 . . 118 F7
Tasmania Ho **4** GL51 . . 132 E2
Tatchley La GL52 . . . . . 134 B4
Tatenhill Cl GL2 . . . . . . 110 B7
Taunton Wlk BS7 . . . . . 19 A7
Taurus Cl GL2 . . . . 126 F5
Taut The GL6 . . . . 148 F6
Taverner Cl BS4 . . . . . . 2 D7
Tavistock Rd BS4 . . . . . . 8 F1
Tavistock Wlk BS4 . . . . . 8 F1
Tawny Cl GL20 . . . . 182 B5
Tayberry Gr GL51 . . . . . 129 F4
Tayler Rd GL54 . . . . . . 168 A1
Taylor Cl BS15 . . . . 10 F8
Taylor Gdns BS13 . . . . . . 1 F4
Taylors Cl SN16 . . . . . . 142 D1
Taylors End GL50 . . . . . 130 B6
Taylors Ground GL2 . . . 117 F2
Taylors Row **28** GL14 . . 176 F4
Tayman Cl BS10 . . . . . . 18 E6
Tayman Ridge BS30 . . . . 5 D8
Taynton Cl BS30 . . . . . . 11 C2
Teagues Wy GL14 . . . . 191 C4
Teal Cl
  Bristol BS32 . . . . 40 D2
  Quedgeley GL2 . . . . . . 117 D1
Teal Wy GL7 . . . . 143 A7
Teasel Cl GL2 . . . . 126 F5
Teasel Mead BS32 . . . . 29 E7
Tebbit Mews **3** GL52 . . 193 C4
Teddington Gdns GL4 . . 119 B6
Ted Preston Cl GL20 . . . 192 D2
Teewell Ave BS16 . . . . . 20 E4
Teewell Cl BS16 . . . . . . 20 E4
Teewell Ct BS16 . . . . . . 20 E4
Teewell Hill BS16 . . . . . 20 E4
Teignmouth Rd BS4 . . . . 8 F1
Telephone Ave BS1 . . . 195 A2
Telford Ho
  Bristol BS8 . . . . 7 E7
  Cheltenham GL51 . . . . . 132 F3
Telford Way GL2 . . . . . 109 F7
Telford Wlk BS5 . . . . . . 20 A1
Tellings Orch SN16 . . . . 142 B2
Teme Rd GL52 . . . . 134 A2
Tempest Dr NP16 . . . . . 60 D8
Templar Rd BS37 . . . . . 43 E3
Temple Back BS1 . . . . . 195 B2
Temple Back E BS1 . . . 195 C2
Temple Circle Gyratory
  BS1 . . . . 195 B1
Temple Cl
  Gloucester GL4 . . . . . . 119 E8
  Lydney GL15 . . . . 147 F6
Temple Cl BS31 . . . . 4 E5
Templefields GL54 . . . . 166 C6
Templefields Cl GL54 . . 166 C6
Temple Gate BS1 . . . . . 195 B1
Temple Gate District Ctr
  BS3 . . . . 8 F4
Temple Guiting CE Prim Sch
  GL54 . . . . 175 A6
Templeland Rd BS13 . . . . 1 F5
Temple Meads Sta BS1 . 195 C2
Temple Rose St BS1 . . . 195 B2
Temple St
  Bristol, Bedminster BS3 . 8 B2
  Bristol BS1 . . . . 195 B2
  Keynsham BS31 . . . . 4 F5
Temple Trad Est BS2 . . . 9 C5
Templeway GL15 . . . . . 147 F6
Temple Way BS2 . . . . . 195 B2
Temple Way Underpass
  BS2 . . . . 195 C3
Templeway W GL15 . . . 147 F6
Tenby La NP16 . . . . 60 F4
Tenby Rd BS31 . . . . 4 D4
Tenby St BS5 . . . . 9 B7
Tennessee Gr BS6 . . . . 18 C5
Tenniscourt Rd BS15 . . . 21 A1
Tennis Rd BS4 . . . . 9 A2
Tennyson Ave GL2 . . . . 118 C4
Tennyson Cl BS31 . . . . . 4 F5
Tennyson Rd
  Bristol BS7 . . . . 18 E5
  Cheltenham GL51 . . . . . 132 E1
  Dursley GL11 . . . . 80 C7
Tensing Rd GL53 . . . . . 130 E4
Tenth Ave BS7 . . . . 29 B1
Tereslake Gn BS10 . . . . 28 D4
Terhill **4** GL52 . . . . . . 133 F2
Tern Cl GL4 . . . . 119 C6
Terrace The
  Nailsworth GL6 . . . . . . 91 A2
  Wotton-u-E GL12 . . . . . 68 D8
Terrell Gdns **14** BS5 . . . 9 D7
Terrell St BS2 . . . . 195 A4
Terris Ct BS34 . . . . 29 E4
Terry Ho BS1 . . . . 194 C3
Terry Ruck Cl GL51 . . . 132 D2
Tesco Rdbt GL2 . . . . . . 117 F1
Tetbury Cl BS34 . . . . . . 29 C7
Tetbury Hill GL8 . . . . . . 140 B8
Tetbury Hospl GL8 . . . . 140 C3
Tetbury La
  Crudwell SN16 . . . . . . 141 B3

Tetbury La continued
  Leighterton GL8 . . . . . . 70 C3
  Nailsworth GL6 . . . . . . 91 C2
Tetbury Police Mus★
  GL8 . . . . 140 B4
Tetbury Rd
  Bristol BS15 . . . . 10 B8
  Cirencester GL7 . . . . . . 150 B3
  Cirencester GL7 . . . . . . 190 E4
  Gloucester GL4 . . . . . . 118 E1
  Sherston SN16 . . . . . . 58 D1
Tetbury St GL6 . . . . . . 148 A3
Teviot Rd BS31 . . . . 5 A4
Tewkesbury CE Prim Sch
  GL20 . . . . 192 D4
Tewkesbury Comm Hospl
  GL20 . . . . 192 D4
Tewkesbury Ind Est
  GL20 . . . . 192 F5
Tewkesbury Mus★ GL20 192 C4
Tewkesbury Rd
  11 Bristol BS2 . . . . . . 19 A2
  Cheltenham GL51 . . . . . 133 A4
  Gloucester GL2 . . . . . . 126 F5
  Newent GL18 . . . . 171 B5
  Northway GL20 . . . . . . 182 B6
  Stow-on-t-W GL54 . . . . 176 C5
  Uckington GL51 . . . . . 132 E6
Tewkesbury Sch GL20 . . 182 B4
Tewther Rd BS13 . . . . . . 2 D3
Texas Cl GL7 . . . . 152 E2
Teyfant Rd BS13 . . . . . . 2 E4
Teyfant Wlk BS13 . . . . . 2 E4
Thackeray BS7 . . . . 19 A8
Thames Cl
  Charfield GL12 . . . . 67 D4
  Cricklade SN6 . . . . 143 E4
Thames Ho **9** BS35 . . . 51 C8
Thames La SN6 . . . . . . 143 F4
Thamesmead Cotts SN6 . 143 E4
Thames Rd GL52 . . . . . 134 A2
Thames St GL7 . . . . . . 153 E2
Thames View **2** SN6 . . 142 F4
Thames Vw GL7 . . . . . . 142 F4
Thanet Rd BS3 . . . . 8 B2
Thatcham Ave
  Gloucester GL2 . . . . . . 118 B1
  Quedgeley GL2 . . . . . . 110 B8
  Quedgeley GL2 . . . . . . 110 B8
Thatcham Rd GL20 . . . . 192 E1
Thatchers Cl BS5 . . . . . 10 B7
Thatchers End GL52 . . . 138 B3
Theatre Royal★ BS1 . . . 195 A4
Theescombe Hill GL5 . . . 91 B6
Theocs Cl GL20 . . . . . . 192 C2
There-and-Back-Again La
  BS1 . . . . 194 C3
Theresa Ave BS7 . . . . . 18 E4
Theresa St GL1 . . . . . . 118 D7
Thessaly Gate GL7 . . . . 190 B4
Thessaly Rd GL7 . . . . . 190 B8
Theyer Cl GL3 . . . . 120 E3
Theynes Croft BS41 . . . . 7 B1
Thicket Ave BS16 . . . . . 20 C3
Thicket Rd BS16 . . . . . . 20 C4
Thicket Wlk BS35 . . . . . 64 C1
Thiery Rd BS4 . . . . 9 C2
Thingwall Pk BS16 . . . . 19 E3
Third Ave
  Bristol, Filton BS7 . . . . . 29 A1
  Bristol, Hengrove BS14 . . 3 B7
  Dursley GL11 . . . . 80 C8
Third Way BS11 . . . . . . 26 C2
Thirlebrook Cotts GL20 . 182 B6
Thirlestaine House Cotts
  GL53 . . . . 193 B3
Thirlestaine Pl GL53 . . . 193 C1
Thirlestaine Rd GL53 . . . 193 C1
Thirlmere Ct BS30 . . . . 11 D6
Thirlmere Rd
  Bristol BS34 . . . . 29 A8
  Cheltenham GL51 . . . . . 129 E7
Thistlebank GL2 . . . . . . 127 B5
Thistledown Cl GL51 . . . 132 D4
Thistle Downs GL20 . . . 182 C5
Thistle St **1** BS3 . . . . . . 8 B3
Thomas Ave BS16 . . . . . 21 B8
Thomas Cl BS1 . . . . . . 195 B2
Thomas Keble Sch GL6 . 148 C7
Thomas La BS1 . . . . . . 195 B2
Thomas Moore Cl GL3 . . 128 A8
Thomas Pring Wlk **1** BS5 20 A1
Thomas St N **12** BS2 . . . 18 D1
Thomas St
  Bristol, Kingsdown BS2 . 195 B4
  8 Bristol, Russell Town BS5 9 B7
  Bristol, St Pauls BS2 . . . 18 F1
  Chepstow/Cas-Gwent NP16 60 E8
  Cirencester GL7 . . . . . . 190 C5
  Gloucester GL1 . . . . . . 196 C1
Thomas Stock Gdns GL4. 119 E6
Thomas Way BS16 . . . . 19 C4
Thomond Cl GL51 . . . . . 133 C4
Thompson Dr GL53 . . . 130 D4
Thompson Rd
  Bristol BS14 . . . . 3 E6
  Siddington GL7 . . . . . . 150 F2
  Stroud GL5 . . . . 99 D8
Thompson Way GL3 . . . 127 E6
Thomson Rd **7** BS5 . . . . 9 B8
Thoresby GL52 . . . . . . 133 E5
Thoresby Ave GL4 . . . . 110 C8
Thornbury Cl GL51 . . . . 133 B2
Thornbury Hospl BS35 . . 64 C1
Thornbury Ind Pk BS35 . 51 B7
Thornbury Mus★ BS35 . . 51 B8

Thornbury Rd BS35...... 51 A5
Thorn Cl BS37 .... 43 D1
Thorncliffe 10 GL51 .... 130 B8
Thorncliffe Dr GL51 .... 130 B8
Thorndale BS8......... 194 A4
Thorndale Mews BS8... 194 A4
Thornhaugh Mews 5
GL51................ 129 E5
Thornhayes Cl BS36.... 31 A8
Thornhill Cl GL11 ...... 118 D5
Thornhills The BS16.... 20 B6
Thornleigh Rd BS7..... 18 E5
Thornmead Gr BS10.... 28 A2
Thorns Farm BS37 ..... 43 E1
Thorn Tree Dr NP16.... 60 F4
Thornwell Prim Sch NP16 60 F5
Thornwell Rd NP16 .... 60 F5
Thornycroft Cl BS7..... 19 B7
Thorpe Lodge 9 BS6 .. 18 D1
Threadneedle St 10 GL5.. 99 C7
Three Ashes La GL18... 171 A6
Three Brooks La BS32... 29 E8
Three Choirs Vineyard★
GL18................ 170 F7
Three Cocks La GL1 ... 196 A3
Three Counties Pk
WR13............... 180 C5
Three Oaks Cl BS16 .... 20 C4
Three Queens' La BS1... 195 B2
Three Sisters La GL52.. 134 D3
Three Trees Wy GL14... 156 E8
Three Wells Rd BS13....1 F4
Thrissell St BS5........ 9 A8
Throat The GL6........ 102 F4
Throgmorton Rd BS4....2 F8
Thrupp La GL5......... 99 E3
Thrupp Sch GL5........ 99 E3
Thrush Cl GL4......... 119 D6
Thurlestone BS14....... 3 A6
Thurlow Rd BS5....... 19 C2
Thurston's Barton BS5.. 19 E1
Tibberton BS15........ 11 A8
Tibberton Com Prim Sch
GL19................ 171 E1
Tibberton Gr GL51 .... 129 B7
Tibberton La GL19..... 165 D6
Tibbiwell Gdns GL6.... 103 F8
Tibbiwell La GL6...... 103 F8
Tibbott Rd BS14 .... 3 D5
Tibbott Wlk BS14...... 3 D5
Tiberius Ave GL15..... 92 B4
Tichborne Rd BS5...... 9 C7
Tide Gr BS11.......... 17 A8
Tidenham Wy BS34..... 39 F1
Tidford Cotts GL7..... 153 E2
Tidling Cnr SN16...... 142 B3
Tidswell Cl GL2....... 109 F8
Tiffany Ct BS1......... 195 B1
Tiger Moth Cl GL3 .... 120 B4
Tilley Cl BS31.......... 5 A2
Tilling Rd BS10........ 18 E7
Tilling Wlk BS10....... 18 E7
Tillis View GL14....... 154 D7
Tilney Rd GL50........ 133 D4
Tilnor Cres GL11...... 87 F4
Tilsdown GL11......... 87 F4
Tilsdown Cl GL11...... 87 F4
Tilting Rd BS35........ 64 B2
Timbercombe Gate GL53 131 B4
Timbercombe La GL53 .. 131 B3
Timbercombe Mews
GL53................ 131 B4
Timber Dene BS16..... 19 D4
Timberscombe Wlk BS14.. 3 C5
Timbrells Ct GL7...... 142 F8
Timbrells The GL7..... 142 B8
Timmis Cl GL4........ 119 C4
Timms Gn WR12....... 188 B2
Timperley Way GL51... 129 E5
Timsbury Rd BS3........8 E2
Timsbury Wlk BS3.......8 E2
Tindell St GL2........ 10 F4
Tinding Dr 3 BS16..... 19 D8
Tinglesfield GL7....... 190 B8
Tinker's Cl 27 GL56... 187 A3
Tinkley La GL10....... 90 B5
Tinmans Gn NP25..... 154 C4
Tintagel Cl BS31....... 4 D4
Tintern Abbey★ NP16 .. 146 C2
Tintern Ave BS5....... 9 D8
Tintern Cl BS30....... 10 F6
Tintern Hts NP16..... 146 A5
Tintern Old Station★
NP16................ 146 C3
Tintern Rd GL4....... 118 E3
Tippetts Rd BS15...... 10 D6
Tirle Bank Way GL20.. 192 F4
Tirlebrook Grange GL20 182 D4
Tirlebrook Prim Sch
GL20................ 192 F4
Tirley Cl GL2......... 117 E1
Tirley Ho BS34........ 39 F1
Tirley Knowle GL19... 172 E8
Tirley St GL19........ 172 F7
Tithe Farm La GL19... 165 E6
Tiverton Cl GL51...... 132 F2
Tiverton Wlk BS16.... 20 A2
Tivoli La GL50........ 193 A1
Tivoli Mews GL50..... 193 A2
Tivoli Pl GL50........ 193 A1
Tivoli Rd GL50........ 193 A1
Tivoli St GL50........ 193 A1
Tivoli Wlk 17 GL50... 130 B8
Toadsmoor Rd GL5.... 148 A5
Tobacco Cl GL54...... 139 F4
Tobacconist Rd GL6... 148 A3

Tobias Gdns BS37...... 43 D1
Tobyfield Cl GL52..... 138 A3
Tobyfield La GL52..... 138 A3
Tobyfield Rd GL52.... 138 A3
Tockington Gn BS32.. 50 B2
Tockington La BS32... 40 A7
Tockington Manor Sch
BS32................ 50 C2
Tockington Park La BS32 40 E8
Tocknell Ct GL11...... 87 F8
Toddington BS37...... 32 D8
Toddington Prim Sch
GL54................ 184 C3
Toddington Sta★ GL54 184 C3
Toghill La BS30....... 13 A8
Toll Down Way SN14... 36 A3
Toll House Ct 5 BS3.... 8 A4
Tolsey La GL20....... 192 C4
Tomlin Pl GL15....... 156 B1
Tommy Taylor's La GL50 133 D4
Tom Price Cl GL52.... 193 C3
Tone Dr GL3.......... 120 F5
Tooke Rd GL6......... 91 E7
Topcliffe St GL2....... 110 B7
Top Rd
Kempsford GL7......... 144 E8
Upper Soudley GL14... 156 C5
Torchacre Rise GL11... 87 F8
Tormarton Cres BS10... 27 F4
Tormarton Intc BS37... 34 B1
Tormarton Rd
Acton Turville GL9 .... 35 E6
Marshfield, East End SN14 . 15 A8
Marshfield SN14 .... 25 A4
Toronto Rd BS7....... 19 A8
Torpoint Rd BS3....... 8 D2
Torrance Cl BS30..... 11 D6
Torridge Rd BS31..... 5 A4
Torrington Ave BS4.... 2 F8
Tortworth Prim Sch GL12. 66 C7
Torwood House Sch BS6 . 18 A3
Totshill Dr BS13...... 2 E4
Totshill Gr BS13.......2 E4
Tottenham Pl BS8..... 194 B3
Totterdown Bridge Ind Est
BS2................. 9 A4
Totterdown La GL7.... 152 E2
Touching End La SN14 . 14 F4
Touchstone Ave BS34.. 29 F5
Tower Cl GL4......... 119 D8
Tower Hill BS2........ 195 B3
Tower Ho
10 Cheltenham GL52... 193 C4
Woodchester GL5...... 98 F1
Tower House Dr GL19.. 179 F2
Tower La
Bristol BS1........... 195 A3
Bristol, Cadbury Heath BS30 11 B6
Towerleaze BS9....... 17 D3
Tower Rd
Bristol BS15.......... 20 C1
Yorkley GL15......... 156 A2
Tower Rd N BS30..... 11 B7
Tower Rd S BS30...... 11 B5
Tower St
Bristol BS1........... 195 B2
Cirencester GL7...... 190 D4
Tower The BS1........ 195 B2
Town Row 21 GL54... 168 A1
Townsend
Almondsbury BS32...... 39 F4
Mitcheldean GL17...... 164 D5
Ruardean GL17....... 163 E4
Townsend Cl
Bristol BS14............3 F5
Dursley GL11......... 88 B1
St Briavels GL15...... 146 F7
Townsend La BS32.... 40 A5
Townsend Rd BS14.....3 F5
Townsend St GL51.... 133 C3
Town St GL19......... 173 A8
Townwell GL12........ 66 B2
Towpath Rd GL2...... 118 C7
Toynbee Rd 2 BS4.....2 E8
Tozers Hill BS4....... 9 C2
Tracy Cl BS14..........2 F7
Tracy Row GL20...... 192 D5
Trafalgar Dr GL3..... 127 F8
Trafalgar Rd GL7..... 190 C5
Trafalgar St GL50..... 193 B2
Trafalgar Terr 3 BS3...8 B2
Traherne Cl 5 HR8... 178 F7
Trajan Cl GL4........ 119 F6
Tralee Wlk BS4....... 8 D1
Tram Rd The 17 GL16.. 155 A5
Tramway Rd
Bristol BS4........... 9 C3
Cinderford GL14...... 156 C6
Upper Soudley GL14... 156 C5
Tranmere Ave BS10... 28 A4
Tranmere Gr BS10.... 28 A3
Transom Rd BS1...... 195 B2
Transport Mus★ GL1. 196 A3
Tranton La GL13..... 76 C4
Tratman Wlk BS10.... 27 F3
Travers Cl BS4........ 2 D6
Travers Wlk BS34.... 29 F5
Tredegar Rd BS16.... 20 B3
Tredington Com Prim Sch
GL20................ 136 B6
Tredington Pk GL20... 173 F8
Tredworth Jun & Inf Schs
GL1................. 118 F7
Tredworth Rd GL1.... 118 F7
Treefield Pl 5 BS2.... 19 A2

Treelands Cl GL53..... 130 D5
Treelands Dr GL53.... 130 D5
Tree Leaze BS37...... 43 F2
Tregarth Rd BS3........7 F1
Trelawney Ave BS5.... 9 D8
Trelawney Pk BS4.... 9 D3
Trelawney Rd BS6.... 18 C1
Trelleck Rd NP16.... 146 B4
Trellick Wlk BS16.... 19 E8
Tremblant Cl GL52... 134 D4
Tremes Cl SN14...... 14 F8
Trenchard Rd
6 Bream GL15....... 147 D8
Saltford BS31........ 5 D3
Stanton Fitzwarren SN6. 145 A1
Trenchard St BS1.... 194 C3
Trench La BS32...... 40 E2
Trendlewood Pk BS16.. 19 E5
Trenley Rd GL11..... 88 F7
Trent Dr BS35....... 51 D7
Trent Gr BS31........ 5 A4
Trentham Cl 7 BS2... 19 A2
Trent Rd GL3........ 120 F5
Trescothick Dr BS30 .. 11 D4
Tresham Cl BS32..... 40 D2
Tresmore 2 GL52.... 133 F2
Tretawn Gdns GL20... 192 F4
Trevanna Rd BS3.......7 F1
Trevelyan Wlk
Bristol, Henbury BS10..... 27 F3
Bristol, Stoke Gifford BS34. 30 A5
Treverdowe Wlk BS10.. 27 D3
Trevethin Cl BS15.... 10 D7
Trevisa Cres GL13.... 85 E3
Trevisa Gr BS10...... 28 C4
Trevor Rd GL3....... 119 F7
Trewint Gdns BS4......2 F8
Trewsbury Rd GL7... 149 E3
Triangle S BS8....... 194 B3
Triangle The
Hewelsfield GL15...... 146 D4
Longlevens GL2...... 127 C3
Triangle W BS8....... 194 B3
Tribune Pl GL4....... 119 E6
Trident Cl BS16...... 31 A1
Trier Way GL1....... 196 B1
Trinder Rd BS20..... 16 B4
Trinity CE Prim Sch GL9.. 36 A6
Trinity Coll BS9...... 17 E4
Trinity Ct 4 BS15.... 10 E8
Trinity Dr GL6....... 148 A3
Trinity La GL52...... 193 C4
Trinity Mews 17 BS2.. 195 C3
Trinity Pl BS8....... 194 A2
Trinity Rd
Bristol BS2........... 9 A7
Cirencester GL7...... 190 C3
Gloucester GL4...... 119 F6
Harrow Hill GL17..... 164 B3
Stroud GL5......... 99 D6
Trinity School La GL52 193 C4
Trinity St
Bristol BS2........... 9 A7
Tewkesbury GL20..... 192 C4
Trinity Way GL14..... 191 D5
Trinity Wlk
Bristol BS2........... 195 C3
Bristol, Newton BS2... 9 A7
Tewkesbury GL20..... 192 C4
Trin Mills BS1....... 195 A1
Tripps Row BS41...... 7 A1
Triscombe Way GL51.. 132 D3
Troon BS37........... 32 E8
Troon Dr BS30....... 11 B6
Troopers' Hill Rd BS5.. 10 A7
Trotman Ave GL11.... 87 F5
Troughton Pl GL20... 192 E4
Trowbridge Rd BS10... 28 C1
Trowbridge Wlk BS10.. 28 C1
Trowscoed Ave GL53... 130 D6
Trubodys Yd BS30.... 11 E7
Trubshaw Cl BS7..... 18 F6
Trubshaw Ct GL3.... 128 C5
Trubshaw Wy 15 GL56. 187 B3
Trull Cotts GL8...... 140 F7
Trumpeter Rd GL51... 129 C6
Trumpet La BS5...... 10 B7
Truro Rd BS3..........8 B3
Tryes Rd GL50....... 130 C6
Trygrove GL4........ 119 D6
Trym Bank BS9...... 17 D7
Trym Cross Rd BS9... 17 C5
Trymleaze BS9....... 17 C5
Trym Rd BS9......... 18 A7
Trym Side BS9....... 17 C5
Trymwood Cl BS10... 27 F2
Trymwood Par BS9.... 17 D6
T T Trad Est BS37.... 44 D1
Tubular Cotts NP16... 73 A1
Tucker St BS2....... 195 C3
Tuckett Ho BS16..... 20 C7
Tuckett La BS16..... 20 C7
Tuckwell Rd GL7..... 144 F7
Tudor Cl
Bristol BS30......... 11 C3
Innsworth GL3....... 127 F7
Tudor Ct
Gloucester GL1 .... 127 A3
Leonard Stanley GL10... 97 E4

Tudor Rd
Bristol, Hanham BS15... 10 C5
Bristol, Lower Easton BS5.. 19 C1
Bristol, St Pauls BS2... 18 F1
Cirencester GL7...... 190 E5
Monmouth/Trefynwy NP25 154 B7
Tudor St GL1........ 118 C6
Tudor Wlk GL16..... 155 A4
Tuffley Ave GL11.... 118 D5
Tuffley Cres GL1.... 118 D3
Tuffley La GL4...... 118 C3
Tuffley Pk GL1...... 118 D3
Tuffley Prim Sch GL4.. 118 D1
Tuffley Rd GL1...... 18 C8
Tuffley Trading Estate
GL2................. 118 B3
Tufthorn Ave GL16... 155 B4
Tufthorn Cl GL16.... 155 B4
Tufthorn Ind Est GL16. 155 B4
Tufthorn Rd GL16.... 155 B4
Tufton Ave BS11..... 17 A8
Tufts The GL15...... 147 C8
Tugela Rd GL13........1 F7
Tug Wilson Cl GL20.. 182 C5
Tulworths The GL2... 127 B5
Tumper Vw GL3...... 120 E4
Tunacre GL2......... 125 D6
Tunbridge Way BS16.. 21 A8
Tuners La SN16..... 141 C3
Tunstall Cl GL9..... 17 E4
Turkdean Rd GL51.. 129 E8
Turley Rd BS5...... 19 D1
Turnberry
Bristol BS30......... 11 B6
Yate BS37........... 32 E8
Turnberry Wlk 3 BS4.. 9 D1
Turnbridge Cl BS10... 28 D4
Turnbridge Rd BS10.. 28 C3
Turner Cl BS31...... 5 A5
Turner Dr BS37..... 43 B1
Turner Gdns BS7.... 19 B6
Turner Rd GL11..... 87 E4
Turners Cl GL2...... 125 D4
Turners Ct 5 BS30.. 10 F4
Turner's Ct 8 GL20.. 192 C4
Turner Wlk BS30... 11 D7
Turnpike Ave GL12... 68 C6
Turnpike Cl
Chepstow/Cas-Gwent
NP16.............. 72 C1
15 Moreton-in-M GL56. 187 A3
Yate BS37........... 43 E2
Turnpike End NP16... 61 B4
Turnpike Gate GL12.. 54 B6
Turnpike Rd SN6.... 145 D3
Turnstone Dr GL2... 117 D1
Turtlegate Ave BS13...1 E4
Turtlegate Wlk BS13....1 E4
Turville Barns GL7... 153 C8
Turville Dr BS7..... 19 A6
Tuscany Ho BS6.... 18 A3
Tusculum Way GL17.. 164 D5
Tuthill Rise GL15.... 92 B3
Tutnalls St GL15.... 92 B3
Tutshill CE Prim Sch
NP16................ 73 A3
Tutshill Gdns NP16.. 73 A1
Tweed Cl BS35...... 51 C8
Tweenbrook Ave GL1. 118 E6
Tweeny La BS30..... 11 D6
Twenties The GL7.... 150 E2
Twenty Acres Rd BS10. 28 B2
Twentyfield BS15.... 18 C5
Twickenham Rd BS6.. 18 C5
Twigworth CE Prim Sch
GL2................. 127 A8
Twigworth Ct GL2... 173 A1
Twinberrow La GL11.. 80 B7
Twinnell Ho 5 BS5.... 9 A8
Twixtbears GL20..... 192 C5
Two Acres Rd BS14... 3 A7
Two Hedges Rd GL52.. 138 A3
Two Mile Ct BS15.... 10 C8
Twomile Hill Prim Sch
BS15............... 10 C8
Twomile Hill Rd BS15.. 10 B8
Two Mile La GL2.... 125 B4
Two Wys Cl GL6..... 148 A9
Twyning Manor GL20.. 181 F8
Twyning Rd WR8.... 180 A10
Twynings The BS15... 20 E2
Twyver Bank GL4.... 119 F3
Twyver Cl GL4...... 119 F3
Twyver Pl GL3...... 120 E5
Tybalt Way BS34.... 29 E5
Tylea Cl GL51....... 129 C7
Tyler Cl BS15....... 10 E5
Tyler Ct 3 BS15..... 132 E2
Tylers Farm BS37... 43 F4
Tyler's La BS16..... 20 D5
Tyler St BS2........ 9 A6
Tylers Way
Chalford GL6........ 148 C6
Sedbury NP16...... 61 B8
Yate BS37........... 43 F5
Yorkley GL15....... 156 B2
Tyndale Ave
Bristol BS16........ 20 A4
Yate BS37........... 43 D3
Tyndale Cl GL11.... 79 E4
Tyndale Ct 7 BS6... 18 B1
Tyndale Mon The★ GL11.. 79 E4
Tyndale Prim Sch BS37. 43 D3
Tyndale Rd
Bristol BS15........ 20 E2
Dursley GL11........ 87 E4

Tyndale Rd continued
Gloucester GL3..... 120 A8
Slimbridge GL2..... 95 B1
Tyndale View BS35... 51 B8
Tyndale Vw GL12.... 67 E5
Tyndall Ave BS8..... 194 C4
Tyndall Ho 6 BS2... 195 C3
Tyndall Rd BS5......9 B8
Tyndalls Park Mews BS2 194 C4
Tyndall's Park Rd BS8.. 194 C4
Tyndalls Way BS10... 18 E8
Tyne Ho 8 BS35..... 51 C8
Tyne Rd BS7........ 18 D3
Tyne St BS2......... 19 A2
Tyning Cl
Bristol BS14........ 3 A7
Yate BS37........... 43 E2
Tyning Cres GL2.... 95 E3
Tyning Rd
Bristol BS13......... 8 F3
Saltford BS31........ 5 E2
Tynings Ct GL3..... 128 D5
Tynings Rd GL6..... 91 A4
Tynings Sch The BS16. 20 E4
Tynings The GL6.... 148 A4
Tynte Ave BS13......2 E3
Tyntesfield Rd BS13... 2 A8
Typhoon Wy GL3.... 120 B4
Tyrone Wlk BS4......2 E8
Tyrrel Way BS34.... 29 E5
Tythe Ct
Dursley GL11....... 87 F5
Marshfield SN14.... 15 A8
Tythe Rd WR12..... 188 A1
Tytherington Rd BS35. 52 A6
Tythe Terr 19 GL54.. 174 A7
Tythings Cres GL18.. 170 F4
Tythings Mews GL18. 170 F4
Tythings The GL18.. 170 F4

U

Uley CE Prim Sch GL11.. 89 C1
Uley Long Barrow (Hetty
Pegler's Tump)★ GL11 .. 89 B5
Uley Rd GL11........ 80 E8
Ullenwood Court Bsns Pk
GL53................ 122 B7
Ullenwood Rd GL4... 119 D7
Ullswater Cl
Bristol BS30......... 11 D6
Yate BS37........... 43 E3
Ullswater Rd
Bristol BS10........ 28 C1
Cheltenham GL51.... 129 E7
Underbanks BS20.... 16 D4
Undercliff Ave GL53.. 130 D3
Undercliff Rd GL53... 130 D3
Underdown Ho BS1... 195 A1
Underhill NP16..... 146 C4
Underhill Cl 12 GL4.. 119 C4
Underhill Rd
Charfield GL12...... 67 A5
Gloucester GL4..... 119 C4
Underwood Cl BS35... 51 A4
Underwood Est NP25. 154 B7
Unicorn Bsns Pk BS4.. 9 D5
Unicorn Pk BS4..... 9 D5
Union Ho GL50..... 193 B3
Union Pl GL20...... 192 D4
Union Rd
2 Bristol BS2........ 9 A6
Coleford GL16...... 155 B6
Union St
Bristol BS1......... 195 B3
Cheltenham GL52.... 193 C4
Dursley GL11....... 80 B8
Gloucester GL1..... 196 C4
Stow-on-t-W GL54.. 176 F4
Stroud GL5......... 99 C7
Unite Ho 1 BS1.... 194 C2
Unity Cl BS31....... 5 A5
Unity Rd BS31...... 5 A6
Unity St
Bristol, Brandon Hill BS1.. 194 C2
Bristol BS2......... 195 C3
Bristol, Kingswood BS15.. 10 C8
University Cl BS9.... 17 E4
University Farm 17 GL56. 187 A3
University Rd BS8... 194 C4
University Wlk BS8... 194 C3
Univ of Bristol BS8... 194 C3
Univ of Bristol Dept of Ed
BS8................. 194 C3
Univ of
Gloucestershire(Francis
Close Hall) GL50.... 133 D3
Univ of Gloucestershire
(Hardwick Campus) GL50,
GL51............... 133 C3
Univ of Gloucestershire
(Oxstalls Campus) GL2. 127 B3
Univ of Gloucestershire
(Park Campus) GL53.. 130 C6
Univ of Gloucestershire
(Pittville Campus)
GL52............... 133 F4
Univ of the West of England
BS3.................7 E4
Univ of the West of England
Faculty of Health & Applied
Science BS16......... 19 E5

Univ of the West of England
Frenchay Campus BS16 . 29 E1
Unlawater Ho GL14 . . . . . 157 A7
Unlawater La GL14 . . . . . . 157 A7
Unwin Cl GL51 . . . . 129 C7
Unwin Rd GL51 . . . . 129 C7
Upcott SN6 . . . . 143 E6
Upfield Cl GL5 . . . . 98 F8
Upfield Prep Sch GL5 . . . . 98 F8
Up Hatherley Way GL51 . 129 E5
Uphill Pl GL1 . . . . 118 D5
Uphill Rd
Bristol BS7 . . . . 18 F5
Upper Lydbrook GL17 . . . . 163 D2
Upjohn Cres BS13 . . . . 2 D3
Uplands Com Prim Sch
GL5 . . . . 99 D8
Uplands Dr BS31 . . . . 5 F2
Uplands Rd
Bristol BS16 . . . . 20 D3
Saltford BS31 . . . . 5 F2
Stroud GL5 . . . . 99 D8
Uplands View Terr GL5 . . . 99 D7
Upper Bath Rd BS35 . . . . . 51 B8
Upper Bath St GL50 . . . . . 193 B1
Upper Belgrave Rd BS8 . . 18 A2
Upper Belmont Rd BS7 . . . 18 E3
Upper Berkeley Pl BS8 . . 194 B3
Upper Bilson Rd GL14 . . . 191 C6
Upper Byron Pl BS8 . . . . . 194 B3
Upper Chapel La BS36 . . . . 31 C7
Upper Cheltenham Pl
BS6 . . . . 18 E1
Upper Church La BS2 . . . 194 C3
Upper Church Rd GL5 . . . . 98 E7
Upper Church St NP16 . . . 60 F8
Upper Comm GL15 . . . . . . 147 D5
Upper Conham Vale BS15 10 A5
Upper Cranbrook Rd BS6 . 18 B4
Upper Cross 8 HR8 . . . . . 178 F8
Upper Dorrington Terr
GL5 . . . . 99 D6
Upper End Ct WR11 . . . . . 188 A6
Upperfield Rd GL51 . . . . . 133 A5
Upperhall Cl 4 HR8 . . . . . 178 F8
Upper Hayes Rd GL6 . . . . . 91 A4
Upper Highfields GL9 . . . . 55 F2
Upper Horfield Prim Sch
Bristol BS5 . . . . 19 A1
Bristol BS7 . . . . 19 A8
Upper Kitesnest La GL6 . 102 F3
Upper Leazes GL5 . . . . 99 D7
Upper Lynch Rd GL6 . . . . 148 D6
Upper Maudlin St BS2 . . . 195 A3
Upper Mill La GL52 . . . . . 134 E5
Upper Mills Ind Est GL10 . 97 F6
Upper Myrtle Hill BS20 . . . 16 C4
Upper Nelson St NP16 . . . . 60 E8
Upper Norwood St GL53 . 130 C6
Upper Park Rd GL6 . . . . 91 C3
Upper Park St GL52 . . . . . 130 F8
Upper Perry Hill BS3 . . . . . . 8 C4
Upper Poole Rd GL11 . . . . 80 B8
Upper Quay Ho GL1 . . . . . 196 A3
Upper Quay St GL1 . . . . . . 196 A3
Upper Queen's Rd 2
GL10 . . . . 97 F7
Upper Rd
Eastnor HR8 . . . . 179 B8
Pillowell GL15 . . . . 155 F1
Upper Rissington Bsns Pk
GL54 . . . . 169 D6
Upper Rodley Rd GL14 . . . 157 F8
Upper Sandhurst Rd BS4 . . 9 D4
Upper Springfield Rd GL5 99 C8
Upper St
Bristol BS4 . . . . 9 A4
Dyrham SN14 . . . . 23 D4
Upper Station Rd BS16 . . . 20 D4
Upper Stone Cl BS36 . . . . . 31 C7
Upper Stowfield Rd
GL17 . . . . 163 C4
Upper Sydney St BS3 . . . . . . 8 B3
Upper Terr BS11 . . . . 27 B1
Upper Tockington Rd
BS32 . . . . 50 A2
Upper Tynings GL6 . . . . 91 A4
Upper Tynings The GL5 . . 98 D8
Upper Washwell GL6 . . . . 111 F1
Upper Wells St BS1 . . . . . 194 C3
Upper York St BS2 . . . . . . 195 B4
Upthorpe GL11 . . . . 88 B5
Upthorpe La GL11 . . . . 88 B6
Upton Cl GL4 . . . . 119 E7
Upton Gdns GL8 . . . . 140 B5
Upton Hill GL4 . . . . 119 D1
Upton La
Brookthorpe GL4 . . . . 111 B6
Gloucester GL4 . . . . 119 F4
Maiden Head BS41 . . . . 1 F1
Upton Rd BS3 . . . . 8 B4
Upton St Leonards CE Prim
Sch GL4 . . . . 119 F3
Upton's Gdn GL2 . . . . 100 E5
Upton St GL1 . . . . 119 A8
Urfords Dr 1 BS16 . . . . 20 C6
Usk Ct 6 BS35 . . . . 51 C8
Usk Way GL3 . . . . 120 F5
Utah Dr GL7 . . . . 152 E2
Uxbridge La GL2 . . . . 110 B8

V

Vaisey Field GL2 . . . . 100 F5
Vaisey Rd GL7 . . . . 190 B8
Vale Bank GL2 . . . . 157 B6
Vale Ct
Bristol BS8 . . . . 194 A4
9 Cricklade SN6 . . . . 143 E4
Vale Foundary La BS3 . . . . . . 7 F2
Vale La BS3 . . . . 2 C8
Valentine Cl
Bristol BS14 . . . . 3 B5
Chepstow NP16 . . . . 61 A4
Vale Rd
Bishop's Cleeve GL52 . . . . 137 F5
Stratton GL7 . . . . 190 B8
Valerian Cl
Bristol BS11 . . . . 16 F6
Gloucester GL4 . . . . 119 E7
Vale St BS4 . . . . 9 A4
Vale The BS16 . . . . 21 F6
Valiant Way GL3 . . . . 120 C7
Vallenders Rd GL20 . . . . . 182 C7
Valley Cl GL5 . . . . 148 A5
Valley Cotts GL51 . . . . 173 F1
Valley Gdns
Bristol BS16 . . . . 20 F8
Gloucester GL2 . . . . 118 A1
Quedgeley GL2 . . . . 110 B8
Valley La GL4 . . . . 120 A1
Valley Pk GL2 . . . . 128 F8
Valley Rd
Bristol, Bedminster Down
BS13 . . . . 2 A8
Bristol, Mangotsfield BS16 . 21 A5
Bristol, Warmley BS30 . . . . . 11 D6
Cinderford GL14 . . . . 191 C3
Leigh Woods BS8 . . . . 7 C7
Lydney GL15 . . . . 92 C2
Upper Lydbrook GL17 . . . . 163 D1
Wotton-u-E GL12 . . . . 68 C8
Valley View
Chedworth GL54 . . . . 159 A6
Dursley GL11 . . . . 87 F4
Valley View Pk GL54 . . . . 168 E7
Valley View Rd GL5 . . . . . . 99 F6
Valls The BS32 . . . . 29 F6
Valma Rocks BS5 . . . . 10 A6
Vanbrugh La BS16 . . . . 19 E7
Van Der Breen St GL6 . . . 105 B1
Vandyck Ave BS31 . . . . 4 F6
Vantage Point Bsns Village
GL17 . . . . 164 D5
Varley Ave GL3 . . . . 120 B6
Varnister La GL17 . . . . 163 F4
Varnister Rd GL17 . . . . 163 F4
Vassall Ct BS16 . . . . 20 B5
Vassall Rd BS16 . . . . 20 B5
Vatch La GL5 . . . . 148 B7
Vatch View GL5 . . . . 103 E1
Vattingstone Ho BS35 . . . . 50 F5
Vattingstone La BS35 . . . . 50 F5
Vaughan Cl BS10 . . . . 27 F3
Vauxhall GL18 . . . . 170 F4
Vauxhall La NP16 . . . . 60 D8
Vauxhall Rd
Chepstow/Cas-Gwent
NP16 . . . . 60 D8
Gloucester GL1 . . . . 196 C1
Vauxhall Terr
3 Bristol BS3 . . . . 8 A4
Gloucester GL1 . . . . 196 C1
Vayre Cl BS37 . . . . 44 C1
Veldt House Barns HR8 . . 178 B5
Velhurst Dr 1 GL6 . . . . 148 B6
Velthouse La GL17 . . . . . . 165 A5
Vennings The GL11 . . . . 87 F6
Venns Acre GL12 . . . . 68 B6
Vensfield Rd GL2 . . . . 117 E2
Vention La GL17 . . . . 163 D3
Ventnor Ave 1 BS5 . . . . 9 F8
Ventnor Rd
Bristol, Filton BS34 . . . . 29 B3
Bristol, St George BS5 . . . . . 19 F1
Venton Ct 5 BS15 . . . . 10 B5
Vera Rd BS16 . . . . 19 F2
Verbena Cl 2 GL4 . . . . 119 E5
Verda Pl GL51 . . . . 129 C6
Vernal Cl GL4 . . . . 119 F5
Vernals La GL12 . . . . 67 C8
Verney Cl GL53 . . . . 130 E6
Verney Rd GL10 . . . . 97 F7
Verneys The GL53 . . . . 130 E6
Vernon Cl BS31 . . . . 5 D3
Vernon Pl GL53 . . . . 193 C3
Vernon St 5 BS2 . . . . 8 F4
Verrier Rd BS5 . . . . 9 C7
Vertican Rd GL3 . . . . 127 D6
Vervain Cl GL3 . . . . 128 A7
Verwood Dr BS30 . . . . 11 C2
Vestry Gdns GL4 . . . . 119 C7
Vetch Cl GL4 . . . . 119 A4
Viburnum Cl 6 GL50 . . . . . 130 B6
Viburnum Rd BS32 . . . . 40 D5
Viburnum View 4 GL4 . . 119 F5
Vicarage Cl
Churchdown GL3 . . . . 128 C4
Lydney GL15 . . . . 92 A2
Shurdington GL51 . . . . 129 E2
Vicarage Cotts
11 Bristol BS16 . . . . 20 D5
12 Chipping Campden
GL55 . . . . 189 A2
Vicarage Ct
Bristol BS15 . . . . 10 B5
Vicarage Ct *continued*
Brockworth GL3 . . . . 120 E5
Vicarage Dr GL17 . . . . 164 D5
Vicarage La
Arlingham GL2 . . . . 157 B5
Brockworth GL3 . . . . 120 E6
Frampton on Severn GL2 . . 157 F1
Highworth SN6 . . . . 145 D3
Hillesley GL12 . . . . 55 D8
Olveston BS35 . . . . 50 B3
Vicarage Rd
Bristol, Bishopsworth BS13 . . 2 A6
Bristol, Hanham BS15 . . . . . 10 B5
Bristol, Moorfields BS5 . . . . . 9 C8
Bristol, Southville BS3 . . . . . . 8 B4
Coalpit Heath BS36 . . . . 31 C6
Gloucester GL1 . . . . 119 A7
Leigh Woods BS8 . . . . 7 D6
Pilning BS35 . . . . 38 C7
Vicarage St GL6 . . . . 104 A8
Vicars Cl BS16 . . . . 20 B4
Viceroy Cnr 7 GL50 . . . . . 193 A4
Vickers Rd GL54 . . . . 169 D7
Victor Ho BS34 . . . . 29 C7
Victoria Ave BS5 . . . . 9 C7
Victoria Cl
Dursley GL11 . . . . 88 B1
Thornbury BS35 . . . . 64 B3
Victoria Cotts
Quedgeley GL2 . . . . 117 E3
4 Stonehouse GL10 . . . . . . 97 F8
Victoria Cres BS35 . . . . 38 A6
Victoria Ct
6 Bristol, Cotham BS6 . . . . 18 D1
Bristol, Redland BS6 . . . . . . 18 A3
Gloucester GL2 . . . . 126 F6
Victoria Dr GL10 . . . . 96 F7
Victoria Gdns 7 BS6 . . . . . . 18 D1
Victoria Gr BS3 . . . . 8 E4
Victoria Ho BS31 . . . . 4 F4
Victoria Mans GL50 . . . . . 193 A3
Victoria Par BS5 . . . . 9 C8
Victoria Park Prim Sch
BS3 . . . . 8 E3
Victoria Pk
Bristol, Fishponds BS16 . . . 20 A5
Bristol, Kingswood BS15 . . . 20 D1
Victoria Pl
Bristol BS3 . . . . 8 C3
Cheltenham GL52 . . . . 133 F1
Victoria Rd
Avonmouth BS11 . . . . 16 B7
Brimscombe GL5 . . . . 99 F1
Bristol, Hanham BS15 . . . . . 10 C5
Bristol, St Philip's Marsh BS2 9 A5
Bristol, Warmley BS30 . . . . . 11 D5
Chepstow/Cas-Gwent NP16 60 F5
Cirencester GL7 . . . . 190 D4
Coleford GL16 . . . . 155 A5
Gloucester GL2 . . . . 126 F6
Ledbury HR8 . . . . 178 E8
Lydney GL15 . . . . 92 A3
Quenington GL7 . . . . 152 D7
Saltford BS31 . . . . 5 D3
Victoria Retreat GL50 . . . 193 B1
Victoria Sq BS8 . . . . 194 A3
Victoria St
6 Bourton-on-t-W GL54 . . 168 F7
Bristol BS1 . . . . 195 B2
Bristol, Staple Hill BS16 . . . . 20 D5
Cheltenham GL50 . . . . 133 D3
Cinderford GL14 . . . . 191 C3
Cinderford GL14 . . . . 191 C4
Gloucester GL1 . . . . 196 C1
Painswick GL6 . . . . 103 F8
Victoria Terr
9 Bourton-on-t-W GL54 . . 168 F7
Bretforton WR11 . . . . 188 A7
15 Bristol, Clifton BS8 . . . . 7 F6
Bristol, St Philip's Marsh BS2 9 B5
Cheltenham GL52 . . . . 133 F1
Victoria Vale GL14 . . . . . . 191 C4
Victoria Wlk BS6 . . . . 18 D1
Victor Rd BS3 . . . . 8 C3
Victor St
9 Bristol, Russell Town
BS5 . . . . 9 B6
Bristol, St Philip's Marsh BS2 9 A4
Victory Cl GL3 . . . . 128 A8
Victory Rd
Gloucester GL1 . . . . 118 F7
Whiteshill GL6 . . . . 103 A3
Victory Villas GL7 . . . . 152 F4
Vigor Rd BS13 . . . . 2 B5
Villa Cl GL14 . . . . 191 C2
Village Ave GL54 . . . . 175 D2
Village Cl BS37 . . . . 43 D1
Village Farm
Elberton BS35 . . . . 50 A6
Preston GL7 . . . . 150 F3
Village Mews GL51 . . . . . . 132 F4
Village Rd GL51 . . . . 132 F4
Village The BS16 . . . . 21 C7
Village The GL14 . . . . 165 C1
Villa The GL14 . . . . 191 C2
Villa Way HR8 . . . . 178 E7
Villiers Rd BS5 . . . . 19 B1
Vilner La BS35 . . . . 51 B7
Vilverie Mead GL52 . . . . . 137 D4
Vimpany Cl BS10 . . . . 27 F3
Vimpennys La BS35 . . . . . . 38 E1
Vincent Ave GL4 . . . . 118 D1
Vincent Cl BS11 . . . . 27 C2
Vincent Ct 2 BS16 . . . . 20 D3
Vine Cotts NP16 . . . . 60 E8
Vinecroft GL13 . . . . 85 E8
Vine Ct GL50 . . . . 133 C3
Vine Hall GL15 . . . . 147 E4
Vineries Cl GL53 . . . . 130 C4
Viner's La GL9 . . . . 36 B5
Vines The GL3 . . . . 120 B7
Vine Terr GL1 . . . . 196 C4
Vine Way GL20 . . . . 192 D1
Vineyard La GL12 . . . . 67 F5
Vineyards Cl GL53 . . . . 131 B4
Vineyards La GL50 . . . . . . 133 B1
Vineyard St GL54 . . . . 174 A7
Vineyards The GL51 . . . . . 133 A1
Vineyard The WR12 . . . . . . 184 E5
Vining Wlk 4 BS5 . . . . 9 B8
Vinney La BS37 . . . . 44 F8
Vinny Ave BS16 . . . . 21 A7
Vintery Leys BS9 . . . . 18 B7
Virginia Ave GL7 . . . . 152 E2
Virginia Cl BS37 . . . . 44 A1
Virginia Rd GL20 . . . . 182 C4
Vittoria Wlk GL50 . . . . 193 B2
Vivian St BS3 . . . . 8 D3
Vizard Cl GL11 . . . . 80 B8
Vorda Rd SN6 . . . . 145 D4
Vowell Cl BS13 . . . . 2 B4
Voxwell La GL52 . . . . 137 E3
Voyager Cl BS34 . . . . 30 A4
Voyce Cl GL4 . . . . 118 D2
Vulcan Way GL4 . . . . 119 F6
Vyners Cl GL7 . . . . 190 C2
Vyvian Ct GL1 . . . . 196 B2
Vyvyan Rd BS8 . . . . 194 A3
Vyvyan Terr BS8 . . . . 194 A3

W

Wade Ct GL51 . . . . 129 C7
Wade Hill SN6 . . . . 145 C3
Wadehurst Ind Pk BS2 . . . . 9 A7
Wade Rd BS37 . . . . 43 A3
Wades La GL6 . . . . 103 C3
Wades Rd BS34 . . . . 29 B3
Wade St BS2 . . . . 195 C3
Wadham Cl GL7 . . . . 153 C6
Wadham Dr BS16 . . . . 30 B1
Wadham Gr BS16 . . . . 21 B5
Wad La GL19 . . . . 180 F2
Waggons La GL19 . . . . 172 C4
Wagtail Dr GL20 . . . . 182 B5
Wainbridge Cres BS35 . . . 38 D7
Wainbrook Dr BS5 . . . . 19 D2
Wainfleet Ave GL2 . . . . . . 110 B7
Wainland Pl GL16 . . . . 154 F3
Wainlode La GL2 . . . . 173 A3
Wakefield Cl GL7 . . . . 144 F7
Wakeford Rd 1 BS16 . . . . . 21 A7
Wakeford Way BS30 . . . . . 11 D7
Wakeman Cl GL20 . . . . 192 E2
Walden Rd BS31 . . . . 5 A4
Waldrist Cl GL51 . . . . 132 F5
Walford Prim Sch HR9 . . 163 C7
Walham La GL1 . . . . 126 E4
Walker Cl
Bristol, Downend BS16 . . . . 21 A7
Bristol, Upper Easton BS5 . . . 9 B8
Walker Ct BS16 . . . . 20 F5
Walkers Gdn 14 GL54 . . . . 168 A1
Walker's La GL17 . . . . 163 F4
Walker St BS2 . . . . 194 C4
Walker Way BS35 . . . . 51 B7
Walkley Hill GL5 . . . . 99 A5
Walkley Rd GL20 . . . . 192 D5
Walk Mill La GL12 . . . . 67 F4
Walk The GL12 . . . . 67 F5
Wallace Apartments 11
GL52 . . . . 193 C4
Wallace Ho GL51 . . . . 129 F6
Wallbank Ho GL1 . . . . 127 A3
Wallbridge GL5 . . . . 99 B7
Wallbridge Ind Est GL5 . . . 99 B6
Wallcroft Ho BS6 . . . . 18 A3
Walled Gdn The
Kingscote GL8 . . . . 82 B5
Ledbury HR8 . . . . 178 F8
Wallingford Rd BS4 . . . . 2 D7
Walliscote Ave BS9 . . . . . . 18 C6
Walliscote Rd BS9 . . . . 18 C6
Wallow Gn GL6 . . . . 90 F2
Wallscourt Farm Acad
BS16 . . . . 19 D8
Wallscourt Rd BS34 . . . . . . 29 B2
Wallscourt Rd S BS34 . . . . 29 B1
Wallsend La SN14 . . . . 24 C5
Wallshut Wood BS7 . . . . . . 19 C8
Wallsworth Hall Nature in
Art Mus* GL2 . . . . 173 A1
Wallwern Wood/Coed
Wallwern NP16 . . . . 72 C1
Walmer's View GL14 . . . . 156 B6
Walmore Hill Prim Sch
GL2 . . . . 165 F1
Walnut Ave BS37 . . . . 44 A2
Walnut Bank Dr GL20 . . . 183 A4
Walnut Cl
Bristol BS15 . . . . 20 F1
Broadway WR12 . . . . 185 B8
Cheltenham GL52 . . . . 133 E4
12 Coleford GL16 . . . . 155 B5
Easton-in-G BS20 . . . . 16 A3
Frampton Cotterell BS36 . . . 31 C6
Gloucester GL3 . . . . 120 B4
Gloucester GL4 . . . . 119 D3
Keynsham BS31 . . . . 4 C4
Thornbury BS35 . . . . 64 D1
Winchcombe GL54 . . . . 139 F5
Walnut Cres BS15 . . . . 10 F8
Walnut Ct GL20 . . . . 183 A4
Walnut Dr SN14 . . . . 15 F6
Walnut La BS15 . . . . 11 A8
Walnut Tree Cl BS32 . . . . . 40 A5
Walnut Wlk
Bristol BS13 . . . . 2 A6
Keynsham BS31 . . . . 4 C4
Walsh Ave BS14 . . . . 3 A7
Walshe Ave BS37 . . . . 44 C1
Walsingham Rd BS6 . . . . . 18 E2
Walter Preston Ct GL5 . . . 98 E7
Walter Rd BS36 . . . . 31 B6
Walter Reynold Homes
GL54 . . . . 176 E5
Walter St BS3 . . . . 8 A4
Walton Ave BS4 . . . . 9 D5
Walton Cl
Bristol BS30 . . . . 11 C1
Keynsham BS31 . . . . 4 D4
Upton St Leonards GL4 . . . 119 E3
Walton Dr GL20 . . . . 192 F5
Walton Gdns GL20 . . . . . . 192 F4
Walton Heath BS37 . . . . . . 43 F1
Walton Ho
Cheltenham GL51 . . . . 132 E2
Tewkesbury GL20 . . . . 192 F4
Walton House Bglws 8
GL54 . . . . 168 A1
Walton House Ct 9
GL54 . . . . 168 A1
Walton Rd BS11 . . . . 16 D6
Walton Rise BS9 . . . . 18 A7
Walton St BS5 . . . . 19 B1
Walwyn Cl GL17 . . . . 164 D5
Walwyn Gdns BS13 . . . . 2 C3
Wandsdyke Prim Sch BS14 . 2 F4
Wansbeck Rd BS31 . . . . 5 A4
Wanscow Wlk BS9 . . . . 18 B6
Wansdyke Ct BS14 . . . . 3 B5
Wansdyke Workshops
BS31 . . . . 5 A6
Wantridge GL18 . . . . 170 B8
Wapley Bank BS37 . . . . 32 D5
Wapley Hill BS37 . . . . 32 E4
Wapley Rd BS37 . . . . 33 B3
Wapping Rd BS1 . . . . 195 A1
Ward Ave GL3 . . . . 127 E6
Ward Cl GL52 . . . . 138 A4
Warden Hill Cl GL51 . . . . . 129 F6
Warden Hill Prim Sch
GL51 . . . . 130 A5
Warden Hill Rd GL51 . . . . 130 A6
Warden Rd BS3 . . . . 8 C4
Ward Ind Est GL15 . . . . 84 A8
Wardour Rd BS4 . . . . 2 D8
Ward Rd GL54 . . . . 168 A1
Wards Rd GL51 . . . . 129 D6
Ware Ct BS36 . . . . 30 D5
Warend Hill
Dursley GL11 . . . . 80 A6
North Nibley GL11 . . . . 79 F6
Waring Ho BS1 . . . . 195 A1
Warman Cl BS14 . . . . 3 F6
Warman Rd BS14 . . . . 3 F6
Warmington Rd BS14 . . . . . . 3 C8
Warminster Rd BS2 . . . . 19 A2
Warmley Park Sch BS30 . . . 11 B7
Warneford Pl 23 GL56 . . . 187 A3
Warner Cl BS15 . . . . 10 F6
Warns Ct 15 GL8 . . . . 140 B4
Warns The BS30 . . . . 11 A4
Warren Bsns Pk GL8 . . . . . . 57 F5
Warren Cl
Bristol BS32 . . . . 40 D3
Cheltenham GL51 . . . . 129 F6
Churchdown GL3 . . . . 128 A7
Warren Croft GL11 . . . . 79 E4
Warren Dr 13 HR8 . . . . 178 F8
Warren Gdns BS14 . . . . 3 F5
Warren La HR9 . . . . 170 A1
Warren Rd
Bristol BS34 . . . . 29 B3
Northway GL20 . . . . 182 B4
Warrens Gorse Cotts
GL7 . . . . 150 B8
Warren Slade NP16 . . . . . . 60 F5
Warren The GL4 . . . . 118 A2
Warren Way BS37 . . . . 43 E3
Warrington Rd BS4 . . . . 9 D2
Warth La
Arlingham GL2 . . . . 157 C6
Northwick BS35 . . . . 48 D3
Warwick Ave
7 Bristol BS5 . . . . 19 B1
Gloucester GL4 . . . . 118 C1
Warwick Cl
Bristol BS30 . . . . 11 B2
Chepstow/Cas-Gwent NP16 60 D6
3 Fairford GL7 . . . . 152 E4
Stroud GL5 . . . . 99 A4
Warwick Cres GL52 . . . . . 131 B6
Warwick Pl
Cheltenham GL52 . . . . 193 C4
Tewkesbury GL20 . . . . 192 D3
Thornbury BS35 . . . . 64 A1
Warwick Rd
Bristol, Baptist Mills BS5 . . . 19 B1
Bristol, Redland BS6 . . . . . . 18 B1
Keynsham BS31 . . . . 4 D4
Washingpool Hill BS35 . . . 50 E1
Washingpool Hill Rd
BS32 . . . . 50 D2
Washingpool La BS11 . . . . . 26 F7
Washing Pound La BS14 . . . 3 B4
Washing's La NP25 . . . . . . 154 C5

Washington Ave BS5 . . . . . 19 C1
Washpool La
 Fairford GL7 . . . . 152 F1
 Kempsford GL7 . . . . 144 F8
Washpool Rd GL52 . . . . . . 138 A5
Wasley Rd GL51 . . . . 132 F1
Waste Dr GL8 . . . . 57 A8
Watch Elm Cl BS32 . . . . 29 E6
Watch House Rd BS20 . . . 16 D4
Watchill Ave BS13 . . . . 1 F6
Watchill Cl BS13 . . . . 1 F6
Waterbridge Rd BS13 . . . . . 1 F4
Watercress Rd BS2 . . . . . . 18 F3
Waterdale Cl
 Bristol BS9 . . . . 18 C7
 Hardwicke GL2 . . . . 109 D8
Waterdale Gdns BS9 . . . . . 18 C7
Waterfield Cl GL53 . . . . . . 193 B1
Waterford GL35 . . . . 51 D8
Waterford Ct GL53 . . . . . . 130 C6
Waterford Rd BS9 . . . . 18 B6
Water Furlongs SN6 . . . . . 143 E4
Watergrip La GL20 . . . . . . 183 A8
Water La
 Brimscombe GL5 . . . . 99 E1
 Bristol BS1 . . . . 195 B2
 Bristol, Hanham Green
  BS15 . . . . 10 B2
 Bristol, Upper Knowle BS4 . . 9 D2
 Bristol, Windmill Hill BS3 . . 8 F3
 Charlton Kings GL52 . . . . 131 B6
 Pill BS20 . . . . 16 C4
 Woodchester GL5 . . . . 98 F3
 Wotton-u-E GL12 . . . . 68 B6
Waterloo Bsns Pk GL17 . . 163 C2
Waterloo Cl GL20 . . . . 182 D7
Waterloo Ho BS20 . . . . 16 D5
Waterloo La GL7 . . . . 152 E3
Waterloo Pl 21 BS2 . . . . . 195 C3
Waterloo Rd BS2 . . . . 195 C3
Waterloo St
 Bristol BS2 . . . . 195 C3
 11 Bristol, Clifton BS8 . . . . . 7 F7
 Cheltenham GL51 . . . . . . 133 B3
Waterloo The GL51 . . . . . . 190 D5
Waterloo Way GL20 . . . . . 182 D7
Watermans Ct 4 GL2 . . . 117 D1
Water Mdw GL2 . . . . 109 E7
Watermead GL15 . . . . 92 A3
Watermill Cl GL12 . . . . 65 E7
Watermoor Cl GL51 . . . . . 132 D4
Watermoor Rd GL3 . . . . . . 128 B5
Watermoor Rd GL7 . . . . . . 190 D3
Watermoor Way GL7 . . . . 190 D3
Watermore Cl BS36 . . . . . . 31 C7
Watermore Gdns BS36 . . . 31 D8
Watermore Prim Sch
 BS36 . . . . 31 C8
Watershoot Cl GL52 . . . . . 134 C4
Waterside 3 GL20 . . . . . . 192 C4
Waterside Cl
 Andoversford GL54 . . . . . 166 D6
 Quedgeley GL2 . . . . 117 D1
Waterside Dr BS32 . . . . . . 40 A1
Water's La BS9 . . . . 18 A7
Waters Rd BS15 . . . . 10 C8
Waters Reach GL2 . . . . . . 118 B6
Water St GL11 . . . . 88 B1
Waters Way NP16 . . . . 60 E7
Waterton Cl GL3 . . . . 120 B6
Waterwells Dr GL2 . . . . . . 110 A6
Water Wheel Cl 7 GL2 . . 117 D1
Watery La
 Doynton BS30 . . . . 13 A8
 Frampton on Severn GL2 . 157 D2
 Gloucester GL4 . . . . 111 F8
 Kinsham GL20 . . . . 182 D6
 Lea HR9 . . . . 164 C8
 Lydney GL15 . . . . 147 F5
 Minsterworth GL2 . . . . . . 117 B7
 Newent GL18 . . . . 170 F4
Wathen Rd BS6 . . . . 18 F3
Watkins Cnr SN5 . . . . 143 E1
Watkins Terr GL11 . . . . 88 E8
Watkins Yd BS9 . . . . 18 A8
Watledge Bank GL6 . . . . . . 91 B5
Watledge Cl GL20 . . . . 192 D4
Watledge Rd GL6 . . . . 91 B5
Watley's End Rd BS36 . . . . 30 F7
Watling Way BS11 . . . . 16 D7
Watson Ave BS4 . . . . 9 D4
Watson Gr GL4 . . . . 119 F5
Watson Ho 5 GL52 . . . . . 193 C4
Watson's Rd BS30 . . . . 10 F3
Watters Cl BS36 . . . . 31 D6
Wattisham Rd GL2 . . . . . . 110 C7
Watts Cl
 Berkeley GL13 . . . . 85 E7
 Gloucester GL3 . . . . 120 B7
Wavell Cl BS37 . . . . 43 D3
Waveney Rd BS31 . . . . 5 A3
Waverley Rd
 Bristol, Cotham BS6 . . . . . 18 C1
 Bristol, Shirehampton BS11 16 E6
 Gloucester GL2 . . . . 127 C2
 Yate BS37 . . . . 43 B2
Waverley St 8 BS5 . . . . . . 19 A1
Waycroft Acad BS14 . . . . . . 3 C5
Wayend Street HR8 . . . . . 179 C7
Wayford Cl BS31 . . . . 5 A3
Wayland Ct 7 BS16 . . . . . 20 A4
Waylands SN6 . . . . 143 F4
Wayleaze
 Coalpit Heath BS36 . . . . . . 31 D7
 Wapley BS37 . . . . 32 F3

Wayridge The GL4 . . . . . . 119 D4
Wayside Cl BS36 . . . . 31 B7
WCA Ho BS1 . . . . 195 A2
Weald Cl GL4 . . . . 119 C5
Weare Ct BS1 . . . . 194 A1
Weavers Cl
 Dursley GL11 . . . . 80 B8
 Kingswood GL12 . . . . 67 F4
Weavers Dr GL11 . . . . 89 B1
Weavers Ho 17 GL5 . . . . . 99 C7
Weavers Rd
 Cirencester GL7 . . . . 190 E4
 Quedgeley GL2 . . . . 117 F2
Weavers Row GL5 . . . . 99 F1
Webber Ho GL20 . . . . 192 B3
Webb Rd GL8 . . . . 140 B5
Webbs Heath BS30 . . . . . . 11 E8
Webb St BS5 . . . . 9 A8
Webbs Wood GL52 . . . . . . 29 F7
Webbs Wood Rd BS32 . . . 29 F7
Webley Rd GL17 . . . . 163 F3
Wedgewood Cotts WR12 184 E5
Wedgewood Cres GL14 . . 191 D6
Wedgewood Rd BS16 . . . . 30 D1
Wedgwood Cl BS14 . . . . . . 3 B5
Wedgwood Dr GL2 . . . . . . 127 C4
Wedlock Way BS3 . . . . 7 F3
Wedmore Cl BS15 . . . . 10 F7
Wedmore Rd BS31 . . . . 5 D4
Wedmore Vale BS3 . . . . . . 8 E2
Weedon Cl 6 BS5 . . . . 19 A2
Weigh Bridge Ct GL55 . . . 189 A2
Weight Rd 2 BS5 . . . . 9 C7
Weir Bridge Cl GL4 . . . . . 119 E8
Weir La SN14 . . . . 14 F8
Welch Ho GL52 . . . . 129 D2
Welch Rd GL51 . . . . 132 E4
Welcomyn 11 GL6 . . . . . . 148 C6
Welland Cl GL52 . . . . 134 A4
Welland Dr GL52 . . . . 134 A4
Welland Lodge Rd GL52 . 134 A4
Welland Rd
 Keynsham BS31 . . . . 4 F4
 Quedgeley GL2 . . . . 117 F2
Wellbrook Rd GL52 . . . . . 137 F5
Well Cl
 Chepstow/Cas-Gwent
  NP16 . . . . 60 F4
 Long Ashton BS41 . . . . 7 B1
 Northway GL20 . . . . 182 C5
Well Cross Rd GL4 . . . . . . 119 A4
Well End GL5 . . . . 99 E8
Weller Bglws GL2 . . . . 118 C4
Wellesley Prim Sch BS37 . 32 D6
Wellesley Rd GL50 . . . . . . 133 E3
Wellesley St GL1 . . . . 118 F6
Wellfield GL20 . . . . 192 F5
Wellgarth Rd BS4 . . . . 9 A2
Wellgarth Rd BS4 . . . . 9 A2
Wellgarth Wlk BS4 . . . . . . 9 A2
Well Hill GL6 . . . . 148 A3
Well House Cl BS9 . . . . . . 17 E3
Welling Cl GL11 . . . . 80 C7
Wellington Ave BS6 . . . . . 18 E1
Wellington Aviation Mus★
 GL56 . . . . 187 A3
Wellington Cres BS16 . . . . 18 E6
Wellington Ct 11 BS6 . . . . 18 E1
Wellington Dr
 Bristol BS9 . . . . 18 D6
 Yate BS37 . . . . 43 B2
Wellington Hill BS7 . . . . . 18 E6
Wellington Hill W BS9 . . . 18 D7
Wellington Ho GL7 . . . . . 190 D5
Wellington La
 Bristol BS6 . . . . 18 E1
 Cheltenham GL52 . . . . . . 133 E3
Wellington Lodge Cl
 GL20 . . . . 182 D7
Wellington Mews BS11 . . . 16 D5
Wellington Par GL1 . . . . . 196 C3
Wellington Pk BS8 . . . . . . 18 A2
Wellington Pl
 Bristol BS16 . . . . 30 B1
 Cheltenham GL52 . . . . . . 193 C2
Wellington Rd
 Bristol BS2 . . . . 195 C4
 Bristol, Kingswood BS15 . . 20 D2
 Cheltenham GL52 . . . . . . 133 E3
 10 Moreton-in-M GL56 . . . 187 B3
 Upper Rissington GL54 . . 169 D6
 Yate BS37 . . . . 43 E3
Wellingtons Gr GL4 . . . . . 191 D2
Wellington Sq GL50 . . . . . 133 E3
Wellington St
 Cheltenham GL50 . . . . . . 193 C3
 Gloucester GL1 . . . . 196 B2
Wellington Terr
 18 Bristol BS8 . . . . 7 F6
 8 Moreton-in-M GL56 . . . 187 B3
 Newnham GL14 . . . . 156 F6
Wellington Wlk BS10 . . . . 18 C7
Well La
 Badminton GL9 . . . . 46 E5
 Drybrook GL17 . . . . 164 A4
 Guiting Power GL54 . . . . 175 B3
 Stow-on-t-W GL54 . . . . . 176 F4
Wellmeadow GL16 . . . . . . 154 D7
Wellmeadow La GL16 . . . 155 A8
Well Pl GL50 . . . . 133 B1
Wells Cl
 Bristol BS14 . . . . 3 C5
 Cheltenham GL51 . . . . . . 129 F5
Wells Gdns 5 WR12 . . . . . 185 C8
Wellsprings Ho GL2 . . . . . 127 C3

Wellsprings Rd GL2 . . . . . 127 C3
Wells Rd
 Bisley GL6 . . . . 148 D8
 Bristol BS4 . . . . 9 B2
 Gloucester GL4 . . . . 119 C8
 Maiden Head BS41 . . . . 1 E1
Wells St BS3 . . . . 8 A4
Wellstead Ave BS37 . . . . . 43 D1
Wellsway BS31 . . . . 4 F3
Wellsway Sec Sch BS31 . . . 5 A5
Well Vale La HR9 . . . . 162 D3
Welsford Rd BS16 . . . . 19 D4
Welsford Rd BS16 . . . . 19 C4
Welsh Back BS1 . . . . 195 A2
Welsh House La GL18 . . . 170 F8
Welsh St NP16 . . . . 72 D1
Welsh Way
 Bagendon GL7 . . . . 158 D1
 Fairford GL7 . . . . 152 B5
 Sunhill GL7 . . . . 151 F7
Welton Wlk BS15 . . . . 20 C2
Welveland La GL4 . . . . 127 E1
Welwyn Mews 4 GL51 . . 129 E5
Wenchford Forest Trail★
 GL15 . . . . 156 C2
Wendling Rd GL2 . . . . 110 B7
Wendover Gdns GL50 . . . 133 E4
Wend The GL17 . . . . 164 F5
Wenlock Rd GL20 . . . . . . 192 D3
Wenmore Cl BS16 . . . . 30 D1
Wentforth Dr 2 BS15 . . . . 20 C2
Wentsfield GL10 . . . . 96 F7
Wentworth
 Bristol BS30 . . . . 11 A6
 Yate BS37 . . . . 43 E1
Wentworth Cl
 Cheltenham GL51 . . . . . . 132 D3
 Gloucester GL2 . . . . 127 B5
Wentworth Rd
 Bristol BS7 . . . . 18 D3
 Cheltenham GL51 . . . . . . 132 D3
Werth La GL19 . . . . 181 B1
Wescott Gr BS11 . . . . 27 C2
Wesley Ave BS15 . . . . 10 D5
Wesley Cl
 Aylburton GL15 . . . . 147 E4
 7 Bristol, Upper Soundwell
  BS16 . . . . 20 D3
 Bristol, Whitehall BS5 . . . 19 C1
Wesley Ct
 Gloucester GL1 . . . . 196 C2
 16 Stroud GL5 . . . . 99 C7
Wesley Hill BS15 . . . . 20 D1
Wesley Ho GL50 . . . . 193 B4
Wesley La BS30 . . . . 11 B5
Wesley Pl BS8 . . . . 18 A2
Wesley Rd
 Bristol BS7 . . . . 18 E4
 Cinderford BS14 . . . . 191 D5
 Leonard Stanley GL10 . . . . 97 E3
 Whitecroft GL15 . . . . 155 F1
Wesley St BS3 . . . . 8 C3
Wessex Ave BS7 . . . . 18 F7
Wessex Ct BS7 . . . . 18 F7
Wessex Dr GL52 . . . . 134 B2
Wessex Ho 11 BS2 . . . . . 195 C3
Westacre Cl BS10 . . . . 28 A2
Westal Gn 15 GL50 . . . . . 130 B8
West Allcourt GL7 . . . . . . 153 E2
Westal Pk GL51 . . . . 130 B7
West Approach Dr GL52 . 133 E4
West Ave GL7 . . . . 164 B4
Westbourne Ave BS31 . . . . 4 E5
Westbourne Cl 2 BS16 . . . 21 A4
Westbourne Ct BS5 . . . . . . 9 B8
Westbourne Dr
 Cheltenham GL52 . . . . . . 133 F2
 Hardwicke GL2 . . . . 109 E7
Westbourne Gr 9 BS3 . . . . 8 C3
Westbourne Ho 12 GL52 . 133 F2
Westbourne Pl BS8 . . . . . 194 B3
Westbourne Rd
 Bristol, Downend BS16 . . . 20 F8
 8 Bristol, Upper Easton BS5 9 B8
Westbourne Terr BS16 . . . 20 B7
West Broadway BS9 . . . . . 18 D6
Westbrooke Ct BS1 . . . . . 194 A1
Westbrook Rd BS4 . . . . 3 D8
Westbury Court Gardens★
 GL14 . . . . 157 C8
Westbury Court Rd BS9 . . 18 A7
Westbury Ct BS9 . . . . 18 A7
Westbury Hill BS9 . . . . . . 18 A7
Westbury La BS9 . . . . 17 C7
Westbury Mews 6 BS9 . . . 18 A7
Westbury-on-Severn CE
 Prim Sch GL14 . . . . 165 C1
Westbury-on-Trym CE Prim
 Acad BS9 . . . . 18 A8
Westbury Park Prim Sch
 BS6 . . . . 18 B3
Westbury Pk BS6 . . . . 18 A4
Westbury Rd
 Bristol BS6 . . . . 18 A4
 Cheltenham GL53 . . . . . . 130 E4
 Gloucester GL4 . . . . 118 D3
West Coombe BS9 . . . . . . 17 D6
Westcote Rd BS4 . . . . 18 E1
West Country Water Pk★
 BS36 . . . . 40 F2
Westcourt Dr BS30 . . . . . . 11 B4
West Croft BS9 . . . . 18 C7
West Dene BS9 . . . . 17 E6
Westdown Gdns GL52 . . . 133 E1

West Dr GL50 . . . . 133 E3
West Dundry La BS41 . . . . . 1 E2
Westend GL11 . . . . 87 D4
West End
 Avening GL8 . . . . 140 A8
 Bristol, Kingsdown BS2 . . 195 A4
 Bristol, Southville BS3 . . . 194 C1
 Coaley GL11 . . . . 96 C1
 Kingham OX7 . . . . 177 F2
 Minchinhampton GL6 . . . 148 A3
 Northleach GL54 . . . . 168 A1
 Oldbury-on-S BS35 . . . . . . 63 C6
 Ruardean GL17 . . . . 163 E4
Westend Cross GL10 . . . . 101 A2
West End Gdns GL7 . . . . . 152 D8
Westend La BS35 . . . . 63 B6
West End La
 Broadway WR12 . . . . 185 B7
 Gloucester GL3 . . . . 120 B6
Westend Par GL1 . . . . 126 C3
Westend Rd GL12 . . . . 53 E5
Westend Terr
 Chipping Campden GL55 . 188 F2
 Gloucester GL1 . . . . 126 C3
Westering Cl BS16 . . . . . . 21 A5
Westerleigh Bsns Pk
 BS37 . . . . 43 B1
Westerleigh Cl BS16 . . . . . 20 F7
Westerleigh Rd
 Bristol BS16 . . . . 20 F6
 Coalpit Heath BS36 . . . . . . 31 D2
 Pucklechurch BS16 . . . . . 22 C7
 Westerleigh BS36, BS37 . . 32 B5
 Yate BS37 . . . . 32 C8
Westerley Cl GL14 . . . . . . 191 D3
Western Approach
 Distribution Pk BS35 . . . 38 C4
Western Ave
 Chepstow/Cas-Gwent
  NP16 . . . . 60 F5
 Frampton Cotterell BS36 . . 42 A1
 Mitcheldean GL17 . . . . . . 164 D5
Western Ct
 Bristol BS34 . . . . 30 A4
 6 Cheltenham GL50 . . . . 133 E3
Western Dr BS14 . . . . 2 E1
Western Grange BS34 . . . . 29 A3
Western Hill Rd GL20 . . . 183 B5
Western Rd
 Bristol BS7 . . . . 18 E6
 Cheltenham GL50 . . . . . . 193 A3
Western Way GL18 . . . . . . 178 D2
Westfield
 Dursley GL11 . . . . 88 A2
 Llangrove HR9 . . . . 162 B6
West Field GL2 . . . . 125 D5
Westfield Ave
 Brockworth GL3 . . . . 120 D6
 Northway GL20 . . . . 182 C4
Westfield Cl
 Bristol BS15 . . . . 10 D5
 Keynsham BS31 . . . . 4 C5
Westfield Cotts GL51 . . . . 136 B3
Westfield Ct GL14 . . . . . . 191 D5
Westfield Gn GL7 . . . . 152 A3
Westfield Ho BS7 . . . . 17 F5
Westfield La BS34 . . . . 29 E3
Westfield Pk BS6 . . . . 18 B1
Westfield Pl BS8 . . . . 7 F7
Westfield Rd
 Bristol BS9 . . . . 18 A7
 Brockworth GL3 . . . . 120 D6
 Cinderford GL14 . . . . 191 D5
Westfields GL12 . . . . 68 A7
Westfield Terr GL53 . . . . . 126 E5
Westfield Way BS32 . . . . . 40 D2
Westgate BS1 . . . . 194 B1
Westgate St GL1 . . . . 196 A3
West Gr BS6 . . . . 18 F1
West Grange Ct GL5 . . . . . 99 B8
West Hay Gr GL7 . . . . 141 F8
West Hill SN26 . . . . 144 D2
Westhill Ct SN6 . . . . 145 C3
West La GL7 . . . . 141 F8
Westland Ave BS30 . . . . . 11 C4
Westland Rd GL2 . . . . 109 D7
West Leaze Pl BS32 . . . . . 29 E6
Westleigh Cl
 Bristol BS10 . . . . 28 D1
 Yate BS37 . . . . 43 C1
Westleigh Ct BS37 . . . . . . 43 C1
Westleigh Pk BS14 . . . . 3 B8
Westleigh Rd BS10 . . . . . . 28 D1
West Littleton Rd SN14 . . 24 E2
West Lodge Dr GL4 . . . . . 119 D6
West Mall BS8 . . . . 7 F6
West Market Pl GL7 . . . . . 190 C5
Westmarsh La BS35 . . . . . . 63 B5
Westmarsh La BS35 . . . . . . 63 B5
Westmead Rd
 Bristol BS5 . . . . 10 B7
 Gloucester GL2 . . . . 127 D5
West Mill La SN6 . . . . 143 E4
Westminster Cl
 1 Bristol BS9 . . . . 18 A7
 Cheltenham GL53 . . . . . . 130 F7
Westminster Ct 3 GL52 . . 127 B2
Westminster Rd BS5 . . . . . . 9 D8
Westmoreland Rd BS6 . . . 18 B3
Westmorland Ho BS6 . . . . 18 A3
Westmorland Terr BS37 . . 34 D7
Weston Ave 4 BS5 . . . . 9 D7
Westonbirt Arboretum★
 GL8 . . . . 58 B8
Westonbirt Sch GL8 . . . . . 58 B8
Weston Cl BS9 . . . . 17 C7

Weston Cotts SN7 . . . . . . 145 E8
Weston Cres BS7 . . . . 18 E6
Westonian Ct BS9 . . . . . . 17 C4
Weston Ind Est WR11 . . . 188 D4
Weston Rd
 Bretforton WR11 . . . . . . 188 B5
 Gloucester GL1 . . . . 196 B1
 Honeybourne WR11 . . . . 188 C6
 Long Ashton BS41 . . . . 7 A1
Westons Brake BS16 . . . . 31 A1
Westons Hill Dr BS16 . . . 31 A1
Westons Way BS15 . . . . . . 10 F7
Westover Cl BS9 . . . . 27 F1
Westover Ct 3 BS9 . . . . . . 28 A1
Westover Dr BS9 . . . . 28 A1
Westover Gdns BS9 . . . . . 17 F8
Westover Rd BS9 . . . . 28 A1
Westover Rise BS9 . . . . . . 28 A1
West Par BS9 . . . . 17 C7
West Park Rd BS16 . . . . . . 20 E5
West Pk BS8 . . . . 194 B4
West Pk BS9 . . . . 17 C7
West Point Row BS32 . . . . 40 C3
Westpoint Trad Est BS15 . . 10 D7
West Priory BS9 . . . . 18 A7
West Ridge
 Frampton Cotterell BS36 . . 31 B7
 Frampton Cotterell BS36 . . 31 C7
Westridge Rd GL12 . . . . . . 68 A8
West Rocke Ave BS9 . . . . 17 D6
Westrop SN6 . . . . 145 D3
Westrop Prim Sch SN6 . . 145 C3
West Shrubbery 5 BS6 . . 18 B2
West St
 Bristol, Bedminster BS3 . . . 8 C3
 Bristol BS2 . . . . 195 C3
 2 Bristol, Kingswood BS15 10 D8
 Bristol, Oldland Common
  BS30 . . . . 11 C4
 Kingham OX7 . . . . 177 F2
 Tetbury GL8 . . . . 140 B4
 Tytherington GL12 . . . . . . 52 B5
West Town Ave BS4 . . . . . . 9 D1
West Town Dr 2 BS4 . . . . . 9 D1
West Town Gr BS4 . . . . 3 D8
West Town La BS4 . . . . 9 D1
West Town Lane Inf Sch
 BS4 . . . . 9 C1
West Town Lane Jun Sch
 BS4 . . . . 9 C1
West Town Pk BS4 . . . . 9 D1
West Town Rd BS11 . . . . . 16 C7
West Tynings GL6 . . . . 91 A4
Westview GL19 . . . . 173 C7
West View
 Alveston BS35 . . . . 50 F4
 Bristol BS16 . . . . 21 A6
 Cinderford GL14 . . . . 191 D3
 Joy's Green GL17 . . . . . . 163 D3
 Newent GL18 . . . . 170 F4
 Newnham GL14 . . . . 156 F7
 Poulton GL7 . . . . 151 F3
 Wotton-u-E GL12 . . . . 68 C7
West View Rd
 Bristol BS3 . . . . 8 B3
 Keynsham BS31 . . . . 4 E5
Westward BS41 . . . . 7 B2
Westward Ct GL5 . . . . 98 D6
Westward Dr BS20 . . . . . . 16 C4
Westward Gdns BS41 . . . . . 7 B2
Westward Rd
 Bristol BS13 . . . . 1 F7
 Stroud GL5 . . . . 98 D6
West Way
 Bristol BS10, BS34 . . . . . . 28 E4
 Cirencester GL7 . . . . 190 C4
 Lechlade on T GL7 . . . . . 153 E3
Westwick Rd GL19 . . . . . . 165 D6
Westwood Cres BS4 . . . . . . 9 D5
Westwood La GL52 . . . . . 134 D3
Westwood Rd BS4 . . . . 3 D8
West Wly GL52 . . . . 137 F5
Wetherby Ct BS16 . . . . . . 30 F1
Wetherby Gr 1 BS16 . . . . . 30 F1
Wetherell Pl BS8 . . . . 194 B3
Wetherleigh Dr GL2 . . . . . 125 E5
Wexford Rd BS4 . . . . 2 D8
Weyhouse Cl GL5 . . . . 99 D5
Weymouth Rd BS3 . . . . 8 D2
Whaddon Ave GL52 . . . . . 134 A2
Whaddon Dr GL52 . . . . . . 133 F2
Whaddon Prim Sch
 GL52 . . . . 134 B2
Whaddon Rd GL52 . . . . . . 134 B2
Whaddon Road (Cheltenham
 Town FC) GL52 . . . . 133 F3
Whaddon Way GL4 . . . . . . 118 D1
Wharfdale Sq GL51 . . . . . 132 F3
Wharfdale Way
 Hardwicke GL2 . . . . 109 D8
 Stonehouse GL10 . . . . 97 C6
Wharfedale BS35 . . . . 51 D8
Wharfings The GL7 . . . . . 144 E7
Wharf La
 Kempsford GL7 . . . . 144 E7
 Lechlade on T GL7 . . . . . 153 E2
Wharf Rd 5 BS16 . . . . 19 F4
Wharfside GL2 . . . . 118 C7
Wharf The GL19 . . . . 173 E6
Wharncliffe Cl BS14 . . . . . . 3 B5
Wharncliffe Gdns BS14 . . . 3 B5
Whartons 8 BS4 . . . . 9 D1

Whatley Ct **9** BS8 . . . . . . 18 B1
Whatley Rd BS8 . . . . 18 B1
Wheal Cl GL20 . . . . 182 C4
Wheal Rd GL20 . . . . 182 C4
Wheat Cl GL56 . . . . 177 A6
Wheatfield Ct GL55 . . . . . 189 A6
Wheatfield Dr BS32 . . . . . 40 D1
Wheatfield Prim Sch
  BS32 . . . . 40 D1
Wheathill Cl BS31 . . . . 4 D5
Wheatland Dr GL51 . . . . . 132 D4
Wheatridge E The GL4 . . . 119 E4
Wheatridge The GL4 . . . . 119 D4
Wheatsheaf Dr GL52 . . . . 137 D4
Wheatsheaf La SN16 . . . . 142 A4
Wheatstone Cl GL20 . . . . 182 C5
Wheatstone La GL17 . . . . 163 C4
Wheatstone Rd GL1 . . . . . 118 F7
Wheatway GL4 . . . . 119 D3
Wheelers Patch BS16 . . . . 21 B5
Wheelers Rise GL5 . . . . . . 98 F8
Wheelers Wlk GL5 . . . . . . 98 F8
Wheelwrights Cnr **3** GL6 . 91 B4
Whelford Rd GL7 . . . . . . 144 E8
Whetstones GL14 . . . . . . 157 A7
Whimbrel Rd GL2 . . . . . . 117 D1
Whimsey Rd GL14 . . . . . . 191 B6
Whinchat Gdns BS16 . . . . 19 F6
Whip La GL6 . . . . 91 B5
Whippington Ct BS1 . . . . 195 B3
Whippington's Cnr GL16 . 154 E7
Whistle Rd BS15 . . . . 21 B2
Whitby Rd BS4 . . . . 9 C4
Whitchurch CE Prim Sch
  HR9 . . . . 162 E4
Whitchurch District Ctr
  BS14 . . . . 3 A5
Whitchurch La
  Bristol, Bishopsworth BS13. . 2 B5
  Bristol, Hartcliffe BS13 . . . 2 C5
  Bristol, Whitchurch BS14. . . 2 E5
  Dundry BS41 . . . . 2 C1
Whitchurch Prim Sch BS14 3 C4
Whitchurch Rd BS13 . . . . . 2 A6
Whitebeam Cl GL2 . . . . . 127 B5
Whitebeam Ct BS55 . . . . . . 9 E8
Whitebeam Ho **7** BS16. . . 20 C6
Whitechapel Rd **8** GL15 155 D1
White Cotts GL5 . . . . 98 E6
Whitecourt GL11 . . . . 89 A1
Whitecroft GL6 . . . . 91 B4
Whitecroft Rd GL15 . . . . 155 E1
Whitecroft Sta★ GL15 . . 155 F1
Whitecroft Way BS15 . . . . 11 A7
Whitecross Ave BS14 . . . . . 3 C6
White Cross Rd GL15 . . . . 92 A2
Whitecross Sq GL53 . . . . 193 C4
Whitecross St **19** NP25 . . 154 A7
White End GL19 . . . . 172 D4
Whitefield Ave
  Bristol, Hanham BS15 . . . . 10 D5
  Bristol, Speedwell BS5 . . . 20 A1
Whitefield Cl
  8 Bristol BS16 . . . . . . 20 D3
  Stonehouse GL10 . . . . . . 97 F6
Whitefield Rd BS5 . . . . . . 20 A2
Whitefields BS37 . . . . 44 C1
Whitefields Rd GL52 . . . . 137 D4
Whitefriars GL5 . . . . 131 B7
Whitefriars La SN6 . . . . . 142 F6
Whitegates BS36 . . . . 30 D6
Whitehall GL5 . . . . 99 D7
Whitehall Ave BS5 . . . . . . 19 E1
Whitehall Gdns BS5 . . . . . 19 D1
Whitehall La GL2 . . . . . . 124 E6
Whitehall Prim Sch BS5 . . 19 D1
Whitehall Rd BS5 . . . . 9 C8
Whitehall Trad Est **4** BS5 19 D1
White Hart GL7 . . . . 152 E3
Whitehart Ho GL51 . . . . . 133 C3
White Hart La **13** GL54. . 176 C1
White Hart St GL51 . . . . . 133 C3
Whitehill La GL17 . . . . . . 164 B4
White Horse La GL6 . . . . 103 F8
White Horse Rd SN6 . . . . 143 E4
White House Bsns Ctr The
  BS15 . . . . 10 D7
Whitehouse Ctr BS13 . . . . 2 C5
Whitehouse Farm GL14. . 165 D1
Whitehouse La
  Bristol BS3 . . . . 8 D4
  Gorsley HR9, GL18 . . . . . 170 C5
  Pilning BS35 . . . . 38 C7
  Tetbury GL8 . . . . 140 C1
Whitehouse Pk GL5 . . . . . 98 E7
Whitehouse Pl BS3 . . . . . . 8 E4
Whitehouse St GL53 . . . . . 8 E4
Whitehouse Way GL52 . . 138 B3
Whiteladies Rd BS8 . . . . 194 B4
Whitelands La
  Little Shurdington GL51 . . 121 C8
  Little Shurdington GL51 . . 121 D8
Whitelands Rd GL7 . . . . . 190 E5
Whiteleaze GL18 . . . . 18 C8
White Lodge Rd BS16 . . . . 20 F4
Whitemarsh Cl GL51 . . . . 132 D4
Whitemead Ho **3** BS3. . . 8 A3
Whiteshill BS16 . . . . 30 D3
Whites Hill BS5 . . . . 10 A6
White St BS5 . . . . 195 C4
Whitethorn Cotts GL51 . . 133 A7

Whitethorn Dr GL52 . . . . 134 C3
Whitethorn Vale BS10 . . . 28 C3
White Tree Rbdt BS6 . . . . 18 A4
White Tree Rd BS9 . . . . . . 18 B4
Whitewall La BS35 . . . . . . 64 F1
Whitewater Rd GL8 . . . . . 70 C4
Whiteway GL11 . . . . 80 C6
Whiteway Cl
  Bristol, St Anne's Park BS4. . 9 E6
  Bristol, St George BS5. . . . 10 A8
  Dursley GL11 . . . . 80 C7
Whiteway Ct
  1 Bristol BS5 . . . . 10 A8
  Cirencester GL7. . . . . . . 190 D6
Whiteway Mews BS5 . . . . 10 A8
Whiteway Rd
  Bristol BS5, BS15 . . . . . . 20 A1
  Gloucester GL4 . . . . 119 B5
Whiteway View GL7 . . . . 190 B7
Whitewell Cl GL4 . . . . . . 119 E7
Whitewood Rd BS5 . . . . . . 19 F1
Whitfield Ho **7** BS15. . . . 10 D8
Whitfield Rd BS35 . . . . . . 64 C2
Whitfield St GL1 . . . . 196 B2
Whitford Cl WR11 . . . . . . 188 A6
Whiting Rd BS13 . . . . 2 A4
Whitland Ave BS13 . . . . . . 2 B5
Whitland Rd BS13 . . . . 2 B5
Whitley Cl BS37 . . . . 43 C3
Whitley Mead BS34 . . . . . 29 E3
Whitley Wy **17** GL56 . . . 187 B3
Whitmead Gdns BS13 . . . . 2 C4
Whitminster CE Prim Sch
  GL2 . . . . 100 E5
Whitminster La GL2. . . . . 100 A6
Whitmore Ave BS4 . . . . . . 10 A3
Whitmore Rd GL54 . . . . . 174 A8
Whitmores The GL54 . . . . 176 C1
Whitson Ho **2** BS2. . . . . 195 C3
Whitson St BS1 . . . . 195 A4
Whitstone Rise GL2 . . . . . 110 A5
Whittingham Hall GL14 . . 156 E5
Whittington Ct★ GL54. . . 166 C7
Whittington Ho GL5 . . . . . 99 A7
Whittington Rd
  Bristol BS16 . . . . 20 C6
  Cheltenham GL51 . . . . . 129 D8
Whittington Way GL15 . . 147 D8
Whittington Wlk **18**
  GL18 . . . . 171 A4
Whittle Ave GL4 . . . . 118 D2
Whittle Cl
  1 Cheltenham GL51 . . . 129 C8
  Stoke Orchard GL52 . . . . 136 D5
Whittles La GL2 . . . . 157 F2
Whittlestone Cl GL54. . . . 176 C4
Whittlestone Hollow
  GL54 . . . . 176 D4
Whittle Wy GL3 . . . . 120 C6
Whittock Rd BS14. . . . . 3 D6
Whittock Sq BS14. . . . . 3 D7
Whittucks Cl BS15 . . . . . . 10 D4
Whittucks Rd BS15 . . . . . . 10 C4
Whitwell Rd BS14. . . . . 3 B8
Whitworth Mews GL3 . . . 120 C6
Whitworth Rd GL7 . . . . . 190 C3
Whornes Orch GL4 . . . . . 119 F3
Whytes Cl BS9 . . . . 18 A8
Wick CE Prim Sch BS30 . . 12 B6
Wick Cres BS4. . . . . 9 D3
Wickets The
  Bristol, Filton BS7 . . . . . . 28 F1
  Bristol, Upper Soundwell
  BS15 . . . . 20 D2
Wicketts The BS7 . . . . 28 F2
Wickfield La GL52. . . . . . 138 F4
Wickham Ct BS37 . . . . 33 D8
Wickham Glen BS16 . . . . . 19 D5
Wickham Hill BS16 . . . . . . 19 D5
Wickham View BS16 . . . . . 19 D4
Wick House Cl BS31. . . . . . 5 D3
Wick La
  Lower Apperley GL19 . . . 173 C6
  Upton Cheyney BS30 . . . . 12 A2
Wicklow Rd BS4 . . . . 2 E8
Wick Rd
  Bristol BS4. . . . . 9 D4
  Oaksey SN16 . . . . 142 A4
  Pilning BS35 . . . . 38 C7
Wickridge Cl GL5 . . . . 99 C8
Wick St GL6 . . . . 103 E4
Wickwar Rd
  Kingswood GL12 . . . . 67 E6
  Rangeworthy BS37 . . . . . 53 B1
  Yate BS37 . . . . 44 B5
Wickwar La GL7 . . . . 143 B6
Wick Wick Cl BS16, BS36. . 31 A2
Widcombe BS14 . . . . 3 A6
Widcombe Cl **3** BS5. . . . 10 A7
Widden Prim Sch GL1. . . 196 C2
Widden St GL1. . . . . 196 C2
Wider Mead **5** BS7 . . . . 19 C8
Widhill La SN26. . . . . 144 D1
Widmore Gr BS13. . . . . 2 B5
Wigeon La GL20 . . . . 192 E5
Wigmore Cl **5** GL4 . . . . 119 E6
Wigton Cres GL51 . . . . . . 28 C2
Wilbye Gr BS4 . . . . 2 D7
Wilcox Cl BS15 . . . . 10 C6
Wildcroft Ho BS9 . . . . 18 B4
Wildcroft Rd BS9 . . . . 18 B4
Wilder Ct BS2 . . . . 195 B4
Wilder Ho BS2 . . . . 195 B4
Wilder St BS2 . . . . 195 B4

Wildfowl & Wetlands Trust
  Slimbridge★ GL2 . . . . . 95 A6
Wilding Cl GL20 . . . . 192 E5
Wildlife Wlk GL3 . . . . . . 120 E4
Wildmoorway La
  South Cerney GL7 . . . . . 143 A8
  South Cerney GL7 . . . . . 143 A8
Wildwood Residential Cvn Pk
  GL7 . . . . 190 F2
Wilkes Ave GL3 . . . . 120 A8
Wilkes Mdw GL16 . . . . . . 155 B6
Wilkinson Rd GL7 . . . . . . 190 D1
Willada Cl BS3 . . . . 8 B2
Willcox Dr GL52 . . . . 138 B3
Willersey Bsns Pk WR12 . 188 B3
Willersey CE Prim Sch
  WR12 . . . . 188 B2
Willersey Rd GL51 . . . . . 129 E8
Willesley Dr GL8 . . . . 57 B7
Willett Gdns GL54 . . . . . 174 A7
William Emes Gdn GL56 . 186 C7
William Gough Cl GL51 . . 132 D5
William Jessop Wy BS13 . . 2 E4
William Mason Cl **5** BS5 . . 9 B7
William Morris Camphill
  Com GL10 . . . . 101 A1
Williams Cl BS30 . . . . 10 F3
Williamson Rd BS7. . . . . . 18 F3
Williams Orch GL2 . . . . . 125 D5
William St
  Bristol, Fishponds BS16 . . 20 B3
  8 Bristol, Moorfields BS5 . . 9 C8
  Bristol, Newton BS2 . . . . . 9 A6
  Bristol, St Pauls BS2 . . . . 18 F1
  Bristol, Windmill Hill BS3. . . 8 E4
Williamstrip Farm Cotts
  GL7 . . . . 160 F1
Willinton Rd BS4. . . . . 2 F8
Willis Est BS2. . . . . 18 F3
Willis Rd BS15 . . . . 20 F2
Willis Wlk GL20 . . . . 182 C5
Willment Way BS11 . . . . . 26 D1
Willmott Cl BS14. . . . . 2 F3
Willoughby Cl
  Alveston BS35 . . . . 51 A4
  Bristol BS13. . . . . 2 B7
Willoughby Rd BS7 . . . . . 18 E5
Willow Ave GL4 . . . . 119 B7
Willow Bank BS10. . . . . . . 18 C7
Willow Bank Rd GL20 . . . 183 D4
Willow Bed Cl BS16 . . . . . 20 B6
Willowbrook Dr GL51 . . . 132 D4
Willow Cl
  Ashton under Hill WR11 . . 183 D8
  Bristol, Patchway BS34 . . . 28 E7
  Bristol, Warmley BS30 . . . 11 D6
  Charfield GL12 . . . . 67 A4
  Chepstow/Cas-Gwent NP16 60 D6
  Dursley GL11 . . . . 88 A3
  Wick BS30 . . . . 12 B6
  Woodmancote GL52 . . . . 138 B3
Willowcroft Cl GL4 . . . . . 119 D3
Willow Ct BS7 . . . . 19 A7
Willow Cvn Site GL2 . . . . 126 D5
Willowdean GL14 . . . . . . 191 C5
Willow Dr
  Bishop's Cleeve GL52 . . . 138 B4
  Tewkesbury GL20 . . . . . 192 F1
Willow Edge GL2. . . . . . . 110 A5
Willow Gr
  1 Bristol BS16 . . . . . . 20 C4
  South Cerney GL7 . . . . . 143 A8
Willowherb Cl GL52 . . . . 134 C3
Willow Ho BS13. . . . . 2 D4
Willow Hts GL15 . . . . 92 B5
Willowleaze GL2 . . . . 127 D3
Willow Park Dr GL52 . . . . 137 F4
Willow Rd
  Bristol BS15. . . . . 10 C3
  Charlton Kings GL53 . . . . 131 C5
  King's Stanley GL10. . . . . 98 A4
  Stonehouse GL10. . . . . . . 97 E7
  Willersey WR12. . . . . . . 188 B2
Willow Sh Ctr The BS16 . . 20 E6
Willows The
  Bristol, Bradley Stoke
  BS32 . . . . 29 D8
  Bristol BS16. . . . . 20 E4
  Bristol, Frenchay BS16 . . . 30 B1
  Coalpit Heath BS36 . . . . . 31 F7
  Dymock GL18. . . . . 178 D2
  Gloucester GL1 . . . . 196 C4
  Highworth SN6 . . . . 145 D3
  Longhope GL17 . . . . 164 F5
  Quedgeley GL2. . . . . 117 E1
  Yate BS37 . . . . 43 D2
Willow Way
  Coalpit Heath BS36 . . . . . 31 C6
  Gloucester GL4 . . . . 119 B7
Willow Wlk
  Bristol BS10. . . . . 28 B3
  Keynsham BS31. . . . . 4 D4
Willsbridge Hill BS30 . . . . 11 A2
Willsbridge Mill★ BS30. . . 11 A2
Wills Dr BS5 . . . . 9 A8
Wills Way BS13. . . . . 8 D4
Willway St BS3 . . . . 8 D4
Wilmot Ct BS30 . . . . 11 A6
Wilmots Way BS20 . . . . . 16 D4
Wilshire Ave BS15 . . . . . . 10 D5
Wilson Pl BS2 . . . . 195 C4
Wilson Rd GL51 . . . . 129 D1
Wilson St BS2 . . . . 195 C4
Wilton Cl
  Bristol BS10. . . . . 28 C1
  Gloucester GL1 . . . . 118 D6

Wilton Rd GL1 . . . . 118 D6
Wiltshire Ave BS37. . . . . . 44 A3
Wiltshire Pl BS15 . . . . 20 E3
Wilverley Ind Est BS4 . . . . 9 E1
Wimbledon Rd BS6 . . . . . 18 C5
Wimborne Cl GL51 . . . . . 129 E6
Wimborne Rd BS3 . . . . . . 8 C1
Winash Cl BS14 . . . . 3 D7
Wincanton Cl BS16. . . . . . 30 F1
Wincel Rd GL51 . . . . 129 E7
Winchcombe Abbey CE Prim
  Sch GL54. . . . . 174 A7
Winchcombe Folk & Police
  Mus★ GL54. . . . . 174 A7
Winchcombe Gdns GL52 . 142 F7
Winchcombe Gr BS11 . . . . 16 F5
Winchcombe Railway Mus★
  GL54. . . . . 174 A7
Winchcombe
  Dumbleton WR11. . . . . . 184 A8
  Frampton Cotterell BS36. . 31 B8
  Gloucester GL4 . . . . 118 E2
Winchcombe Sch GL54. . . 174 A8
Winchcombe St GL52 . . . 193 C4
Winchcombe Sta GL54. . . 174 A7
Winchester Ave BS4 . . . . . 9 D3
Winchester Ct BS16. . . . . . 19 E6
Winchester Dr GL4 . . . . . 118 E3
Winchester Ho **5** GL50. . 133 B1
Winchester Rd BS4 . . . . . . 9 D3
Winchester Way GL51 . . . 129 E7
Wincombe Trad Est BS2 . . . 9 A4
Wincroft BS30 . . . . 11 C4
Windcliff Cres BS11. . . . . . 16 E7
Windermere Cl GL51 . . . . 129 E7
Windermere Rd
  Bristol BS34. . . . . 29 A8
  Cheltenham GL51. . . . . . 129 E7
  Gloucester GL2 . . . . 127 C4
Windermere Way BS30 . . . 11 D6
Windfall Way GL2. . . . . . 127 C2
Windmill Cl BS3 . . . . 8 E4
Windmill Cotts GL18 . . . . 82 A6
Windmill Field GL4 . . . . . 119 D7
Windmill Hill BS3. . . . . 8 D3
Windmill La
  Bristol BS10. . . . . 27 D3
  Kingscote GL8 . . . . 82 A6
Windmill Rd
  Kemble GL7 . . . . 141 F8
  Minchinhampton GL6. . . . 91 E6
Windrush SN6 . . . . 145 C3
Windrush Ct
  Temple Guiting GL54 . . . 175 A8
  Thornbury BS35. . . . . . . 51 C8
Windrush Gn BS31. . . . . . . 5 A4
Windrush Rd
  Cheltenham GL52 . . . . . 134 A2
  Gloucester GL4 . . . . 118 E2
  Keynsham BS31. . . . . 5 A4
Windrush View GL54 . . . . 175 D2
Windscreens Ave BS2 . . . . 9 A7
Windsor Ave
  Bristol BS5. . . . . 10 B6
  Keynsham BS31. . . . . 4 E4
Windsor Cl BS34 . . . . 29 E4
Windsor Cres BS10. . . . . . 27 C4
Windsor Ct
  14 Bristol, Clifton BS8. . . 7 F6
  Bristol, Downend BS16 . . . 20 E7
  Wick BS30 . . . . 12 C7
Windsor Dr
  Lydney GL15. . . . . 92 B6
  Yate BS37 . . . . 43 D2
Windsoredge La GL6 . . . . 91 A6
Windsor La GL11. . . . . 81 A8
Windsor Pl
  Bristol, Clifton BS8 . . . . . . 7 F6
  Bristol, Mangotsfield BS16 . 21 A5
  Stroud GL5 . . . . 103 B1
Windsor Rd
  Bristol, Longwell Green
  BS30 . . . . 10 F2
  Bristol, Montpelier BS6. . . 18 E2
  Dursley GL11 . . . . 88 B1
  3 Tetbury BS35 . . . . . 140 B4
Windsor St GL52 . . . . 133 F3
Windsor Terr
  Bristol, Clifton BS8 . . . . . . 7 F6
  Bristol, Windmill Hill BS3. . . 8 F4
  Cirencester GL7. . . . . . . 190 E4
Windward Wlk BS10 . . . . . 18 E7
Windyridge GL6 . . . . 105 A1
Windyridge Gdns GL50 . . 133 C5
Windyridge Rd GL50 . . . . 133 C5
Wineberry Cl BS5 . . . . . . 19 D1
Wine St BS1 . . . . 195 A3
Winfield GL18 . . . . 170 F4
Winfield General Hospl
  GL2 . . . . 126 E5
Winfield Rd BS30 . . . . 11 C7
Winford Ct BS6 . . . . 18 A5
Winford Gr BS13 . . . . 2 A8
Winford La BS41. . . . . 1 C1
Winford Terr BS41 . . . . . . 1 C1
Wingfield Rd BS3 . . . . 8 E2
Wing La GL20 . . . . 182 E8
Winkworth Pl **4** BS2. . . . 18 F1
Winniecroft Cotts GL4. . . 119 D2
Winnycroft La GL4 . . . . . 119 C1
Winsbury Way BS32. . . . . 40 D1
Winscombe Cl BS31. . . . . . 4 D6
Winsdor Dr GL4. . . . . 118 C2

Winsford St **2** BS5 . . . . . 9 A8
Winsham Cl BS14. . . . . 3 B5
Winsley Cl **10** GL4. . . . . 119 C4
Winsley Rd
  Bristol BS6. . . . . 18 D1
  Gloucester GL4 . . . . 119 C4
Winstanley Ho **4** BS5. . . . 9 B6
Winston Cl **1** HR8 . . . . . 178 F7
Winstone St BS2. . . . . . . 194 C3
Winstone Gdns GL7 . . . . . 190 F5
Winstonian Rd GL52. . . . . 133 F2
Winston Rd GL3. . . . . 128 B5
Winterbotham Rd
  Cheltenham GL51. . . . . . 132 C1
  1 Dursley GL11 . . . . . . 87 F4
Winterbourne Hill BS36. . . 30 D5
Winterbourne Rd BS34. . . 29 E6
Wintersfield GL7. . . . . . . 144 F8
Winterspring La GL12 . . . . 68 F3
Winterstoke Cl **5** BS3. . . . 8 B3
Winterstoke Ctr **1** BS3 . . . 8 B3
Winterstoke Ho **1** BS3. . . 8 A2
Winterstoke Rd BS3. . . . . . 8 A2
Winterstoke Underpass
  BS3 . . . . 7 F4
Winterway GL56 . . . . 186 C6
Wintles Cl GL17 . . . . 164 D5
Wintle's Hill GL14 . . . . . . 157 D6
Wintles La GL14. . . . . 165 C3
Winton Cl GL51 . . . . 130 A7
Winton Rd GL51 . . . . 130 A7
Winton St BS2. . . . . 8 F4
Wintour Cl NP16 . . . . 72 D1
Wirewood Rd NP16 . . . . . 73 A2
Wirewood Cres NP16. . . . . 73 A2
Wishford Cl GL2 . . . . 127 E4
Wisloe Rd GL2. . . . . 95 F2
Wistaria Ave BS37 . . . . . . 44 A1
Wistaria Rd **1** GL8. . . . . 140 B4
Wisteria Cl GL51 . . . . 130 A4
Wisteria Way GL3 . . . . . . 128 A7
Wistley Rd GL53 . . . . 131 B5
Witchell Rd BS5 . . . . 9 C7
Witch Hazel Rd BS13. . . . . 2 D1
Witcombe BS37 . . . . 32 C7
Witcombe Cl BS15 . . . . . . 20 F1
Witcombe Pl GL52 . . . . . 193 C3
Witham Rd BS31. . . . . 5 A3
Witherlies Rd BS16 . . . . . 19 E6
Withers La **1** BS13 . . . . . 2 C4
Withers The GL52. . . . . . . 137 F4
Withey Cl W BS9. . . . . 17 F5
Witheys The BS14. . . . . . . 3 C3
Withington CE Prim Sch
  GL54. . . . . 166 E2
Withington Cl BS30 . . . . . 11 C3
Withleigh Rd BS4 . . . . 9 B2
Withybridge Gdns GL51 . . 132 B2
Withybridge La GL51. . . . . 132 A6
Withy Cl E BS9. . . . . 17 F6
Withyfield Rd GL52. . . . . . 138 A4
Withyholt Ct GL53. . . . . . 130 F5
Withyholt Pk GL53 . . . . . 130 F5
Withy La BS34. . . . . 29 A7
Withymead Rd SN14. . . . . 15 A3
Withy Mews GL4 . . . . 119 B5
Withypool **7** GL51 . . . . 129 E5
Withypool Gdns BS14 . . . . 3 B5
Withys The BS20. . . . . 16 D4
Withy Trees Rd WR11 . . . 188 B3
Withy Way GL11 . . . . 87 F5
Withywood Gdns BS13 . . . . 1 F1
Withywood Rd BS13. . . . . . 1 F1
Witley Lodge Cl GL51 . . . 129 D5
Witney Cl BS3 . . . . 5 D3
Witney Ct GL50 . . . . 193 A3
Witney Mead BS36. . . . . . 31 B8
Witpit La GL7 . . . . 150 F4
Woburn Ave GL4 . . . . . . 118 C1
Woburn Cl BS30 . . . . 10 F5
Woburn Rd BS5. . . . . 19 B3
Woefuldane Bottom GL6 148 A3
Wolds End Cl **2** GL55. . 189 A2
Wolferton Rd BS7. . . . . . . 18 F2
Wolford Rd GL56. . . . . . . 187 D6
Wolfridge Gdns BS10. . . . 28 A4
Wolfridge La BS35 . . . . . . 50 F4
Wolfridge Ride BS35 . . . . 50 F4
Wolseley Lodge GL2 . . . . 127 B2
Wolseley Rd
  Bristol BS7. . . . . 18 D3
  Gloucester GL2 . . . . 127 C2
Wontley Dr GL52. . . . . . . 138 A3
Woodbine Cl GL4 . . . . . . 119 E5
Woodbine Rd BS5. . . . . 9 D8
Woodbines Park Mobile
  Home Pk GL51 . . . . 129 C6
Woodborough Cl GL6 . . . 103 F7
Woodborough St BS5 . . . . 19 B1
Woodbridge La GL54. . . . 166 E1
Woodbridge Rd BS4 . . . . . 9 A2
Woodbury La BS8 . . . . 18 A2
Woodchester
  Bristol BS15. . . . . 20 D4
  Yate BS37 . . . . 32 C6
Woodchester Endowed CE
  Aided Prim Sch GL5 . . . . 99 A2
Woodchester Mansion★
  GL10 . . . . 89 F7
Woodchester Park Walks★
  GL10 . . . . 89 D7
Woodchester Pk★ GL10 . . 90 B7
Woodchester Rd BS10. . . . 18 C2
Woodcock Cl
  Gloucester GL4 . . . . 119 D5
  Stonehouse GL10. . . . . . 101 F1

Woodcock La GL10....... 97 F8
Woodcote
Bristol BS15............. 10 D6
Gloucester GL2........127 B5
Woodcote Rd BS16..... 20 B3
Woodcote Wlk BS16.... 20 B2
Woodcroft Cl
Bristol BS4............. 9 E4
Woodcroft NP16......73 A4
Woodcroft La BS4......73 A4
Woodcroft Rd BS4.....9 E4
Woodcroft Terr NP16...73 B4
Wood Edge Rd GL16....155 B3
Woodend BS15.........10 D6
Woodend Cl GL4.......119 E8
Woodend La
Awre GL14............157 B2
Dursley GL11..........87 D7
Dursley GL11..........87 F6
Gorsley HR9...........170 A4
Rockhampton BS35.... 76 E1
Woodend Rd
Frampton Cotterell BS36... 31 C7
Harrow Hill GL17.....164 B3
Wood End St GL18 ....179 B4
Wood End Wlk BS9.....17 C6
Woodfield Rd
Bristol BS6............. 18 B2
Dursley GL11..........87 E4
6 Ledbury HR8........178 E2
Woodford Ct GL4.......119 B7
Woodgate Cl
Charlton Kings GL52....131 C5
Gloucester GL4........119 E8
Woodgate Rd
Cinderford GL14.......191 D5
Mile End GL16.........155 B7
Woodgrove Rd BS10... 27 D2
Woodhall GL14.........20 F6
Woodhouse Ave BS32... 40 D7
Woodhouse Cl
Cirencester GL7.......190 B3
Woodhouse Down BS32... 40 D6
Woodhouse Dr GL5.... 99 B6
Woodhouse Gr BS7.... 18 E6
Woodington Ct **1** BS30.. 10 F4
Wood La
Down Hatherley GL2....173 D1
Gorsley GL18.........170 D4
Horton BS37...........55 A1
Nailsworth GL6........91 C3
Woodland Ave
Bristol BS15...........20 D2
Dursley GL11..........88 A2
Woodland Cl BS15.....20 C2
Woodland Ct BS9......17 C3
Woodland Dr GL11.....88 A2
Woodland Gn GL4......119 E3
Woodland Gr BS9......17 D6
Woodland Pl GL15.....156 B2
Woodland Rd
Berry Hill GL16........155 A7
Bream GL15...........155 D1
Bristol BS8............194 C4
Coleford GL16.........154 F8
Drybrook GL17........164 B4
Leyhill GL12...........66 B4
Parkend GL15.........155 E3
Woodland Rise
Lydney GL15...........92 B4
Parkend GL15.........155 E3
Woodlands
Bristol, Downend BS16... 20 E6
Bristol, Patchway BS32... 40 D3
Bristol, Sneyd Park BS9... 17 E3
Leonard Stanley GL10... 97 E3
Narth The NP25........154 B1
Tytherington GL12.....52 B6
Woodlands Cl
Eastcombe GL6........148 C7
St Arvans NP16........72 B6
Whitecroft GL15.......155 E1
Woodlands Ct BS32... 40 B3
Woodlands Dr GL5.... 99 E8
Woodlands La
Berkeley GL13..........85 A1
Bristol BS32...........40 C3
Woodhouse Down BS32... 40 E5
Woodlands Park Cvn Pk
GL50.................133 D5
Woodlands Pk
Bristol BS32...........40 C3
Quedgeley GL2........117 D1
Woodlands Rd
Charfield GL12.........67 A4

Woodlands Rd *continued*
Cheltenham GL51.......130 B5
Cirencester GL7........190 B2
Tytherington GL12.....52 B6
Woodlands Reach GL14.191 D4
Woodlands Rise BS16... 20 D6
Woodlands The
Llandogo NP25.........146 B7
Stroud GL5............99 D8
Woodland Terr
Bristol, Kingswood BS15... 10 E7
Bristol, Redland BS6.....18 B2
Woodland View
Joy's Green GL17.......163 D3
Leonard Stanley GL10... 97 F3
Monmouth/Trefynwy
NP25................154 A4
Ruspidge GL14........156 C6
Woodmancote GL7.....158 B4
Woodland Way BS15... 20 C2
Woodleaze BS9........17 B6
Woodleigh BS35.......64 C1
Woodleigh Cl **9** HR8...178 E8
Woodleigh Field GL2....125 E6
Woodleigh Gdns BS14... 3 C6
Woodleigh Rd HR8.....178 E8
Woodmancote
Dursley GL11..........80 B7
Yate BS37.............32 D8
Woodmancote Rd **7** BS6. 18 E1
Woodmancote Sch GL52.138 B4
Woodmancote Vale
GL52.................138 B3
Woodmans Cl BS37.....33 B8
Woodmans Rd BS37.....33 C8
Woodmans Vale BS37... 33 C8
Woodmans Way GL52... 137 F3
Woodmarsh BS14......3 A4
Wood Mead BS16, BS34... 19 D8
Woodmead Gdns BS13... 2 C4
Woodmead La BS30.....23 A1
Wood Mews GL2........126 A4
Woodnook GL5.........28 C2
Woodpecker Cres BS16... 22 C4
Woodpecker Rd GL4....9 A4
Woodpeckers Cl GL19...172 D5
Woodpecker Wlk GL6... 90 F5
Wood Rd
Bristol BS15...........10 D8
Mile End GL16.........155 B6
Woodrow Way GL2......118 A3
Woodruff Cl GL4.......119 B4
Woodrush Rd GL20.....192 E2
Woodside
Bristol BS9............17 D3
Stroud GL5............99 F8
Turkdean GL54........167 F4
Woolaston GL15.......147 B3
Woodside Ave GL14....191 D3
Woodside Gr BS10.....27 D3
Woodside La GL10.....97 F2
Woodside Prim Sch
GL17.................163 F3
Woodside Rd
Bristol, Downend BS16... 20 C7
Bristol, Kingswood BS15... 10 C7
Bristol, St Anne's Park BS4... 9 E6
Coalpit Heath BS36.....31 E6
Woolaston GL15.......147 B3
Woodside Sch GL10.... 27 E2
Woodside Terr GL6.....102 F3
Woods Orch GL4.......118 C2
Woods Orchard Rd GL4.118 E2
Wood St
Bristol BS5............19 B2
Bristol BS34...........28 F7
Bristol BS34...........29 A7
Bushley GL20..........181 C5
Stroud GL5............99 D7
Woodstock Ave BS6.... 18 C1
Woodstock Cl
Avening GL8...........148 A1
Bristol BS15...........10 F8
Woodstock Rd BS14....148 A1
Woodstock Rd
Bristol, Kingswood BS15... 10 F7
Bristol, Redland BS6......18 C2
Woodstock Sch GL10... 27 E2
Woodstock Terr GL11... 89 C1
Woodvale
5 Gloucester GL2....118 A1
Quedgeley GL2........110 A8
Woodview
Four Oaks GL18........170 D7
Frampton Mansell GL6... 148 E5

Woodview Cl BS11..... 16 E7
Woodview Rd GL11..... 88 A4
Woodville Ave GL16....155 C6
Woodville Rd
Cinderford GL14.......191 E4
Tewkesbury GL20......192 D1
Woodville Rd W GL14...191 E4
Woodward Ave BS37.... 43 B1
Woodward Cl GL8......140 B5
Woodward Dr BS30.....10 F4
Woodwell Rd BS11.....16 E5
Woodyleaze Dr BS15... 10 D6
Woolaston Comm GL15..147 C3
Woolaston Prim Sch
GL15.................147 C3
Woolaway Bglws GL56... 187 A6
Woolcot St BS6........18 B2
Woollard La BS14......3 E1
Woolley Rd BS14.......3 E5
Woolmarket The GL7....190 D5
Woolpitch Wood/Coed
Woolpitch NP16.......60 C8
Woolridge Hill GL19....172 C2
Woolstone La GL52.....137 F8
Woolstrop Way GL2....118 A3
Woolthorpe La GL2.....157 C6
Wootton Cres BS4.....9 E6
Wootton Pk BS14, BS4... 9 B1
Wootton Rd BS4.......9 F6
Worcester Cl BS16.....20 B2
Worcester Cres BS8....194 A4
Worcester Ct BS8......194 A4
Worcester Par GL1.....196 B4
Worcester Rd
Bristol, Clifton BS8....194 A4
Bristol, Kingswood BS15... 20 D1
Cinderford GL14.......191 E5
Corse GL19............172 B6
Ledbury HR8...........178 F8
Worcester St GL1......196 B3
Worcester Terr BS8....194 A4
Worcester Wlk GL16... 155 C6
Wordens The GL5......98 D8
Wordings Mount GL6...104 E8
Wordsworth Ave GL51... 132 E1
Wordsworth Cl BS34... 29 A8
Wordsworth Rd
Bristol BS7............19 B7
Dursley GL11..........80 C7
Working La GL54.......183 E1
Workmans Cl GL11.....87 E4
Workshop Rd BS11.....26 C4
World of Mechanical Music
Mus★ GL54...........168 A1
Worldsend La GL13.....76 E7
Worlds End La GL12....68 C7
World's End La BS31....5 C5
Worley Ridge GL6......91 A4
Wormwood Hill GL6.....91 A1
Worrall Mews **10** BS8...18 A2
Worrall Pl **11** BS8......18 A2
Worrall Rd BS8........18 A2
Worrel's La BS16......30 D3
Worsley St BS5........9 D7
Worthing Rd BS34.....28 F8
Worthy Cl BS15........10 F6
Worthy Rd BS11.......26 D7
Worthys The BS34.....30 A6
Wortley Rd GL12.......68 C6
Wortley Terr GL12.....68 C6
Wotton Cres GL12.....68 C6
Wotton Ct GL4.........127 D1
Wotton Elms Ct **4** GL2...127 B2
Wotton Heritage Ctr★
GL12.................68 B7
Wotton Lawn Hospl GL1.127 A2
Wotton Rd
Charfield GL12.........67 B5
Iron Acton BS37.......42 F5
Kingswood GL12.......67 F5
Wragg Castle La GL6...103 C6
Wragg Ct GL11.........88 A5
Wraggs Row **22** GL54...176 F4
Wraxall Gr BS13.......2 A8
Wraxall Rd BS30.......11 A6
Wrenbert Rd BS16.....20 D5
Wren Cl
Bristol BS16...........19 E7
Gloucester BS4........119 B6
Wren Dr BS16..........20 A6
Wren Terr GL3.........127 D6
Wright Cl GL54........169 D7
Wright Rd GL54........169 D7
Wright Way BS16......19 E8
Wrington Cl BS34......29 C7
Wrington Cres BS13....2 A7

Wroughton Dr BS13.... 2 D4
Wroughton Gdns BS13... 2 D4
Wroxham Dr BS34......29 C8
Wyatt Ave BS13........1 F5
Wyatt Cl BS13.........1 F5
Wyatt Ct GL54.........166 E5
Wyatts View BS4.......43 B1
Wychbury Cl GL53......130 D5
Wychwood BS15........10 E6
Wyck Beck Rd BS10.... 28 A3
Wyck Rissington GL54... 169 C8
Wycliffe Coll GL10.....97 F6
Wycliffe Rd BS9.......18 B7
Wycliffe Row **9** BS3....8 F4
Wycombe Gr BS4......9 D2
Wycombe Rd GL2......110 A7
Wydelands GL56.......186 E6
Wyebank Ave NP16.....73 A1
Wyebank Cl NP16......61 A8
Wyebank Cres NP16....61 A8
Wyebank Dr NP16......73 A1
Wyebank Pl NP16......61 A8
Wyebank Rd NP16......61 A8
Wyebank Rise NP16....61 A8
Wyebank View NP16....61 A8
Wyebank Way NP16....61 A7
Wyebridge St **17** NP25... 154 A7
Wye Cres NP16.........60 E7
Wye Croft Cl BS10.....28 D3
Wyedale Ave BS9......17 C7
Wyedean Cl BS15......51 C8
Wyedean Sch & 6th Form Ctr
NP16.................61 A8
Wyelands Pk GL17......163 D3
Wyelands View NP16....60 B4
Wye Rapids Cotts HR9... 162 E2
Wye Rd GL3...........120 F5
Wye's Gn NP25.........154 C4
Wyesham Ave/Rhodfa
Wyesham **4** NP25....154 A7
Wyesham Inf Sch NP25..154 A7
Wyesham Jun Sch NP25.154 A7
Wyesham La (Sky Farm La)
NP25.................154 B7
Wyesham Rd NP25......154 B7
Wyeside Commercial Ctr **25**
NP25.................154 A7
Wyeside Pk HR9........163 C5
Wye Valley Link Rd NP16. 60 E5
Wye View Ho NP16.....61 A7
Wye View La HR9.......162 E3
Wye View Terr NP25....154 C4
Wykis Ct BS15.........10 E5
Wylington Rd BS36.....31 B6
Wymans Ct GL50.......133 C5
Wyman's La GL51......133 B6
Wyman's Rd GL52......134 A3
Wymbush Cres BS13... 2 C5
Wymbush Gdns BS13... 2 C5
yndbrook La GL19......179 F4
Wyndcliffe View NP16... 72 B5
Wyndcliffe Ho NP16....61 A7
Wyndham Cres
Bristol BS4............10 A3
Easton-in-G BS20......16 B4
Wyndham Ct BS2.......195 B4
Wyndham Wy GL54.....174 A8
Wynford Villas GL19....171 C1
Wynols Cl **6** GL16.....155 B5
Wynols Ct **7** GL16.....155 B5
Wynols Hill La GL16....155 B5
Wynols Rd GL16.......155 B5
Wynstones Dr GL4.....110 F5
Wynstones Sch GL4....110 E8
Wynstones The BS15... 10 C7
Wyntour Ho NP16......61 A8
Wyntour's Par GL15....92 A2
Wynyards Cl GL20......192 D4
Wyvern Rd NP16.......61 B1
Wyvern Villas BS9.....18 A8

Y

Yalland Cl **8** BS16..... 20 A4
Yalta Cl **16** GL51........ 132 E2
Yanleigh Cl BS13........1 D6
Yanley La BS41, BS13... 1 C1
Yard The BS2..........19 A3
Yarlington Cl GL52......137 E4
Yarnells Alley **14** GL20... 192 C4
Yarnolds GL51.........129 E1
Yarnold Terr GL51......133 A4
Yarrow Cl GL4..........119 A4

Yartleton La GL17......165 A7
Yate Her Ctr★ BS37....43 E2
Yate Rd BS37..........42 F3
Yate Rocks BS37.......43 F7
Yate Sta BS37.........43 C2
Yatton Cl BS13.........1 F8
Yeaman's Ho BS1......195 B1
Yeldham Mews GL52... 133 F4
Yellow Hundred Cl GL11. 80 C8
Yelverton Rd BS4......9 E1
Yeomans Cl BS9.......17 D5
Yeomanside Cl BS14... 3 C5
Yeomeads BS41........7 A1
Yetts The NP16........61 B8
Yewcroft Cl BS14......3 A4
Yewtree Cl GL11.......87 D3
Yew Tree Cl
Cheltenham GL50......133 C5
Shipton GL54.........166 E5
Whitchurch HR9.......162 D4
Yew Tree Cotts **16** GL54. 176 F4
Yew Tree Ct
Bristol BS14..........3 B5
8 Broadway WR12...185 C8
Yew Tree Dr
Bristol BS15..........20 F3
Gotherington GL52.... 138 A8
Yew Tree Gdns BS20... 16 C4
Yew Tree Rd GL3.......120 B4
Yew Tree Way
Churchdown GL3......128 A5
Thrupp GL5...........99 E3
Yew Tree Wood NP16... 60 B8
Yokehouse La GL6......104 A6
York Ave BS7..........18 F4
York Bldgs BS3........8 E4
York Cl
Bristol, Bromley Heath
BS16...............30 F1
Bristol, Stoke Gifford BS34. 29 D4
Yate BS37............43 E4
York Ct BS2...........195 B4
York Gdns
Bristol BS8...........7 F6
Winterbourne BS36....30 F8
Yorklea GL15..........156 A1
Yorkley Prim Sch GL15. 156 A1
Yorkley Rd GL54.......134 C2
Yorkley Wood Rd GL15. 156 A1
York Pl
Bristol, Brandon Hill BS1. 194 C2
Bristol, Victoria Park BS8. 194 B3
York Rd
Bristol, Lower Easton BS5. 19 C1
Bristol, Montpelier BS6... 18 E1
Bristol, Staple Hill BS16... 20 E4
Bristol, Windmill Hill BS3... 8 E4
Cinderford GL14.......191 E5
Gloucester GL4........119 C8
Tewkesbury GL20......192 C2
York Row GL52.........134 A4
York St
Bristol, Baptist Mills BS2... 19 A2
2 Bristol, Clifton BS8... 18 A2
9 Bristol, Redfield BS5... 9 C7
Bristol, St Pauls BS2... 195 B4
Cheltenham GL52......193 C4
Youngs Cotts GL6......148 B4
Youngs Ct BS16.......21 B8
Youngs Orch
Brimscombe GL5.......148 A5
Gloucester GL4........119 D6
Y Paddgau/The Paddocks **6**
NP25.................154 A7
Yr Hen Heol/The Old Rd **22**
NP25.................154 A7

Z

Zetland Rd BS6........18 D2
Zinc Rd BS11..........26 C3
Zinnia Cl GL3..........127 F7
Zion Apartments **12**
GL16.................155 A4
Zion Hill GL6..........102 F3
Zoons Rd GL3..........120 A8
Zura Ave GL3..........120 B4